The Photographer's Guide to Adobe Lightroom

Learn industry-standard best practices and techniques to get the best out of the latest version of Lightroom Classic

Marcin Lewandowski

<packt>

BIRMINGHAM—MUMBAI

The Photographer's Guide to Adobe Lightroom

Group Product Manager: Rohit Rajkumar
Publishing Product Manager: Rohit Rajkumar
Senior Editor: Keagan Carneiro
Content Development Editor: Adrija Mitra
Technical Editor: Joseph Aloocaran
Copy Editor: Safis Editing
Project Coordinator: Sonam Pandey
Proofreader: Safis Editing
Indexer: Tejal Daruwale Soni
Production Designer: Aparna Bhagat
Marketing Coordinator: Teny Thomas

First published: July 2022

Production reference: 1220722

Published by Packt Publishing Ltd.
Livery Place
35 Livery Street
Birmingham
B3 2PB, UK.

978-1-80107-010-2

www.packt.com

To Kinga and Jolan.

– Marcin Lewandowski | soundofphotography.com

Contributors

About the author

Marcin Lewandowski is a professional photographer based in Cork, Ireland. His work has been exhibited around Europe in places such as the Getty Images Gallery and the Brighton Photo Biennial, and he is on permanent exhibition in the Cork City and County Archives, among other locations. In addition, some of the projects he was involved in were exhibited as far as Bangkok and Istanbul.

Marcin has worked with clients ranging from major magazines such as France's *Le Point* and *The Irish Times*, through corporate clients such as DC Shoes and Lionsgate Films, to many businesses, organizations, and venues around Ireland and Europe.

Marcin always photographs personal projects as a creative outlet, trying new approaches and techniques to become a better photographer.

About the reviewers

Soumyadeep Paul has led an impressive career as a professional photographer in his 10 years working in the media industry, based in Kolkata, India. Although he is a specialized landscape and travel photographer, he has also worked in many other fields, such as architecture, event, and wedding photography. In 2014, he worked on a book project celebrating 200 years of the Indian Museum, Kolkata. Prior to his current role as a photo editor at Dream Touch Visual Pro, Soumyadeep worked as a professional photographer for Google Business View Team at 1neclick Online Pvt. Ltd. Soumyadeep is a balanced freethinker and a hardworking and passionate photographer, and he loves to work in a team, as he believes there is always something to be learned from others.

"Thank you to everyone who has helped me throughout my journey, and thanks in advance to those in the future. A very special thanks to my mother for being supportive throughout my journey and to my beloved wife for having trust in me and being fully supportive throughout my career. Nothing would be possible without them. Thanks to my teachers, fellow photographers, and everyone who helped me grow."

Liz Staley is a visual artist and blogger who loves horses, animation, comics, and true crime. She began her digital art journey using Adobe Photoshop and then learned how to use Clip Studio Paint. She currently writes a weekly blog for *Graphixly.com* with art and Clip Studio Paint tips. Although she still loves the medium of comics and animation, her personal art now mostly consists of animal portraits that combine education with conservation. Liz loves horses, dogs, horror movies, anime, and learning the Japanese language.

Table of Contents

3

Tools Available within the Library Module 53

4

Folders and Collections 103

Section 2: Developing Photographs in Lightroom Classic 123

Preface

It takes talent to be a great photographer, but in the digital era, it also takes a level of technical proficiency. Adobe Photoshop Lightroom Classic was designed as a one-stop solution for photographers to perfect their final products in a desktop-focused workflow, which includes local storage of photos as files and folders on your computer. Knowing how to navigate through Lightroom efficiently means that you'll be able to concentrate on being creative instead of wondering "what does this button do?"

Complete with step-by-step explanations of essential concepts and practical examples, you will begin by importing photographs into Lightroom. Next, you'll focus on how to sort through, sequence, develop, and export your photographs in various formats, or even design a book and create gallery-ready prints. Finally, you will learn how to make informed decisions within Lightroom and understand how to approach your work depending on the type of photographs you are working on. This guide also illustrates real-life usage and presents workflow examples that are not just for aspiring professionals but also for artists and amateurs who are still getting to grips with the technical side of photography.

So, welcome to this journey that will take you through the wonders that are possible with Lightroom, as is evident from the photographs that you will find in the chapters and the front cover of the book itself. All these photographs are the author's creations, and he hopes to pass on some of his passion to you! By the end of this book, you'll be confident in importing, editing, developing, and delivering your photos like a professional.

Who this book is for

This is a book for photographers who are new to Lightroom and also for those who've tried it already and need a more structured approach to start making the most of its advanced features. Essentially, this photography book is aimed at everyone who wants to become proficient enough in Lightroom to make better decisions and focus on creativity and productivity instead of the software.

What this book covers

Chapter 1, An Overview of Lightroom Classic, briefly discusses where Lightroom came from, what sets it apart from other software, and how it helps photographers streamline their work. It also looks at how all the tools are laid out throughout the modules and touches on how we can personalize its layout.

Chapter 2, Bring It All In – Importing Photographs into Lightroom, starts with an explanation of what to do upon turning on Lightroom for the first time and follows that by focusing on the functionality of the Import dialog, sharing a few tips and tricks for an uninterrupted and well-managed workflow.

Chapter 3, Tools Available within the Library Module, introduces the Library module and different approaches to editing collections of photographs. It also shares a few tips for the editing workflow.

Chapter 4, Folders and Collections, discusses managing the ever-growing library that every photographer will have. You will see the differences between distinctly different approaches to storing and managing a library of photographs and learn how to work with folders and collections in a seamless way. This chapter also looks at the sorting, filtering, and searching capabilities of Lightroom Classic.

Chapter 5, An Introduction to the Develop Module, introduces a few simple tweaks such as straightening and cropping, through making basic Exposure and Saturation adjustments, to complete overhauls of how a photo will look with Profiles and Color Grading: Lightroom is a one-stop-shop. In this chapter, we will briefly look at the Develop module's functionality before deep diving into more details in the next chapter.

Chapter 6, A Detailed View of the Develop Module's Functions, takes an in-depth look at each of the Develop module's tabs. Whether we are aware of adverse conditions that caused the "straight out of the camera" photograph to need a bit of tweaking or maybe we can see with the eyes of our imagination coloring variants we would like to try out. Whatever might be the case, the Develop module is a natural extension of a photographer's imagination and in this chapter, you will learn how to use its tools to your advantage.

Chapter 7, Get Them All Out of Lightroom – Exporting for Work and Leisure, addresses the questions do you want your camera settings to be added to final files? Do you want the print house to receive optimized files for a large canvas print? Do you primarily work with social media? There are many different requirements placed on photographers regarding file formats. This chapter will deal with these questions and many more.

Chapter 8, Get Them All Out – Using the Print and Book Modules, looks at the streamlined way Lightroom offers to get our pictures from the screen into the physical world. This chapter explains how to achieve the best results in preparing files for printing at home, how to work on designing a photo book layout, and how to prepare it for optimal printing. We will also look at how using the Print module can give you an edge in creating your social media posts.

Chapter 9, Slideshow, Map, and Web Modules, shows how to create presentations with the ease of clicking one button. You'll learn how to utilize the features in the Map module, even if you don't use geotagging, and how to build a website without subscribing to any website building services.

Chapter 10, Final Notes and Summary, looks at everything we have learned, including all of the Lightroom Classic modules discussed. It also glances at the other versions of Lightroom that come with it as a package, adding an additional screen, and tethered shooting.

To get the most out of this book

You will need Lightroom Classic installed on your computer. Regardless of whether you work on a Mac or PC, Adobe recommends at least 16 GB of RAM with a minimum requirement of 8 GB. Having a high-resolution monitor will also make learning about and using Lightroom much more enjoyable.

Software/hardware covered in the book	Operating system requirements
Lightroom Classic	macOS – macOS Catalina (version 10.15) or later Windows – Windows 10 (64 bit) 1909 or later

Download the table of keyboard shortcuts

In the chapters, we have given the keyboard shortcuts for macOS only. However, please don't worry if you are more familiar with Windows, as you can always refer to this table where you will find all the Lightroom shortcuts for both Mac and Windows: `https://packt.link/qN41C`.

```
The full table is also provided after the last chapter of the
book.
```

Download the high-resolution images

We also provide a PDF file that has the high-resolution images of the screenshots and diagrams used in this book. You can download it here: `https://packt.link/gA91L`.

Conventions used

There are a number of text conventions used throughout this book.

`Code in text`: Indicates code words in text, database table names, folder names, filenames, file extensions, pathnames, dummy URLs, user input, and Twitter handles. Here is an example: "Please keep in mind that any adjustments discussed in this chapter work best on RAW files, and you will reach the full potential of neither the tools nor your photographs when working on `.jpg` files."

Bold: Indicates a new term, an important word, or words that you see onscreen. For instance, words in menus or dialog boxes appear in **bold**. Here is an example: "With **Tool Overlay** switched to **Always**, we can toggle various types of overlay grid with the keyboard shortcut "*O*".

> **Tips or Important Notes**
> Appear like this.

Get in touch

Feedback from our readers is always welcome.

General feedback: If you have questions about any aspect of this book, email us at `customercare@packtpub.com` and mention the book title in the subject of your message.

Errata: Although we have taken every care to ensure the accuracy of our content, mistakes do happen. If you have found a mistake in this book, we would be grateful if you would report this to us. Please visit `www.packtpub.com/support/errata` and fill in the form.

Piracy: If you come across any illegal copies of our works in any form on the internet, we would be grateful if you would provide us with the location address or website name. Please contact us at `copyright@packt.com` with a link to the material.

If you are interested in becoming an author: If there is a topic that you have expertise in and you are interested in either writing or contributing to a book, please visit `authors.packtpub.com`.

Share Your Thoughts

Once you've read *The Photographer's Guide to Adobe Lightroom*, we'd love to hear your thoughts! Scan the QR code below to go straight to the Amazon review page for this book and share your feedback.

`https://packt.link/r/1801070105`

Your review is important to us and the tech community and will help us make sure we're delivering excellent quality content.

Section 1: Importing Images into Lightroom and Exploring the Library Module's Structure and Tools

Every journey starts with a first step. Our first step will be to take a look at how and where our photographs are stored. We will learn how to sieve through everything to get to the juicy ones. This will get us nicely primed for the *Section 2* chapters.

In this section, we will cover the following topics:

- *Chapter 1, An Overview of Lightroom Classic*
- *Chapter 2, Bring It All In – Importing Photographs into Lightroom*
- *Chapter 3, Tools Available within the Library Module*
- *Chapter 4, Folders and Collections*

1

An Overview of Lightroom Classic

Lightroom was first introduced as a beta release back in 2006 and almost immediately revolutionized how photographers work with their pictures. Its biggest "out-of-the-box advantage" over everything else was the ability to manage, edit, and develop photographs in one place—all of that without needing to go to Camera Raw or Photoshop, editing photographs by opening them one by one, and saving them as new images. Lightroom offers a non-destructive approach to working with our photos. We can see and work on seemingly infinite copies of photographs with different looks. In reality, we are only creating additional "develop recipes" applied to the original photograph. All visual changes made to pictures are saved in Lightroom's database as a text "recipe." This approach nullifies the need for multiple copies of any stored photos. You will learn a little bit more about this when we will talk about the Library module in later chapters. The main thing to know about the advantages of this type of editing is that it takes up less storage space and allows better performance for both the software itself and us—the photographers.

This chapter will briefly discuss where Lightroom comes from, what sets it apart from other software, and how it helps photographers streamline their work. We will look at how all the tools are laid out throughout the modules and understand how much we can personalize its layout.

In this chapter, we will cover the following areas:

- Introducing Lightroom
- Looking at a simple sample of a Lightroom Classic workflow
- Getting familiar with the Lightroom interface
- Customizing Lightroom

Introducing Lightroom

In its first iteration, Lightroom was missing many features such as watermarking or localized corrections. Year after year, Adobe listened to photographers and added all "missing" functions, plus many more. Expanding Lightroom's functionality cemented its position as an industry standard and a go-to tool for professionals and amateurs alike. The amazing thing about Lightroom is that its **user interface (UI)** looks almost the same since its inception, which says a lot about how well designed it is. All that Lightroom needed was the addition of more tools and expansion of already available ones. The principle of using sliders as controllers for most adjustments proved both intuitive and easy to master.

Adobe Photoshop Lightroom Classic is an all-in-one tool for photographers, providing a simple solution to everything from management of a photography collection to the detailed post-production stage. Lightroom Classic also provides tools for printing, designing photo books and slideshows, and publishing simple web galleries—all from within the same software. By reading this book, you will learn how to make working with photographs as simple, pleasurable, and fun as possible. Lightroom helps photographers to get the best out of photos. Whether you are a professional looking for a tool to help you in streamlining your workflow or an amateur who wants to improve their approach to editing and developing photos, Lightroom has it all. In my opinion, a great thing about Lightroom is that there is no one right way to use it. Specific patterns can increase productivity and make a photographer's life easier and more enjoyable, but there is a lot of flexibility to work the way anyone might like.

Most of the Lightroom's tools are available through various "access points". By different "access points", I mean that the same function can be accessed through an onscreen button, menu option, or keyboard shortcut, allowing users to choose the most convenient way to use them and, with time, to streamline workflows in a very personalized and convenient manner.

Looking at a simple sample of a Lightroom Classic workflow

You might say, "*That sounds great, but how does all this work?*" In this section, you will find a small example of how a Lightroom workflow can be used in a real-life situation. This is a "quick and dirty" example of how I might use Lightroom on a daily basis. To make this as real as possible, I grabbed my pocket camera and went out to make a few photos—luckily, it had just started to snow, which hardly ever happens here. As you will see in this example, a Lightroom workflow is a very organic process, and as you read this book and practice a bit, it will become a very natural process for you as well.

Let's get started:

1. The first step is to move photographs from a memory card into Lightroom by importing them. We will be covering this in *Chapter 2, Bring It All In – Importing Photographs into Lightroom*, but please also see the following screenshot:

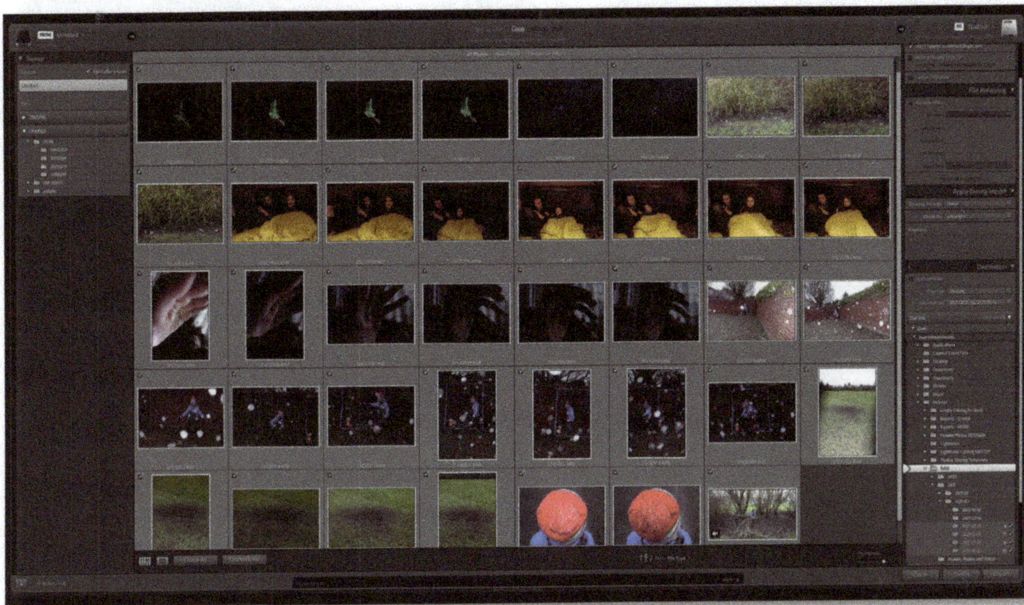

Figure 1.1 – Importing images: sub-module view

It's a fairly simple process where we will choose where to save our photographs, in which structure, and how to rename them. We will also choose any presets that we might want to see applied, add keywords, and more.

2. Once all images are imported, it's a matter of selecting our favorites, which is quickly achieved with a very flexible built-in system for rating and filtering—you will learn all about this in *Chapter 3, Tools Available Within the Library Module*, but in a nutshell, while looking through each important image, we will apply a star rating of one to five stars, add "pick/reject" flags, and include color labels. We will apply filters to see our top picks and further narrow down our selection with additional ratings. Here, you can see the Library module view after filtering for images rated with one star:

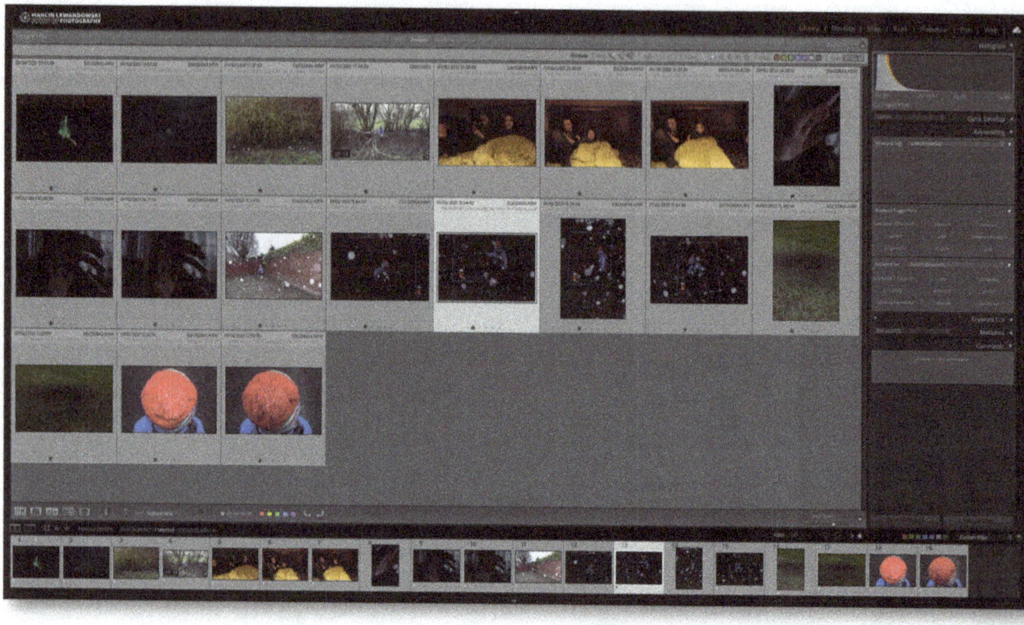

Figure 1.2 – Library module view after filtering for images rated with one star

3. Once all of the "looking through" is done and we have a selection of our absolute favorites, it's time to give them the desired look. For that, we move to the Develop module (covered in detail in *Chapter 5, An Introduction to the Develop Module*). In this module, we will make adjustments, compare different looks, and pick the one we like most.

   First, let's have a peek inside the Develop module, where we can make all desired adjustments and later compare the finished version to the original file. You can see an overview of this here:

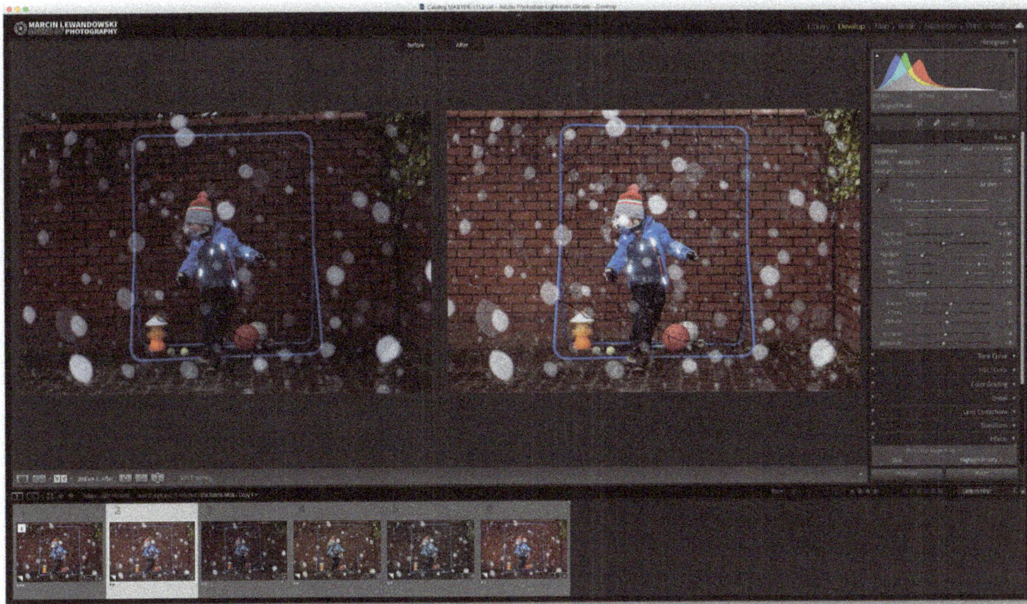

Figure 1.3 – Comparing finished/developed photograph to the original file (please note all the adjustments I made on the right side and multiple versions with a different look in the filmstrip)

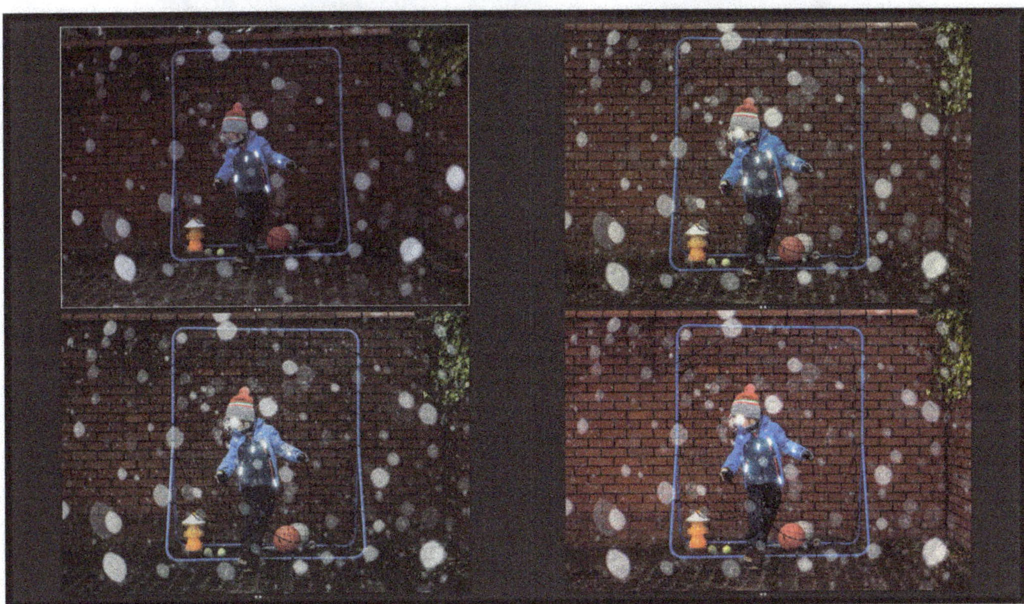

Figure 1.4 – Comparing a few different versions in Survey mode to pick a favorite

4. Options within the Develop module are vast; we will cover all of this in *Chapter 5, An Introduction to the Develop Module*, and *Chapter 6, A Detailed View of the Develop Module's Functions*. Once we are finished, there is also a lot of flexibility regarding what can be done next. Let's say that we want to post this photograph on Instagram. In that case, we can sync with Lightroom for mobile devices, which is included in the package, by simply marking them for syncing (which is covered in *Chapter 10, Final Notes and Summary*) and from there, share to Instagram, as illustrated in the following screenshot:

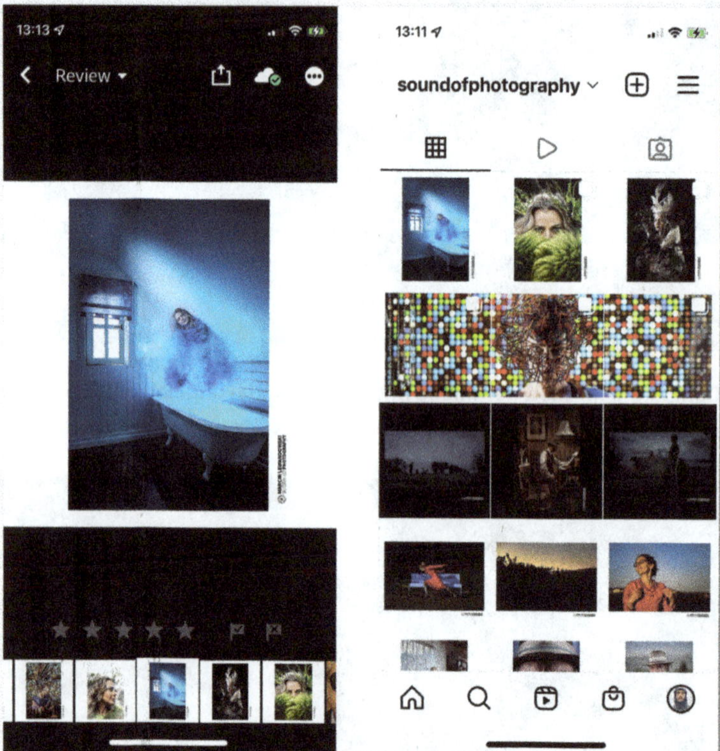

Figure 1.5 – On the left is a screen from Lightroom Mobile showing the synced photo; on the right is my Instagram feed where I posted this photo directly from within Lightroom

Figure 1.5 is just a simple workflow example that I based on a small series of photographs quickly made to illustrate this chapter. As you can see, working within Lightroom is simple to follow once we know what we are doing. There are many options to choose from along the way to get to the desired final result. Whatever this final result might be for everyone, the principle always remains the same: import, edit, develop, and go from there.

You should now have a better idea of what Lightroom can do for you and what you can do with Lightroom. Please read on to learn a little bit more about how to control all of this functionality.

Starting with the Library module, Lightroom's layout revolves around photographs that are always the central point of all operations, regardless of whether we choose to view one photo or a selection of them. For example, please see the following screenshots of the same selection of photographs viewed in a few different ways within the Library module:

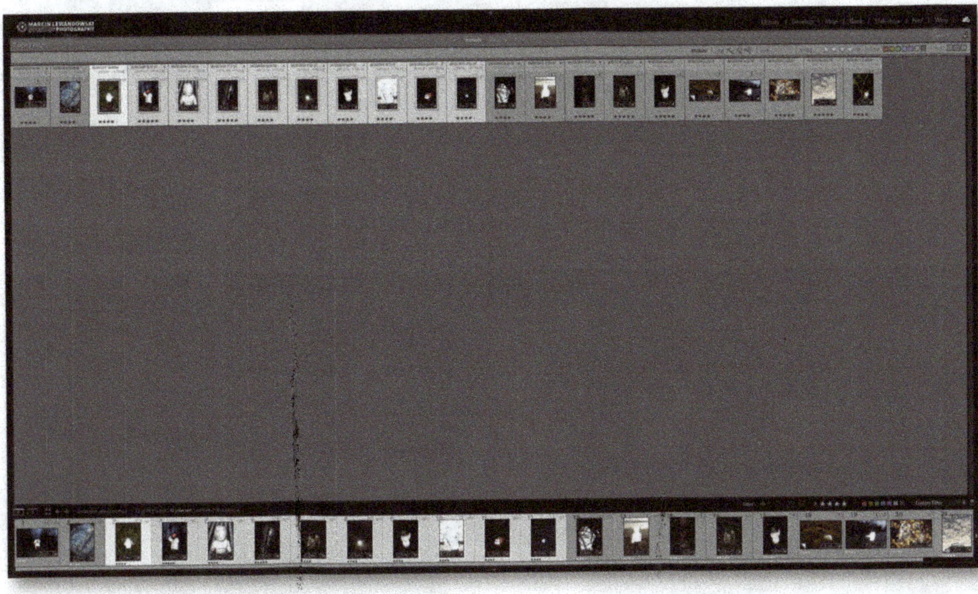

Figure 1.6A – Tiny cells in grid view with filmstrip and no side panels

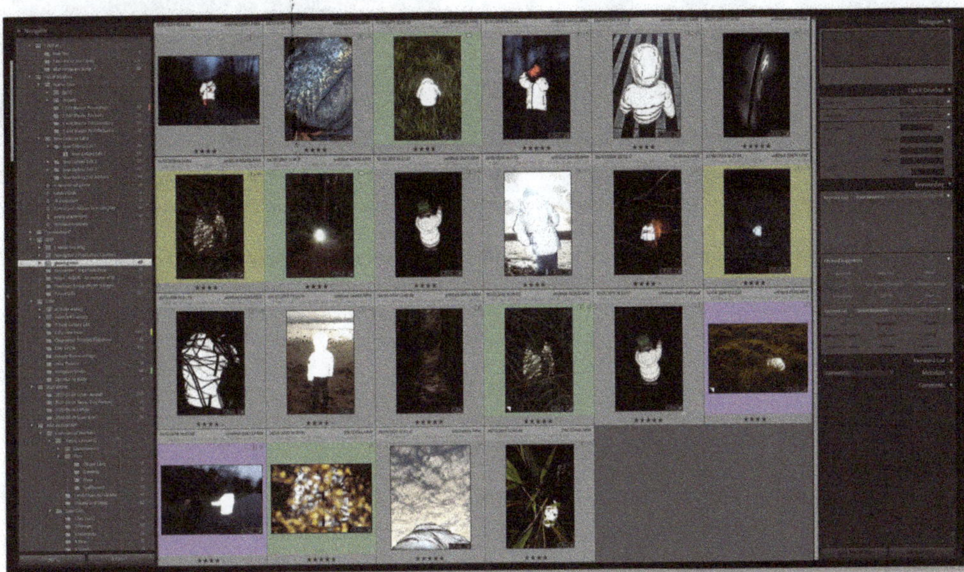

Figure 1.6B – Bigger cells in grid view with color-label tinted cells, side panels, and no filmstrip

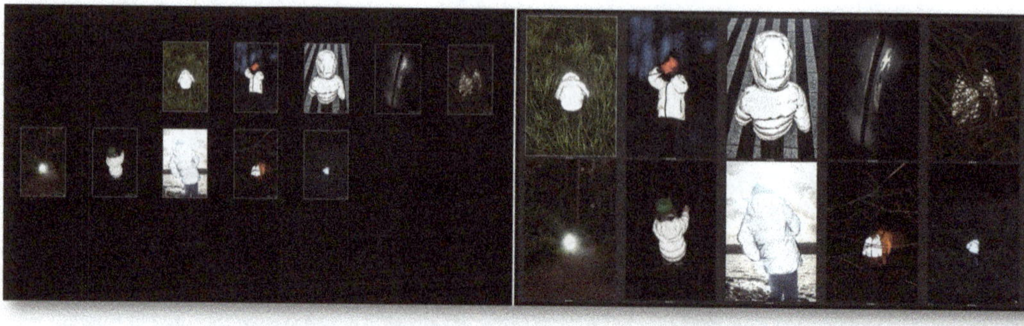

Figure 1.6C – Selected photographs only with "lights out"; Selected photographs in Survey mode, all panels closed

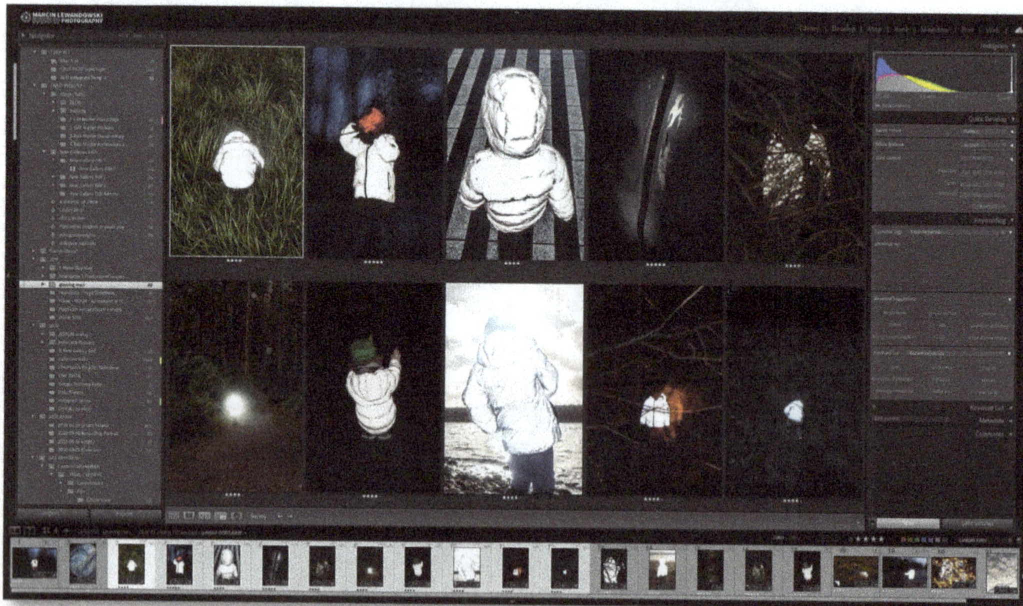

Figure 1.6D – Selected photographs in Survey mode, all panels opened

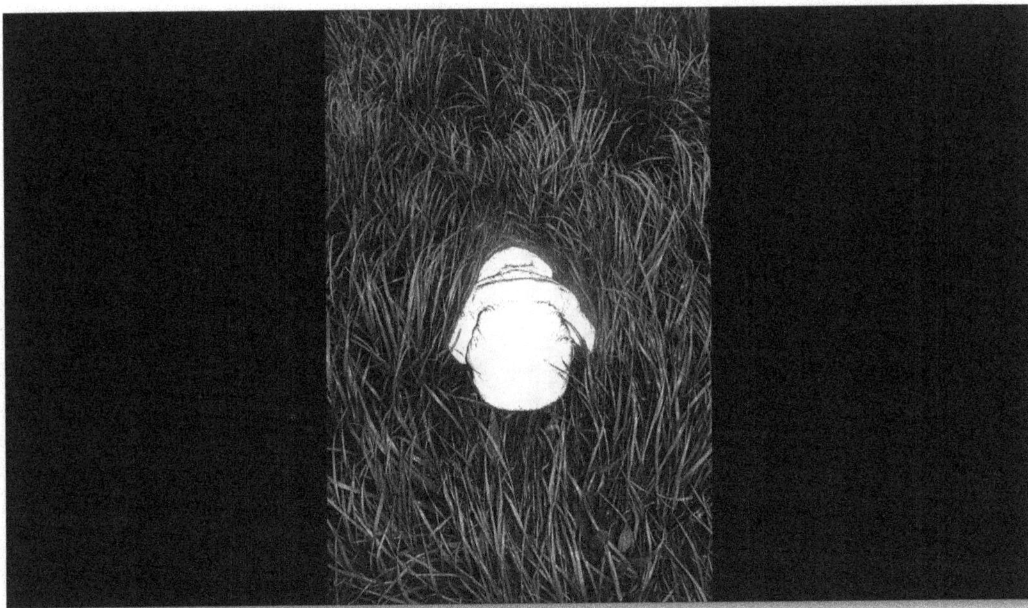

Figure 1.6E – Selected photograph in fullscreen mode

All these different views are only a click of a mouse button or a simple keyboard shortcut away. By the end of this book, you will be moving effortlessly between all viewing options, knowing exactly how to tailor each of them to your needs. You will understand their advantages and recognize differences in using each of them. Most of this information is available in *Chapter 2, Bring It All In – Importing Photographs into Lightroom*, and some module-specific options will be distributed throughout the book.

Whether we work on an extensive edit from a multiple-day photoshoot or choose a selection from a family meeting, Lightroom provides several tools to make this as easy as possible. We will cover this and more in the next section.

Getting familiar with the Lightroom interface

Lightroom consists of seven main modules, additional sub-modules for importing/exporting images, and different popups for preferences and syncing photos with Adobe cloud storage (included with Lightroom Classic).

The UI of Lightroom revolves around an idea of a workspace surrounded by tools. That workspace is where we will see the effect of any actions taken with the said tools. Each module contains side panels, and these panels are split further—into tabs.

The left-side panel is used to move around our collections and folders or to apply module-specific presets; the right-side panel contains all module-specific tools. The bottom part of each panel is always occupied by a filmstrip with our photographs. This filmstrip remains in the same spot between modules and is always accessible. You can see a representation of this in the following screenshot:

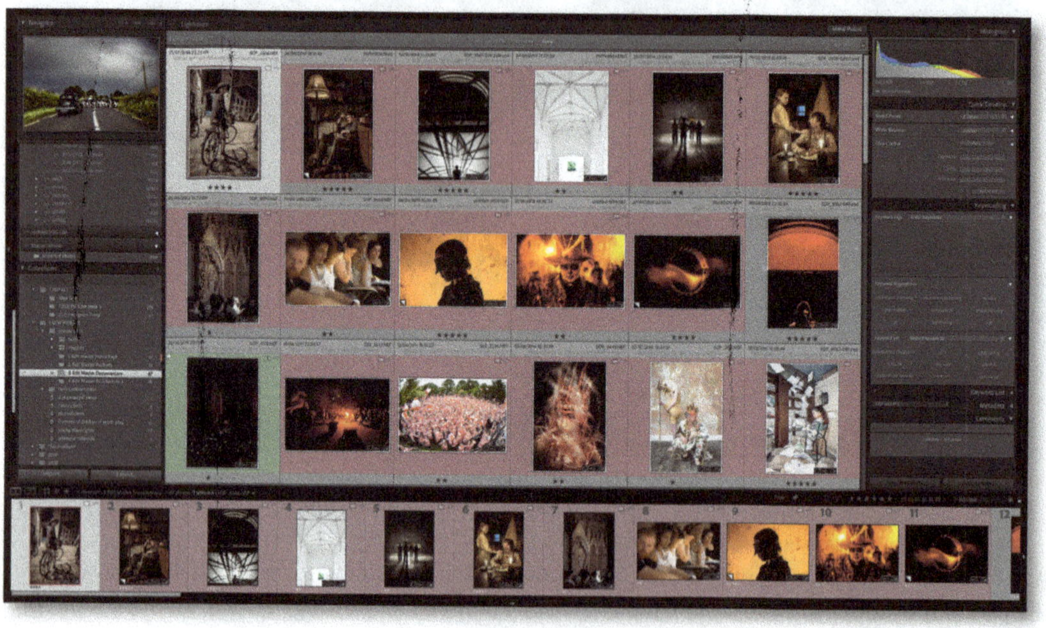

Figure 1.7 – Filmstrip along the bottom of Lightroom is always accessible from within all modules

Even if you haven't imported any photographs into Lightroom so far and it's the first time you are turning it on, I encourage you to look at the different modules as you progress through this chapter to get more familiar with their layout.

Access to all of the modules is always located on the top-right side of the screen as a **Module Picker**, as illustrated in the following screenshot:

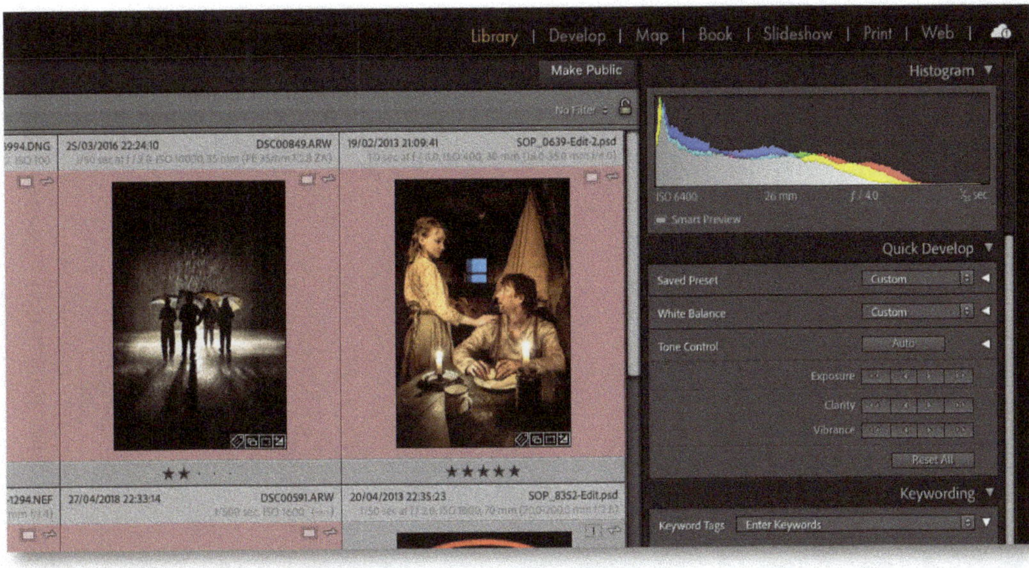

Figure 1.8 – Module Picker in the top-right corner

It's possible to change the appearance of this menu and even hide modules we don't use or don't need; they will always be accessible in other ways. I will describe how to do this toward the end of this chapter. For the moment, let's go through each panel and look briefly at their functions in Lightroom Classic.

First, take a look at the following screenshot:

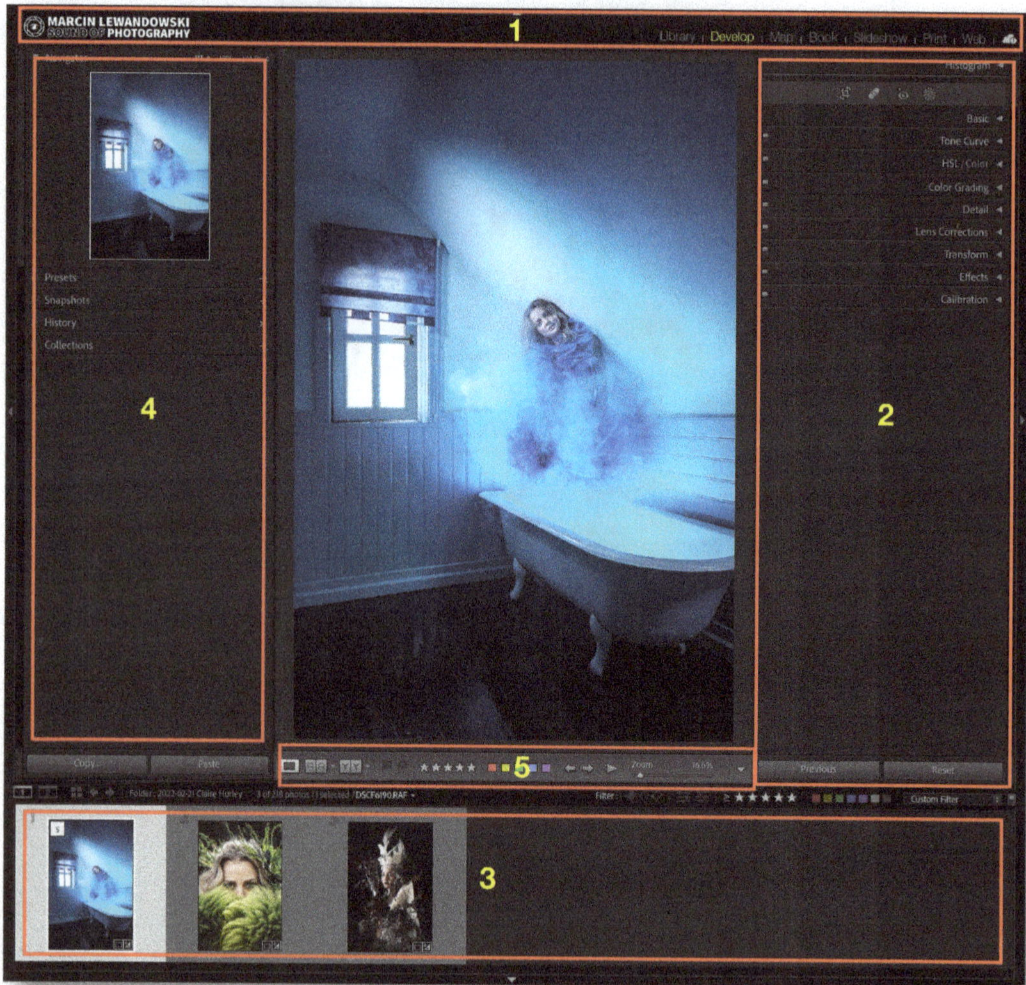

Figure 1.9 – Develop module with all panels opened and all tools and tabs within panels closed

The preceding screenshot illustrates all panels opened, as follows:

1. Module Picker (top panel)
2. Right Modules panel
3. Filmstrip (bottom panel)
4. Left Modules panel
5. Toolbar (above the filmstrip)

All of the tabs and panels within Lightroom Classic can be opened and closed to simplify the layout and make it better suited to our needs. The first important part of the UI—to help us with it—is the small arrows located in the middle of the external edge of each panel, as illustrated in the following screenshot:

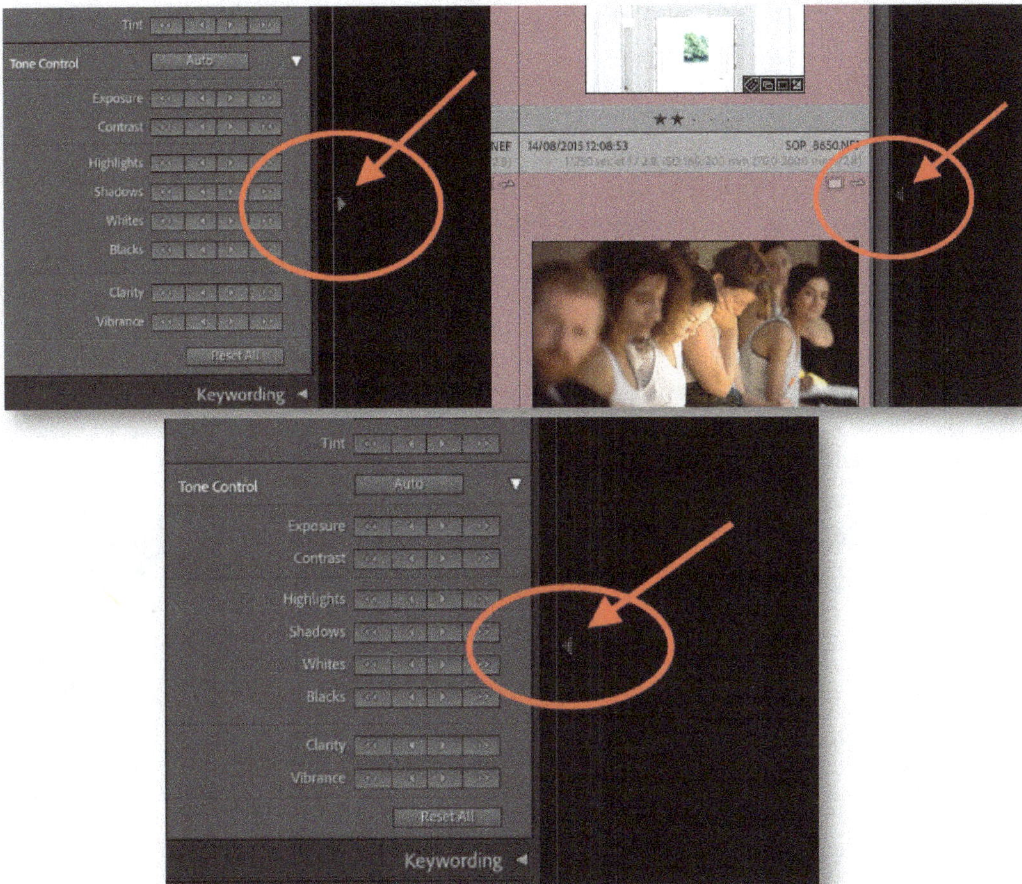

Figure 1.10 – Small arrows on the side of each panel, for opening and closing panels

When the little arrow is gray, this means that the panel is currently open, and you can click on it to close the panel. You can also click on the narrow frame where the arrow is located to do the same. When the little arrow is made of white dots, the panel is closed, and you can open it up. Instead of opening it back up, you can also just hover on the narrow frame where the arrow is. This will temporarily preview the panel and keep it in Preview mode as long as the cursor is hovering over it. As long as this preview is initiated, we can access all of the functionality of the panel. The same rule applies to each of the four panels located around the central area of Lightroom. It's a handy thing to remember later when you want, for example, a photograph that you are working on to occupy a larger part of the screen.

Handy Keyboard Shortcuts to Remember

"*Tab*": Show/hide both side panels

"*Shift* + *Tab*": Show/hide all panels

"*F5*": Show/hide Module Picker (top panel)

"*F6*": Show/hide Filmstrip (bottom panel)

"*F7*": Show/hide Left Modules panel

"*F8*": Show/hide Right Modules panel

The second type of small arrow you will notice within each module's panels is the one responsible for opening and closing tabs. You can open and close these at will by clicking on the arrow, tab title, or the narrow frame where it is located. The same principle applies to opening tools within tabs and folders/collections, except that to expand the tools within tabs, we need to click directly on the small arrows. There are keyboard shortcuts for many of these functions, and they will be mentioned throughout the book and available as a "cheat sheet". Try opening and closing everything you see to feel more comfortable with this functionality, and take a look at the following screenshot to guide you further:

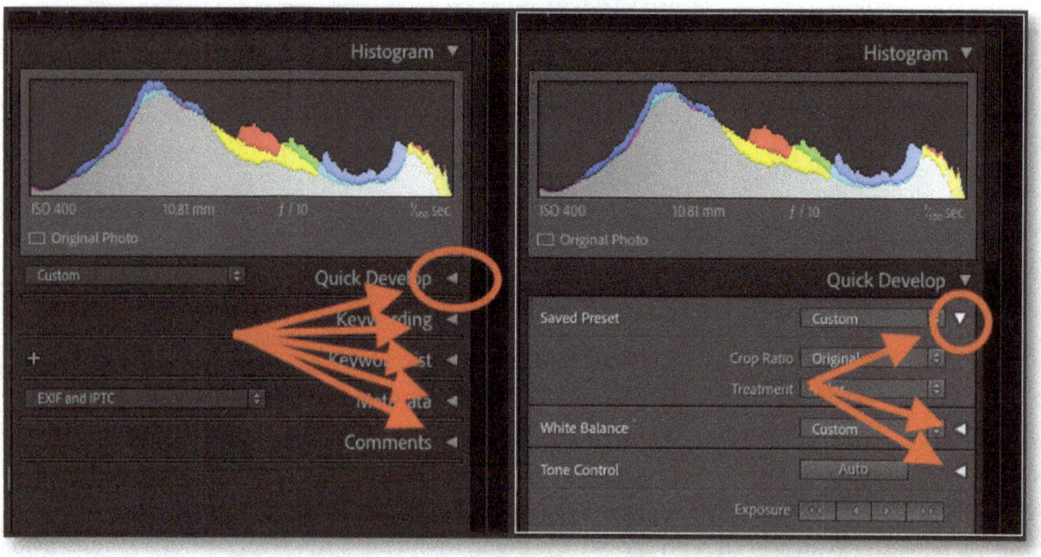

Figure 1.11 – Left: click these to open tabs; Right: click these to open tools within each tab

As we look through all the modules in this chapter, I encourage you to open and close each of the tabs to get a better sense of moving around Lightroom's workspace.

Without further ado, let's have a quick look through all the available modules.

Library module

This is our HQ within Lightroom. From here, we are managing our whole photography collection imported into Lightroom (importing is covered in *Chapter 2, Bring It All In – Importing Photographs into Lightroom*).

The left panel starts with the Navigator, but beyond that, it's essentially a list of all our imported folders and collections. The left panel also contains a few handy publishing tools for services such as Adobe Stock (yes—there is an option to earn some money through it as well), Facebook, or Flickr (the Library module is covered in *Chapter 3, Tools Available Within the Library Module*).

You can see an overview of the Library module in the following screenshot:

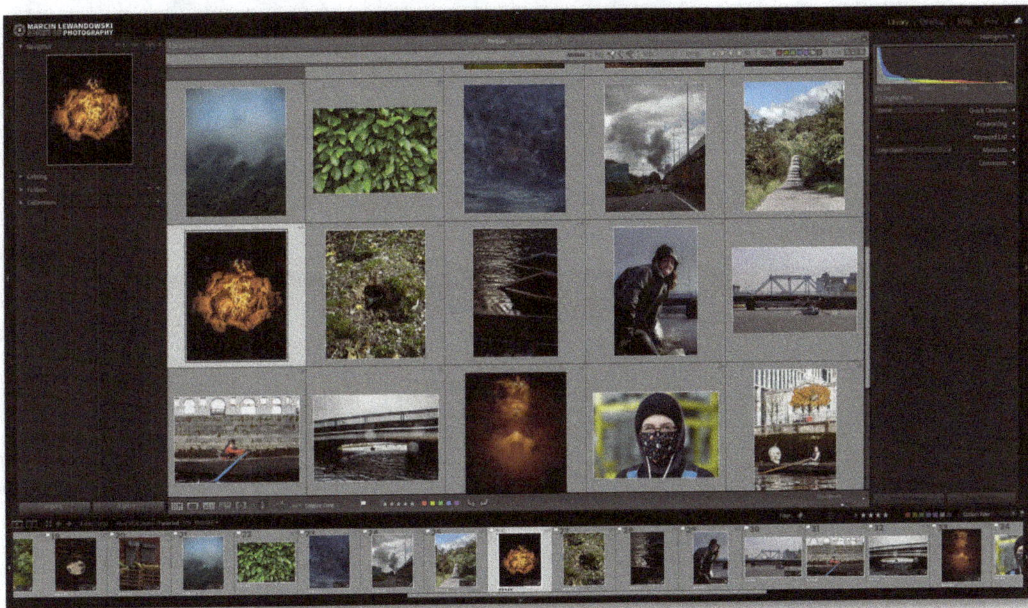

Figure 1.12 – Library module with all panels and tabs enabled: grid view

The Library module's right panel includes Histogram, Quick Develop tools that allow simple adjustments to be made to reviewed photographs, and tools for editing a picture's metadata. These right-side panel tabs are where we can add and manage keywords, captions, and copyright notices, change the time when photos were made, or add and amend **Global Positioning System (GPS)** data. All available information about each photograph can be accessed and changed through this panel, including mass changes applied to groups of photos.

The Library module's top part contains a panel with a powerful search tool to make queries based on fields available within photographs' metadata. The same top panel also includes a search engine based on the text and rating we applied to our photographs. You can see a metadata filter example in the following screenshot:

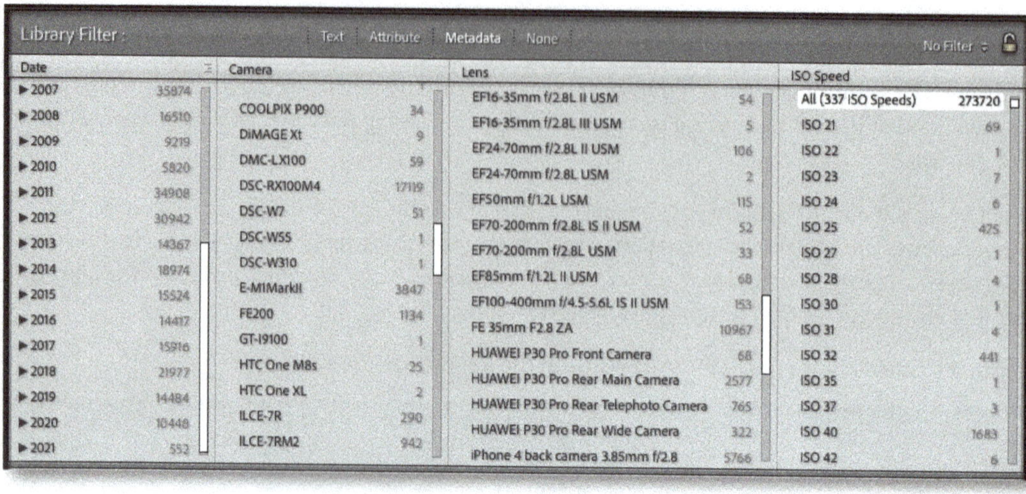

Figure 1.13 – Metadata filter example of query columns

On the bottom part of the screen, we can always find the filmstrip (also see *Figure 1.7*), as illustrated in the following screenshot:

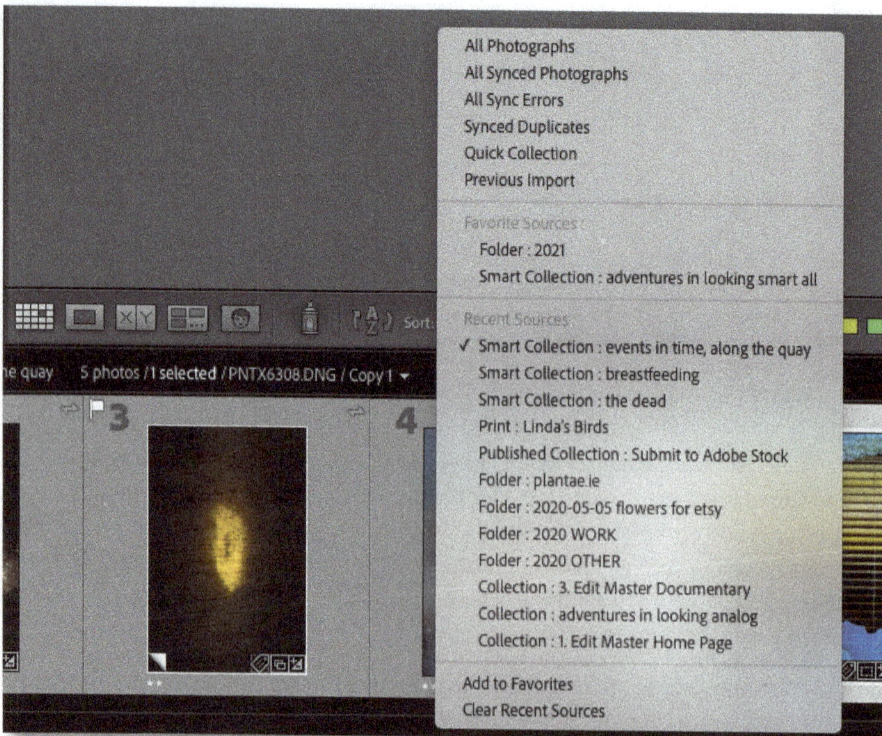

Figure 1.14 – Right-clicked toolbar reveals access to folders, collections, and so on

Directly above the ever-present filmstrip is a toolbar with access to a personal selection of folders, collections, and customizable filters to see only the images we choose. Again, the filmstrip is the only panel that remains unchanged throughout Lightroom and is accessible within every single module. The Library module offers us also an ad hoc slideshow functionality and control over the potential second screen.

Folders are a mirror image of a file-and-folder structure on the hard drive. When we import into Lightroom, we can choose how and where photographs import to keep everything structured. Suppose we already have an extensive library of images in perfect order. In that case, we can add them to Lightroom without changing their position on the hard drive. From that moment, Lightroom folders will reflect the folder structure of our hard drive. We can naturally choose different approaches for different files and folders. We can even edit the folders' content when external drives are not connected—that is a whole other topic, though described in detail later in this book.

Collections, on the other hand, do not have any significant physical presence on the hard drive. They are simply a visually presented database containing references to actual files. Collections can be made up of photographs present in folders located on various hard drives, and we will still be able to browse, reorder, and edit collections, even when our external hard drives are not connected.

This is an example of the Compare view, available in the Library module:

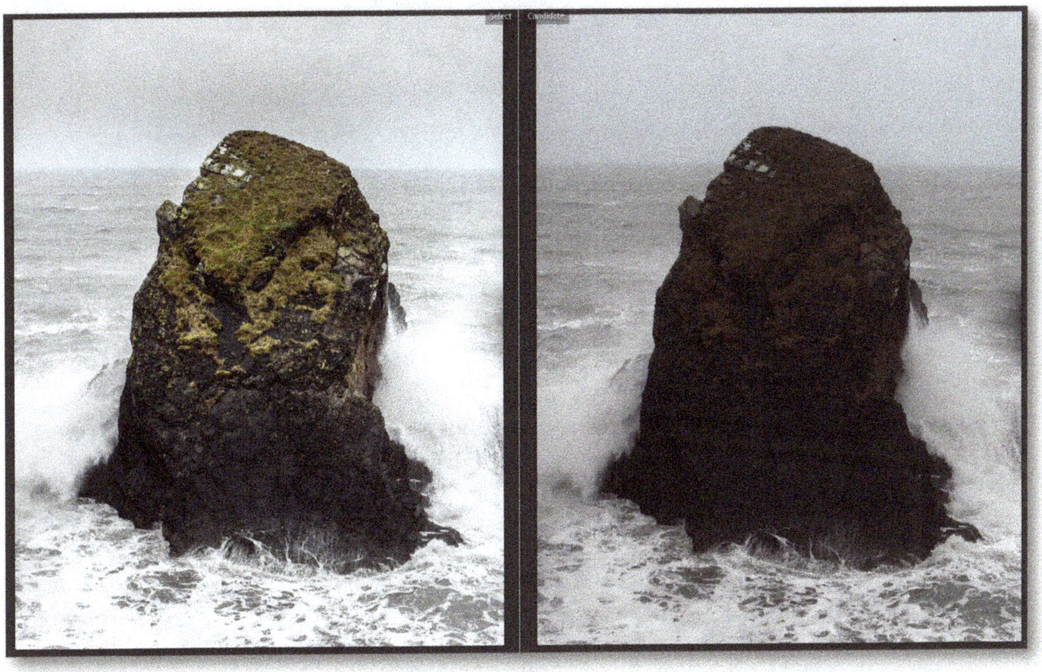

Figure 1.15 – Compare view with the developed photograph on the left and the original photo on the right

Develop module

This is the heart of Lightroom's workshop where most of the magic happens (we will be learning all about the Develop module in *Chapter 5, An Introduction to the Develop Module* and *Chapter 6, A Detailed View of the Develop Module's Functions*). You can see an overview of it here:

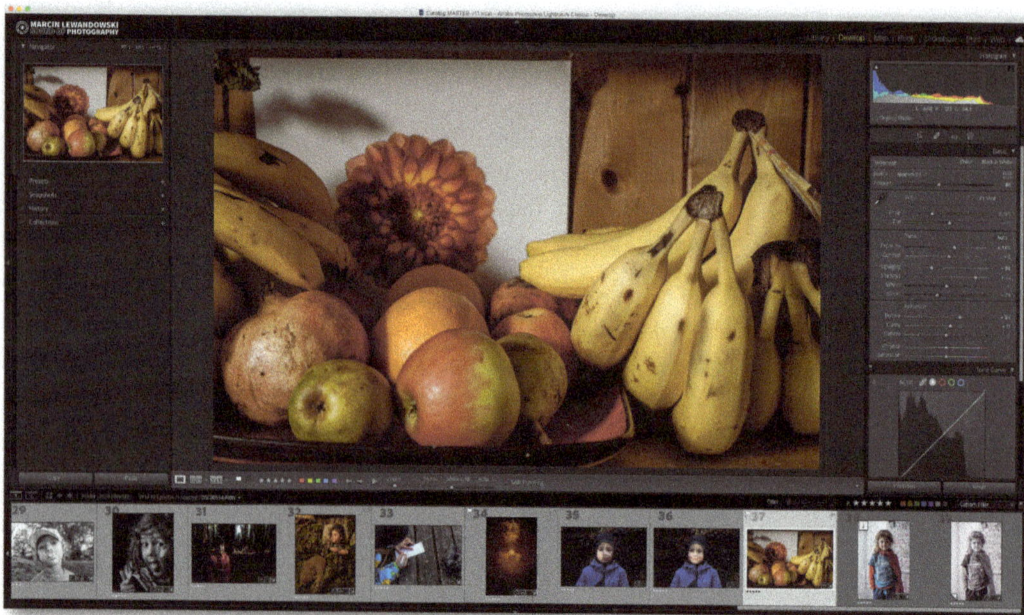

Figure 1.16 – Develop module with all panels enabled

The top-left corner starts again with the familiar Navigator. The three following tabs are exclusive to the Develop module and are outlined in more detail here:

- **Presets** is where you will store all different "looks and recipes" that can be later applied to any photographs.
- **Snapshots** will keep various versions and different looks of the same picture that we can choose from later when we cannot decide which definitive version to go for.
- The **History** tab is a time-machine type of tool. Lightroom keeps every single change we ever made to our photographs, and all this history is always accessible to us. We have unlimited undos always available to us. We can revisit each photograph to see how it looked at any stage of being developed.

We also have a tab called **Collection**. It is a familiar tab that we can access without leaving the Develop module.

The right-side panel starts with the familiar sight of the Histogram, which is by default in the same position as within the Library module. In the default view, the Histogram is followed by a collection of all available tools that we will use to adjust our photographs and give them the desired look.

The first tab contains all basic tone-correction tools, from exposure and contrast through more nuanced controls over shadows and highlights to photo enhancers such as clarity or vibrance. This is just a peek at all available tools; going further into menus and opening subsequent tabs, we will be able to do the following:

- Correct an image's tonality with the Curves tool.
- Adjust the colors of a photograph with **Hue, Saturation, and Luminance** (**HSL**).
- Colorize highlights and shadows of a picture with Color Grading.
- Work on sharpness, reduce noise, and apply lens-specific corrections.
- Transform the geometry of our photographs.
- Add vignetting or grain.
- Apply camera-specific color calibration.

> **Note**
>
> Let's not forget about the Crop overlay, Spot removal, Red eye correction, and Masking tools just below the Histogram at the top of this panel. We will be using adjustment brushes for dodging, burning, and other localized work, from darkening a sky that is too bright to removing blemishes and softening the skin on portraits. That is an extensive list of capabilities, and all of them are provided in a package that is easy to use and instantly gratifying. All adjustments and effects are visible straight away and easily changed, adjusted, or completely reversed. All changes can be immediately applied to all the photographs we choose in just one click, which is an incredibly powerful feature, saving hours of work. We will look in detail at each of these functions in *Chapter 5, An Introduction to the Develop Module,* and *Chapter 6, A Detailed View of the Develop Module's Functions.*
>
> **Tip**: The fastest way to enter the Develop module is to press the "*D*" key on the keyboard.

Map module

This one is quite self-explanatory—all photographs in your library containing geographical coordinates will be distributed on a map to help us find photographs that we might be looking for. The task of pinpointing "that one" photograph might sound easy when our library is still small, but after years of photographing, the library builds up and makes things harder to find.

You can see an overview of the Map module in the following screenshot:

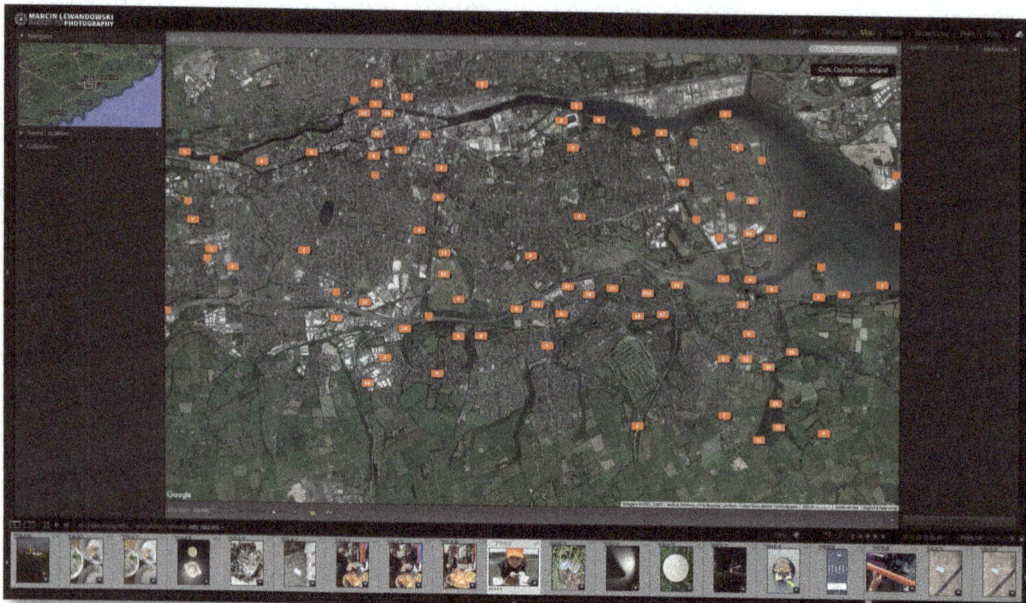

Figure 1.17 – Map module with all panels enabled: synced smartphone folder view

The Map module can help us to locate folders we are searching for. The familiar tab with all collections is at our disposal on the screen's right side—more about the Map module in *Chapter 9*, *Slideshow, Map, and Web Modules*.

Book module

This is the best tool for creating book layouts without the need to learn any additional graphic software.

You can see an overview of the Book module here:

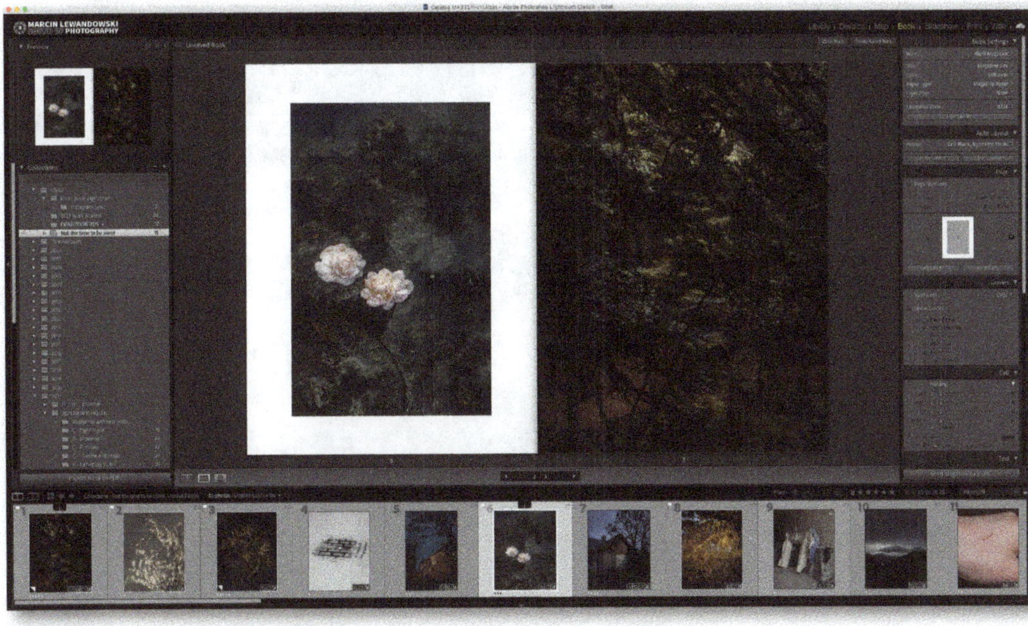

Figure 1.18 – Book module with all panels enabled with sample layout

It is as easy as "choose-place-print", with all adjustments to the layout that you might think of in-between. Once the design is finalized, it can be saved as print optimized files or sent directly to Blurb for printing as a book or magazine in multiple sizes and aspect ratios. More about the Book module can be found in *Chapter 9, Slideshow, Map, and Web Modules.*

Slideshow module

Forget PowerPoint or Keynote. The process of creating visually striking slideshows within Lightroom is as simple as choosing the right collection and pressing **GO**.

You can see an overview of the Slideshow module in the following screenshot:

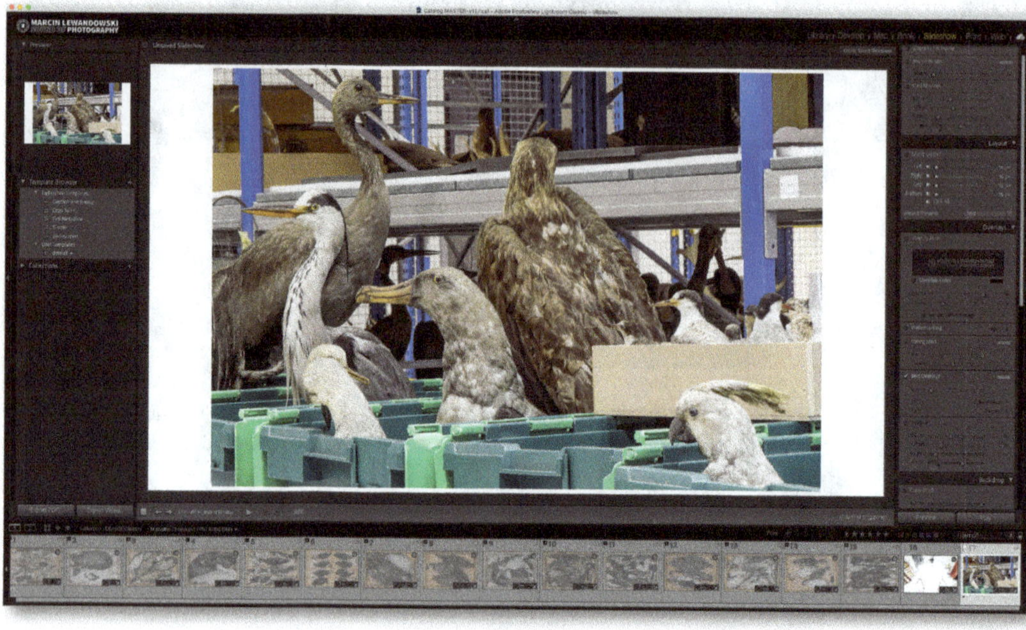

Figure 1.19 – Slideshow module with all panels enabled

As with most other modules, we are greeted with a large view of selected work accompanied by the **Collections** tab on the left and current panel-specific adjustments on the right. We can use the slideshow module to export **Portable Document Format** (**PDF**) files or videos, and we can run a slideshow on a secondary screen while we work on our photographs. We'll learn all about this module in *Chapter 9, Slideshow, Map, and Web Modules,* of this book.

Print module

Just as with all other modules, Print also has the Collections module available on the right-side panel, and a template browser accompanies it to save our print-specific layout designs.

You can see an overview of the Print module here:

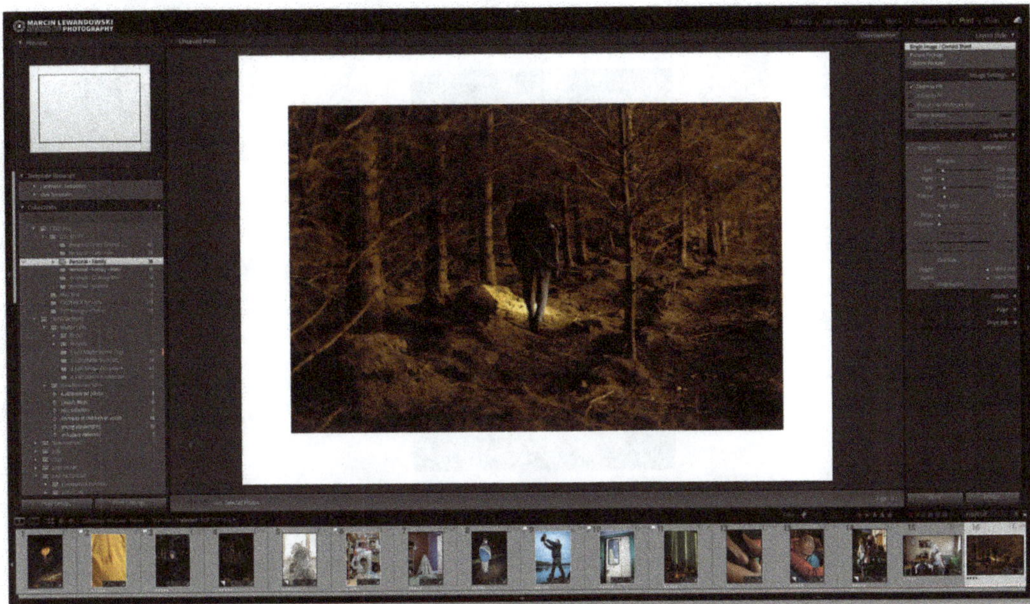

Figure 1.20 – Print module with all panels enabled

As with each module, it also offers the ever-present filmstrip on the bottom of the panel. The right-side panel has all the necessary tools to adjust the size, placement, and appearance of images we print. Adjustments include everything from margin sizes, multiple-copies picture packages, borders, watermarking, and color management, down to the use of **International Color Consortium** (**ICC**) profiles. It is a precise and very flexible module to work with. We can prepare print files in any chosen specification for printing with an outside service as much as we can do it ourselves. We'll learn about this module in *Chapter 8, Get them All Out - Using the Print and Book Modules.*

Web module

If you do not have a website, this module has everything you need to build one. Simple customization and the ability to create templates mean that you can build a website in no time at all, including direct upload via the **File Transfer Protocol** (**FTP**).

You can see an overview of the Web module here:

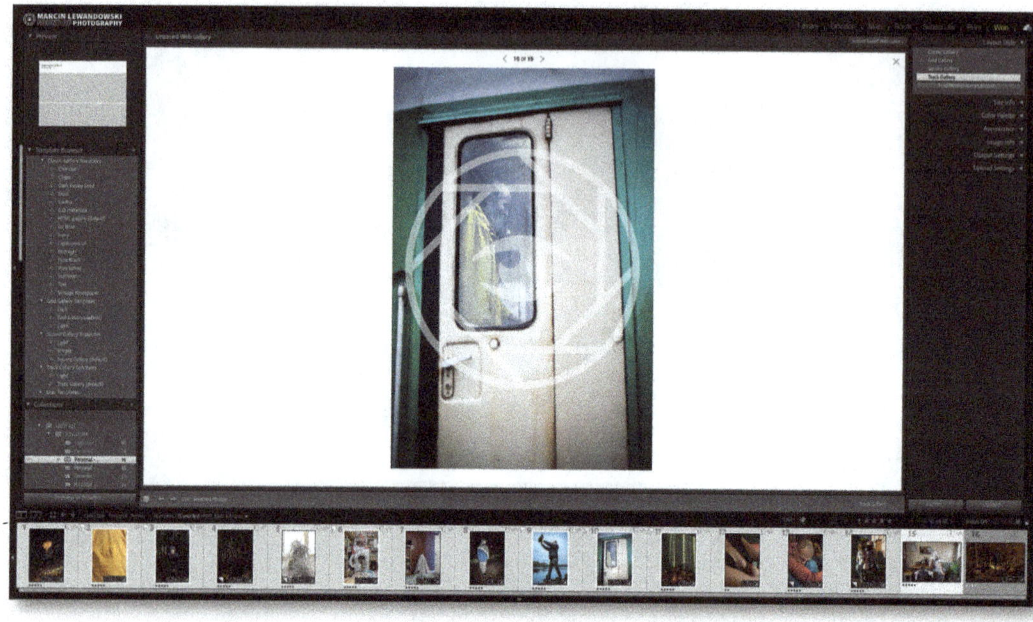

Figure 1.21 – Web module with all panels enabled

We can access all Lightroom modules from the menu in the top-right corner through the **File** menu and multiple keyboard shortcuts. Please see a handy reference sheet with all keyboard shortcuts at the end of this book.

Customizing Lightroom

This is an excellent place to mention the possible customization of Lightroom, which can be done on many levels—from purely aesthetical to functional. Regarding the practical part, we will be mentioning all of its aspects as we go through each panel. However, in a nutshell, practically everything can be temporarily disabled and removed from our view to create a clutter-free environment that suits our needs. Some tabs can even be moved around, especially within the Develop module. Please look at the following example with the default Module Picker and Develop module layout versus an example of a simplified Module Picker and changed layout and content of the Develop module's right panel.

See the following screenshot and read on to learn how to change it yourself:

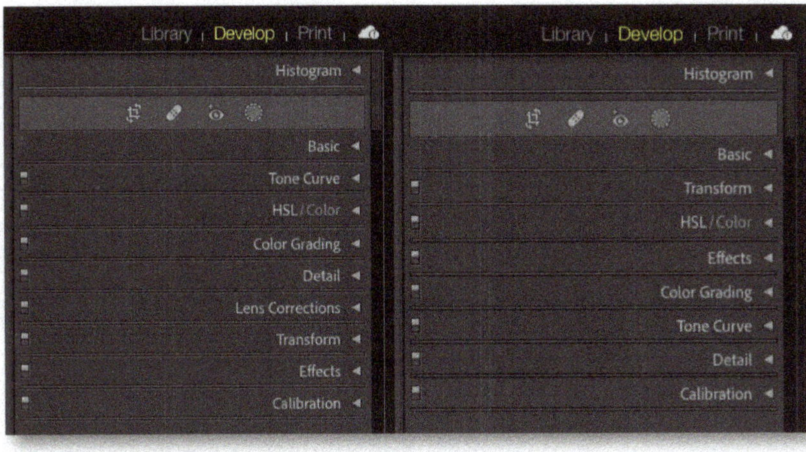

Figure 1.22 – Default Module Picker layout on the left and customized version on the right

When it comes to visual customization, we can change end panels and identity plates. Both of these are fairly simple operations.

We can access the end panels' settings through the **Preferences** menu (also accessed by "⌘"). Just go to **Lightroom Classic** > **Preferences** > **Interface** > **End Marks** > **Go To Panel End Marks Folder**. This folder is by default empty, but once you save any `.png` files in there, they will be available to use as end marks. We can use something purely aesthetical such as a logo or something more functional, such as a reminder about keyboard shortcuts or keywording principles; our imagination is the limit!

We have the same freedom with the identity plate, which will be populated with our Adobe **identifier** (**ID**) by default. This can be changed by right-clicking anywhere on the Module Picker's left side. From the pop-up menu, we choose the **Edit Identity Plate...** option, which gives us full control over its look. You can see an illustration of this in *Figure 1.23*.

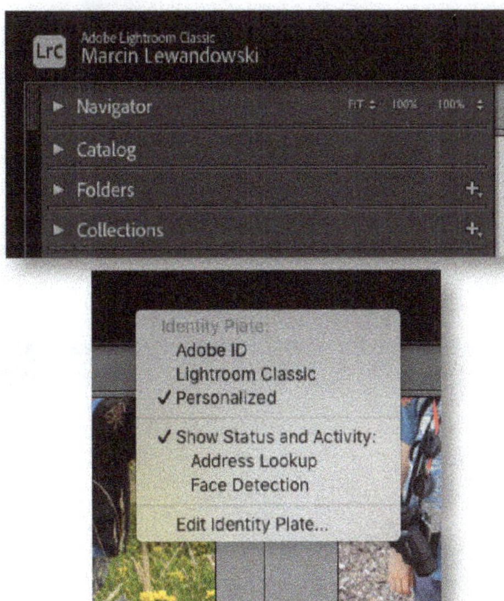

Figure 1.23 – Default Identity Plate example and Accessing Identity Plate Editor menu

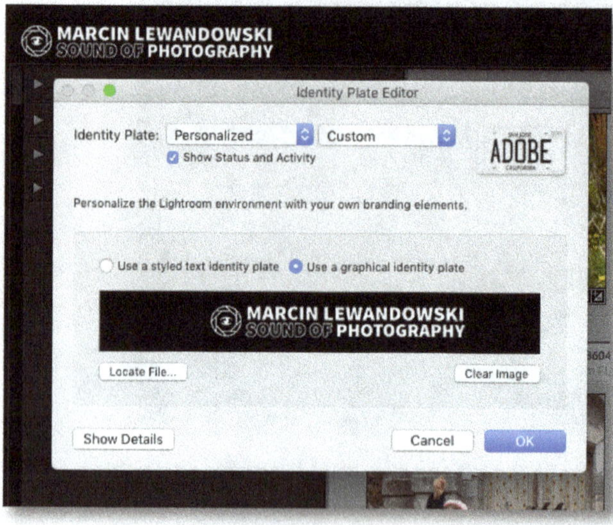

Figure 1.24A

Just as with end marks, the files you want to use must be in `.png` format, and once you decide what you want to use, just click **Locate File...** and choose the image you want. I suggest you start experimenting with a picture that's not taller than 250 **pixels (px)** so that it can fit snuggly in the corner. Once we pick our branding, this is also the place to change the font face and font size for the Module Picker. If you can't see it, click on the **Show Details** button in the bottom-left corner, as illustrated in *Figure 1.24A*.

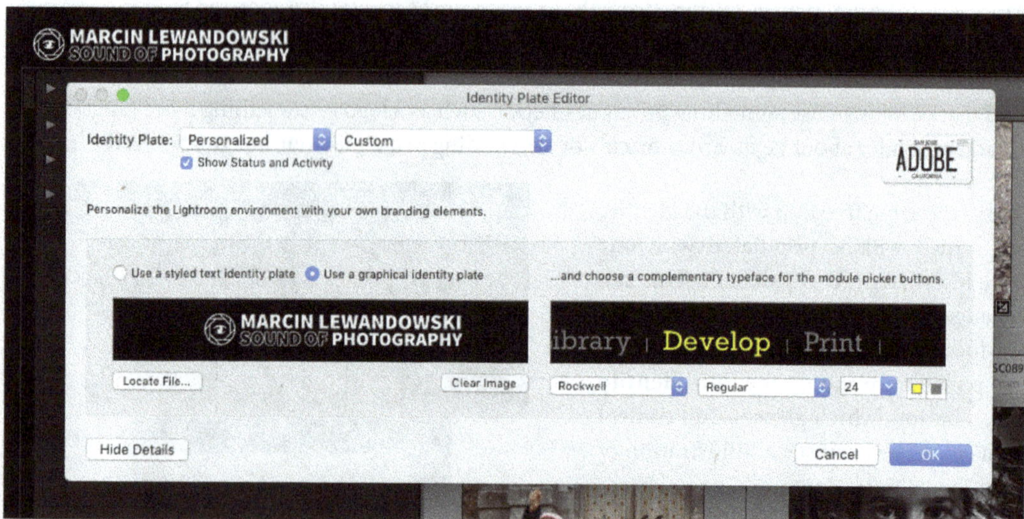

Figure 1.24B – Identity Plate Editor

Summary

Even though we didn't go into much detail in this chapter, you can see that it is a very comprehensive tool that will help any photographer in their work or hobby. Even if you only use Lightroom for asset management, which we will cover in the next two chapters describing Import dialog and the Library module, you will save a ton of time and develop a way of thinking about your collection that is impossible outside of Lightroom. If you travel a lot, Lightroom will help in tracking your trips. If you print your photographs, Lightroom will help you manage that process, just as it will if you are designing books or presentations. Even simple touches such as the customization of your logo can be beneficial—think about showing your work to a client on your laptop/tablet and always having your name and the name of your website present; this can be a powerful branding tool. The remote usage capabilities and syncing can be advantageous, too—Lightroom offers it all within the same package and without the need for any plugins or additional software. Saying all this, the true power of Lightroom lies in its Develop module, where we will polish our photographs and make them stand out from the crowd, quite often with just a few simple clicks.

As you can see, Lightroom is a very capable piece of software designed for photographers to make their work easier and more enjoyable. Now, it's time to learn how to utilize all of these tools to the photographer's benefit.

2

Bring It All In – Importing Photographs into Lightroom

If, by this point, you are using only your computer's native software to browse files or maybe work with something such as Photoshop or Bridge, you will have to develop a new way of thinking about managing your assets. To work on any photographs in Lightroom, we must first import them, which means that we need to tell Lightroom where they are. By doing this, we will create a database with our files' locations, and from that point, we will be able to not only work on them using Lightroom but also move folders or delete images from within Lightroom itself. As we mentioned earlier, Lightroom offers a non-destructive process of working with photographs. By creating a database called Catalog, Lightroom leaves our original files untouched, adds a description of what we want to do with them, and visually displays the results. We need to create this library by importing images into Lightroom and pointing it to the files we want to edit.

The topics we are going to cover in this chapter are as follows:

- Opening Lightroom for the first time
- Understanding the import dialog functionality
- A few tips and tricks to remember

Opening Lightroom for the first time

When we start Lightroom for the first time, it asks us to either create a new catalog or locate an existing one. Whether you have put any thought into this decision or not, we will go through the whole process so that everyone understands the aftermath of this choice.

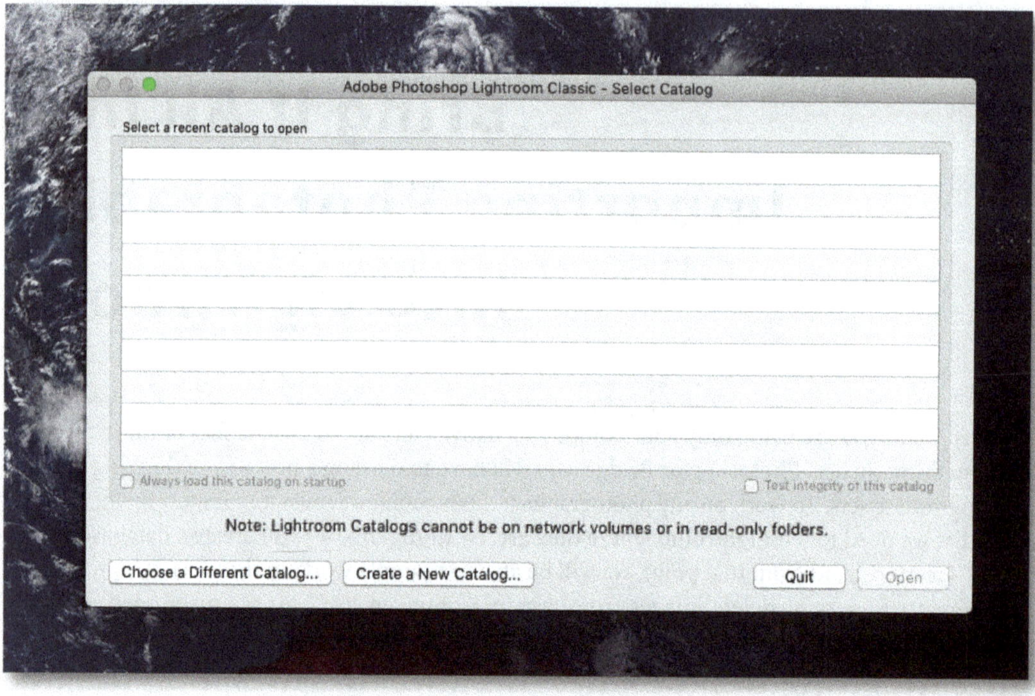

Figure 2.1 – The Select Catalog dialog

This catalog that Lightroom asks us to create is a database that will house references to all the photographs we will ever import into Lightroom in the future. Once we create our catalog, which will have the `lrcat` file extension, Lightroom will also create a few additional files with the same base name and added words – `Sync`, `Previews`, `Smart Previews`, and `Helper`. These files will hold information that helps us to keep Lightroom working as smoothly as possible.

This is how it looks on my computer.

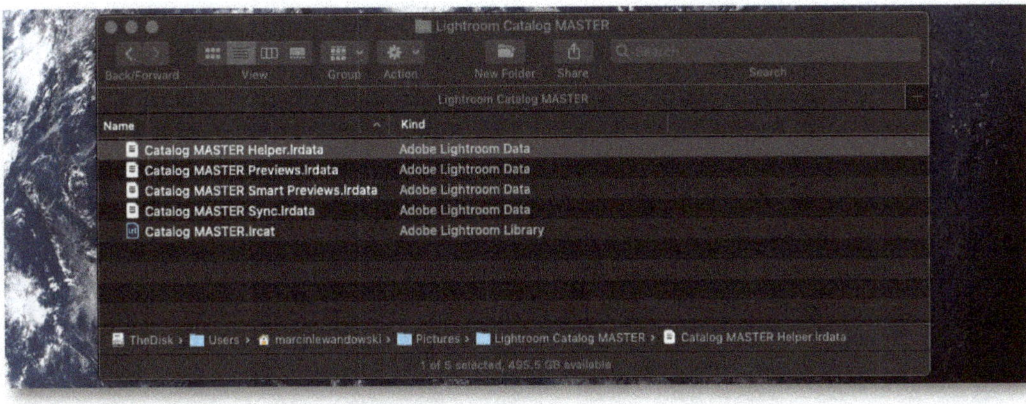

Figure 2.2 – The catalog structure

Our first and last catalog

I use just one catalog to house all of my photographs, and after testing various catalog combinations over the years, I found it most efficient for the way I work. I tried separate catalogs for work and personal photographs, which was not ideal because some personal photos may crossover to work and vice versa – especially things that I planned to use solely for blogging, Instagram, or other social media. I tried a setup with a catalog named OTHER for these "crossover" category images, but this just proved to add unnecessary work to my workflow. Other experiments involved creating separate catalogs year by year and even different catalogs for large projects. Again, it all proved to be just a waste of time, causing a lot of switching between catalogs when I wanted to find a particular picture or move something across. Now, I structure everything inside Lightroom in a way that reflects my work. I have separate folders for personal photographs, folders for commissioned work, and different folders for anything that doesn't fit into these two categories – that is, multi-year projects or things destined only for social media use. I always have everything in one catalog, and as long as I maintain good housekeeping within that catalog, it all works smoothly.

Whatever you might decide works best for you at a later stage when you know Lightroom better, for now, let's start with the single catalog structure and import the first set of photographs into Lightroom Classic.

Setting up general preferences before starting the import dialog

There is one more thing I would like you to know before we go into the actual import module. Please go to **Menu** > **Lightroom Classic** > **Preferences** > **General**.

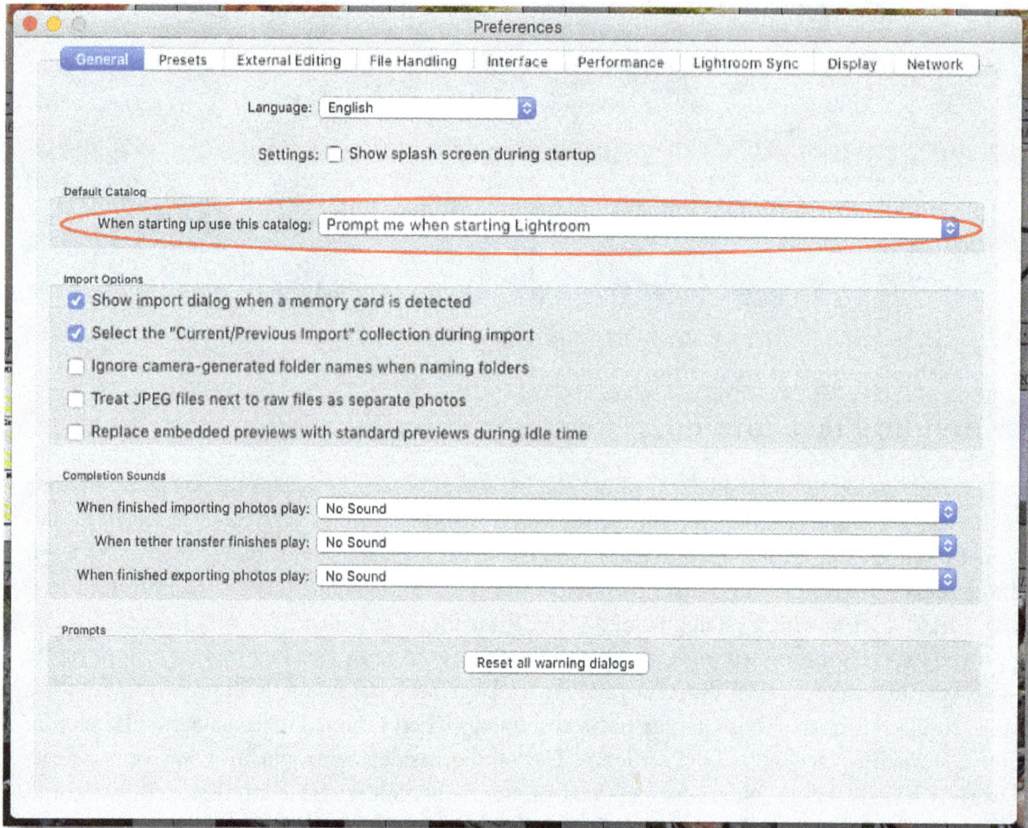

Figure 2.3 – General preferences

At the very top, you can change the language and turn off the splash screen during startup – this is entirely up to you. After that, we have an option to choose the catalog that Lightroom will open during startup. I suggest that at this time, you choose **Prompt me when starting Lightroom** to use it as a reminder that Lightroom works with catalogs, folders, collections, and so on. You can change it later to suit your style of work.

In the second paragraph of this window, you will see an option called **Show import dialog when a memory card is detected**. If the box next to this sentence is checked, it means that each time we insert a memory card into our computer's reader, Lightroom will automatically open the import dialog.

The same box's second line reads **Select the "Current/Previous Import" collection during import**. With this box checked, Lightroom will go automatically to the collection of currently imported photographs upon the start of the import process; if we don't check this box, Lightroom will stay within the selection we viewed before starting the import process, and we will have to navigate to this collection manually. I almost always keep it checked when importing anything because I usually look at the photographs straight away, but your workflow might be different; I just want to make you aware of it.

The third option is **Ignore camera-generated folder names when naming folders**. There is no significance to this box as long as we understand what's happening during the import process and set everything we want in the import panel. Checking this box means that if you import everything at once without proper management, Lightroom will import all images on a memory card regardless of the folder structure created by the camera. For some camera systems, new folder creation can be set in intervals of hundreds or thousands of photographs, by date, and so on. I never have it checked and always set everything manually in the import module itself. For now, let's keep it unchecked – you can always come back here and change it.

The fourth option is **Treat JPEG files next to RAW files as separate photos**. If you shoot RAW and JPG and want to keep both files during import, you have to keep this option checked; if you keep it unchecked, Lightroom will treat JPG files as duplicates and discard them.

Lastly, for this part, we have the **Replace embedded previews with standard previews during idle time** option. It is a great function, but its potential usability will be impacted by choosing how we import the photographs; thus, we leave this unchecked for the moment and come back to it later.

Having the preceding covered lets us slot that memory card into the reader or attach the camera to our computer and bring our photographs into Lightroom.

Understanding the import dialog functionality

If you checked the box for **Show import dialog when a memory card is detected**, then the import module will open automatically. If you didn't tick that box earlier, click on the **Import** button in the bottom left corner of the Library module's bottom left corner.

Alternatively, you can even drag images from outside of Lightroom and drop them into the Library module to open the import dialog. I find the last option helpful when I want to bring into Lightroom a particular image I just downloaded and I don't feel like browsing folders on my computer from within the import module. Still, I'm getting ahead of myself here.

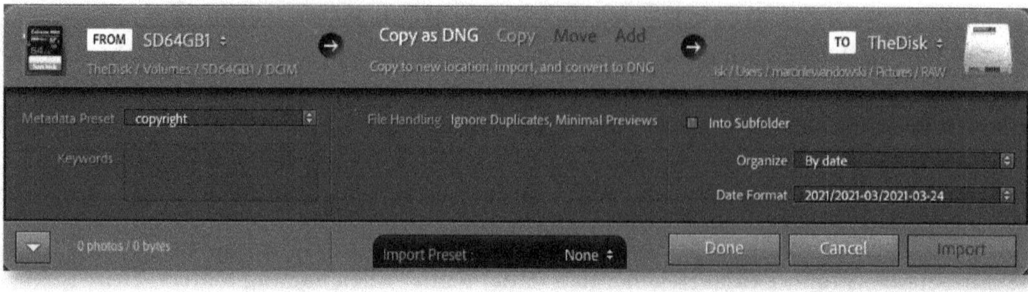

Figure 2.4 – A miniature version of the import dialog

Default view

If you see the miniature version of the import dialog, like the one illustrated in *Figure 2.4*, then click on the arrow in the bottom left corner to open it up to the full view. And voila, we are in, and we'll see that it's all simpler than it might look right now. Let's start at the beginning.

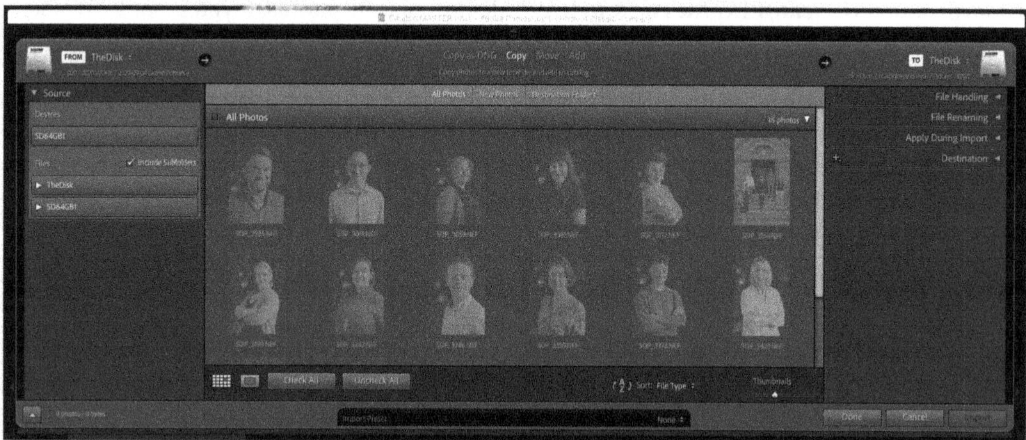

Figure 2.5 – The full import dialog

The import dialog is split into three main parts, as are all Lightroom modules. The left-side panel is where we choose our source, from where we want to import our photographs. The middle of the import dialog shows photos that we will be importing and a few associated tools. The right panel is where we choose our photographs' destination and any additional settings to apply during import.

The left panel

We start off with the left panel and the options we have under it that help us choose our source.

Source

Starting with the left panel, we have a few ways to choose where to import from.

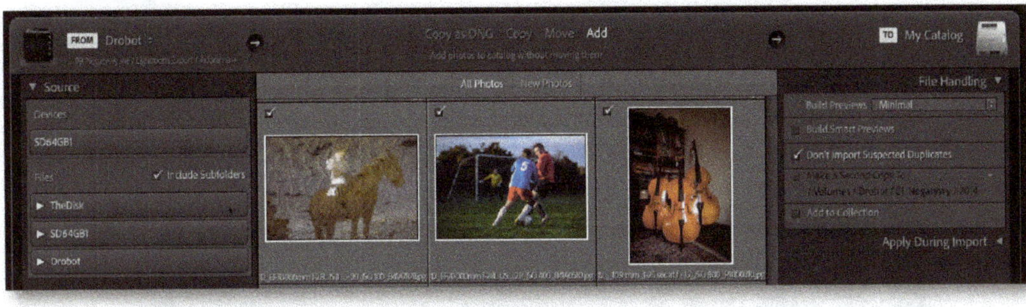

Figure 2.6 – The import dialog top part with an external drive named Robot chosen

Even though Lightroom will automatically choose the inserted memory card as a default source, we have a choice and can change it by clicking on the memory card symbol. You will notice that the corner changes color to a slightly brighter hue when we hover the cursor over it; we can click that to choose any source currently present or attached to our computer, memory cards, hard drives, and so on. I never use that for access and prefer to go directly to the **Source** tool placed directly below. Typically, you will see your freshly inserted memory card at the top, above other locations.

I say typically, as, now and then, your computer might not see the inserted memory card. In a scenario like that (and after making sure you have correctly ejected the card if necessary), re-insert the card into your card reader or turn on your camera; this should show the new source on top in a matter of seconds in the **Devices** field. By clicking on the memory card name (it will change hue to a lighter gray), we choose it as a source from which to import.

Devices versus files

Instead of choosing our memory card from the devices, we have an option to select it from **Files** just below it. Choosing from the **Files** tab will add an **Include Subfolders** option. It is needed to cover the fact that some of us choose cameras that split files on memory cards in folders of hundreds or create a new folder each day. Some cameras, such as Sony models, hide files in unusual places; by checking this box, we can make sure that Lightroom sees them all as ready for import.

We can also, by "*CTRL* clicking", choose multiple folders to import from a few of them. In addition to the memory card, we can also choose to import files we already have on our computer's hard drive. To do that, we select our hard drive tab and then find the folders we want to import. It is handy for importing already existing collections of photographs. One more thing to notice in this section is the

Eject after import box - checking it will eject our memory card after importing all photographs, so we don't have to think about manually ejecting it later. We can remove the memory card straight away after the import finishes. It is a tiny but convenient option, working well whenever I need to import multiple memory cards, when it speeds up the process, or when I forget to pull the card out and it's sitting in the reader, ejected. This way, I don't need to worry about accidentally frying the card and irreversibly damaging it a few hours later when pulling it out in a hurry.

At any time during this process, we can right-click on one of the sources to get more info about them, show their location on our hard drive, and choose to include/exclude subfolders. We can also eject the memory card/external memory or even change its icon, which is what I just did to illustrate it in the following screenshot. You can change this icon by right-clicking on your device (in this case, a SanDisk 64GB card) and saving a `.png` file of your choice in the **Device Icons** folder, which that action will open. You also need to rename this file to match your device's name.

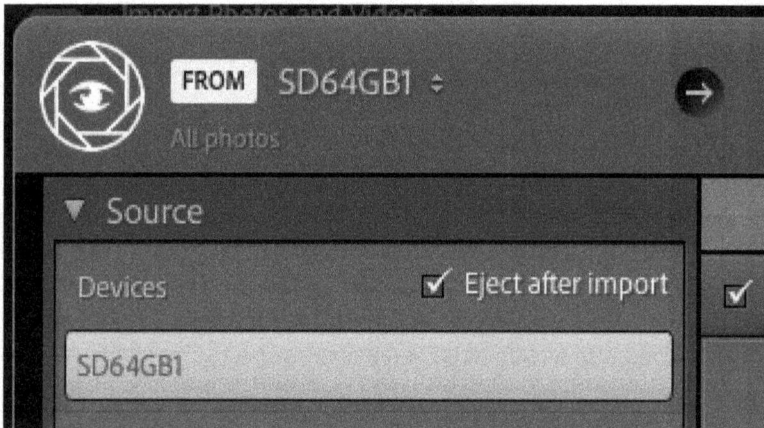

Figure 2.07 – The changed icon of the memory card

The top panel

Continuing clockwise from the left panel we just discussed, we arrive at the top part of the import dialog, which gives us a few options on what to do with the files we want to bring into Lightroom.

Copy or move – that is the question

The most common choice is **Copy**.

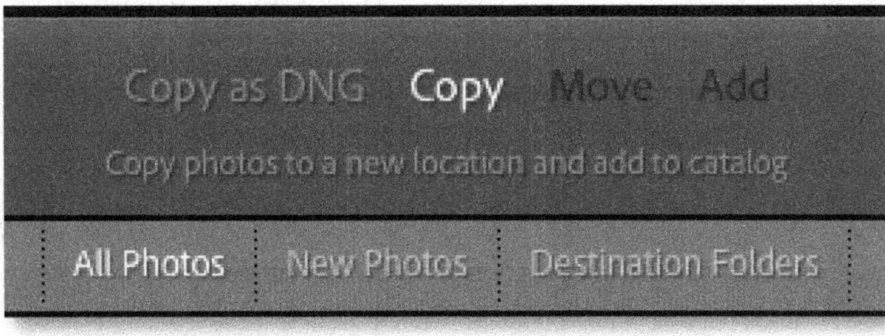

Figure 2.8 – The Copy option highlighted

This option is for copying images we pick from the location of our choice (in this case, a memory card) to another location of our choice (in this case, a folder on a hard drive). Just before that, we have a **Copy as DNG** option.

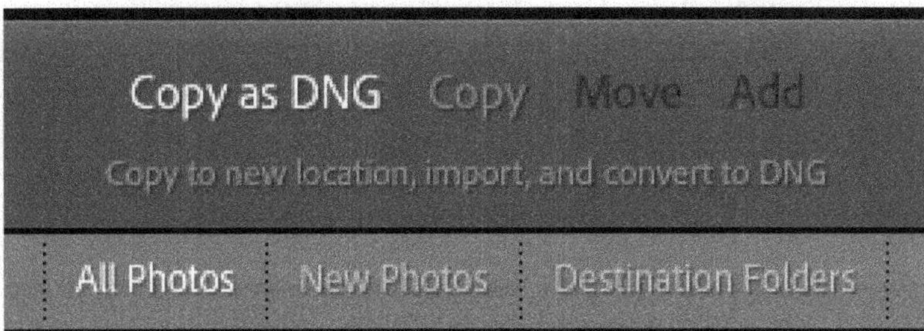

Figure 2.9 – The Copy as DNG option Highlighted

DNG files

DNG might need a few words of explanation, so let me go into detail; if you already know all about it, you can skip to the next paragraph. **DNG** means **Digital Negative**, and it's an Adobe-made and patented open source, lossless RAW file format. There is a short list of advantages and disadvantages that we need to consider when thinking about choosing this option. First of all, here are some benefits:

- DNG files are slightly smaller than our initial RAW pictures, and so we will be saving about 2–3 MB on a file from a 26 MP camera. In the long run, that is a lot of space.
- DNG is an Adobe-made format, so Lightroom and Photoshop handle these files better.
- Some actions within Lightroom will work much faster compared to RAW formats, especially within the Library module.

Here are the disadvantages:

- Converting files into DNG might be time-consuming, especially on slower computers, and with a large number of pictures, you will have to test your particular setup to see the difference. Another disadvantage is that some of the metadata might get lost.
- As you can imagine, each camera manufacturer has a different idea about storing different picture data. Things such as the focus point or other manufacturer-specific details might get lost in translation. It is not a deal-breaker for me, but it might be for you.
- Lastly, what I think is the most significant difference is how DNG stores any Lightroom edits versus RAW edits. As we already mentioned, Lightroom is non-destructive editing software, and all changes are stored as additional data. In the case of RAW files, this data is stored as `.xmp` (sidecar) files, containing all the changes we made. In the case of DNG files, these changes are stored within the file itself, which means two things – we will have far fewer files to manage on the hard drive, but there is a slightly larger possibility of these files being corrupted during the read/write processes. It is a puzzle that you will have to resolve to decide which option is better for you.

For now, I suggest we go with the RAW files, and if you later decide to work with DNG format across the board, no worries – there is a tool within Lightroom to convert already existing files en masse. You can access it by going to **Library** > **Convert Photos to DNG**; for now, let's get back to the import dialog.

Move and add

We looked at the **Copy as DNG** and **Copy** options, but there are two more – **Move** and **Add**. These two options are only available when we are working on files already present on the hard drive. When importing photos from a memory card, these two options will be inaccessible.

Figure 2.10 – The Move option highlighted

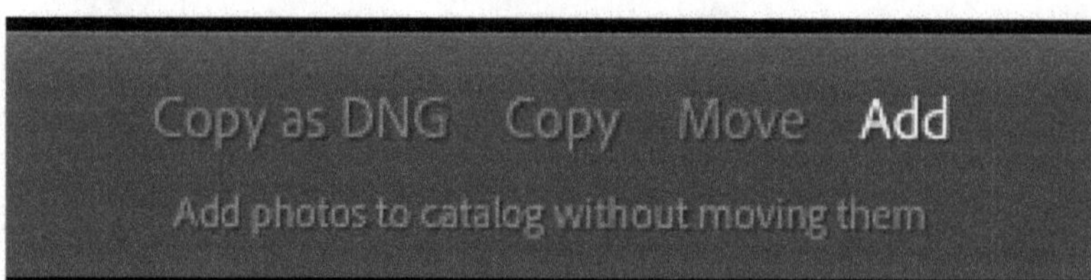

Figure 2.11 – The Add option highlighted

Choosing the **Move** option will move all images from the source folder we just picked on the left into the destination folder we will select on the right side. It is an excellent option if we want, for example, to bring structure to this library and turn a big folder of unsorted photographs into a group of day-by-day folders. In that scenario, we can use Lightroom to create these new folders depending on the photographs' creation date and move them into their new location. I think it is a great function; however, I don't use it myself. It is probably professional paranoia of not being in total control of everything that's happening on my hard drive. In any scenario, I always let Lightroom copy all the files, check whether Lightroom copied everything, and then delete them from their source.

The **Add** function imports photographs we choose into Lightroom but leaves them in their original location. Remember when we mentioned earlier about importing into Lightroom a library of images where we might have a structure of folders that we want to keep and be available in the same arrangement within Lightroom – this is the place to do it. There are also other scenarios when you might find this function helpful – that is, I use the **Add** function when importing files from the downloads folder and don't want to interfere with my main structure of files. In that scenario, Lightroom will "take note" of the downloads folder's location and make it available in our library.

Viewing options

Under these four options, and still above the photographs that we are importing, we find three options for how they are displayed as follows.

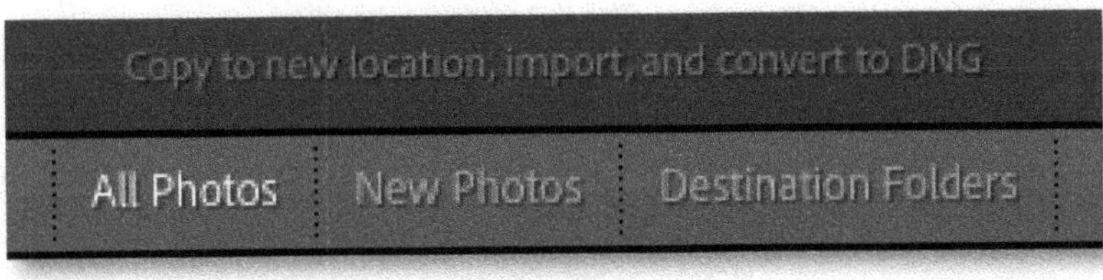

Figure 2.12 – The viewing options

The **All Photos** function does what it says on the tin – it shows all photographs present in the source medium we chose to import from. They will be all visible without any folder structure and sorted in the order we choose in the bottom bar, just below the actual photographs. When importing from a memory card, I most often keep this sorted by **Capture Time** unless I know I have some video files mixed in with photographs; then, I sort it by media type to work with them separately. Some of the photographs in our source location might appear dimmed; this happens when we choose the **Don't Import Suspected Duplicates** option. It looks for pictures with the same original filename, same capture time, and the same file size as photos already in our Lightroom library. It's a great option if we, for example, forget to format the memory card and shoot more new photographs on it. The **Don't Import Suspected Duplicates** function will ensure that the photos we already imported are not imported again.

The **New Photos** view will ignore all duplicate photographs grayed out in the previous view and display only photos that are not yet on our hard drive.

Destination folders will display the same photos as **All Photos**, but it will split the view into sections, reflecting the structure we are choosing in the right-side panel, which we will discuss in the next paragraph.

The right panel

The right-side panel splits into four tabs, and we will look at them in order of their appearance.

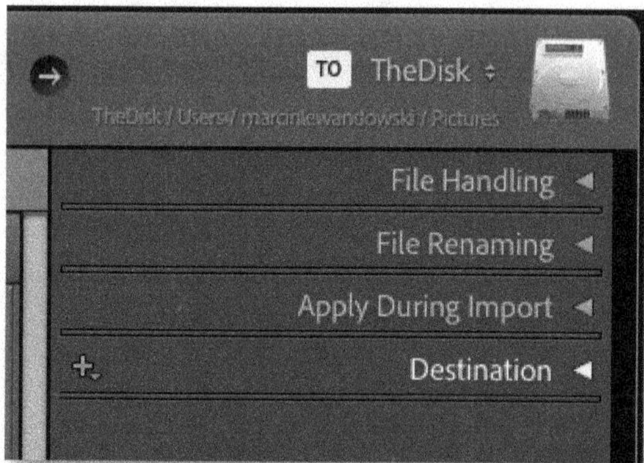

Figure 2.13 – The right panel tabs

File handling – building previews

To access this option, go to **File Handling** > **Build Previews**. This option will hugely impact our workflow with the imported set on a few different levels:

- If we want absolute performance in terms of availability to scroll through thumbnails, then **Build Previews** > **Minimal** is the way to go. With this option chosen, Lightroom will make the smallest possible previews of our photographs and only start rendering larger-size previews when required.

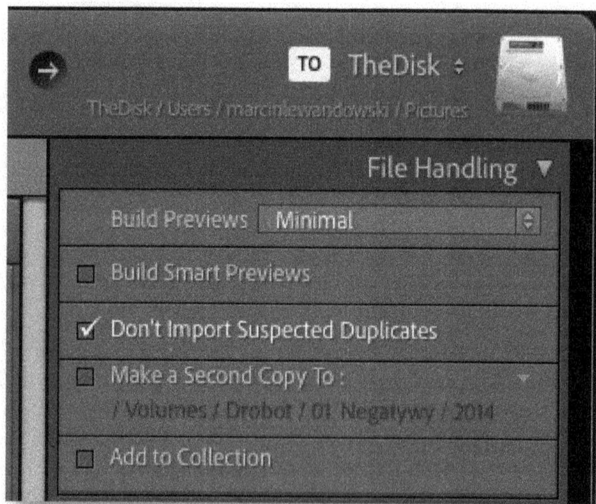

Figure 2.14 – The File Handling tab

- **Build Previews** > **Embedded and sidecar** – this option renders the largest previews generated by the camera. It's a slightly slower process but still much faster than the next ones we will mention.
- **Build Previews** > **Standard** – this option renders images ready for viewing at the *fit* zoom level, which is almost a full-screen view. We can easily adjust the size of standard previews in Lightroom Classic by going to **Catalog Settings** > **File Handling** > **Standard Preview Size**. A smaller size equals a faster rendering speed, while a larger size equals a slower rendering of each photograph.
- The last option is **Build Previews** > **1:1**, which builds previews at a 100% view of the actual pixels. This process will take the most time, but once completed, zooming each photograph to a 100% view will be readily available at the click of a mouse.

I approach these differently, depending on the situation, but when I need to start working on images straight away, standard previews are my preferred way. Having them available, I can run through them in a full-screen size, with Lightroom rendering 1:1 previews only for the images, which I'm zooming in on during the editing process. It is not the fastest way to import images, but it is the fastest way to review work. I look at it as an investment in saving time down the line during the editing process.

Build Smart Previews

Smart previews are miniature yet fully editable versions of our RAW files that we can edit even when original files are not accessible. They are made based on Adobe's lossy version of their DNG format. To give us a size perspective, the RAW file from a 26 MP camera is about 30 MB in size, so, after a full day in the field, we might have about 1,500 images to go through; that's approximately 40 GB and often more, especially for sport and wedding photographers, but I'm digressing here. The same files in their smart preview versions will take up about 1.5 GB. It is a huge difference, especially when we plan to work with these photographs on the go, using a smartphone, tablet, or even a laptop with a small-size **SSD** (short for **solid state drive**). The part about it that I like is that we can export developed pictures – up to a specific size, that is. We can import images to our "master computer" and then work on them on a different device without the need for access to the originals. It is also a great way to work on photographs that we might have stored on an external hard drive. All smart previews are stored within a smart previews file assigned to our catalog. This way, we can work and edit/develop photographs that are not physically present on our computer, and once we reconnect our external hard drive, all changes will sync to the original RAW files.

Don't Import Suspected Duplicates

As we already mentioned, by enabling this function, we ask Lightroom to look for pictures with the same original filename, same capture time, and the same file size as photos already in our Lightroom Library. Lightroom will not import any of these duplicates to our Library again.

Make a Second Copy To:

This quite self-explanatory function will appeal to the most cautious of us. In principle, it works similarly to the secondary backup memory card in many cameras. When **Make a Second Copy To:** is enabled, Lightroom will create a duplicate copy of the currently imported photographs in a location we specify. I, personally, never use this option due to how I manage my library, but I can see its use, especially if we created this second copy on an external hard drive that we use for backups.

Add to Collection

This function will make much more sense once we go through the following two chapters, where we will dive deep into working within the Library module, which includes collections. In short, once we have any collections in our library, choosing this option will present us with a list of all of them, and we will be able to decide where we want them.

File Renaming

With this tool, we can automatically rename all of the files during the import process. When enabled, Lightroom gives us a prepopulated list of renaming templates to choose from and an edit function just under the list, which opens an all-inclusive menu for renaming photographs.

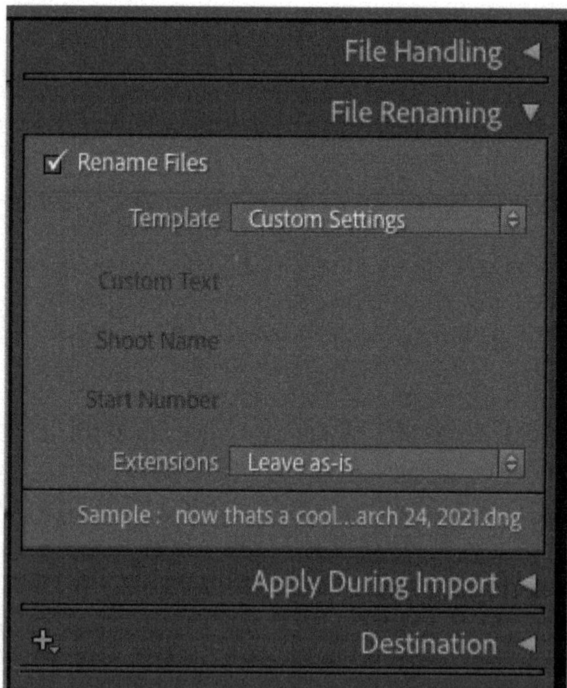

Figure 2.15 – The File Renaming tab

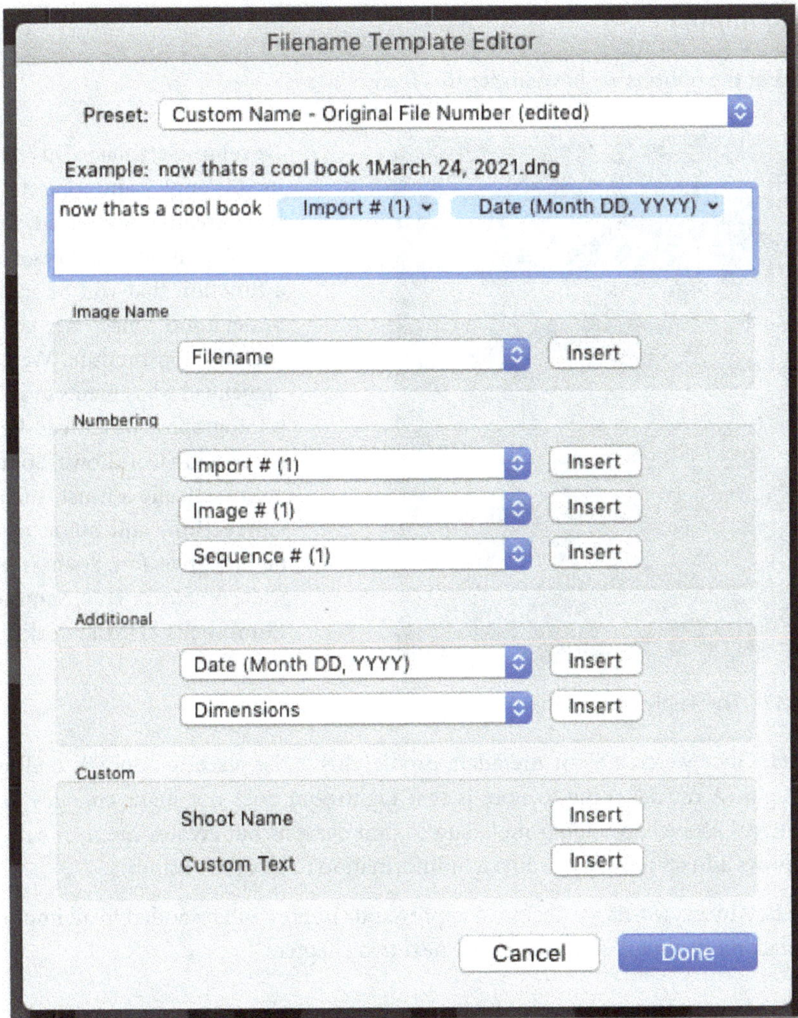

Figure 2.16 – The File Renaming tool

There is no right or wrong way of doing this, but my suggestion is to keep everything simple. We can rename our exports from Lightroom in the same way, and I see no need to rename original files elaborately.

Apply During Import

Let's take a look at the options we have under this feature:

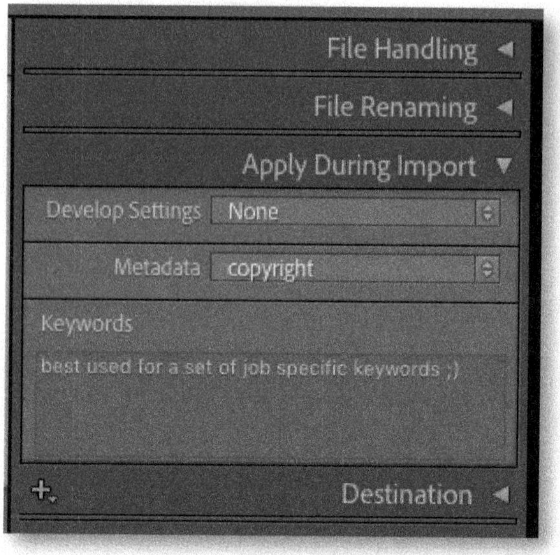

Figure 2.17 – The Apply During Import tab

- **Develop Settings**: This tab allows us to apply any presets that we have created and saved within our Develop module's **Presets** tab. It's a function that will be much better understood once we go through the Develop module. We can apply predefined adjustments to all imported photographs, which can be massive for specific workflows. Some presets are practically a must, such as **Lens Correction**, and some presets can be just great fun, such as black and white profiles or **Hue, Saturation, and Luminosity** (**HSL**) tweaks.

- **Metadata**: Once we create our metadata profile, this is the place to apply it to all imported photographs. A crucial thing to note is that Lightroom does not make changes to original camera RAW files when adding metadata to photographs but creates them in sidecar XMP files. I always add all necessary copyright information to all of my imports.
- **Keywords**: Any keywords we decide to apply to our import will be added to all imported files. We will talk more about keywords in the next two chapters.

Destination

This is the moment we were all waiting for – choosing where to import our new photographs so that we can finally bring them inside Lightroom and start some real work with them.

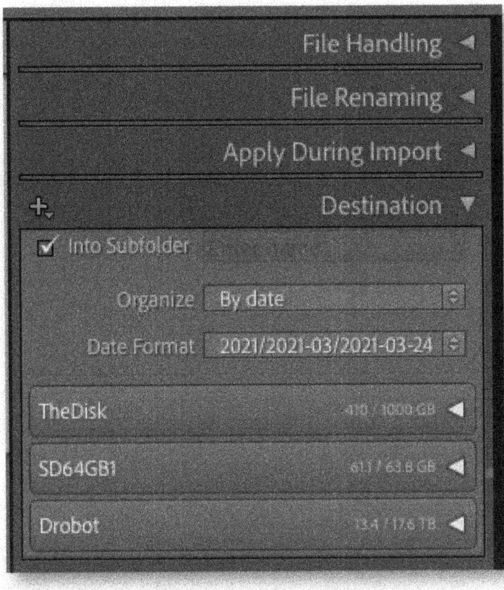

Figure 2.18 – The Destination tab

The first choice we have to make is to decide whether we want photographs to import into a subfolder. Once we tick the **Into Subfolder** box, Lightroom will create a folder in the location we choose as a destination for our photographs and save them into that folder, using a structure we pick in the next step.

Organizing imported files

We have three straightforward options here – we can either save and import all our photographs into one folder chosen as a destination, a subfolder in that location, or order them by the creation date. I always import my photographs ordered by date, using a few variations when choosing locations. My basic structure looks more or less like this – I create separate folders for `WORK`, `PRIVATE`, `VIDEO`, `PROJECTS`, and `OTHER` for each year. Within each of these folders, I split photographs by date using the YYYY-MM-DD format – that is, when I'm importing from memory cards that have strictly "work images" on them, I choose the `WORK` destination folder and organize by date (`YYYY-MM-DD`). I will usually add a description to this folder's name once I start reviewing the newly imported photographs. When I import from a memory card that is a mixture of everything, then I always import into a day-by-day structure (`YYYY/YYYY-MM/YYYY-MM-DD`) and later sort images manually into their final destination folders. There are naturally many ways to organize the Library in Lightroom, and when we get to collections, there will be even more things to consider. The default idea of importing everything into `Pictures/YYYY/YYYY-MM/YYYY-MM-DD` is a perfect starting point and helps us keep track of our photographs. It provides the basis for a good structure and a system in which it will be hard to get lost. As long as we are smart about keywords during review and rename folders by giving them custom names, Lightroom will help us stay organized with the organize-by-date structure.

The Bottom Tool tab

As we go from left to right, let's continue clockwise to the bottom of the import dialog, where we have a few different viewing options.

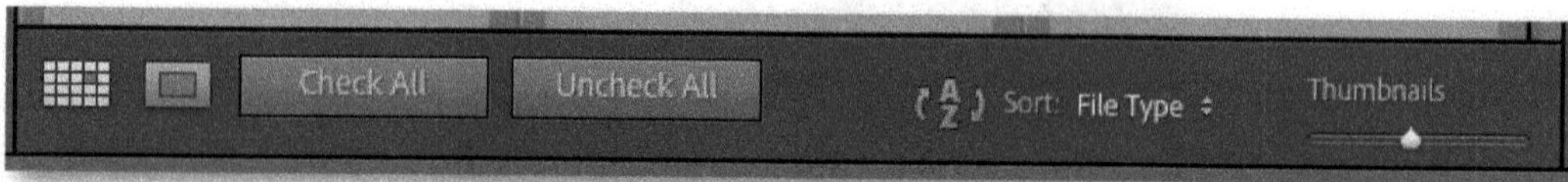

Figure 2.19 – Viewing options – the Bottom Tool tab

We will ignore for the moment the **Done** / **Cancel** / **Import** buttons and come back to them in one of the following paragraphs.

Starting from the left, we can choose Grid (the "*G*" keyboard shortcut) or Loupe view (the "*E*" keyboard shortcut). These two viewing options are followed by the **Check All** and **Uncheck All** buttons, which will do exactly that – check or uncheck to import all photographs from our current import source. The **Check All** behavior will depend on whether we chose **Don't Import Suspected Duplicates**, ignoring or including these for import depending on our choice.

Next on the right is the **Sort** option and the choice of ascending or descending order. I usually have this set to ascending by capture date, but there are moments where other options are more beneficial. For example, when I have video files mixed in with stills, I will sort by media type. You might also want to separate RAW and JPG images by sorting by the import file type, and so on.

Please look at the available options because once you are aware that they are here and remember it, there will be a time when they come in really handy.

Lastly, we have a slider to adjust the size of the thumbnails we are currently viewing.

On that thought, let's continue and look at the pictures in our view. We can check and uncheck all the tick boxes for import manually by clicking on them directly in Grid View or choosing the **Include in Import** checkbox in Loupe View. We can do this not only with single pictures but also with more extensive selections of them. We make these selections in the same way we select files and folders on the computer by either "*Ctrl*-clicking" multiple items or selecting an area with "*Shift*-clicking". Once we choose and click **Check/Uncheck** for one of the photographs within our pick, the same option will apply to all selected photos. In addition to that, we can also check/uncheck these boxes by using the "*X*" keyboard shortcut for unchecking and the "*P*" keyboard shortcut for checking.

> **Tip**
>
> You might think about this as e"*X*"clude from import and "*P*"ick for import to remember it better.

Hitting that Import button

Finally, we are ready to click the **Import** button:

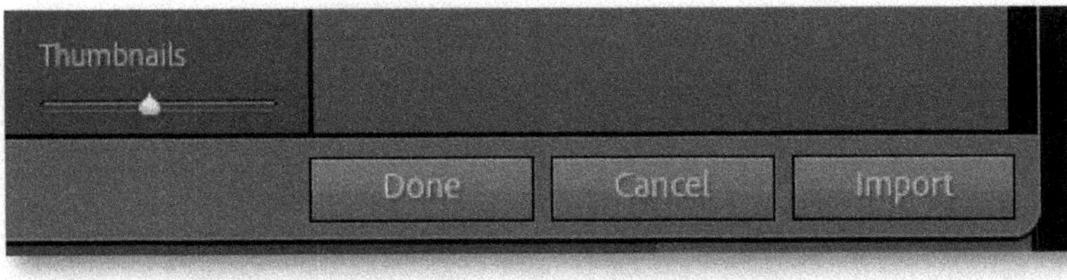

Figure 2.20 – The bottom right corner buttons

Just in case we don't want to do it, we can always hit **Cancel**, which will revert all settings to their state from our previous import, or choose **Done**, which will also cancel the current import but save all our current settings.

Here's one last reminder on the basic workflow of importing photographs:

1. Choose where to import from, and make sure to include subfolders.
2. Choose what to import, what to do with duplicates, and manually exclude or pick any photos for import.
3. Choose how Lightroom will import images – by adding, copying, moving, or converting to DNGs.
4. Choose the destination.
5. Choose the import folder structure.
6. Hit that **Import** button.

The import dialog's top tab is a friendly reminder of how our workflow within this panel will look. It reminds us of the three decisions we will be taking to get images into Lightroom:

- Where to import from (source)
- How to import (copy, move, add, or convert)
- What their destination is on our hard drive

Import Preset

All the hard work we did setting everything up is not lost as we can save it as a preset that can be used in our future work.

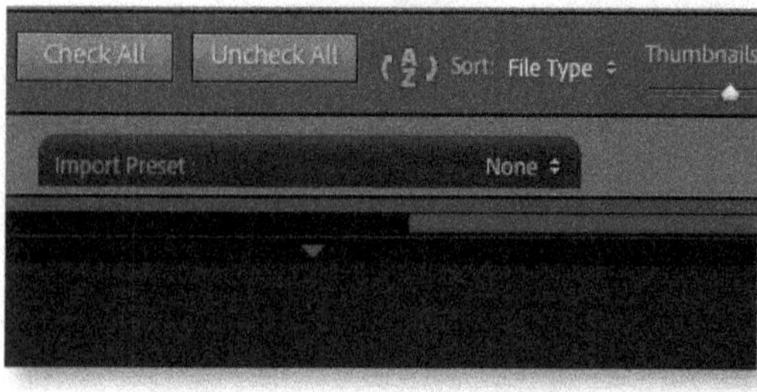

Figure 2.21 – Import Preset

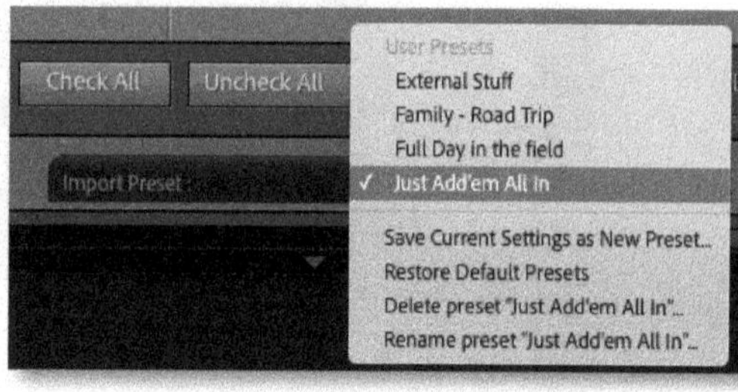

Figure 2.22 – All my import presets

Lightroom always opens the import dialog with the same settings we used for our previous import. If you think you might use different settings for different kinds of imports, there is an exquisite solution tucked away at the very bottom of the import dialog called **Import Preset**. If we want to approach, for example, wedding imports differently from our hiking treks, photographs from a busy festival, or maybe a portrait session, saving our settings for later can be a real time saver. I suggest you wait for a while and complete at least a few imports to think about setting this up. As we already mentioned at the beginning of this book, there is no one set way of working with Lightroom. Once we know what every tool does, it is up to us to utilize them most conveniently and wrap Lightroom around our workflow, not the other way around. After using Lightroom for about 15 years, I still don't use these presets too much.

As you can see in the screenshot, there are a few different settings. I usually have it set as **Just Add'em All in**, which is my default setting, created to ensure that I have all options turned on in the way I like, even after making some changes. I will always modify it slightly anyway, especially in terms of keywords and destination.

Now that we have understood the whole process of importing and bringing our photographs into Lightroom, let's look at some tips and tricks that will make this process a little easier to work with.

A few tips and tricks to remember

Once we initialize the import dialog, we can toggle between its miniature and full version by clicking on the small arrow in the bottom-left corner.

If we can't see pictures on the inserted memory card, it's good to make sure that the computer can see it, and if it does, remember to tick **Include Subfolders**.

Remember to check whether photos will be copied, moved, or added upon import to avoid unnecessary cleanup work later.

Remember to set **Don't Import Suspected Duplicates ON** or **OFF**, depending on your preferences.

If you shoot RAW and JPG and want to keep both files, remember to check the **Treat JPEG files next to RAW files as separate photos** box in **Menu** > **Lightroom Classic** > **Preferences** > **General**.

Use the "*Shift* + ⌘ + *I*" keyboard shortcut to initialize the import dialog from any Lightroom module.

Keyboard Shortcuts within the Import Dialog

"*G*" – enter Grid View (the same shortcut works in the Library module).

"*E*" – enter Loupe View (the same shortcut works in the Library module).

"*X* "– exclude a photo from import (in the Library module – used to flag a photo as rejected).

"*Shift* + *X*" – exclude a photo from import and go to the next photo.

"*P*" – pick a photo for import (in the Library module – used to flag a photo as a pick).

"*Shift* + *P*" – pick a photo for import and go to the next photo.

The preceding covers the import dialog; we will pop back here when discussing other modules when there is a crossover between any functions.

Summary

In this chapter, we learned how to create a catalog, what it means, and then imported a batch of photographs into Lightroom. It's a relatively simple process that follows a simple path *from (where we import)* > *to* (where we save), which we can translate as *source* > *path* > *destination*. The whole chapter contained quite a lot of information regarding a seemingly straightforward process. However, most of the options we discussed are set up only once in a while and for many photographers only once. It will all depend on your process and approach. As with everything, it takes a bit to get used to this process, and I encourage you to get into the habit of having a quick circular look each time you import images, following the guidance of this chapter. Even if it's only a glance, it will help you imprint the image of import dialog options in your head. This way, every import that follows will be more intuitive, and you won't become complacent, make a simple mistake, and waste time reorganizing everything again.

This brings us to the topic of our next chapter, which is the Library module, where we will look through and potentially reorganize images we just imported.

3

Tools Available within the Library Module

Lightroom's Library module is the foundation of a lot that happens when we work on our photographs. The Library module's design helps us to find and choose our best shots quickly and conveniently. With each new edit, the experience of using the Library module turns more organic and intuitive, allowing us to focus on the photographs without overthinking the tools that we are using. There is no one right way to use Lightroom for creating our edits. Each of us does photography differently, focusing on different topics, and has a different process. We also have a varying level of "trigger happy"; landscape photographers will approach editing their work differently to wedding photographers or a hobbyist collecting memories from family trips. The good news is that the Lightroom's Library module is built in a way that will speed up and simplify the editing process for any and every type of photographer, streamlining our methods and keeping it enjoyable.

In order to approach all of that in an intuitive way, we must learn how to move around the Library module freely and understand where everything is. When I say everything, I mean Lightroom Library's tools as well as all of our photographs and their locations within the Library as well as on our hard drives. We will do just that in the first part of this chapter, later learning more about keywording and metadata. We also need to know the tools to give us a good idea of how our final edits look, both as a part of a sequence and as singular photographs.

In the second part of this chapter, we will explore many different viewing and selection modes but also dip into developing our photographs with the **Quick Develop panel** (**QDP**), which will also give us a great teaser of Lightroom's capabilities when it comes to adjusting our photos. Without further ado, let the fun begin.

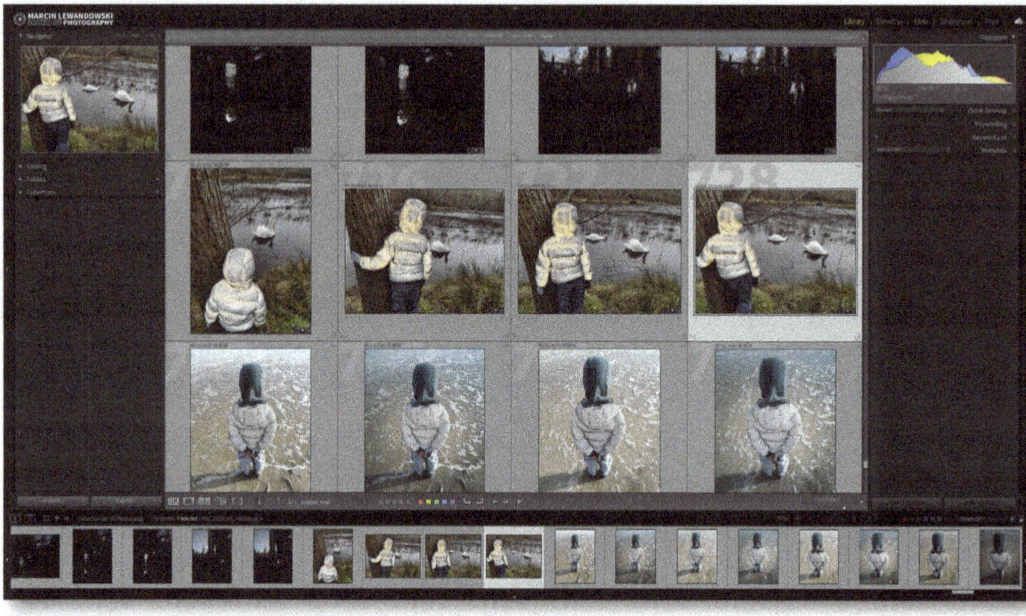

Figure 3.1 – The Library module

The main topics we'll cover in this chapter are as follows:

- An introduction to the Library module and its workspace
- Editing photographs – all the tools you'll ever need
- How I edit and my editing workflow

An introduction to the Library module and its workspace

We will start with the Library module's left side, which lists all our available photographs in their physical locations. By available, I mean all the pictures that we already imported into Lightroom.

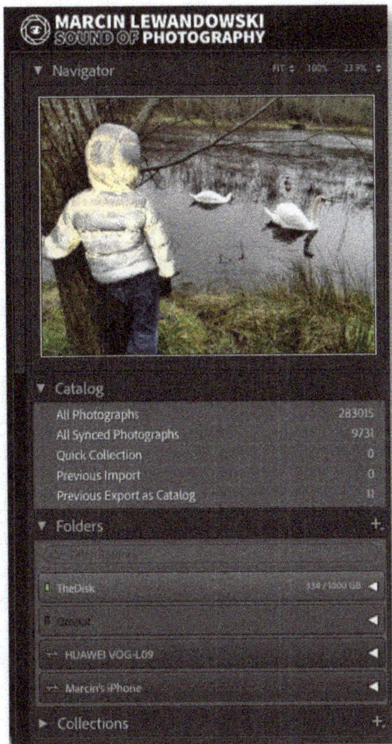

Figure 3.2 A

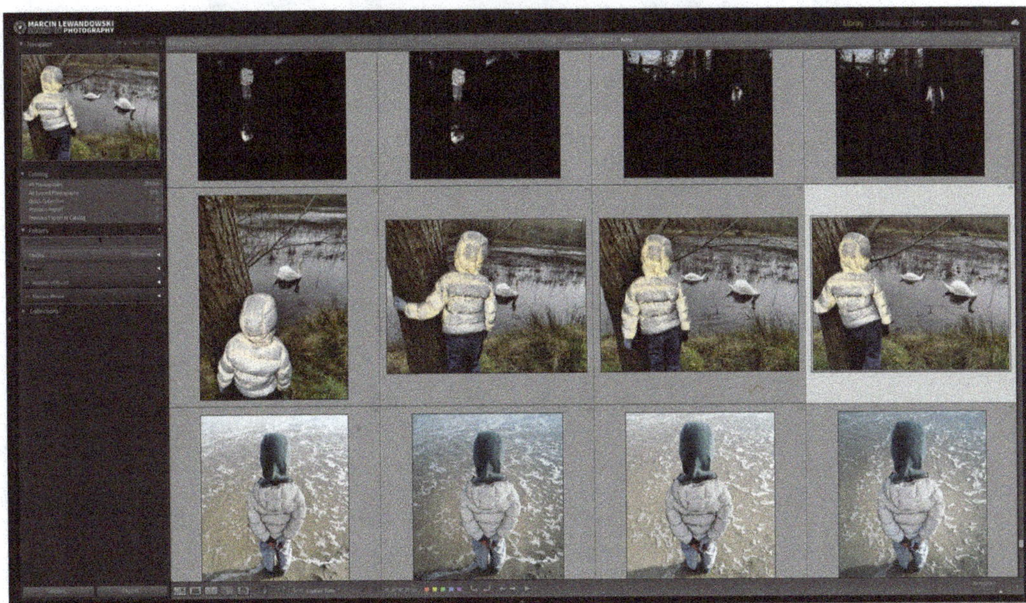

Figure 3.2 B – Detail of the left side panel in Library Module

The left-side panel

This is where we will learn how to make our life easier and explore all the tools helping us to manage our collection, making sure everything is easy to find even after years of collecting.

Navigator

The first tool we have at our disposal is **Navigator**.

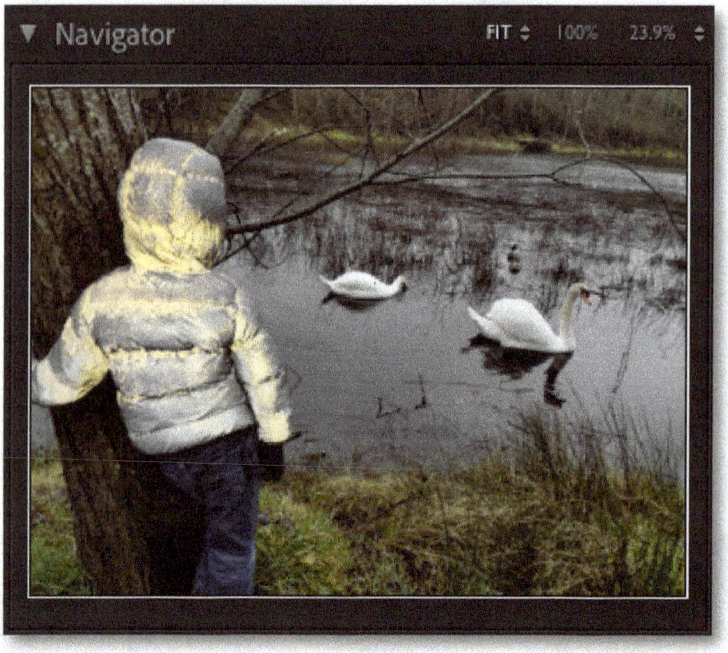

Figure 3.3 – A Navigator close-up with the FIT option chosen

This is a miniature version of the currently selected photograph. If we choose so in the preferences, Navigator will also always show the first photograph in each folder we are hovering over with the mouse cursor, which is handy when we skim over hundreds of folders. This is how to do it – **Lightroom Classic** > **Preferences** > **Interface** > **Show photos** in Navigator on mouseover. Preferences are also available with a keyboard shortcut, "⌘". With Navigator, we can choose how the currently selected photograph is displayed. We can do so by clicking the small up/down arrows to select the **FIT/FILL** option, the **100%** view next to it, or the custom magnification level as a third option, which we can adjust with the small up/down arrows.

You might find Navigator handy and fitting for the way you work, but I personally don't use it and most of the time have this tab closed. All of the functions I just mentioned are accessible from different and, in my opinion, more convenient places when looking directly at and through photographs. We will get to these later.

Catalog

The next tab on the left side is the **Catalog** tab:

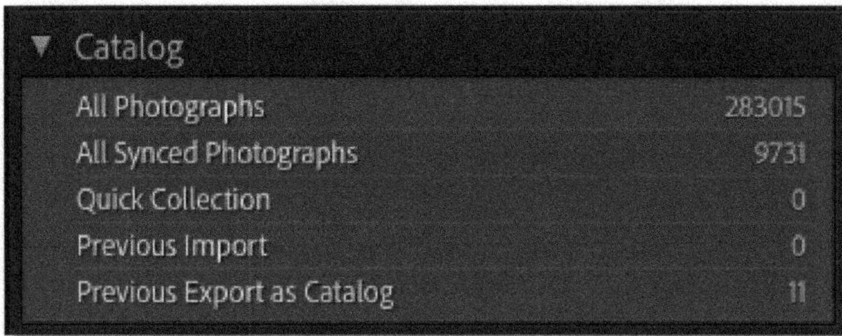

Figure 3.4 – The Catalog tab detail

Initially, if you are new to Lightroom, it will contain four options – **All Photographs**, **All Synced Photographs**, **Quick Collection**, and **Previous Import**. Once we export our photographs as a catalog, the contents of the last export will be visible at the bottom of the **Catalog** tab under the **Previous Export as Catalog** heading, but that's a detail to look at later; first, we will learn about the main four sections.

All Photographs

This function does precisely what it says. With one click, Lightroom will display thumbnails of all photographs we have so far imported into Lightroom, regardless of whether they are available on a computer's hard drive or unavailable because we store them on an external drive. The number next to it is the total number of photographs we currently have present in our Library. With a right-click, we can access additional functions of this option, which are in the order of appearance as follows:

- **Import Photos and Videos**: This will lead us to the menu we discussed in detail in *Chapter 2, Bring It All In – Importing Photographs into Lightroom*, so I won't go into any additional explanation – it's just another way to import our images.
- **Import from Another Catalog**: We only need this option if we have another catalog, other than the one we are using at the moment, and want to add images from it to the current one. It is an excellent function if we're going to merge separate catalogs into one at some stage, but as I mentioned in *Chapter 2, Bring It All In – Importing Photographs into Lightroom*, don't think about it until you really know your way around Lightroom and have a good reason to do it.

- **Import a Photoshop Elements Catalog**: If so far you used Photoshop Elements for working with your photographs, Lightroom will help you to easily transfer this work. To do this, go to **Photoshop Elements** > **File** > **Manage Catalogs** > **Optimize**. Once you complete this process, come back to Lightroom and choose the **Import a Photoshop Elements Catalog** option, and then follow the instructions on the screen. This is a one-off event, and once completed, you can continue to work on your photographs from within Lightroom.

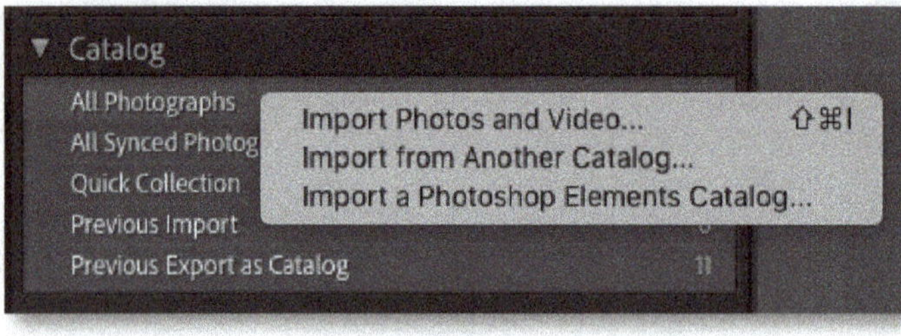

Figure 3.5 – Right-clicking All Photographs

Quick Collection

Any images we view and work with can be added to the quick collection with the "*B*" keyboard shortcut as long as **Quick Collection** is our target collection. Choosing **Quick Collection** as the target collection can be done by right-clicking it and picking the third option from the list or with a keyboard shortcut, "⌥ ⇧ ⌘ B".

We have access to another two options after right-clicking – **Save Quick Collection** and **Clear Quick Collection**. With **Save Quick Collection**, we can create a collection (we will talk about collections in the next chapter) with all photographs that are currently present in the quick collection. Please keep in mind that if we add any photographs to the quick collection after using the **Save Quick Collection** option, they will not be automatically added to that saved collection.

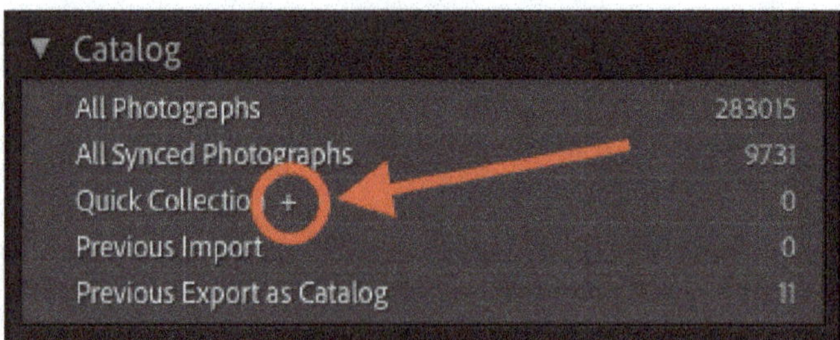

Figure 3.6 – The small plus sign next to a collection means that it's a target collection

Previous Import

Here, we can always find images from our latest import. If you imported a set of photographs while going through the second chapter, this is where you will find all the images from that import. It's as simple as that, and there is no additional layer of functionality on top of this one.

Previous Export as Catalog

After we export a catalog, this is where we will find the contents of that latest export. You will notice that right-click gives a **Remove This Temporary Collection** option, which is how I keep it – there's no need for me to have a function that I rarely use. If you choose to remove this option, it will be back when you export any of your images as a catalog. Other than that, you will never have to think about it again.

You might ask whether there are any benefits to exporting a catalog. Yes. All functions within Lightroom can be beneficial; some are just not for everyone. Imagine this situation – you have an extensive edit to complete or want to work on your personal project, but you are going on a 2-week trip where you know you will have no access to the internet or, at most, just a patchy connection.

With a reliable connection, you can sync images to your cloud storage and access them via the Lightroom app on your mobile device – problem solved.

Without that connection, we can work around the problem by going to the folder/collection we want to take with us, exporting it as a collection, including the original files, and saving it on a memory card. Once done, we need to transfer this new catalog to a laptop with installed Lightroom, and voila – we can edit, including work on the original files. If space and speed are of utmost importance, then including only Smart Previews will be sufficient, especially if we will import an edited catalog back to our Library. As long as we don't change filenames and their location, and basically keep the file structure untouched, we can import from another catalog into our master Lightroom catalog, and we are all set. I know I'm digressing, but it's good to be aware of this functionality.

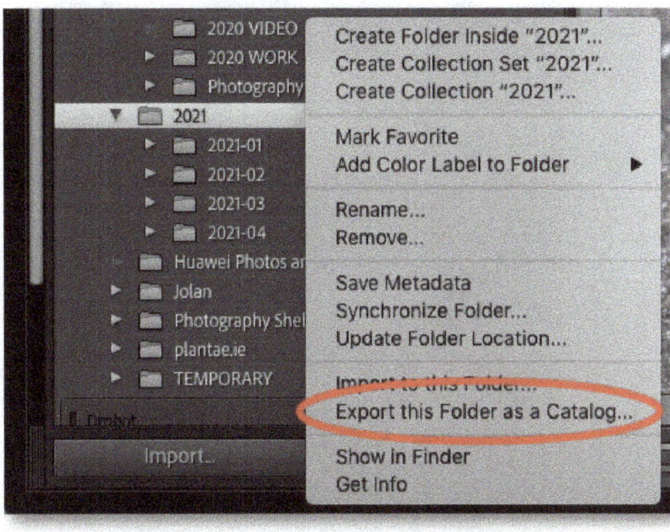

Figure 3.7 A

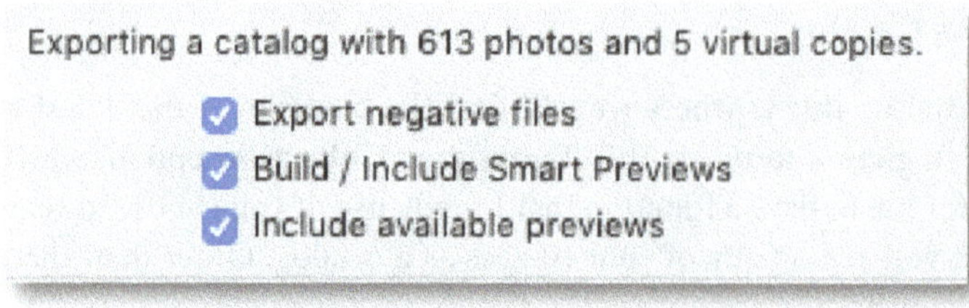

Figure 3.7 B

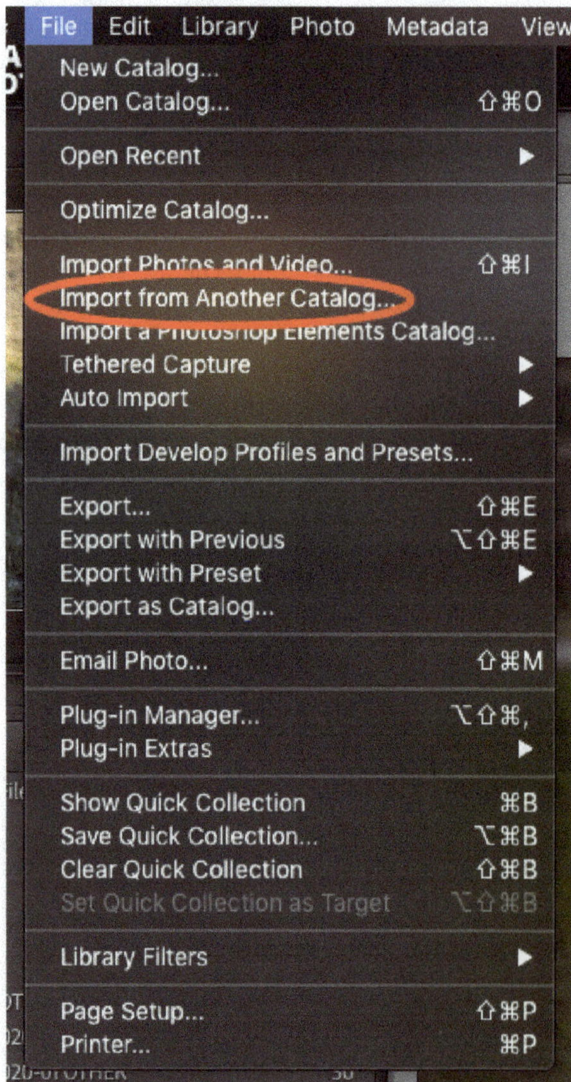

Figure 3.7 C – Exporting and importing a catalog

Folders

The third panel in this column is called **Folders**, and as you would expect, it is just that – a panel containing all the folders with images we have imported into Lightroom so far. This panel splits into different physical locations where we store our pictures. In my case, it's the hard drive of my computer, Drobo storage (which I use as my primary backup), and two virtual folders that contain photographs and automatically sync pictures from my phone via the Lightroom mobile app. When we open any of the drive's tabs, we can see only folders where our photographs are. We can expand this view by right-clicking any folder and choosing **Show Parent Folder**. We undo this by right-clicking again and selecting **Hide This Parent**.

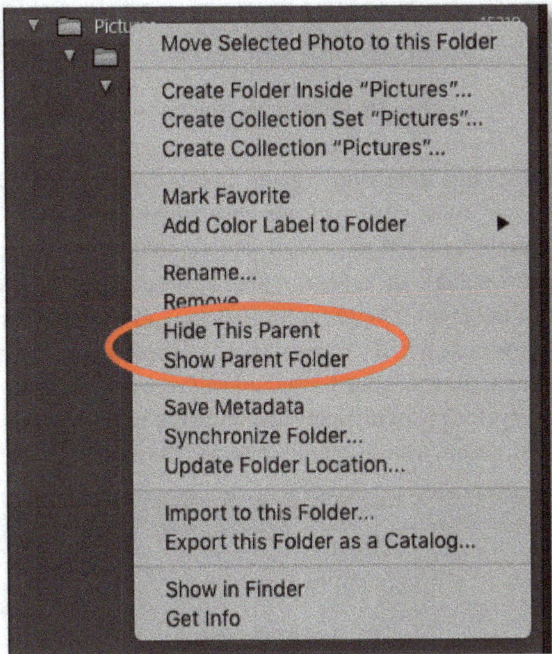

Figure 3.8 – Hide This Parent and Show Parent Folder

The right-side panel

The **Collections** panel is a whole thing in itself, and we will talk about it (and the **Folders** panel) in the next chapter. Right now, we will jump across the screen to the right side of our display, which in its default state starts with the histogram. I will digress here and explain it simply for those who are not too familiar with the concept of histograms.

Histogram

Histograms are graphic representations of data, and in the case of Lightroom, the histogram represents the intensity of tones from dark to bright.

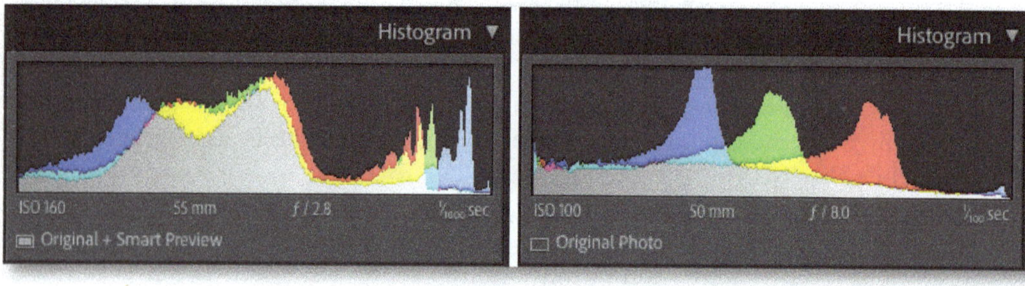

Figure 3.9 – Histogram examples

On the left side of the chart are blacks and shadows going through mid-tones in the middle to highlights and whites located on the right-most edge – please have a look at *Figure 3.08* to see two sample histograms. There are 256 levels from left to right, 0 representing black (shadow clipping) and 255 representing white (highlight clipping). The taller the chart at any of the levels, the more we have pixels at that particular intensity. If the graph's height is more than 0 on the left-most or right-most edge, it means that we have unrecoverable details in one or both of these areas. The more darker tones we have in our selected photograph, the more our histogram will veer to the left, and the opposite applies to the lighter tones. The same principle of intensity applies to the RGB channels, represented by their respective colors. Note the visual hint, with the graph changing from darker to lighter from left to right.

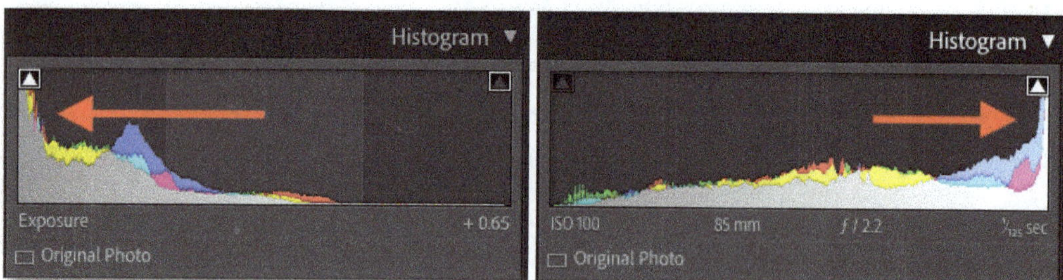

Figure 3.10 – Left – clipped shadows and right – clipped highlights

Quick Develop panel

This panel contains a simplified version of the Develop module, giving us the ability to make small changes "on the fly" while editing our current batch of photographs– all without the need to go to the Develop module.

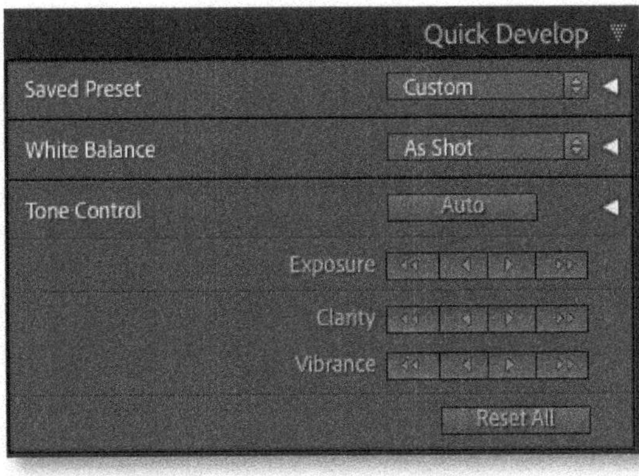

Figure 3.11 – The Quick Develop panel with all the tabs closed

The QDP is divided into three separate tabs, each offering a different set of functions – **Saved Preset**, **White Balance**, and **Tone Control**. The QDP tabs are independent of each other, and we can open or close them separately to suit our needs and, most of all, keep the workspace uncluttered. This way, we can focus on the photographs, not on everything around them. Let's take a look at each of the tabs in the QDP and what they contain:

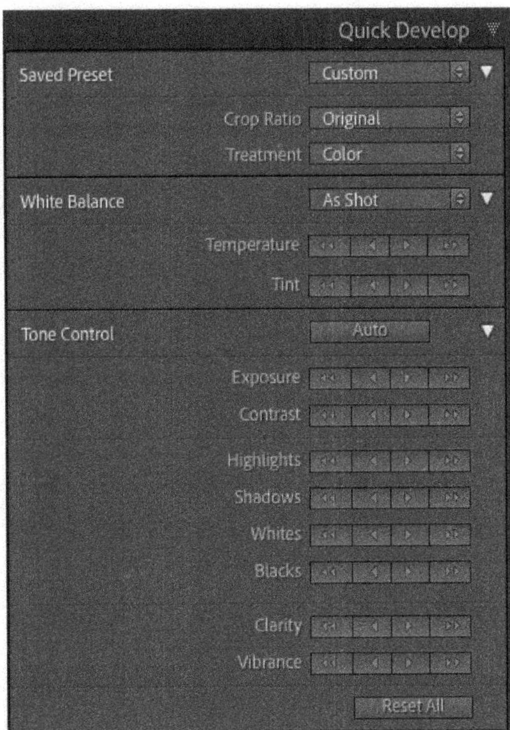

Figure 3.12 – The Quick Develop Panel with all the tabs opened

Saved Preset

When we start working with Lightroom, this section will contain only a handful of default presets, but over time, we can save our own, buy custom-made presets on the internet, swap them with friends, and even find some really cool free stuff if we look around. Clicking on the pop-up menu of **Saved Preset** allows us to apply any preset that we have to the currently viewed photograph, and if we are working in Grid View, then that preset will apply to all highlighted photos. Using presets in this way allows us to see how our edit might look after we develop it and is an opportunity to try something "*on the fly*" while we are still choosing our favorites. We can quickly check out an idea without breaking out of editing mode by going into the Develop module and changing the framing with **Crop Ratio** or having a glance at how our photo might look in black and white:

- **Crop Ratio**: If we want to check how the photos will work as a square, make sure that the series of portraits will fit nicely into Instagram's 8x10 format, or whether the landscape will look good in the CinemaScope aspect ratio, this function will help us do it. Again, if we are viewing in Grid View, then the chosen aspect ratio will apply to all highlighted photographs.
- **Treatment**: This offers just two choices but profound ones – color or black and white. With this function, you can quickly switch it here and immediately find out whether the series or single you are looking at will work well in timeless black and white.

White Balance

We are slowly getting into developing our photographs. If you don't shoot with the RAW file format, the possibility to tweak the white balance post-shoot is one of the good reasons to start. The top option is a drop-down menu, and the next two start a repeated pattern for all remaining tools in the QDP. Singular arrows pointing left and right change settings by 1/3 of a stop, in the case of white balance; the left arrow will make the photo cooler and the right arrow warmer, respectively decreasing and increasing the light temperature in Kelvin units. We can also deal with the balance of the tint with the magenta versus cyan slider – aka the struggle between too much green versus too much pink. The double arrow is where things get interesting, as we can adjust settings by a full stop; see *Figure 3.12*.

Tone Control

This is the last tab in the QDP, and it gives us a real teaser of what we can expect in the Develop module. Just as with the **White Balance** tool, with single arrows, we can adjust settings in 1/3 of a stop and with double arrows in full-stop increments.

Settings in the Develop module will reflect all the changes we will make in the QDP, and all sliders, which replace the arrow buttons, will be moved to reflect the changes we made. All of the changes we made in QDP will also appear in the develop history in the Develop module.

As with a few other things earlier – let's not get ahead of ourselves; there is just so much interlinked functionality in Lightroom that it's hard not to mention specific things along the way.

The **Reset All** button at the bottom of the QDP will reset settings for all three tabs, reverting our photograph(s) to their original state. At the top of this tab, we can also try the **Auto** settings button. Its accuracy, however, is highly dependent on the type of photograph we are trying to adjust. It will work great on evenly lit photographs but usually get it wrong for tricky light or high-contrast work. See for yourself; try it on a few entirely different photos, and remember – everything happening within Lightroom is a non-destructive process, and Lightroom will never alter our original pictures.

We can always click on **Reset All** and return to the beginning. Note that holding the "⌥" button will change the **Clarity** and **Vibrance** tools to **Sharpening** and **Saturation** respectively. Also, collapsing the QDP tabs doesn't close it completely. We always have access to the presets, white balance presets, auto/manual exposure, Clarity/Sharpening, and Vibrance/Saturation controlled with the "⌥ *(Alt)*" button.

Keywording

Keywords are one of the foundations of an easily searchable library. When I started my adventure with Lightroom, and even with photography in general, it was hard for me to get a perspective on how and where it might progress. Some 10 years and 500,000 photographs later (about 5 years ago), I found my collection in a bit of a mess, spread across multiple hard drives, separate catalogs, and hundreds of DVDs. When I started compiling a better-organized body out of it and consolidating everything into one catalog, I realized how badly a lot of what I had was keyworded. So, if you can afford the time, keyword your photographs carefully; it will come in very handy with many tasks within Lightroom.

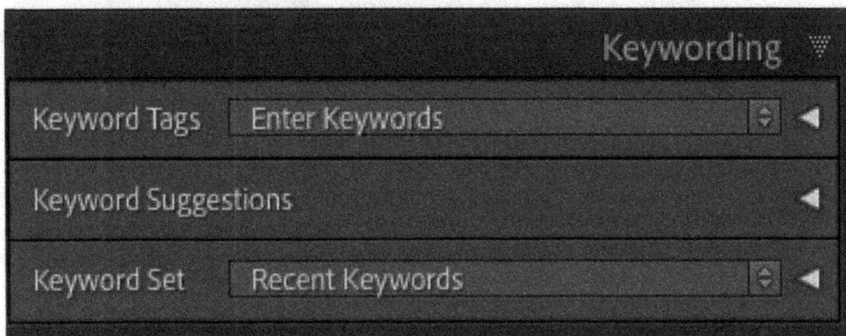

Figure 3.13 – The Keywording panel with all the tabs closed

Keyword Tags

Starting with the pop-up menu next to **Keyword Tags**, we have three options after we click on it – **Enter Keywords**, **Keywords & Containing Keywords**, and **Will Export**.

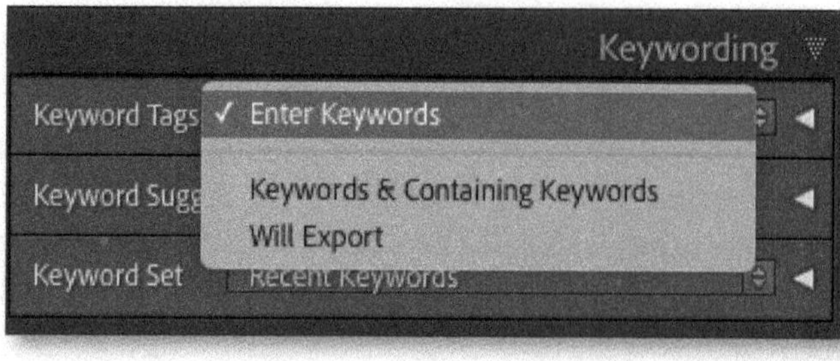

Figure 3.14 – Keyword Tags

Enter Keywords is an easy concept – we write keywords, which I think about as tags, and separate them by commas to create separate keywords. There is another trick you can use for your keywording, which is creating keyword hierarchies, and you can do this by separating keywords with greater than (">") and less than ("<") symbols. Whatever keyword is at the open end of the symbol will be the master keyword for the other one. The same rule will apply if you use the vertical bar (|) after a keyword. Suppose you write the keywords `dead zoo>bird taxidermy`, `bird taxidermy<dead zoo`, and `dead zoo|bird taxidermy`; here, `bird taxidermy` will be nested below the `dead zoo` keyword in the following keyword list. I can see how this might be beneficial for some of you, and for certain types of work, it might be a great time saver down the line, but I don't use it too often and only for specific projects. You can check your hierarchies by choosing **Keywords & Containing Keywords** or going to the keyword list in the next panel.

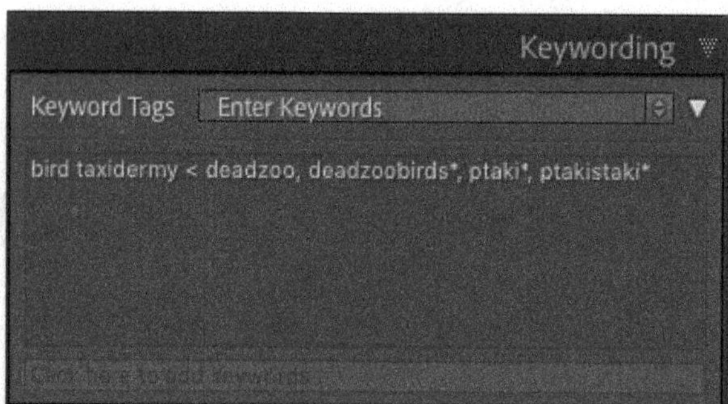

Figure 3.15 A

Figure 3.15 B – Example of nested keywords

Will Export simply presents all keywords' which will be written into pictures' metadata upon export if we choose to do so in the export settings. We will learn all about the exporting process in *Chapter 8, Get Them All Out – Using the Print and Book Modules.*

Keyword Suggestions

This selection of nine keywords is based on several different criteria such as other keywords already associated with the photograph, photographs captured at a similar space and time, and possibly others, as shown here:

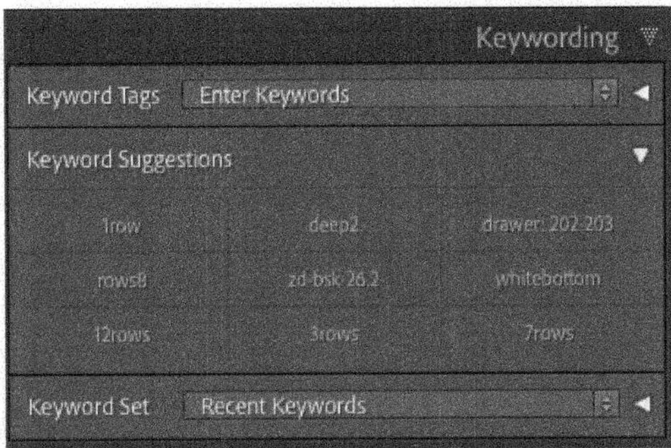

Figure 3.16 – Keyword Suggestions

I could never pinpoint exactly how this works, and Adobe stays vague about it too. I find this function a hit/miss feature. Sometimes, it works great and lists exactly what we need; sometimes, it's just hilarious trying to be helpful, especially when it has no reference points in other keywords. I think about it as a tool that's always there; I keep it open but rarely use it. It's quite different from the following one.

Keyword Set

This is where keywording becomes more straightforward, especially when we are not used to doing it. The pop-up menu offers a few helpful options, as shown here:

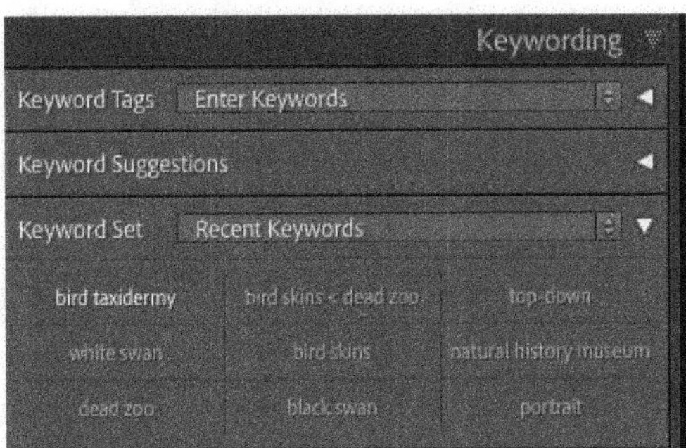

Figure 3.17 – Keyword Set

In my experience, there is a lot that we can do with nine keywords, but what's great about this list is the option to use all nine of these keywords with simple keyboard shortcuts. Once we press the "⌥" key, next to each keyword appears a number from one to nine. When we press any number while holding the "⌥" key, we assign the keyword next to that number to our chosen photo or a set of images. If you think that is an excellent functionality, you will like the following paragraph even more.

When we click on **Recent Keywords**, a pop-up menu will open, giving us access to create our custom lists of nine keywords with the same keyboard shortcuts assigned to them. Whatever type of edit we might be working on will have a related set of keywords at our fingertips. We only need to choose **Edit Set...**, add up to nine keywords that we need to work on, pick **Save Current Settings as New Preset...** from the preset list above, choose an easy-to-decipher title, and we are all set. As a default, we have three lists at our disposal called **Outdoor Photography**, **Portrait Photography**, and **Wedding Photography**. Even if we never worked extensively with keywords, these should give us a pretty good idea of how we might start approaching the making of our lists. I create them *as required* and clean up afterward using the **Restore Default Presets** option.

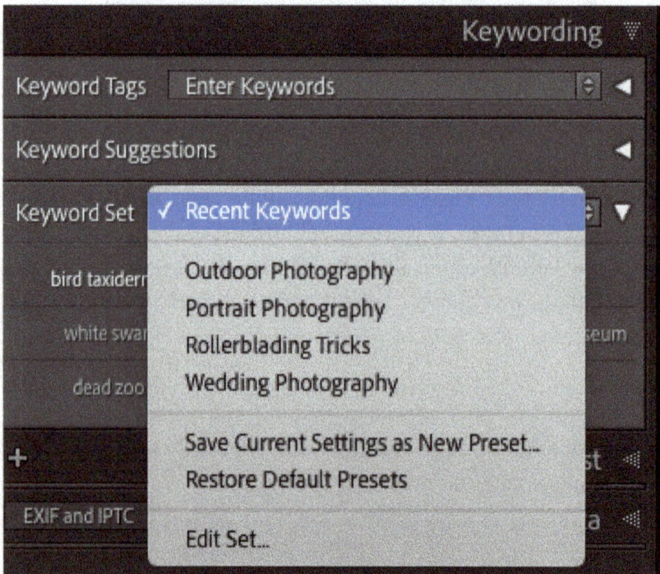

Figure 3.18 – Customizable keyword sets

Keyword List

One more function we have at our disposal to help us with keyword management and also add a powerful keyword-based search engine is **Keyword List**, a list of all keywords we have ever used in our Library. Keywords that we don't have assigned to any photographs anymore will also be visible on that list and available for us to use again in another way. By ticking the box on the left side of each keyword in the keyword list, we assign that keyword to the currently chosen photograph (or a group of photographs). As for the search engine, once we hover over a keyword that we assigned to at least one shot, we will notice a small arrow appearing on the right side of that keyword. Clicking on the arrow will open, in the Library view, all the photographs with that keyword. It might not seem that powerful at first sight, but imagine that you have photographed your dog for 15 years and want to find all of the photos that include your friend across all the different created folders and drives over all of these years. If we were diligent enough to keyword his name along the way, then with a single click of a button, all of them will appear in front of us. Just think about the options.

At the top of the keyword list, we have a very efficient filter to search for any keywords. Once we start typing, Lightroom will filter out from the keyword list any keywords that do not match the combination of letters we just typed. As we go through the filter keywords, please also note a small arrow on the right side. Once we click on it, a small three-word sub-menu will appear, listing **All**, **People**, and **Other**:

- **All** is a default setting, listing all the keywords we have ever created (and not deleted) in Lightroom.
- **People** limits the list of keywords to people whom we keyworded using the **People** view (which we will come back to in a few paragraphs).
- **Other**, which covers the **All** keywords except confirmed people.

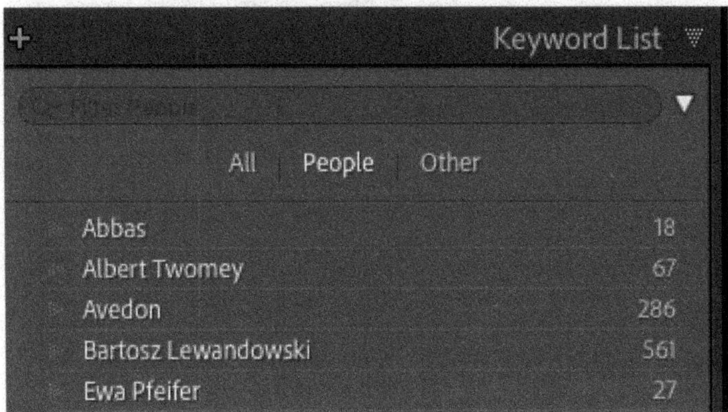

Figure 3.19 – Keyword List | People

Metadata

All of the core metadata sits within EXIF and IPTC. I always took these for granted and used them whenever needed without giving them a second thought, but for clarity, let me briefly explain what both of these are and dive into a few other available settings.

EXIF is an abbreviation of **Exchangeable Image File Format** and contains all information generated by our cameras. EXIF includes the camera model, photograph creation date, exposure mode, lens used, aperture, and focal length, and takes into account and calculates a 35mm equivalent for all crop sensors. It's a great tool when we want to experiment with manual settings, serving as a journal of all the different settings we tried, displaying them next to the effects of our experimentations. We can also display a specific portion of these settings over the viewed photographs, both in Loupe View and Grid View. One extra tip to take from this - when we are hovering over the metadata in this panel, some of it will become highlighted (most of these lines are also represented by an arrow on the right side of them). When we click on the highlighted setting, Lightroom will filter the currently viewed selection of photographs using the value we clicked - that is, if we are browsing through our pictures and our attention is caught by a photo made with a specific lens, we can click on the **Lens** field and Lightroom will filter for all images made with that lens.

IPTC means **International Press Telecommunications Council**, and it is a format developed by "old media" to organize the process of sharing information. The IPTC standard was adopted by "new media" in a more or less unchanged form, and search engines widely use it. Any field that you hover over will slightly brighten up, which means you can edit its contents. We can create a preset with all copyright information that we want to have included with our photographs and either sync it here in Grid View or apply it when importing our photos. Here is how it's done.

To create a metadata-related preset, click on the pop-up **Preset** menu in the **Metadata** Panel, choose **Edit Presets**, fill in any information you want, click **Done**, and save the changes as a new preset:

Figure 3.20 – Creating a metadata preset

In Grid View (the "*G*" keyboard shortcut), click on one of your currently visible photographs and then choose all of them ("⌘*A*"). Once we highlight all the photos, we need to select **Sync Metadata...** and ensure that the image we have highlighted and synced with has all the required details filled in. Alternatively, you can also choose one of the presets you created and apply it to all the selected photographs.

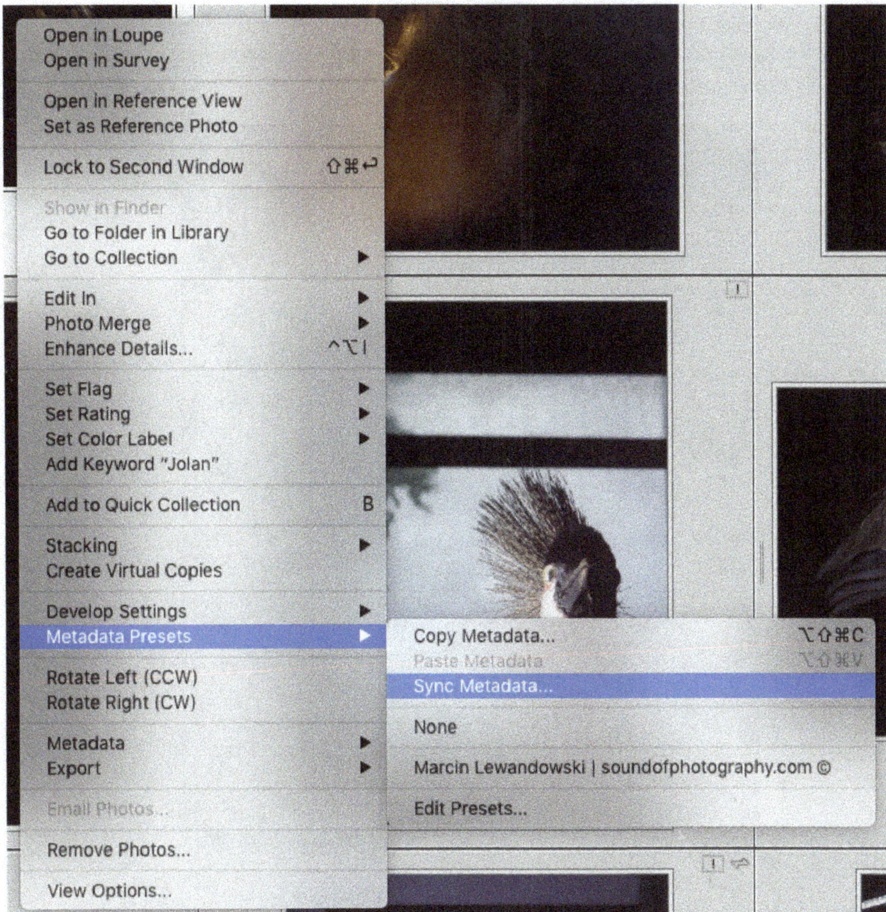

Figure 3.21 – Sync Metadata..., available on a right-click

Note

We'll learn more about Grid View and different view types in the *Getting to know the toolbar* section.

We can also apply our newly created presets while working in the import dialog, which we covered in the previous chapter. In the right-side panel, make sure you choose **Apply During Import** > **Metadata**, and from there, your chosen preset will stay selected as default for all your imports until you decide to change it.

The field I use the most in the **Metadata** panel is **Large Caption**. Anything we write here will populate as a caption on most websites, and when we send it to a newspaper or magazine, they will be able to see it as a caption.

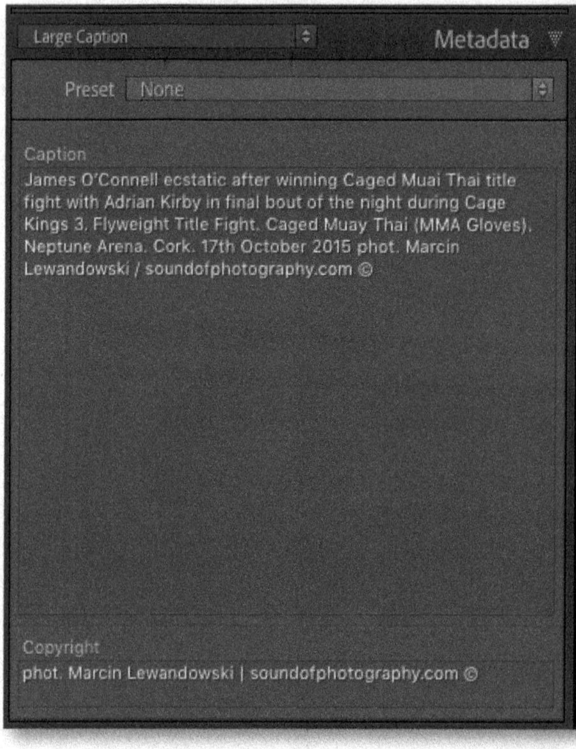

Figure 3.22 – The Large Caption field

Comments

The very last panel here is **Comments**, but you can't use it from within Lightroom. It will show comments that other users write on your photographs if you sync them and share collections via Lightroom Mobile. I honestly never saw this feature being used by anyone.

It feels like we've had a very long introduction without mentioning the crucial part of this chapter, editing our work, but before that, here's just one last tip regarding work with panels in general. When we click on any tab in the side panels, we will activate a pop-up menu to choose which tabs are visible, creating a workspace to suit us better. Any tabs can be turned on or off by clicking on them. The **Show All** option can also restore them. My favorite option here is **Solo Mode** – when enabled, only one tab remains open at a time; when we click on any other tab to open it, the previously active tab will close. This function works in all panels, and it comes in handy if we switch between tabs often and don't want to keep scrolling up and down all the time.

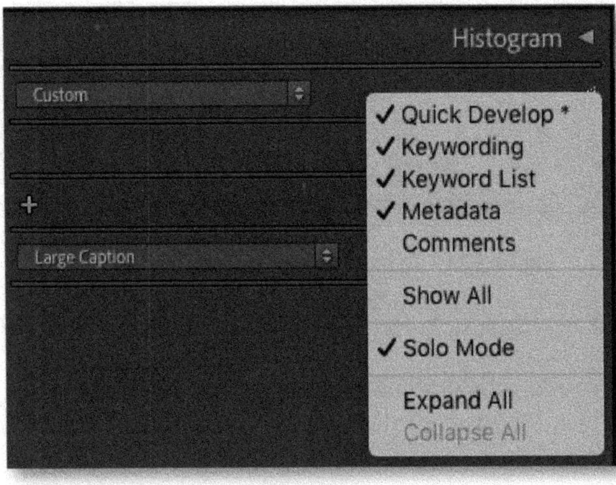

Figure 3.23 – Solo Mode

Now that we have a good idea of the panels available in the Library module and their functions, we are now ready to start editing our work.

Editing photographs – all the tools you'll ever need

I might owe you an explanation. I know that some of you think about editing in terms of picture postproduction and retouching. I come from a school of thought where "*to create an edit*" is to choose the best photographs from a created body of work and sequence them, especially if they will not be presented in chronological order. However, the most important thing is to sift through everything to make a selection that is interesting to look through and hopefully leaves the viewer hungry for more. Anything to do with postproduction or retouching, I will always call developing photos, which is appropriate for the Lightroom Develop module. I hope this makes things a bit clearer.

We have at our disposal a great variety of tools to suit any type of workflow, but first, let's make our workspace look the way we want.

Getting to know the toolbar

We will start with the toolbar at the bottom of the Library window and activate all available tools. To do that, we need to click on the down-pointing arrow and choose, one by one, all the unchecked options. These tools will now be visible on the left, each separated by a vertical bar.

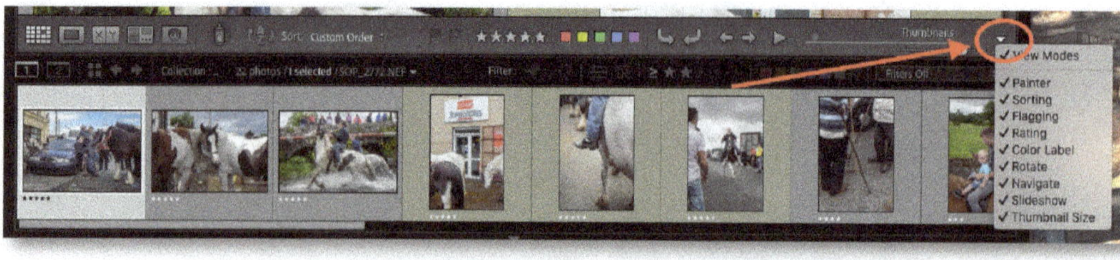

Figure 3.24 – The toolbar – all tools activated

Starting on the left, we can choose between the available view modes.

Note that when you hover over each view for a moment, it will display the tool's name and, what's even more critical, a keyboard shortcut for that tool. This mouseover to see the tool's name and its potentially associated keyboard shortcut works across all Lightroom tools. Try to remember this when using Lightroom. Sometimes, these shortcuts are just great as reminders. Sometimes, we might learn about a shortcut that we wished existed and were not aware of, but let's get back to the **View Modes**.

Grid View

This is where we can view our images as, well, a grid.

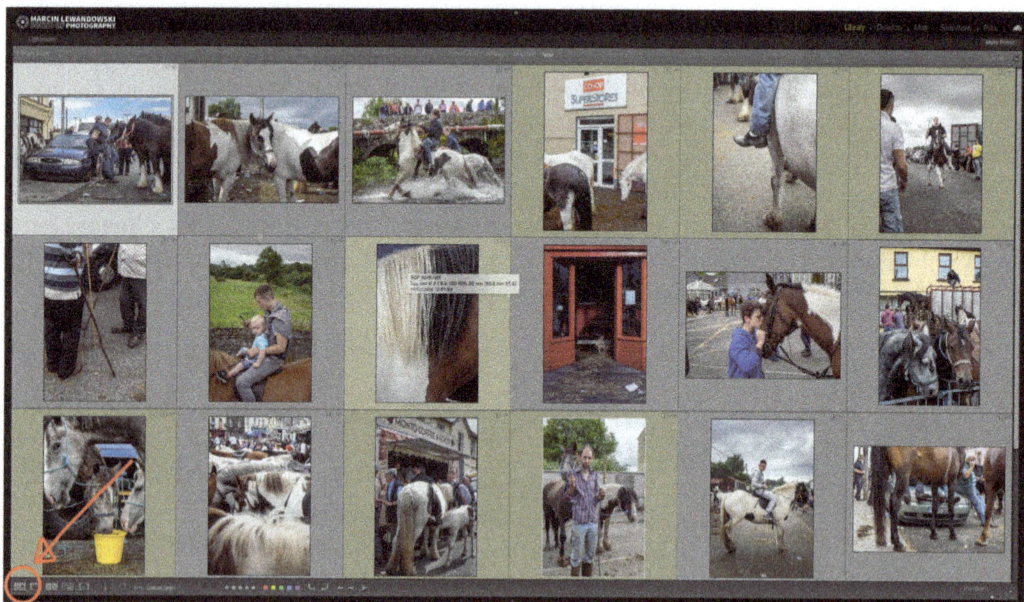

Figure 3.25 – The Library in Grid View mode – all panels collapsed

It's an entirely customizable grid too. First and foremost, we can change the size of viewed thumbnails with the slider on the right of our toolbar. We can do the same using the "+" and "-" keyboard shortcuts to increase and decrease the size of thumbnails. As we already mentioned in the introduction, all panels can be collapsed, and we can do this in a few ways:

1. We can click on the small arrows on the side of each panel.
2. We can press "*TAB*" on the keyboard to collapse/open both side panels.
3. We can press "*Shift TAB*" to collapse/open all panels.
4. We can press "*T*" to show/hide the toolbar.
5. Finally, we can press "\" to show/hide the **Library Filter** bar on top of our Grid View.

Hiding/collapsing everything gives us a very clean workspace that might become a default view for editing once you get to know the basic keyboard shortcuts. It is for me, with various tweaks, depending on what I edit at any particular time.

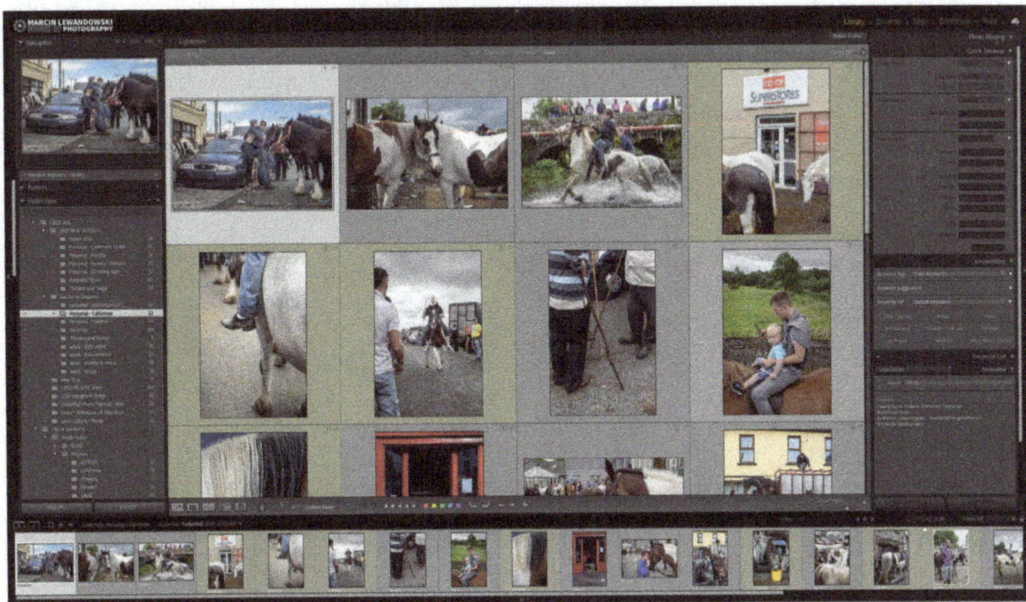

Figure 3.26 – The Library in Grid View mode – all panels opened

The next step is understanding what information we can display over each photograph in Grid View. We have three customizable views to choose from – **Compact Cells**, **Expanded Cells**, and what I call **Clean Cells** (Adobe does not call it anything):

- **Compact Cells** give us little information, but what we can choose is quite flexible. Additionally, we have the availability of a large index number at the top-left corner of each cell.
- **Expanded Cells** provides much more information, and we can adjust the type of displayed information by clicking directly on different info fields in Grid View. I encourage you to play around with choosing various options that you might think will work for you. The settings I use as default are **Capture Date/Time**, **File Name**, and **Common Photo**.

  This way, I get a quick overview of when I made a picture, what lens I was using, and my settings for the photo. The filename is always handy and is a quick reference for finding photographs at a later stage; as you possibly noticed, I have a habit of not renaming any photos and always keeping them under their original names. When we want to reset to defaults, we can go to **Library View Options** and click on **Restore Defaults**.
- **Clean Cells** – this is just the photo with the cell not containing any information. If I can get away with it and don't need any info, I just go through the edit visually and use this view. Nothing on the screen draws my attention away from the photographs, and I can focus just on the pictures.

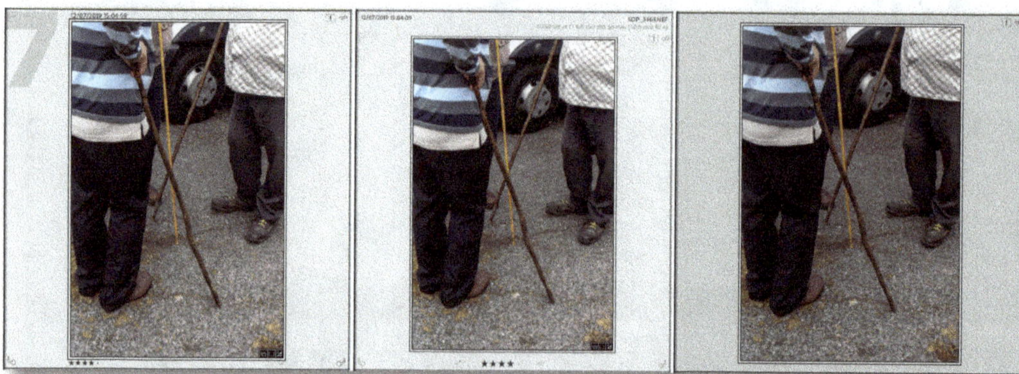

Figure 3.27 – Settings from left to right – Compact Cells, Expanded Cells, and Clean Cells

To manage any of the preceding cell views, we need to right-click on any photograph and choose **View Options...** from the very bottom of the appearing menu, go to **View** > **View Options**, or click the "⌘ + *J*" shortcut.

We can cycle through these three views with a shortcut, "*J*".

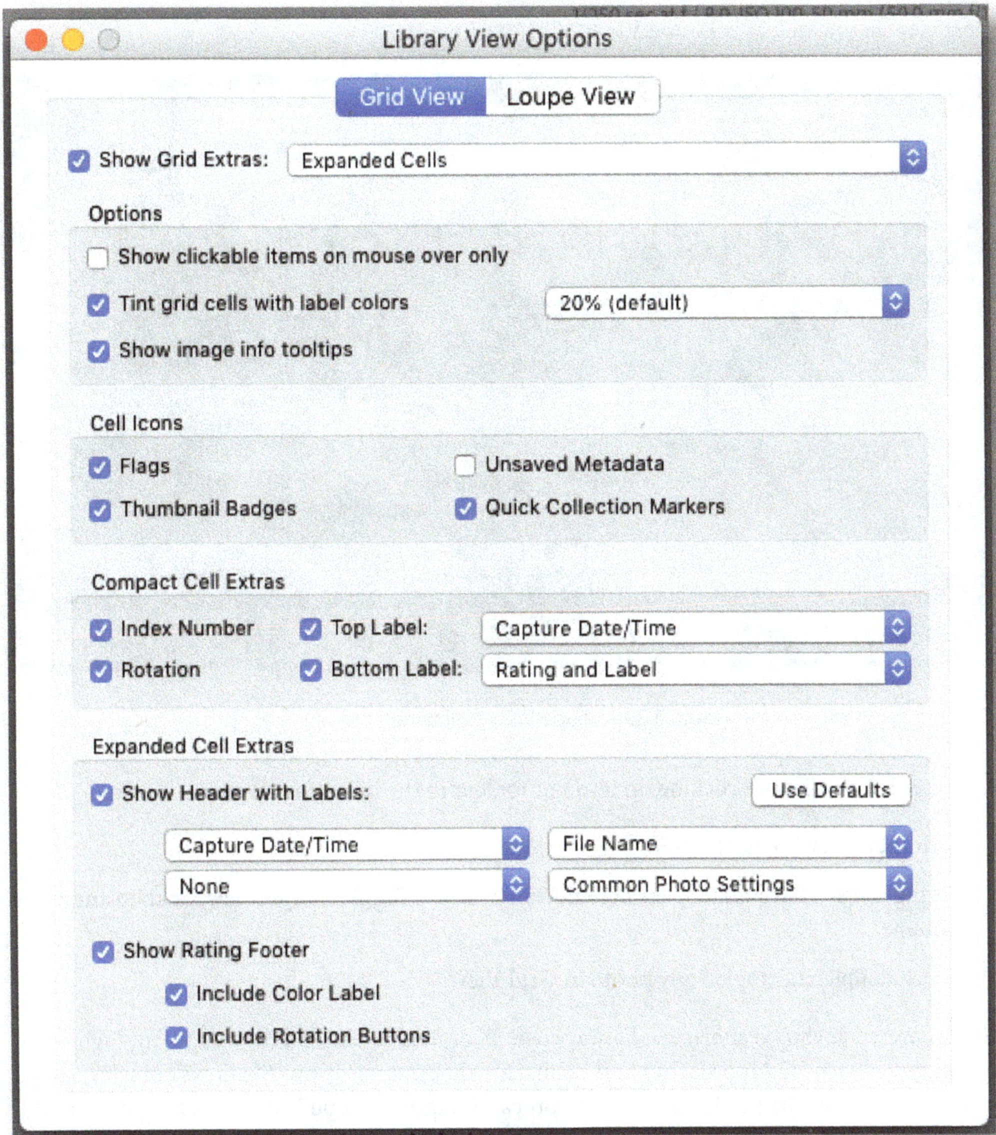

Figure 3.28 – The author's preferences for Grid View

Loupe View

The next view in the toolbar is **Loupe View**.

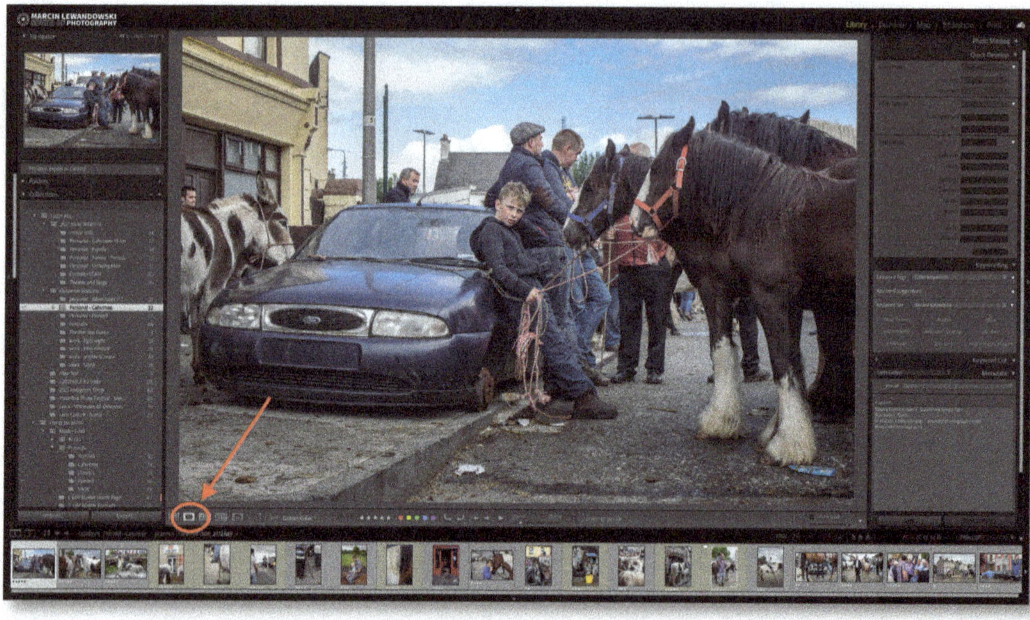

Figure 3.29 – Loupe View – all panels open

We can enter Loupe View by clicking on it in our toolbar in the following ways:

- With the "*E*" keyboard shortcut
- Hitting "*Enter*", hitting the space bar choosing **View** > **Toggle Loupe View**, or choosing **View** > **Loupe**
- By just double-clicking on any photo in Grid View

Since I discovered keyboard shortcuts, I always use "*E*" or double-click on the image, but Lightroom can accommodate various approaches and habits, as you can see. Using "*E*" allows entering Loupe View from any place within Lightroom. As you can imagine, Loupe View can also present vital information about the photograph we are viewing. When we press "*I*", it does so. Pressing that shortcut again will cycle to the second set of info, and on the third keypress, it will disappear again. We can choose what information is displayed in the same way as in Grid View by going to **View** > **View Options** or pressing "⌘ + *J*". Once we are in Loupe View, we can zoom in on any area of the photograph. Note that our cursor became a small loupe. Once we click anywhere on a picture, we will be zooming it to 100% of its size. We can change that by adjusting the value with the zoom slider located on our toolbar. When we click on the photo again, it will return to its default size, fitting the view area.

Compare View ("C")

With this view, we can compare two photographs side by side, as shown here:

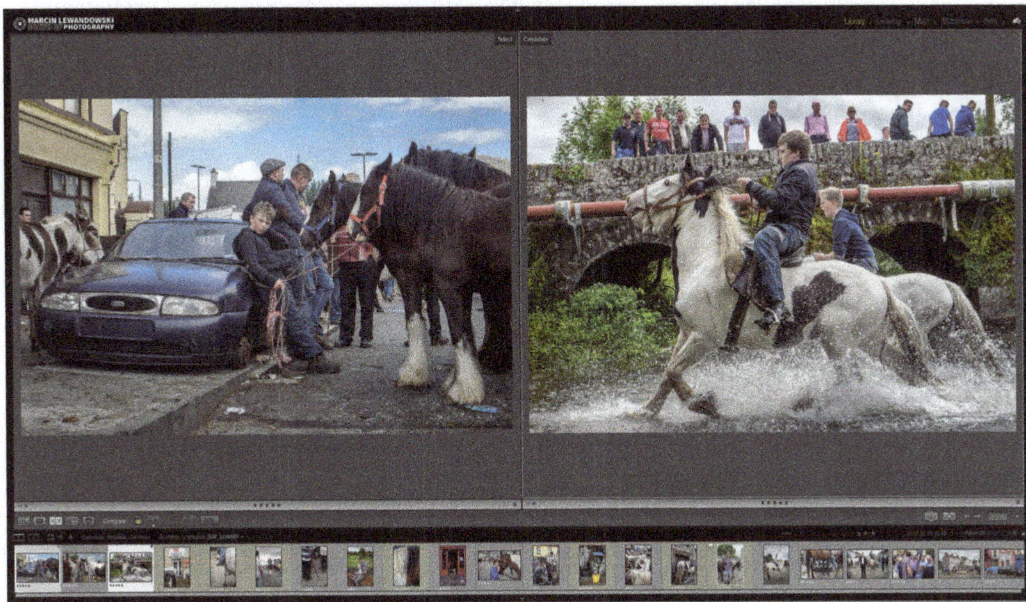

Figure 3.30 – Compare View with the side panels collapsed

Once you enter this mode, Lightroom will automatically assign the currently viewed photograph as **Select** and another one as **Candidate**. The picture we can actively change has a thin white frame around it, which by default is around the photo marked as **Select**. We can change the active photograph to a different one by clicking on any other photograph in our Filmstrip. Note that using left and right arrows will not change the **Select** photo but instead the **Candidate** photo – this is to help us choose the best photographs in a series.

While in Compare View, we can zoom in on both images simultaneously or separately; we control this by linking and unlinking focus with a small lock icon on the toolbar. When the photographs are not linked, and we would like to see the same zoomed area on **Select** and **Candidate**, we click **Sync**, and this will zoom to the same area which we are viewing without changing the Link Focus setting. The following tools after the zoom settings are **Swap** and **Make Select**.

The swap will exchange **Select** and **Candidate**, while **Make Select** will upgrade our current **Candidate** to the status of **Select** and choose the following available photograph as **Candidate**. Both sections, **Select** and **Candidate**, have all necessary rating tools underneath them, including flags, stars, and color labels. Once we are finished with this Compare View, we can either click **Done** or press "C" to exit to Loupe View. We can also use any other keyboard shortcut and jump to a different panel or different module.

Survey View ("N")

This is also a tool for comparing photographs, but not only can we choose our favorites among a selection of pictures; we can also change their sequencing by manually moving around our photographs.

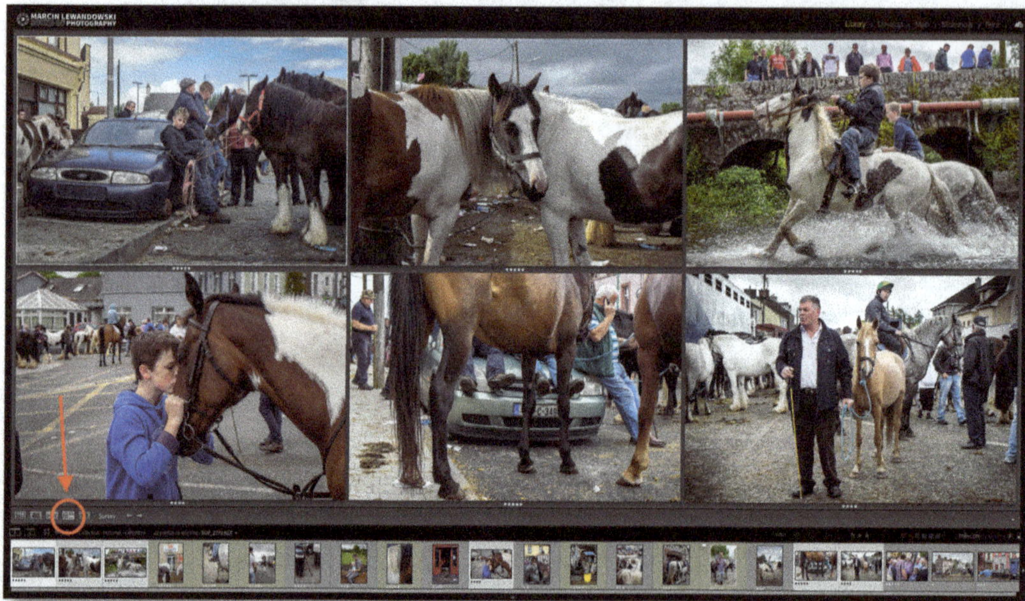

Figure 3.31 – Survey View with the side panels collapsed

Survey View works even with just one photo, and there is an upper limit on how many photos we can choose for Survey View, but it's a large number, dependent on the screen size. For me, this is the ultimate tool for choosing photos that fit in a series. In the name of "*less is more*," I always try to edit out any photos that are not, in my opinion, simply the best. I use Survey View more often than Compare View, even for choosing from a series of similar photographs. I find it easier to pick one of four or five than constantly focusing on just two and picking the better one. Survey View is also handy for comparing various virtual copies, but we will get to that in the chapter about the Develop module. As with other tools in Lightroom, this view supports star rating, flagging, and color labels. What I like the most about this view is that we can shuffle photographs around and see how they look next to each other.

People ("O")

When we activate People View, Lightroom will open a new tool and start the process of recognizing faces on all photographs in the location we are currently viewing (a folder, a collection, all photographs, and so on).

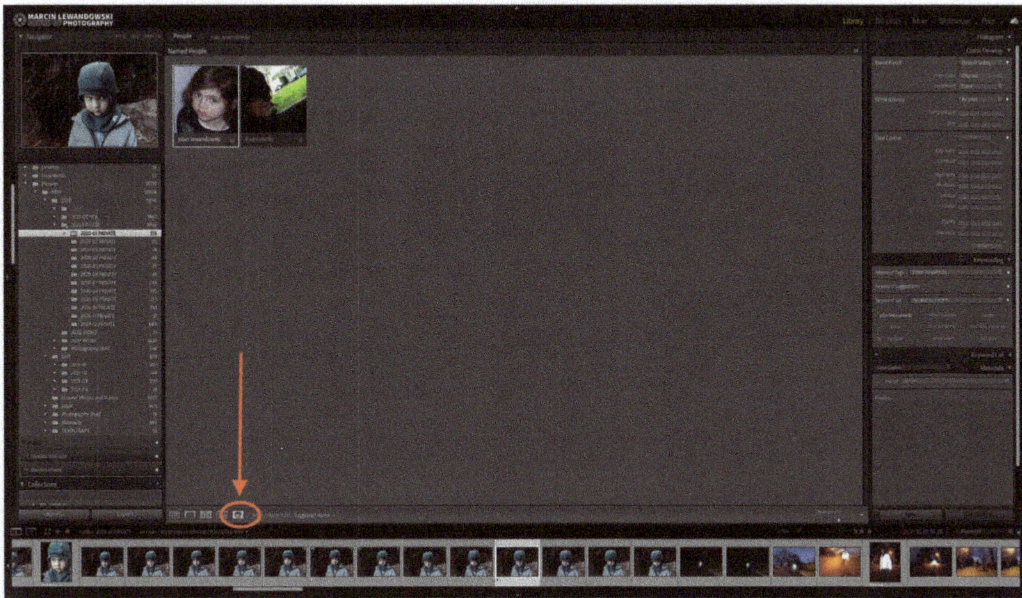

Figure 3.32 – A People View example with opened panels

If we choose in **Catalog Setting** ("⌥⌘,") **Metadata** > **Automatically detect faces in all photos**, then People View will be populated with Lightroom's best guesses. I say best guesses, as sometimes Lightroom's AI's attempts are hilarious or simply odd, such as a road sign or a piece of fabric; sometimes, it will just be completely wrong and guess the wrong person. It's an interesting feature, especially if your photographs are full of faces which you want to be all clearly defined and searchable. I'm experimenting mostly with family photographs at the moment and with varying levels of success, but the more I use People View, the more I like it. I urge you to try it, especially if you are just starting your journey with Lightroom.

Painter

Imagine a spray can that you can load with whatever you want – Painter is a realization of that idea within Lightroom. To turn on the Painter tool, we need to click the spray can icon or use the "⌥⌘K" shortcut. This will open a menu with the list of available "paints."

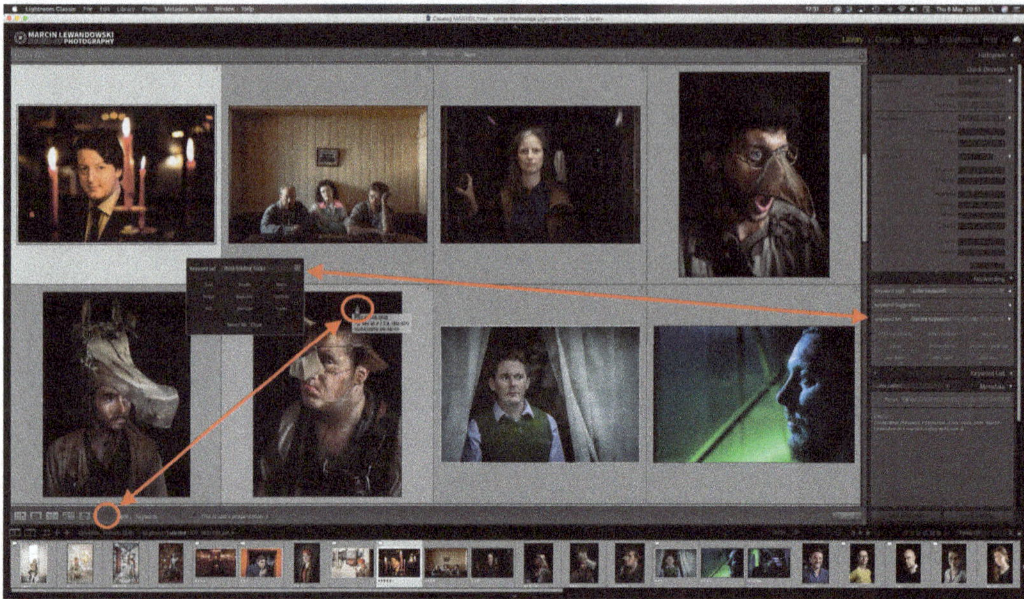

Figure 3.33 – The Painter feature turned on with a custom keyword set in use

First and foremost is the keywording paint, which I use most often. To work with keywords in Painter mode, I make my thumbnails very small but large enough to recognize the person, object, or anything else that I want to assign a keyword on each photograph, and I start spraying. Just as with an actual spray can, as long as we hold the mouse button down as we move across pictures, we will be assigning our chosen keyword to each of the pictures we go over. The same principle applies to spraying pictures with labels, settings, rotations, and so on. To disable Painter mode, we simply "put the can back from where we took it" by clicking the empty gray circle, where we activated the Painter tool on the toolbar, or by pressing *Esc*. We can also temporarily activate Painter mode by holding "⇧⌥" – this will change our cursor into a spray can, allowing us to paint with the most recently used settings.

Sorting

I think that of all the available tools in Lightroom, this is the one that does not require explanation. The letters **A>Z** or **Z>A** sort by ascending or descending, and a pop-up menu provides us with a plethora of options.

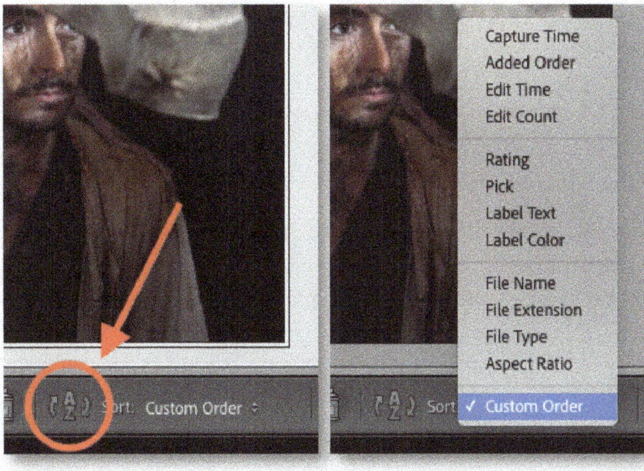

Figure 3.34 – Sorting – descending and ascending on the left, and the available fields to sort on the right

Flagging

We have a choice of three flag statuses – **Flagged** ("*P*"), **Rejected** ("*X*"), and **Unflagged**; two of them are available here as buttons, and not choosing any of them leaves a photograph with the **Unflagged** status. As a default, all photographs have the **Unflagged** status.

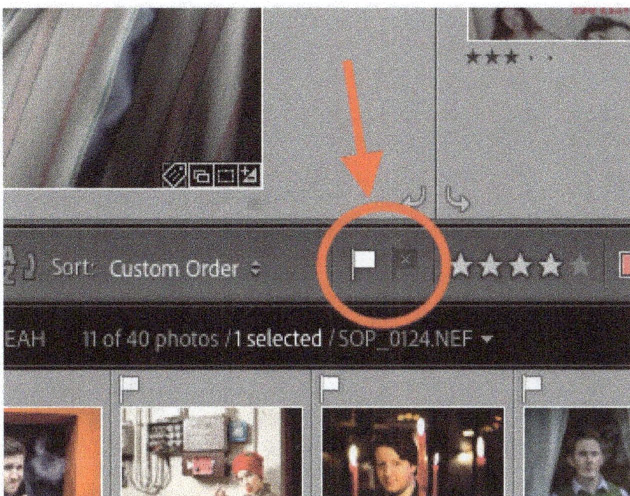

Figure 3.35 – Flags – pick (P) and reject (X)

We can filter our Library for all three statuses, separately and in combinations, and there are many ways to use the flagging system:

- *Example 1* – After we import all images and we need to send out a few samples, we can quickly skim through all the imported photographs, assigning a few the **Flagged** status with the "*P*" keyboard shortcut, which is easy to remember with the mnemonic **pick this photo**.
- *Example 2* – After we create the final edit and send samples to our client, they might come back with a choice of five photos they would like to see in black and white. We can quickly locate the photographs in question in that scenario, filtering for their filenames and marking them as **Flagged**.
- *Example 3* – When we are working on an edit, we can mark all out-of-focus, closed-eyes, and unusable pictures as **Rejected** with the "*X*" keyboard shortcut (as a mnemonic, think about "crossing" them out and checking them for deletion). Once we are done, we can filter the folder we are working on for **Rejected** and delete all the filtered photos.

Rating – stars (0–5).

The star rating is probably the tool I use most often, not counting the Develop module, of course. From complete amateurs to professional photographers, everyone faces the same problem – out of all the photographs I took today (during the event, concert, hike, holidays, project, and so on), which ones are the best and good enough to show my client? The star rating helps us with that, and I'll show you how I do it in practice later on in this chapter. Each photograph in Lightroom has a default rating of 0 stars. By clicking on a toolbar star, we apply a rating of that many stars; they add up as we go left, and so the first star is one, and the last one is five.

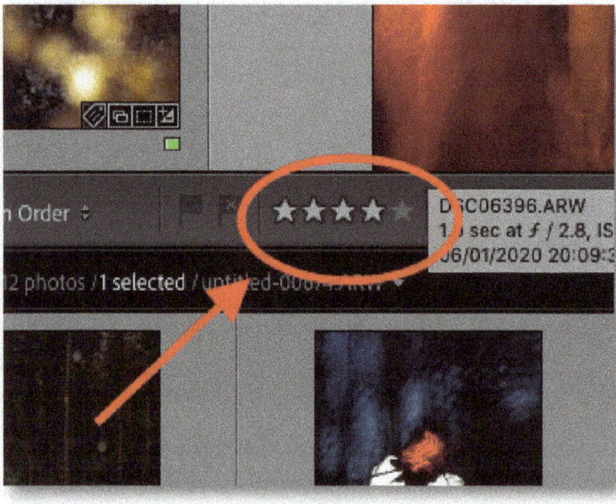

Figure 3.36 – The star rating tool set to four stars

To do this with keyboard shortcuts, we can simply use digits "1" through "5" on our keyboard to do the same. When in Grid View, all selected photographs will receive a star rating, and it's a technical fact worth remembering. I made a mess a few times when I started my journey with Lightroom, applying a rating to the whole folder without noticing it after spending a few hours rating and flagging everything. We can always use "*Ctrl* + *Z*" to undo the last edit (or many of them; keep pressing), but we can't do it after closing Lightroom so remember that a rating will always apply to all selected photographs when we are in Grid View. When we use Loupe View or Survey View, only the currently viewed photo will receive the rating (or flag/color label for that matter), even if we have multiple photographs selected.

Color Label (6–9)

This is another way to distinguish a selection of photographs, this time with color labels. To use it, we can either click on the five different colorful squares in our toolbar or use numbers on the keyboard. Numbers 6 through to 9 represent colors in the same order as they appear in the toolbar.

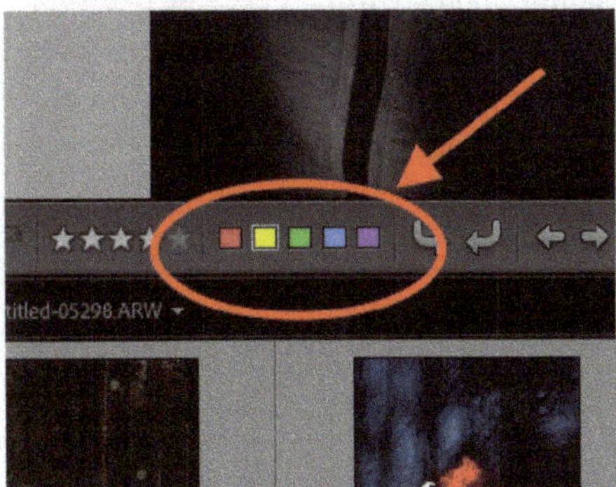

Figure 3.37 A

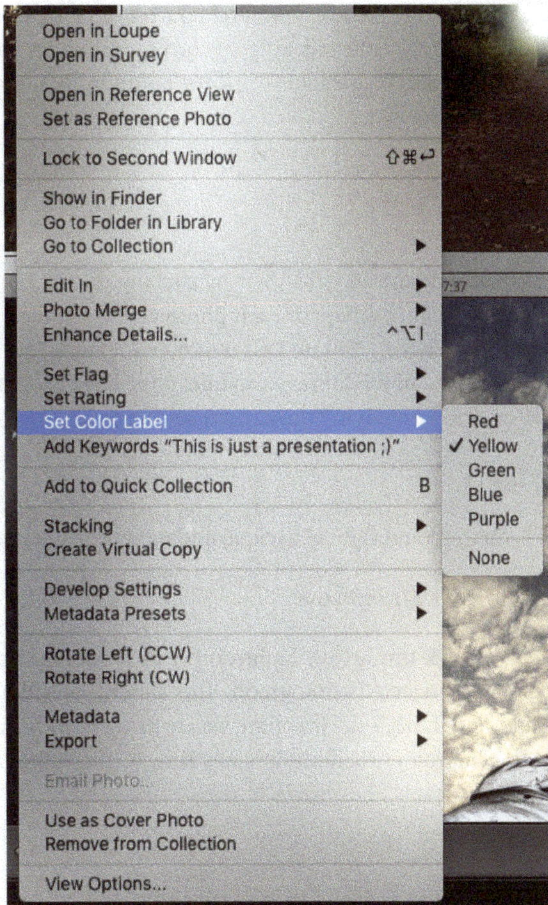

Figure 3.37 B – Images showing the Color Label tool set to Yellow and right-click to set the color label

Unfortunately, there is no keyboard shortcut for the purple label. The only way to apply purple is by choosing one of the squares, going to the photo > **Set Color Label** > **Purple**, or clicking on the photo and choosing **Set Color Label** > **Purple**. We can remove applied color labels by using toolbar colors or the same keyboard shortcut. All numbers toggle an assigned color on/off. Remember when we looked at **View Options** a few pages ago ("⌘ + *J*")? One of the available options to pick was **Tint grid cells with label colors** – with this option enabled, all cells will be colored with an assigned color and, when selected, have a thin frame in the same color around the photograph.

Rotate

You can rotate the picture counterclockwise or clockwise. You can do this by either clicking on corresponding arrows or with a keyboard shortcut – "⇧*]*" for counterclockwise and "⇧*[*" for clockwise.

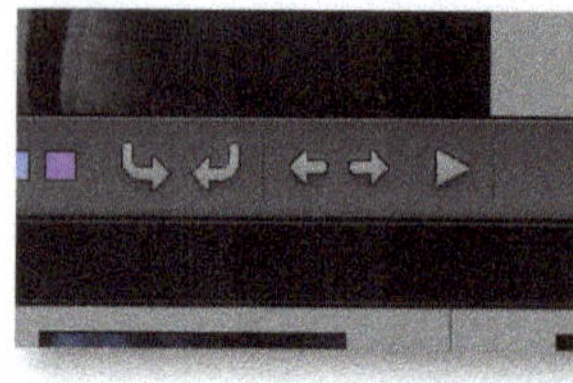

Figure 3.38 – The Rotate, Navigate, and Impromptu Slideshow tools

You can also do this in Grid View by clicking on one of the corresponding arrows in the bottom-left and bottom-right corners of each photo cell. As you can imagine, you can also access this function by choosing **Photo** > **Rotate Left** (counterclockwise) and **Photo** > **Rotate Right** (clockwise). As with everything else in the Library module, if we have more than one photograph selected while in Grid View, we will be applying the chosen setting to all of the selected photographs.

Navigate

Left is forward and right is back, just like our keyboard arrows. But we already knew that...

Impromptu Slideshow

When we click this arrow, Lightroom will render and play an impromptu slideshow, starting with the currently selected photograph. This slideshow will use settings we have picked in the Slideshow module, and if this is the first time we are using it, they will be default Lightroom settings. We can also start this impromptu slideshow at any time by using the *"Enter"* and *"Esc"* keyboard shortcut to stop it.

Zoom

While in Loupe View, with "*E*", we can use the **Zoom** function, which can zoom in as far as 1600%. We can either click anywhere on our photograph to zoom into 100% detail, use the "*Z*" shortcut, or use the slider directly.

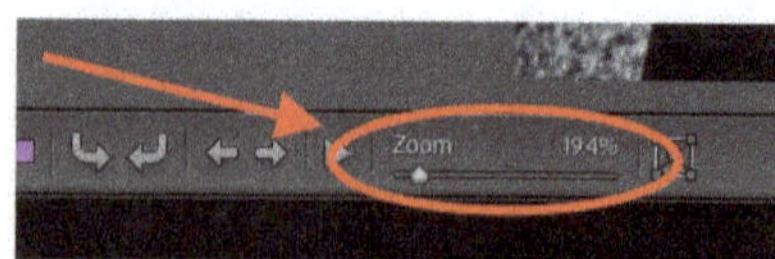

Figure 3.39 – The Zoom tool in Loupe View

After we press "Z" to zoom into 100%, adjust the zoom level to any value other than 100%, and press "Z" to zoom out. Next time we press "Z", Lightroom will use the adjusted zoom setting. We can reset the setting to 100% by double-clicking on the **Zoom** slider's arrow.

Draw Face Region

Activating this function will allow us to associate a face with a name. If you didn't activate **Automatic Detection of Faces** in **Catalog Settings** ("⌥⌘"), then you might want to assign names to some faces within your Library manually.

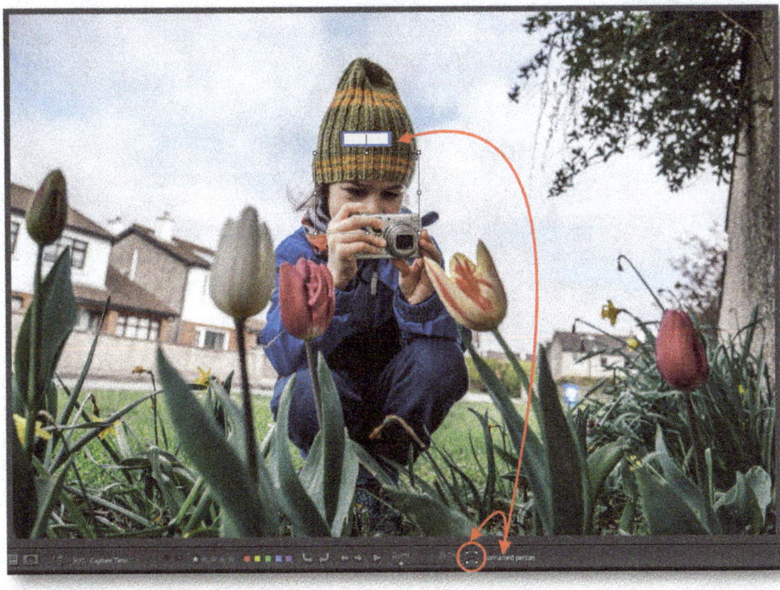

Figure 3.40 – The Draw Face Region tool activated and ready for name input

These names will now be accessible for search functions and visible in the panel on the right in **Keyword List** > **People.**

Grid (not to be confused with Grid View)

This function overlays a grid over our selected photograph, and we can adjust its density with the **Grid** slider. We can also hold the "⌘" key to access a small menu that will appear on top of our selected photo.

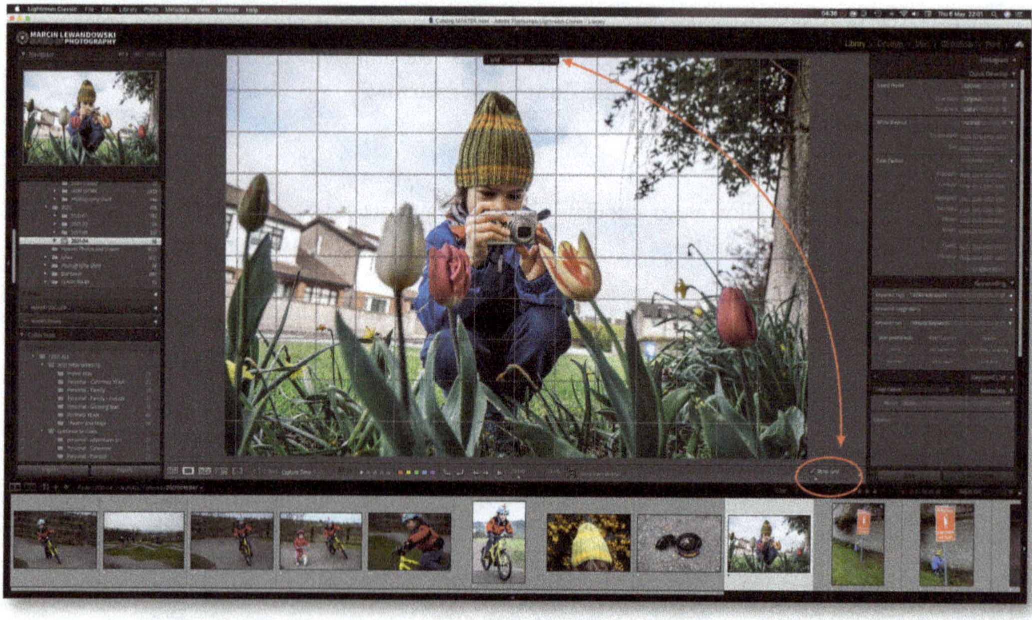

Figure 3.41 – The Grid Overlay tool activated

By left-clicking on the **size** or **opacity** words, we can move left and right to change the grid size (density) and opacity.

Thumbnails

While we are in Grid View, the aforementioned three options are unavailable (Zoom, Draw Face Region, and Grid will be unavailable). They are replaced by the **Thumbnail Size** slider, which we can move left and right to adjust the size of displayed thumbnails to our heart's content.

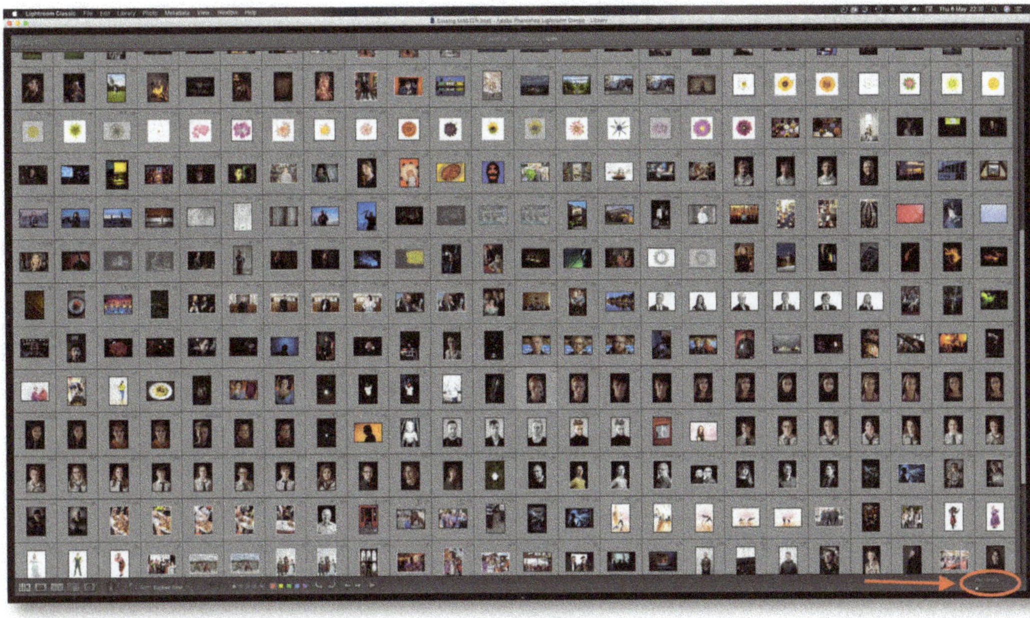

Figure 3.42 A

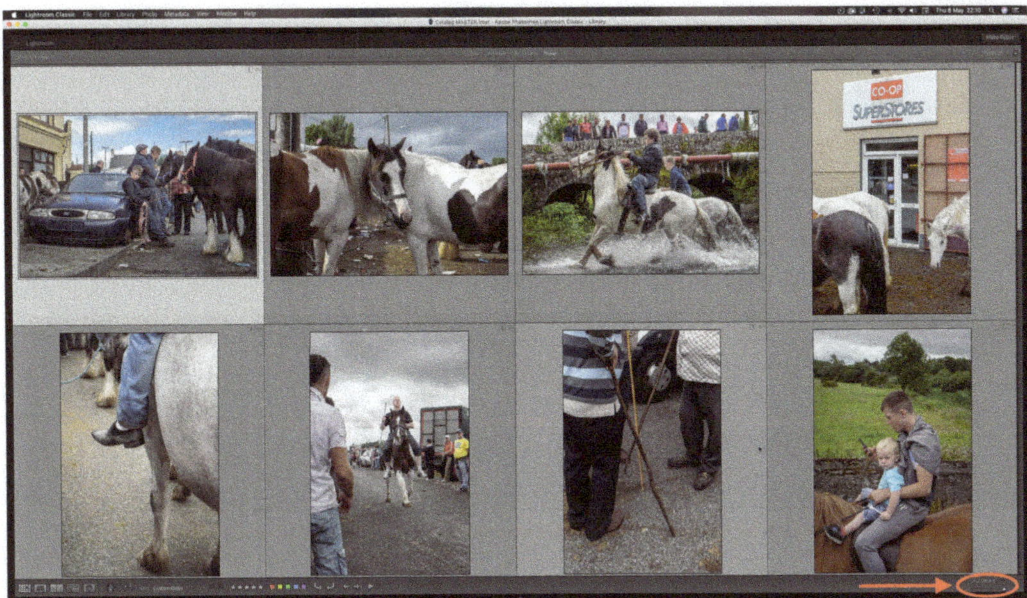

Figure 3.42 B – The smallest and largest possible thumbnails

Getting to know the Filmstrip toolbar

The next available toolbar is under the one we just learned about. It runs over the whole length of the Filmstrip, and it is available in the same form within each module, being an integral part of the Filmstrip. This toolbar contains some of the most valuable tools for making edits.

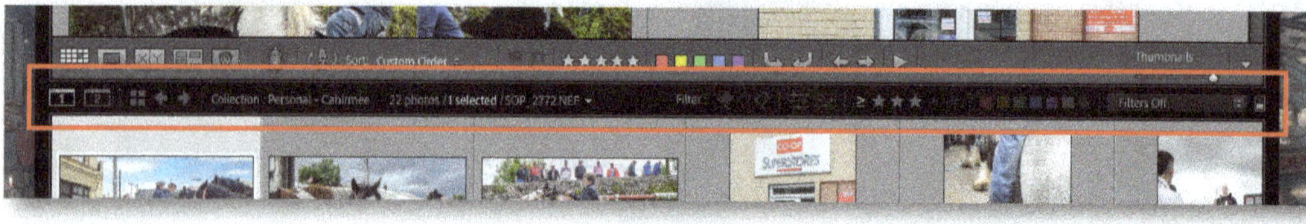

Figure 3.43 – The Filmstrip toolbar

The first tool on the left is for managing additional displays – there will be more about it in *Chapter 10, Final Notes and Summary.*

The next button opens Grid View – here, it's called Library Grid. The following two arrows are forward and backward and only work for locations, so we can jump there and back between folders, collections, and so on.

Source Location is a set of valuable information about what we are viewing. It shows us the following:

- The type and name of the location we are currently looking at
- The total number of items in this location and the number of images displayed after we applied any filters
- The count of presently selected images
- The filename of the now highlighted image (if we hover over other photos in the Filmstrip, then this will be the name of whichever photograph we are hovering over)

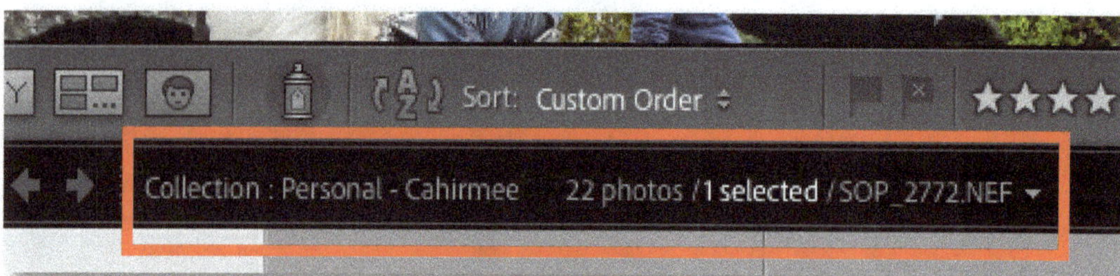

Figure 3.44 – Source Location

We can click anywhere on this toolbar, as far as the word **Filter**, to open a handy location sub-menu.

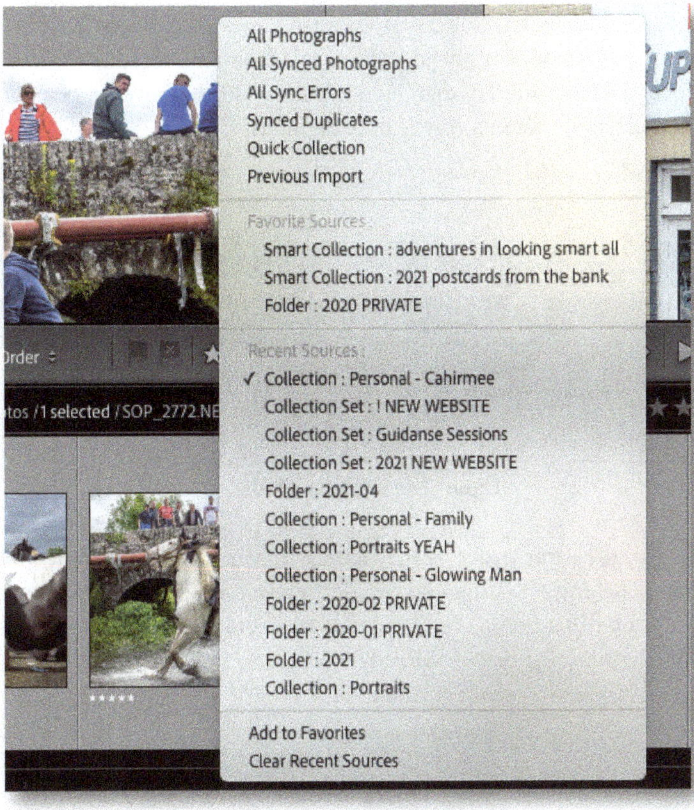

Figure 3.45 – Source location sub-menu

The first set of locations is always the same and provides us further access to a few handy default locations and collections that we usually overlook. With **All Sync Errors** we can check for any issues we might have with Sync. Once in a while, something will get stuck for various reasons, and here is always a good place to start our investigation. In case of an unknown failure, we can go to **Lightroom Classic** > **Preferences** (or "⌘") > **Lightroom Sync** to try to figure it out, or reset Sync by pressing "⌥" and choosing **Rebuild Sync Data**.

The second set is what makes this sub-menu worthwhile, in my opinion – **Favorite Sources**. We can add to this list and easily remove from it a shortcut to any location within Lightroom we want. To do this, we must go to the location we would like to have on this list and choose the **Add to Favorites** option in the relevant menu. If the location is already referenced in **Favorites Sources**, that menu position will change to **Remove from Favorites**.

The third and last set is **Recent Sources**, which doesn't need an introduction. It is a list of our 12 most recently visited locations – we can clear it in the following, the last part of this menu.

Filters

Finally we are going to dive into Filters! Filters are accessible from two places. The first is this toolbar we are currently discussing, and this is my go-to filter selection for everyday work. We must fire up the second filter bar for a deeper kind of digging – it is located just above the photographs while in Grid View mode; we will get to that in a couple of paragraphs.

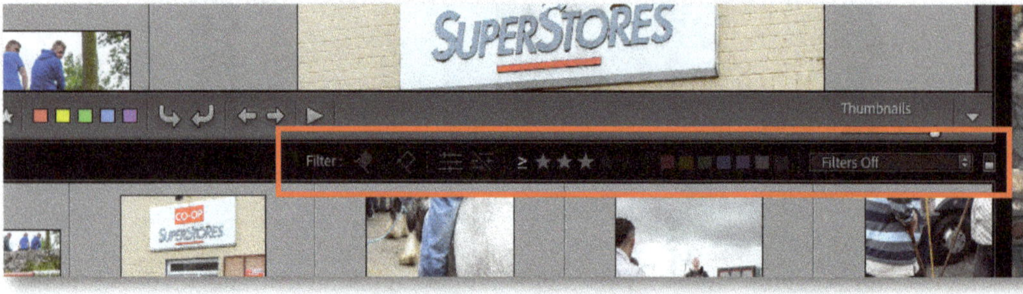

Figure 3.46 – Toolbar filters

Filters on this tab are in the same order as they appear in the toolbar above it, which is initially confusing. I remember clicking on rating and wondering why it filters images, or maybe it was the other way around. One filter that doesn't have a tool equivalent is **Filter based on edit status**, which allows us to look for photographs that we already worked on in the Develop module or original, unedited files.

Figure 3.47 – The Filter tool based on edit status

We can combine all filters on this tab with each other. When we choose multiple conditions, then all conditions will have to be met for Lightroom to display a photograph – that is, if we select **Flagged Photos** and two stats, then Lightroom will display only photographs that meet both these conditions.

The only slight variation is with the color labels – when we choose one color label, Lightroom will only display photographs with that color label. When we choose more than one color label, then Lightroom will display all photographs with either color.

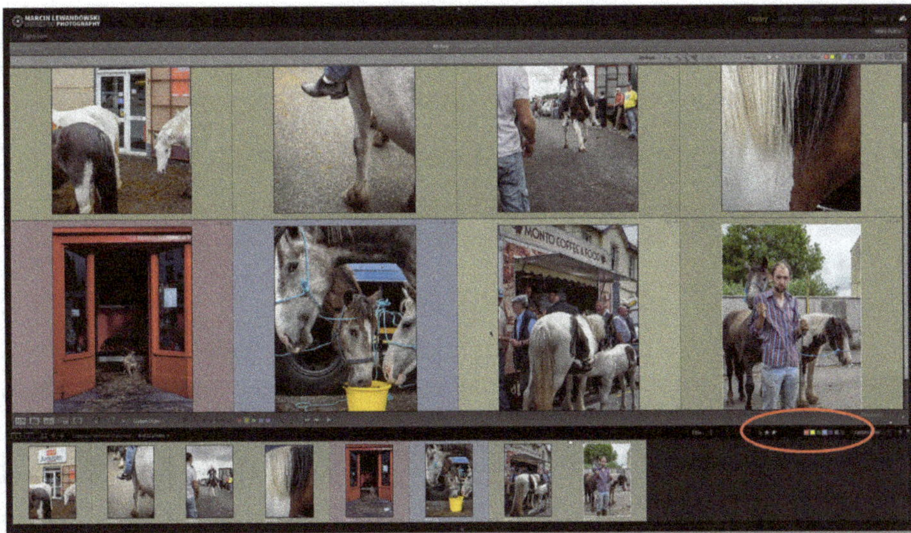

Figure 3.48 – The toolbar filter enabled for images with a rating equal to or greater than two stars and a red, yellow, or blue label

Filters based on a flag, rating, and color are usually enough for any day-to-day work, but if we want to dig deeper, there is an absolute mine of information in the filter bar above our Library. We can switch it on by choosing one of the few default modes available in the pop-up menu next to the filters we just mentioned or choosing one of the modes in the filter Bar itself. If you can't see the filter bar with the **Text**, **Attribute**, **Metadata**, and **None** words, make sure that you are in Grid View, and if it's still not there, press "\" on your keyboard – it's the shortcut to toggle the visibility of the filter Bar on and off.

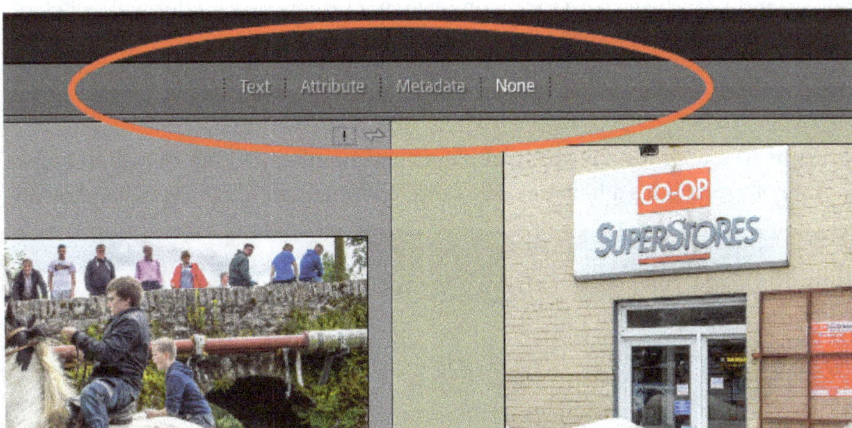

Figure 3.49 – The filter Bar on top of our Library

Before we jump to the filter bar, note a small toggle at the very end of this row – it's an on/off switch for filters, and when turned on, it will apply the latest filter setting we used.

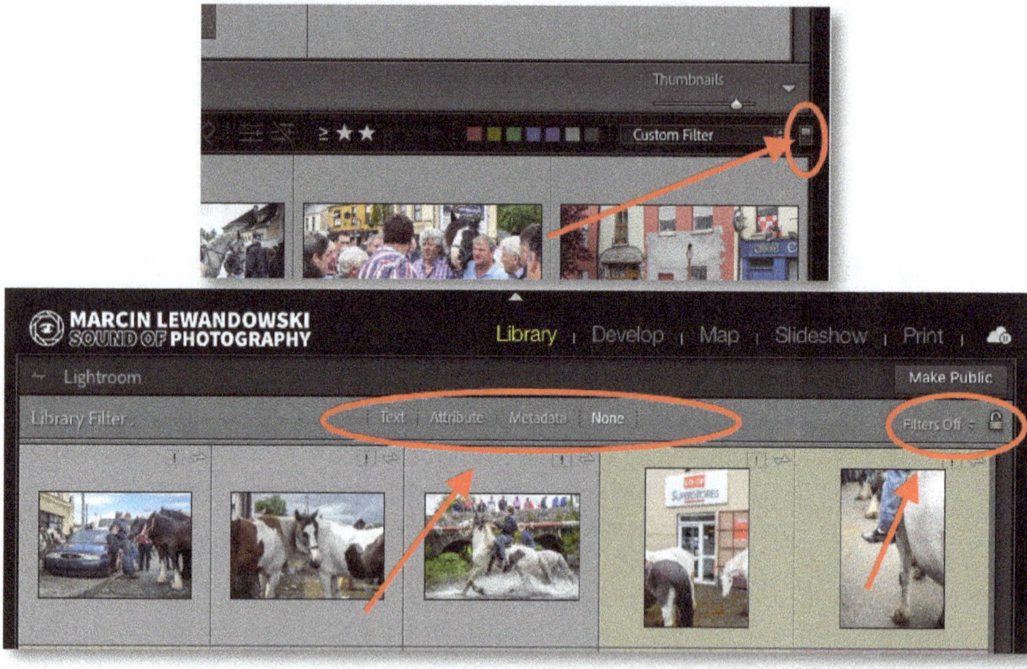

Figure 3.50 – The filter on/off toggle switch and the filter bar tools view

The filter bar offers four categories to choose from, and they can all be combined and are all visible in the middle of this bar. At the end of the bar, we can access the same pop-up menu that is on the Filmstrip toolbar, and lastly, we have a lock icon – when it's opened, the filter will switch off when we will change sources, and when locked, filters will not be disabled when we change sources.

Text

This field allows us to search for any string of letters and numbers within our photographs' data. Here is a good way to start if it's a filename, keyword, comment, or EXIF detail, as shown here:

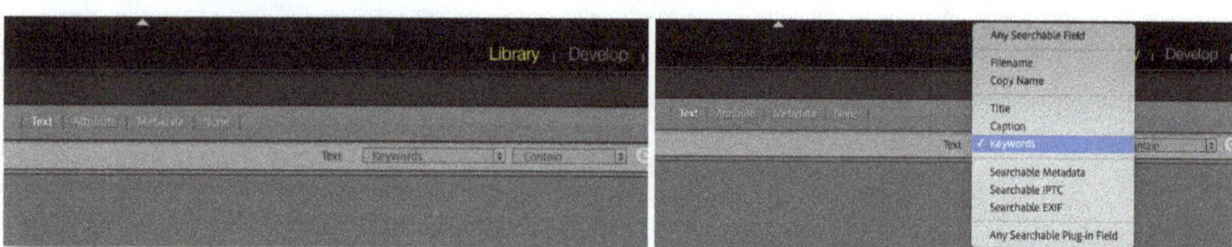

Figure 3.51 A

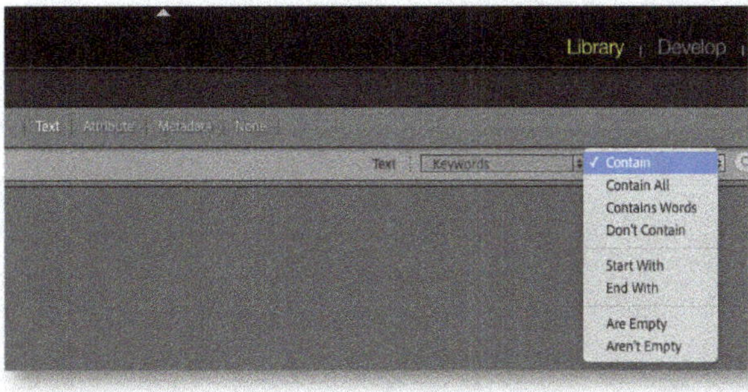

Figure 3.51 B – Setting pop-up menus available from the filter bar

From the first menu, we can choose which parts of data we want Lightroom to crawl; the second menu allows us to specify conditions. The more specific we can be, the faster we will receive the results – that is, if we look for a string of digits in any searchable field, we will receive results with items pulled from keywords, EXIF, IPTS, locations, and so on. For example, **1,000** can be part of a filename, focal length, ISO, shutter speed, or detail of the name of our camera. If we, however, specify that we want to look for the same string just in the filename, the results will include only photographs with filenames that contain the searched-for string.

Attribute

This part of the Library Filter matches almost precisely the content of the Filmstrip Filter with the addition of the **Kind** function, which will allow us to display three "top-level" kinds of files – master photos, virtual copies, and videos – separately or in any combination.

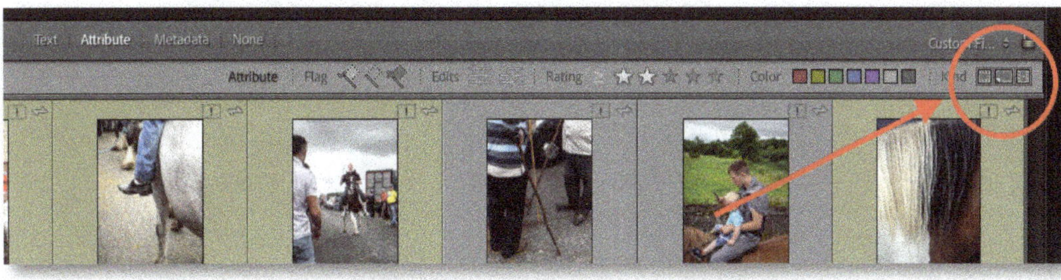

Figure 3.52 A – The filter for the three types of files to be displayed – left to right – master photos, virtual copies, and videos

Metadata

This filter gives us the most impressive set of possibilities, and we can add up to eight different queries, one per column, when using it. The top of each column always has two switches, one in each corner:

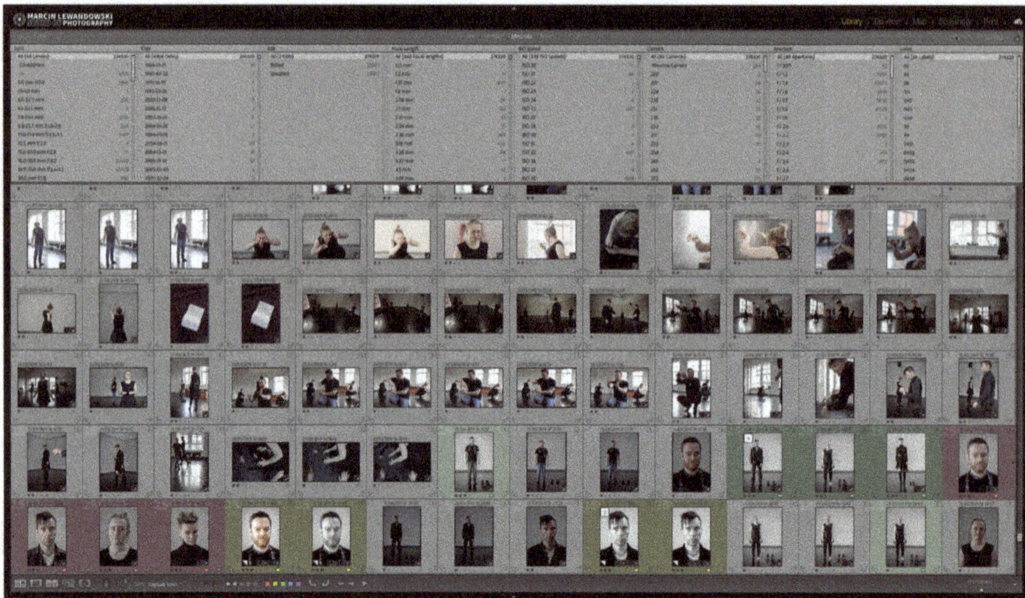

Figure 3.53 – Metadata filters turned on with maximum columns and no filters enabled

The top left gives us a choice of all available filters we can apply, while the right is responsible for adding and removing columns. In the case of the date, the right switch allows us to choose sort order and view type; the hierarchical view shows all the top-level folders we can open, and flat view, which shows only the folders containing actual photographs.

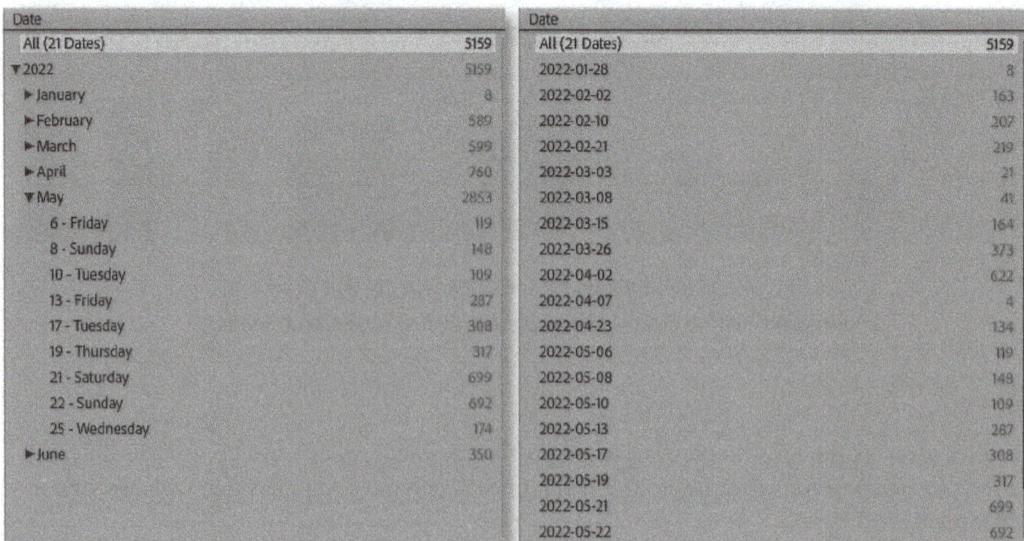

Figure 3.54 - Hierarchical and flat view examples of the same selection

Filtered results are displayed on an "and" basis, meaning that results will be narrowed down with each column, starting on the left. For example, if we have a date as our first column and click on a date within it, all the following columns' results will narrow them down to only show results from the chosen date. Similarly, if we, for example, select **Lens** as our first column and pick one, then all following columns will narrow down their search results to only show images made with that lens, and so on. One thing to remember is that picking different results to be displayed in any of the columns will do the following:

- Reset all results in columns on the left side.
- Filter results in the columns on the right to reflect the new query.

Again, we can combine all three filters. Any active filter will have its name highlighted. We can deactivate all filters by clicking **None**.

How I edit

They say, "lead by example," so the following sections are some examples of my editing workflow.

The big one – editing a large selection of photographs

Here is a system which I use to approach large edits, especially when I need to work fast, there are many images, and I don't have time to dilly dally:

1. After importing a new set of photographs, I quickly run through them in Loupe View and mark as rejected any unusable photos.

   This action not only allows me to prepare a reasonably clean collection to work with, but it is also an opportunity to skim through the whole body of images. I can see anything that stands out, and these "standout" images will get five stars straight away. It needs to be an organic process at this stage, without too much thinking involved. At this stage, I would be working primarily in Grid View, sporadically turning on Loupe View, confirming treasures and rubbish alike.

2. Once that's done, I will run through the photographs again, one by one, and mark anything vaguely interesting with one star. At this stage, it's still a very intuitive process – that is, suppose I have a burst series of 5, 10, or even more images, and while clicking through them, most seem good. In that case, I will mark all of them as one star and worry about it later; this is all about a gut feeling and simply choosing images that might be candidates for the final selection.

   After this second stage, I do something that might feel counterintuitive for some of you, but here it is anyway.

3. I filter for all of the photos marked with one star, go to Grid View and mark them all as two stars, and then I filter through for the two star-rated photos and get rid of any weaker images by giving them one star.

   By editing this way, removing the weaker images from the overall selection first, I have all of the photos that potentially create my final edit always on the screen. It is a process that also reminds me of working with tangible prints. When small prints are laid down on a table, we can shuffle them around, getting rid of photographs that don't fit in the sequence.

4. I repeat this process the same way, up to five stars or until I think I have picked only the best frames.

I found that having a target number of final photographs at the back of my head while editing can be a helpful way to stay focused and ruthless when getting rid of weaker images. The tricky question that might come to your mind at this moment might be, *what is the magic number*?

As with most things in creative practice, this includes photography, there are no correct answers, but as a rule of thumb, I'm happy to hit a 10% mark when editing any large commission. Thinking in these terms, and just as an example, let's assume we spent a day at a wedding and made 2,500 frames. Probably 10–20% will get an automatic "*boot out the door,*" and another half or more will be parts of a burst/series or any other images shot in quick succession. That's already around up to 1,500 images rejected from the final edit after the two-star run. If we can keep every fourth photo from what's remaining after that, all is good, and we did a great job.

The easiest way to eliminate weaker images when looking at similar photographs is by comparing them in Survey View and downgrading them there.

After all of this is done, I will usually revisit the lower ratings for one more run-through to find any possible gems that might be hiding somewhere and, in the end, delete anything with zero stars. There will be some exceptions that I will flag or assign color labels to, but that's a whole different topic.

This leads us directly from easily manageability to enjoying perusing our collections. Once you have fewer photographs, you will pay more attention to them. It will be easier to find what you are looking for, and instead of searching for a needle in a haystack, you will simply open a gallery of images you already liked in the first place so that you can then choose your absolute favorites.

Handy shortcuts to use here are view (the "*E*" keyboard shortcut) and delete (the "*X*" keyboard shortcut). Once this is done, I filter for the rejected photos and delete all the original raw files.

The not-so-big one – everyday edits from shorter commissions

As much as I would love all of my jobs to be multi-day sessions, lots of work consists of quick 1–2 hour callouts, sometimes half-a-day jobs. I will often approach editing these smaller commissions differently – here is an example of how I might do it:

1. After importing a new set of photographs, I'll glance through them in Grid View, and if I remember any unique frames that I know I want to see first, I'll make sure to do so and give them a high star rating, often five stars. I do this to ensure that I will not miss the intuitive "likes," even if some of them won't make the final cut. At this stage, if I want to send the client a sample, I will choose one or two of the images I just rated, do a "quick develop" job on them, export, and send an email/message to the client.
2. Once I have done that, I will make sure the photographs are in capture time order, and I will go to the first photo from the session and choose Loupe View ("*E*"). I will, at this stage, hide all panels using the "*Shift Tab*" keyboard shortcut.
3. The first run should be very intuitive, and so I quickly look through all of the photographs, rating everything that catches my attention with one star. If the pictures I initially rated with five stars still stand out when I get to them, I will leave them at a five-star rating; if they don't stand out, they will get a one-star rating in the process and be ready for the second round.

   When I say that I do a quick, intuitive run, I also mean that I don't linger too long on picking favorites from multiple frames within sets of bursts but instead choose from them on the fly. Sometimes, I might have a burst of similar photos from the same situation with only minor details making the difference – that is, closed eyes, someone moving head or hands, or objects and colors leaving or entering my frame. In that case, I might go down to the bottom of the screen to open Filmstrip and do a bit of "mini-editing" of the burst.
4. I will start by selecting all photos in the burst – this way, when I get to the last one, Lightroom will "*wrap around*" the selection and go to the first photograph in this burst.
5. Once selected, I will skim through them quickly a few times, marking favorites with one star.
6. Once I have a smaller selection, I will choose only the one-star images from this burst by filtering or manually by using "⌘ click".
7. From here, I press "*N*" to enter Survey View and rate the ones that stand out as weaker with zeros. After that slight digression, I will come back to all photographs and continue the one-star rating process.
8. After the one-star round, I'll filter for all images with a one-star rating and turn on Grid View again. I will now scroll up and down in this view to find pictures that I definitely like and want to include in the final selection, rating them with two stars. Once I'm happy with my picks, I'll filter for images with a one-star rating, change to Loupe View, and quickly run through all ones to make sure I didn't miss anything.

From here, it is just downhill, as by this stage, I should have a pretty well-defined edit rated two stars. If photos come from a 1 hour-ish session, it's probably already a final edit, which I might reduce by downgrading a few images to a one-star rating. If I have more photographs from a more extensive session, I will do a third, sometimes fourth, and fifth run, with an increased star rating each time, until I get to a selection I'm happy to present to the outside world.

Special treatment of edits with additional requirements

Quite often, edits will require special treatment, and this is where I usually deploy a color rating.

Let's say I want to make my final edit available in black and white (or even in a few different variations). In that case, I do the following:

1. I select all photos in the final edit, right-click on any of them, and choose **Create Virtual Copies**.

   Once we create our virtual copies, our selection will switch to the newly created copies. This is a great under-the-radar Lightroom feature.

2. From here, I simply apply a color label with the following keyboard shortcuts – "6" for red, "7" for yellow, "8" for green, "9" for blue, or if I really want purple, I'll right-click on one of the photos and choose **Set Color Label** > **Purple**.

From here, we can do a few things:

- To keep working only with the newly created virtual copies, I filter for **Color Label**, which I just applied to them.
- To stay only with my originals, I'll go to **Edit** > **Invert selection**. Another way to filter for originals is to filter for whatever was our final edit's star-rating value and select **Show photos with "Unlabeled" label** – it's the seventh color label filter's value.

As for flags, I use them in several different ways. One would be to mark during editing my personal favorites – sometimes what we like most might not be what a client will like most; sometimes, I flag things I want to include in a blog/Instagram.

Summary

After going through this chapter and experimenting with Lightroom itself, you should be confident enough to handle any edit using ratings, labels, and flags. My musings in the *How I edit* section are by no means a definite solution, nor will they be suitable for all photography and editing styles. For example, in my early years with Lightroom, I used flags as my go-to tool, and only after flagging did I start rating photographs, which I found constraining and more time-consuming. Additionally, it was taking away the usability of flags on larger-scale projects. I bet that by now, you already have your ideas on how to deploy available tools, and I would love to hear how you use them in your workflow.

We just looked at the extensive list of options available within the Library module. The critical point to take away from here is that we don't need to complicate our workflow by understanding all the combinations of the available tools but instead start small – pick the type of labeling that feels natural and start using it. All of these tools are here to make our choices more straightforward and more intuitive. The same goes for comparing photographs and using different types of views. Even though we have extensive keywording and querying capabilities, the main thing is to keyword our images descriptively so that when the time comes, we can quickly pinpoint the right ones. Lightroom exists to make photographers' time more easily manageable. Even the simple act of editing our selection by an increased rating to find favorite shots should be enough to start with; the rest will come naturally when we need it. Simply being aware of the availability of more complicated options will make it easy to find them when we need them.

In the next chapter, we will look at the management of our collection, structure the Library to help us find everything faster, and prepare Lightroom to be a reliable photographers' companion for years to come.

4

Folders and Collections

A big part of Lightroom Classic is its excellent selection of asset management tools. We will learn about the differences and similarities between **collections** and **folders**, how we might use them, and what different approaches can mean for our workflow, both in the short term and when planning for the future.

When I mention "asset management," it is just a fancy way to think of how digital evolution replaced sticking labels on bags with negatives held in shoeboxes. By assets, I mean our precious photographs. Even if they don't mean much financially, they can be of great emotional or historical value. So, we want to be able to pinpoint the photograph we are looking for quickly and accurately. If you are only just starting a photography career, you will appreciate neat management of your photo collection when a client comes back to you 10 years after you made a photo for them, asking for a full-resolution copy. If you are trying to clean up many years of unsorted folders and files, you will learn a few tricks to make your life easier. Again, asset management means knowing what is where and how to get there.

This chapter will cover the following topics:

- What are folders?
- What are collections?
- Creating and copying folders and collections
- Editing folders and collections
- Sorting, filtering, and other useful actions
- Ideas for using folders and collections to our advantage

A brief overview of folders and collections

Folders and collections are two distinctly different approaches to storing and managing a library of photographs, but we can work with them in a seamless way. The most important thing is to develop a new way of thinking about how we can access our photographs.

Folders

The most significant difference between folders and collections is that folders are referencing the actual locations of photo files on our hard drives. We learned in the previous chapter that by right-clicking on any folder and choosing the **Show Parent** option, we can display the exact path to the location of any folder on our hard drive. If we delete or move a photograph from a folder within Lightroom, the same will happen with the referenced file on our hard drive. Lightroom is as much an asset management system as it is a tool for making our photographs look better through the development process.

Access to all of the folders and collections is located in the left panel of Lightroom:

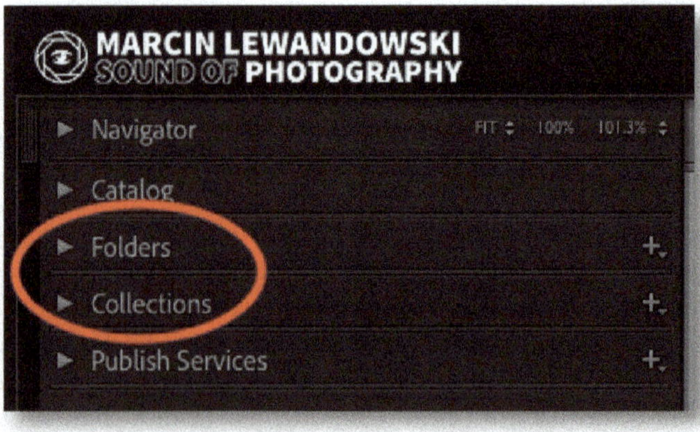

Figure 4.1 – The left panel, including Folders and Collections

Folders reflect the file structure on our hard drive, and if we are good at housekeeping, the structure within Lightroom and on the hard drive will be an exact match. The following screenshot shows the folder structure on Lightroom and the hard drive:

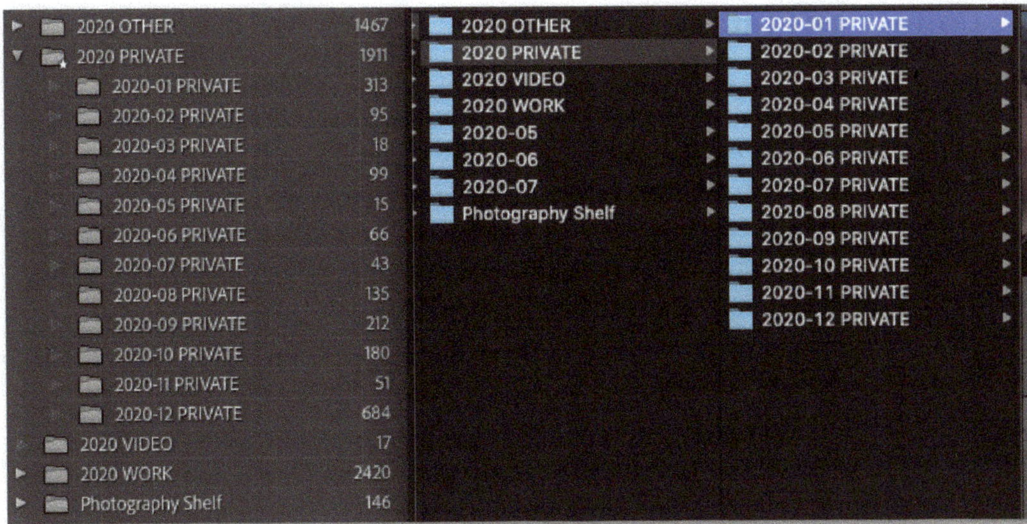

Figure 4.2 – The folders structure on Lightroom (left) and the hard drive (right)

Collections

On the other hand, collections are not related to the location of our files and are only possible within Lightroom. Imagine having a library housing thousands of photographs that you have made so far. They are all neatly structured by year, day, month, and event; all are star-rated, flagged, color-labeled, keyworded, captioned, and searchable through any camera setting. Imagine that you would always like to have quick access to all photographs rated with five stars, green-labeled, keyworded **night**, and photographed with a fast 50 mm lens.

The first thing that springs into mind is to go to **Catalog** > **All Photographs** and filter for these specific terms, but these results are only temporary and only available as long as we stay within these search terms. Instead, we can create a collection containing photographs with the chosen search terms and give it a title. Once we create a collection, it will be available to us on a permanent basis within the **Collections** tab.

Creating a collection will never make copies of any files; it will work as a visual reference of the list of files we just filtered. Both retrospectively and going forward, it will catch all photographs with the parameters we just used for the search. To better understand this concept, we will dive directly into the **Collections** tab and look at its offerings. One of the central things to remember is that working with folders is like working with files on the computer, and any changes made to a folder's structure within Lightroom will be reflected on our hard drive. Collections, on the other hand, are virtual copies that do not create extra versions of picture files on our hard drive.

The Collections tab

The first thing to notice on this tab is the small + sign on its right side. It is there to create new collections. Once we click on +, a small pop-up menu will appear, giving us access to a list of options that is split into three small groups. The first group of three options allows us to create collections, and we will come back to these in the next paragraph. Let's get the other two out of the way first:

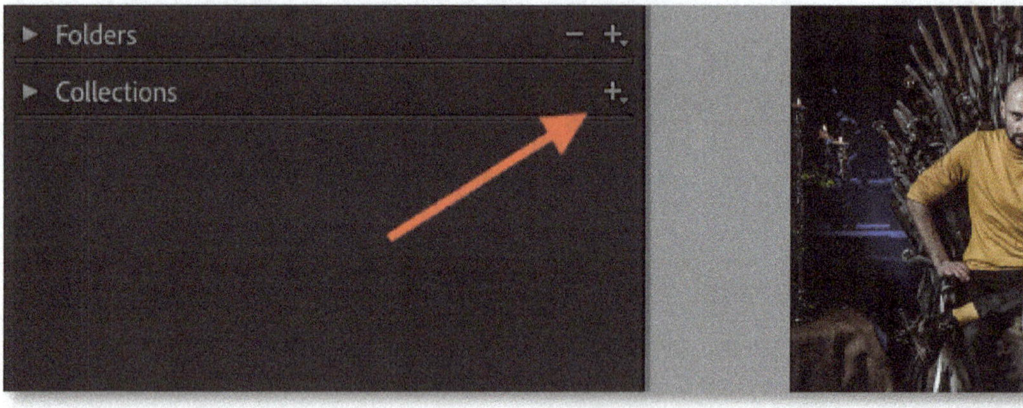

Figure 4.3 – The Collections plus sign

Note that once you select any collection, a small - sign will appear on the left of the + sign. It is there for deleting collections. Remember that deleting collections does not delete the photographs; they will remain in their original locations:

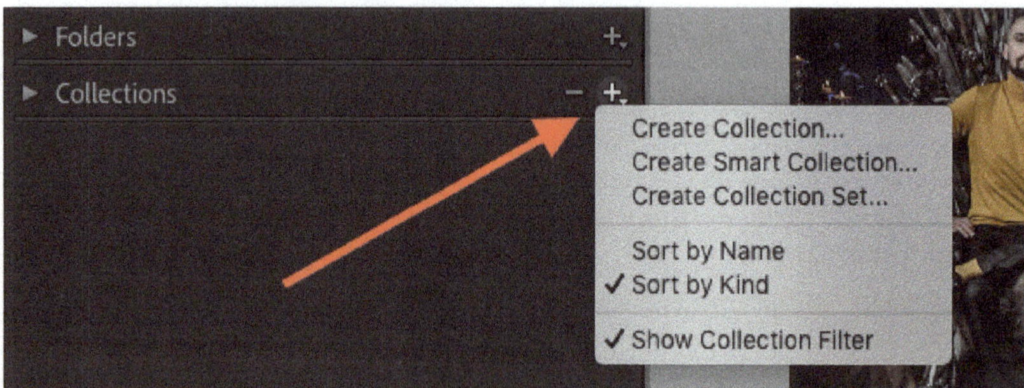

Figure 4.4 – The Collections plus and minus signs

In the following sections, we will see how to filter collections using different methods.

Sort by Name versus Sort by Kind

As seen in *Figure 4.4*, **Sort by Name** disregards the types of collections and sorts all our collections in alphabetical order, looking at names only. **Sort by Kind** is a two-tier sort order. It first splits all our collections into groups by different types of collections and then orders them alphabetically within each group. Different collection types are collections, smart collections, saved prints, saved slideshows, and so on. Sorting by kind is the way I always do it; this way, I have collection sets always at the top of my **Collections** section.

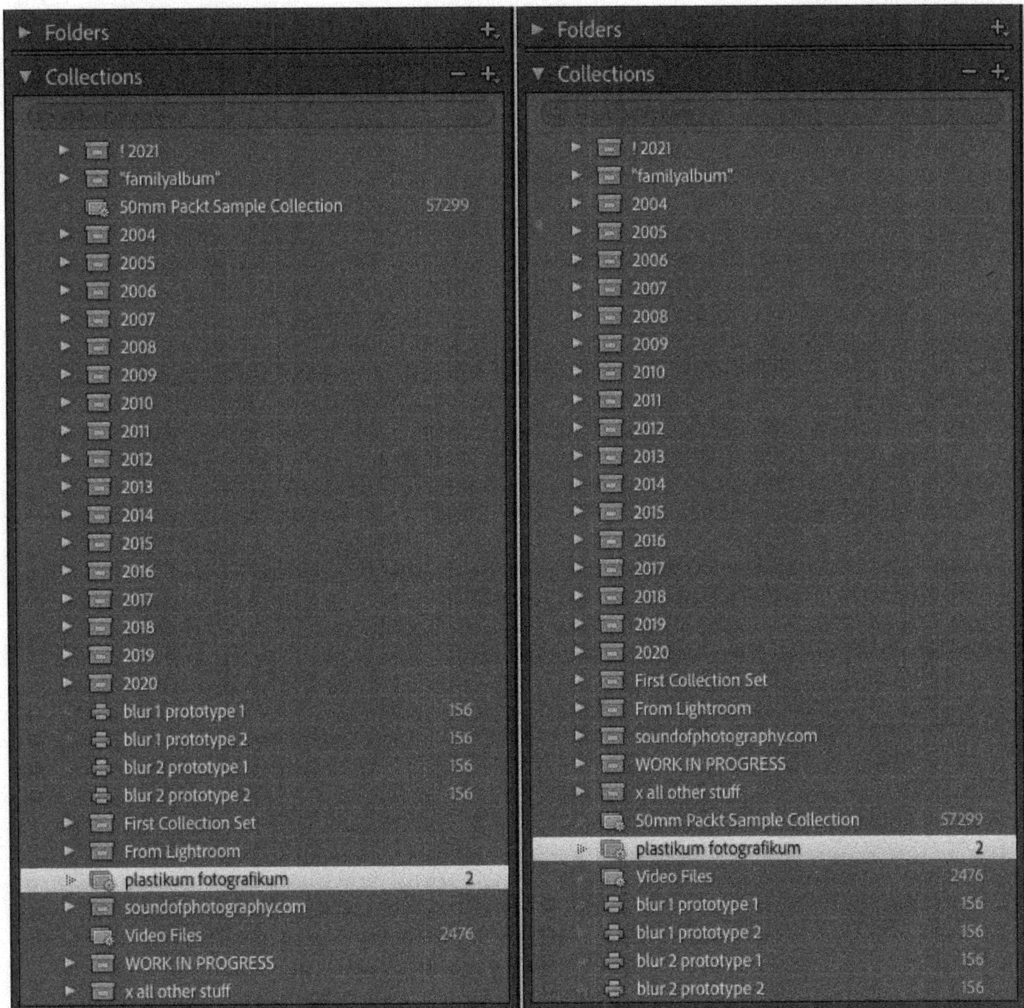

Figure 4.5 – Sort by Name (left) versus Sort by Kind (right)

Show Collection Filter

While this tool is enabled, we will have access to the search toolbar at the top of our collections. I leave it on as a default, to have it at hand if I need it at any stage. `Show Collection Filter` is a phrase search and will look within the names of collections. It's crucial to give collections meaningful names when we create them to find them later. So, even if we remember only part of any collection's name, when we search for it, Lightroom will narrow down results to only those containing the string we search for. You can see how the collections look when this option is disabled versus enabled in the following screenshot:

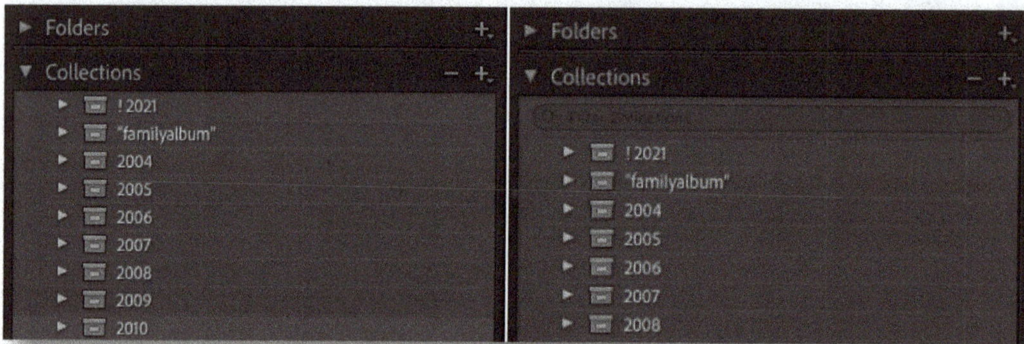

Figure 4.6 – The collection filter disabled (top) and the collection filter enabled (bottom)

Create Collection...

This is a very straightforward sub-menu where we will create our first collection. Start by clicking on the + sign at the top-right corner of this tab.

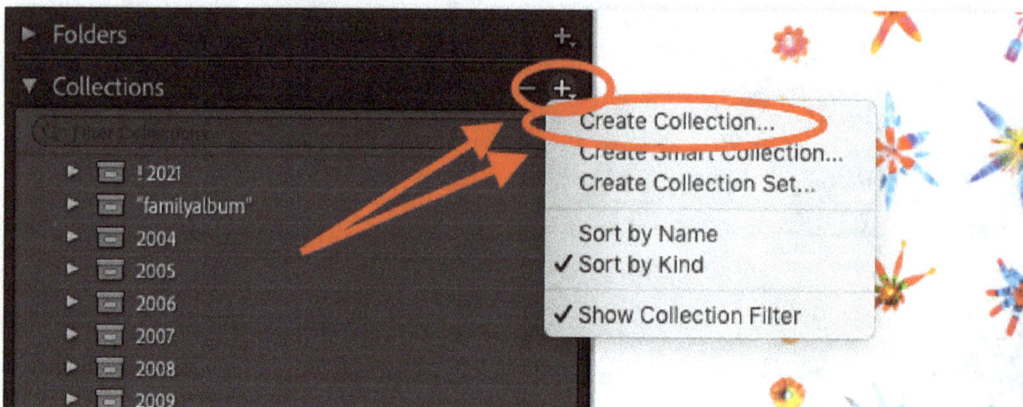

Figure 4.7 – Create Collection...

Then, in the pop-up menu, we are presented with a minimal number of options, but all of them can significantly influence our later workflow:

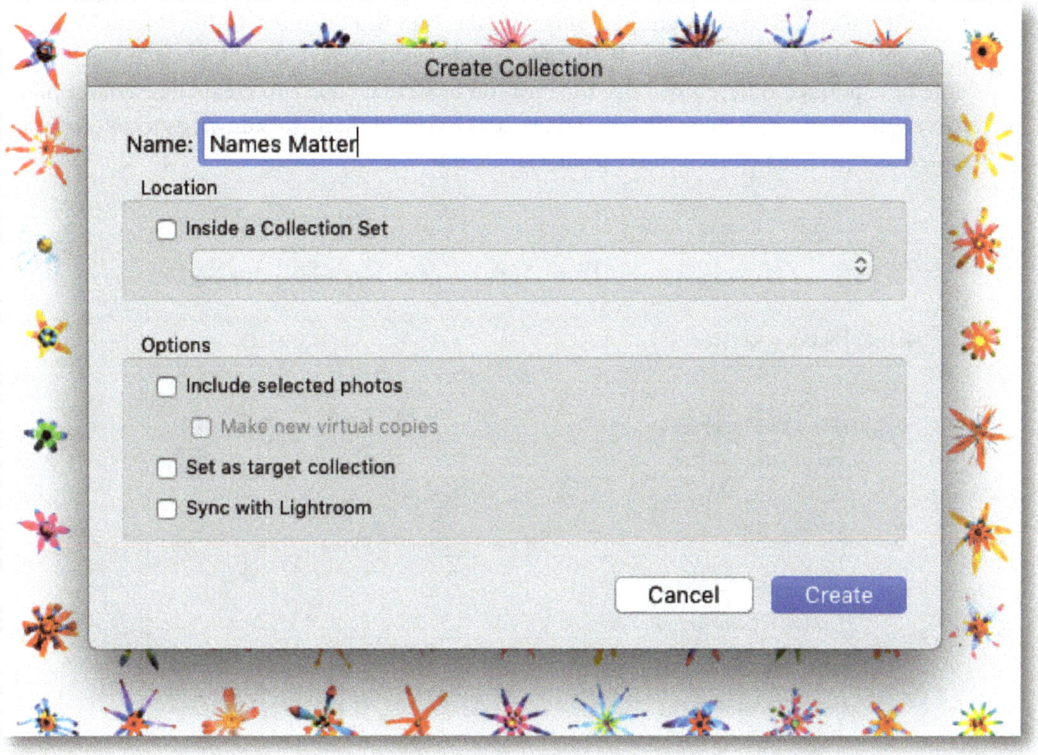

Figure 4.8 – Create Collection menu

Let's look at the options in the pop-up menu:

- **Name**: It's a good habit to name folders in a way that is descriptive and easy to search. I'm guilty of naming some collections in the past with rushed, random names such as `Collection1`, `Collectionsasdgwerg`, `Collection1345`, and so on. Doing it this way, I created more unnecessary work for myself, as I would have to click through all similarly named collections to find the one I'm really looking for and sooner or later rename it anyway. The takeaway from this is that naming everything in a meaningful way will save you a lot of time and frustration. For this exercise, you can call this collection `First Collection`.
- **Inside a Collection Set**: Once we have our name ready, we can house this new collection inside a collection set – this pop-up menu will be populated with all the collection sets we already have in our collections library.

- **Include selected photos**: The next section allows us to choose whether we want to include selected photos in this new selection. It's a very useful function once we are aware of it, and consider it before creating a collection. If we include selected photos, we can also choose to create virtual copies. This means that only virtual copies will be found within this collection. Again, this is a very useful option if we, for example, want to have the whole set in black and white or captioned differently. I use the creation of virtual copies to create new collections sparsely, but I know photographers who use it as a core of their workflows, especially when created as a part of a collection set from a single job:

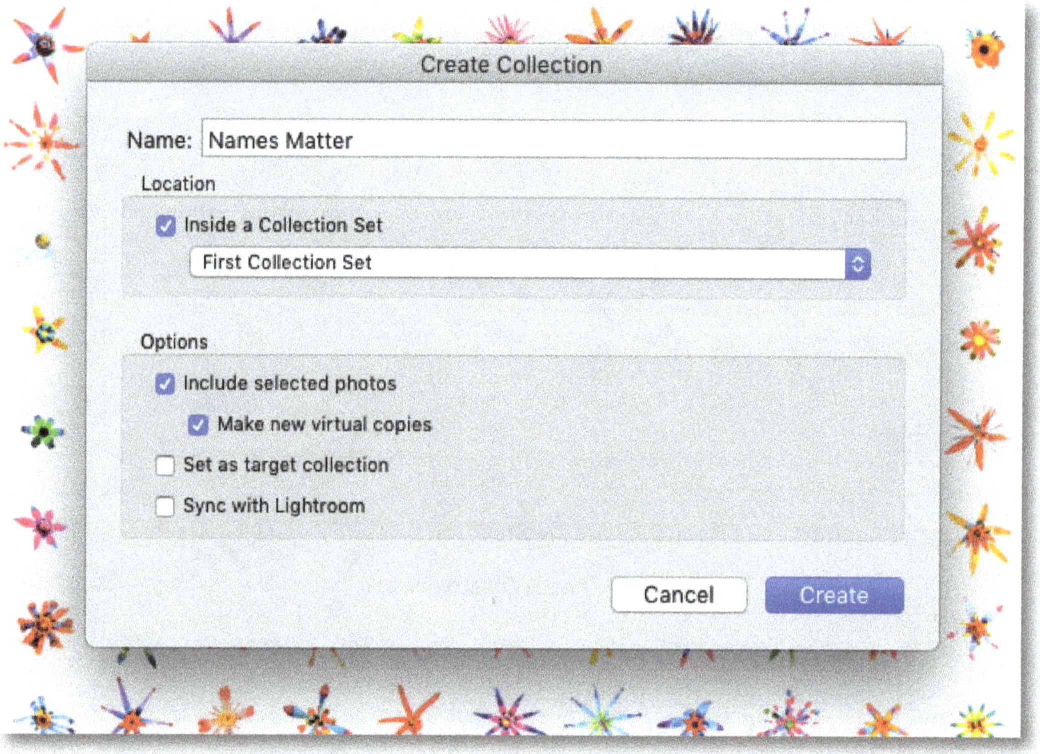

Figure 4.9 – Create Collection menu with Make new virtual copies option selected

All that we have left to choose from are the two **Set as target collection** and **Sync with Lightroom** options.

- **Set as target collection**: We will have this choice each time we create a new collection. Once we mark any collection as the target collection, we can add any images to it using the "*B*" keyboard shortcut. This shortcut, in fact, will always add pictures to any collection set as our target collection from within every module. We discussed the idea of a "*quick collection*" in the previous chapter – have a look at the paragraph before *Figure 3.5* for reference. We will tick this box for this exercise and make **First Collection** our target collection. From now on, and until we assign a "target collection" marker (symbolized as a tiny + symbol) to a different collection, we can use the "*B*" keyboard shortcut on any selected photograph to add it to this collection. Of course, we can always add pictures to any collection by dragging selected images from the grid or the strip on the bottom to the collection of our choice.

Figure 4.10 – The target collection icon

- **Sync with Lightroom**: If we tick this box, all photographs present in the currently selected collection will be automatically synchronized with our Adobe Lightroom account and available within the Adobe Creative Cloud environment to be edited online. The small "left-right" arrow next to the collection in the **Collections** tab identifies the synced collections. Any changes in collections are always happening in real time. There might be a bit of a delay when we delete or add a new photograph to our collection, but that's primarily dependent on the speed of our internet connection. It's also worth remembering that any edits we do in any mobile version of Lightroom will be reflected in Lightroom Classic on our desktop as well. Mobile versions of Lightroom will be working on the *smart preview* versions.

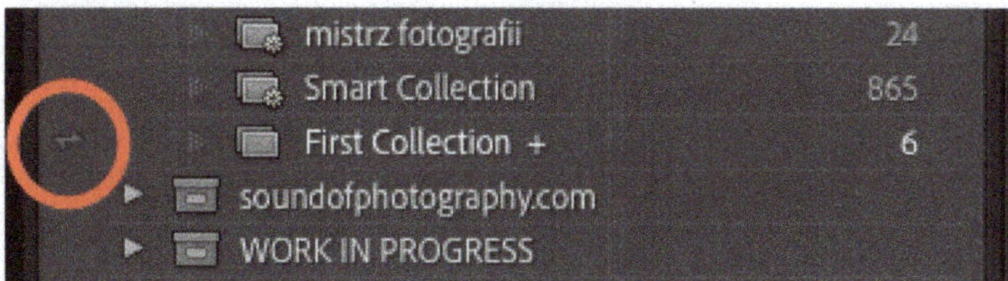

Figure 4.11 – Sync with Lightroom icon

Create Smart Collection...

Now, let's go back to the collections pop-up menu seen in *Figure 4.4* and talk about the **Create Smart Collection...** option. Once we choose the **Create Smart Collection...** option, we are presented with an almost empty window, where we can create a "rule" in the same way as creating a query in the **Metadata** tab. One huge advantage is that this search will stay permanent within this collection and be updated by Lightroom each time any new image matches our set criteria. The first two options are the same as in the **Create Collection...** menu; we need to name the collection and decide where it will be located. For this exercise, let's call it `First Smart Collection`. Once we choose the name, start by setting the other fields, just as shown in the following screenshot (*Figure 4.12*). Under the **Match** dropdown, select **all of the following rules**, with the only rule being a rating that is greater than or equal to zero. Not clicking on any of the five small dots leaves the rating set as zero, similar to how it is in the Library module:

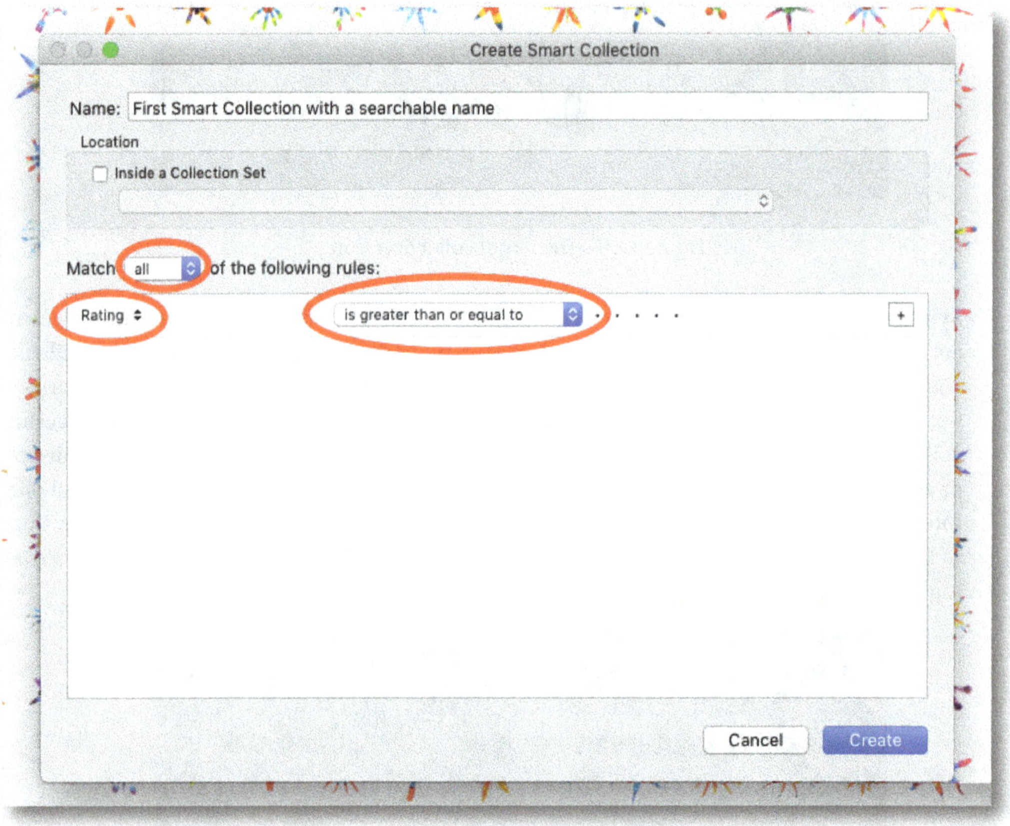

Figure 4.12 – Create Smart Collection menu

Once we click **Create** with these settings, our first smart collection will contain all photographs we currently have in Lightroom. This is because the default rule is set to search for all pictures with a rating greater or equal to zero stars, and that rule catches everything in our Lightroom library. We go into this in more detail in the *Options unique to smart collections* section.

Create Collection Set...

A collection set is a group of collections. A collection within Lightroom can't have sub-collections (such as folders and subfolders on our computers). To house multiple collections under one roof, we need a collection set. As you can also see from the sub-menu, a collection set can accommodate multiple collection sets. I can only guess that this can be pretty deep if we want, but after getting nine levels of collection sets deep, they stop being visible in the left-side panel. I just tested this out of curiosity for those of you that might need it. That invisible collection set will still be accessible, but we will just have to guess whether we picked the right one:

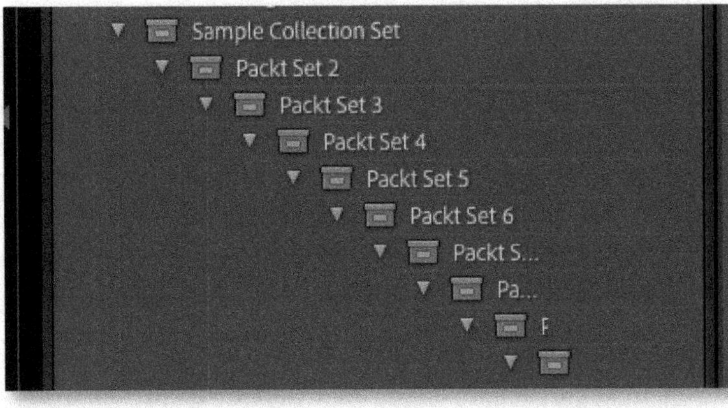

Figure 4.13 – Sample Collection Set 10 levels deep

Now that we have learned about what collections are and how collections are grouped into sets, in the next section, we will look at what options we have available for our collections and what options are only available for specific collection sets.

Right-click menus – an overview of functionality for different collection types

Whether we click on a collection, smart collection, or collection set, all three types of collections open a similar pop-up menu once right-clicked, except for minor differences.

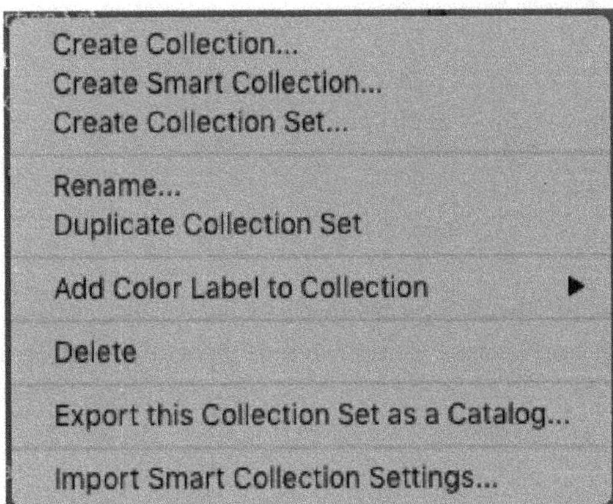

Figure 4.14 A

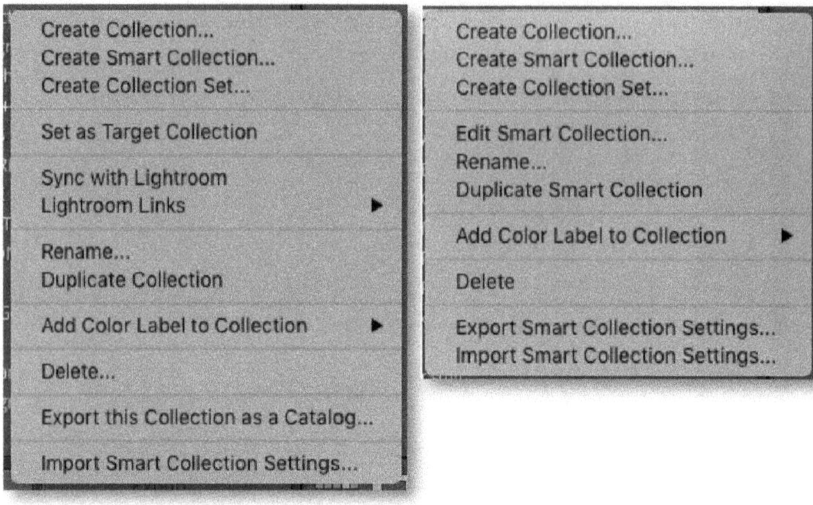

Figure 4.14 B – The right-click menus: collection set, collection, and smart collection

The top three entries give us precisely the same functionality as the + button previously discussed.

Starting with the collection set, right-click for the pop-up menu; the following options are available:

- **Rename...**: This option opens a small window, allowing us to rename our selection. The title will be automatically highlighted and ready to change.

Figure 4.15 – Renaming

- **Duplicate Collection Set**: This function will create a duplicate copy of our selection, with the name extended by the word `copy`, and place it in the same location as the collection set we are copying.

- **Add Color Label to Collection**: Picking a color will add a narrow band of the color we chose at the end of the row for the folder we right-clicked. It might not seem like much, but once there are hundreds of collections in our library, this tiny color label can make a big difference, especially when used sparsely and in an easily recognizable way – that is, to color specific types of collections, and so on. I use it mainly for the collections I'm working with at any given time, so I can spot them, almost without looking, when scrolling up and down the **Collections** tab:

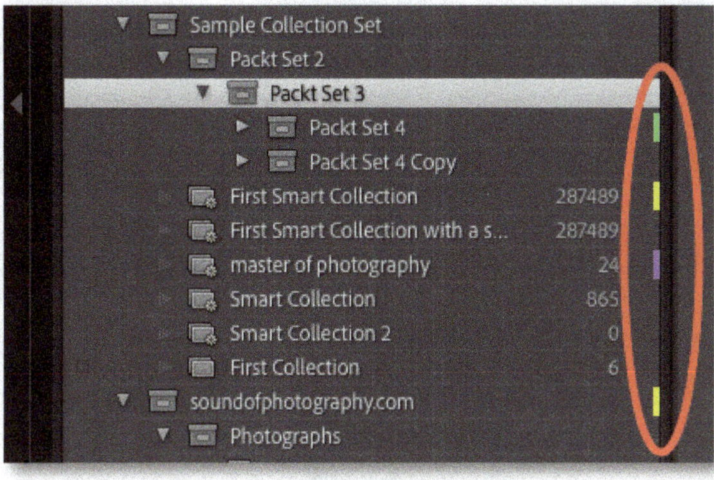

Figure 4.16 – Color labels

Right-click options for collections

Now, we'll start looking at the options available for collections:

- **Set as Target Collection**: We already discussed this in smart collections. This option will be unavailable for smart collections for the simple reason that they are based on the results of rules we set up for any particular smart collection (see *Figure 4.14*).
- **Sync with Lightroom**: We can sync any content available from within Lightroom Classic into the Adobe cloud. By doing so, we can edit it in any mobile version of the app but also share it with others. Once we choose **Sync with Lightroom**, we will have a **Make Collection Public** option and can share it. The easiest way to do so is to click **Copy Public Link**, and if we want to check how it looks first, we can use the **View on Web** option. This function is not available for the smart collections.

Once we share any collection, the **Comments** field available in the Library module will get populated with comments and "likes." It's a way to get feedback or share with family and friends. As with any collection, all changes made within Lightroom will be almost instantly reflected in the online version. This means that we can work on an edit with someone co-editing from a completely different place and see the same results practically in real time. At any stage, we can make a connection private from within the same pop-up menu:

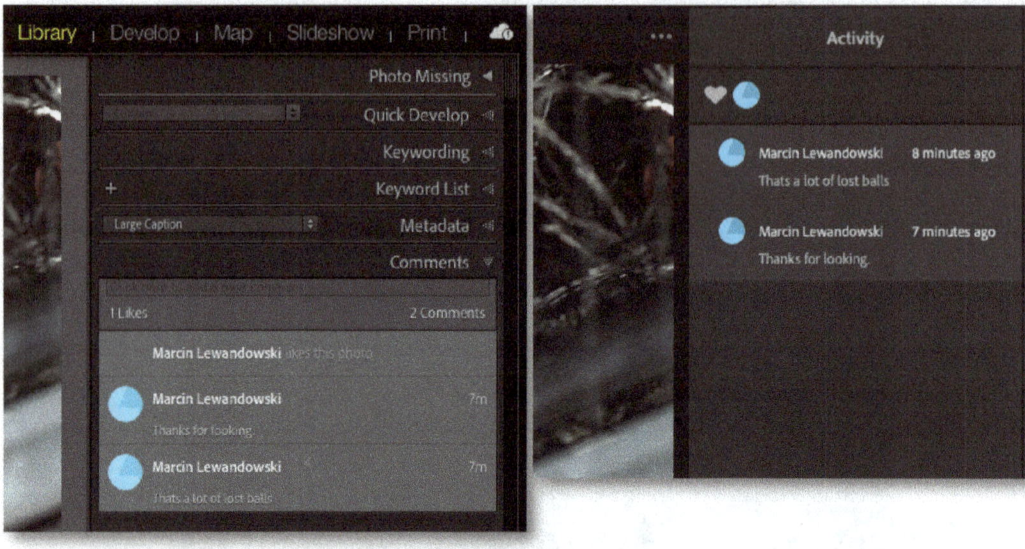

Figure 4.17 – Public collection comments seen on Lightroom (left) and online (right); you can add yours at https://adobe.ly/3iX458j (you must have an Adobe account to comment)

Options unique to smart collections

Here, we will see the options that are specific to smart collections. They are as follows:

- **Export Smart Collection Settings...**: Once we have a smart collection with predefined rules, we can export these settings as a "preset" to import later.
- **Import Smart Collection Settings...**: This works in the same way as duplicating a smart collection, and we place a smart collection made with parameters in the imported smart collection settings. Lightroom will place this new smart collection within the currently selected location.
- **Export this Collection as a Catalog...**: We mentioned exporting a catalog in the previous chapter, and this is where we do it. This option is available for all types of collections, including sets. Once chosen from the list, it will present us with a simple pop-up menu, where we pick the name and location for the catalog to be created. The other available options are as follows:
  - **Export negative files**: When we choose this option, Lightroom will copy all original files associated with the catalog we are exporting to a new location of our choice. Exporting negative files is very useful when we want to transfer our work in the same structure to a different computer and still be able to access original files.

- **Build/Include Smart Previews**: When enabled, Lightroom will create Smart Previews for all original files associated with our catalog or use already existing ones if available. This is an excellent way to speed up a workflow or take a collection to work on a different computer without the need for the original files.
- **Include available previews**: When this option is selected by default, Lightroom will only export previews of all the original files associated with a catalog. We will be able to edit any collections within it but not the actual photographs; for that, we need at least one of the aforementioned:

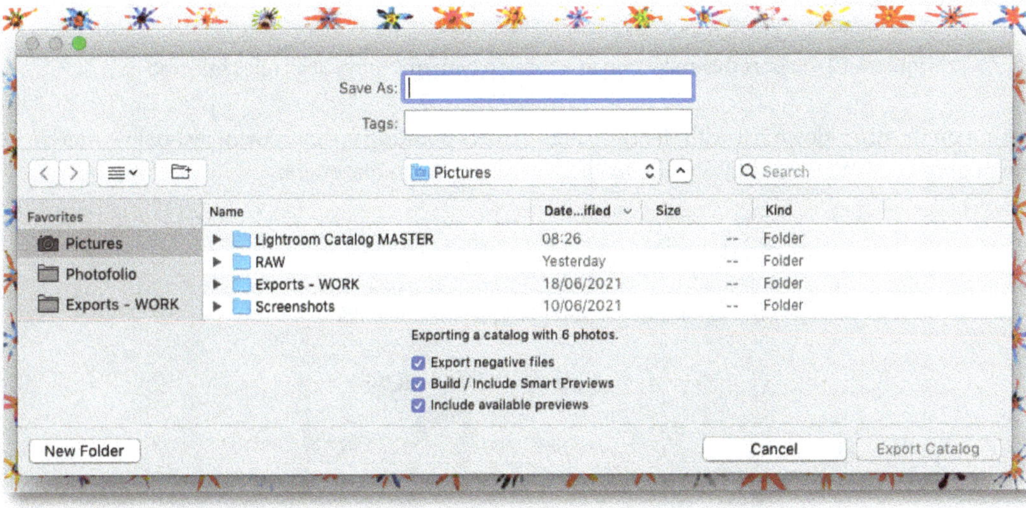

Figure 4.18 – Export this collection as a catalog menu

Edit Smart Collection

The first thing we can change is the name, but after that, it's all about specifying rules that work as filters. In the **Match** drop-down menu, we can choose between **any**, **all**, and **none**, with **all** always being a default choice. The meaning of the **Match** option applies to the rules listed in the dropdown below, and the results will depend heavily on which one we choose. This means that every rule we set in the dropdown below must be satisfied for the photograph to find its way into this collection. By selecting **any**, we specify that just one rule needs to be matched. The **none** option means that we want to see photographs that do not match any rules we specify:

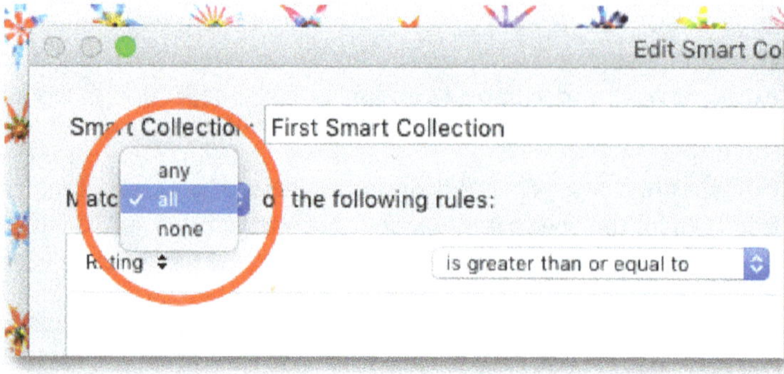

Figure 4.19 – Export this collection as a catalog with matching of all rules selected

Clicking on the drop-down list with the two small arrows pointing up and down, just below **Match**, opens a menu with all the available rules to choose from to form our query.

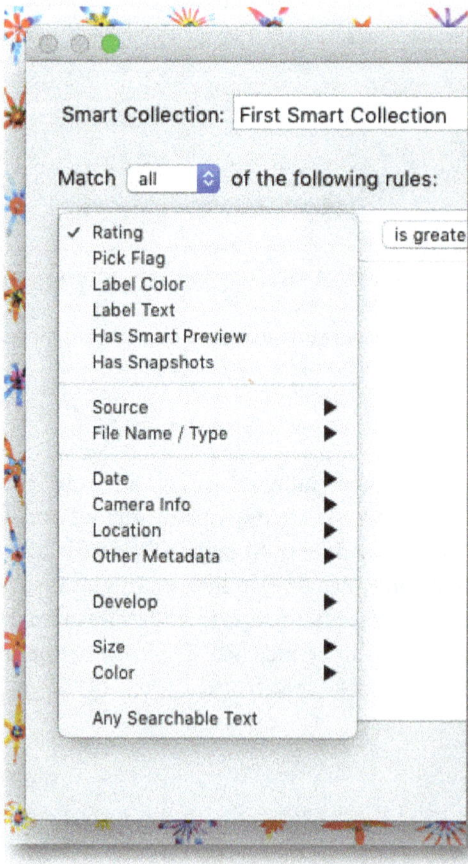

Figure 4.20 – The list of available rules

Each query has a subset of rules in the form of drop-down menus or textboxes to specify the details of our query. For example, **Rating** has the **is**, **is not**, **is greater than**, **is less than**, **is greater than or equal to**, **is less than or equal to**, and **is in range** parameters. Creating a **Rating** rule on its own will match all appropriately rated images from our entire library, which can be handy for some uses. Its biggest strength comes through when we match it with other terms, such as a specific keyword or location. Some rules, such as **Has Smart Preview** or **Has Snapshots**, will only have a choice between **is true** and **is false**, while text-based rules will give us a choice between **contains**, **contains all**, **contains words**, **doesn't contain**, **starts with**, and **ends with**.

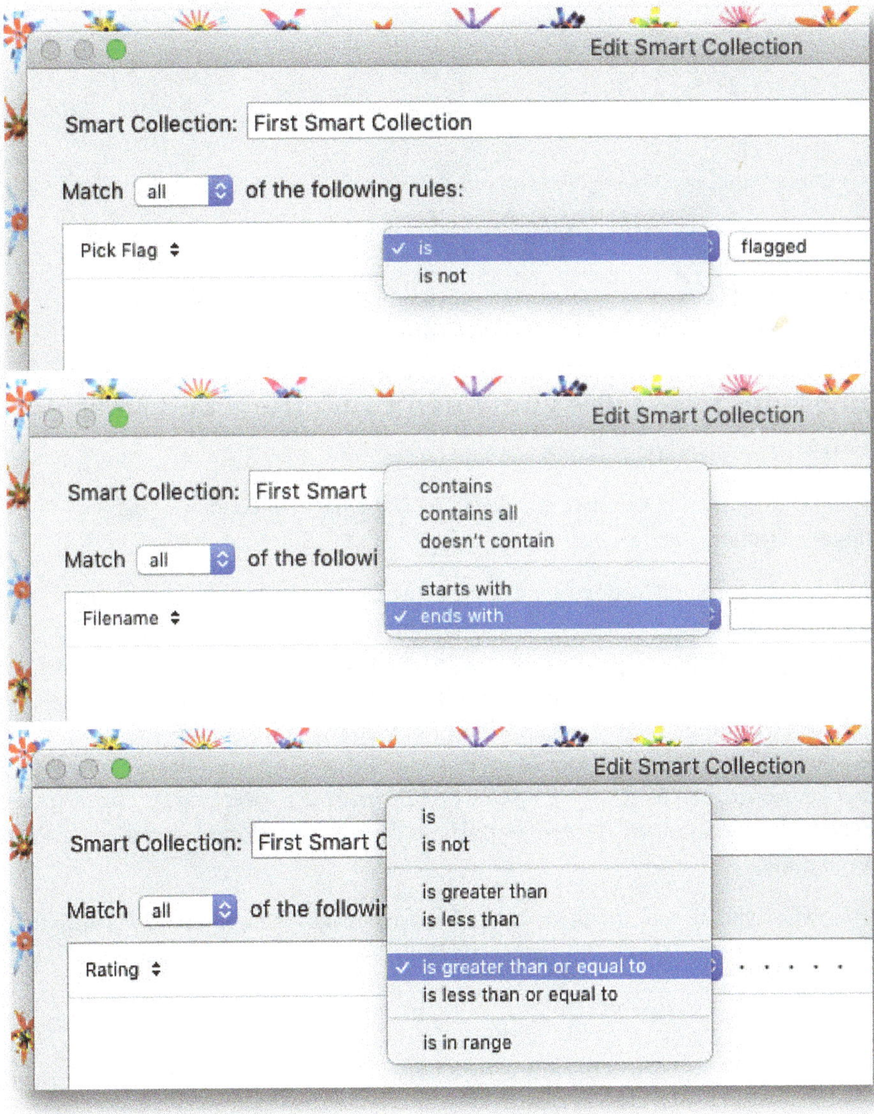

Figure 4.21 – Rules' subsets examples

We can combine multiple rules by adding them with the small + sign at the end of each rule. Then, their behavior will differ, depending on what we chose in the **Match** drop-down menu – **any**, **all**, or **none**.

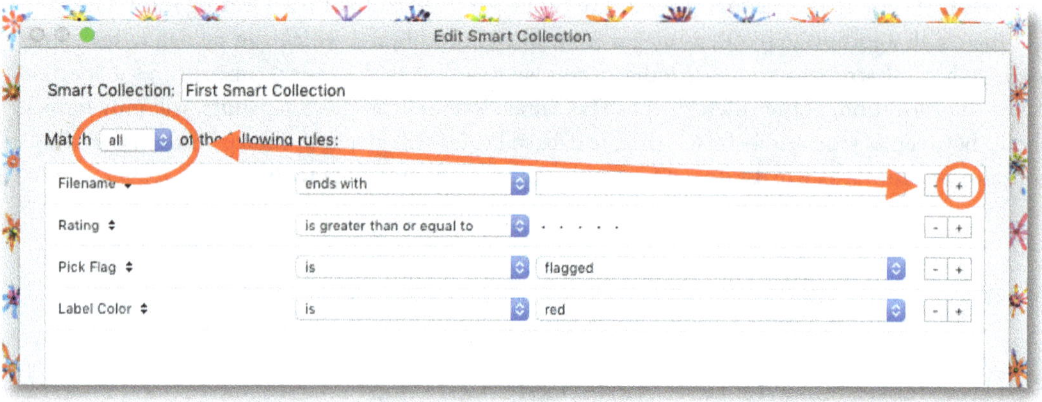

Figure 4.22 – Adding rules

Once we create a smart collection, we can right-click on it to duplicate it. Once duplicated, we can click on the copy and edit its name, rules set, and so on.

Differences and similarities between collections and smart collections

One of the significant differences between collections and smart collections is that we can't set the latter as a target collection... or can we?

In a way, many of the smart collections are like permanent target collections. Let me explain. All of the smart collections are always kept up to date by Lightroom. Suppose we have, for example, a smart collection with rules set to pick up images keyworded `beautiful day on the beach`, with a rating of five stars. From now on, whenever we will add the `beautiful day on the beach` keyword and five-star rating to any image, it will be immediately added to this smart collection. We can create a practically infinite number of smart collections that can gather all types of photographs – think about keywords such as `add to portfolio` or `2022 portrait showcase`. The number of varieties is vast and will depend as much on your imagination as on a workflow idea you already have in mind.

We just learned what types of collections can be created, what makes them similar, and which functions are unique to each of them. In the closing summary, I will discuss the possible usage of the knowledge you just acquired.

Using collections

There are as many "definite" solutions to the question of how to use collections as there are photography blogs on the internet, but few lines of thought stand out. One of the workflows I find interesting advocates using collections in a similar way we use filters.

The idea is that we import our photographs and create a collection set with a few collections inside that we can name, such as `All Photos`, `Picks`, and `Final Selection`. The first collection inside that set contains all photographs from the said job. After we flag/rate our initial favorites, we add them by dragging and dropping them into another collection containing only these picks. The third collection is for the final selections. We can expand the number of these collections with another one for images that we want to use in our portfolio or that we want to print. Just as with all Lightroom functionality, it will strongly depend on our workflow.

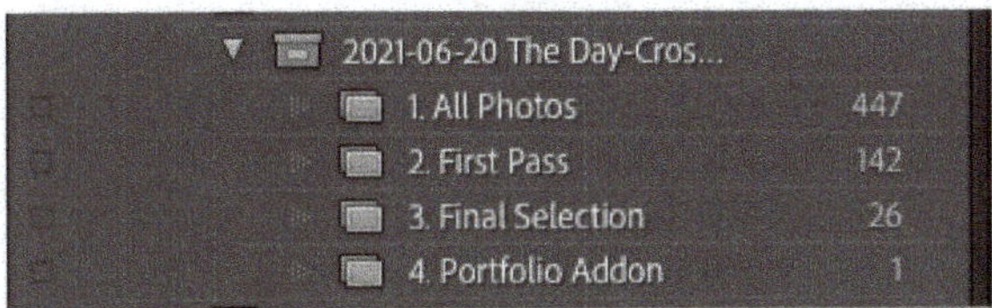

Figure 4.23 – A sample manual collection set workflow structure example

I understand the appeal of this method, but it feels like unnecessary work to me, so I prefer to work within folders by rating, filtering, rating, filtering, and so on. That way, I know I have everything in one place and can always increase and decrease the rating to include or exclude photographs from my final edit, which I can easily get to by filtering for the maximum rating, and I can narrow it down even further by color labels and flags with virtual copies on top of that.

Another idea is for an automated process based on a similar workflow. Let's say we photographed an independent gig on August 15th. We create an appropriately named collection set and create additional smart collections inside it, named in the same way we did in the previous example (`All Photos`, `Picks`, and `Final Selection`). `All Photos` will have the rule to pick up all images from August 15th. `Picks` will have the rule to pick up all images from August 15th with a rating of one or more. `Final Selection` will have all photos from August 15th with a rating of five, and so on. Following this chain of thought, another smart collection will pick up images that are additionally keyworded `print`, another one will pick `portfolio highlights`, and so on.

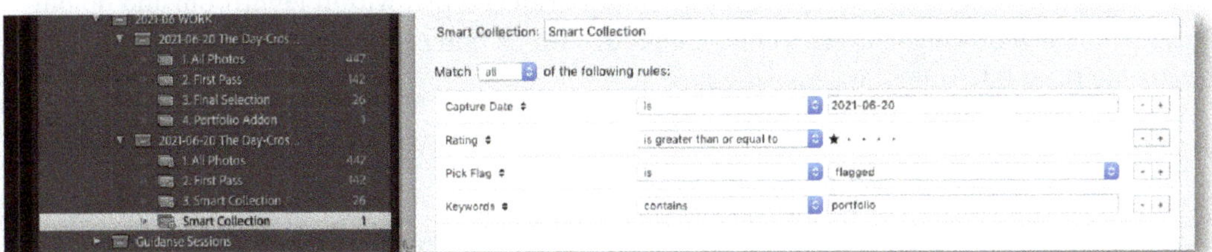

Figure 4.24 – A sample smart collection set workflow structure

From the Author

After years of using Lightroom collections, I found it fundamental to keep its overall structure tidy. Tidiness will have many benefits, especially in terms of time-saving. Just as with most other Lightroom options, there is no golden rule that will work for everyone; how you build your collections and their structure will very much depend on how you work as a photographer and what you expect from Lightroom. If you use one of the methods that we just mentioned (creating collections or smart collections with each job), then keeping a chronological structure might be the most intuitive and convenient way to do it. I have collections split by years and projects. Within each year, I have many different subsets. I have separate collection sets for completed jobs, old portfolios, images I might want to come back to, ongoing projects, and so on, but you might like to do it in a completely different way. In my experience, having a clear folder structure followed by consistent rating, flagging, labeling, and, of course, keywording is a big part of achieving success. Collections are there to reinforce and complement that.

Summary

I remember that when I was just a kid in the late '80s, all I had to look through files and folders on a PC was the text command interface of DOS. Then, one day, Norton Commander entered the picture, allowing me to navigate through files more visually – that was the first revolution. The second revolution took place in the late '90s when I got the ACDSee image viewer, allowing me to browse pictures on a hard drive without the need to open each one separately. The third and final revolution (so far anyway) came with Lightroom – I could forget about everything not photo-related when working on pictures and focus purely on managing my ever-growing collection of digital photographs. Folders and collections are a unique approach to data management that's ideal for photographers, and we just learned a lot about it. By using collections, we can create multiple versions of edits without ever affecting original files and folders. We can use smart collections to gather photographs from within our library by creating queries that can be very basic, using just a keyword. We can also elaborate using multiple match rules, from GPS data, our cameras' serial numbers, to dates and times, together in one permanently running query. Lightroom will do a lot of hard work for us when we ask it. At the same time, we can create a practically endless number of manual edits within collections and collection sets without ever having to deal with multiple copies of the same photographs, keeping everything clean and tidy within Lightroom and on our hard drive. The following chapter will dive directly into working with singular photographs and developing them into something visually special.

Section 2: Developing Photographs in Lightroom Classic

Even though this section contains only two chapters, they are a lot to chew through. Upon completion of this section, you will know about every available Lightroom tool that can change the look of your photographs and have them ready to share with the rest of the world.

In this section, we will cover the following topics:

- *Chapter 5, An Introduction to the Develop Module*
- *Chapter 6, A Detailed View of the Develop Module's Functions*

5

An Introduction to the Develop Module

Here we are, in the area of Lightroom that is its very core, almost the defining part of it. Before Lightroom was developed by Adobe's software engineers, we photographers had to separately open each photograph and develop it, very often in Bridge or Photoshop. Many of us used other pieces of software, from free to open source, but they were often hard to use and quite unintuitive. I remember attending a photography trade show where someone from Adobe was introducing Lightroom to the gathered photographers. We all were in awe of the idea that we wouldn't need to open and save each photograph. Once we develop a photo, we can simply move on to the next one and then export the final results in multiple formats, even watermarked. What was a revolution in working with photography almost 15 years ago became a standard and is now used across the whole spectrum of photography software. I can't imagine working with photographs without the availability of Lightroom anymore. The following screenshot shows what a photograph in the Develop area might look like:

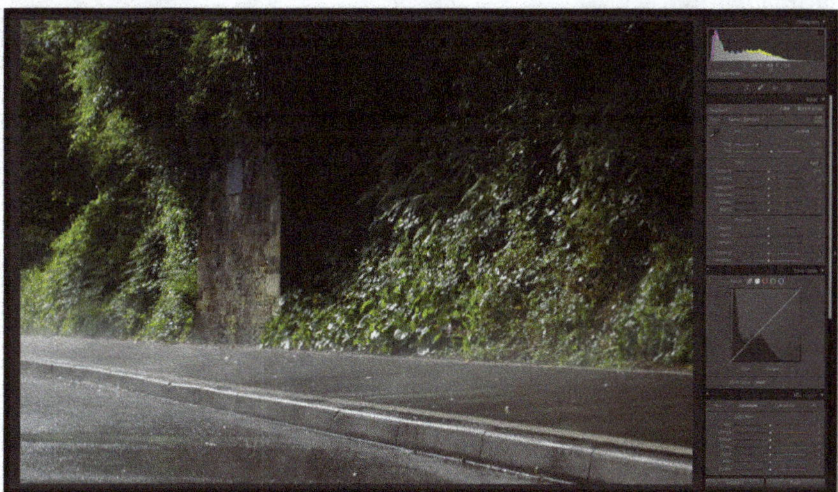

Figure 5.1 – Quick glance at an unedited photo in the Develop module

In previous chapters, we learned how to make getting our photographs into Lightroom and choosing our favorites as easy as possible. Now we will dive head-first into making our work shine. However proficient we are with the camera, getting the best possible image in the camera is still the key to excellent final results. Current industry standards and most clients' expectations require us to apply a certain level of post-production before photographs are delivered to our clients, friends, or family. From simple tweaks, such as straightening and cropping, through retouching basics, such as Exposure or Saturation adjustments, to complete overhauls of the look with Profile and Color Grading - Lightroom is a one-stop shop. As long as we don't need to "photoshop someone in," we can do it; it will often be possible to even "photoshop someone out." This can be seen in the following screenshot. We have removed the building shown in *Figure 5.01*:

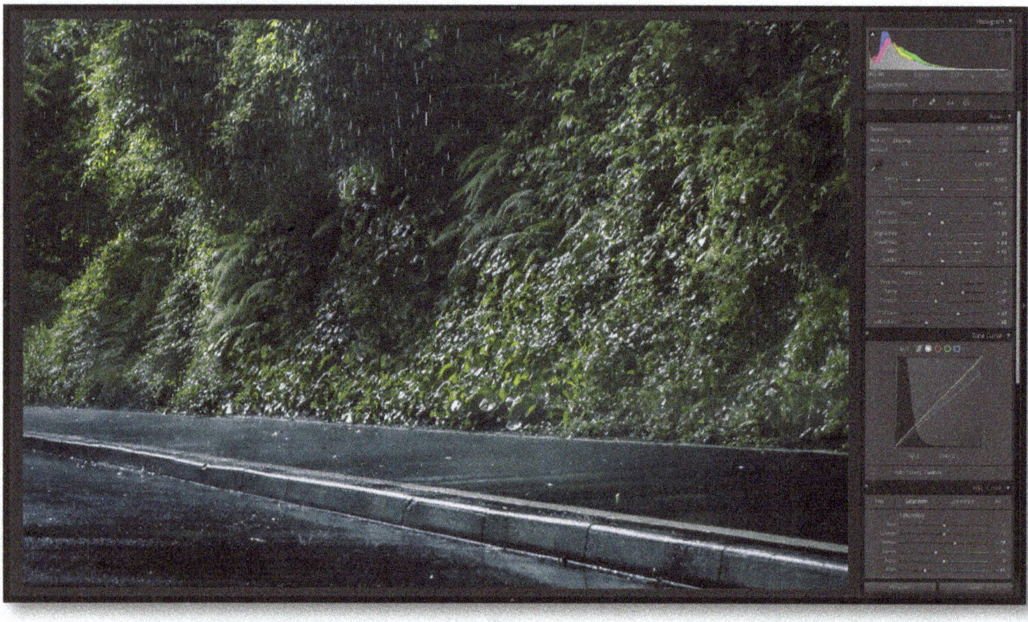

Figure 5.2 – A few tweaks and a minute of work to remove the building from the previous figure

This chapter will cover the following topics:

- Looking at the Develop module options
- Tools available within the Develop module's right-side panel
- Tools available within the Develop module's left-side panel

Let's get started!

Looking at the Develop module options

This section will explain what functions are available to us within the Develop module and briefly look at how they work without delving into details.

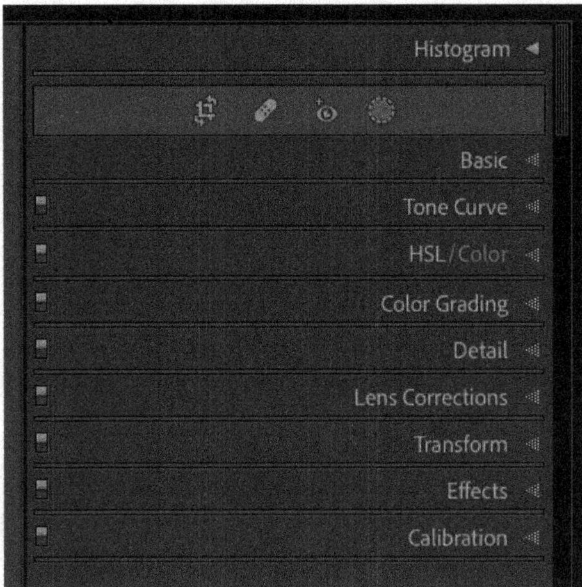

Figure 5.3 – Develop module's right-side panel tools

Practically all of the tools we need to work on photographs are located on the right side of the Develop module. However, the left side (*Figure 5.04*) has a few new tools we haven't yet discussed as well. They will become more relevant once we learn more about the actual Develop panel tools on the right. Therefore, we will come back to the left-panel tools toward the end of this chapter:

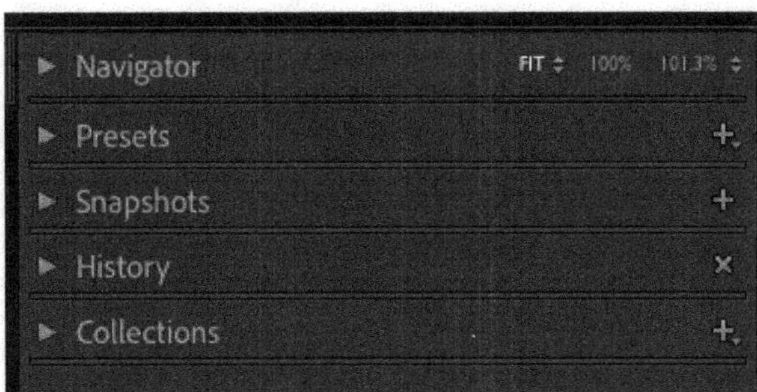

Figure 5.4 – Develop module's left-side panel tools

Let's start with the tools on the right-side panel of Lightroom in the next section.

Tools on the right-side panel

The right-side panel is where all the tools affecting the look of our photographs are, and in the following subsections, we will learn what each of them can do.

Histogram

Just like with the Library module, our default view starts with **Histogram**, but this time, it is one of the tools to change the look of our photo, not just a window with information. If we hover our mouse cursor over the histogram, we will notice that from left to right, **Histogram** is split into five distinct areas, as follows:

- **Blacks**
- **Shadows**
- **Exposure**
- **Highlights**
- **Whites**

This can be seen in the following screenshot:

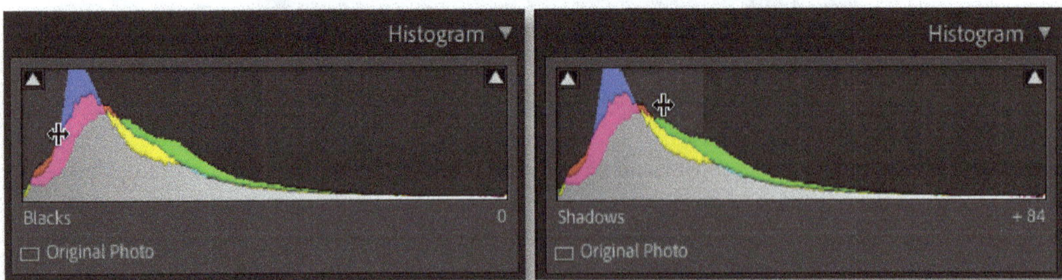

Figure 5.5 A

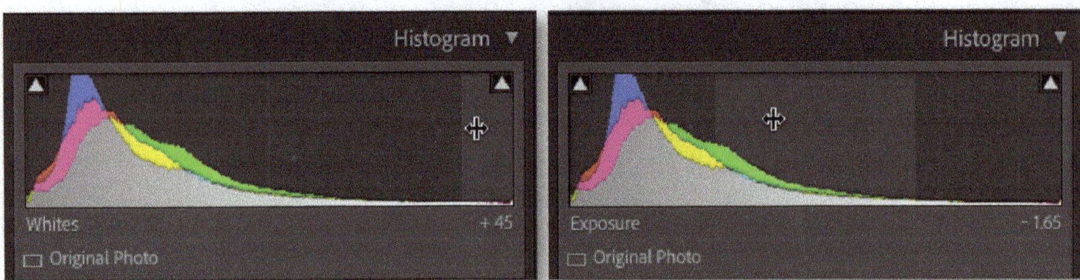

Figure 5.5 B

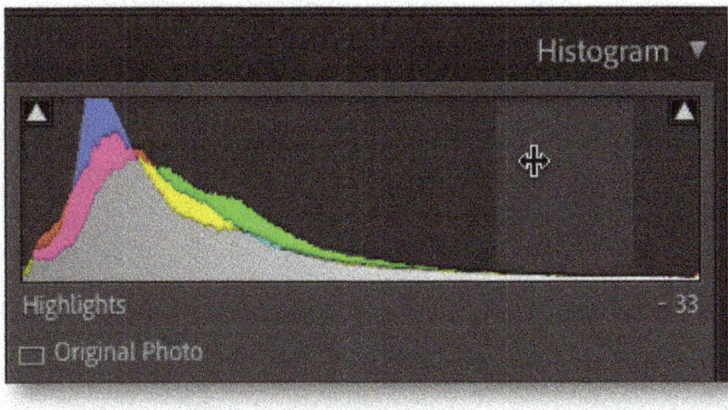

Figure 5.5 C – Adjustable Blacks, Shadows, Whites, Exposure, and Highlights

The mouse cursor changes to "left/right" arrows with a bar in the middle when we hover over the histogram. We can now adjust five major areas directly in the histogram by clicking and moving our cursor left and right. This tool is powerful enough to do all of the preliminary development that we will be doing with the tools available in the next section. All changes done within the **Histogram** tool will be reflected in the automatic movement of the **Basic** tab sliders.

Local adjustment tools

A crucial toolbar with local adjustment tools is located just between the histogram and the **Basic** toolbar. It contains all available local adjustment and correction brushes plus the Crop tool. A set of four local adjustment tools following the histogram includes the following:

- Crop Overlay ("*R*")
- Spot Removal ("*Q*")
- Red Eye Correction
- Masking

You can see this in the following screenshot:

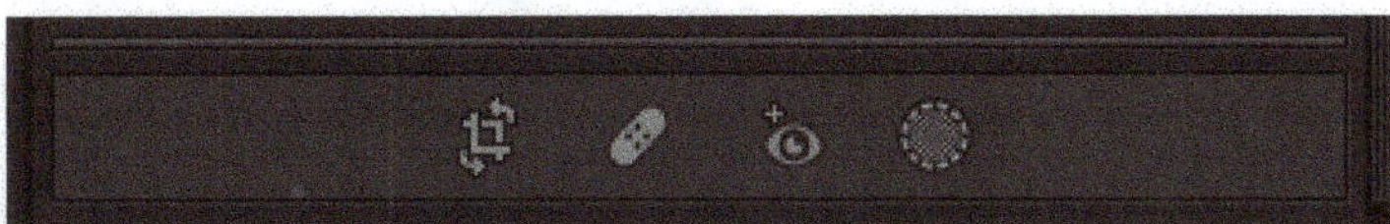

Figure 5.6 – Local adjustment tools

Crop Overlay should be familiar to all photographers. When using it, we can also change the picture's aspect ratio or just straighten it. Next in line is Spot Removal. We can use it for simple tasks, such as cleaning up a few spots made by dirt on our sensor or removing distracting bits on the photographs that lurk behind our main subject. The third is Red Eye Removal, which is caused by some cameras' flash.

With the Masking brushes, we can paint with the tools available in the **Basic** tab. We can also make localized color and sharpness tweaks, fix local fringing, and even paint with color. Masking includes a graduated filter that works by applying settings, gradually transitioning from 100% to 0% in the line and direction of our choice. Radial Filter does so in a circular form, inside or outside of the circle we drew. AI masks will choose the sky or subject. Lastly, we have the most powerful of all, Brush, which we can use to "paint in" any available Lightroom settings to gently retouch or completely change the photograph.

Basic

This tab provides a set of tools we will use to do the majority of our work when developing photographs within Lightroom. The first option we can choose is whether we want to work with color or in black and white. It might seem a little bit unintuitive to get this choice straight away but think about it in terms of how global this tool is, and we can't get more global than changing from color to black and white. Treatment is followed by a choice of profile, which is an option that can completely change the look of our photographs before we go near adjustments sliders and change anything. Finally, before we get into some serious tweaking, we can adjust the white balance of our photos, mainly if we shoot RAW. White Balance changes will dramatically alter any photograph. Whether you want to fix or change the photograph, you will appreciate its clear positioning at the very top of the first module.

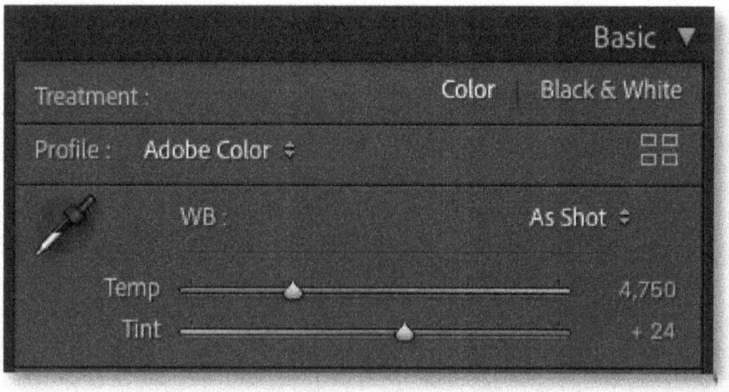

Figure 5.7 – Treatment, Profile, and White Balance tools

White Balance is followed by **Tone** adjustments, all of which, excluding **Contrast**, can be worked on within the histogram. Whenever we change anything with the **Tone** sliders, it's always reflected in the histogram, and the other way around. All changes we apply by adjusting the image directly in the **Histogram** area will change the positioning of the **Tone** sliders:

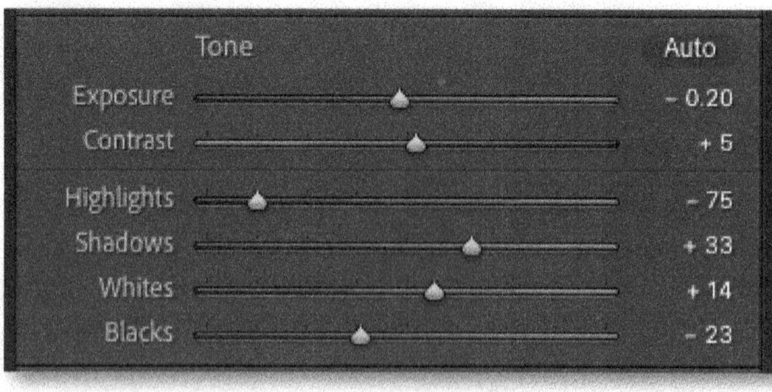

Figure 5.8 – Tone tools

Presence is a set of tools that will help us in defining and refining edges in our photographs. I look at these as a group of more elegant contrasting tools, ranging from the crude **Clarity** to the more intricate **Texture** tool and **Dehaze**, which lies somewhere between them but in a parallel universe. We will cover these options in detail, in the next chapter. **Vibrance** and **Saturation** are responsible for color intensity, and they vary in terms of how and which colors they affect.

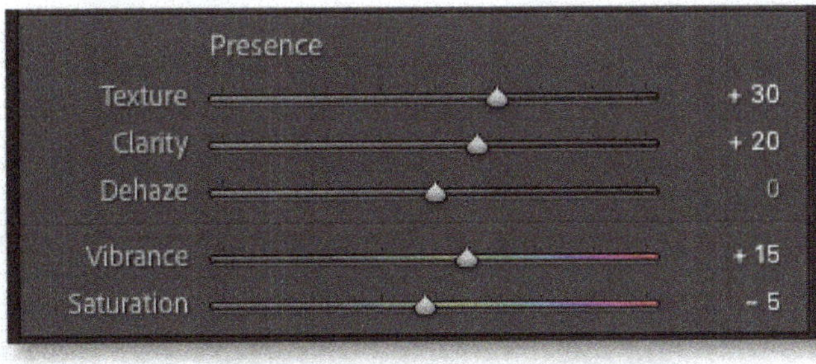

Figure 5.9 – Presence tools

With **Tone Curve**, we can affect the overall brightness and contrast of the image. However, it is much more targeted and precise than the **Presence** collection mentioned earlier. We can control the image in a similar way as we do with the tools in **Tone**, and they work great together, complimenting each other. **Tone Curve** can also be used to colorize images and work on split toning. Overall, it's a much easier tool to understand than it seems at first glance. As a result, it can be very beneficial to our workflow, even if used only sporadically.

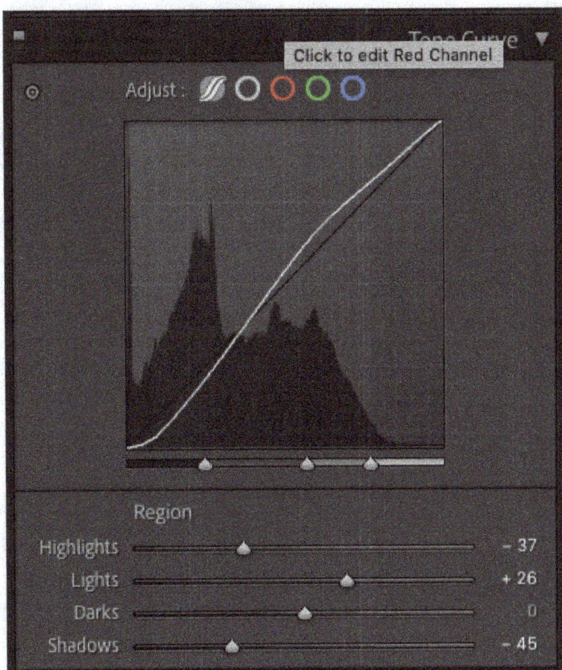

Figure 5.10 – Tone Curve tool

HSL/Color

HSL stands for **hue**, **saturation**, and **luminance**, and as you can imagine, it will help control colors in our photographs. With the set of available sliders, we can affect any color range on the picture separately. From simple tasks, such as darkening the sky or changing the hue of grass, to more elaborate changes that can help fix or exaggerate mixed light color conditions, this is our primary color mixing toolbox.

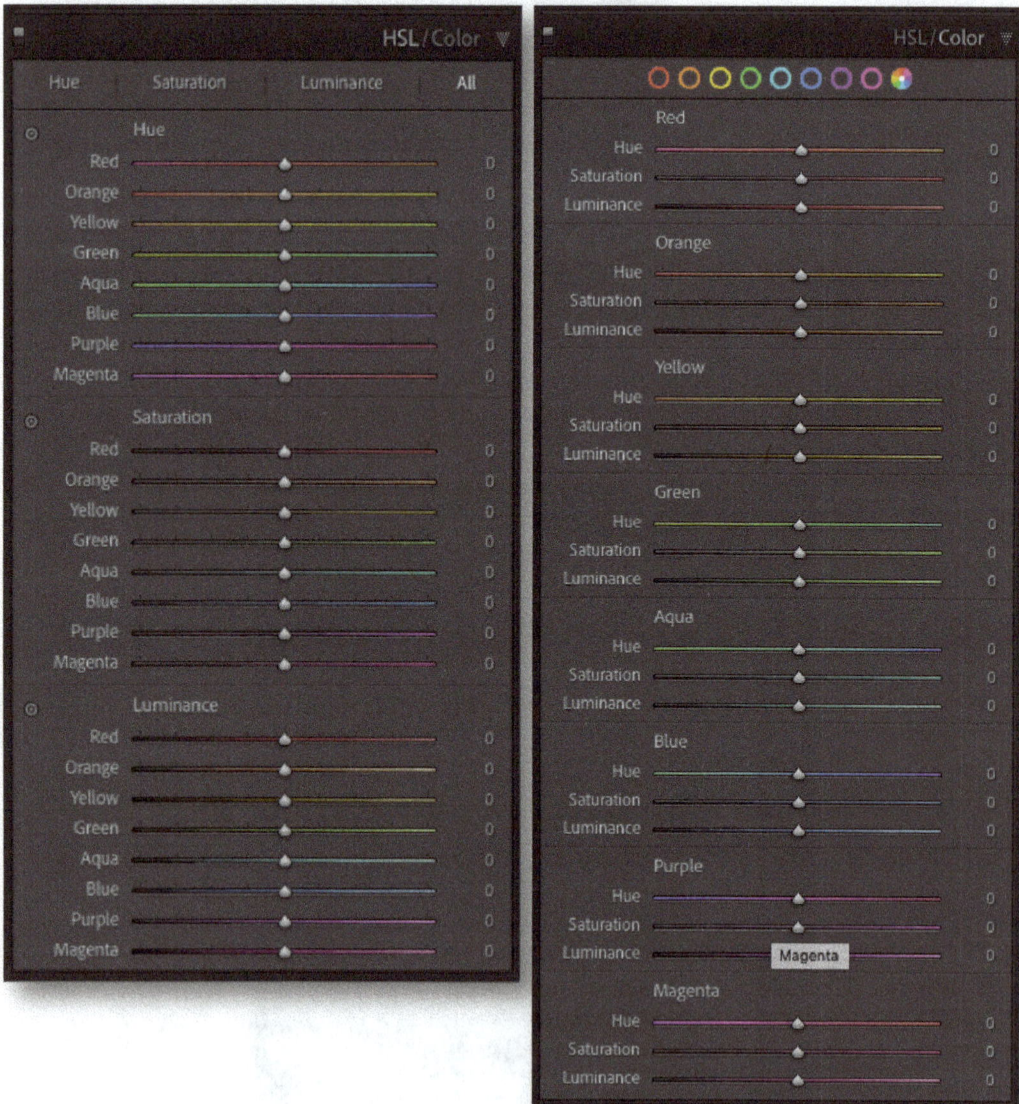

Figure 5.11 – Hue, Saturation, Luminance, and Color tools

Color Grading

Have you ever wondered how to create a signature look or tonality resembling old film photographs? This is the place. Toward the end of 2020, Adobe replaced a few simple sliders with a comprehensive set of controls provided by color wheels, enabling us to precisely apply the desired look to midtones, shadows, and highlights separately or globally to the whole photograph.

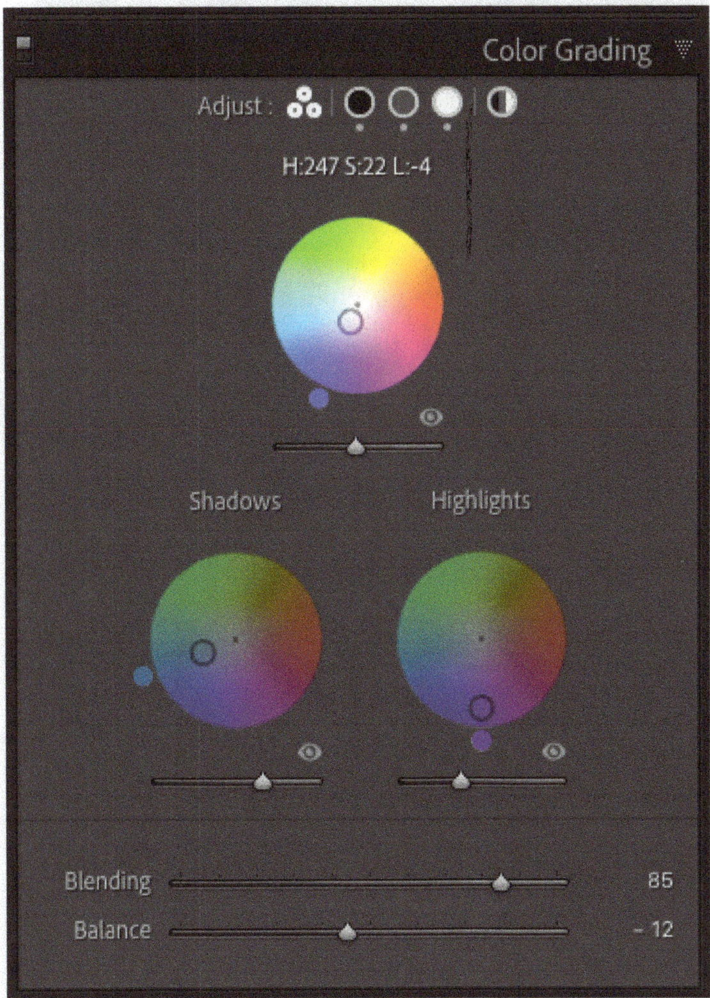

Figure 5.12 – Color Grading tools

Detail

I rarely let my images leave Lightroom without applying at least a bit of sharpness to them. We can control how sharpness is used in our photographs and work on noise reduction with six dedicated sliders in the **Detail** tab.

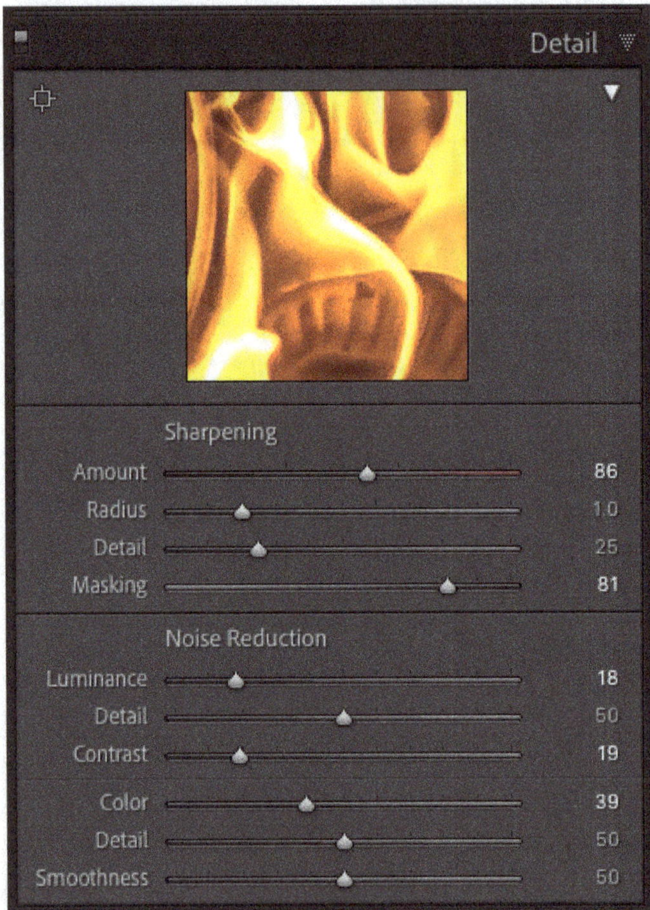

Figure 5.13 – Detail tools

Lens Corrections

One of the benefits of working with digital photography is fixing some of our lens's deficiencies after the photographs are already taken. Each lens has a specific build that can cause some distortion, chromatic aberrations, and unwanted vignetting. With Lightroom's built-in, quite-comprehensive set of lens profiles, we can get rid of these problems automatically. If the lens we are using is not listed, we can still fix fringing and other aspects I just mentioned manually.

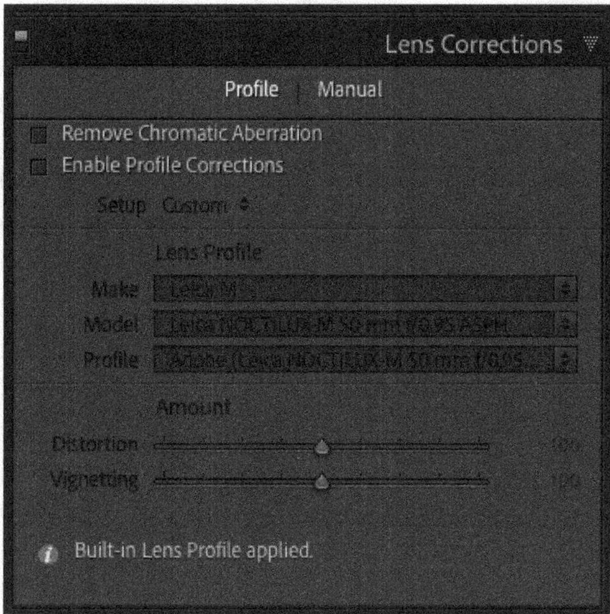

Figure 5.14 A

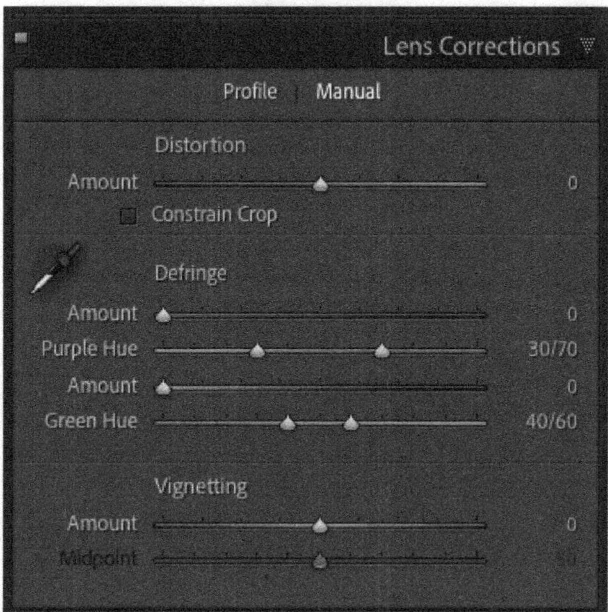

Figure 5.14 B – Lens Corrections tools – Profile and Manual views

Transform

This is the single tool that initially made me switch from the stand-alone version of Lightroom to the subscription model. **Transform** is a compelling set of tools that helps us in fixing crooked perspectives in our images, from very light tweaks straightening our rushed shot to all-powerful, guided, manual control over vertical and horizontal lines, all within our crop's boundaries.

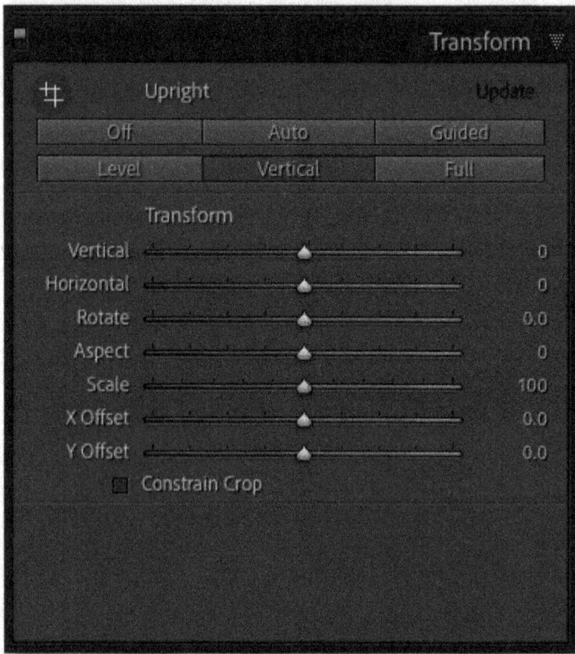

Figure 5.15 – Transform tool

Effects

As much as all of the preceding tools allow us to create a unique look, sometimes a bit of gentle vignetting is simply a must to compliment the image. As for the **Grain** tool, I mostly use it to sharpen some older images… yes, you read that right, and you'll learn all about this trick too.

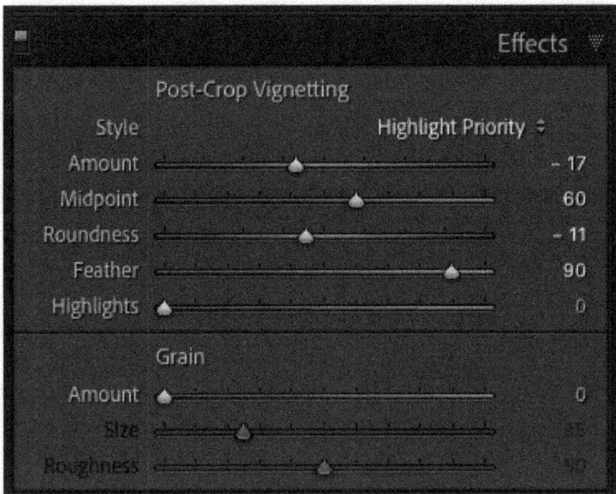

Figure 5.16 – Effects tool

Calibration

This is probably one of the most underrated, overlooked features and, simultaneously, the most potent color-altering tool in Lightroom. Changes made with **Calibration** affect every pixel of our photograph, changing the balance of the RGB mixture for each pixel. As a result, it is a very powerful coloring and grading tool. It is less intimidating than it might look.

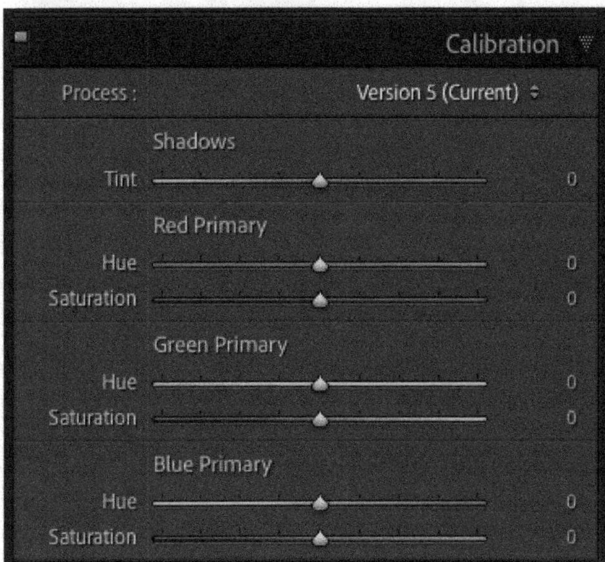

Figure 5.17 – Calibration tool

Previous and Reset

The last two available tools are the **Previous** and **Reset** buttons. The **Previous** button copies all settings from the most recently viewed photograph and applies them to the currently developed photo. The **Reset** button reverts a photograph to its original state directly after import.

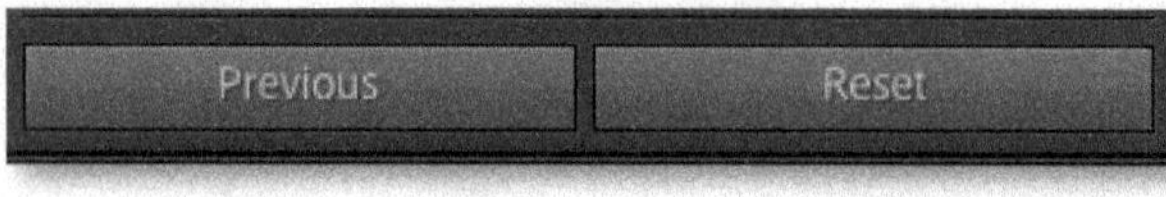

Figure 5.18 – Previous and Reset buttons

Now that we have learned about what options are available to us in the right-side panel of the Develop module, it's time to start looking at the options present in the left-side panel as well.

Tools on the left-side panel

The left panel works in a very similar way as it did in the **Library** module. It's still responsible for asset access but offers it on a more in-depth level for singular photographs.

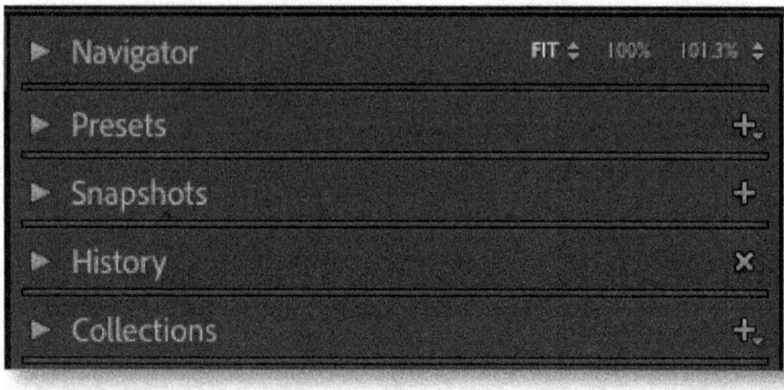

Figure 5.19 – Closed set of left-side panel tabs

The following is a list of the left-side panel tools:

- **Navigator**: This is a familiar tool that accompanies us throughout Lightroom. The Develop module is no different; it also has the same functionality across all the panels.
- **Presets**: Presets are the various settings we choose from the right-side panel saved as templates to be applied to photographs. We can create simple presets to quickly use something such as multiple levels of sharpness or elaborate with settings encompassing multiple changes across many tools within several tabs. Lightroom comes with an excellent selection of presets split thematically into a few different groups.

- **Snapshots**: At any stage of the developing process, we can create a snapshot; this will save all current settings and a history of changes as a new starting point to which we can come back. There is no limit to how many snapshots we can create. It's a valuable tool to track different ideas we might have along the way without the need to make virtual copies.
- **History**: As long as we don't delete it, Lightroom will make a note of and store each change we make indefinitely in every photograph in Library. Think about it for a moment; every saturation nudge, aspect ratio change, export, produced print, brushstroke, spot removal, and camera profile: we can access any of these points and start from there.

  We already discussed **Collections** in the previous chapter; it is available across all Lightroom modules. The same rule applies to the filmstrip at the bottom of our screens.
- **Copy...** and **Paste**: The left panel ends with two buttons: **Copy...** and **Paste**. These can be used to copy and paste any settings that we choose across photographs.

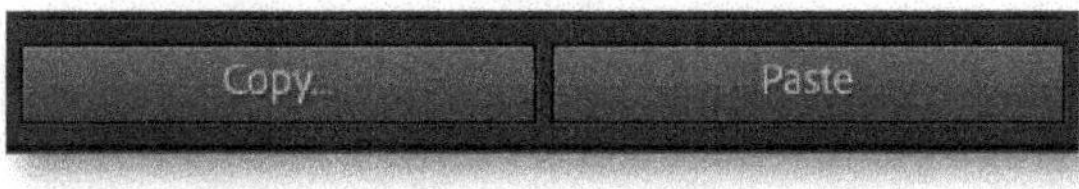

Figure 5.20 – Copy... and Paste buttons

Summary

We just had a quick glance at all the tools in the Develop module.

In the next chapter, we will explain each of the sliders and buttons within each of these tools and learn how they affect our photographs, from pixel level to a gut feeling. We will also look at tool combinations and see how different or similar to each other some of them are. Finally, we will work our way through multiple examples and understand the development process in detail.

6

A Detailed View of the Develop Module's Functions

From its very inception, Lightroom has been the digital equivalent of photography darkrooms, allowing everyone to develop photographs without the use of chemicals at instant speed and with great sophistication – from global adjustments to tiny tweaks, from detailed brush adjustments to batch processing large bodies of work. Lightroom offers photographers all the tools to make images look better (and more) without ever going near Photoshop or other post-production software. Lightroom is an end-to-end solution that's used to polish photographs and it unleashes the potential of photographers.

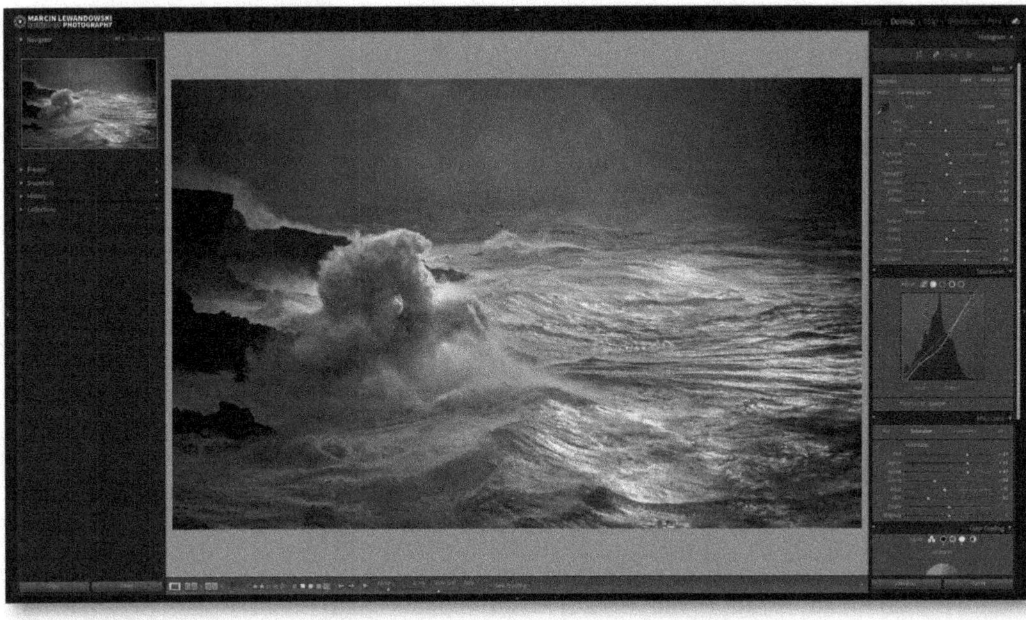

Figure 6.1 – Photograph in the Develop module

In the previous chapter, we briefly looked at each available tool in the Develop module – in this chapter, we will learn how they work and how they can help us. Postproduction is an integral part of photography and we will often think ahead to it when pressing the shutter of our camera – whether we are aware of adverse and unideal conditions that will cause the "straight out of the camera" photograph to need a bit of tweaking or whether we can see various black and white variants with our imagination. Whatever might be the case, the Develop module is a natural extension of any photographer's imagination…

A Little Disclaimer

Please keep in mind that any adjustments discussed in this chapter work best on RAW files, and you will reach the full potential of neither the tools nor your photographs when working on `.jpg` files. `.jpg` files don't hold enough data to take full advantage of Lightroom's capabilities. You will be able to significantly change the look of the photographs but not to the same extent as when working with RAW files. If your camera can't produce RAW files, then don't worry; you will be making the best of what you have and will future-proof your process for the time when you can work with RAW.

In this chapter, we will look at the Develop module by covering the following topics:

- Histogram
- Basic
- Tone Curve
- HSL/Color
- Color Grading
- Detail
- Lens Corrections
- Transform
- Effects
- Calibration

Histogram

The Histogram tool is on the top-right panel, and straight away, it's something so comprehensive that we can use it as our primary adjustment tool. Visually pleasing photographs are usually balanced in tone and color - Histogram adjustments can help us understand this dynamic. The Histogram tool visually represents how many pixels are present in the photograph at each different brightness level. The taller the graph is at any place, the more pixels at a certain brightness are represented in our picture. So, photographs with many dark areas will peak on the left-hand side of the Histogram.

Figure 6.2 A

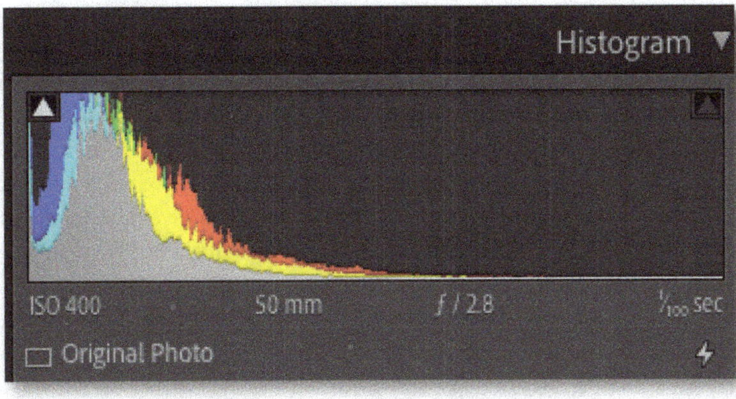

Figure 6.2 B – Photograph with many dark areas; a Histogram of the photograph with mostly dark areas

On the other hand, photographs with many bright regions will peak on the right-hand side of the Histogram.

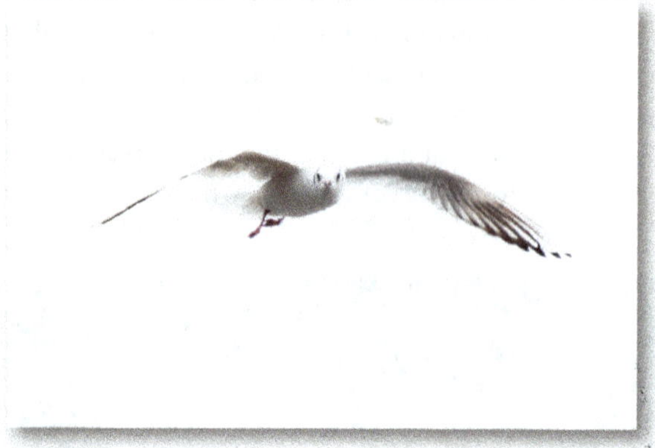

Figure 6.3 A

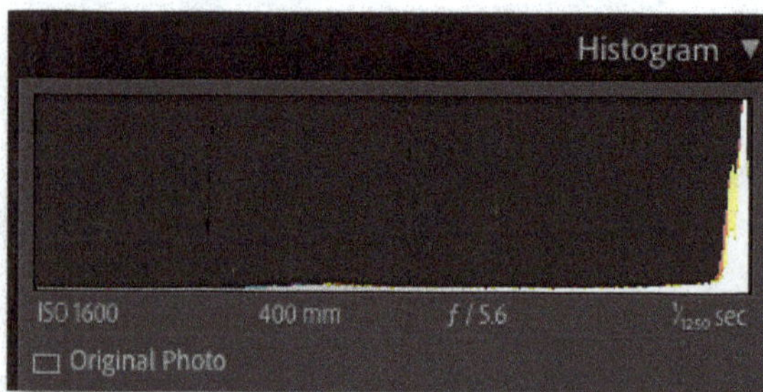

Figure 6.3 B – Photograph with many bright areas (left); a Histogram of the photograph with mostly bright areas (right)

An integral and essential part of this tool is its clipping warning, which is represented by two small arrows in the top corners of the Histogram tool. They warn us about clipping in dark and light areas. Areas affected by black clipping contain no visual information in the shadows; they are pure black. Regions affected by white clipping include no information in highlights, only pure white. Have a look at the preceding examples again. We can see many dark areas and indicators that we may have to deal with black clipping. The first clue is that we can see many pitch-black-looking areas in the picture. We can confirm our suspicion when the top-left histogram's arrow changes from dark gray (the same color as the Histogram's background) to a lighter shade of gray. Next, we can click on the discussed arrow to see areas that have been affected by black clipping. All the pixels that have been affected by black clipping will be highlighted in blue. The same principle applies to white clipping. We can confirm this by clicking on the top-right arrow to color all the areas affected by white clipping. We can also turn it on and off, highlighting both regions of clipping with the "*J*" keyboard shortcut. Please note that if clipping occurs in only one of the colors, it will be tinted in that color within the Histogram tool.

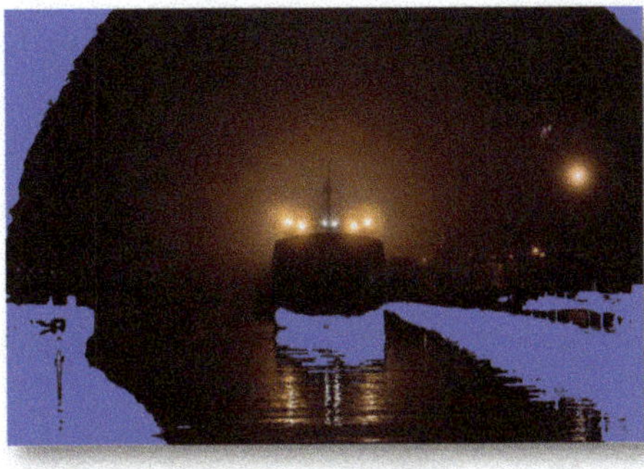

Figure 6.4 A

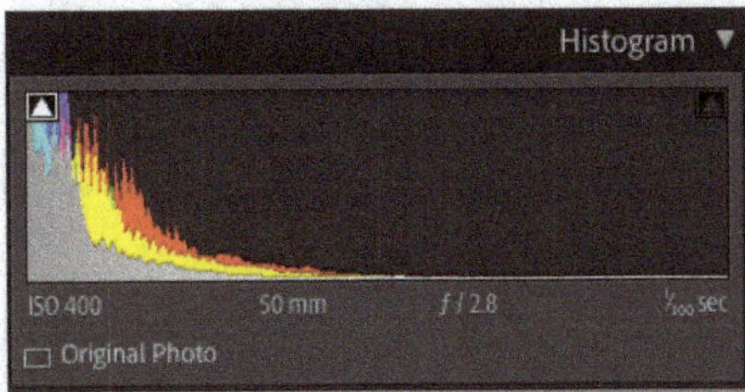

Figure 6.4 B – Black clipping areas in blue, and the Histogram tool with black clipping areas

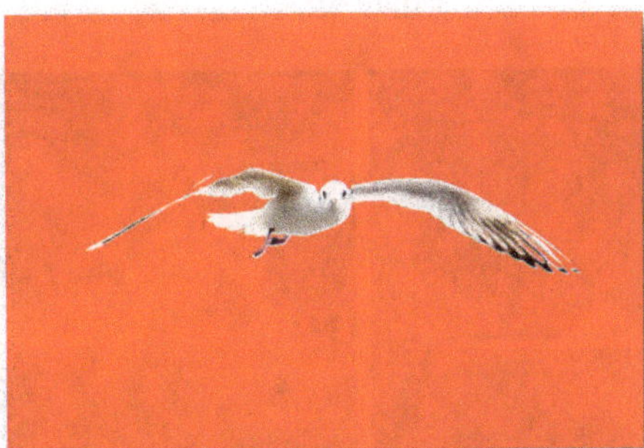

Figure 6.5 A

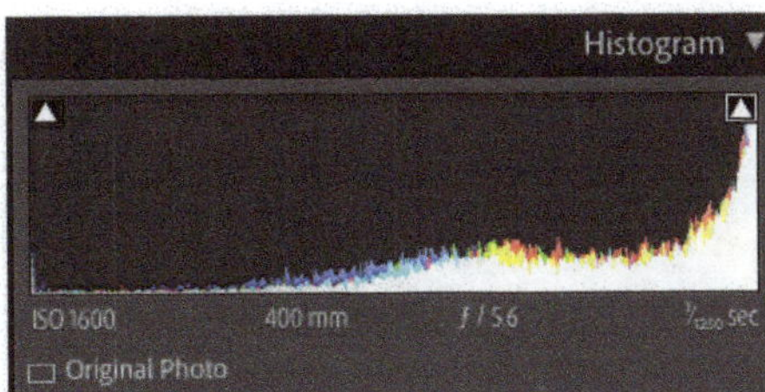

Figure 6.5 B – White clipping areas in red, and the Histogram tool with white clipping areas

Hovering our mouse cursor over the Histogram tool will highlight five distinct areas that match the tone adjustments. From left to right, these are as follows:

- Blacks
- Shadows
- Exposure
- Highlights
- Whites

These can be seen in the following screenshots:

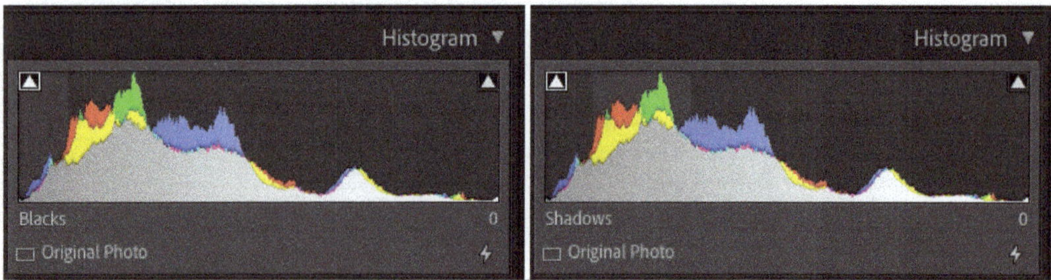

Figure 6.6 A

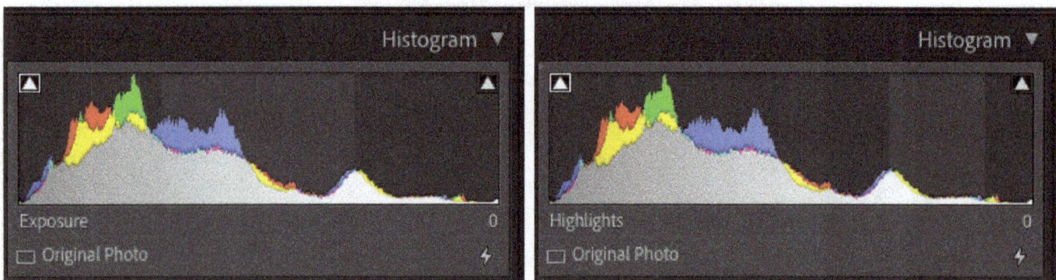

Figure 6.6 B

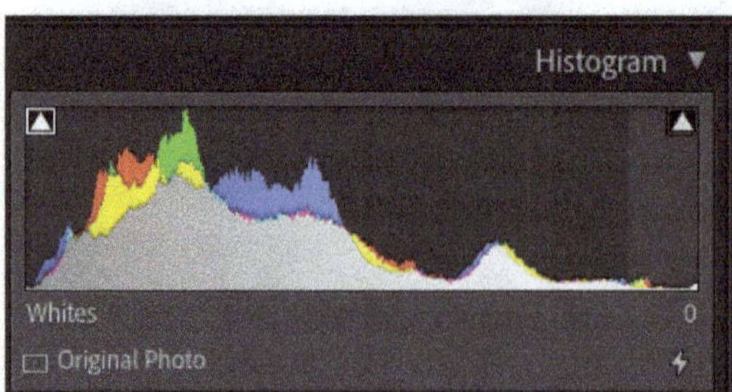

Figure 6.6 C – The Histogram tool showing all five different adjustment areas – Blacks, Shadows, Exposure, Highlights, and Whites

We can adjust our photograph within the Histogram tool by dragging highlighted areas left or right. So long as we don't have a very extreme clipping situation, as shown in the previous examples, we can balance almost any photograph. For example, if we start with a very dark or very bright picture, we can balance it by making a few histogram adjustments.

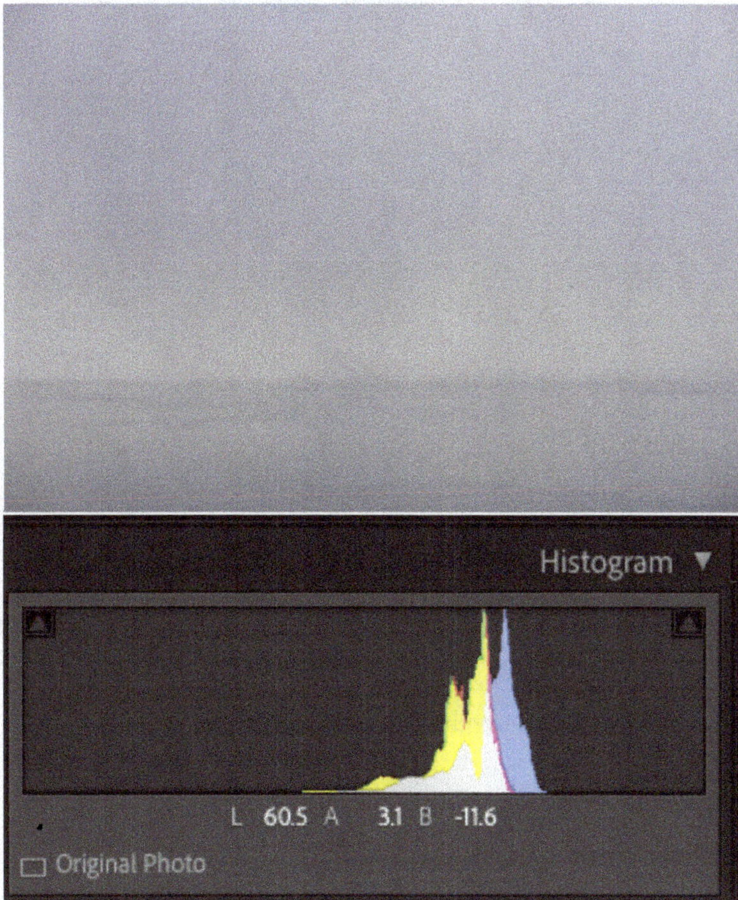

Figure 6.7 A

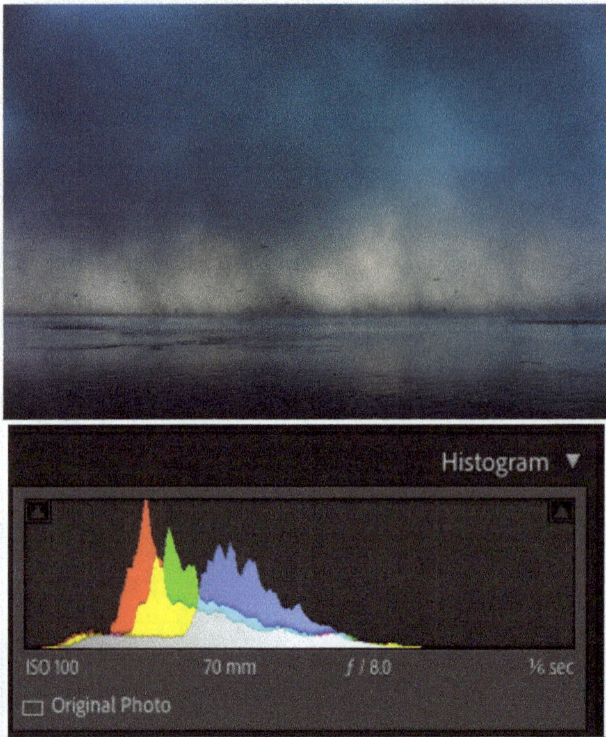

Figure 6.7 B – Balancing an overexposed photograph with the Histogram tool showing the original state (first and second screens) and the final state (third and fourth screens)

Starting with Exposure, I will drag it to the right or left until it fills the Histogram's center area. Once I'm happy with the results, I will drag the highlights to the left to recover details in the highlighted area. When there are dark areas in the photograph, I'll pull Shadows a tiny bit to the right and then pull Blacks to the left to make the darks more defined. Then, I may play with Exposure again to make it look "just right." We can treat this newly balanced photograph as a starting point or even a final result. The main thing is to understand how powerful adjusting directly within the Histogram tool can be. Most photographers, including myself, prefer to work with **Tone** sliders, but once we are aware that this option of working directly with the Histogram tool is available, there will be moments when it will feel just right.

The next section will focus on applying the aforementioned settings locally, within selected areas of the photograph.

Local adjustment tools

A set of four local adjustment tools follows the Histogram tool:

- Crop Overlay ("*R*")
- Spot Removal ("*Q*")
- Red Eye Correction
- Masking

These can be seen in the following screenshot, in the order they were mentioned:

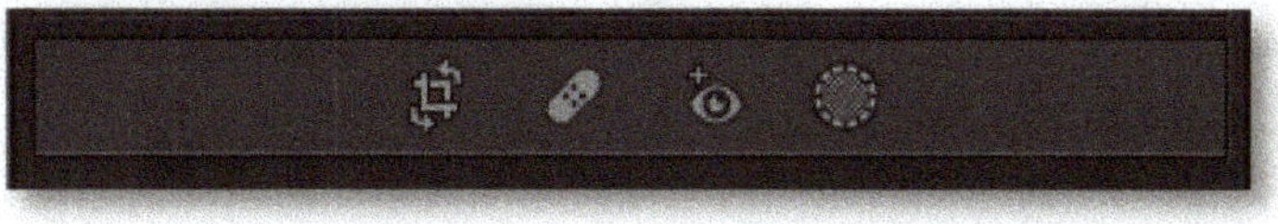

Figure 6.8 – Local adjustment tools

Let's look at these in more detail.

Crop Overlay

We can use Crop Overlay by clicking on the first tool in the line or using the "*R*" keyboard shortcut. Both options will open the **Crop & Straighten** panel.

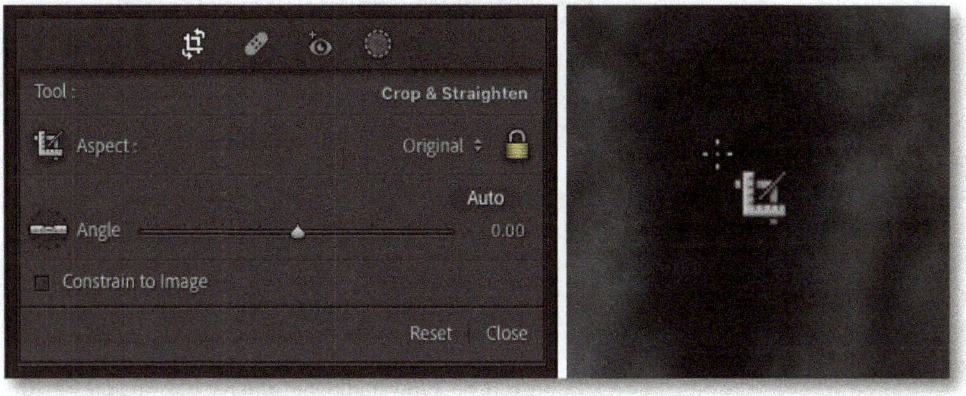

Figure 6.9 – The Crop & Straighten panel and the Crop Frame tool

Clicking next to the word **Aspect** will change the cursor to the **Crop Frame** tool. With the cursor changed to the Crop Frame tool, we can draw our desired crop within the photograph or adjust it to our liking by dragging the corners and edges of the Crop Frame tool. By default, the crop ratio will be the same as the original photograph, but we have a few options to change it. Using the "*X*" keyboard shortcut, we can switch between portrait and landscape orientation of the Crop view. By opening the **Aspect** pop-up menu, we can access a list of preset aspect ratios. The list consists of the most popular aspect ratios – from the **1X1** square to large formats such as **8X10** (which is used by Instagram for vertical photos) to the most popular and widely used **3X2**, which is often referred to as **6X4**. Lastly, we can click on the little padlock at the end of this row to toggle it between locked and unlocked; we can also toggle it with the "*A*" keyboard shortcut. When the padlock is closed, Lightroom will lock the crop ratio to the current setting, regardless of whether we leave the original orientation or change it. Opening the padlock gives us complete creative freedom, whether it's for drawing a new crop frame or adjusting the existing one by dragging its sides and corners.

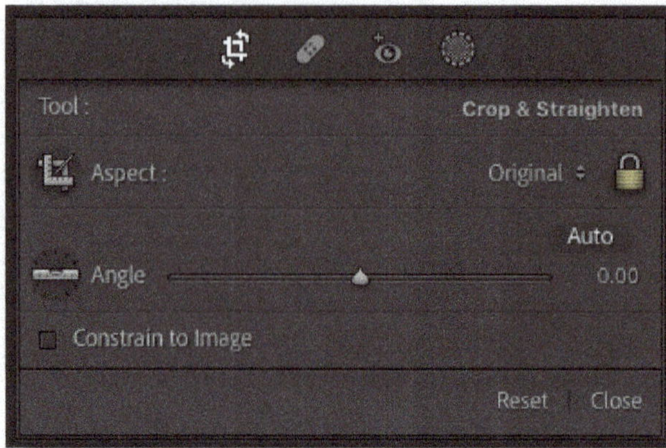

Figure 6.10 A

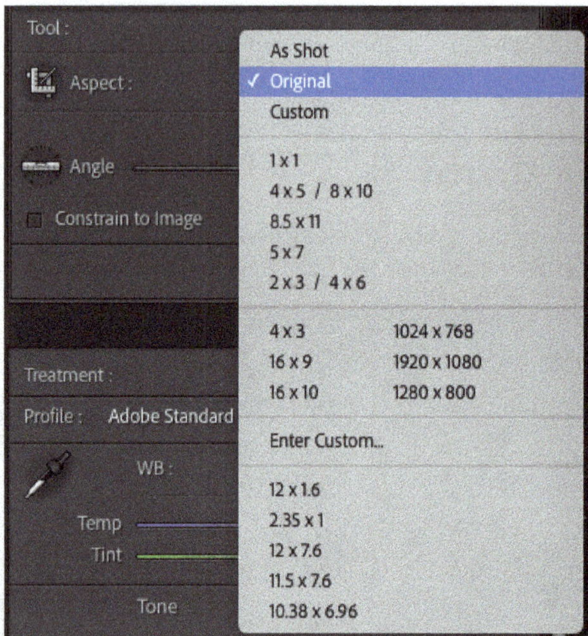

Figure 6.10 B – Crop Frame tool and Aspect ratio presets list

Quick Note

When we toggle the padlock, the first state that we will change it to and make settings with will be the padlock state when we open the Crop Frame tool next time - that is, if we open a photo with a locked aspect ratio, change it to unlocked and adjust it, when we open the Crop Frame tool the next time, it will start in its unlocked state. It's worth remembering this to avoid frustration when working on a batch of photographs that need cropping.

The next slider is for straightening photographs. We can change the angle of our photograph in three different ways:

- The **Auto** button is usually accurate if there are visible straight lines in the pictures, but it can be unreliable.
- Using the **Liner** tool, we can draw the desired horizontal or vertical line that the photo will be aligned with or play with the slider to straighten the image.
- We can also manually adjust the angle by working directly with our Crop Frame tool by using an angle cursor around all of the edges and corners of the crop frame.

Lastly, we have the option to **Constrain to Image** and avoid white areas around the photograph when we work with the Transform tool later.

While using the Crop Overlay toolbar at the bottom of the active window, below the photograph we are working on, we will get the option to turn **Tool Overlay** on or off. It displays different grids, which are helpful while cropping, rotating, and straightening images. When **Tool Overlay** is set to **Auto**, it will only display a grid while we actively work with the Crop Frame tool for rotating, changing the photograph's size, and so on. **Always** and **Never** should be self-explanatory. With **Tool Overlay** switched to **Always**, we can toggle various types of overlay grids with the "O" keyboard shortcut. For the **Fibonacci spiral** and **4X5** grids, we can also change the orientation of the grid with the "⇧O" keyboard shortcut.

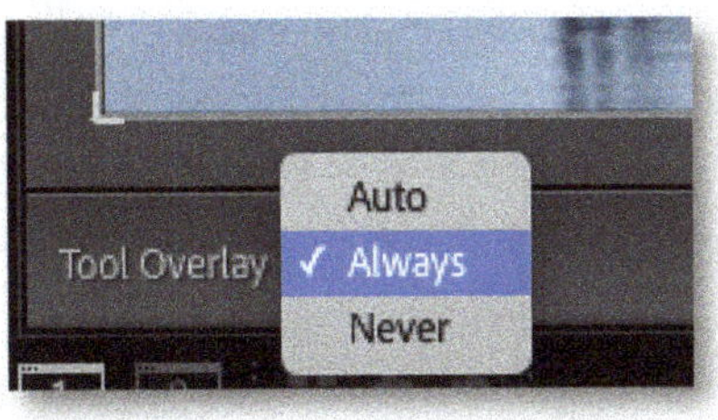

Figure 6.11 – Tool Overlay menu

To confirm and apply our changes, we need to click **Done** at the bottom right, below the edited image, and press "*Enter*" on our keyboard or use the "*R*" keyboard shortcut. Finally, we can discard all changes and return to where we started by pressing "*Esc.*"

At any time, we can use the "⌥⌘*R*" keyboard shortcut to Reset Crop or "⌥⇧⌘*R*" to return our photograph to the originally shot aspect ratio.

Spot Removal

Spot Removal is an essential tool that we can use for anything, from removing sensor dirt to getting rid of whole chunks of landscape or even random people we don't want in our photo. We can also use it to make any silly changes that we want to try, and in that case, our creativity will dictate what is possible. As a photographer, from time to time, I'm asked to "Photoshop" things in and out of pictures. The Spot Removal tool allows me to provide this service at the most basic level.

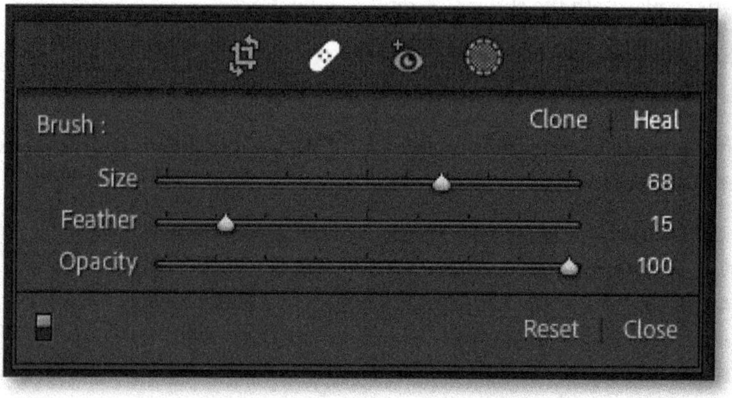

Figure 6.12 – Spot Removal menu

First of all, the Spot Removal tool gives us the option to work in one of two modes: **Clone** or **Heal**. The **Clone** setting will copy anything from the sampled source into the brushed area. At the same time, **Heal** will fill the brushed area seamlessly using the source's lighting and texture. Once we brush any area, we can move both the brushed area and the source. We can also change between the **Heal** and **Clone** functions.

We can adjust the brush itself in a few different ways by controlling three sliders: **Size**, **Feather**, and **Opacity**. This change will also be reflected in the sampled area. To easily pinpoint spots of dust, we can enable the **Visualize Spots** option on the bottom toolbar, which will help highlight any concentrated black irregular spots. We can control the sensitivity of the Visual Spots tool with the slider located next to the checkbox. This overlay can also be enabled/disabled with the "*A*" keyboard shortcut.

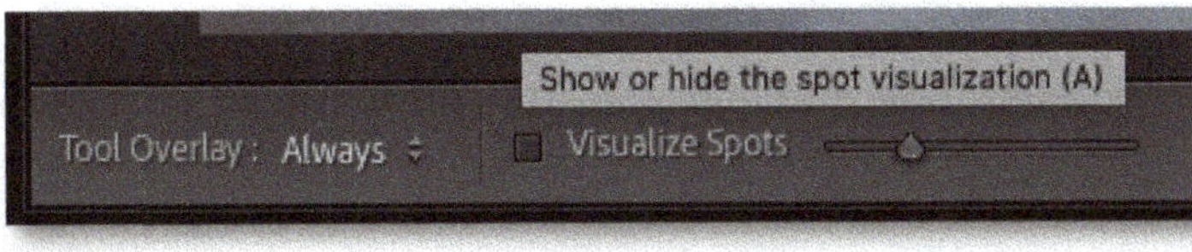

Figure 6.13 A

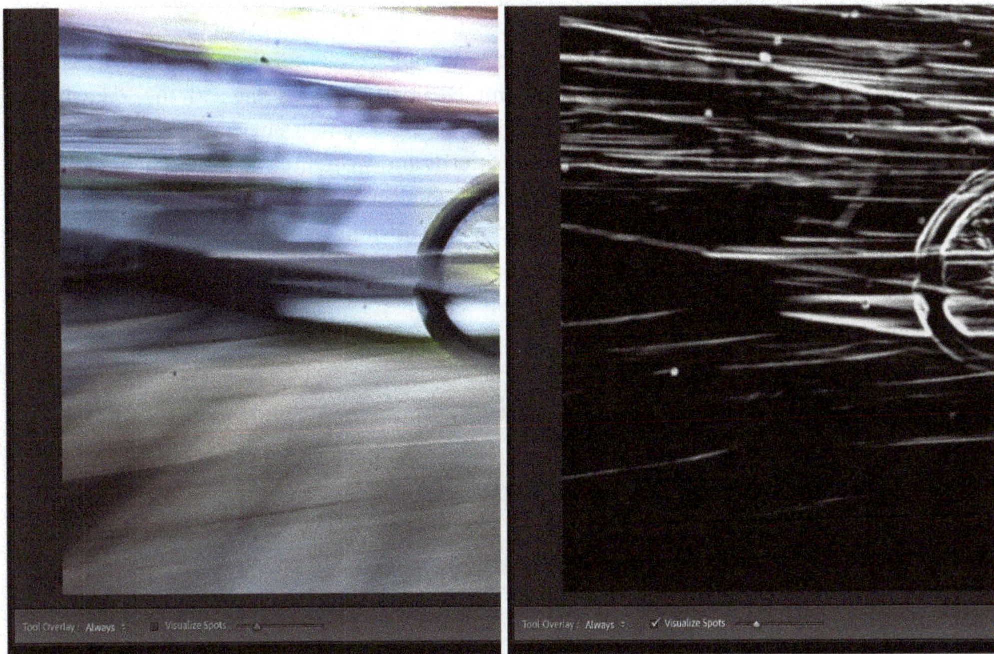

Figure 6.13 B – The Visualize Spots tool and example usage

Let's have a closer look at the **Size**, **Feather**, and **Opacity** settings of the brush:

- **Size**: The size of the brush can be changed with the assigned slider. Alternatively, you can use the "*[*" keyboard shortcut to decrease it and the "*]*" keyboard shortcut to increase it. We can also change the size of the brush by scrolling our mouse up and down. It's good to keep the brush size slightly bigger than the object we want to get rid of from our photograph and be precise when brushing. When we work in that way, Lightroom can easily recognize what we are trying to get rid of and won't have to replace any areas that don't need to be replaced.
- **Feather**: This specifies the blending margin's width. Anything within the feather margin of our brush will blend from 100% cover at the inside margin of the brush's feather to 0% on the outside of the margin of the brush. Therefore, when we change the **Feather** setting, the inside border of our brush will change its circumference without affecting the brush's size. Lightroom will cover anything within the inner circle entirely; the outside circle's coverage will change between the inner and outer edge of the feathered area from 100% to 0%.

- **Opacity**: When **Opacity** is set to **100**, the Spot Removal tool will cover the brushed area with 0% transparency of the brush. In comparison, when **Opacity** is set to **50**, the tool will cover the brushed area with 50% transparency. Usually, we want **Opacity** to be set to **100** so that the brushed area is not visible under the brush and is entirely replaced by the **Heal** or **Cone** layer.

An unwanted person in a landscape picture, blemishes on a headshot, or any dust spots on the sensor can often be quickly dealt with, but we need to be smart about it and remember that this is not magic, just an algorithm trying to patch things up. Brushing will work perfectly most of the time, especially for obvious things, but sometimes, it will get it wrong. We can remedy this in a couple of ways. The fastest and most efficient involves cycling through sampled areas after brushing with the "/" keyboard shortcut. If, after a few cycles, Lightroom still can't pick the right spot, it's best to move the sampled area to one that looks like it should work. Aligning patterns and structure will always help make the effect look more realistic. Making a few brush strokes to achieve natural-looking results will often be necessary. Our eyes will be the best judge, and if we can't see obvious signs of changes within the just brushed area, then nobody will.

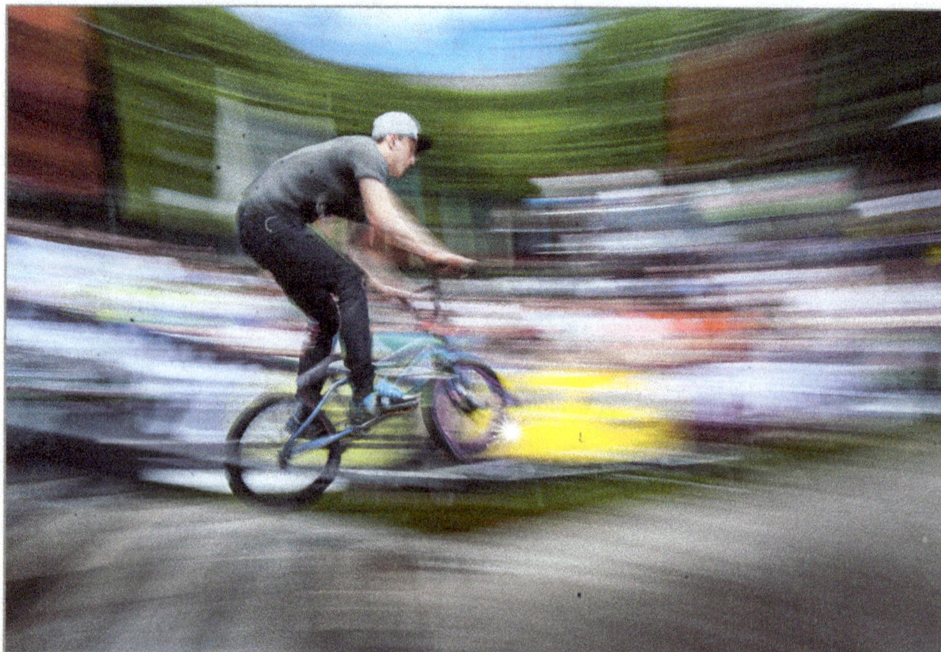

Figure 6.14 A

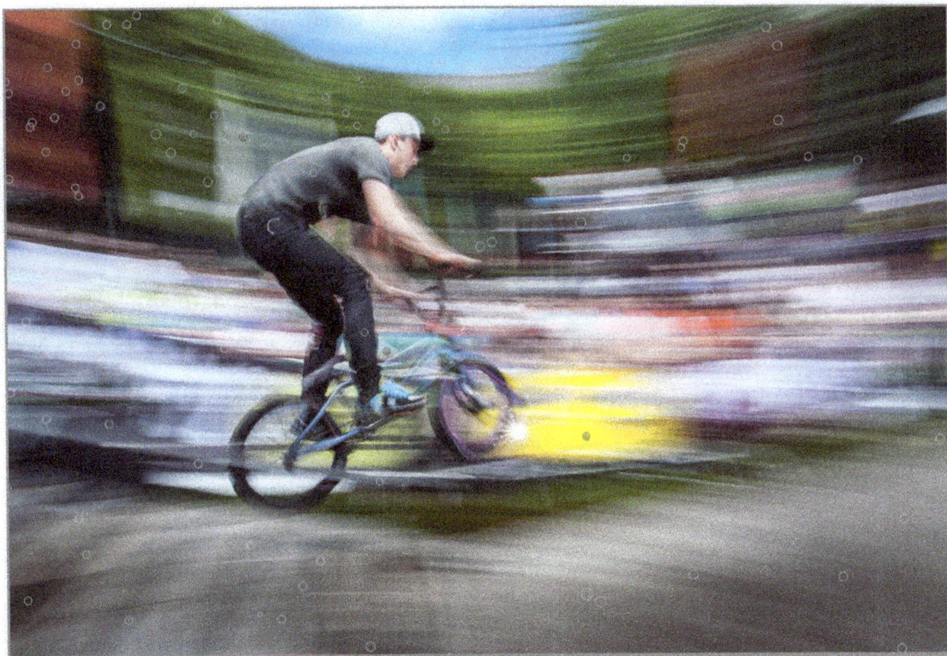

Figure 6.14 B

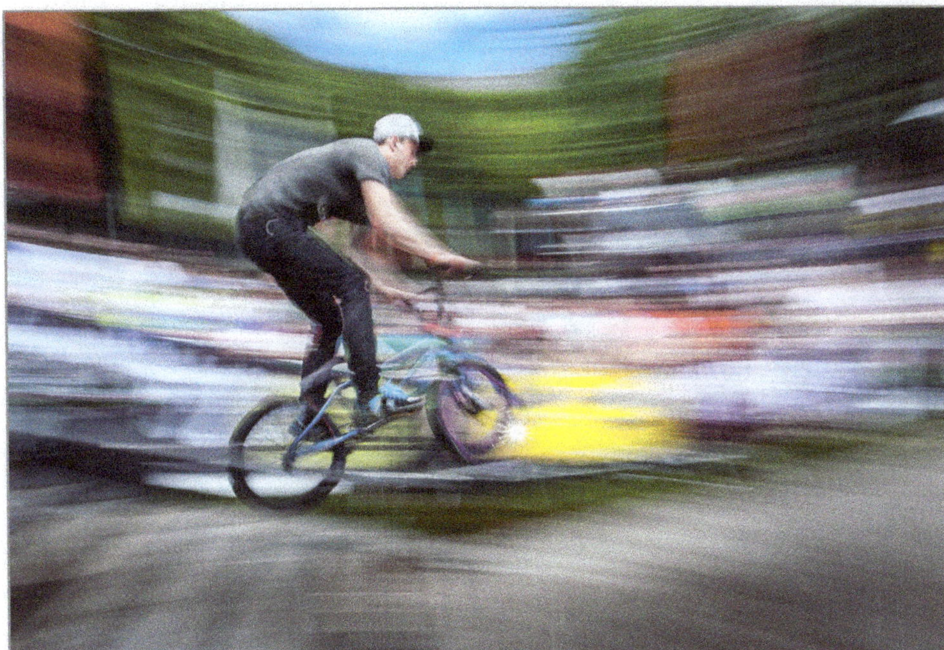

Figure 6.14 C – An example of extensive dust removal – before, during, and after

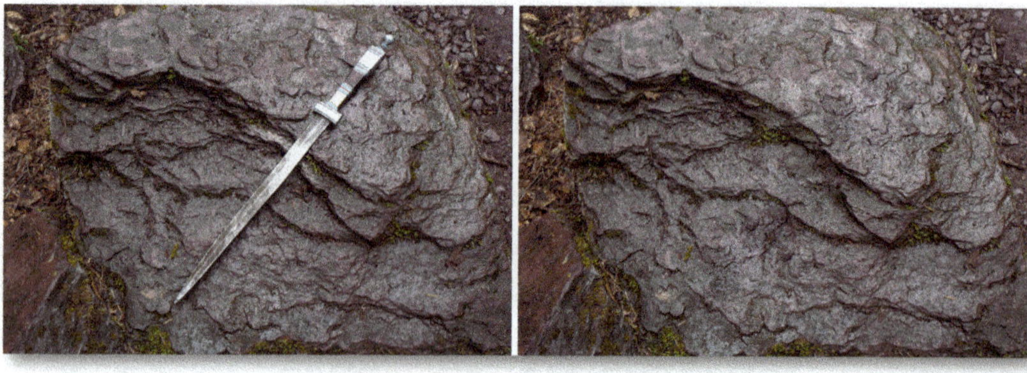

Figure 6.15 – An example of object removal – before and after

Now let's look into **Red Eye Correction.**

Red Eye Correction

Using a camera with an on-camera flash, especially up close, will produce the unfortunate "red-eye" effect, which renders human pupils (and some animals' as well) red by bouncing some of the light back into the lens through the eyes' blood vessels. This tool can help us fix this effortlessly. Click on the tool, click in the middle of a pupil, and drag to cover the whole eye. Once we let it go, Lightroom will change the selected area to circular and blacken its center to eliminate the red-eye effect. If we miss the center, we can move the area – you will notice that the cursor will change to a hand over the chosen location. If the "dark patch" of red-eye correction is too big or too small, we can change it with the **Pupil Size** slider and make it darker or lighter with the **Darken** slider. After switching to the **Pet Eye** function, our choice of working sliders will be limited to only **Pupil Size**, but we will get the option to **Add Catchlight**. This is a straightforward and potentially helpful tool!

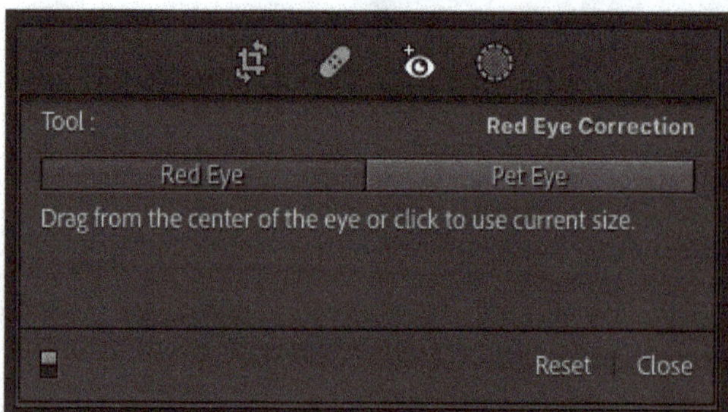

Figure 6.16 A

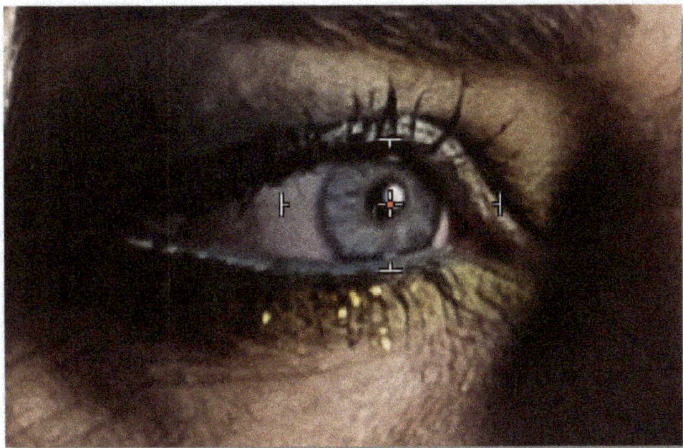

Figure 6.16 B

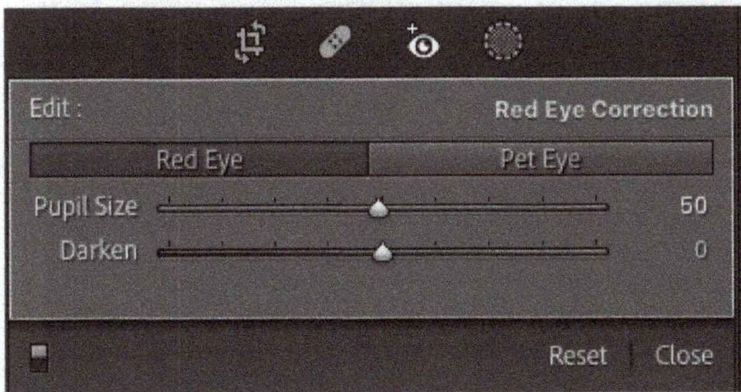

Figure 6.16 C – The Red Eye Correction tool's panel (top) and the Pupil Size cursor and sliders (bottom)

If we use a camera with an on-camera flash in a dark room and the subject is looking directly into the lens, we are almost guaranteed to get the red-eye effect; **Red-Eye Correction** will eliminate this problem.

The tools under the **Masking** icon are for making local adjustments and for using masks and layers. We will learn what they are capable of after learning about the **Basic** tab.

Basic

This section will cover how to globally manipulate photographs without applying masks. We will learn, among other things, how to recover details that have been lost in the shadows, bring back an overexposed sky, or warm up a chilly autumn morning. Turn on your computer, turn on Lightroom, choose a nice variation of photographs you like, and let's get to it.

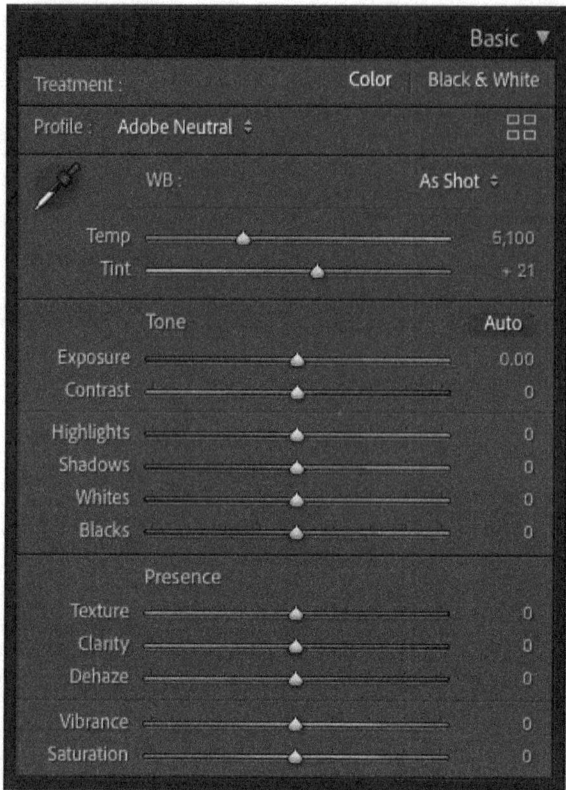

Figure 6.17 – The Basic tab's toolset

Treatment

The **Treatment** option gives us the choice to immediately start working with a black and white version of our image. It might be a creative choice to begin with a black and white photograph, but we will focus on starting in color and discuss working with black and white afterward. Still, this might be an option that some of you may want to come back to at a later stage. We can quickly check what any photograph will look like while using **Black & White** by using the "*V*" keyboard shortcut.

Figure 6.18 – The Treatment tab

Profile

The **Profile** option allows us to completely change the look and feel of our photographs with one click. **Profile** uses a technology called 3D **Look Up Tables (LUTs)**. When we apply a profile, Lightroom replaces the color values of our photographs with different values from custom-built tables of values. Profiles can do wild things and replace color palettes in a way where blues become reds and yellows become pinks. Most of the time, these changes are much more subtle and only add a bit of tint and shift the hues around. With all of these changes to the look of our photographs, profiles do not affect any of the sliders within the **Develop** panel; they simply change the foundations that we can work with. From my perspective, it is not only a great work tool that delivers consistent and predictable effects but is a source of inspiration. Sometimes, you may feel like you want to change something but can't quite put your finger on it. The **Profile** tool can help in situations like this, allowing you to skim through many variants without committing to anything.

Once we open **Profile Browser**, by clicking on the icon with four rectangles, we will be welcomed by a list of available profiles. Unless we have already imported any custom profiles, Lightroom will welcome us with a list of default profiles split into separate categories.

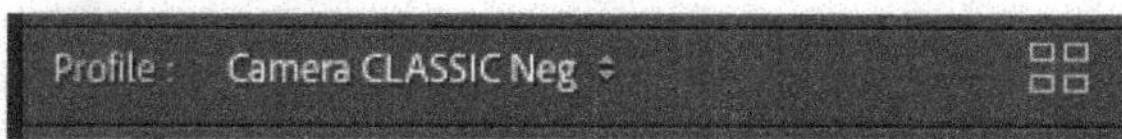

Figure 6.19 A

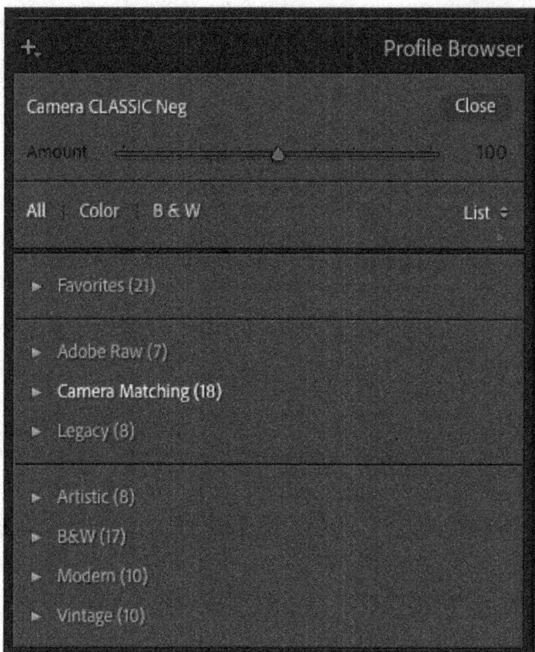

Figure 6.19 B – Profile Chooser and the Profile Browser default view

At the very top of **Profile Browser**, we can see the name of the currently applied profile and an **Amount** slider. With the **Amount** slider, we can change the intensity that many profiles are applied with; we can't adjust the intensity of the **Adobe Raw**, **Camera Matching**, or **Legacy** profiles, but we can adjust most of the other ones. To choose which profiles are displayed, click on the + icon in the top-right corner of **Profile Browser** or right-click anywhere within it. This will open a pop-up menu where we have an additional option called **Reset Hidden Profiles**. This shows all the profiles we chose to hide in the **Manage Profiles** menu. I work with the **Grid** view as I find it convenient. The three categories under the slider are profile filters. Depending on our choice, it will display only **Color**, only **B&W**, or **All** profiles. Remember that any sepia-type profiles will be under the **Color** filter. On the right-hand side of these three categories, we can choose how profiles are displayed by clicking on the name of our current display setting.

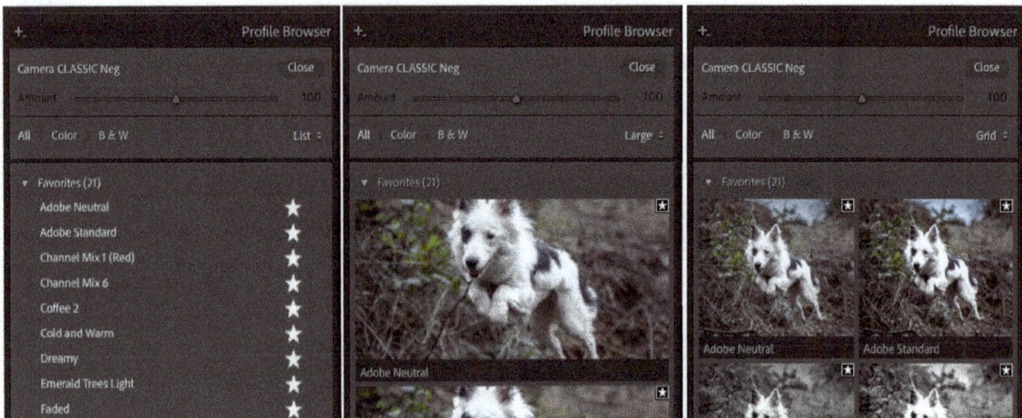

Figure 6.20 – Different profile views – List (left), Large (middle), and Grid (right)

When we hover over any of the profiles, we will immediately see its effect on the currently developed photograph. This preview nullifies any guesswork while we're choosing profiles and allows us to quickly decide on the direction we would like to take with the photo's look, even if we don't apply it.

We can add profiles to our favorites by clicking on the small star in the top-right corner of the **Profile** preview in the **Grid** and **Large** view or by clicking the star next to the profile's name in the **List** view.

You can find profiles online – there are often some free samples, with larger packs available for purchase. My suggestion is to first get a good hold on what's available by default and then decide if you may need more.

White Balance

White Balance is a tool that allows us to change or fix the color cast of any lighting we encounter while photographing. From the cold, blue shadows through the green haze of fluorescent light to the oranges of tungsten bulbs, we can eliminate unwanted color shifts with the **White Balance** tool or use it creatively to, for example, change the day into night or a dull day into a warm and sunny summer's day.

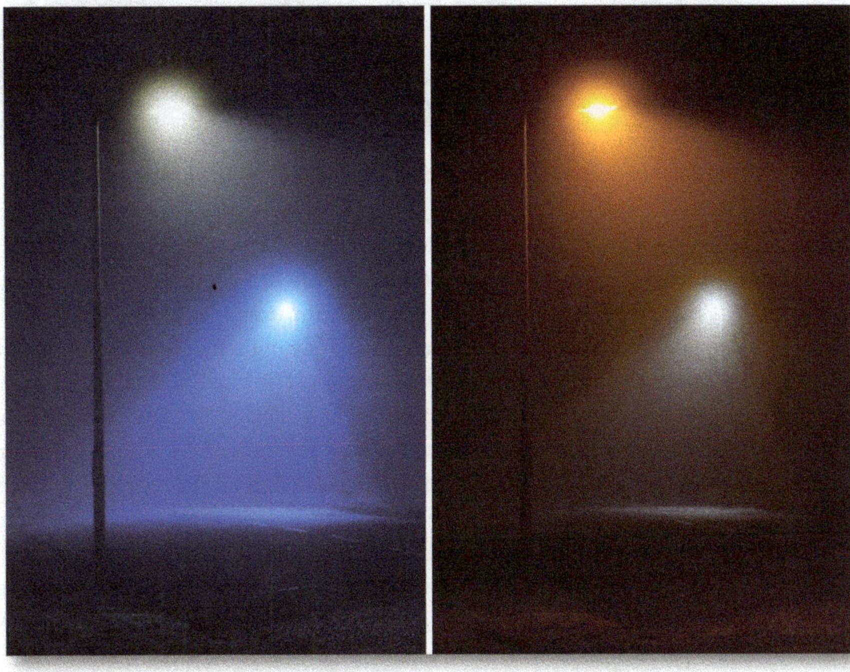

Figure 6.21 A

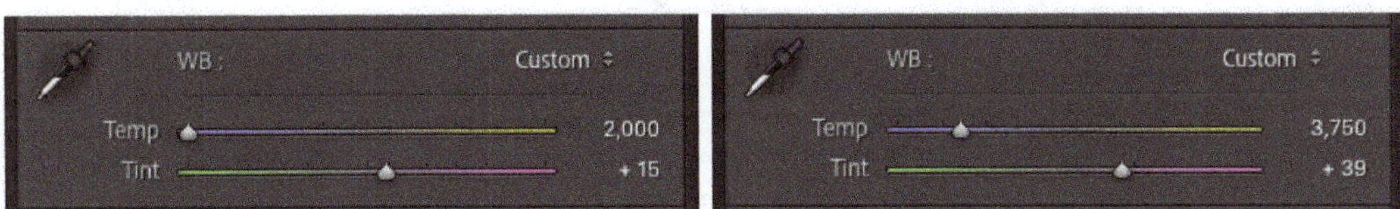

Figure 6.21 B – The same photograph with White Balance corrected for the sodium streetlight in the foreground and with White Balance corrected for the LED streetlight in the background

White Balance Selector

Once you know of the existence of this tool, it becomes an integral part of any workflow, just like one of the blades in a good Swiss Army knife. We can activate **White Balance Selector** by clicking on its icon or by using the "*W*" keyboard shortcut.

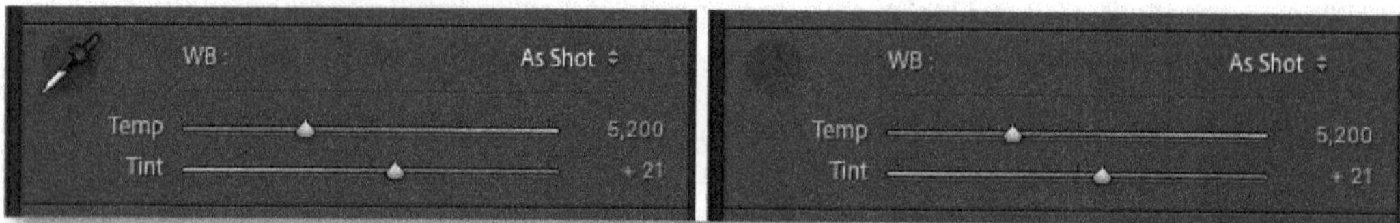

Figure 6.22 – White Balance Selector in its spot on the left and its empty holder on the right

The mouse cursor will change to the selector icon as it leaves its spot, leaving just an empty circle to put it back in. The beautiful thing about this keyboard shortcut, as with most shortcuts within Lightroom, is that we can activate it from within any module. If we are, for example, browsing images in the library and would like to quickly change the white balance on one of them, pressing "*W*" will take us directly to the **White Balance Selector** tool. The optimal way to use **White Balance Selector** is to find a neutral gray area in the photograph with an unwanted tint and click on it. Lightroom will shift the hues to get this area back to neutral gray and, by doing so, shift the hues of the whole photograph. In the perfect scenario, we will have a neutral gray card photographed in all the lighting conditions we encounter. However, in reality, we may not have even a smidge of neutral gray within the frame. In a situation like that, I always try white areas affected by the unwanted White Balance tint, and more often than not, it will work just fine. I may also try black areas that have some color detail, and on many occasions, it will work too. Finally, try clicking on random color areas within a picture to see what happens. With time, you will intuitively understand what works and what doesn't, sometimes looking at surprisingly attractive, though entirely unnatural, colors.

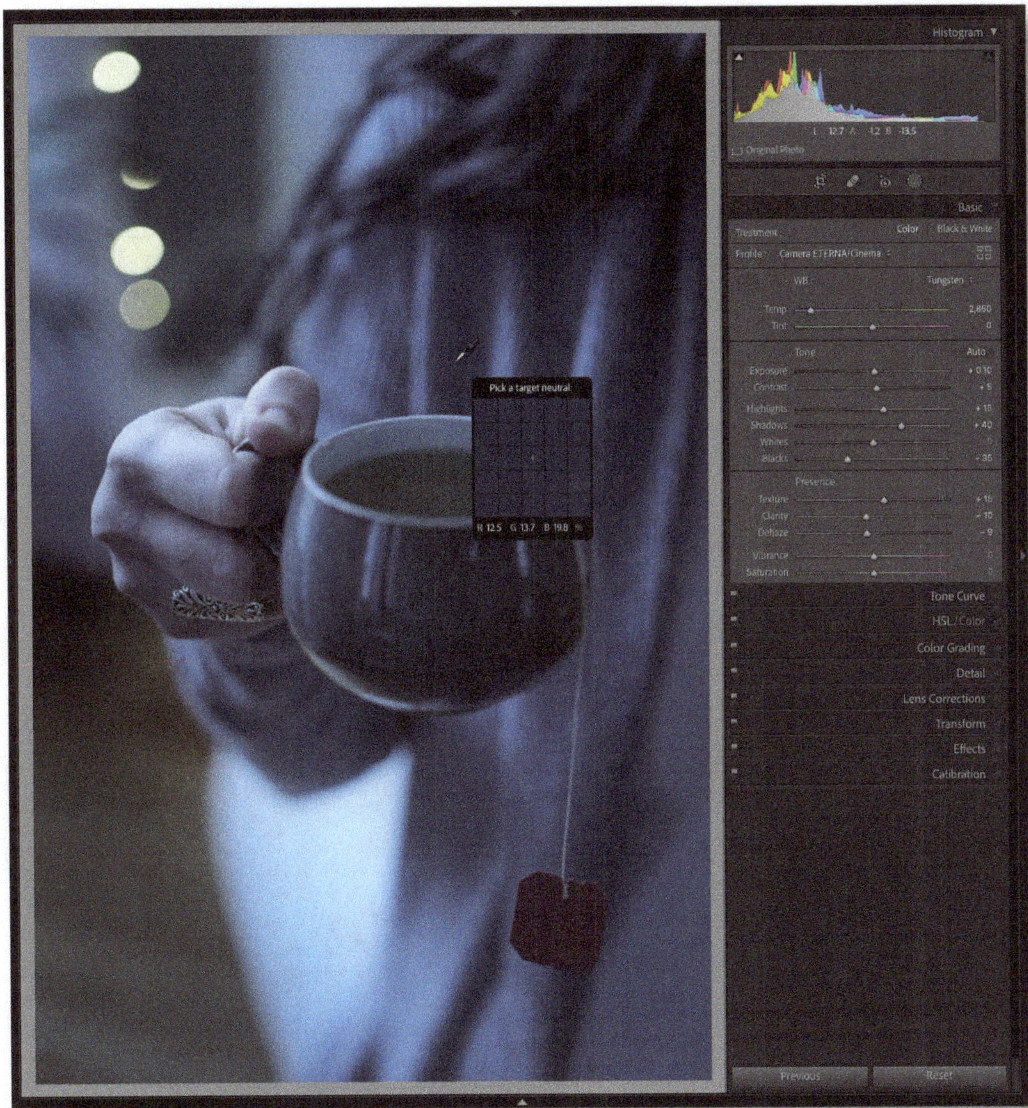
Histogram
Original Photo
Basic
Treatment
Color
Black & White
WB
Tungsten
Temp
Tint
Tone
Auto
Exposure
Contrast
Highlights
Shadows
Whites
Blacks
Presence
Texture
Clarity
Dehaze
Vibrance
Saturation
Pick a target neutral:
R 12.5 G 13.7 B 19.8 %
Tone Curve
HSL / Color
Color Grading
Detail
Lens Corrections
Transform
Effects
Calibration
Previous
Reset

Figure 6.23 A

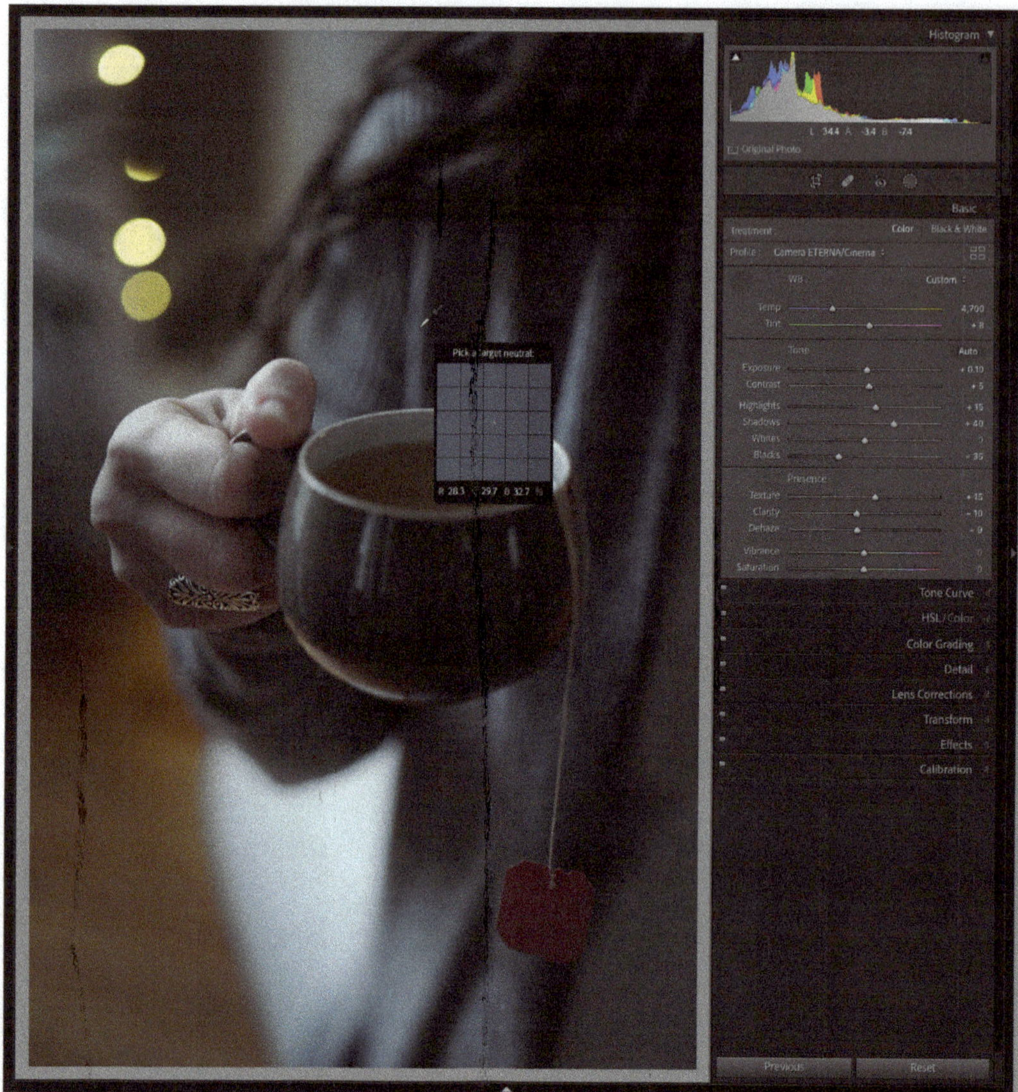

Figure 6.23 B – Choosing a neutral gray color with White Balance Selector on a photo that was taken with Tungsten White Balance settings

In the same line as White Balance Selector, we have a few very handy presets that broadly cover the most common white balance settings. Any of these presets work in a way that counteracts the chosen lighting conditions. If we click on, for example, **Tungsten**, it doesn't re-color photographs in the Tungsten palette; it shifts the color palette as if the picture lit by tungsten light was instead lit by white light. This means that if we change the **White Balance** property of an overcast afternoon scene to **Tungsten**, it will change everything to blue, not the tungsten orange. We pick the lighting conditions we photographed in, and Lightroom will do the rest. We can always try the **Auto** function if none of these matches, which can be very accurate on many occasions. If none of this works, we have sliders to control the **White Balance** settings manually.

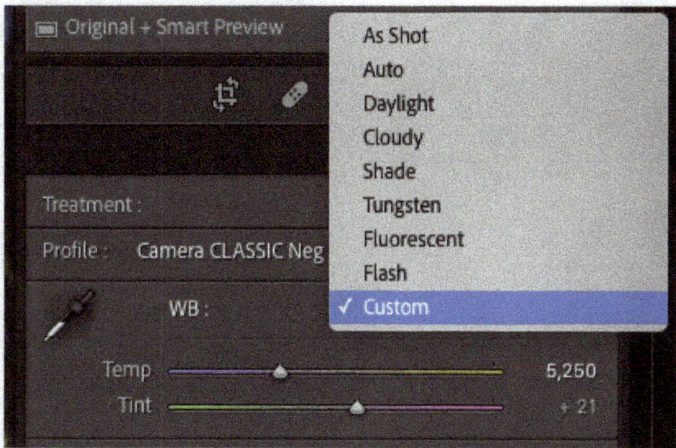

Figure 6.24 – White Balance presets

The top slider, **Temp** (temperature in Kelvins), will change the look of the photograph from cold blue on the left to warm yellow on the right. This change happens on a scale from 2,000 K to 50,000 K, but situations where you will use the edges of this slider will be rare. Most pictures will look very unnatural in both of these most extreme settings. Often, moving within a 2,000 K range will be dramatic enough to change the look of our photo from a cold morning to a warm, summer evening.

The second slider and last tool in the White Balance toolset is the **Tint** slider. Sometimes, when photographing through a tinted window, the photograph may have a greenish cast – we can counteract this by moving the slider slightly to the right. But, again, even though the arbitrary scale of movement is quite broad, ranging from -150 to +150, changes of about 50 units will dramatically influence the photograph's look.

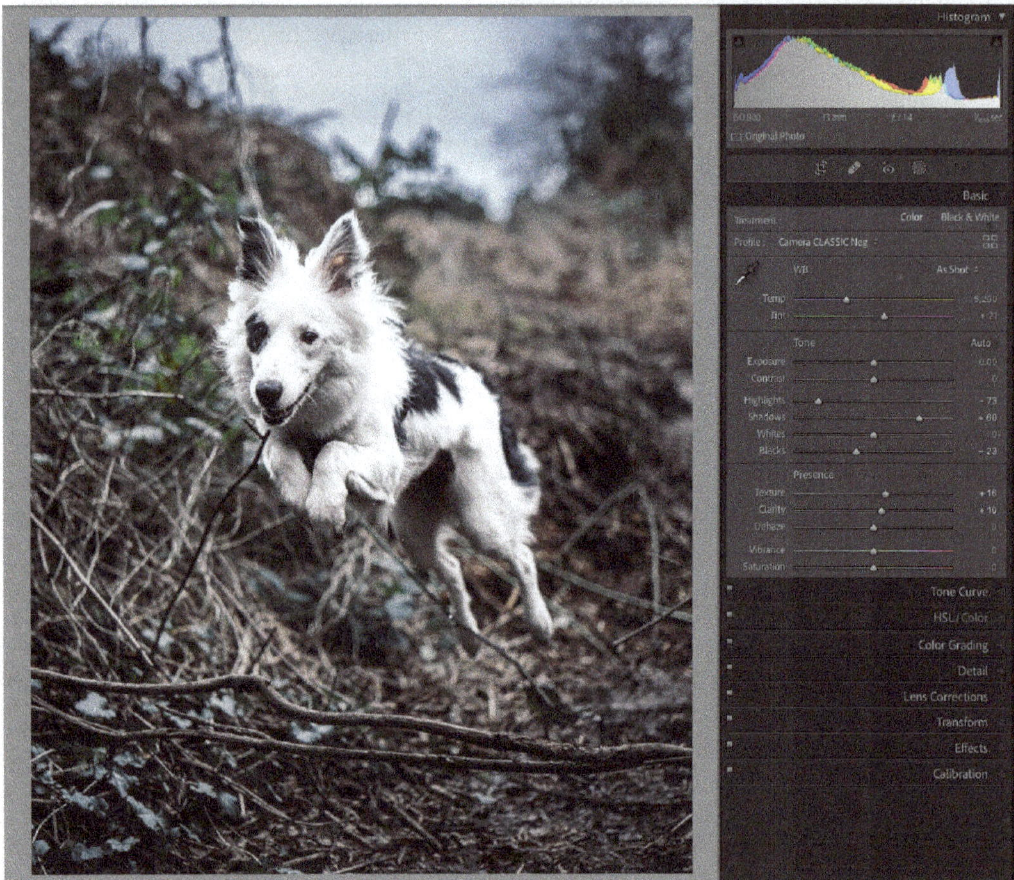

Figure 6.25 A

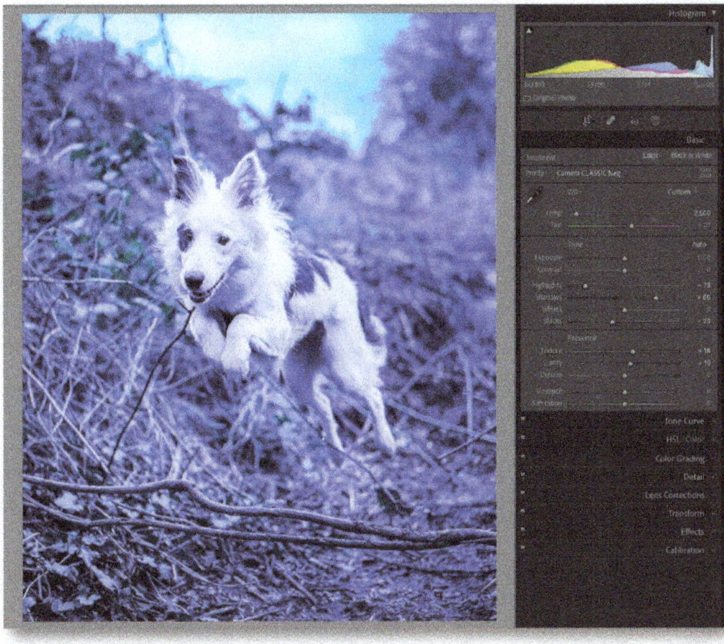

Figure 6.25 B

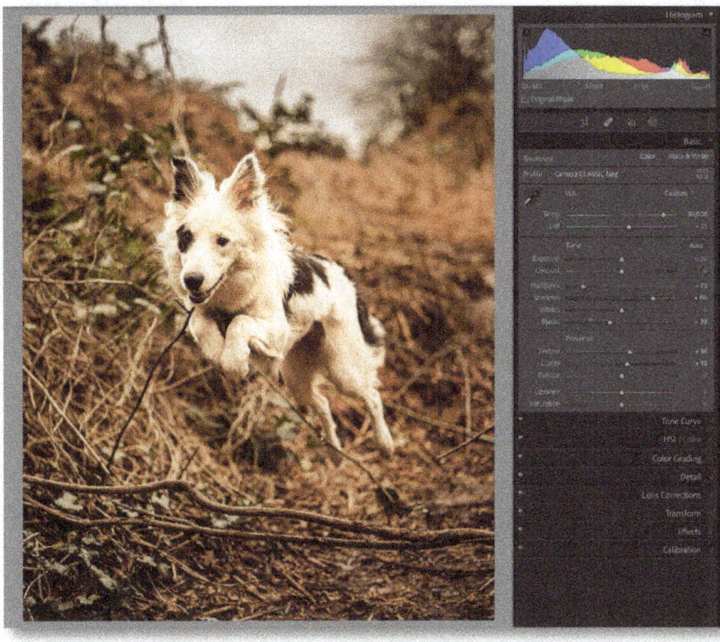

Figure 6.25 C

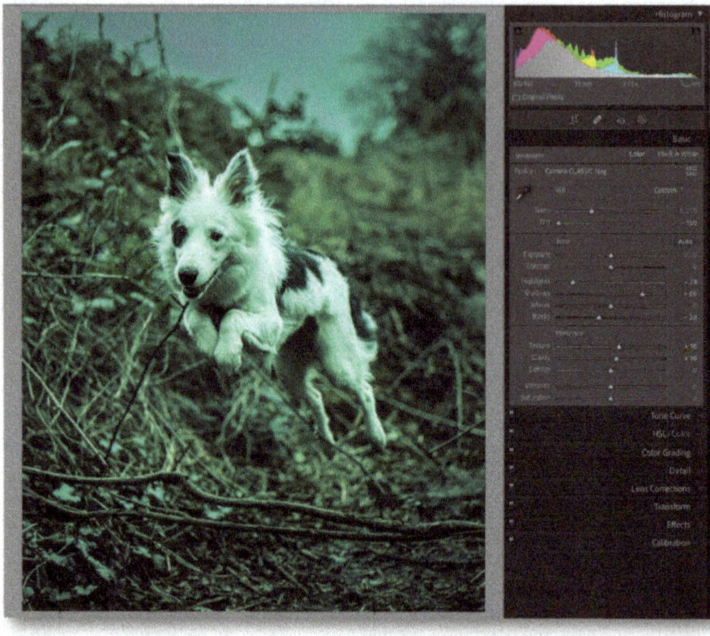

Figure 6.25 D

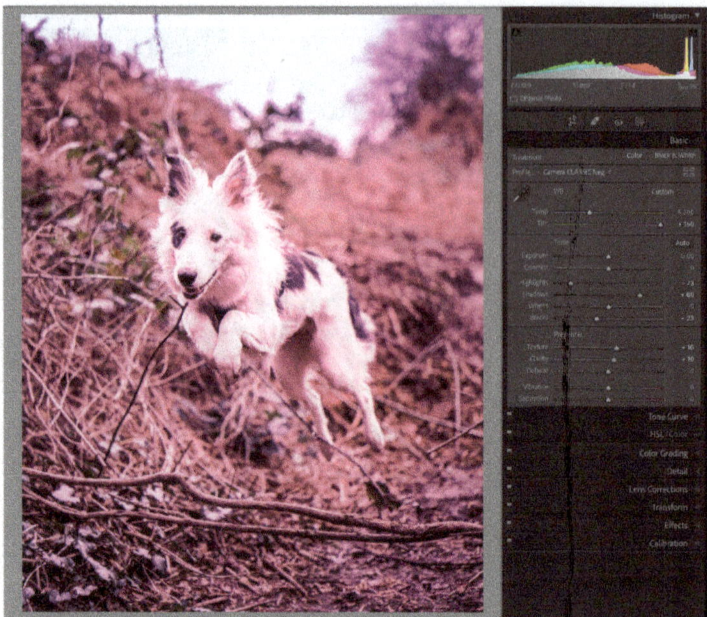

Figure 6.25 E

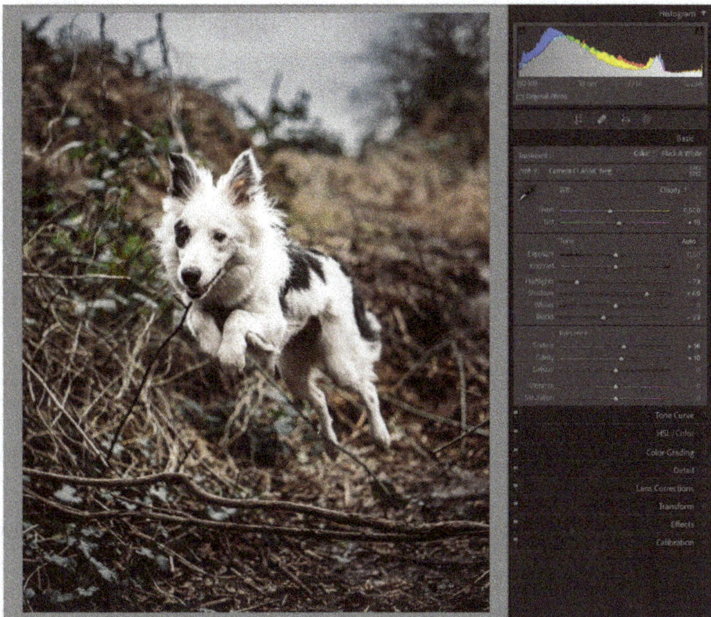

Figure 6.25 F – A photograph with the original White Balance temperature set to 5,200 – "As Shot"; a photograph with the White Balance temperature set to 2,500; a photograph with the White Balance temperature set to 30,000; a photograph with the original White Balance temperature set to 5,200 and -150 Tint; a photograph with the original White Balance temperature set to 5,200 and +150 Tint; a photograph with the White Balance temperature set to 6,500 – Cloudy to warm up the original look a little bit

Tone

The **Tone** tab is where we will be spending most of our time while working on photographs in Lightroom, as most RAW files need a bit of tweaking.

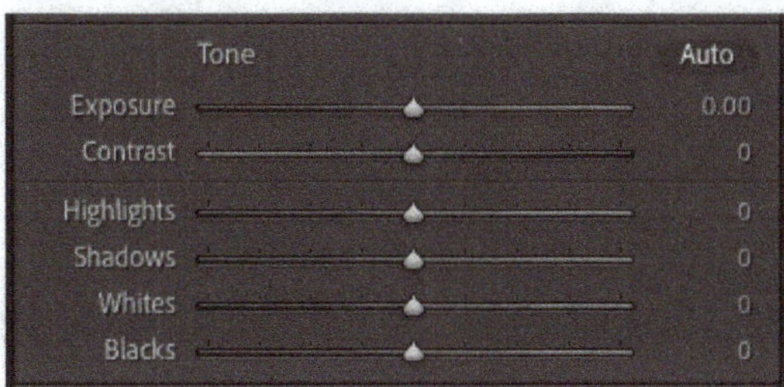

Figure 6.26 – The Tone tab's sliders

It's a toolset for adjusting how bright and dark our pictures will be. I'm simplifying a lot, but even by looking at the names next to the sliders without knowing how they work, intuition tells us that "light" is what we will be dealing with. Light is the key to the look of our photographs.

At the beginning of this chapter, I mentioned that adjusting directly by dragging the Histogram tool left and right is reflected in the **Tone** tool tab. The five areas we can directly affect in the Histogram tool are as follows:

- Blacks
- Shadows
- Exposure
- Highlights
- Whites

In the **Tone** tab, we have sliders to adjust the corresponding areas with one additional slider: **Contrast**.

Just as with adjusting photos directly within the **Histogram** tab, a good rule of thumb is to have the Histogram evenly spread, with "a hump" in the middle, and avoid clipping on either side.

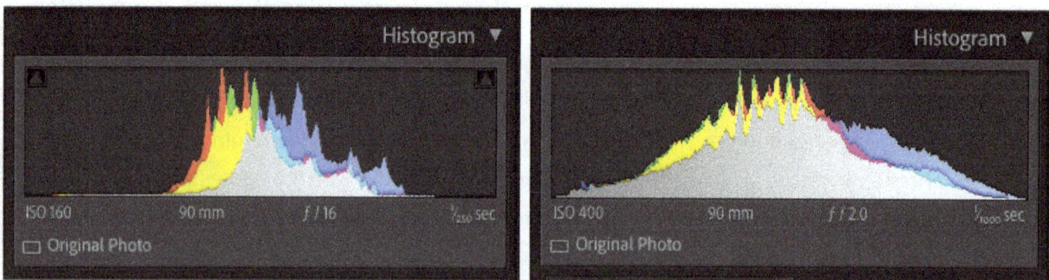

Figure 6.27 A

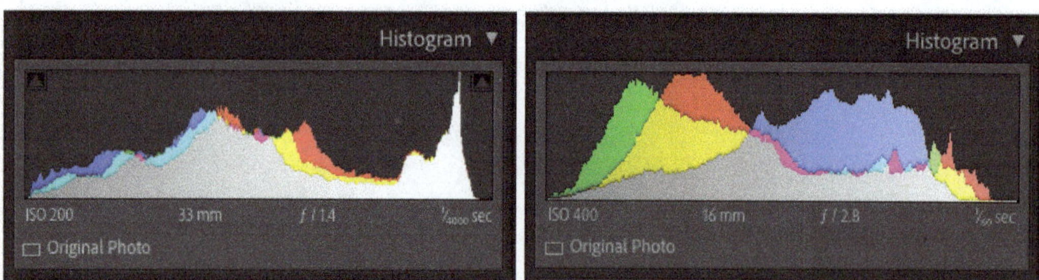

Figure 6.27 B – Examples of histograms with the "middle hump" and no black or white clipping

Whether we prefer working with the **Histogram** or **Tone** sliders, the same rules apply to the adjustments, which will produce a good starting point for a photograph destined for further tweaking. One additional tool available to us in this set is **Contrast**, which, in the simplest of terms, makes bright areas brighter and dark areas darker. Low contrast leads to more details in the shadows but without crispness. And while stronger contrast can hide some of the details, it can be seen as more attractive and better at drawing attention to the photograph. I'm using vague terms here, but we need to remember that fashions change and taste or style are a personal matter.

As a rule of thumb, I suggest working on any photo *from the middle* of the Histogram tool and in the following order:

1. Exposure
2. Highlights
3. Shadows
4. Whites
5. Blacks

Exposure

When we decide to press the shutter release on a camera, exposure time is one of the main factors of the photograph's look. Besides the fact that we may want to capture movement through panning or be creatively free, the overall "exposure" or "brightness" of the image will be a deciding factor when setting up the shot. Whether we use automatic or manual exposure settings, we often face scenarios when we can't achieve "perfect" exposure. Maybe saving details in bright areas will force us to underexpose, or perhaps quite the opposite, we may want to expose shadows to capture what's hiding in the dark. On occasions, we will underexpose to keep the images sharp by using a faster shutter speed when shooting in dark conditions; we will be limited by using an already cranked-up ISO and wide-open aperture. Whichever scenario might be the case, the **Tone** panel will help us fix it.

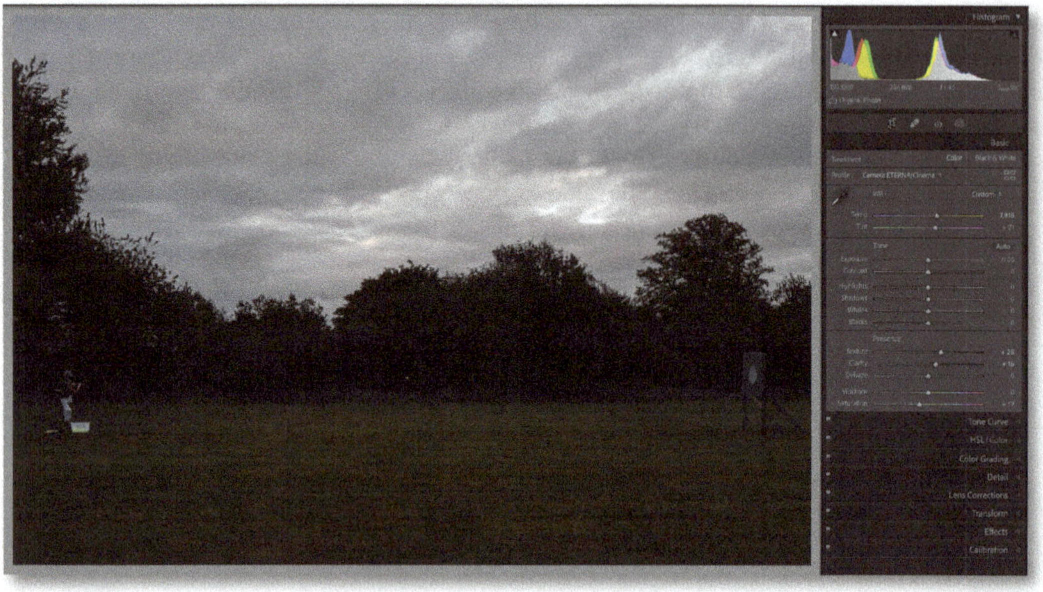

Figure 6.28 A

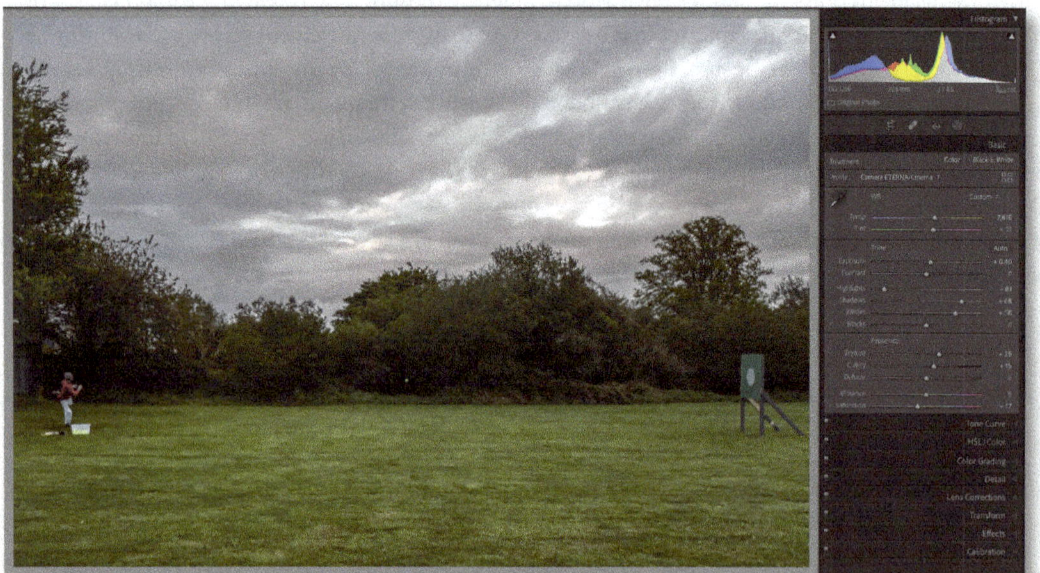

Figure 6.28 B – Original exposure set to save details in highlights (top); the same photograph with balanced Highlights and Shadows areas (bottom)

This slider is responsible for the middle 40% of the range of tones within the picture. Adjusting **Exposure** has the most significant impact on the look of our photograph. When setting up the initial exposure fixes, we need to watch out for highlights and shadows being clipped and not move too much into these two areas. Large regions with strong clipping will be hard to recover.

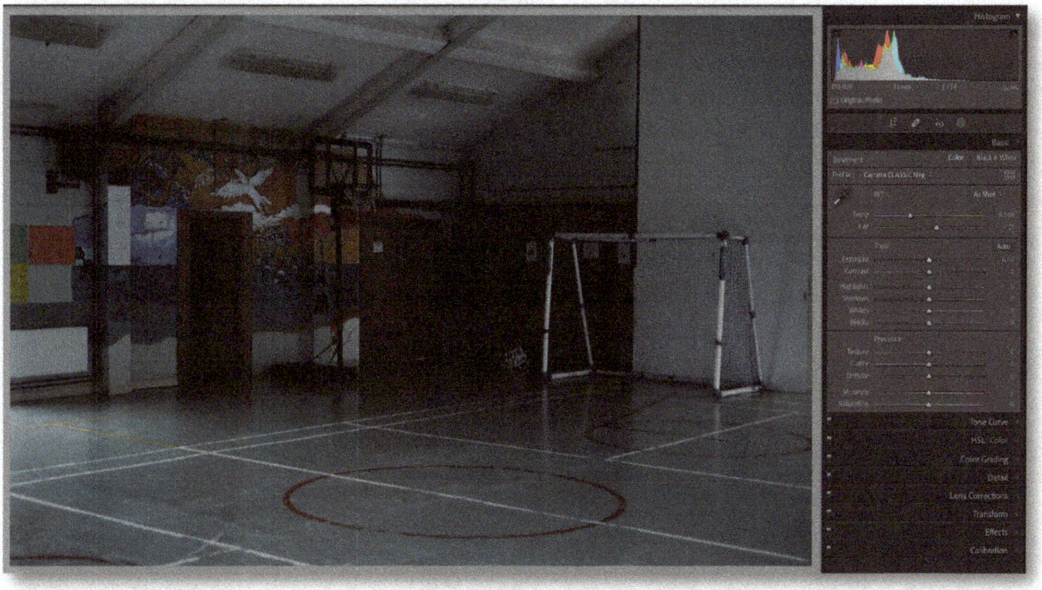

Figure 6.29 A

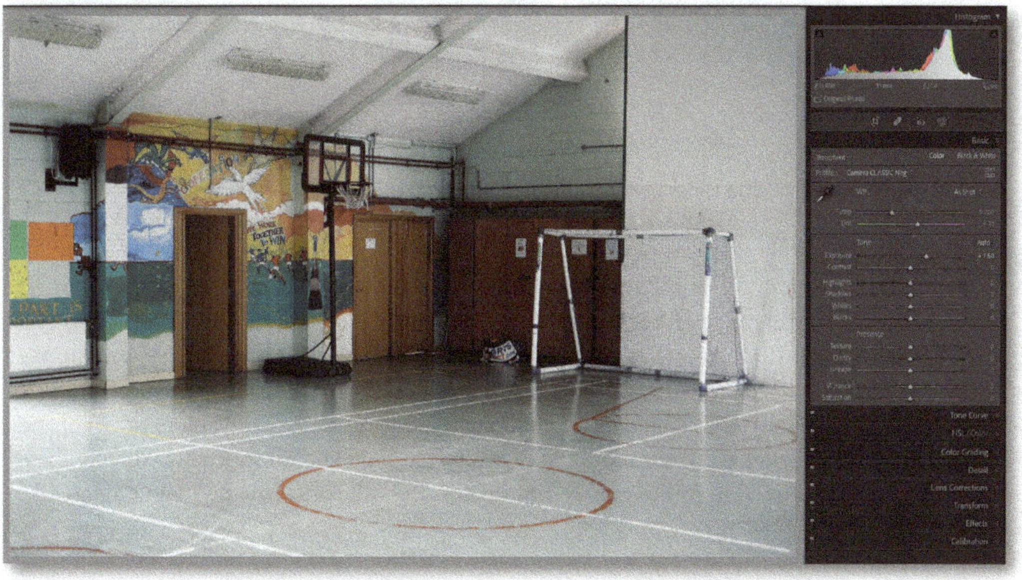

Figure 6.29 B – A photograph without any corrections (top) and a photograph with its exposure corrected by +1.5 (bottom)

Highlights and Shadows

Recovering Highlights and Shadows goes hand in hand and will test our camera's dynamic range capabilities. To create a balanced look, you need to aim at a roughly equal amount of recovery in Highlights and Shadows. For example, let's move Highlights to about the -25 mark. Shadows will need approximately the same amount of recovery and must be moved to about +25 of its respective slider. Start by finding a place where you are happy with the highlights, make an opposite adjustment on the Shadows slider, and treat this as your starting point for balancing the Tone adjustments. Remember that you can highlight clipping in Shadows and Highlights at any time by using the "*J*" keyboard shortcut. This equal amount of movement in Highlights and Shadows is very mathematical. We must judge the look of the photograph with our eyes and decide on the final values for both scales.

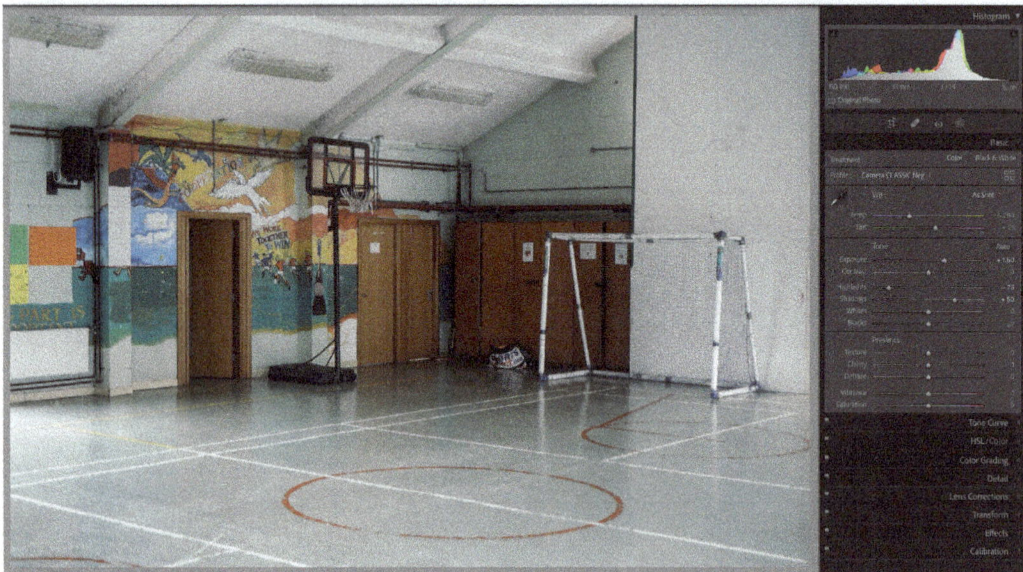

Figure 6.30 – The same photograph with adjusted Highlights and Shadows

Whites and Blacks

A 10% margin of the tonal range on each side of the Histogram tool is reserved for the darkest and lightest of tones, which will turn into pure black and pure white clipping if we are not careful. We can use this 10% to our advantage and add more contrast to our photograph without using the actual **Contrast** slider. If the photo looks a bit dull, try nudging the **Whites** slider a little bit to the right and the **Blacks** slider to the left, keeping in mind the clipping (the "*J*" keyboard shortcut). Moving these sliders in the opposite direction to the one we just mentioned will soften the photograph and take away its contrast.

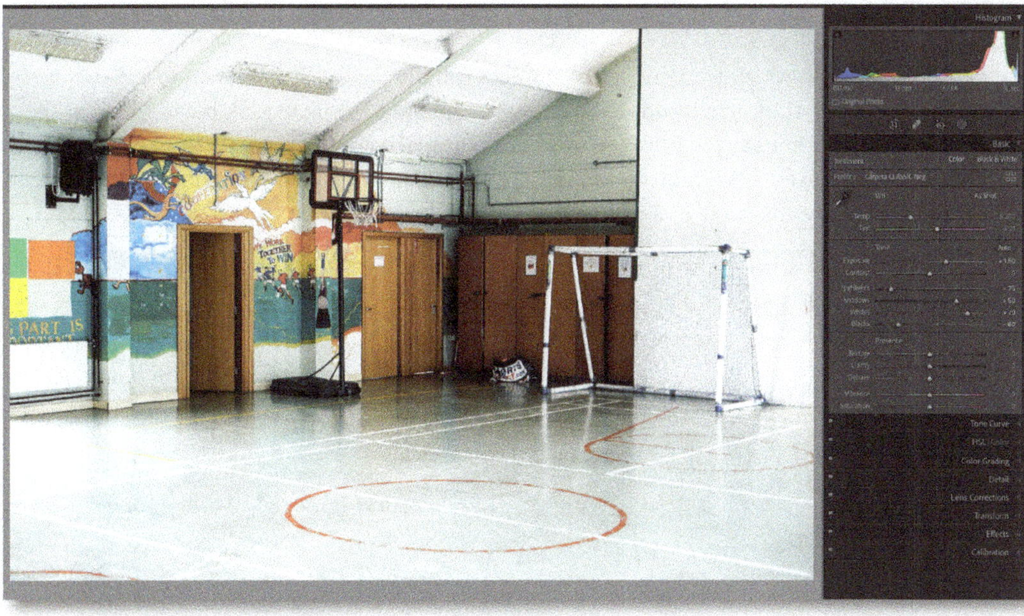

Figure 6.31 A

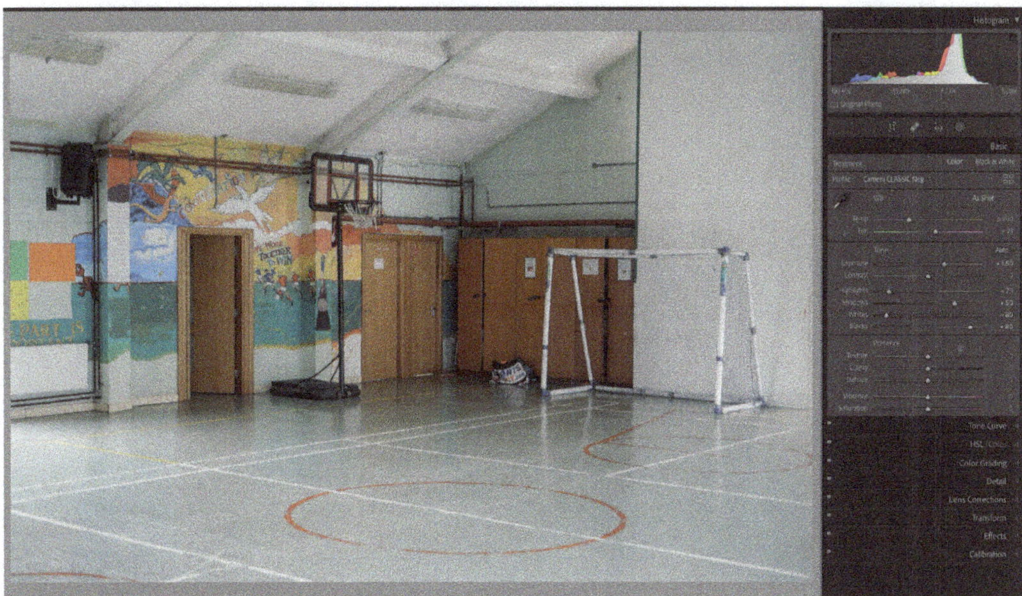

Figure 6.31 B – Increasing and decreasing contrast with the Whites and Blacks sliders

Contrast

Once we are happy with our adjustments, we may want to add or take away some contrast. Too much of it and we will start losing details; not enough and the photograph may look bland. Moving the **Contrast** slider even within a range from **-10** to **+10** can make a huge difference. We can also recover some detail in **Shadows** and **Highlights** by moving the slider into the negative area. If the photograph is already very contrasty, we can use **Blacks** or **just** Whites to add more crispness.

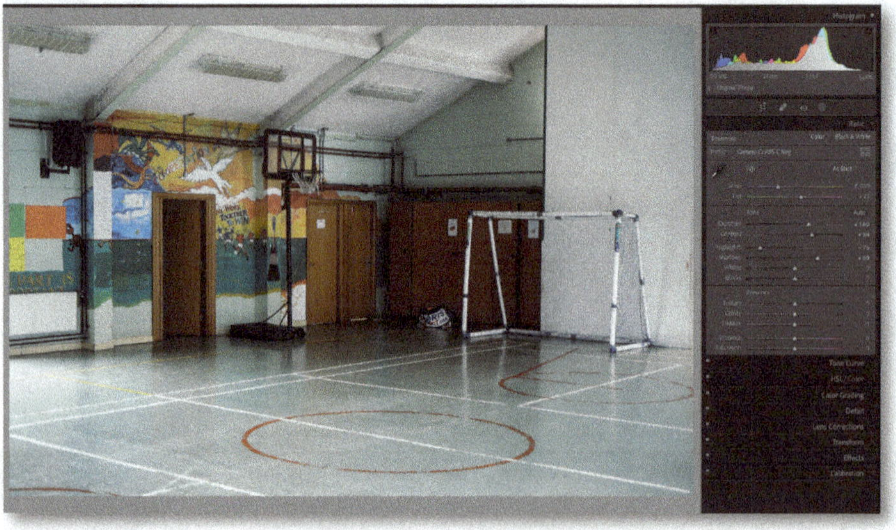

Figure 6.32 A

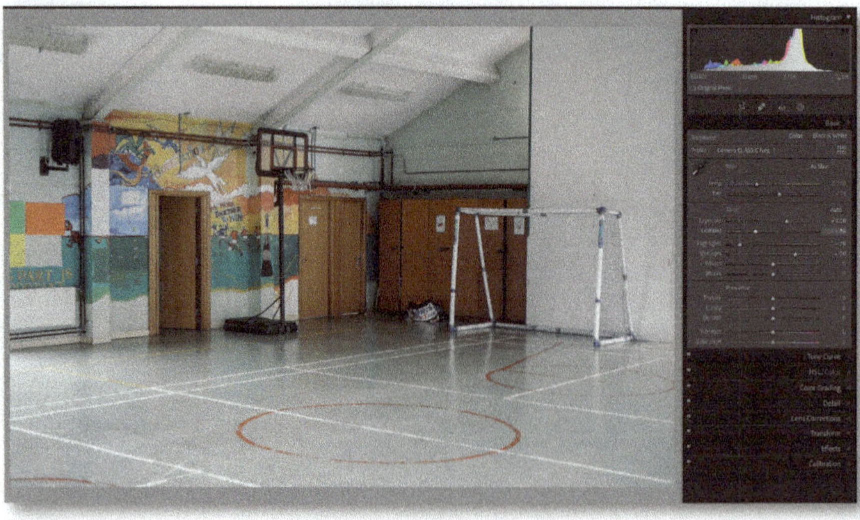

Figure 6.32 B – Increasing and decreasing contrast with the Contrast slider

Going through this procedure is what I call the first pass, and just like with making our edits, it doesn't stop at the first pass. After we make all these adjustments, it's good to go back to our photograph and keep making changes until we are satisfied with the look of our photo. Remember that it's better to make many small changes than a few big ones. The final impact might be similar, but we won't lose as many details.

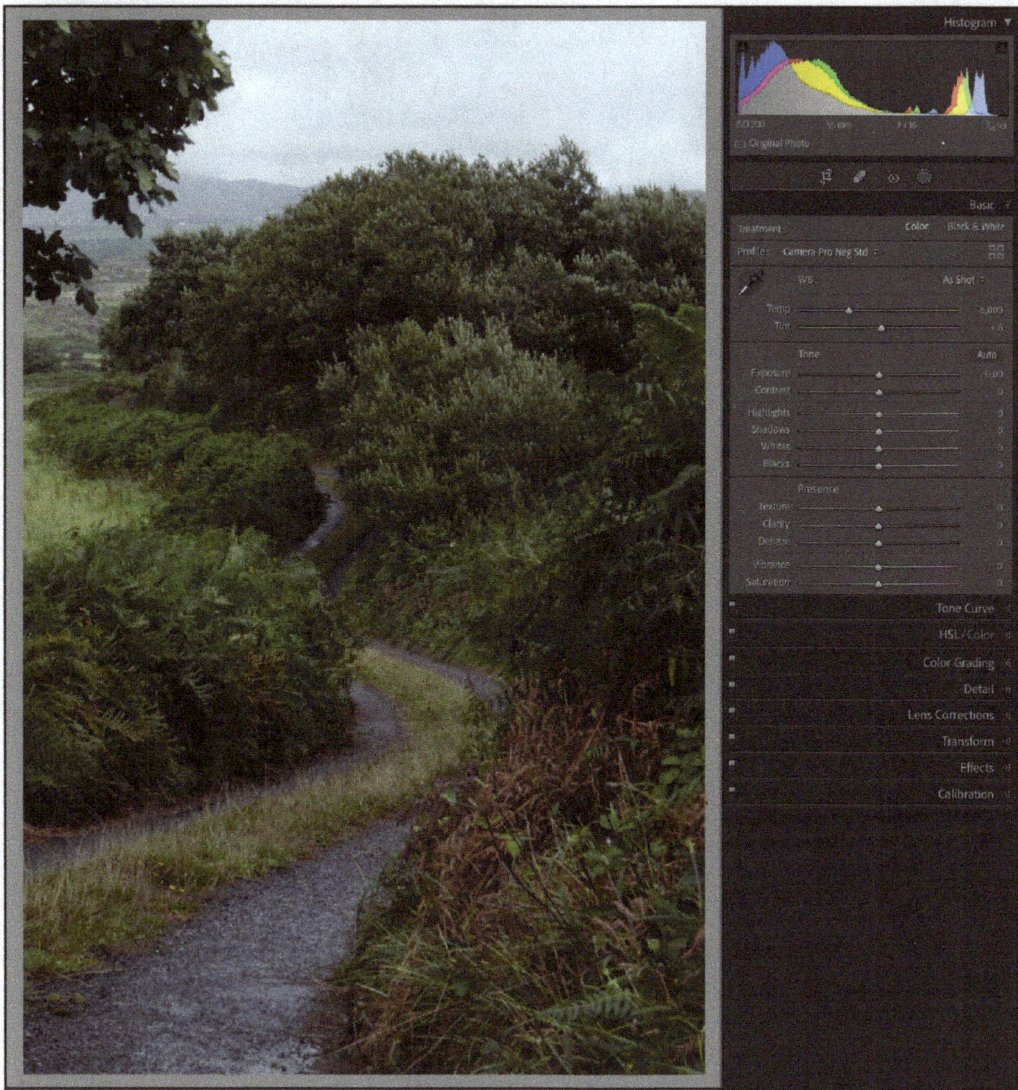

Figure 6.33 A

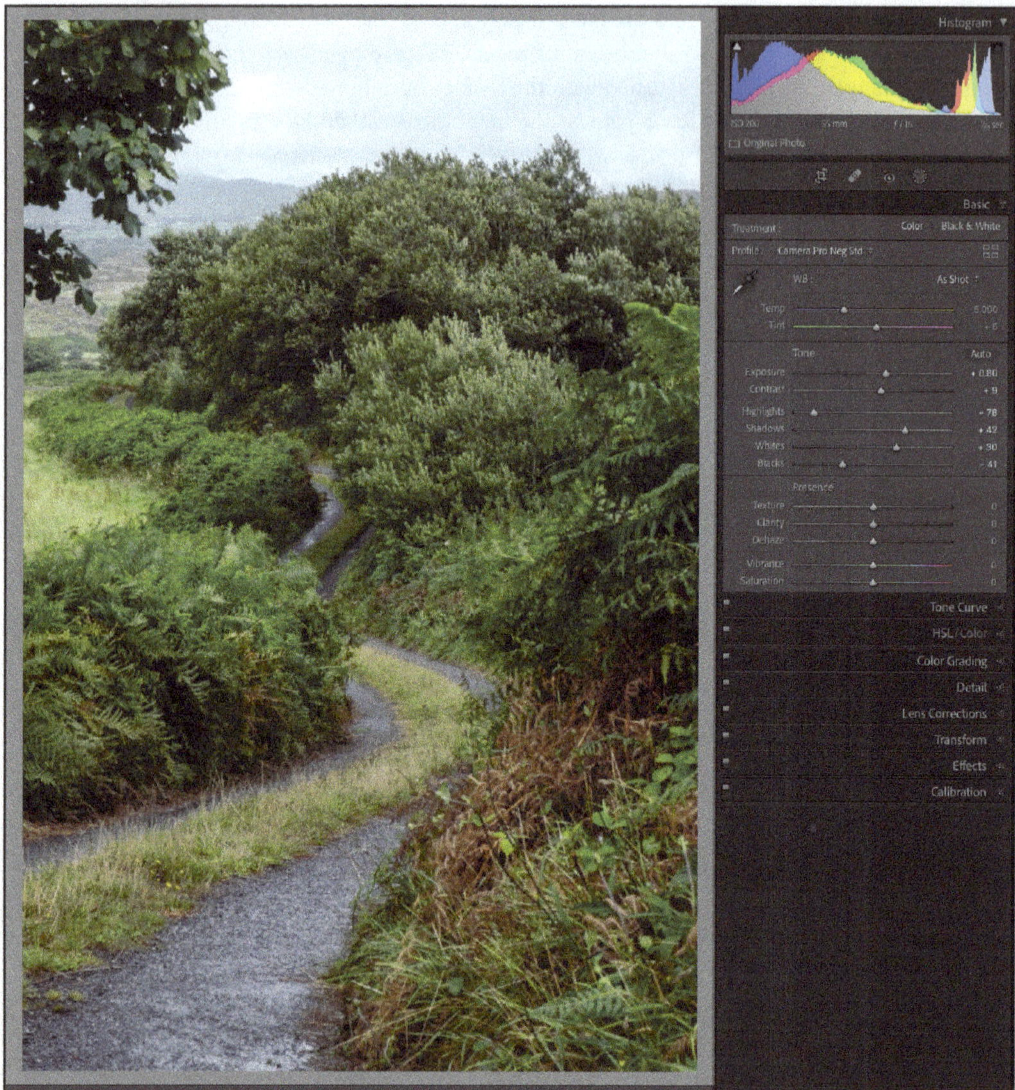

Figure 6.33 B – Another example of working with the tone sliders – the original photograph (top) and the photograph adjusted with basic sliders (bottom) without any local adjustments (masks)

When we are speed developing large edits photographed in balanced conditions, it's worth checking the **Auto** button in the **Tone** panel. Suppose we have a well-balanced photograph that we've just taken with our camera. In that case, Lightroom can do a pretty good job adjusting our picture and bringing it to a point where only minor changes might be necessary. Keep in mind what sort of look you want to achieve. Some of us will look for opposite results than others, and specific scenarios will require us to look outside the box and work in a way that doesn't produce a balanced photograph. For example, developing pictures of cars will be approached differently from people's portraits or documenting a gallery exhibition. In the end, we will want to find our personal touch. Starting with a tonally balanced photograph allows us to see its strengths and weaknesses. It will also show its potential for further changes, especially local adjustments, which we will get to shortly.

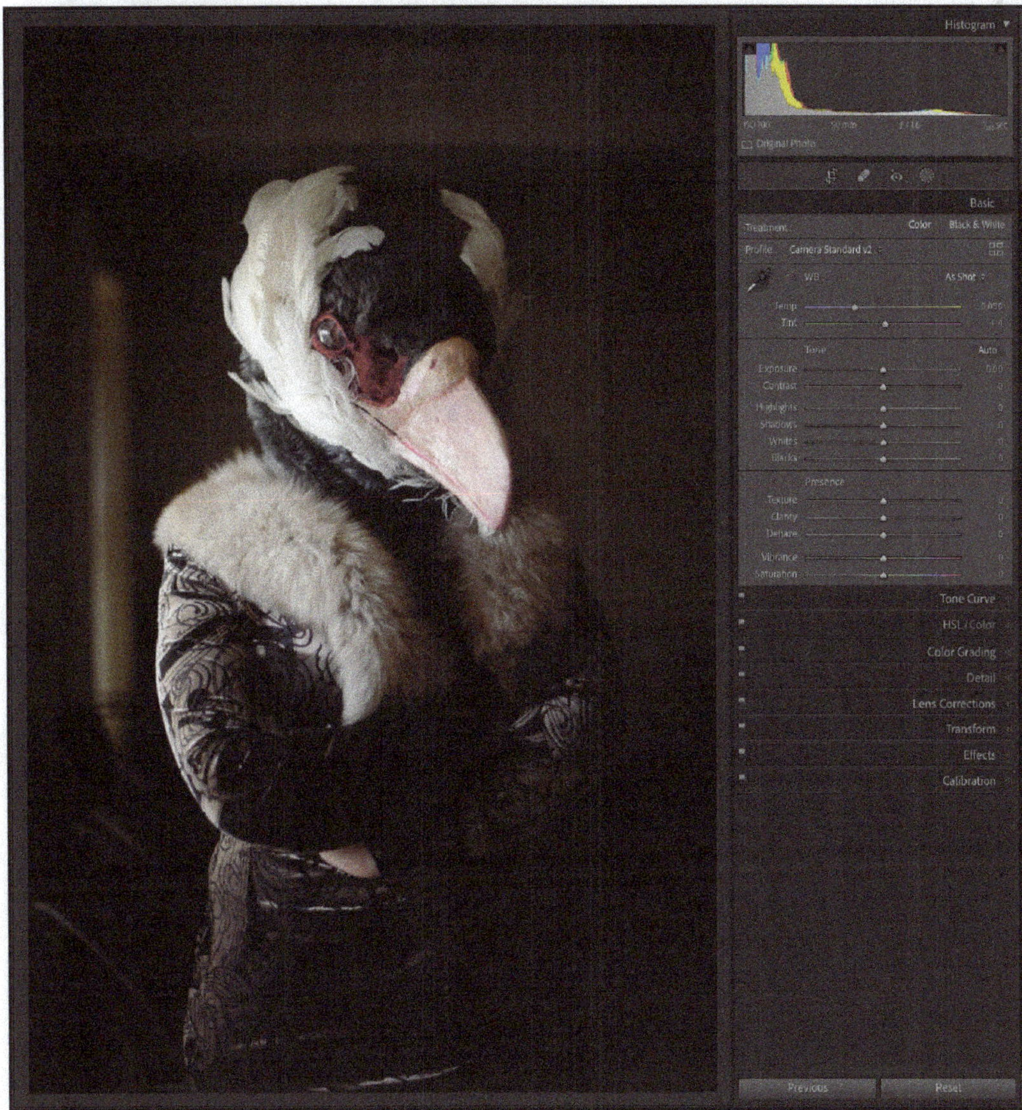

Figure 6.34 A

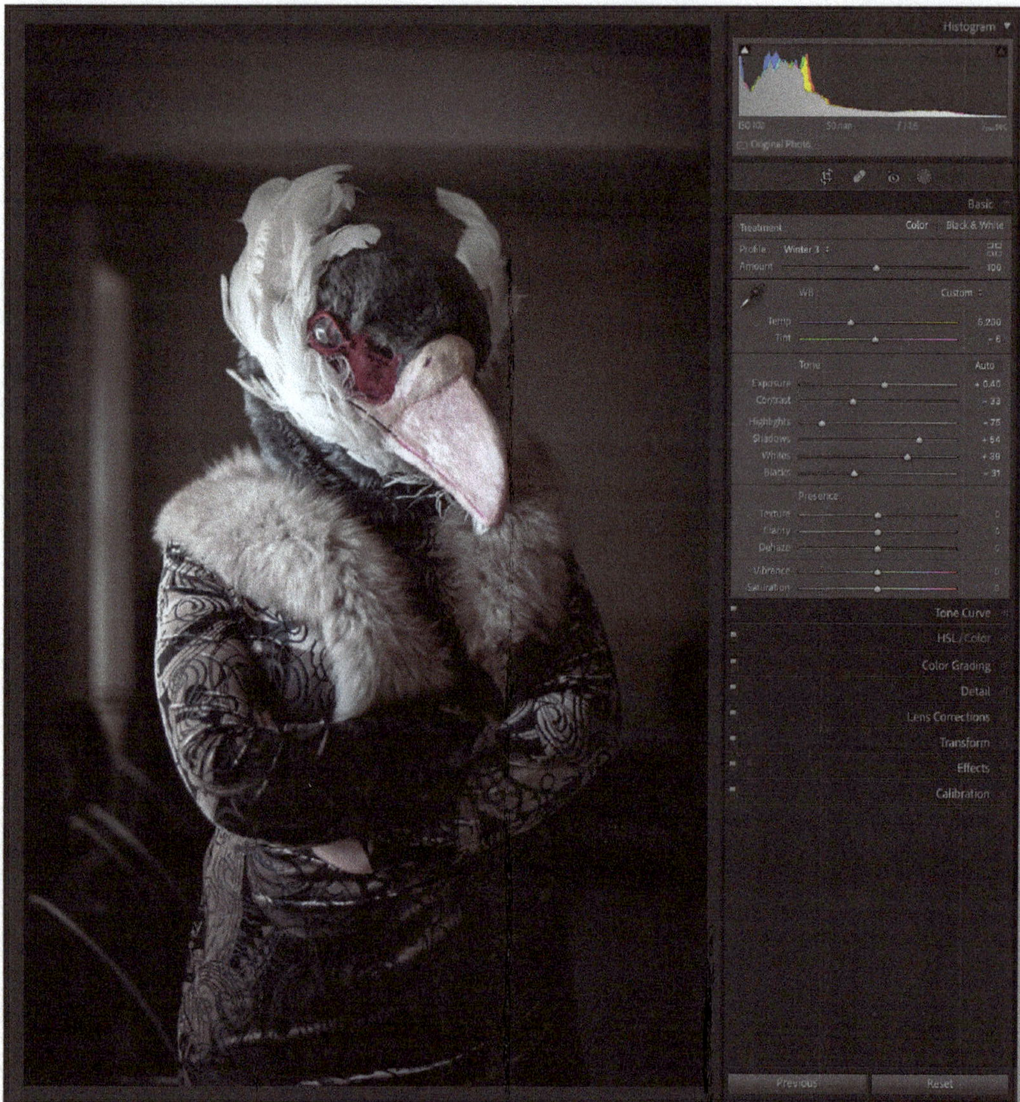

Figure 6.34 B – One more example of working with the Tone sliders – the original photograph (top) and the photograph adjusted with Basic sliders (bottom) without any local adjustments (masks)

Presence

Texture, **Clarity**, and **Dehaze** are three contrast tools that are more sophisticated than the **Contrast** tool itself. All three of them work based on darkening the dark areas and brightening the bright areas of our photographs but with different thresholds and while focusing on different areas.

Texture

Texture works best on very defined details that we want to be more prominent, such as the texture of fabrics, flaking paint, tree bark, or sharp needles on an animal. It also works excellently for hiding skin imperfections and smoothing areas we want to look less rough. It works best at a small scale, so it's good to work with this tool with an image magnified to **100%** to see how it influences the small details. The way I work with it is to apply some texture globally with a picture that fits my screen and then zoom in and out of areas, adjusting the texture in a way that feels right.

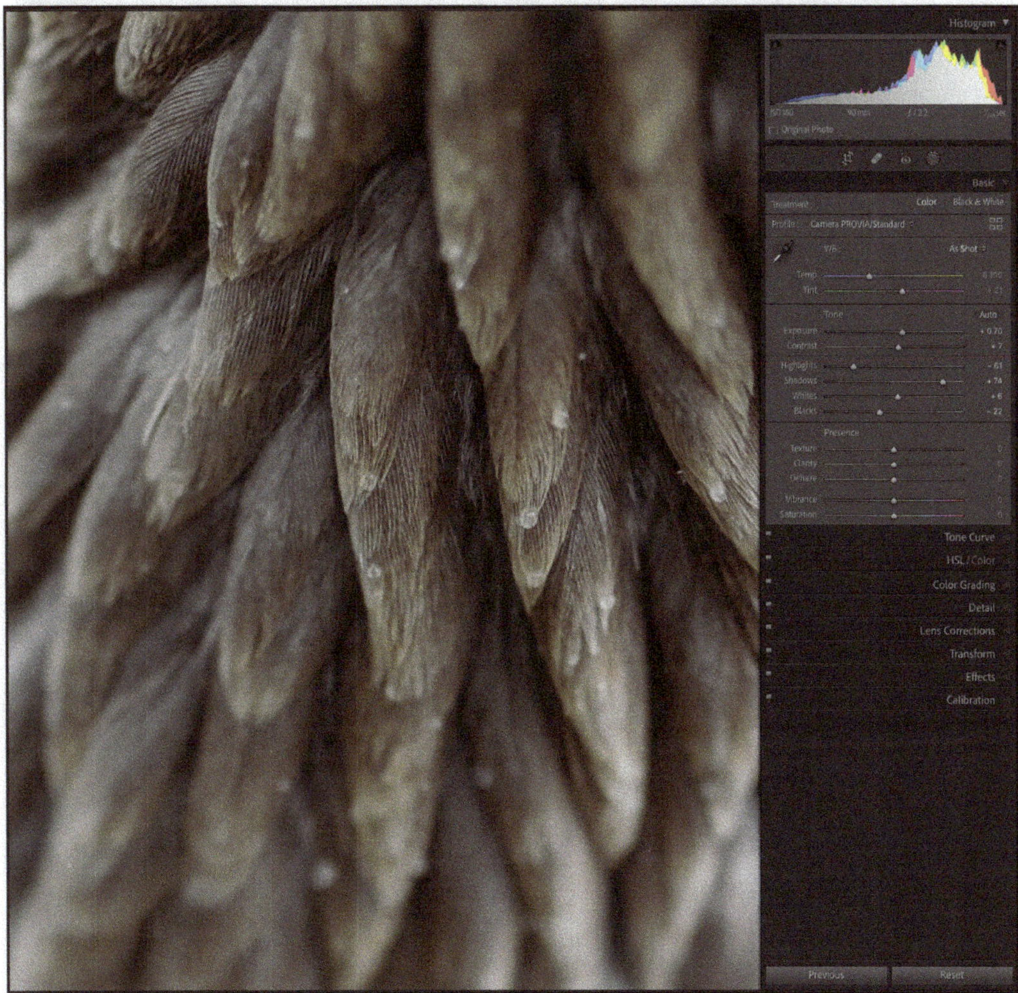

Figure 6.35 A

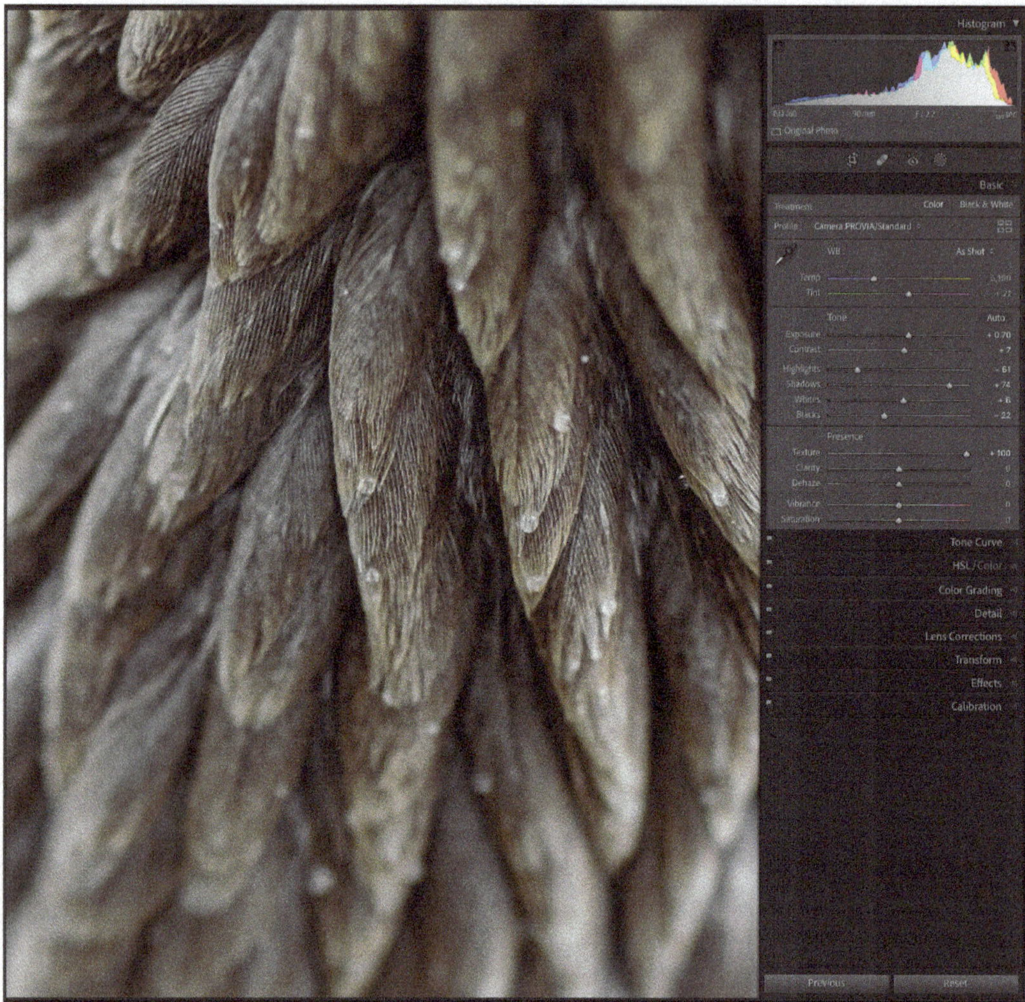
Histogram
Basic
Color
Black & White
As Shot
Tone
Auto
Presence
Tone Curve
HSL / Color
Color Grading
Detail
Lens Corrections
Transform
Effects
Calibration

Figure 6.35 B

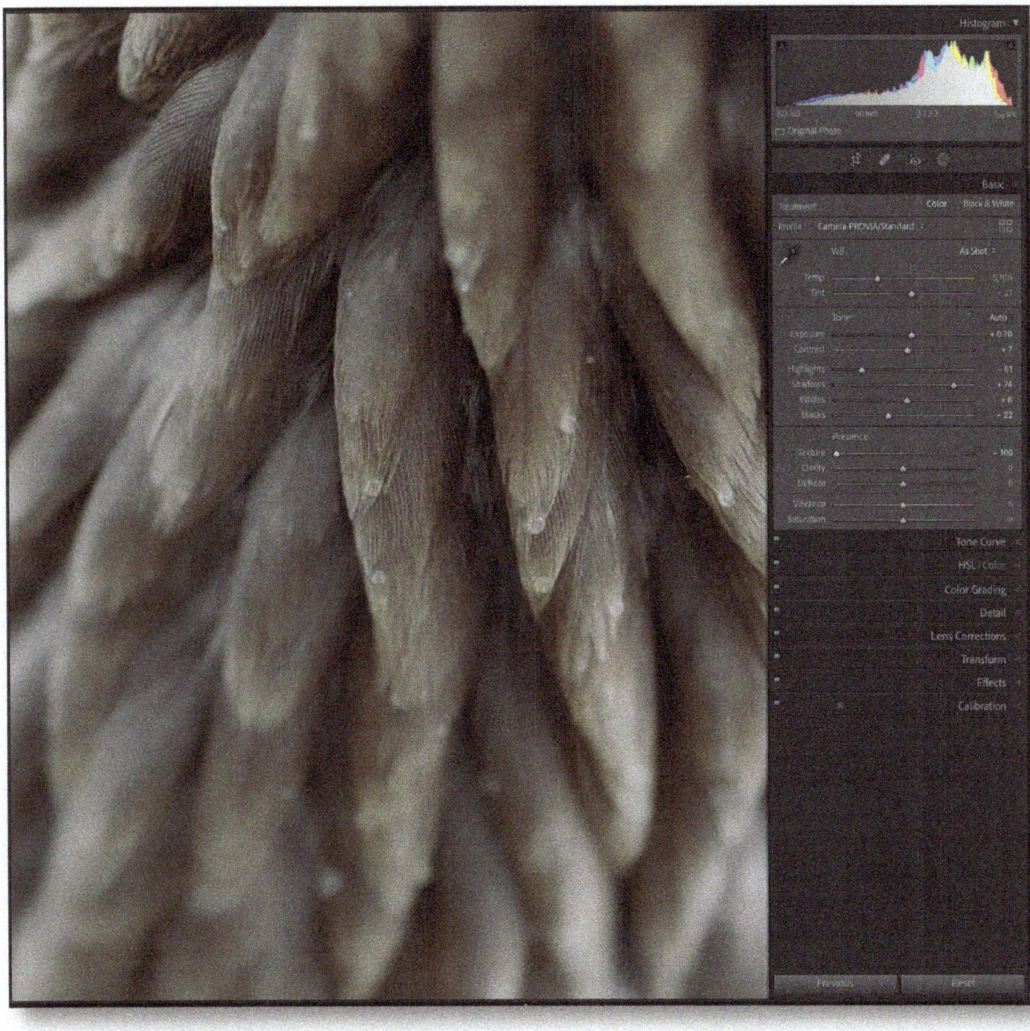

Figure 6.35 C – Picture detail at 100% magnification, with the tone adjusted to taste. From top to bottom – no Texture, no Clarity adjustments; Texture +100; Texture -100

Clarity

Clarity increases contrast and sharpness within the mid-tone areas and works best with inanimate objects. I suggest that you start working with the **Clarity** tool in a range between **+10** to **+20** and go from there. Even with these settings, you should notice a big difference. At first glance, it may look like we are just adjusting contrast, but **Clarity** is more sophisticated, and by working with mid-tones, it recognizes the edges of objects. Contrast is applied globally, treating the whole tonal range in the same way.

If we apply too much **Clarity** to human features, they quickly look artificial and unnatural. You can use this to your advantage, but it's one of those tools that can be easily overused. Understanding **Clarity** is essential to keeping things looking natural, even if slightly exaggerated.

Another way to use **Clarity** is to smoothen things, and human skin is one of the first things that come to mind. Start around **-10** to **-20** and see how it works on a portrait. You will notice that going beyond these values will start making things glow. Applying it sporadically to get a unique look isn't a bad thing, but I would refrain from overusing it.

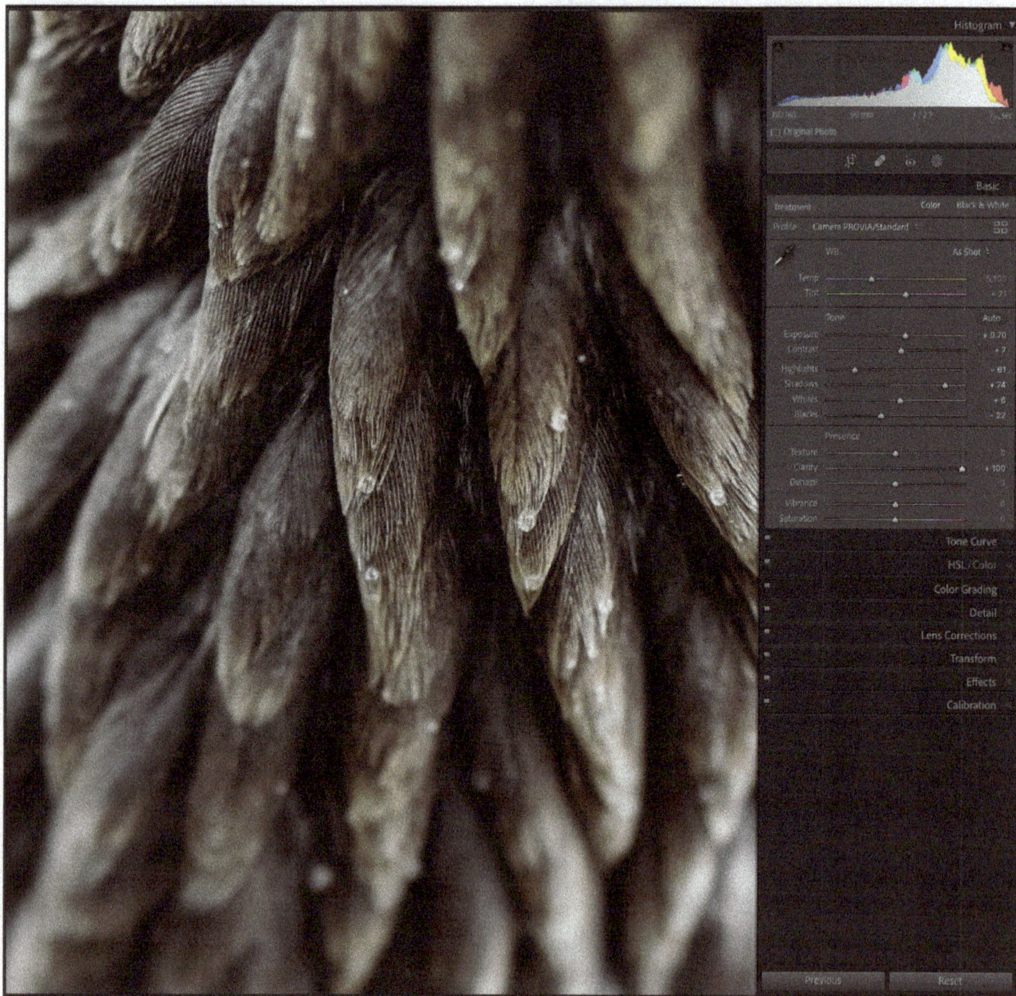

Figure 6.36 A

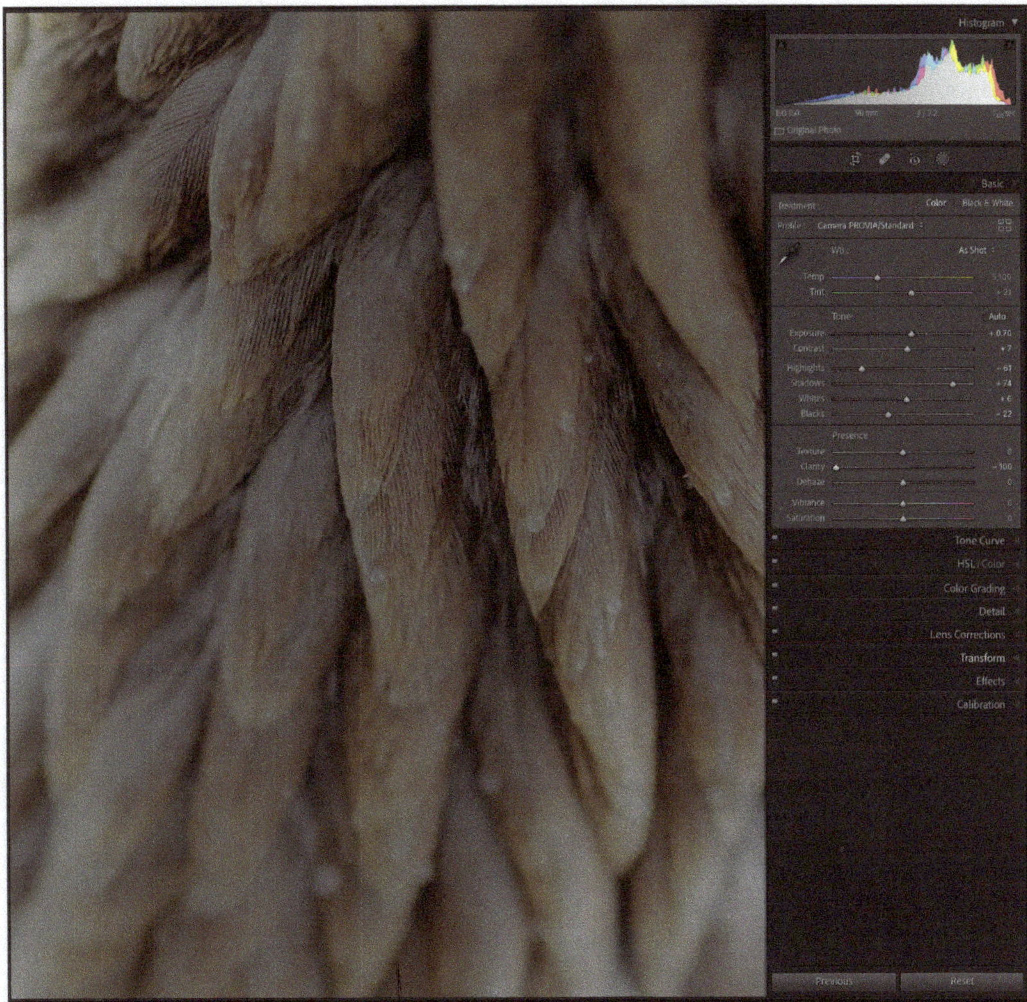

Figure 6.36 B – Picture detail at 100% magnification, with the tone adjusted to taste. Clarity +100 (top) and Clarity -100 (bottom)

Dehaze

Dehaze was designed to deal with fog and haze in landscapes where they can be most prominent. Haze is an effect that softens the photograph and derives its contrast. Dehaze can deal with this very efficiently, but its margins, which will start making photographs unnatural, are relatively thin.

Even though **Dehaze** is targeted toward landscape photographs, it can be used in other scenarios. Like **Texture** and **Clarity**, **Dehaze** works mainly with **Contrast**, but it also increases saturation and lowers luminance, especially within the blues. I would explain it as a **Clarity** tool with added saturation and more overall contrast. It also creates more contrast throughout the picture, not just on the object's edges like **Clarity**.

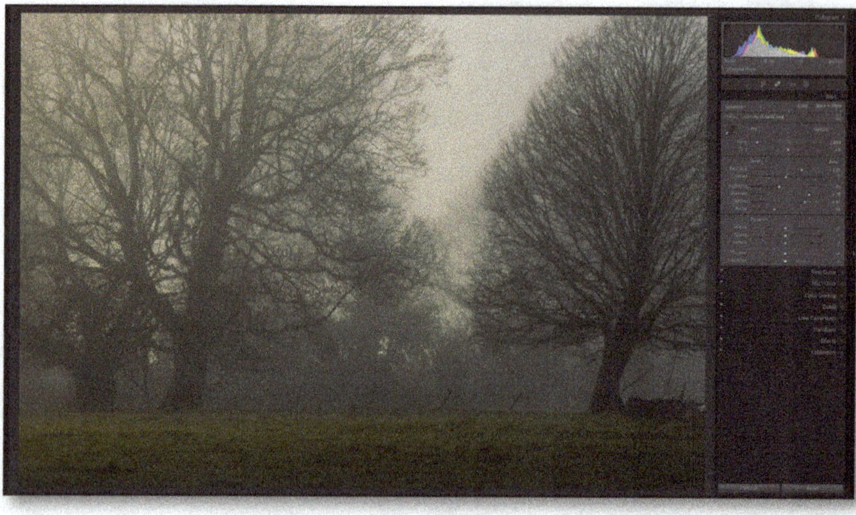

Figure 6.37 A

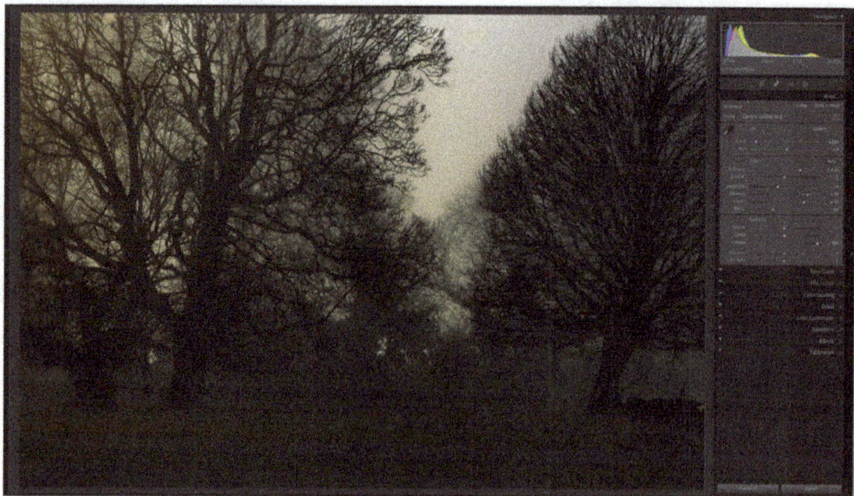

Figure 6.37 B

Figure 6.37 C – Photo of trees in fog, adjusted to taste without the use of Dehaze, with Dehaze set to +100 (top), and Dehaze set to -100 (bottom)

Vibrance and Saturation

It's best to describe these two tools in tandem as unbreakable parallels run between them. **Vibrance** increases **Saturation** in the less saturated areas and decreases **Saturation** in the most saturated areas. **Saturation** is more linear and increases saturation across the whole photograph. Whenever you feel that a picture needs more saturation, start by increasing **Vibrance** – it's more subtle, and often, nudging it by **+10** or **+15** will be enough to make a difference. As a second step, increase **Vibrance** even more and then decrease **Saturation** by about 30-50% of the **Vibrance** increase value. For example, if you increase **Vibrance** by **+30**, decrease **Saturation** by **-10** to **-15**. I will repeat myself here, which will happen throughout this book when it comes to preferences – you need to find balance. Even though some images could be developed simply with advanced mathematics, that's what the **Auto** button does. You need to rely on your creative instincts and experiment; it's just easier to experiment when you know what a tool does.

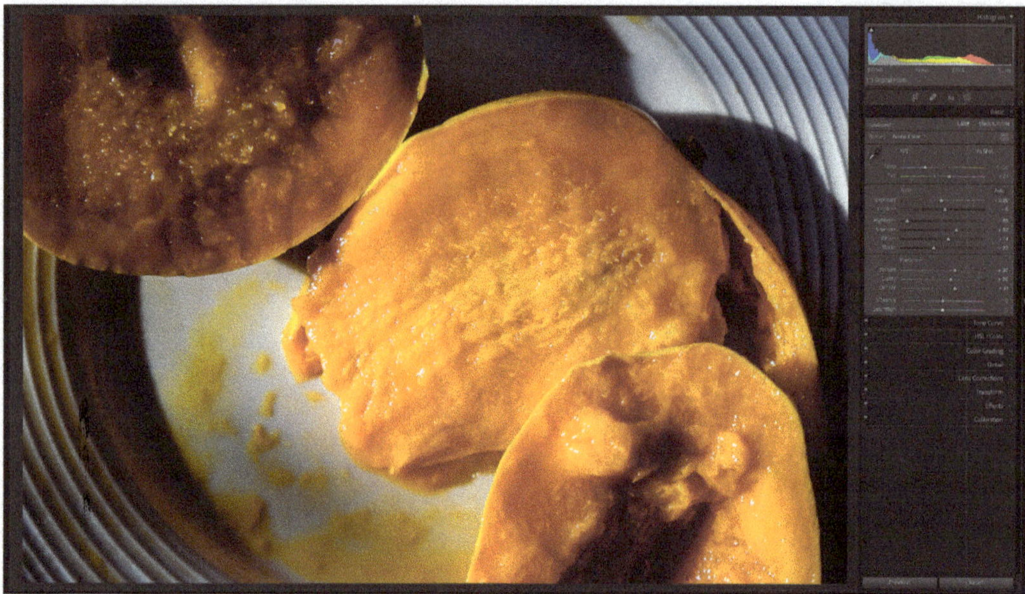

Figure 6.38 A

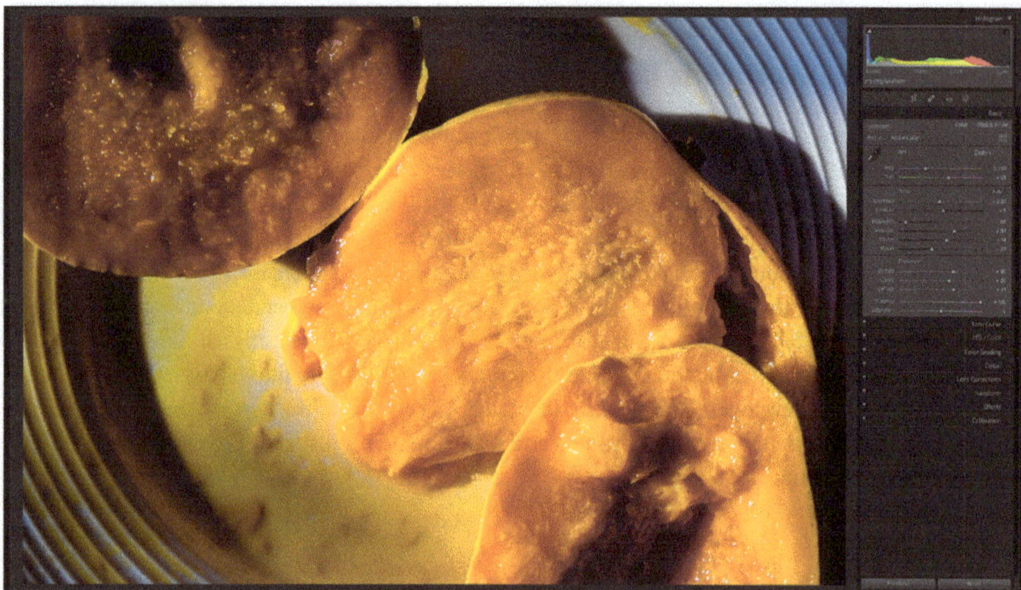

Figure 6.38 B

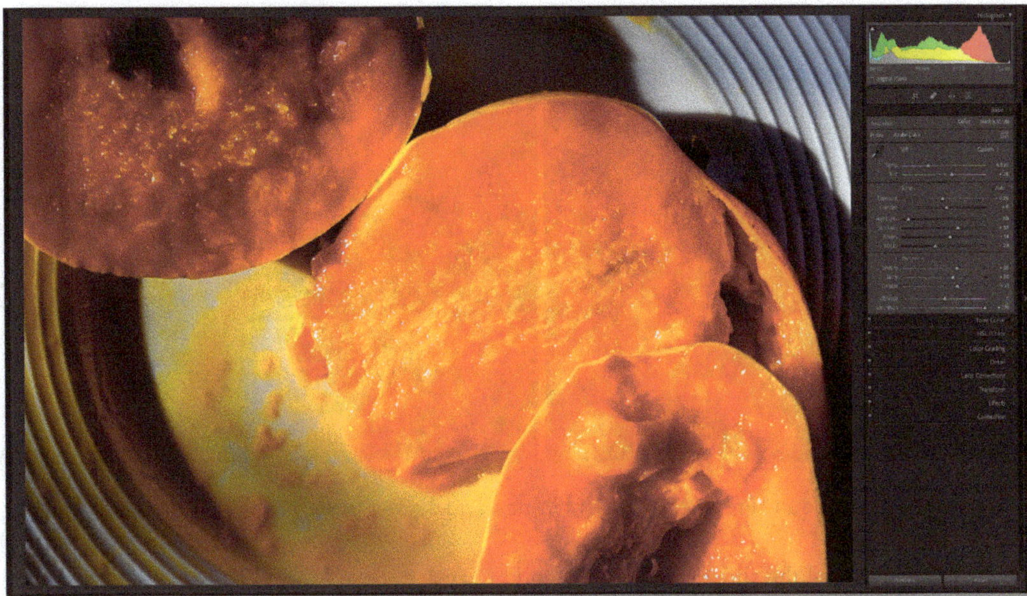

Figure 6.38 C – From top to bottom – a picture with rich colors. Notice what happens to the blue tinge of the cold White Balance that's visible on the plate in the shadow of the mango in the top-right corner when the picture is adjusted without the use of Saturation and Vibrance; Vibrance +100; Saturation +100

Tips for adjusting sliders

These tips may come in handy while you're adjusting the tools in the **Basic** tab:

- Double-clicking on any tool's slider head or name will reset that adjustment. For example, when we double-click on **Exposure** next to its slider, or the slider head of the **Exposure** setting, it will reset it to its default value, which is **0**.
- Double-clicking on the name of a group of adjustments will reset all the tools within that group. For example, double-clicking on **Presence** will reset all five sliders from **Texture** to **Saturation** to their default values.
- We can also reset each group by holding the "*Alt*" key, which will change the name of each group by adding the word "*Reset*" to it, and clicking on the name of the group.

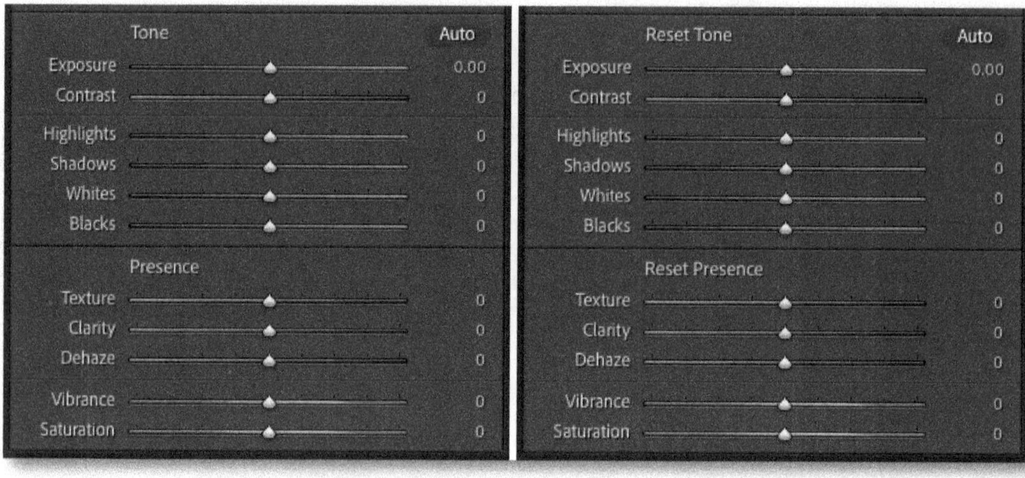

Figure 6.39 – Tone and Presence – the default view and the view with the "Alt" key pressed

- We can adjust all the sliders with the "-" and "+" keys to decrease and increase the value of each slider, respectively. By default, this shortcut is set to adjust the **Exposure** setting, but we can change it by using the "<" and ">" keys. This will cycle through all the settings by going to the previous or the next one. For example, after we've modified **Exposure** with the "-" and "+" keys, pressing "<" will take us to **Tint**, while pressing ">" will take us to **Contrast**. Pressing ">" again will take us to **Highlights** and so on.
- When adjusting some of the sliders, we can press and hold the "*Alt*" key to see the thresholds of that tool. For example, adjusting **Highlights** while holding the "*Alt*" key will show us the highlight clipping areas, while adjusting **Shadows** while holding the "*Alt*" key will show us the shadow clipping areas, and so on. This trick only works with sliders that have easily identifiable thresholds. It applies to sliders on other tabs, which we will discuss later in this chapter.

This brings us to the end of the **Basic** tab and also back to the very top of it. At this point, we understand the capabilities of local adjustments, which allow us to apply the effects we've discussed, but only in selected areas of our photographs.

Local adjustments - Masking

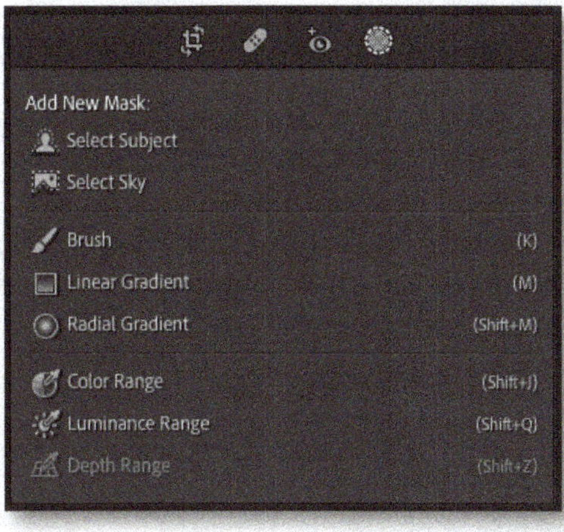

Figure 6.40 – The Masking panel's default view

Often, we want to make some changes locally – that is, only in particular areas. We want to achieve a specific look that is impossible with global adjustments. The **Masking** tool can help us achieve this goal.

Let's start with a brief description of how masking works within Lightroom.

Mask is a user-defined area where we can locally apply settings from a predefined pool of tools, including all **Basic** sliders and a few others. The following screenshot shows the complete list of tools that are available with the **Masking** tool:

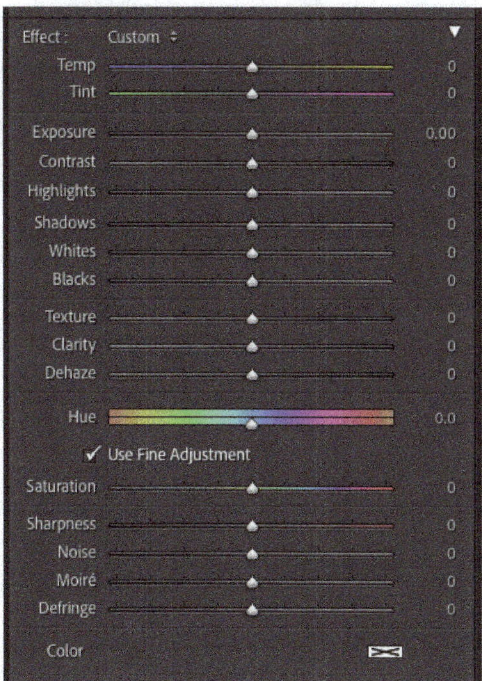

Figure 6.41 – The adjustment tools that are available with the Masking tool

Activating the **Masking** tool opens a "hidden" menu that's split into three categories.

The first two types of masks (**Select Subject** and **Select Sky**) are AI-driven, and all we can do with them is click and wait.

The **Select Subject** tool will pick up the subject of the photograph. While testing various pictures, I found it very accurate. It will pick up people and groups – the same goes for animals, cars, or objects. It has its limitations, but so long as the subject is clearly defined in the photograph, Lightroom should pick it up. I learned to trust it, but from time to time, the mask will require a bit of tweaking, which involves either adding to it or subtracting from it. This is what the two buttons at the bottom of this tool do. Before we discuss these details, let's look at the remaining available tools.

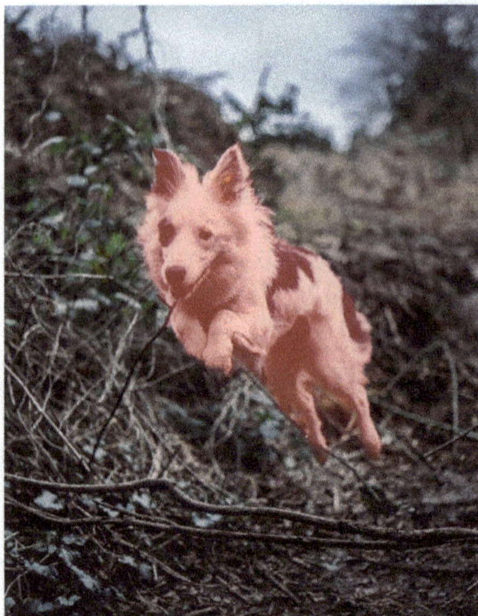

Figure 6.42 A

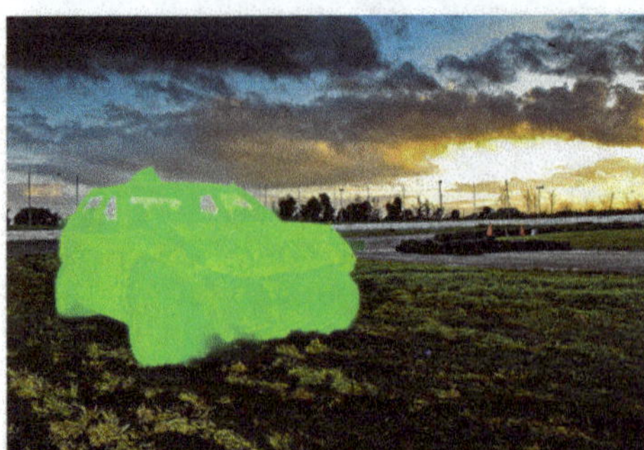

Figure 6.42 – Accurate AI subject mask examples with different mask colors

We can choose the color of the mask by clicking the colored square next to the **Show Overlay** checkbox. This will become visible once we select/create a mask.

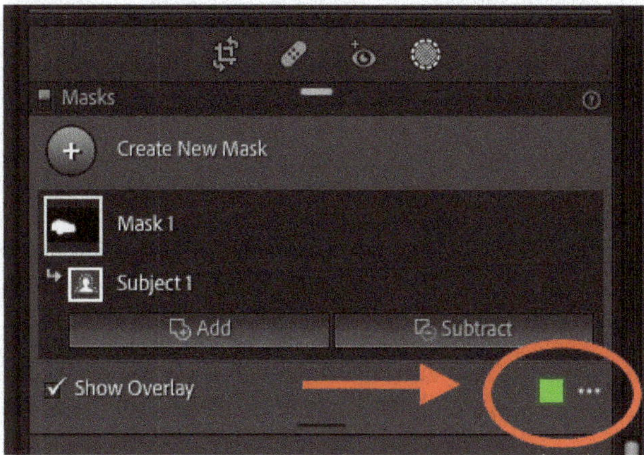

Figure 6.43 A

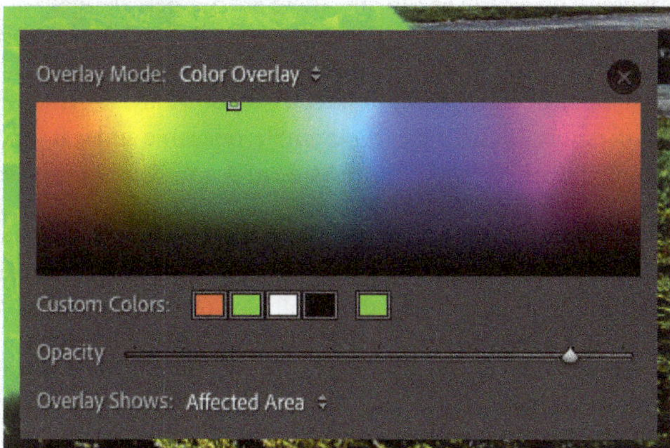

Figure 6.43 B – Choosing a mask overlay color

The **Select Sky** tool is as self-explanatory as it can be. It will find the sky in our photograph and create a mask to edit it.

The **Brush**, **Linear Gradient**, and **Radial Gradient** tools are used for creating masks and are manual. Let's take a look.

Brush

Brush (the "*K*" keyboard shortcut). This is probably the most commonly used mask within Lightroom. Once we activate **Brush**, Lightroom will create an empty new mask. All we have to do now is click and drag the mouse cursor over the areas we would like to affect. We can set up a few characteristics of **Brush**:

- **Size**: This is the size of the brush. We can change it with the slider, with the "*[*" and "*]*" keyboard shortcuts, and by scrolling the mouse up or down.
- **Feather**: This works just like the **Feather** settings in **Spot Removal** and represents the transition between **100%** on the edge of the inner circle to **0%** at the outer edge, creating various transition levels. The higher the **Feather** setting, the softer the edge of the brush.
- **Flow**: This setting represents how fast Lightroom will apply the brush. Imagine that instead of a brush, we are using a spray can; the stronger we press on the spray cap, the stronger the flow will be.
- **Density**: With this setting, we can control the level of transparency of our brush strokes.

Even though all four settings are on a scale of 1 to 100, these are not percentages but rather an arbitrary scale that we need to get a feel for.

In addition to these four sliders, we have the option to set Brush A and B. This is useful when we're working with two utterly different brush settings – for example, one large and soft for overall changes and one small and hard for detailed work. On the opposite side of A and B are the erasing brush's settings.

We also need to address two boxes. **Invert** will invert the mask we just created, changing the selected area with the unselected area. **Auto Mask** will only paint over pixels in color similar to what's directly under the brush's crosshair in the middle (that's the small plus (+) symbol).

These brush settings will stay as we set them, even after turning off the tool, and they will be the same when we turn on the brush next time.

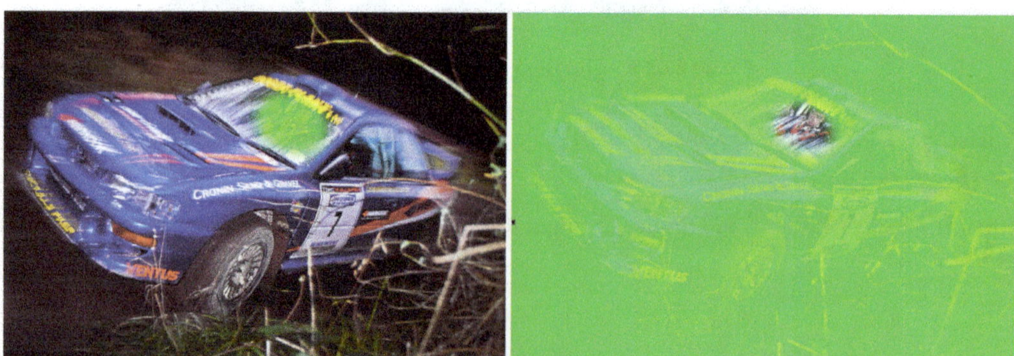

Figure 6.44 A

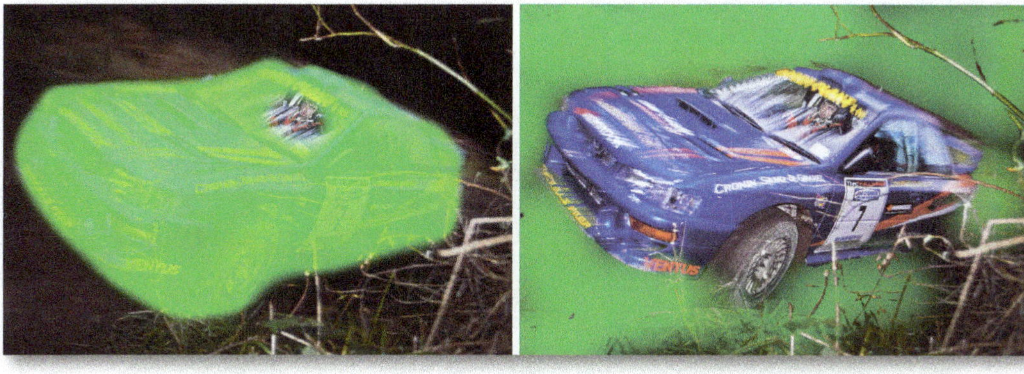

Figure 6.44 B – From top left to bottom right – the mask painted with a brush; the same mask inverted; the same inverted mask painted with the Erase brush around the car; the mask painted with the Auto Mask brush around the car

Linear Gradient

To activate **Linear Gradient**, we need to either click on its name or use the "*M*" keyboard shortcut. **Linear Gradient** works by applying settings we choose gradually, from **0** to **100**, in a straight line. We draw the gradual filter by clicking, dragging, and releasing the mouse cursor. Each of these three simple actions will trigger different behaviors. Upon clicking, the gradual filter will place the margin with 100% of its strength, dragging with the mouse button pressed down will direct and expand the area where the power of the applied filter is spread from 100% to 0%, and finally, releasing the mouse button will set the point where our gradual filter will reach 0%. To test this, I suggest that you set the **Exposure** setting of the gradual filter to something substantial, such as **-4**, and then draw the gradual filter.

Figure 6.45 A

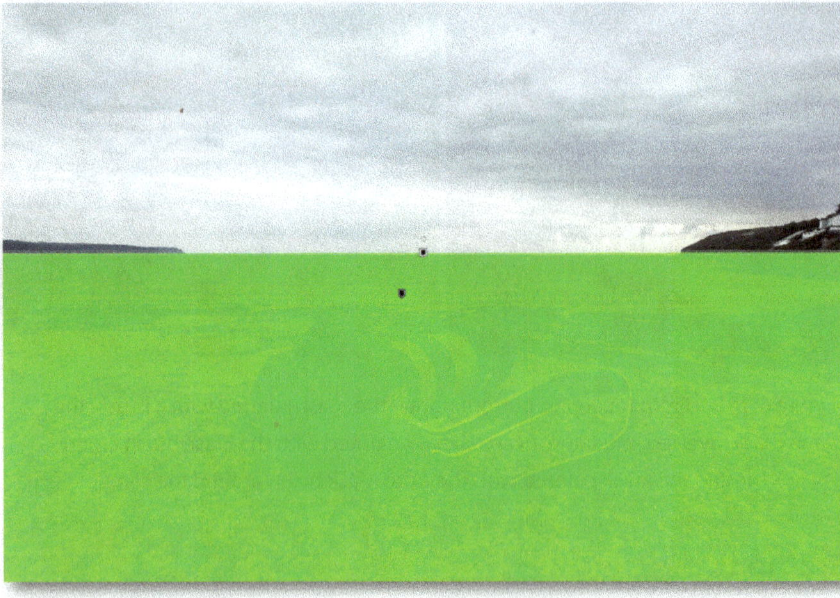

Figure 6.45 B – Linear Mask with a very broad margin/high Feather value (top) and Linear Mask with a very narrow margin/low Feather value (bottom)

Once we've drawn the filter, we can change its positioning, spread, angle, and the values of any sliders.

When we hover over the **Edit** pin, our mouse cursor will change to a small glove, allowing us to move the filter's position. The mouse cursor will also change into said glove when we move it over the edge lines of the currently adjusted filter, allowing us to modify its spread. Last but not least, we can change the angle of our gradual filter, which we can enable by hovering over the middle line. The mouse cursor will change to a double-headed arrow bent at a 90° angle – clicking with it on or close to the midline will allow us to modify the angle of our filter. Right-clicking on the middle black square of the **Linear Gradient** tool will open a small menu that allows us, among a few other self-explanatory functions, to invert the mask.

Radial Gradient

Radial Gradient works on the same basis as **Linear Gradient**, but instead of creating a line, we will be creating an oval shape. The transformation tools that are available for **Linear Gradient** will also be available here. If you would like to draw this mask, start in its corner and do so while holding down the "*Alt*" key. If you want to create a perfect circle, then hold down the "*Shift*" key. When we edit and change the Radial mask's shape and size, "*Alt*" and "*Shift*" will affect how this happens. Holding down the "*Shift*" key will allow you to work with a circle, while the "*Alt*" key will extend the edited mask in only one direction. You can hold both keys down to extend the circle mask in one direction. One additional function is available by clicking and dragging the red dot located on the bottom of the inner ring, which will change the **Feather** value.

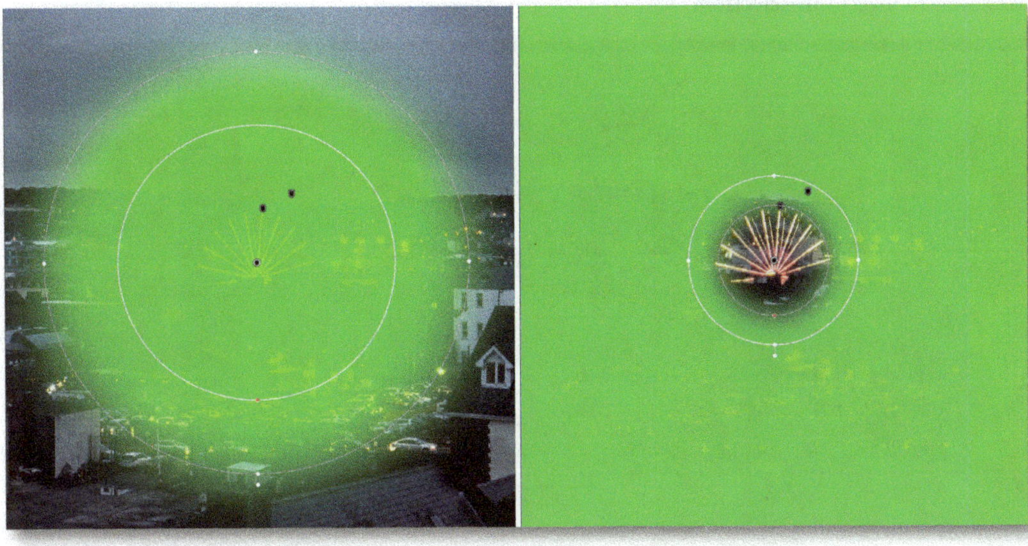

Figure 6.46 – Circular mask examples

Color Range

We can quickly create a mask based on a color choice with the **Color Range** tool ("*Shift* + *J*"). Once we've activated the **Color Range** tool, the mouse cursor will change into a color picker that we can use in a couple of different ways:

- Click on any color to choose it.
- Click and drag over any part of the image to choose all the colors within that selection.
- "*Shift*" and click up to five locations within the image. We can remove any picked locations by using "*Alt*" and clicking on them with the scissors-shaped cursor.

We can adjust all of these ranges later with the **Refine** slider. Moving it into higher values will pick up more similar hues while sliding it to the left will narrow our selection. Just as with the previous masks, we can invert this selection.

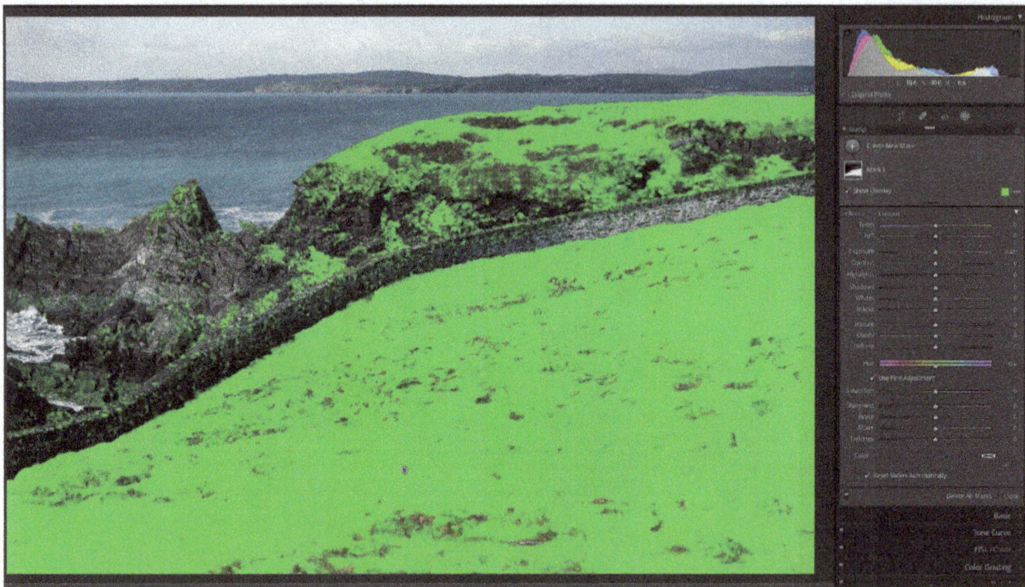

Figure 6.47 A

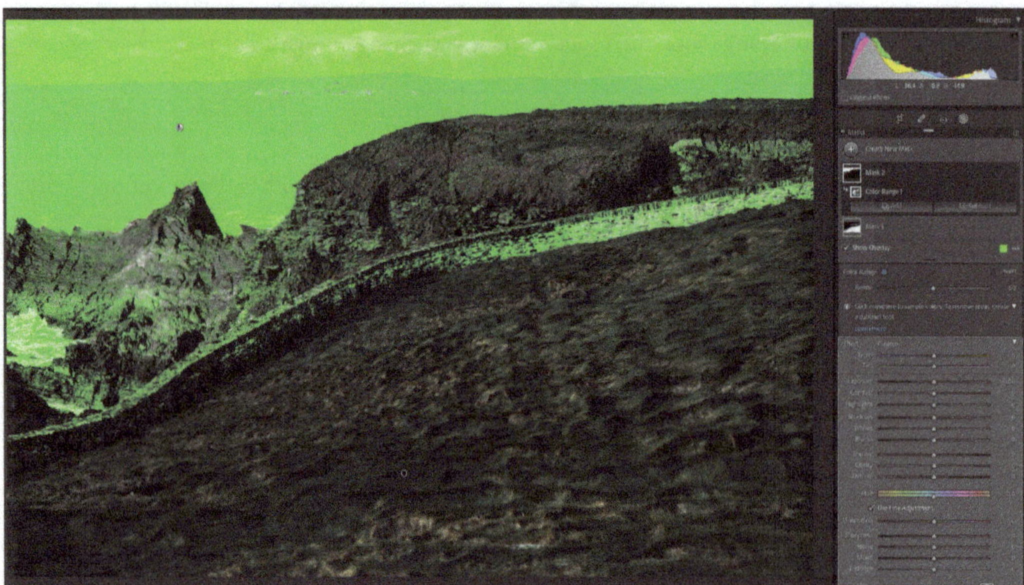

Figure 6.47 B – Color Range mask examples

Luminance Range

Luminance Range is for creating masks based on the selected brightness range. We can choose the level of brightness that we want to work with in a few different ways:

- Click on any point in the photograph to choose it.
- Click and drag over any part of the image to choose all the brightness levels within the selection.
- Manually drag both edges of the **Luminance Range** slider and choose a range to work with. We can also use this slider to adjust and tweak the choices that we have made with the picker.

You can click on **Luminance Map** to see the brightness levels represented on a black and white photograph; the red areas show our selection.

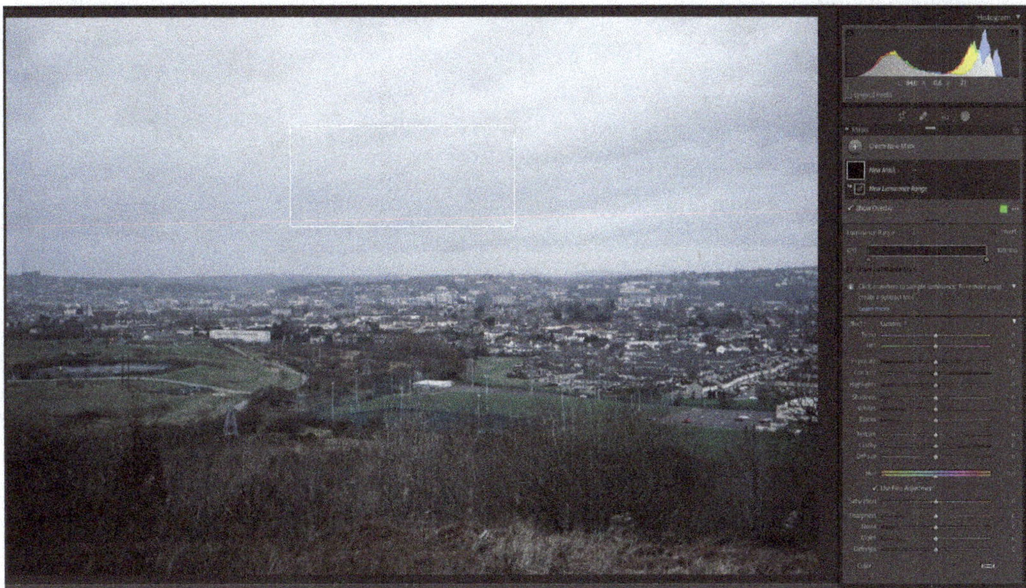

Figure 6.48 A

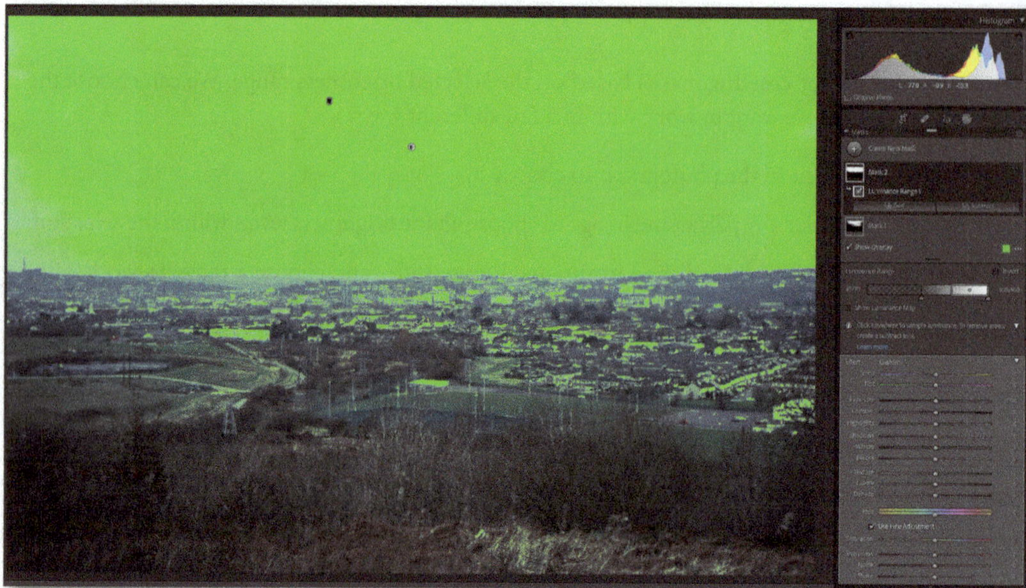

Figure 6.48 B – Luminance Range mask example

Depth Range

The last range-based mask that's available to us is the **Depth Range** mask. Its usage is quite limited as it can only work with files that store depth information – that is, the distance of each object within the photograph from the camera. Like the previous two range-based masks, we can click or click and drag to choose a range to work with and later tweak it with the **Depth Range** slider. For some reason, Adobe decided to reverse bright and dark areas, which are represented on the slider, compared to the Histogram tool. Here, bright areas are on the left while dark areas are on the right.

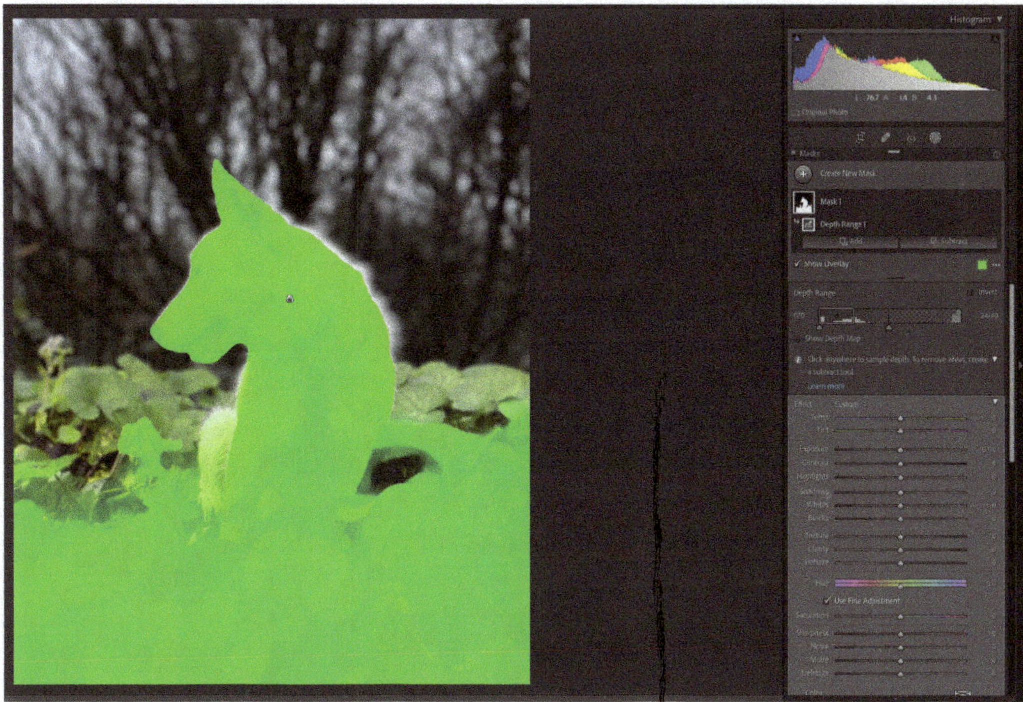

Figure 6.49 – Depth Range mask based on the foreground subject

The only files that work with this tool are iPhone's `.heic` photos, which can be made in *Portrait mode*, and photos made with Lightroom Mobile's camera. For these two, it works like a charm. You just need to enable **Depth map capture**.

Additional masking tools

Now that we know how all of these masks work, it's time to tweak them to perfection with a range of additional masking tools available in Lightroom.

Each mask has a list of possible tweaking options, and they are available as a menu after you click on the little three dots that are in line with the name of each mask.

We can rename each one, which is a good habit to get into and will make things easier when we have a lot of masks to work with or come back to edit them after a while.

With **Intersect Mask With**, after creating any mask, we can narrow the selection by intersecting it with any other type of mask. Think about it as creating a mask within a mask. This option will also be available on the bottom of the **Masks** panel when we press the "*Alt*" key. It will replace the **Add** and **Subtract** buttons, which allow us to add to or subtract from our selection with any type of masking.

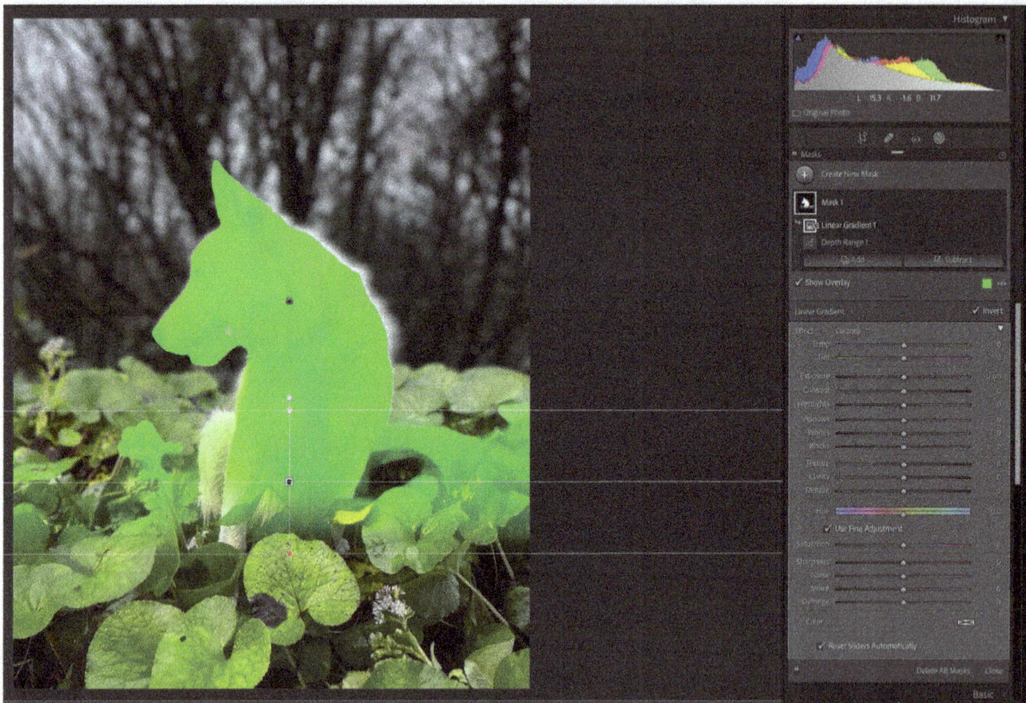

Figure 6.50 – The same photo as in Figure 6.49 intersected with a gradient mask drawn from the top of the photograph

We can naturally also duplicate the mask, delete it, and delete all masks at once.

In addition to this, once we turn on any mask tool, the toolbar directly under the photograph we are working on will change to display two masking-related options:

- **Show Edit Pins** with drop-down menu choices of **Auto**, **Always**, **Selected**, and **Never**.

  Here is what these options are for:

  - **Auto**: This will show adjustment pins when we hover over the picture. Once we move the cursor outside of the picture area, the pins will disappear.
  - **Always**: The pins will stay visible until we turn this off.

  - **Selected**: Only the pin of the adjustment we are currently working on will be visible.
  - **Never**: All of the pins will stay invisible, even when we are drawing a new mask.
- The second added option is **Show Selected Mask Overlay**, which will enable or disable the view of the currently chosen mask in a variety of ways.

If combining these tools doesn't give us the expected results or we just want to delve deeper into bending light to our will, then **Tone Curve** will provide amazing capabilities.

Tone Curve

Tone Curve is probably one of the most feared tabs in Lightroom. However, I hope that after reading this section, you will be more confident in using its capabilities to your advantage.

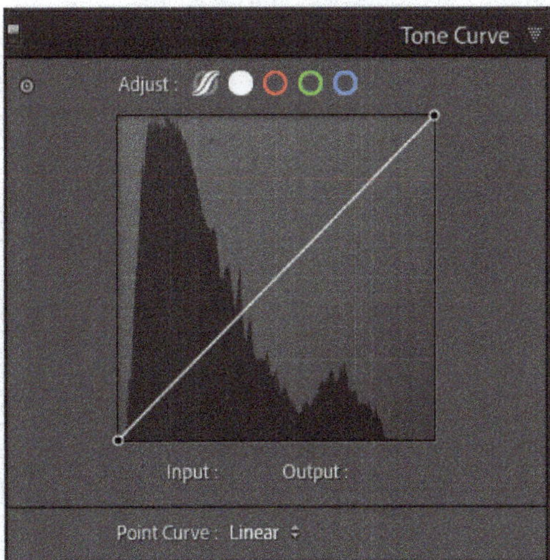

Figure 6.51 – Tone Curve's default settings

Tone Curve represents the tonality of photographs. When you look more closely, you will notice it's a squeezed version of the Histogram tool, representing tones from left to right – dark to light.

If the line is straight and at 45 degrees, then no changes have been made to the tonality of our photographs. If the line isn't straight after you've just imported the photograph, this means that Lightroom applied default changes while importing it; this might be directed by the camera profile, for example.

Parametric Curve

There are four tonal regions that we can adjust in **Parametric Curve** mode – **Highlights**, **Lights**, **Darks**, and **Shadows**. Once we move our cursor over the curve line, we will notice Lightroom displaying the names of affected areas and graphically representing them in a lighter gray color. We can drag the line up and down to adjust the selected areas. Dragging the curve up will brighten the area while dragging it down will darken it. The adjustable scale just below the curve is for changing the range of each tonal area. By default, tonality is split into four equal areas – we can affect this by moving each of the arrowheads. We can reset them by double-clicking on each arrowhead. Moving these sliders will affect the size of each tonal area. For example, if we move the last slider, which represents the beginning of highlights, to the right, we will decrease the size of the highlights area that's affected by any changes that are made to the curve.

Lastly, we can affect the tonal areas by adjusting the sliders for each tonal region that's reflected in the curve's up-down movement of the relevant areas. As with all sliders within Lightroom, we can reset them by double-clicking on a chosen arrowhead or by pressing "*Alt*" and resetting the tool or part of it. We can also adjust any area by choosing the **Targeted Adjustment** tool. When we move the mouse cursor around the photograph, Lightroom will highlight the appropriate part of the Tone Curve. We can affect the curve by clicking and dragging any point within the photo.

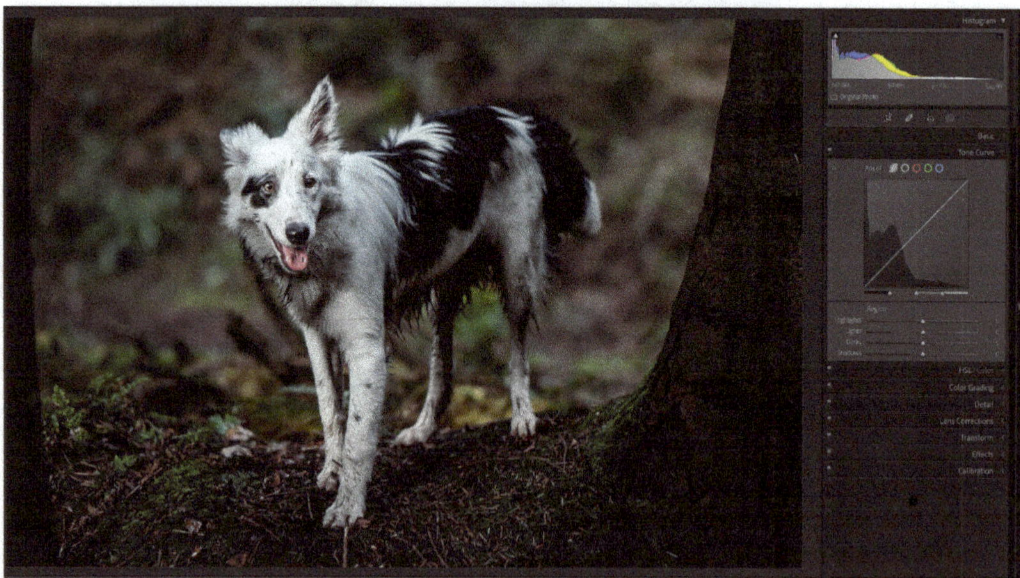

Figure 6.52 A

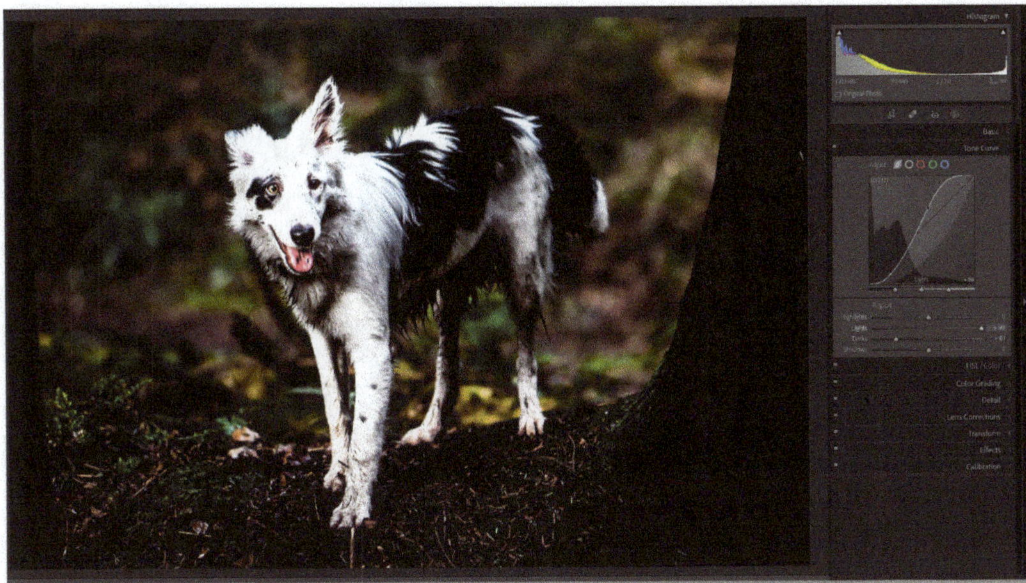

Figure 6.52 B – Flat Parametric Curve and Parametric Curve adjusted to extremely increased contrasts by darkening dark tones and brightening bright ones

Point Curve

To have more flexibility over the tonal adjustments, we can change from **Parametric Curve**, which affects predefined areas, to **Point Curve**. Now, we can be more specific with our adjustments. Once we click on any place within the curve, we create a point that can be dragged up and down to brighten or darken pixels. Two points on the Curve which are located around, and closest to the point which we are adjusting, create "anchors" around the adjusted point. These anchors will not change position when we adjust the point between them. We can also choose one of the presets on the bottom of the tab or save our own. Creating and adjusting the points on the curve can be done by clicking on the curve itself and anywhere around the photograph with the **Targeted Adjustment** tool. When we click anywhere on the photo, we mark its tonal equivalent on the curve. From here, we can click and drag directly on the photograph or adjust the point within the **Tone Curve** tab itself.

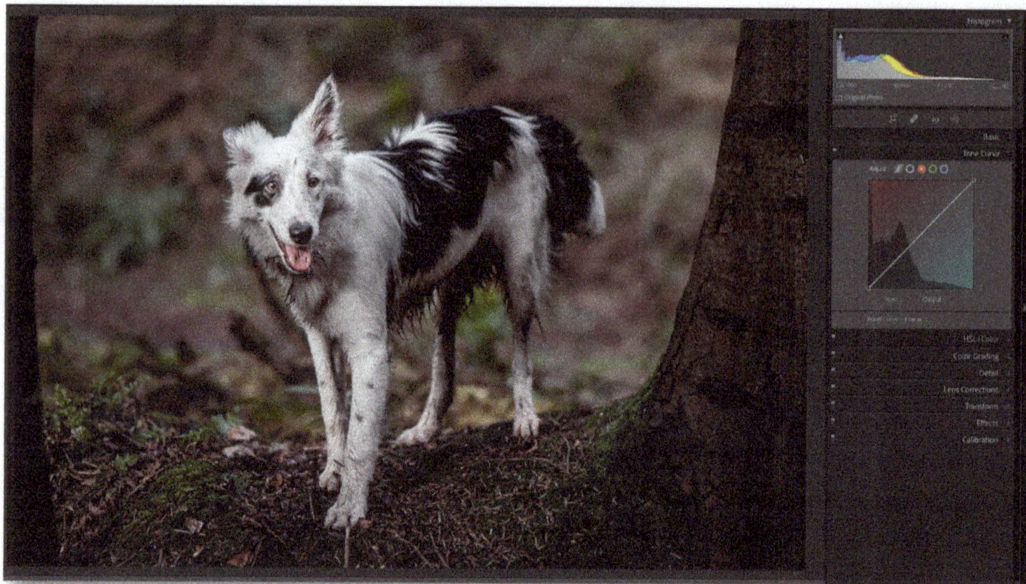

Figure 6.53 A

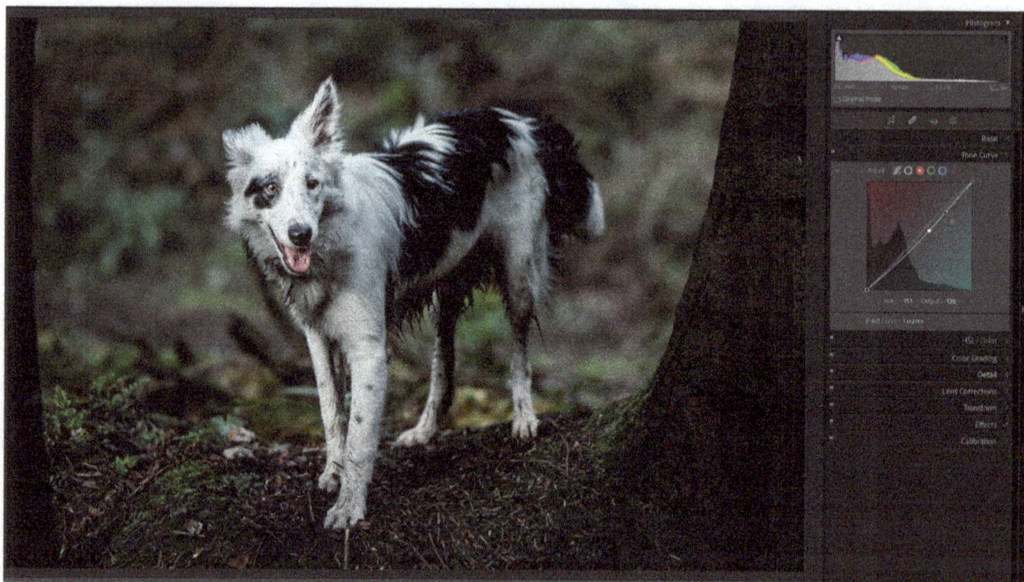

Figure 6.53 B – The Flat Tonal Curve and Tonal Curve of reds adjusted to make the highlighted areas green – notice the slight change in the red-tinted background and the dog's fur shift into greens

Making tonal changes is not everything as we can affect how the colors behave within the photograph. For every point on the curve, we can shift each RGB color into a different color space. Once we click on one of the three RGB-colored rings, the space above and below the curve line will turn into opposite colors. Dragging it up and down will shift the color within the picked tonal range into the shown color space. For example, for the red channel, it's cyans and magentas.

Examples of usage

There are two areas where I use **Tone Curve** the most. First of all, I use it for contrast, adding either more punch to photos or making them flatter. Even though there are many tools we can use to affect the luminosity/brightness of photographs within the **Basic** tab, **Tone Curve** has a unique ability to carve out and separate particular areas within the image. We can, for example, grab one of the curve's ends and change where blacks and whites begin, changing the whole histogram's scale. Shifting the bottom left end to the right will change where the blacks begin; every brightness level on the left of the chosen point will turn darker. The opposite will happen when we move the top-right corner to the left.

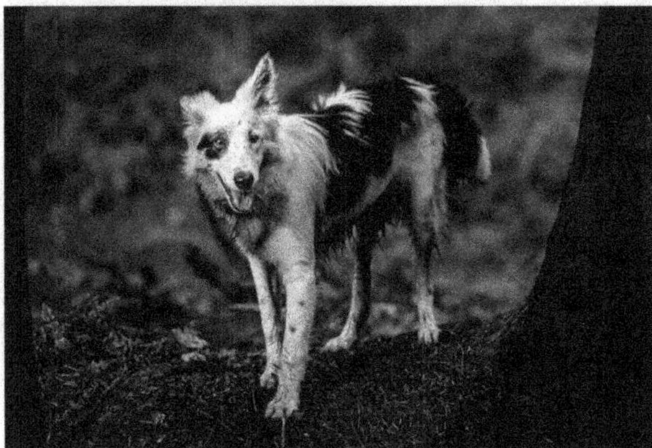

Figure 6.54 A

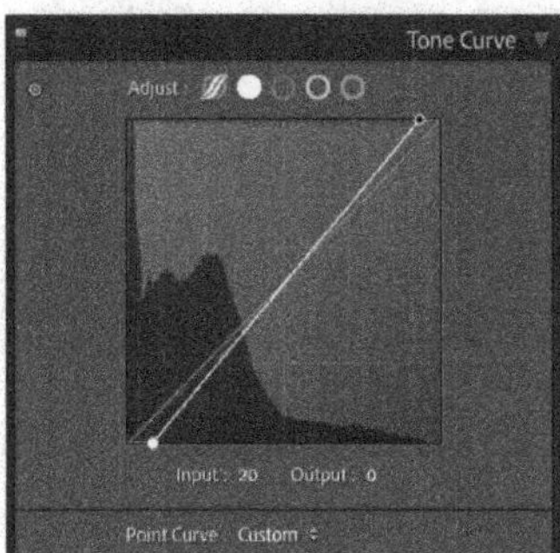

Figure 6.54 B – Creating a more "punchy" look by applying the aforementioned adjustments

To create a punchy, contrasty photograph, we can use an S-Curve. We can place two points on the Tone Curve – one in the **Highlights** area and one in the **Shadows** area. Now, drag **Highlights** up and pull **Shadows** down until you get a satisfying look. Remember to check for clipping and avoid it unless it's the effect you are looking for. Another widely used curve is M-shaped. This is used to open up shadows and punch highlights slightly. To work with an M-Curve, we need to place points in **Highlights** and **Shadows**, just like in the preceding example, plus an additional point in the middle. Now, we must pull up both Shadows and Highlights. Again, check for clipping and move them around until you achieve the desired effect.

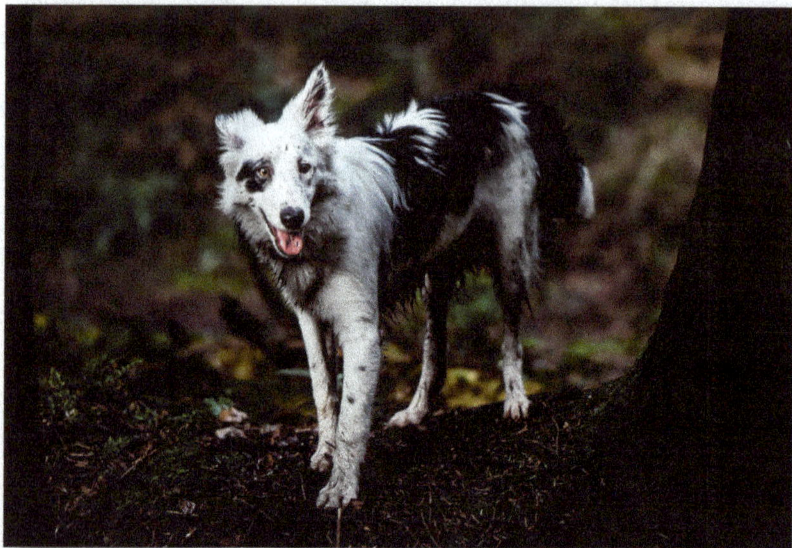

Figure 6.55 A

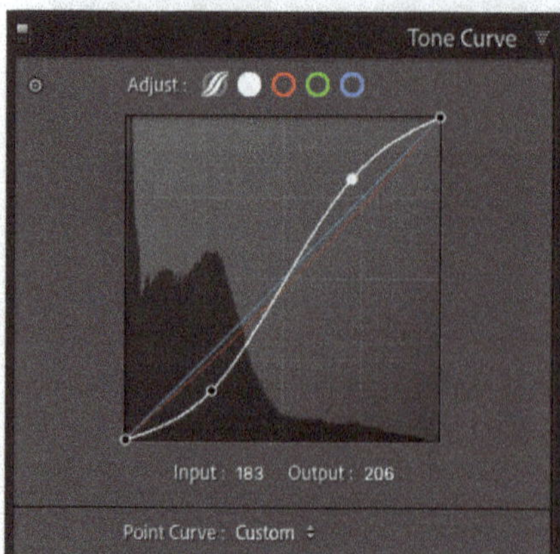

Figure 6.55 B – Creating a more "punchy" look by applying the S-Curve

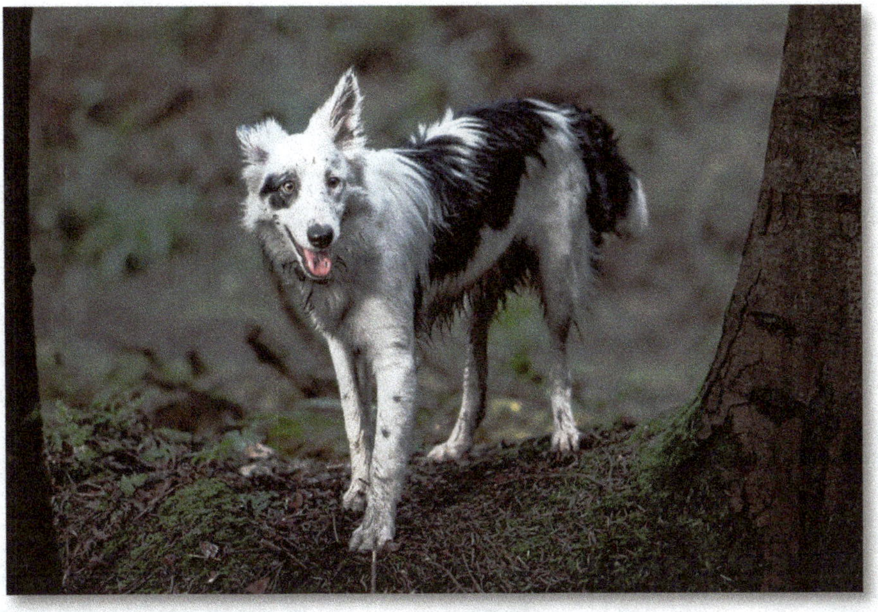

Figure 6.56 A

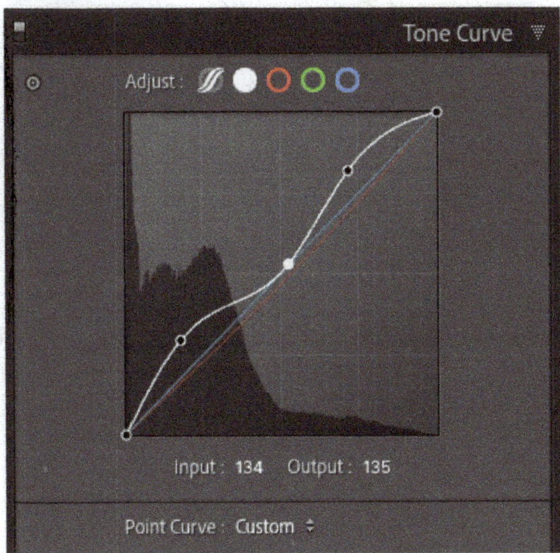

Figure 6.56 B – M-Curve example

You can also use **Tone Curve** to counter color cast from time to time. Have a look at the following example – I nudged the blues into yellow to counter the blue cast in the background without affecting the blues of the jacket. Of course, we can do the same for any color cast by nudging the required area into a desired color space opposite to the cast.

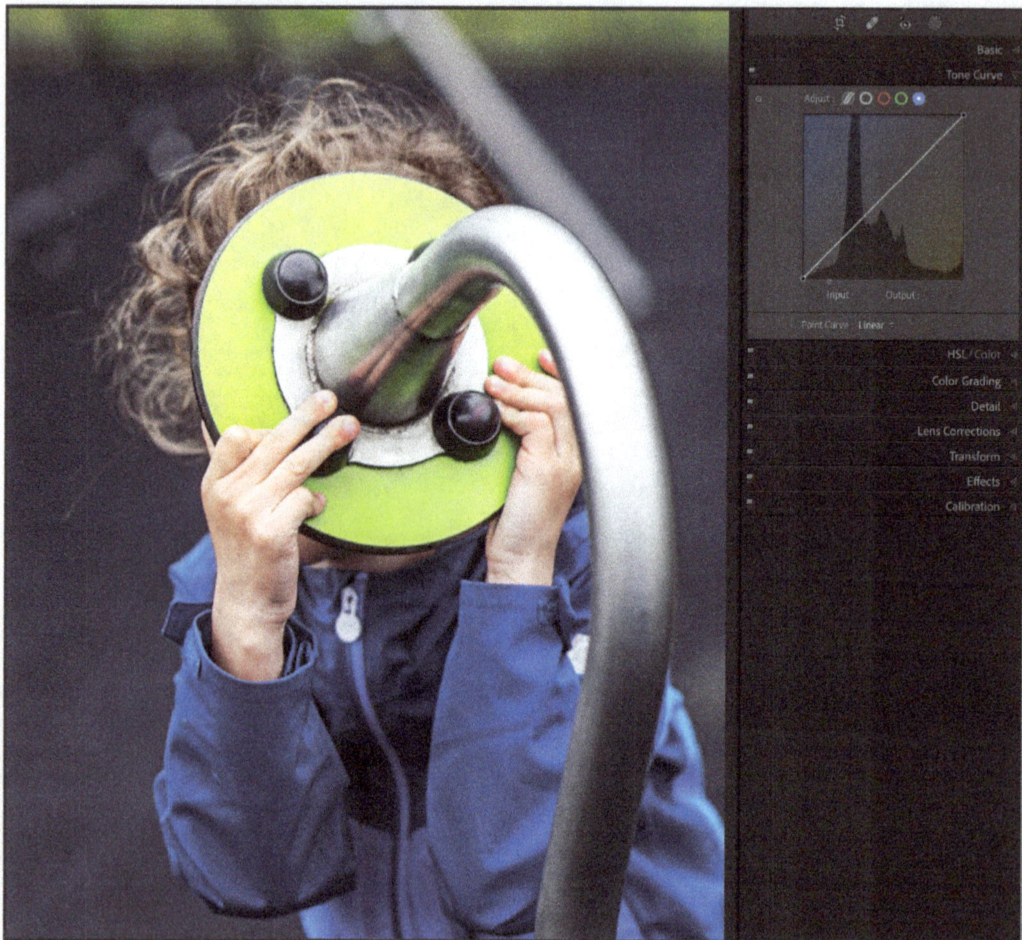

Figure 6.57 A

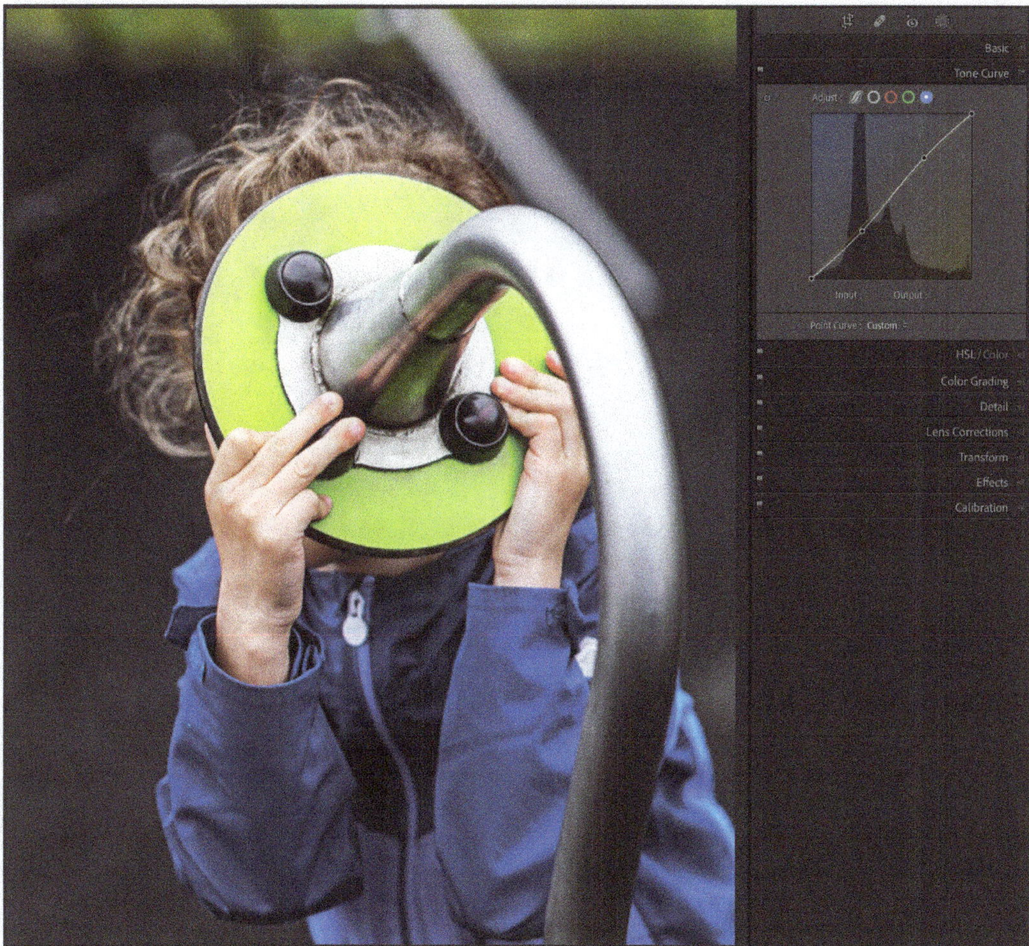

Figure 6.57 B – Nudging the color-targeted curve to counteract the unwanted color cast

In the next section, we will work with color.

HSL/Color

Hue, Saturation, and Luminance (HSL) are what make color photographs come to life. Within this tab, we can change many aspects of color behaviors. They have been placed into eight basic groups that cover the whole color palette and can be found around the color wheel.

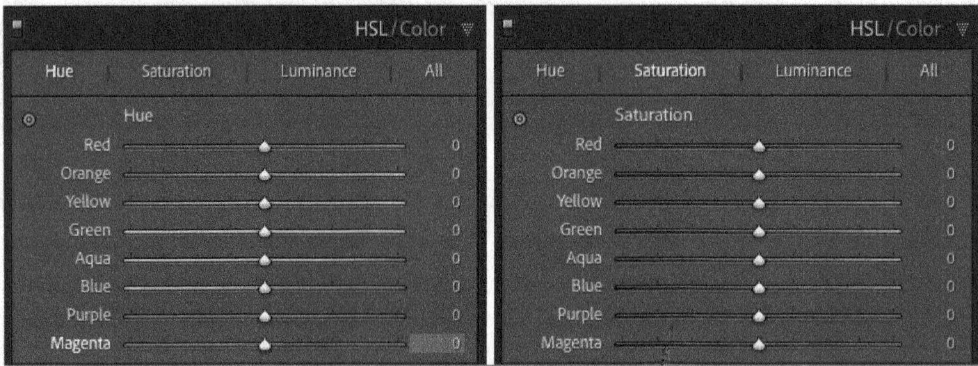

Figure 6.58 A

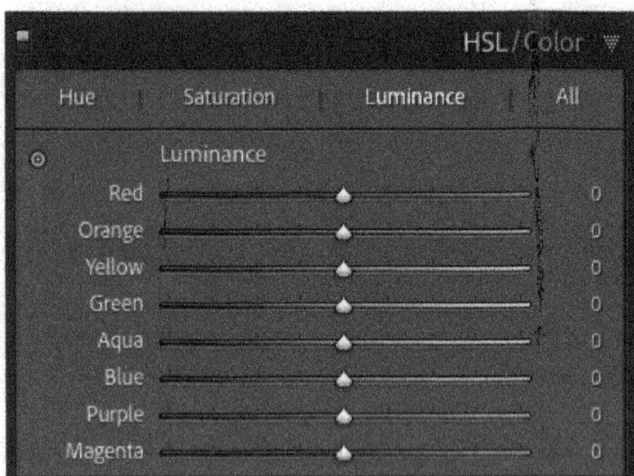

Figure 6.58 B – Hue, Saturation, and Luminance sliders

HSL/Color tool controls

We can control all the sections of this tool in three different ways:

- By moving the sliders left and right
- By using the **Direct Adjustment** tool and then clicking and dragging colors within the photograph
- By double-clicking on any value next to the sliders and entering a numerical value

Hue

To make things simple and not get bogged down in the color theory, let's just say that **Hue** allows us to change how each color looks within the photograph. Let's say that we don't like the shades of green and red that the grass and leaves in our photo have, or the sky has the "wrong" shade of blue. Even after all the adjustments we've already made within **Basic** and **Curve**, there might be some other shades that we may want to have different tints. Just with a few moves of the sliders, we can make changes that will make everything look the way we want it to.

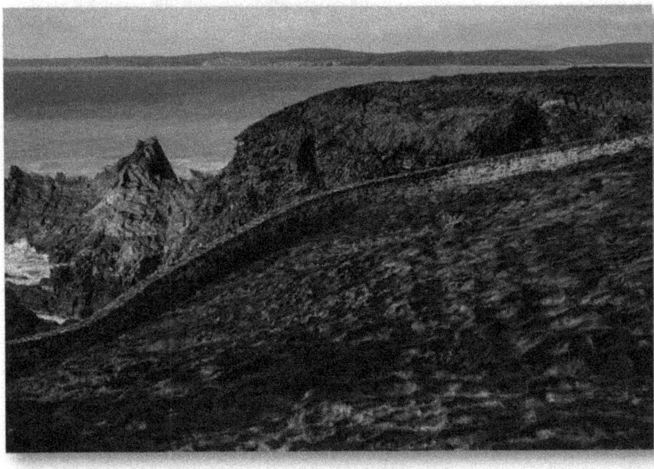

Figure 6.59 A

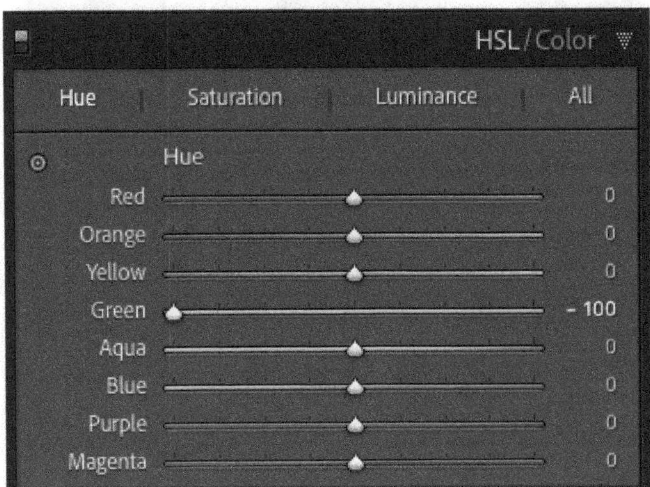

Figure 6.59 B – Example of using the Hue sliders – shifting Green into the Yellow area

Saturation

Here, we can adjust the intensity of each color within our photographs. Ever wanted to have just one color stand out while everything else is muted? This is the right tool for the job.

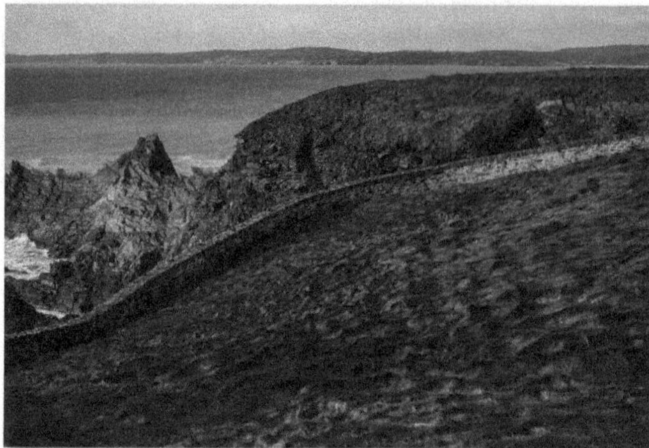

Figure 6.60 A

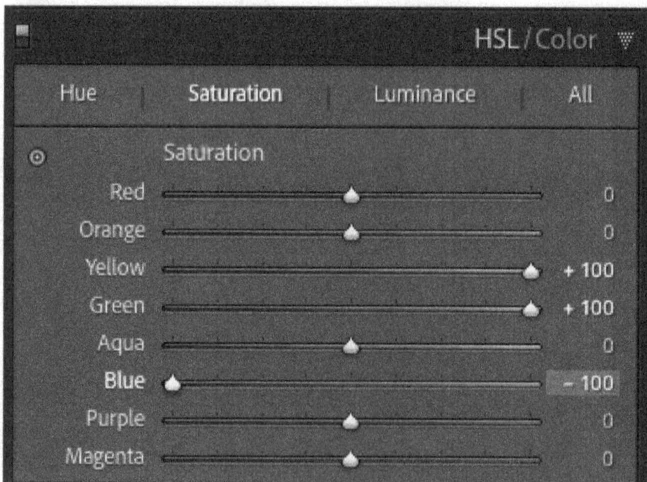

Figure 6.60 B – Saturation sliders – extreme usage example

Luminance

Just as **Saturation** represents the intensity of color, luminosity represents the brightness of that color. We can affect how dark or bright each color appears in the photograph by moving the sliders.

HSL also provides us with a **Black & White** mix when we change **Treatment** in the **Basic** tab to **Black & White**, allowing us to make each color appear darker or lighter. This is where we can make skies black by pulling blues down or even creating an infrared-like look by pushing greens and yellows into bright areas.

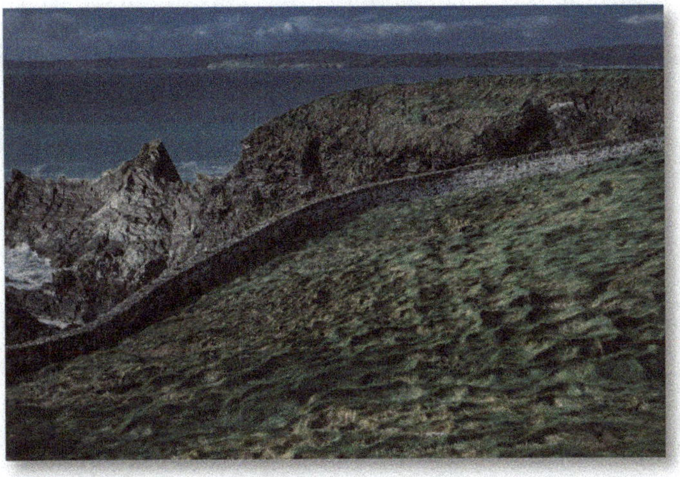

Figure 6.61 A

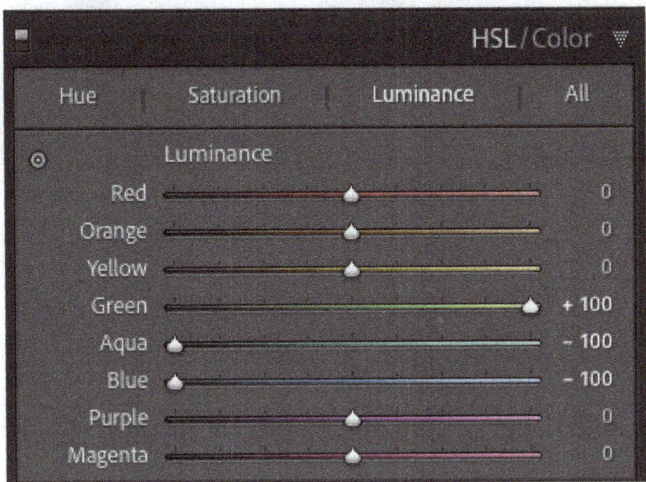

Figure 6.61 B – Luminance sliders – extreme usage example

If the changes that have been applied to color in this panel have left you wanting more, then move on to the next section, where we will look at the **Color Grading** tool. This could be just what you are looking for.

Color Grading

Color Grading is a capable tool that can help us create anything from very subtle color effects to complete recolorization of the photograph. Similar to other Lightroom tools we've discussed, **Color Grading** works on different areas of luminosity; that is, **Shadows**, **Midtones**, and **Highlights**.

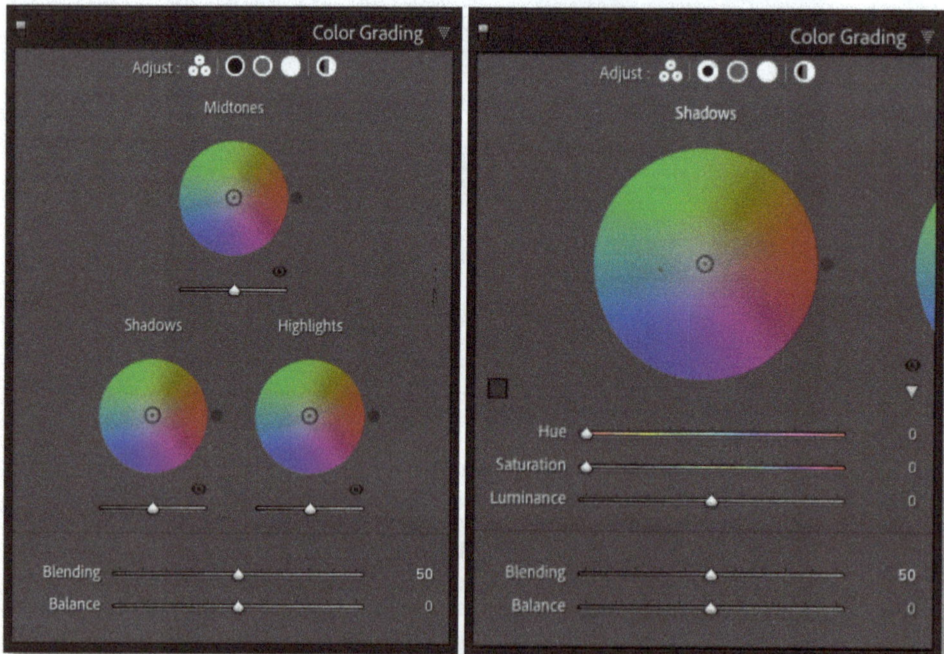

Figure 6.62 A

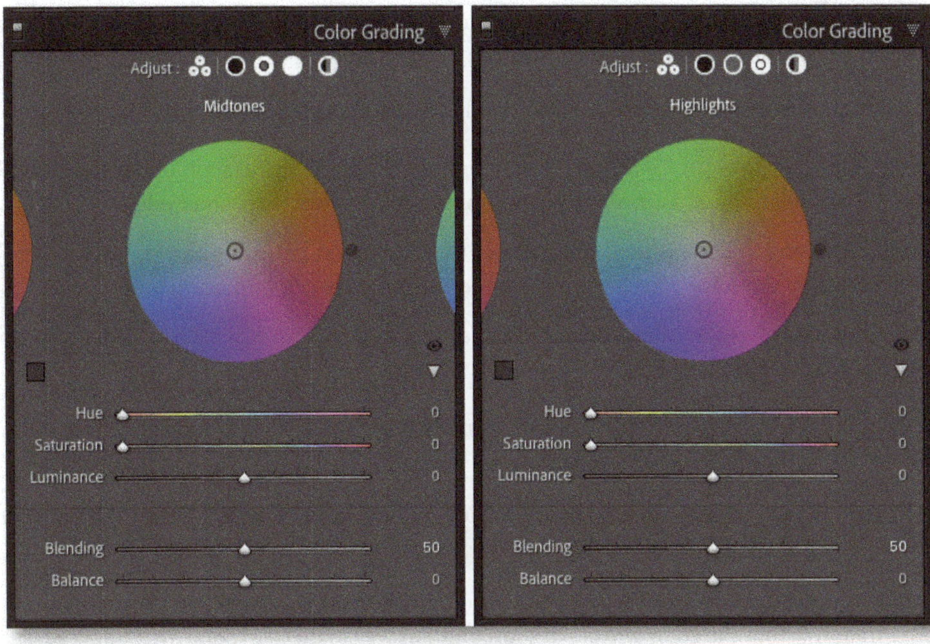

Figure 6.62 B

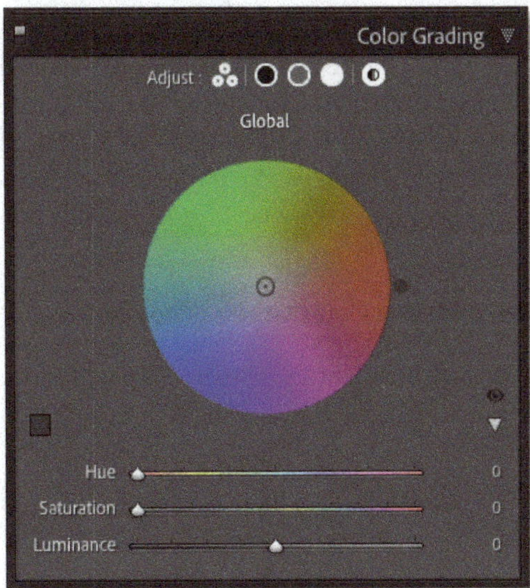

Figure 6.62 C – Color Grading controls – three-Way, Shadows/Midtones/Highlights, and Global

We can add color at a specific hue and saturation for each of these three areas. We can adjust hue and saturation by choosing the desired color on the color wheel. We can work by adjusting the values within the three-way panel, going to each luminosity level separately, or making global changes (the last circle). I will focus on the single luminosity wheels as I find them easier to work with due to their size.

To control our choice of colors, we have three great keyboard shortcuts at our disposal:

- "*Shift*": Once we press the "*Shift*" key, we can only work with the saturation of the chosen color. This is symbolized by a line from the center of the color wheel to its outer edge.
- "*Cmd*": Pressing the "*Cmd*" key only allows us to work on choosing the right hue. This is symbolized on the color wheel by a ring at the currently chosen saturation level.
- "*Alt*": This enables a fine adjust mode where any movements we make are scaled-down for a more precise selection.

Under each of the color wheels, we will find an expanded selection of tools to further help us control the color.

First on the right is an eye icon – clicking on it disables grading for the time it is pressed. It's a before/after view.

Directly under the eye icon is a small arrow. Clicking on this arrow opens two more sliders that control hue and saturation within the color wheel – it's just another way to do so as some users may prefer to work with sliders. But let's close it for now.

On the opposite side is a small square in the color we picked. Clicking on it opens a bubble with a small menu for choosing the color either from swatches or a color picker. We will be offered a set of default swatch colors that we can easily change by right-clicking on any of the five color squares and choosing **Set this Swatch to Current Color**. We can reset the swatch colors at any time by choosing **Reset This Swatch** or **Reset all Swatches** in the same right-click menu. Lastly, we can manually enter values for Hue and Saturation by double-clicking the numbers under the color square. The **0-359** value symbolizes 360 degrees of the color wheel for Hue, while the **0-100** value symbolizes the percentage of Saturation.

Three more sliders are available within the **Color Grading** tool:

- **Luminance** specifies how dark or bright the chosen color will appear. Moving it to the right (values above **50**) will make it lighter while moving it to the left (values below **50**) will make it darker.

  The last two sliders are responsible for how **Shadows, Midtones, and Highlights** (**SMH**) will interact with each other.

- **Blending** is the level of overlap between SMH. In the case of **Color Grading**, it is the overlap of grading within each of these three luminosities. Therefore, moving the **Blending** slider to the right will create a more defined and harsher transition between SMH colors. Moving it to the left will create a less defined, more diffused transition.

- **Balance** affects the balance between the SMH areas. While in the middle, SMH is split into three equal parts. Moving the **Balance** slider to the left will increase the size of the **Highlights** area in comparison to the other two while moving it to the right will increase the size of the **Shadows** area.

Once we have adjusted all the colors to our liking, it's time to sharpen the photograph in the **Detail** panel.

Detail

Lightroom's **Detail** tab is split into two seemingly unrelated categories – **Sharpening** and **Noise Reduction**.

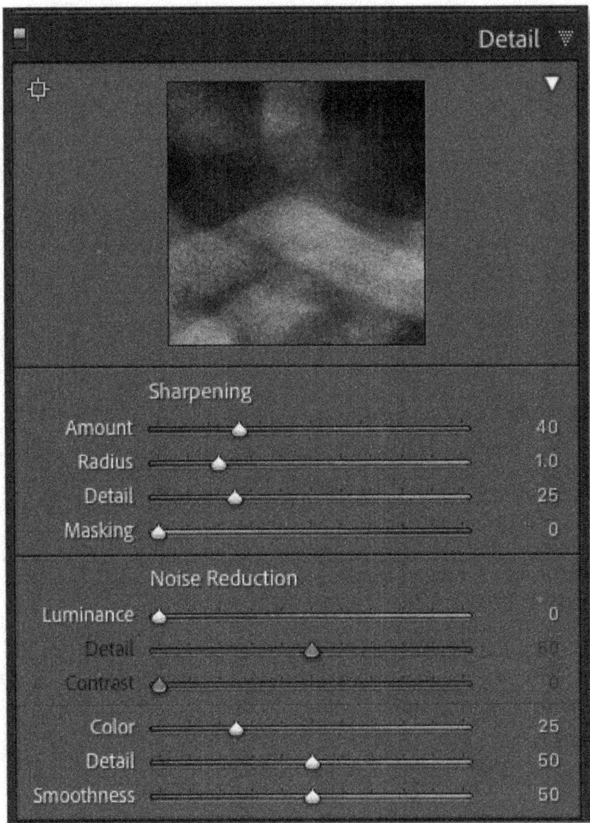

Figure 6.63 – The Detail tab and its default Sharpening and Noise Reduction settings

Sharpening

As you probably know, it is us – the photographers – who are responsible for making sharp photographs. However, because raw, digital images can never match the sharpness of analog photos, tools such as **Sharpening** in Lightroom can help us add a bit more definition. Before we talk about the tool in detail, let's briefly explain how **Sharpening** works. Like any definition-enhancing tool in Lightroom, **Sharpening** is also all about tweaking contrast; it just does so in a different way. **Sharpening** is not a magic wand that can retrieve details or recover a photograph; all it does is look for edges in the photo that are defined by varying contrast and increases the contrast alongside them, making dark areas darker and bright areas brighter. To the human eye, they become more defined and seemingly sharper. This explanation also comes with a word of warning – **Sharpening** will not fix a photograph that's out of focus and won't work miracles on shots with even the slightest motion blur. Sure, combining **Sharpening** with **Clarity**, **Curves**, and **Texture** tweaks may help make it viable for viewing on a mobile phone, but once it's viewed at 100% magnification, the spell will break...

First of all, click on the small down-pointing arrow. This will open a square 100% preview of a fragment in our photograph. We can choose that detail by clicking on the little picture square and then clicking again in a chosen area. To be more accurate with our choice, click on the little square viewfinder – this will turn the mouse cursor into a small square; click with that square anywhere on the currently viewed photograph in the **Navigator** panel, and the chosen area will appear in the small preview within the **Detail** tab. We can also click and drag that detail to see the desired detail. One way or another, always look at **Sharpening** at 100% magnification; otherwise, you may not get the results you expected once you get to exporting and printing.

Let's look at the options/sliders inside **Sharpening**:

- **Amount**: This is probably the most self-explanatory slider within the **Sharpening** part of the tool; it controls how much sharpness we would like to add to our photograph. To see a real difference, it's enough to just move it by about 20 units, especially at 100% magnification. I strongly suggest looking at 100% magnification before confirming any changes – Adobe advises the same approach. Once we sharpen beyond a certain number, which varies from photograph to photograph, we will start seeing a halo along the edges of objects in the photograph, which is a clear signal to dial down.
- **Radius**: To narrow sharpened edges and limit the creation of halos or widen sharpened edges, we need to reduce or increase the size of the radius. **Radius** is the width of the area that's affected by the **Sharpening** slider. The larger the radius, the wider the edge areas will be affected by **Sharpening**. Therefore, using a high value of **Radius** correction will often lead to unnatural-looking effects with a stronger halo effect.

- **Detail**: Increasing the **Detail** slider's value will boost the visibility of textures within the photograph, making them look more enunciated.
- **Masking**: Using a higher value of the **Masking** setting will tell Lightroom to look at more pronounced edges and ignore the details. At low settings, **Masking** treats all the areas in the photograph in the same way, while increasing it restricts the **Sharpening** effect for more pronounced edges.

Adjusting any of these sliders while holding the "*Alt*" key will show us a black and white image with affected areas of the image colored in white and masked, unaffected areas colored in black.

The default Lightroom settings for **Sharpening** will be sufficient to add enough crispness to the photographs we are working on. However, if we need a bit more definition, let's remember about working at 100% magnification or higher to avoid potential halos and an unnatural look.

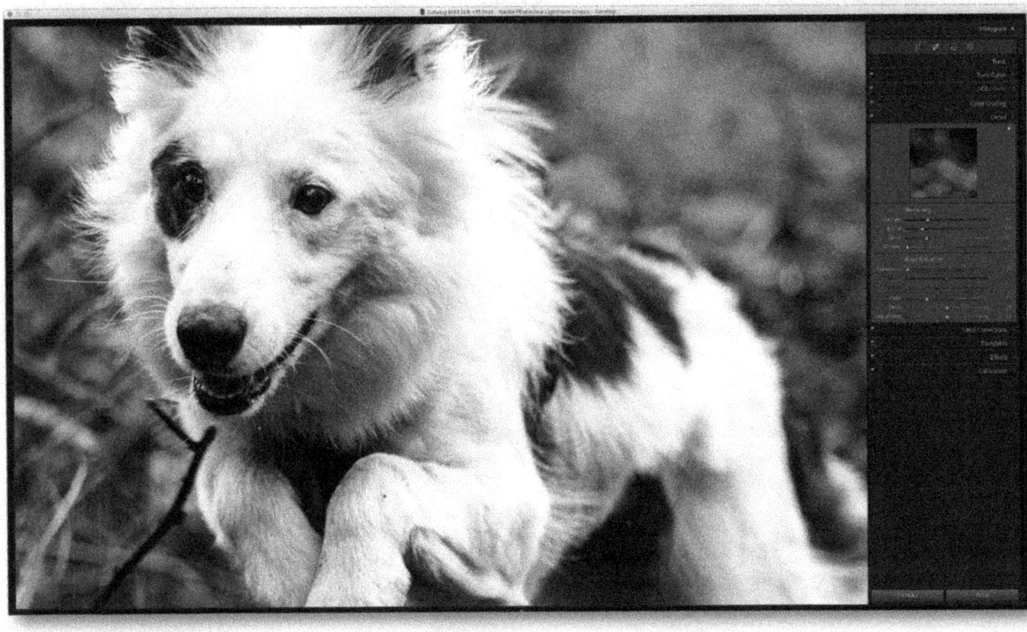

Figure 6.64 – Sharpening at its default settings

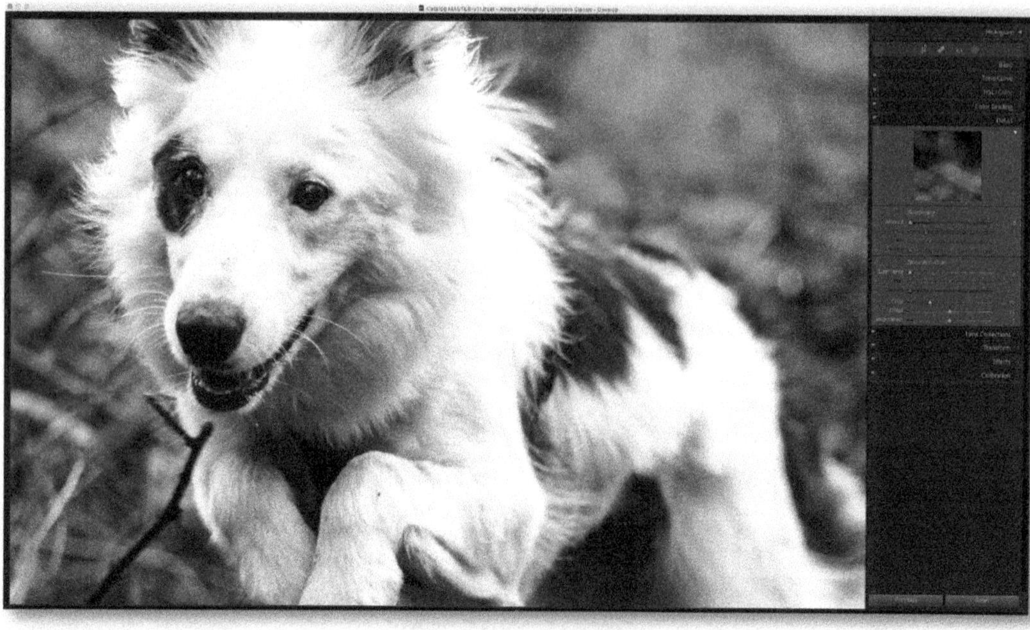

Figure 6.65 – Sharpening reduced to 0

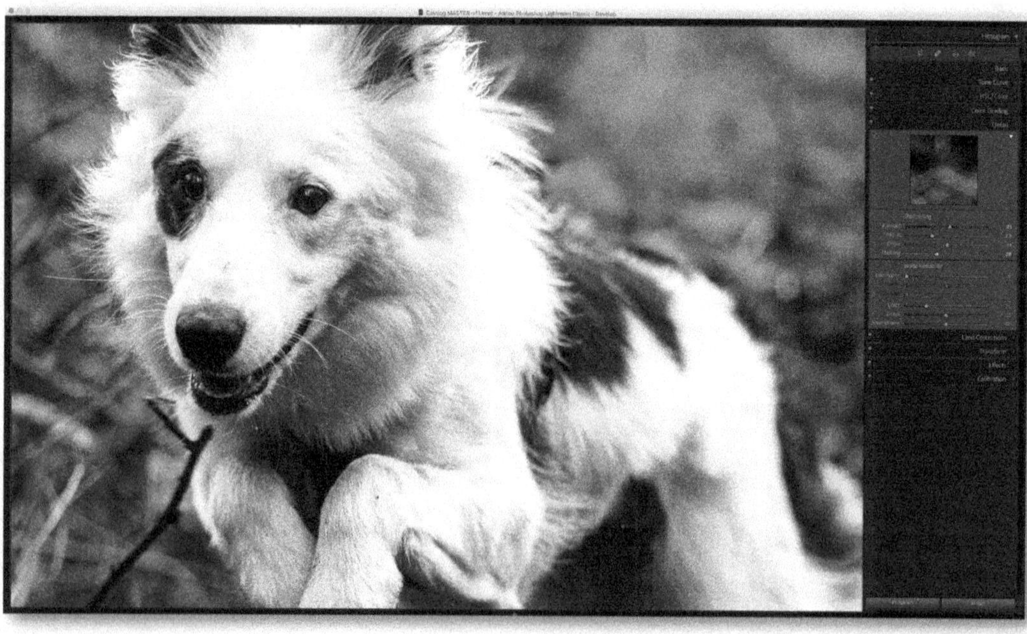

Figure 6.66 – Sharpening at a satisfying level

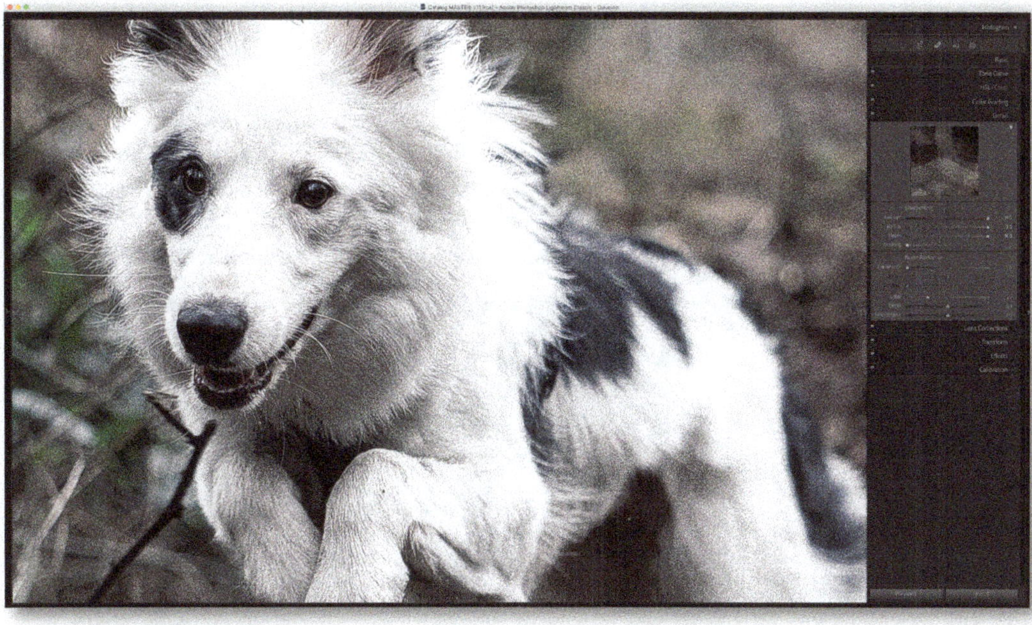

Figure 6.67 – Photo sharpened to its maximum

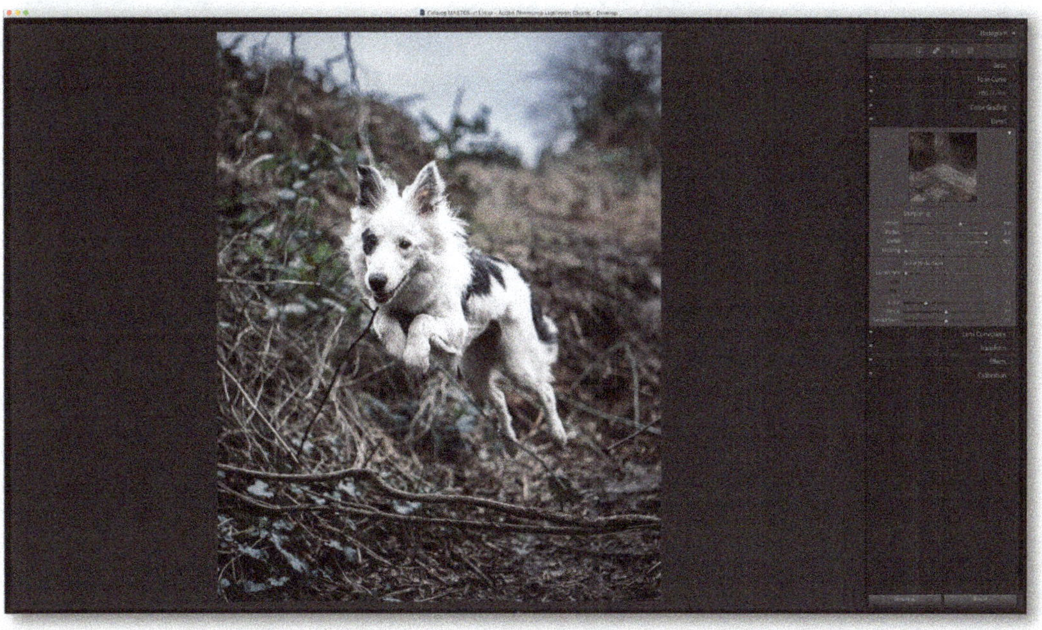

Figure 6.68 – Photo sharpened to its maximum – full picture view

Digital noise has accompanied us since the dawn of digital photography. Even though there has been a gigantic quality leap in this field, most cameras will still produce some noise in higher ISO settings. These will also be pronounced by the **Sharpening** tool. We have two types of noise to deal with – **Luminance** noise, which will be visible as a grainy effect, and **Chroma** noise (represented here by the **Color** set of sliders), which will be visible as color artifacts. We have six sliders at our disposal to counteract these effects. Just like when working with the **Sharpening** tool, 100% magnification is advisable to gauge its effect on the photograph. Completely removing noise is practically impossible, so I suggest focusing on making it as little distracting as possible.

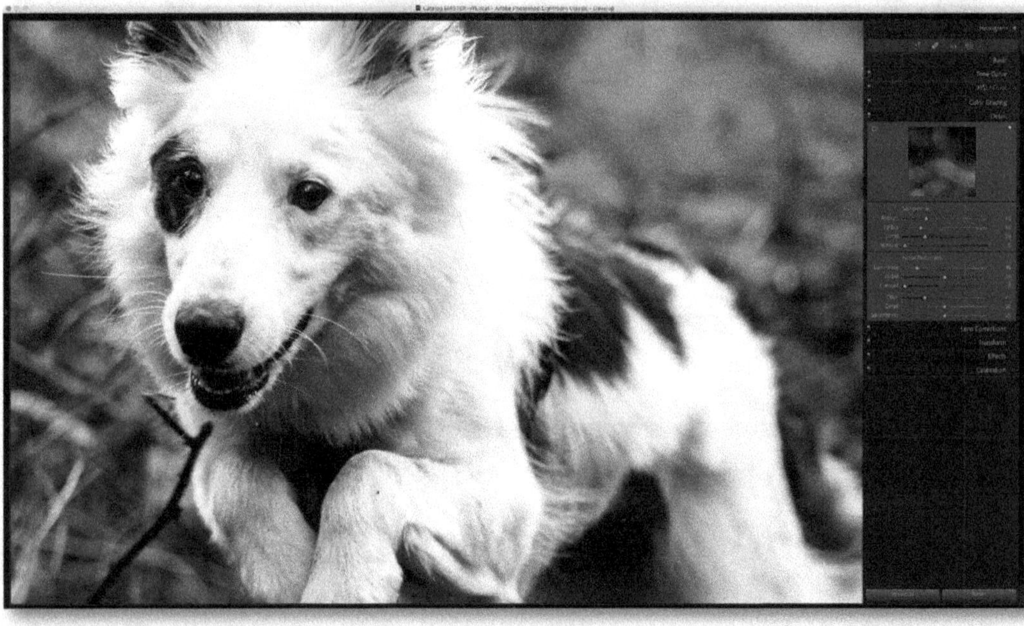

Figure 6.69 A

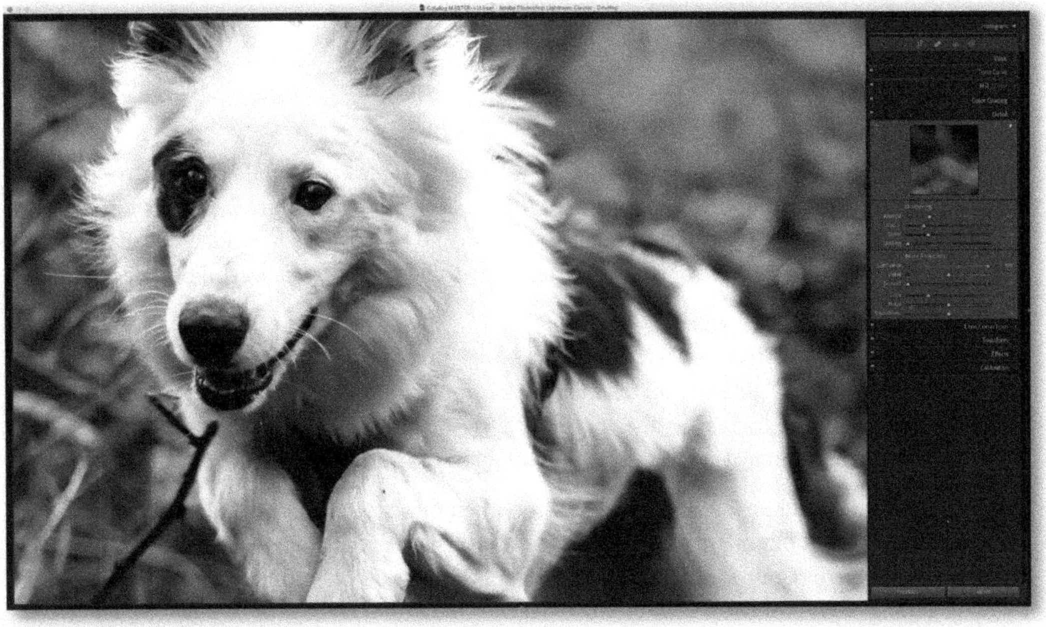

Figure 6.69 B – Gentle Noise Reduction and max Noise Reduction – notice the loss of details

With sharpening done, let's take a closer look at the **Noise Reduction** menu.

Noise Reduction

Let's take a quick look at the sliders in the **Noise Reduction** section:

- **Luminance**: The **Luminance** slider is the main tool to counteract noise in our photos, but we will start losing a lot of details at higher values. Using the **Luminance** tool is all about balancing between getting rid of unpleasant, digitally grainy-looking photographs and retaining or losing details. Working with high **Luminance** values will smother detail and make photographs look "plasticky-smooth" and unnatural. On the other hand, it may work in our favor once in a while and be a creative choice to run **Luminance** at a very high setting. Still, for most applications, it's all about being reasonable, especially when developing photographs of people.
- **Detail**: We can counteract detail being removed by the **Luminance** setting by cranking up the **Detail** slider, which will help us retain a bit more detail at the price of more visible noise.

- **Contrast**: The **Contrast** tool can help us retain contrast in "de-noised" photographs, but as with the previously mentioned sliders, it is a balancing act. High values will retain more contrast in the photographs but also create noisy spots in some areas, which will look like a badly overcompressed `.jpg`. This is something to be avoided.
- **Color**: With the **Color** slider, we can adjust how much unwanted color noise is removed – mostly colored red. It can be another color as well. I have seen color noise in all principle RGB and CMYK colors. This will vary from camera to camera and heavily depend on the ISO, **Exposure**, and other settings that have been used. The **Color** tool is the most powerful of the lot, in my opinion, and it's the least destructive.
- **Detail**: Just like **Luminance Detail**, this is a slider that's designed to help us find a balance between noise removal and detail retention. We can use the **Detail** slider to set a threshold for color noise removal. Increasing the value of the **Detail** slider will protect details and edges in the photograph but may lead to the creation of color noise blotches.
- **Smoothness**: Because noise reduction can smoothen the images where detail becomes flat and unnatural, Lightroom offers us a way to counteract this in yet another way. **Smoothness** will get rid of some blotching, but it's the least potent of the tools offered here, working mostly as a balancing device for the previous two sliders.

The devil is in the details, as the saying goes, and the **Detail** tab can help us retain a bit more of it, similar to how we can lose it when it's overused. My suggestion is to work with it in moderation and always check many photograph areas at 100% magnification before committing to the changes you've made.

I feel like the next section should be at the very top of this module and it covers fixing imperfections that have been created by the hardware, namely lenses.

Lens Corrections

Most lenses need some amount of correction in post-production. Various unwanted effects such as barreling or chromatic aberrations may appear at certain apertures, focal lengths, and focal distances. Different camera brands have varying approaches to fixing it, and not all lenses are made equal. This panel is where we will be controlling all aspects of these corrections.

Lens Corrections, especially in **Auto** mode, will work best on RAW files. They can be applied to `.jpg` files as well but may produce unexpected and unsatisfying results, in which case we need to apply **Profile** in **Manual** mode.

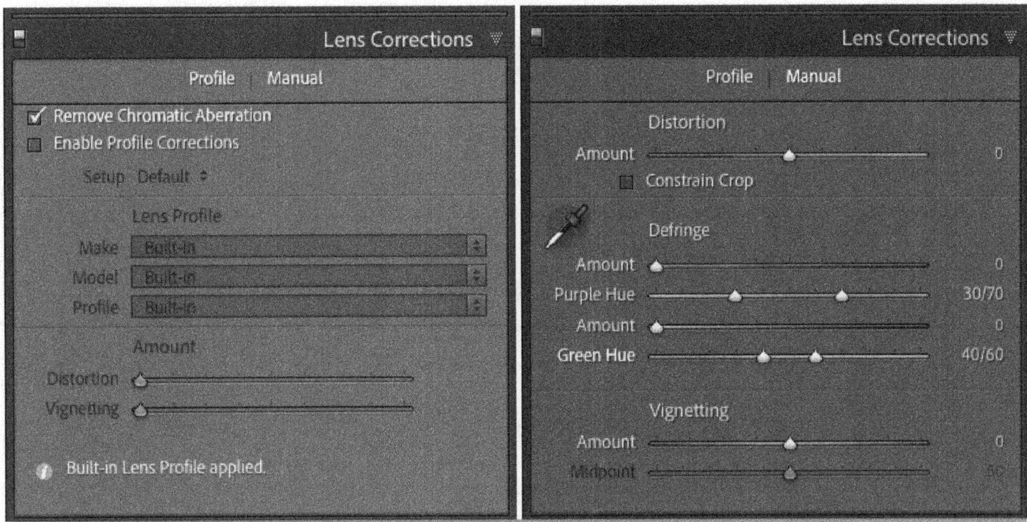

Figure 6.70 – Lens Corrections – Profile and Manual settings

Profile mode

The first box to check is **Remove Chromatic Aberration**. It's not a secret that many lenses create some level of chromatic aberration, especially very fast ones in bright conditions. This tool will get rid of it to a certain degree, but usually, we will want to tweak it, which I'll get back to after explaining the **Profile** tab's other functions.

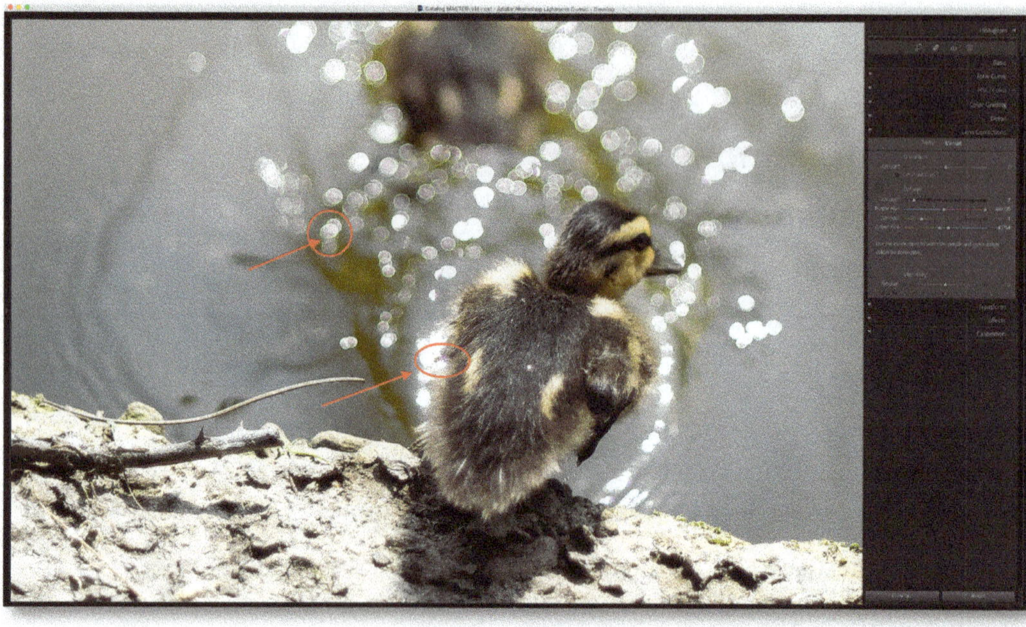

Figure 6.71 A

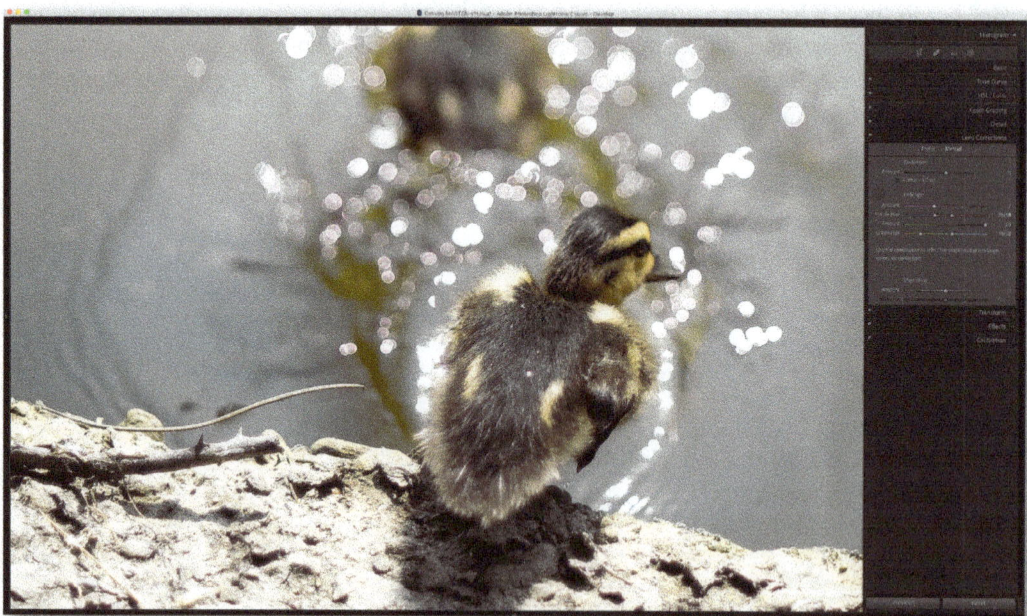

Figure 6.71 B – Lots of green and some purple fringing removed

The next choice we face is between automatic (**Profile**) and manual correction. Some camera brands embed lens correction data in the photo files. In that case, we will see a message saying **Built-in Lens Profile applied** at the bottom of the **Lens Corrections** tab. To confirm the lens/camera combination that's being used, we can click on the icon with the letter **i** next to the message.

If our lens is not supported in this way, then our next step is to **Enable Profile Corrections**. Many branded lenses will pick up the correct profile immediately from the raw data, displaying the make, model, and profile that was used.

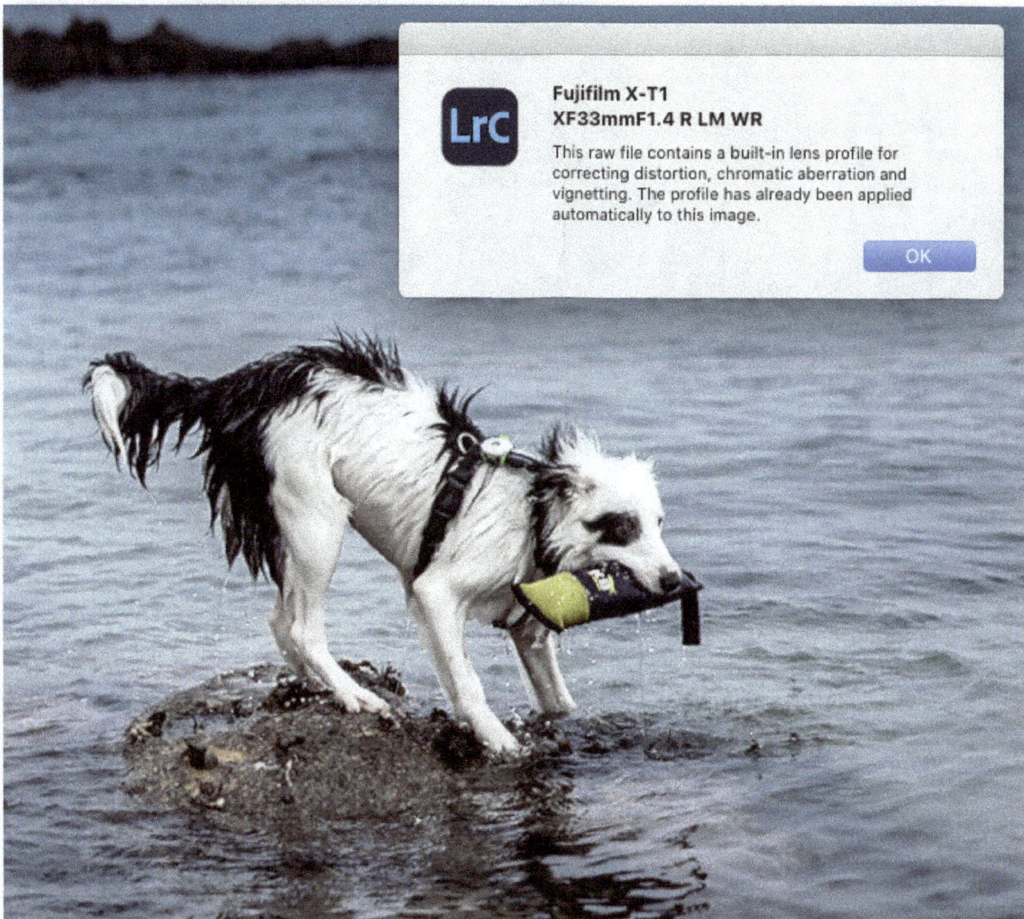

Figure 6.72 – Example of built-in lens profile data

Suppose the lens we used to create the photograph is not automatically found. In that case, we can check the extensive list of available profiles and choose the one that applies to our photograph. Even if we are using something obscure, there is a good chance we will find it in the ever-growing list of supported lens/camera combinations.

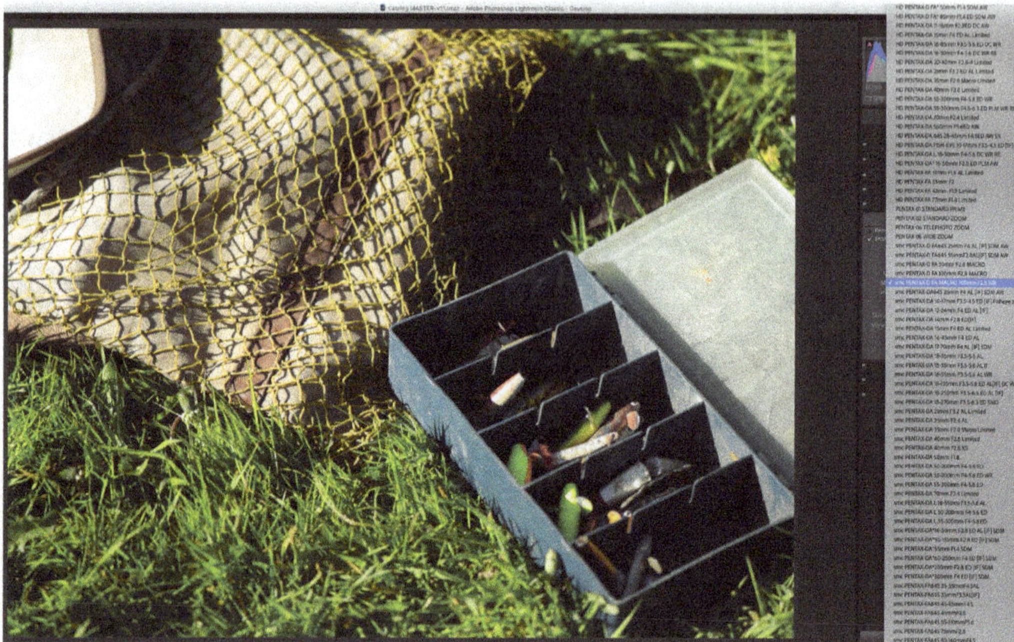

Figure 6.73 – Example of a fragment of the list of lenses for Pentax

Once an appropriate profile has been enabled, we can fine-tune it with the **Distortion** and **Vignetting** sliders on the bottom of the tab. **Distortion** is responsible for barreling and pincushion effects. **Barreling** is an effect that occurs mostly when using wide-angle lenses; the wider the lens, the more it may become pronounced. For example, imagine a large barrel and placing a print on it; the center of the image will be closer and "inflated," while the corners will be further away and "outwards." Additionally, all of the lines in the image will be slightly rounded, like ripples in water, with the center of the image being the central point of the distortion. The preceding screenshot shows a wildly exaggerated example but paired with the following screenshot, this should give you a good idea of how barreling works. Pincushioning is the opposite. Instead of placing an image on the outside of the barrel, imagine putting it on its inside wall. The third picture in *Figure 6.74* illustrates this. **Vignetting** is self-explanatory. Even though these two manual sliders are available, I have rarely had to use them as **Lens Corrections** always matched my expectations. Saying this, I understand there is a reason for their availability, and you can make use of them for creative reasons or to compensate for something I'm yet to encounter. If you deem these changes necessary, you can save them as a new profile; simply choose **Save New Lens Profile Defaults** in the **Setup** menu within the **Lens Corrections** tool.

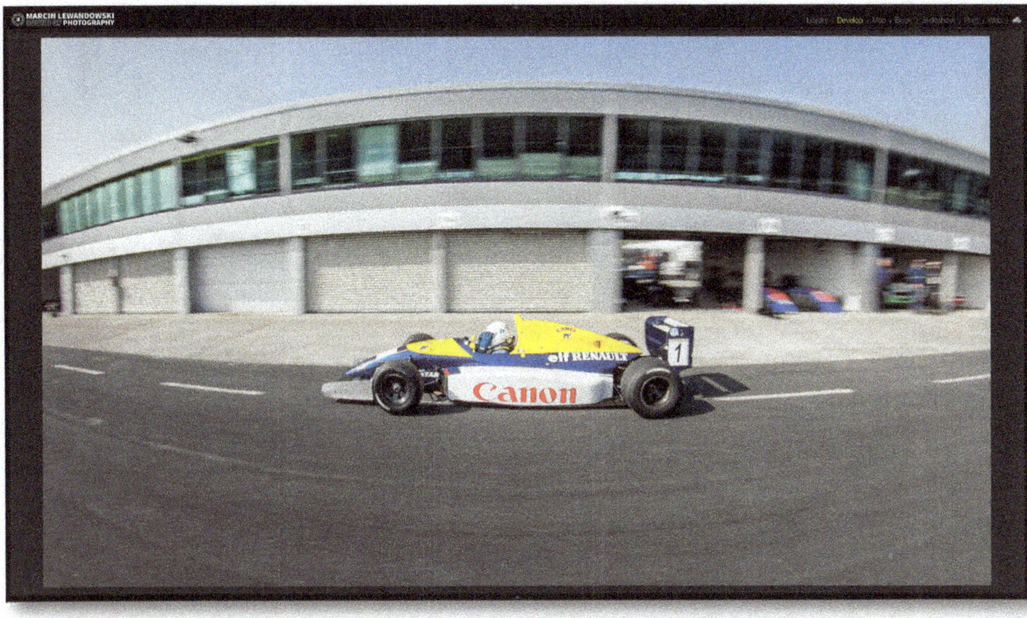

Figure 6.74 A

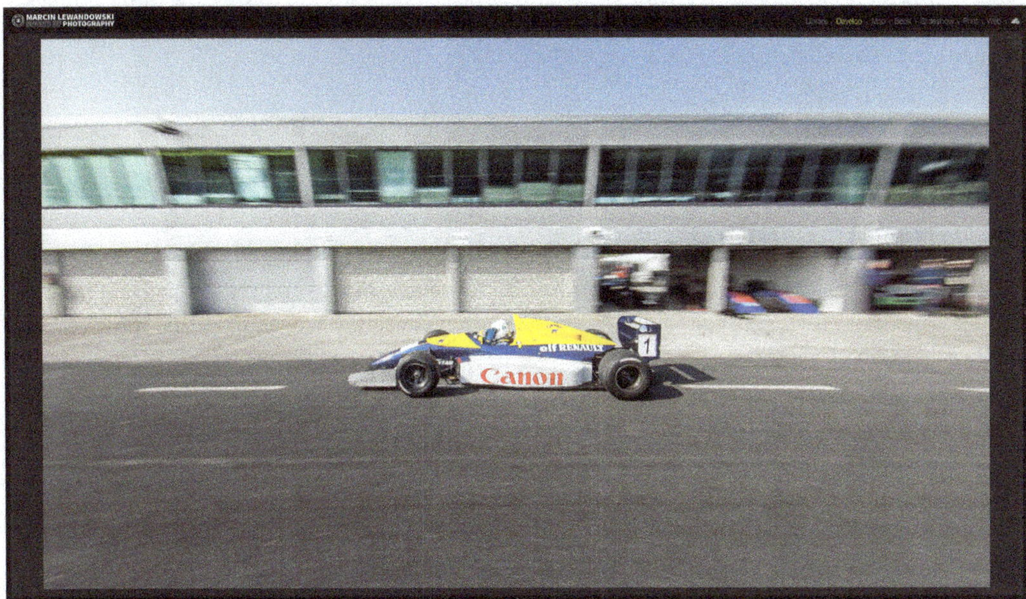

Figure 6.74 B

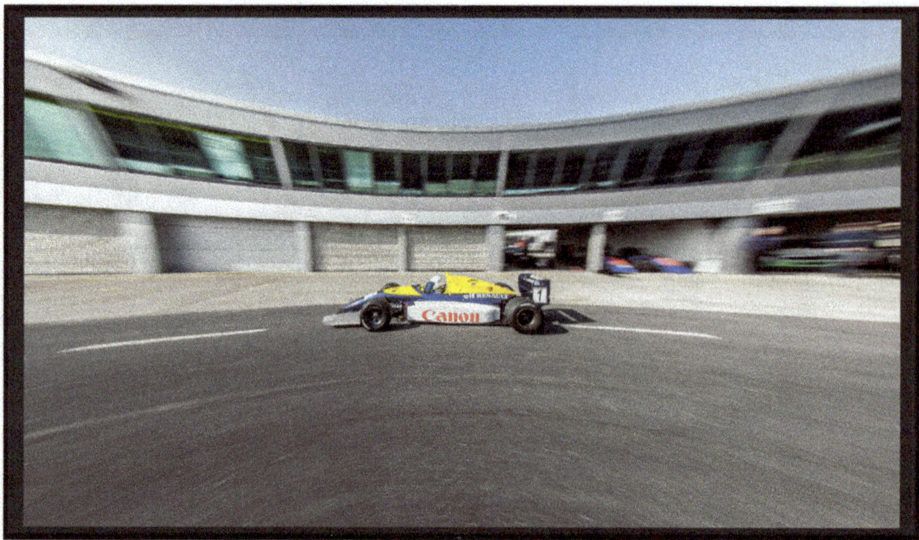

Figure 6.74 C – Image without corrections, image with barrelling and vignetting corrected, and an image with exaggerated pincushioning

We can always try applying profiles from a similar lens or just play around to see how other profiles work. It's an interesting way to see how various lenses need to be corrected, but I won't be geeking out here.

Manual mode

If Lightroom cannot locate a matching lens automatically and it does not have an associated profile, we need to hop into **Manual** mode.

With the **Distortion** slider, we can counteract any barreling and pincushioning – this is especially useful for wide-angle lenses. I suggest always checking the **Constrain Crop** box – this way, we can make sure there are no white borders around our photograph after counteracting barreling or rotation.

The next tool is **Defringe**. If we encounter any purple or green, **Defringe** will work wonders. First, zoom in to 200% or more to be more accurate, click on **Fringe Color Selector**, and choose a fringe color within the photograph. Don't worry if you miss the color; you will simply get a message saying that the chosen color is outside of the fringing hues, and you can try again. In 9 out of 10 situations, this will eliminate any fringing, and we can go back to editing. If this doesn't work as expected, we will be able to tweak it with the four range picking sliders below. Some fringing may remain if we only picked one of two fringing colors or, on rare occasions, **Defringe** may pick up colors from the photographed subjects. This can happen from time to time if we photograph something with a particular purple or green hue, but it's very rare, and the ranges of both fringing hues are set to protect natural colors, such as foliage.

Increasing the **Amount** sliders will apply a stronger defining effect. The sliders below the **Amount** sliders control the fringing color range we want to neutralize. Below them are sliders for broadening the range of color to defringe. These are called **Purple Hue** and **Green Hue**, respectively. Always make sure to not neutralize areas of the photograph outside of the fringing edges.

The last two sliders control the amount of **Vignetting**, which most often happens when photographing with wide-open apertures. Moving the amount sliders to the right will brighten the photograph's edges while moving it to the left will darken the edges. Moving the **Midpoint** slider to the right will reduce the area affected by the **Amount** slider. Moving it to the left will increase the size of the affected area and move the applied **Vignetting** counter-effect deeper into the photograph.

Now that we've fixed the problems that are caused by the insufficiencies of our gear, let's delve into correcting vertical and horizontal lines.

Transform

This is one of those tools that changed my workflow, and I can't imagine working without it anymore. It's practically impossible to always photograph with vertical and/or horizontal lines straight. **Transform** can help us correct any mistakes we make, straighten buildings, interiors, and more.

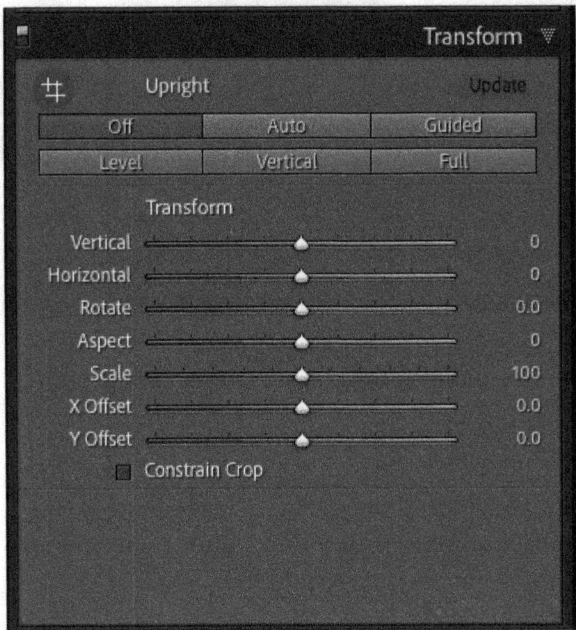

Figure 6.75 – The Transform panel

Let's look at what's available in the **Transform** panel in more detail:

- The **Level** function will do its best at fixing photographs by finding dominating horizontal lines within and leveling them.
- **Vertical** will work like the **Level** function but for the vertical lines, fixing the upright lines.
- **Auto** will analyze our image and try to straighten both horizontal and vertical lines, keeping our photograph's overall look and structure intact.
- **Full** is a combination of all of the aforementioned functions – **Level**, **Vertical**, and **Auto**.

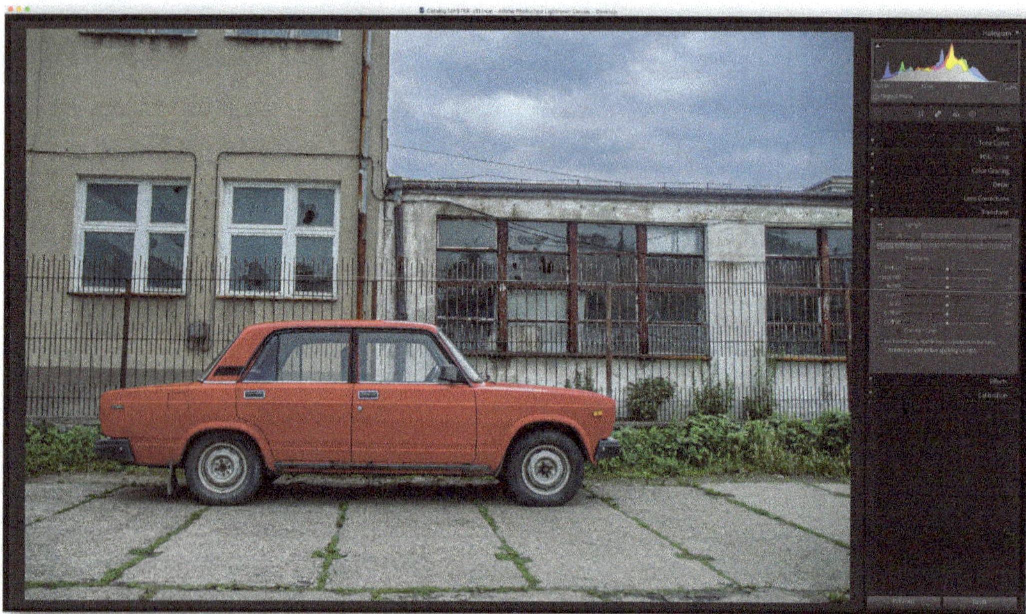

Figure 6.76 A

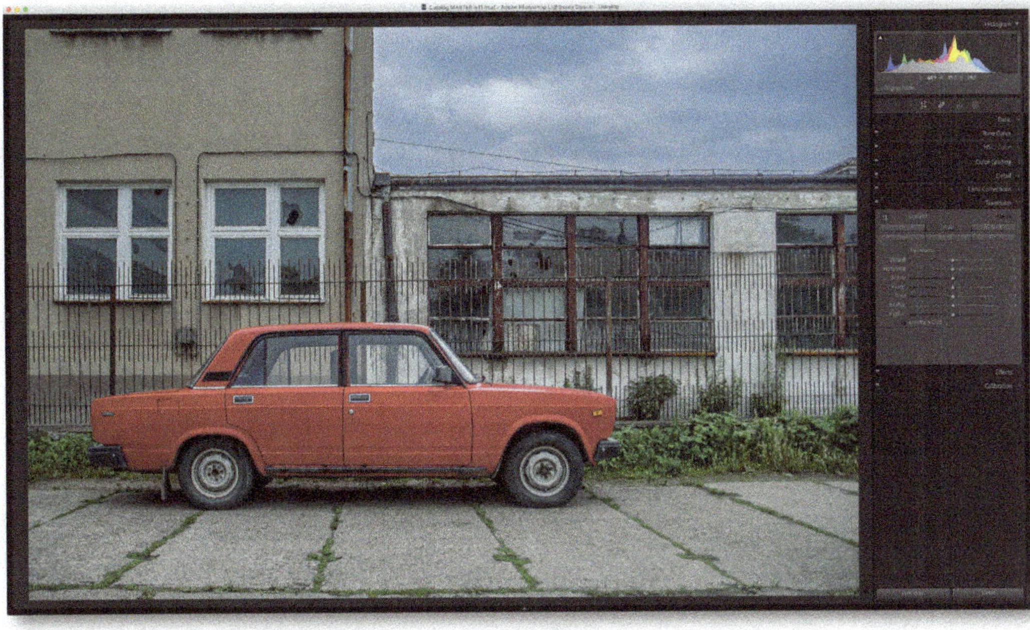

Figure 6.76 B – Original and Auto transformed photo

If there are many straight lines within the photograph, Lightroom may struggle to choose the right ones to follow, and the best course of action is to turn on the **Guided** function. Turning it on will allow us to draw up to two horizontal and up to two vertical lines to straighten the photograph. Now, we can decide which lines we would like to be vertical and/or horizontal and click-drag to draw a line along any of them. Notice that Lightroom will display a small square, magnifying the area where our mouse is currently pointing. Once we draw our line, we can adjust their anchor points or move them in any direction. We can even adjust the anchor points in Zoom (**Z**) mode. We will get the best results by drawing four lines (two vertical and two horizontal). The wider they are distributed, the more accurate the final result will be. Checking the **Constrain Crop** button will keep the crop within the photograph, ensuring there is no white area around it, keeping the photograph's original aspect ratio.

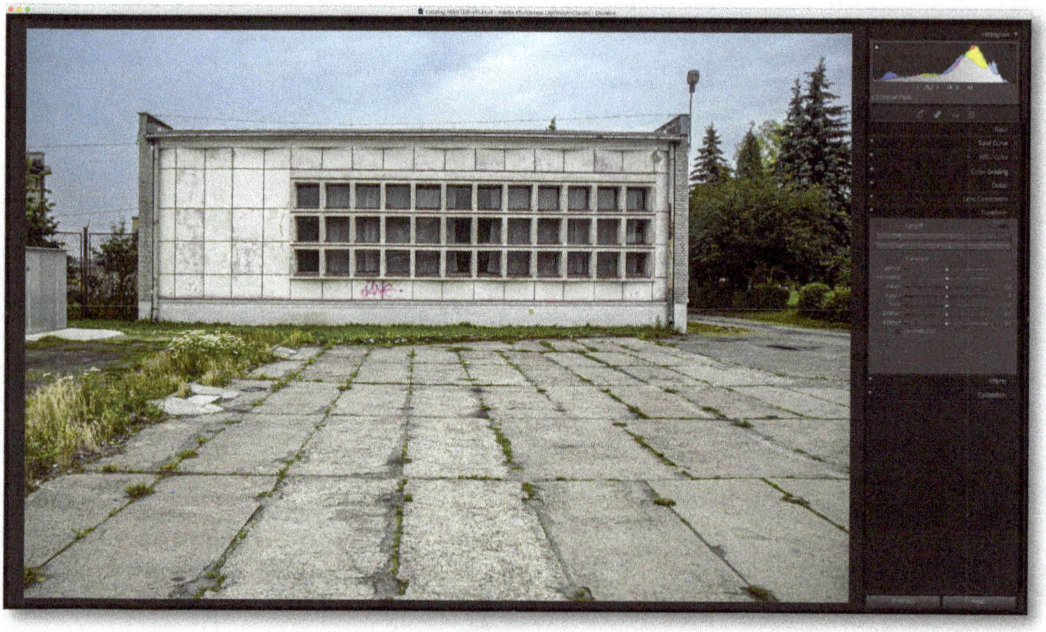

Figure 6.77 – Transformation guides applied to outline straight lines of the pictured building

If none of these functions work for us or we want to do any manual tweaking, we can use the seven available sliders (see *Figure 6.77*) and manually adjust the perspective in our photograph.

Effects

The **Effects** tab provides us with two very nice visual effects, called **Post-Crop Vignetting** and **Grain**, which provide us with an extra bit of creativity.

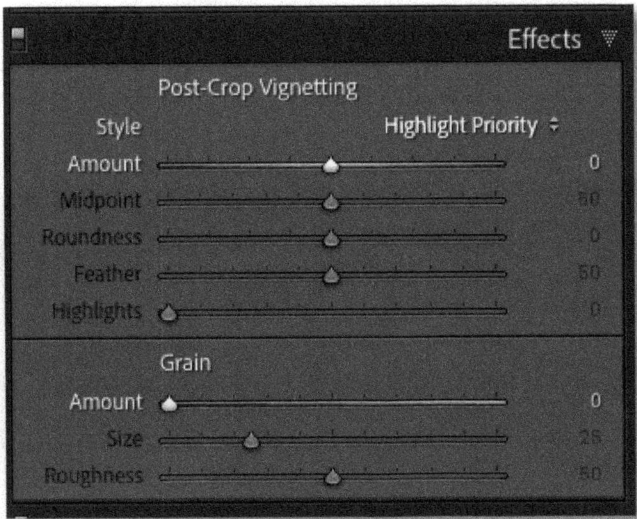

Figure 6.78 – The Effects panel

Post-Crop Vignetting

In the **Style** menu, we can choose three modes that will apply the vignette effect, each in a slightly different way. **Highlight Priority**, which is also our default **Style**, will try to recover some of the highlights around the edges under the vignette effect. **Color Priority** will ensure no color shifts in the edges after **Post-Crop Vignetting** is applied. Finally, **Paint overlay** will only apply a dark overlay that looks dull, especially on printed photographs. Let's have a look at the sliders under **Post-Crop Vignetting**:

- **Amount**: Moving the slider to the left or right controls how strong our vignette will be. The left-hand side of the slider makes our vignette darker, while the right-hand side of the slider makes the vignette white.
- **Midpoint**: This slider controls how deep into the image our vignette will fall. Moving **Midpoint** to the right will shift the strength of the vignetting effect into the photograph's corners, while moving the slider to the left will bring the effect deep into the picture.
- **Roundness**: Adjusting this slider to the right will make the vignette round up to a perfectly circular shape when at a **+100** setting. Moving the slider to the left will make it more rectangular, with only the edges rounded.
- **Feather**: With this slider, we can adjust the softness of the vignette edges, from a harsh look when at **0** to a very soft one at **100**.
- **Highlights**: This allows us to recover highlights from under the vignette effect.

Using **Vignetting** requires a bit of practice, but as with many tools, sometimes, "less is more." You will have to follow your gut feeling on this one. I tend to make it barely visible, just a visual hint leading the viewer's attention to the center of the photograph. Now and then, I may choose something much stronger if it fits the purpose, especially when it's my creative choice.

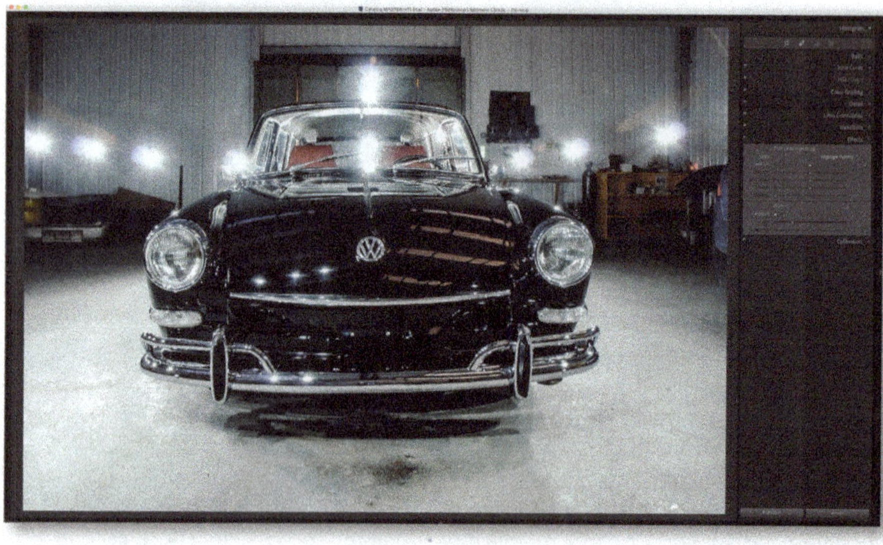

Figure 6.79 A

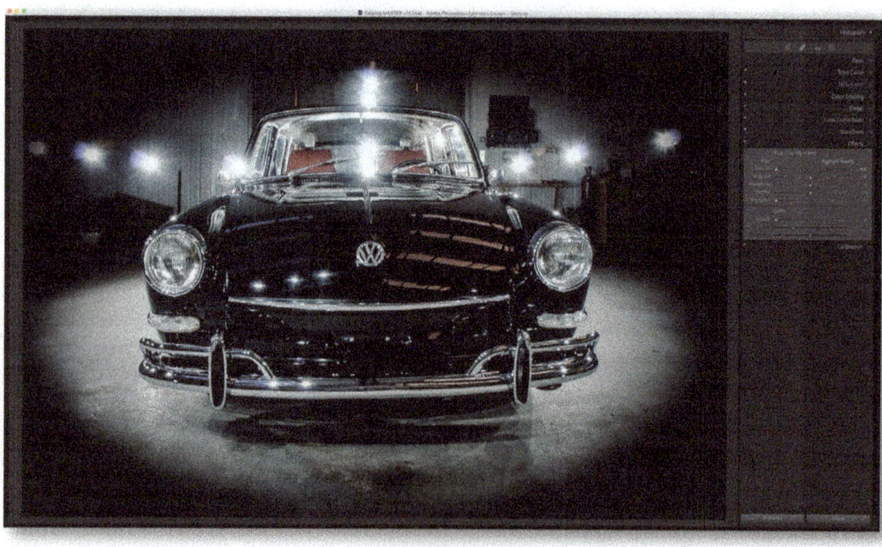

Figure 6.79 B

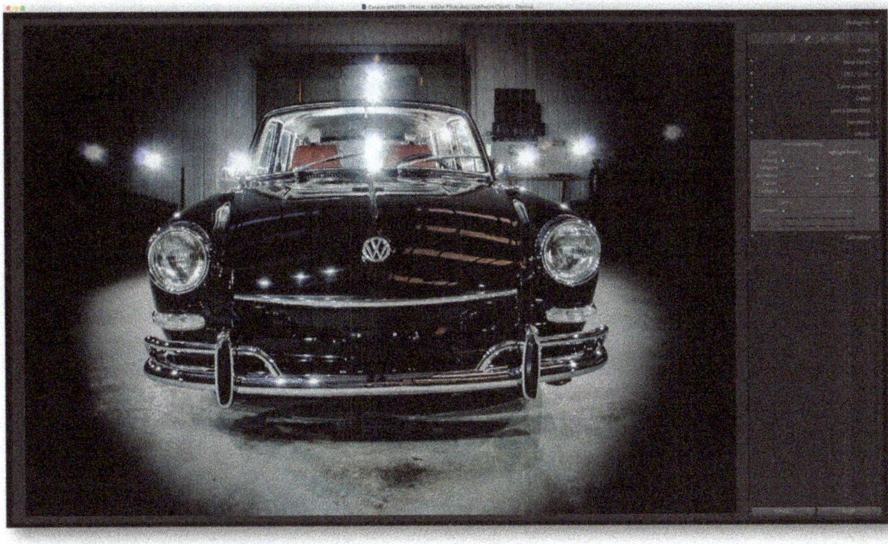

Figure 6.79 C

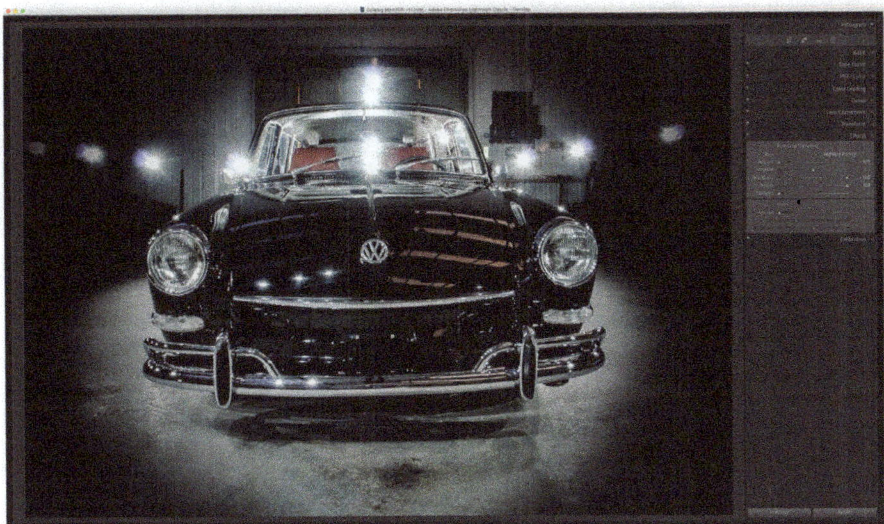

Figure 6.79 D

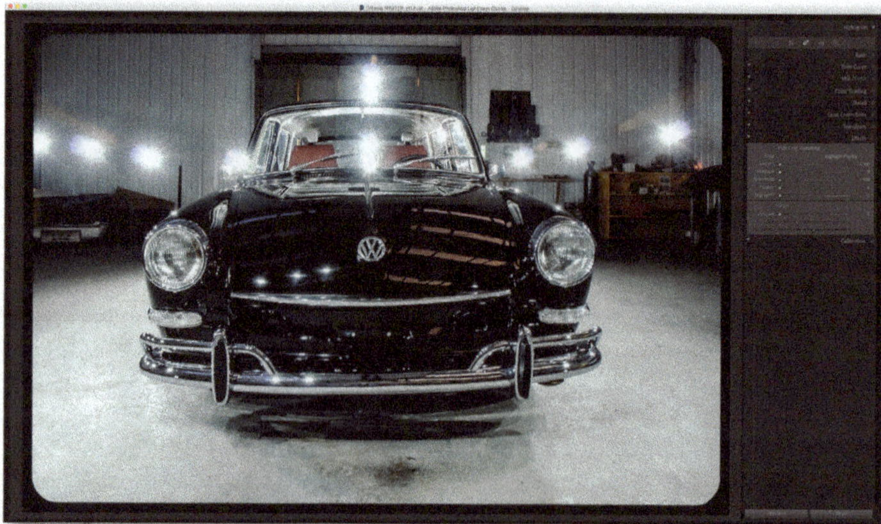

Figure 6.79 E

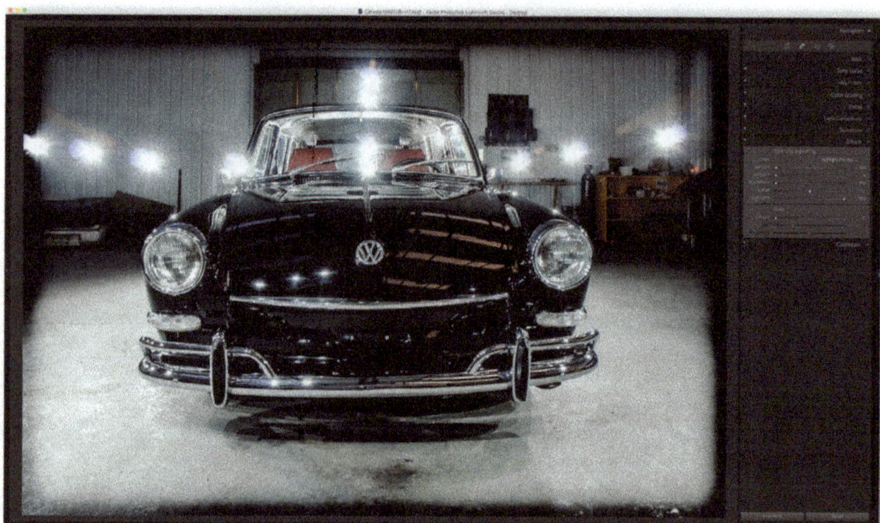

Figure 6.79 F – The original photo and examples of different types of possible vignettes

Grain

This set of sliders allows us to simulate the grain effect of negative/film/analog photographs. Grain is much different from digital noise and has a much more organic look and feel, even when artificially generated.

Just as with working on sharpness, I advise you to use it at 100% magnification to see how it's applied. I also suggest looking at a sharp image area while adding the **Grain** effect. Here are the sliders under **Grain**:

- **Amount**: Moving it to the right will gradually apply a stronger grain effect to our photograph and increase the strength of the grain's contrast.
- **Size**: This will increase the physical size of the added grain, and it will also start visually softening it once we move beyond the default value of **25**.
- **Roughness**: This controls how uniform the distribution of the **Grain** effect is. It looks the most natural and organic around a value of **50**.

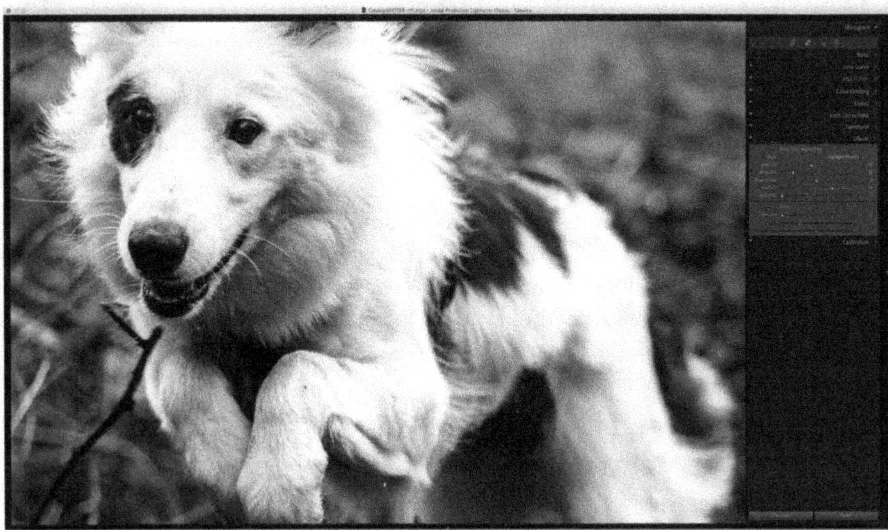

Figure 6.80 A

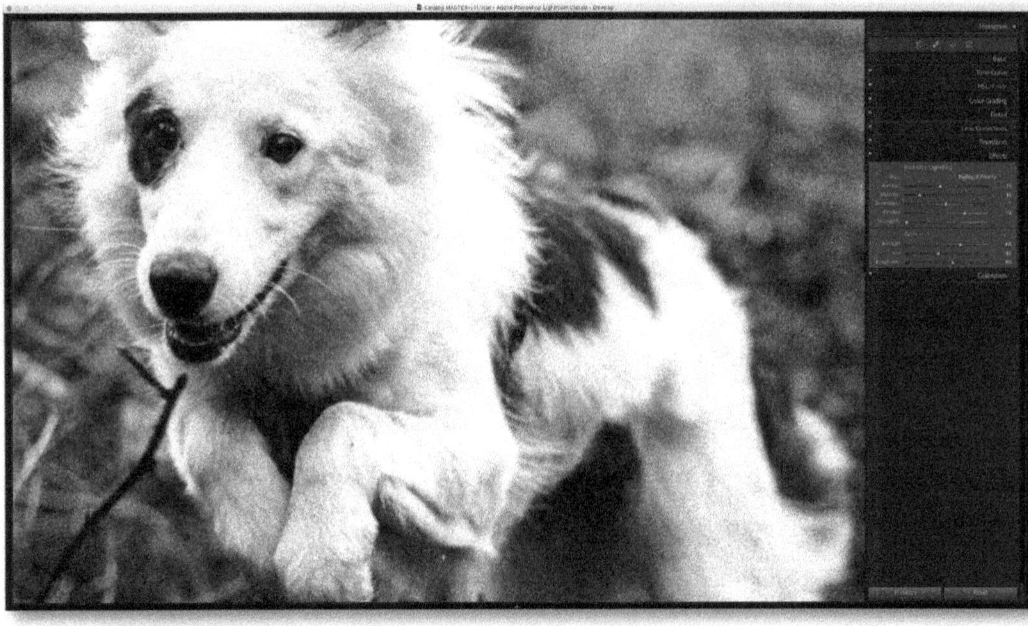

Figure 6.80 B – A photo with no Grain applied and an example of the Grain effect

> **Tip**
>
> If you have a slightly soft photograph with a considerable amount of digital noise, instead of trying to excessively counteract that within the **Detail** panel, first, dial any changes that have been made in the **Detail** tab down by about 60-80% of what you did. Then, go back to the **Effects** tab and apply a little bit of Grain until you see the image look more uniform and sharper. It works best on high ISO, low-MP images, and it's great when working on older images, so knowing this trick may come in handy from time to time.

Calibration

Remember when I mentioned that **Tone Curve** is the most feared tab? Welcome to **Calibration**, the most overlooked tab of them all.

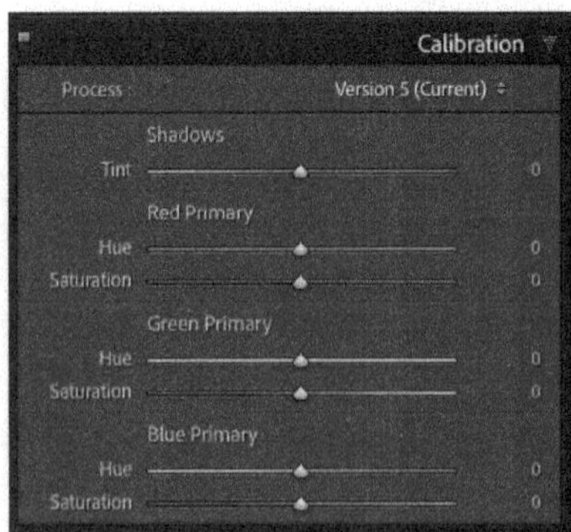

Figure 6.81 – The Calibration panel

Version tells us which Adobe Camera Raw engine our version of Lightroom is using for the currently opened image. If you are on Lightroom Classic, then it should always be set to the latest version. This setting is applied to all newly imported images. Suppose you, however, look through your archives, coming back to edit older photographs that have been sitting in Lightroom for a while. This might be set to an older version, which means that some functionality will be limited or even unavailable. When you update the version, some images may look like they were processed slightly differently, but you will notice less fringing and noise, especially in the shadow areas. Suppose you are planning to update the process version for a large number of photographs. In that case, I strongly suggest that you familiarize yourself with the visual impact this update will have on your images. Don't do it by syncing large numbers but one by one until you can understand the impact of the version change.

The seven sliders under **Process** give us powerful color controls that we can use for anything, from color and tint corrections to very potent grading options.

The **Shadows** slider is responsible for the tint in shadow areas. We can nudge it into the same two areas as **White Balance**, but it has a more subtle effect.

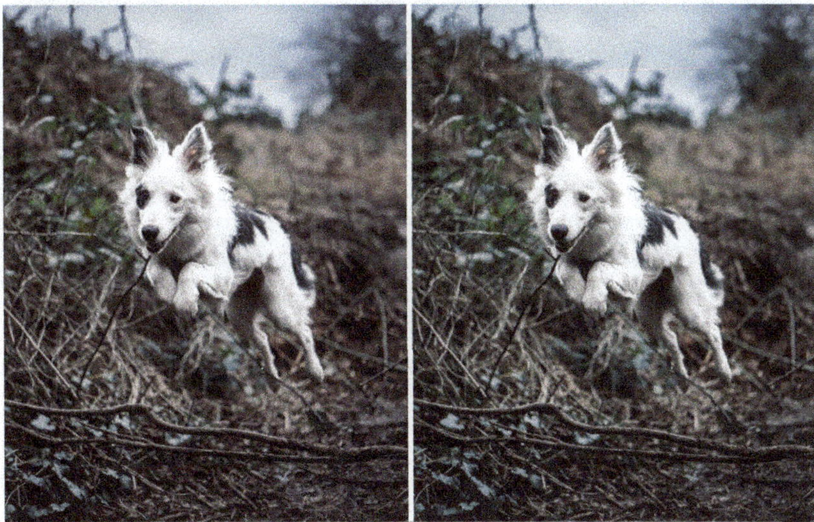

Figure 6.82 – The original photo adjusted to taste (left) and the same photo (right) with Shadows Tint moved -24 into greens to remove the slight purple coloring

We unlock real power with the next three pairs of sliders, which control how the primary RGB colors are mixed. We can change the hue and saturation of each of the three primary colors to create a foundation for all of the other edits. By increasing or decreasing the **Hue** and **Saturation** values, we can affect how a mixture of RGB colors is represented within the photograph. This gives us great potential for new possibilities and experimentation to create interesting color recipes for our pictures.

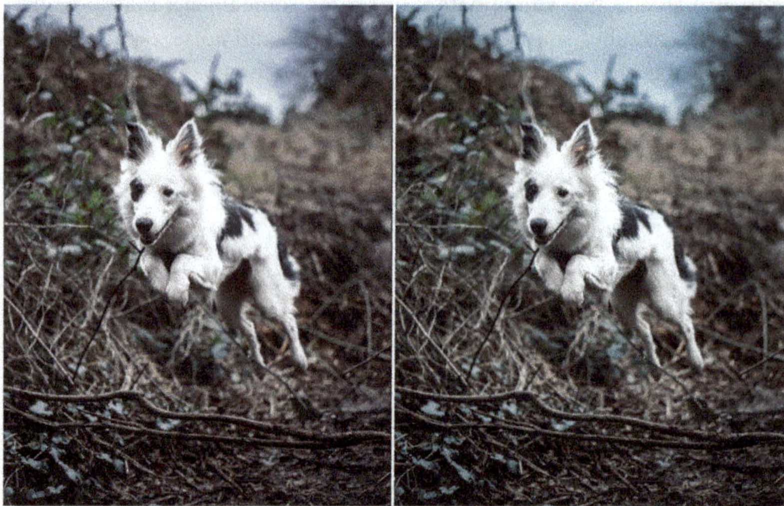

Figure 6.83 A

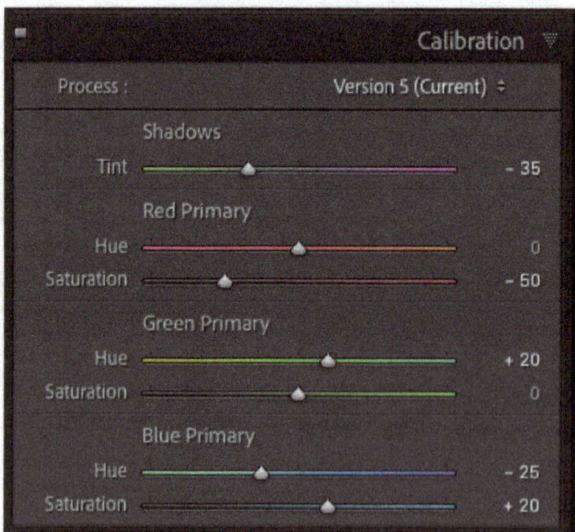

Figure 6.83 B – The original photo adjusted to taste and the photo with the base color values changed in the Calibration panel

Additional information and functions outside the right panel

There are two additional buttons on the bottom of our right panel in **Develop module** – **Previous** and **Reset**.

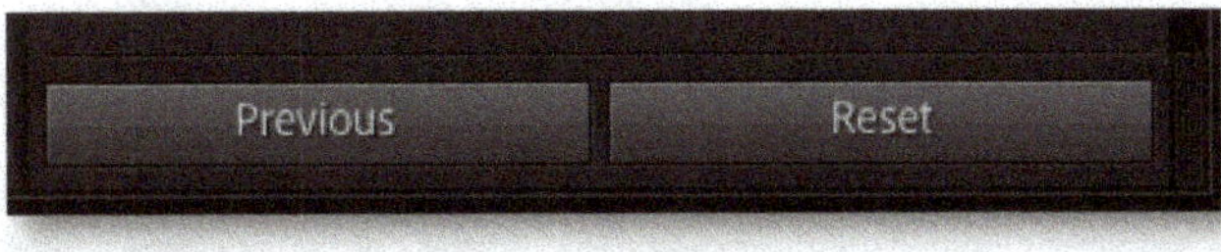

Figure 6.84 – The Previous and Reset buttons

The **Previous** button copies all of the settings from the last photograph and applies them to the currently viewed one. The only settings that aren't copied are the AI masks: **Select Sky** and **Select Subject**. We can also use the "*Alt* + *Cmd* + *V*" keyboard shortcut.

Clicking **Reset** will bring the photograph to its original state. We can also use the "*Shift* + *Cmd* + *R*" keyboard shortcut.

If more than one photograph is selected, Lightroom will replace the **Previous** button with the **Sync...** button. **Sync...** will copy all the settings we have from the highlighted photograph to all the other selected photos. Once we click on **Sync...**, we can choose which settings we would like to synchronize between the selected photographs.

Notice that when more than one photo is selected, the photo with a lighter gray frame is the photo that we will be copying our photographs from.

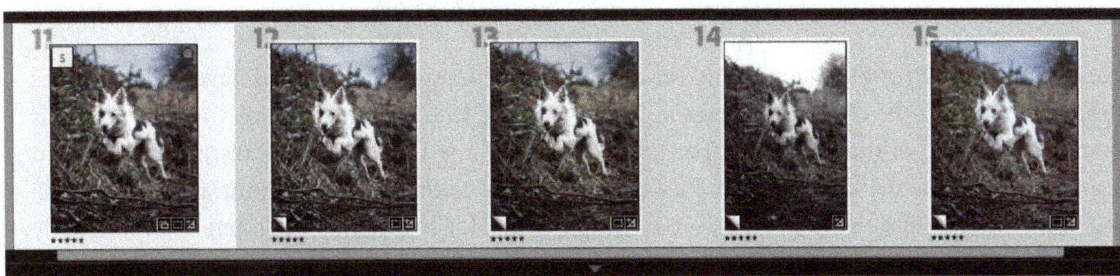

Figure 6.85 – The first photo is a lighter gray

If you are sure about your choice of settings and don't want to choose which ones will be used for syncing again, hold down the "*Alt*" key – this will change **Sync...** into **Sync** (notice the disappearance of the ellipsis). This will automatically sync the settings we chose when we were using the **Sync...** feature.

Lastly, while holding down the "*Cmd*" key, **Sync...** will change into **Auto Sync**. Clicking on **Auto Sync** will lock the little switch next to it, which is, by the way, available to us all the time while we are in the Develop module. Once **Auto Sync** is enabled, and we have more than one picture selected, all the adjustments that have been applied to the currently developed photograph will also be applied to each other selected photograph.

Following the **Develop** panel's functions in a clockwise motion, we stumble upon **Soft Proofing**, which is located at the very end of the **Tools** tab under the photograph we are working on. It's one of those functions that opens the doors to another dimension.

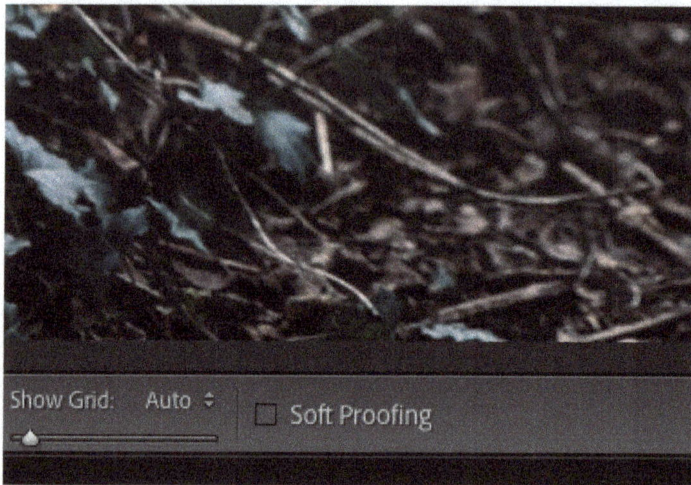

Figure 6.86 – The Soft Proofing checkbox

Once enabled, **Soft Proofing** allows us to see a good approximation of how our image will look once we print it, based on the chosen ICC profile. Without going into too much detail, the ICC profile is like an identity card of the printing paper and will adjust how Lightroom will print each color on the specific paper/printer combination. Lightroom displays colors using the monitor's color profile; using different color profiles is a simulation of the paper's color space. This will often be significantly different from the one we view on our screen.

Every professional paper manufacturer provides ICC profiles for all combinations of their papers on all different major printers. Once you have profiles installed on your computer, you can choose them from the **Profile** menu, located under **Histogram**. This function is only available while we are in **Soft Proofing** mode. If the profile we would like to use is not on the list, simply click **Other...** and check the boxes next to the profiles you would like to use. They will be added to the list and available to choose from for **a Soft Proofing** preview.

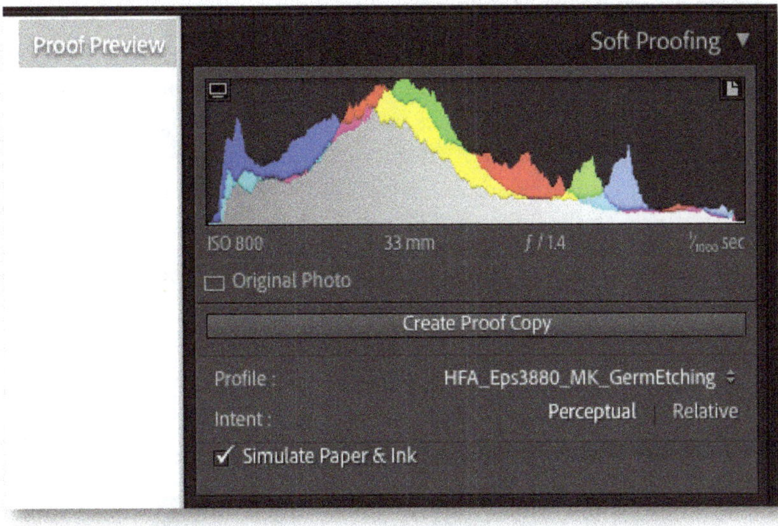

Figure 6.87 – The Soft Proofing panel with an assigned ICC profile

While we are working with the **Histogram** tool, please notice that the clipping icons changed to different ones. **Black Clipping Warning** has been replaced with **Monitor Gamut Warning**, while **White Clipping Warning** has been replaced with **Destination Gamut Warning**:

- **Monitor Gamut Warning** indicates which areas of the photograph are outside our monitor's display capabilities by highlighting them in blue.
- **Destination Gamut Warning** highlights areas of the photograph that are beyond the printer's capabilities to render in red.

By choosing a different profile than the one in our display, we can simulate how the photograph will look in a different color space. There are three other settings here, as follows:

- **Intent** specifies how Lightroom will convert the color space.
- **Perceptual** converts the colors so that they will look as natural as possible to the human eye. Some colors may change slightly, but we will perceive the relationships between colors as natural. **Perceptual** works especially well with highly saturated hues.
- **Relative** converts all out of gamut colors into the closest values that can be reproduced within the chosen destinations' color space.

Some profiles will also have the option **Simulate Paper & Ink**, which will turn all of the whites in our photograph into the color of the paper we will be printing on. Blacks will turn to shades of gray, simulating the look of a printer's black ink on our chosen paper.

From here, we can tweak our photograph further to match our expected printing results. By moving any sliders within the Develop module, Lightroom will immediately ask if we would like to **Undo**, **Make This a Proof**, or **Create Proof Copy**. I advise choosing the third option and creating a new copy to work with. Any changes we make to the photograph will be reflected in a different-looking, re-adjusted photograph after we exit **Soft Proofing** mode. I suggest always choosing **Create Proof Copy** and keeping the **Don't show again** option unchecked. This way, we will avoid nasty surprises in the future.

We just covered all of the functions that are available on the right-hand side of the Develop module. However, there is much more to work with on the left-hand side.

The left-hand side of the Develop module

Let's dive deeper into the left-hand side of the Develop module:

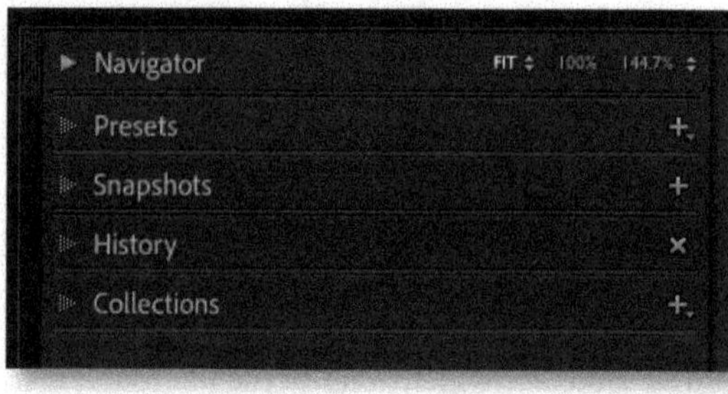

Figure 6.88 – The panels that are available on the left-hand side of the Develop module

Let's look at the options in more detail:

- **Navigator**: **Navigator** has the same functionality as the **Navigator** tool within the Library module.
- **Presets**: Presets are predefined combinations of settings that we can use to quickly develop our photographs or something to skim through for inspiration when we are trying to find the look for our photograph. The presets that come with Lightroom Classic range from very basic, applying only small changes to color and luminosity, to very elaborate ones that shift primary colors in **Calibration** combined with **Color Grading** and **Tone Curve** modifications. What's more important is that we can create our own presets and do so on a completely practical level to help us work quicker and more efficiently. You can create your own preset by clicking on the plus (+) sign on top of the **Presets** tab and choosing the settings you would like to include in it. You may, for example, create a set of presets to control different sharpening/noise control combinations or create signatory **Color Grading** recipes that you can use in various scenarios. Some photographers use it sporadically; for some, it's their go-to solution when working on large sets of photographs. Whichever way you decide to use them, it's a great asset to have at your disposal.

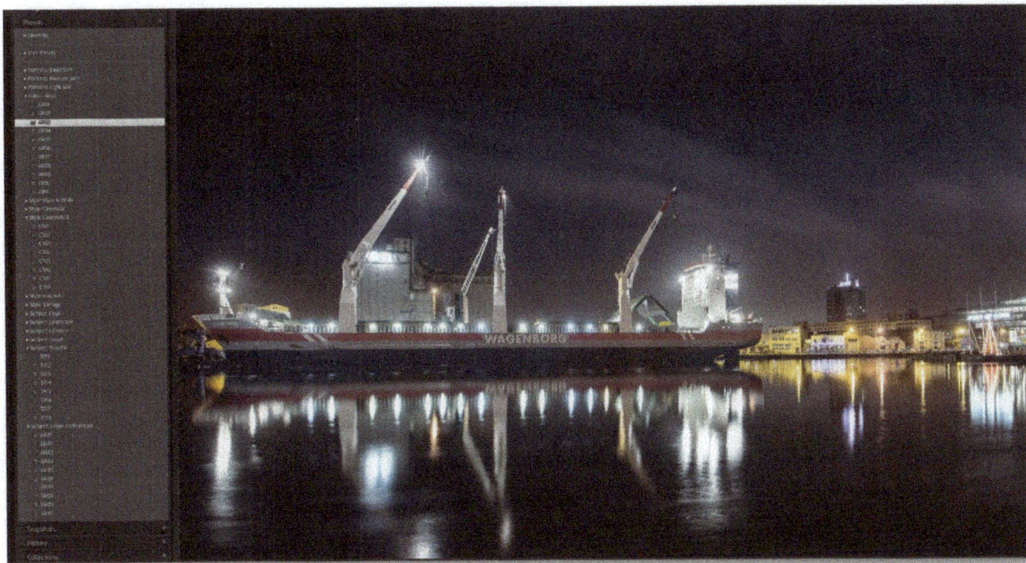

Figure 6.89 A

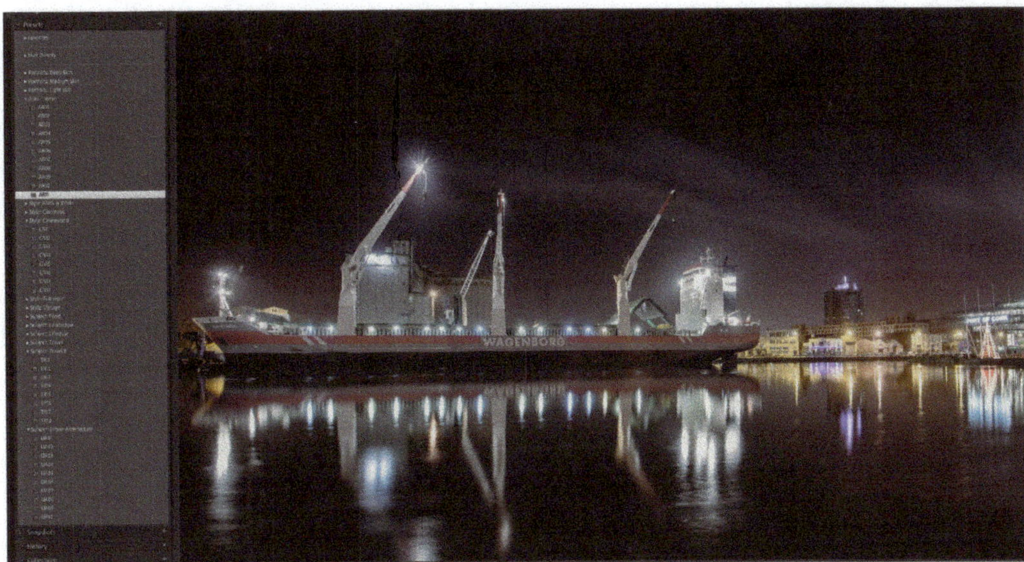

Figure 6.89 B

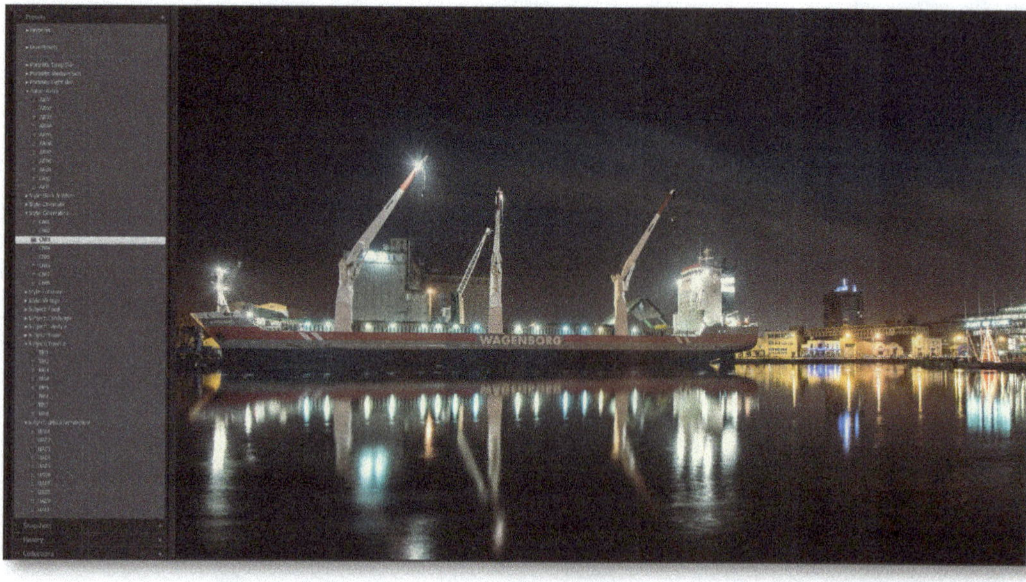

Figure 6.89 C

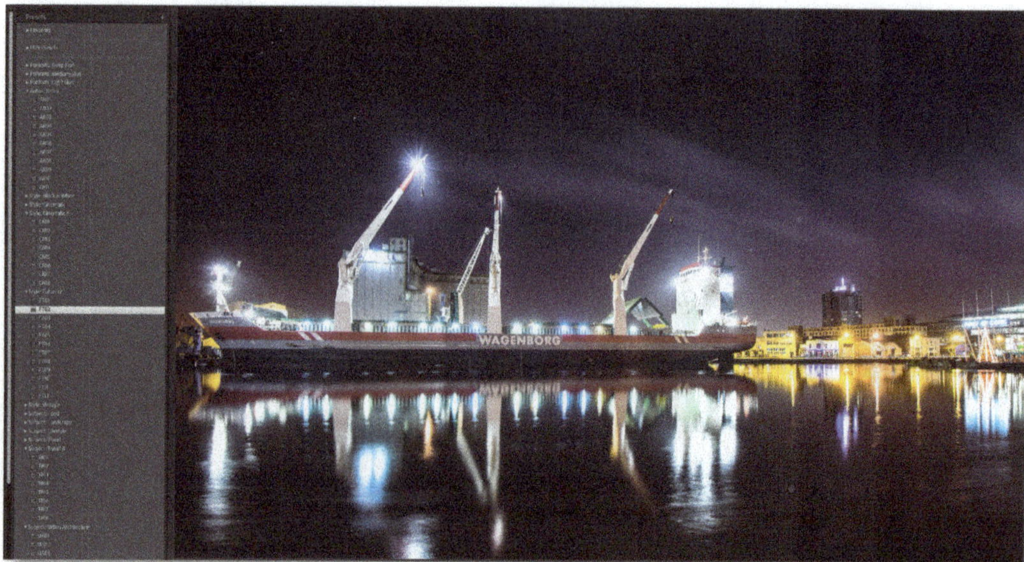

Figure 6.89 D

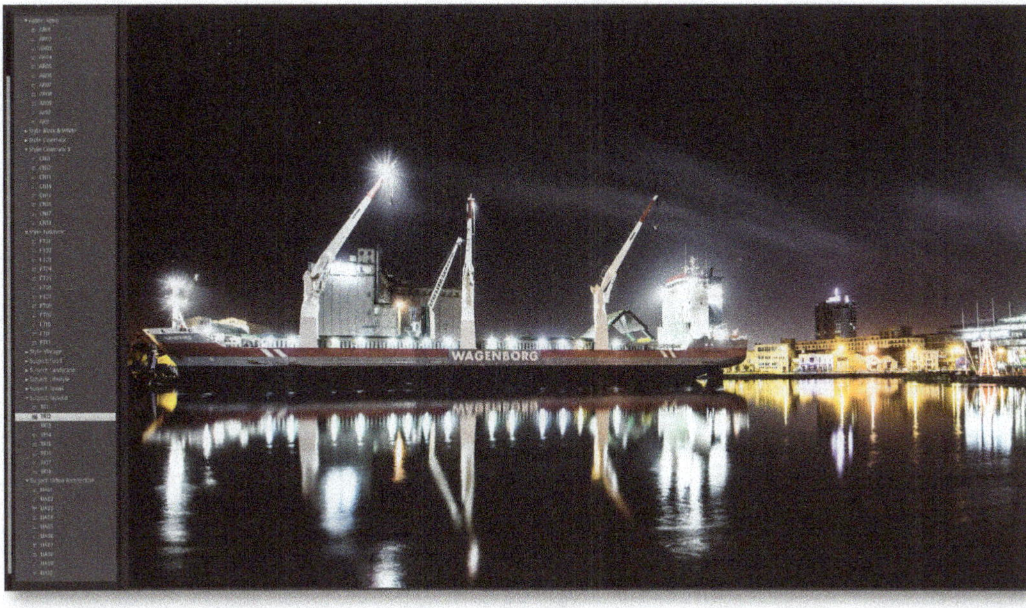

Figure 6.89 E

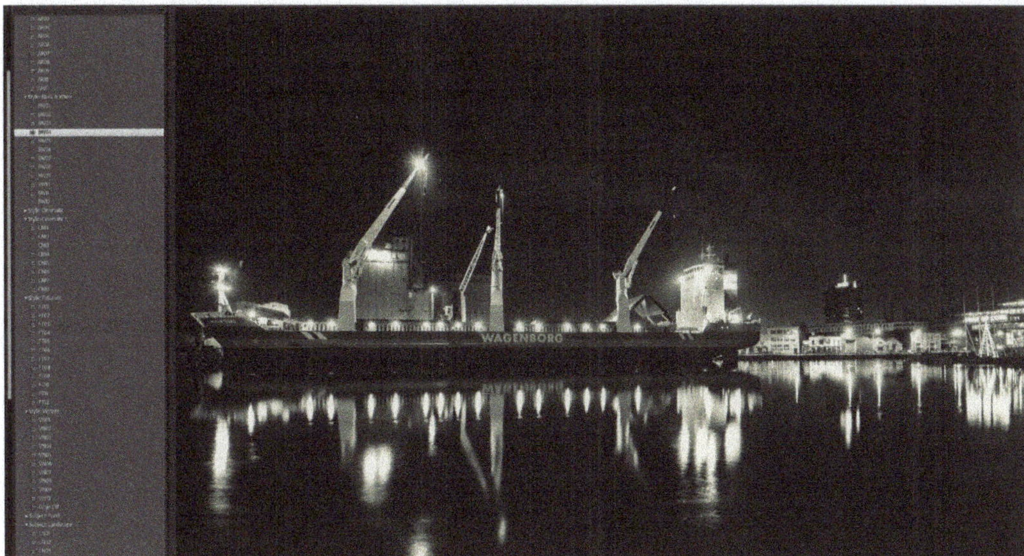

Figure 6.89 F – Examples of built-in presets

- **Snapshots**: This allows us to save the state of our photograph during any stage of the development process. Let's say that we have an idea – a new direction we would like to test. Instead of creating a new virtual copy or remembering where in **History** (the tab below **Snapshots**) we branched out, we can create a snapshot of the current status by pressing the + button or using the "*Cmd* + *N*" keyboard shortcut. This action will open a small popup that states the current date and time and the snapshot's name. We can – and should – change this name to something more descriptive that fits our workflow and the way we think. Once we've created a new snapshot, we can continue working and come back to it if we don't like the new look and want to continue where we left off. I prefer working with Virtual Copies, but many photographers love using **Snapshots** – it's a matter of your workflow and preference. If we are aware of it, it may come in handy; if not, we can even remove this tab from the menu.
- **History**: This is an immensely powerful feature, and it stores each developed state of every single photograph in the Lightroom library. We can go back to any point of the editing process and create a **Virtual Copy** or a **Snapshot. History** will also store other important events, such as printing and exporting, as well as the date and time of each such event.
- **Collection**: Last but not least, we have access to the **Collections** tab, which has the same functionality that it does within the Library module.

At the very bottom, there are an additional two buttons that we can use to **Copy** and **Paste** settings from and to any photograph. Clicking on the **Copy** button will open a pop-up menu that looks exactly like the **Sync** menu. We can choose all the settings we would like to copy and, after switching to another image, click the **Paste** button. These two options have the "*Cmd* + *C*" and "*Cmd* + *V*" keyboard shortcuts, respectively.

With that, we have covered the functionality of the Develop module.

Summary

Even the best captures require some level of development. For example, if we shoot `.jpg` images, the development process might be as simple as making contrast and sharpness fixes, but for those who decide to save photographs in their native RAW format, the **Develop** panel opens doors to creating something truly unique. I always looked at it like I looked at polishing gemstones. Even a simple rock, which I use here as a metaphor for a photograph that is not unique, can be polished to look in the best possible way. Now, imagine a real gem, such as an uncut diamond; the **Develop** panel is our workshop to bring the best out of it. Digital cameras store a lot of information that we can work with later, and just the **Shadows/Highlights** recovery in the **Basic** panel can be a game-changer in terms of the photograph's look. When we stack this with the capability to work with masks, color grading, spot removal, or fixing perspective, Lightroom becomes a tool that is inseparable from our photography workflow.

In the next chapter, we will look at the various **Export** settings and get our carefully edited images out of Lightroom and into the world so that they can be shared with our audience.

Section 3: Exploring the Export, Print, Book, and Slideshow Modules

What would be the point of all the hard work we did in *Sections 1* and *2* if we kept it all hidden in our computer? Even if all we want to do with the photographs is to share them with our closest family members, Lightroom will help us to do so on a number of different levels, from a simple export in a social-media-friendly format to creating photographic prints and designing a photobook. We will also look at a few additional bits of functionality and then finally, wrap the book up with a concise summary.

In this section, we will cover the following topics:

- *Chapter 7, Get Them All Out of Lightroom – Exporting for Work and Leisure*
- *Chapter 8, Get Them All Out – Using the Print and Book Modules*
- *Chapter 9, Slideshow, Map, and Web Modules*
- *Chapter 10, Final Notes and Summary*

7

Get Them All Out of Lightroom – Exporting for Work and Leisure

You did all the hard work to capture the images, edit them, and develop them to perfection. Now it's time to share them with the world and to do that, we need to *get them out of Lightroom*.

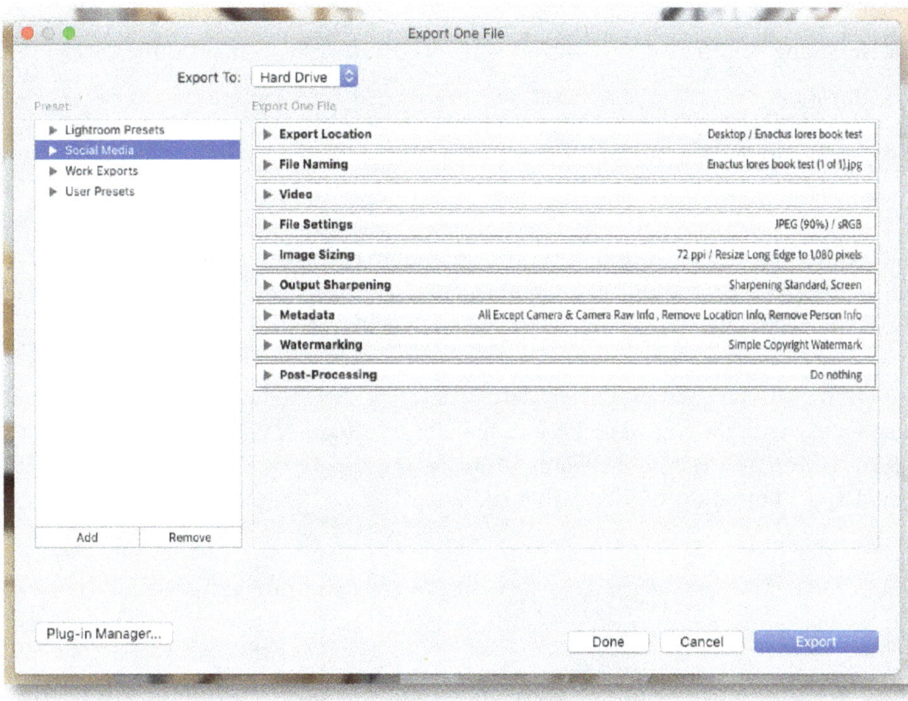

Figure 7.1 – Export dialog

There are many different requirements placed on photographers regarding the final file format. Press photographers will look for different settings from fine art photographers; Instagram has optimal file requirements, and all competition submissions have file requirements. Do you want your clients to know what camera and settings you used or not? Do you want the print house to receive optimized files for that large canvas print? This chapter will deal with all of these questions and a few more.

In this chapter, we will cover each of the nine tabs plus one additional menu, followed by a section on the presets:

- Exporting images
- The Export Location tab
- File naming
- Video
- File settings
- Image sizing
- Output sharpening
- Metadata
- Watermarking
- Post-processing
- Watermark editor
- Creating presets

By the end of this chapter, you will be able to comfortably export your photographs into desired formats and adhere to any requirements given by external services, clients, or even friends and family.

Exporting images

To learn about exporting, we must go back to the Library Module. When we learned about it in *Chapter 3, Tools Available Within the Library Module*, and *Chapter 4, Folders and Collections*, we skipped the **Export** button to come back to it later.

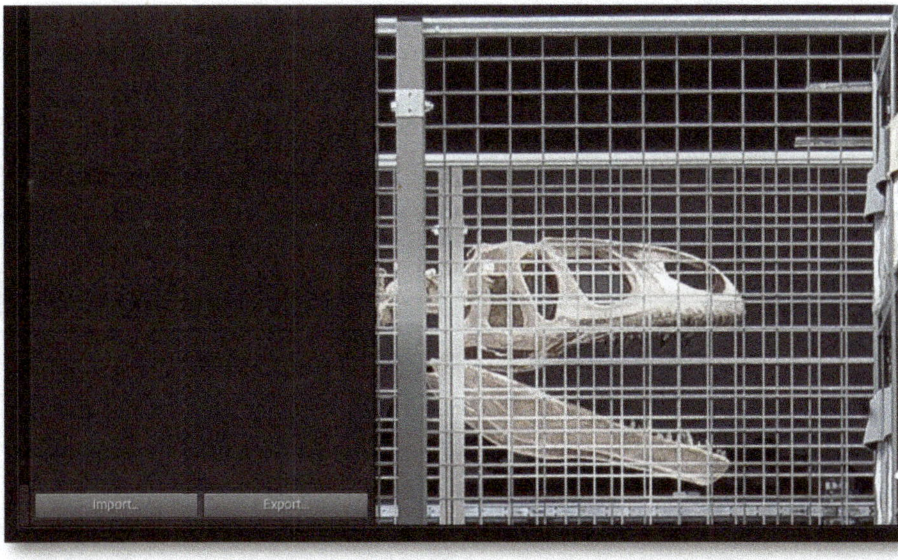

Figure 7.2 – Export button

As you can imagine, using the **Export** button at the bottom of the left panel is not the only way to access the **Export** dialog. We can open it by right-clicking on a photograph or group of pictures in the ever-present filmstrip.

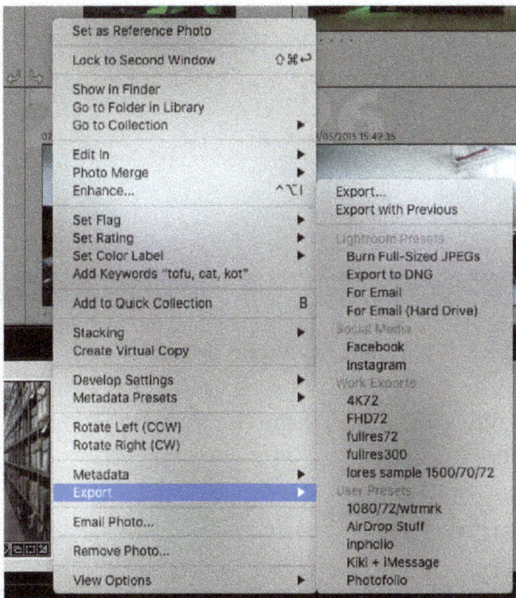

Figure 7.3 – Right-click the Export menu

The **Export** button will open a new window with all export-related settings. Right-clicking on a picture will allow us to either open the **Export** dialog, use the settings we used during our previous export (**Export with Previous**), or use one of the presets. We will return to it once we know more about the different export options. Lastly, we can use the keyboard shortcut "*Shift⌘E*".

The **Export** dialog is split into two panels. The left panel lists all available presets, from the few default ones that come with Lightroom (listed under **Lightroom Presets**) to our personal ones, which we will learn to create towards the end of this chapter.

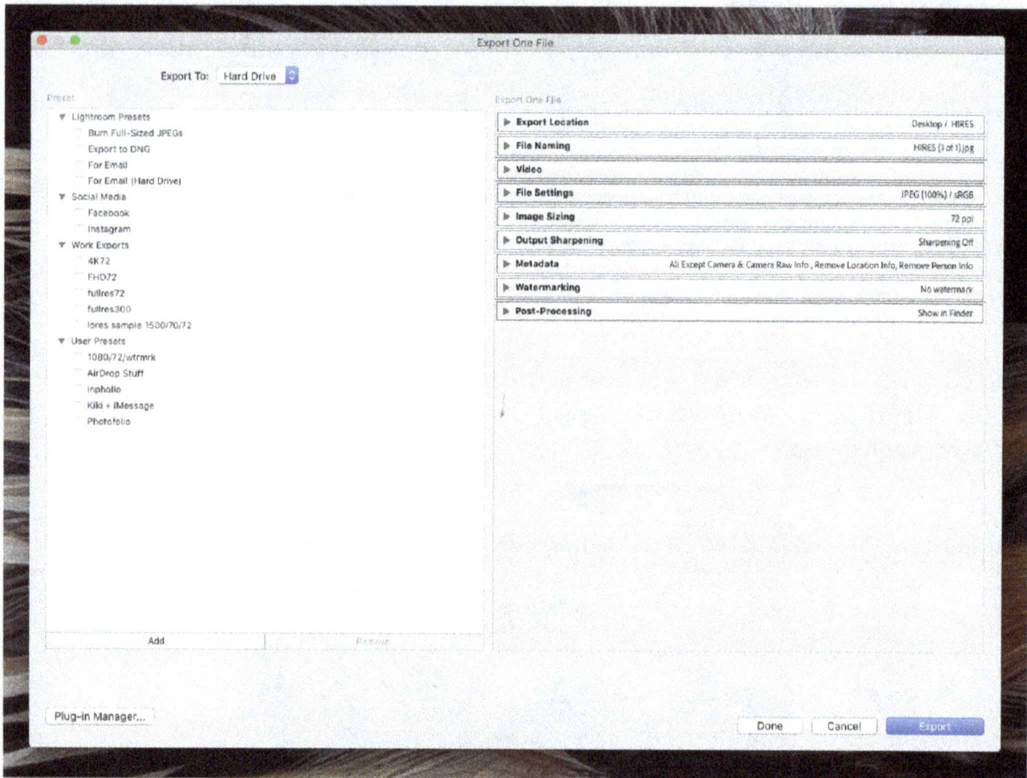

Figure 7.4 – Export dialog

The right panel divides into nine tabs with all the necessary options. We will start from the top and look at them from top to bottom.

The Export Location tab

Let's delve into the **Export To** and **Existing Files** menus inside the **Export Location** tab.

Export To

Depending on your workflow and preferences, there are a few different paths we can take when we choose where we want to export our images.

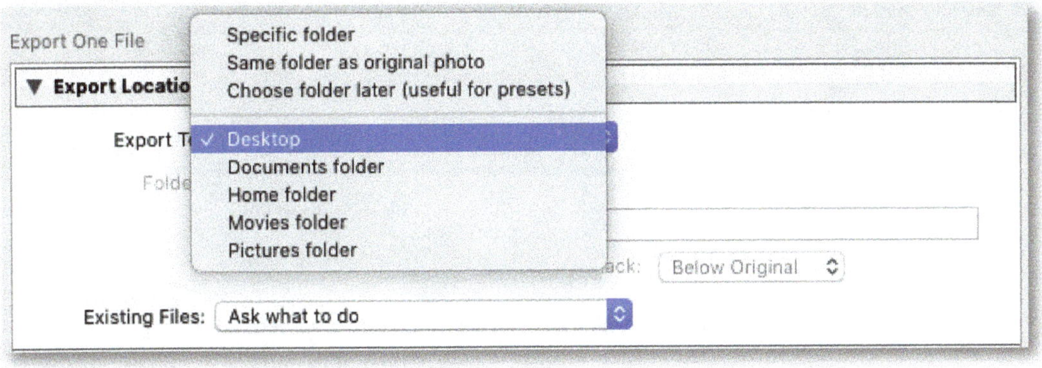

Figure 7.5 – Export To menu

Here, we can specify the export of images to a predefined and existing location or create a new one. The **Export To** menu is where we can choose between the main three options.

Specific folder

Firstly, we can export to **Specific folder** – this will enable the **Folder** function with a drop-down list populated with the most recently used locations. Next to that menu with recent locations, we are offered to **Choose…** any location on the hard drive. Keep in mind that if you choose your desktop as the final destination, without creating or choosing any specific folders on it, Lightroom will export all files directly onto your desktop. This will cause a mess, especially if it is a few hundred photographs. The option **Put in Subfolder** just below the **Folder** menu is a great way to mitigate that potential problem and, most of all, is a way to keep things tidy.

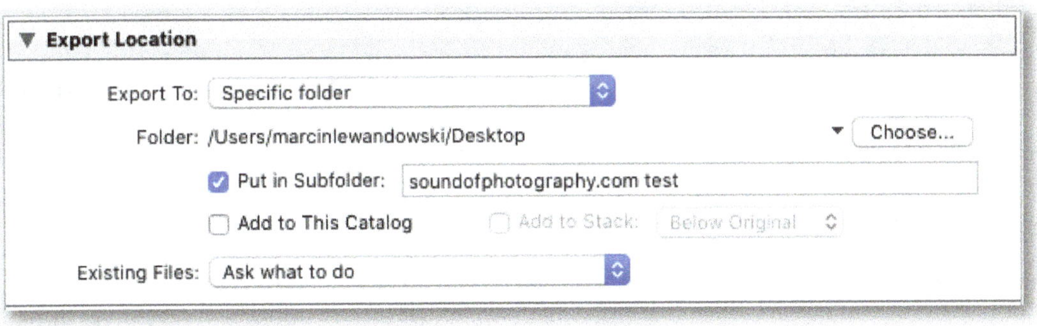

Figure 7.6 – Specific folder

By checking the box and typing anything, Lightroom will create a folder with the name "anything" in the chosen location.

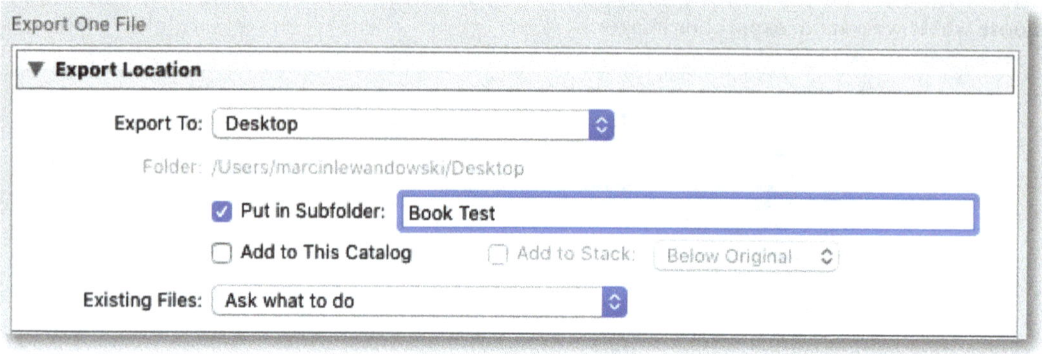

Figure 7.7 – In this example, Lightroom will create a folder named "Book Test" on the desktop and export selected photographs into it

Same folder as original photo

The next option in the **Export To** menu is **Same folder as original photo**. Using this function will export all images into the exact location where the original photographs we are exporting are located. Just as with the first option, we have a chance to not only specify the destination folder but also to create a new folder with a specified name inside it. I personally never use this option as I like to have a clear separation between "negatives" and "prints," but I think it will strongly depend on everyone's personal preferences and approach to "housekeeping." Choosing **Same folder as original photo** also gives us an opportunity to **Add to This Catalog**, which will reimport created images into their original catalog in Lightroom. By checking the **Add to Stack** option, Lightroom will add them to the original exported images in the form of a stack. We have a choice to add them **Above Original** or **Below Original**, which translates to before and after in the filmstrip.

Choose folder later (useful for presets)

The third and last option in the **Export To:** menu is **Choose folder later (useful for presets)**. If we choose this option, Lightroom will ask us where to export files. We will be able to select locations via our computer's operating system dialog (via Finder on Mac). As the actual description says, it is a good choice for presets. When we precisely set all of the options available below and finally commit to **Export**, Lightroom will ask us where we want to save our newly created files. Choosing this option will gray out the option to create a subfolder, which we can do on the operating system level.

The remaining few choices located under the thin line in the **Export To** menu are standard system folders that will slightly differ depending on the operating system you are using. Choosing one of these locations will allow us to create subfolders, which might be handy for quick exports.

Existing Files

The last remaining option of the **Export Location** tab is labeled **Existing Files**. This relates to exporting files with the exact same name already present in the location we chose for the export. As the default, this option is set to **Ask what to do**, which means that instead of choosing specific behavior straight away, we will have a chance to do it after clicking the **Export** button. The choices we will be given match the three options in the **Existing Files** menu.

These three choices are as follows:

- **Choose a new name for the exported file**: It will append our chosen filename with a number. If it's the first copy, it will append the name with **-2**, the next one **-3**, and so on.
- **Overwrite WITHOUT WARNING**: Just the capitalization of this warning signals that we need to be careful when using this option, *especially* if your workflow includes exporting to **Same folder as original photo**. Choosing this option might overwrite our originals, which will be forever lost!
- **Skip**: If you choose this option, the export will not include files with the same name as already existing ones in the location of the export. It's a *safe choice* option, but you will face *a little nightmare* if this happens for a small number of files randomly distributed in a more extensive export, and you will have to manually compare the contents of your export folder with the final selection in Lightroom Library. It happened to me; I do not recommend this experience.

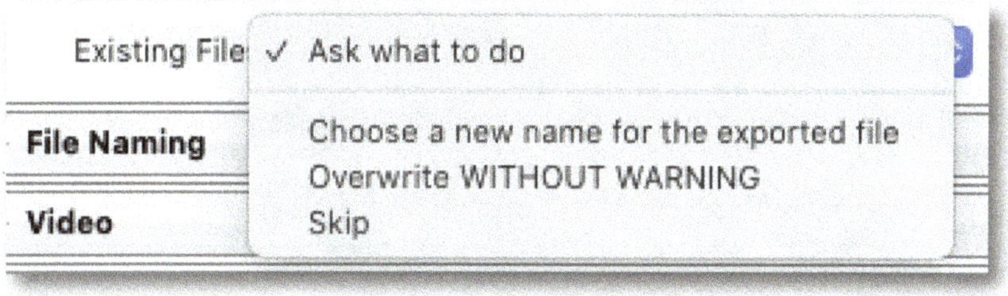

Figure 7.8 – Existing Files

I *always* have the **Existing Files** function set to **Ask what to do** – it potentially adds a choice. In 99% of cases, I will pick **Choose a new name for the exported file**. This way, I don't have to worry about anything being lost or overwritten.

File Naming

The first choice we need to make is simple: **Rename To** or not.

If we choose not to rename the exported files, they will have the same name as our source files. The remaining functions in this tab will be unavailable, and the only choice we can make will be between the uppercase and lowercase extensions. You might have your reasons to change from the default lowercase to uppercase, but I always leave it as is. It is one of those Lightroom options I have never changed since I first used it.

Suppose we, however, choose the **Rename To** function. In that case, we are not only welcomed with a great selection of renaming presets but also a fully customizable **File Template Editor**. Once we click on the list of options, we will see seven presets: four that will use our set **Custom Name** and three that will use the original filename. I usually choose **Desktop** and the same name for **Put in Subfolder** and **Custom Text** when exporting images. This way, I can keep track of what goes where to easily keep track of exported photographs and later distribute them to other locations.

The example (**Example**) on the bottom of this tab will always show us how the chosen name will look after the export depending on the **Rename To** option and **Custom Text** we choose.

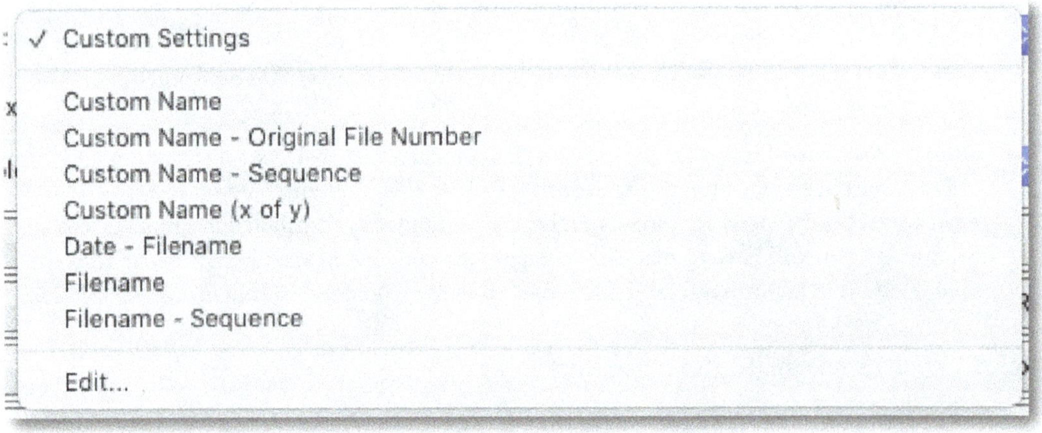

Figure 7.9 A

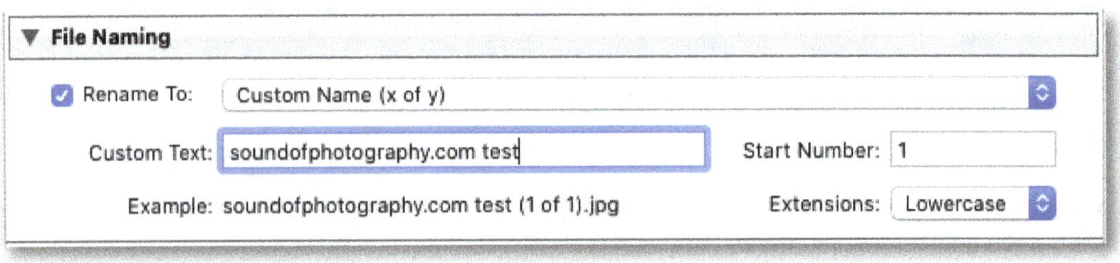

Figure 7.9 B – Seven presets and the File Naming menu

If we need more options, so the names are more specific, we need to choose **Custom Settings** or **Edit…** to open **Filename Template Editor**.

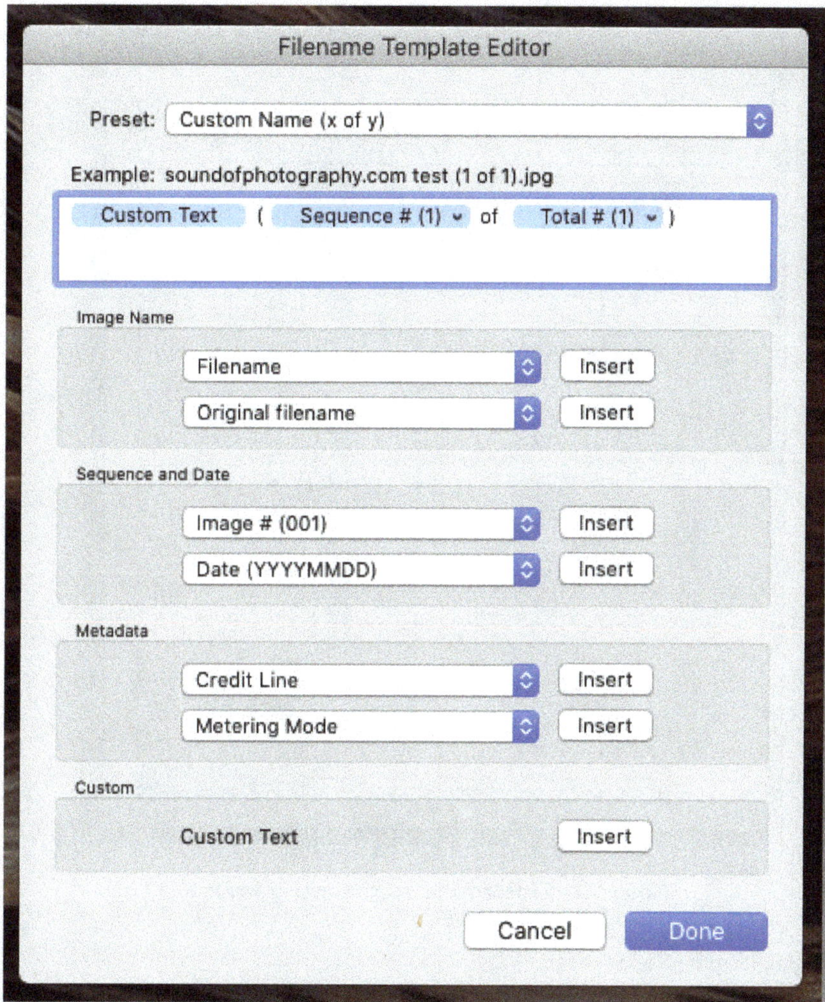

Figure 7.10 – Filename Template Editor

File Template Editor has two sections: a blue framed window where we can type in the custom text, including symbols, and four blocks: **Image Name**, **Sequence and Date**, **Metadata**, and **Custom**.

Once we choose any options from the drop-down menus, they will immediately appear in the blue framed editor's window. We can move things around by click-dragging them to create the desired name. We can also add symbols such as an underscore and so on. Depending on our needs, we can create something very basic or really elaborate, including camera settings and more. Once we have what we need, we can either click **Done** or click the **Preset** menu at the top of this menu and choose **Save Current Settings as a New Preset**.

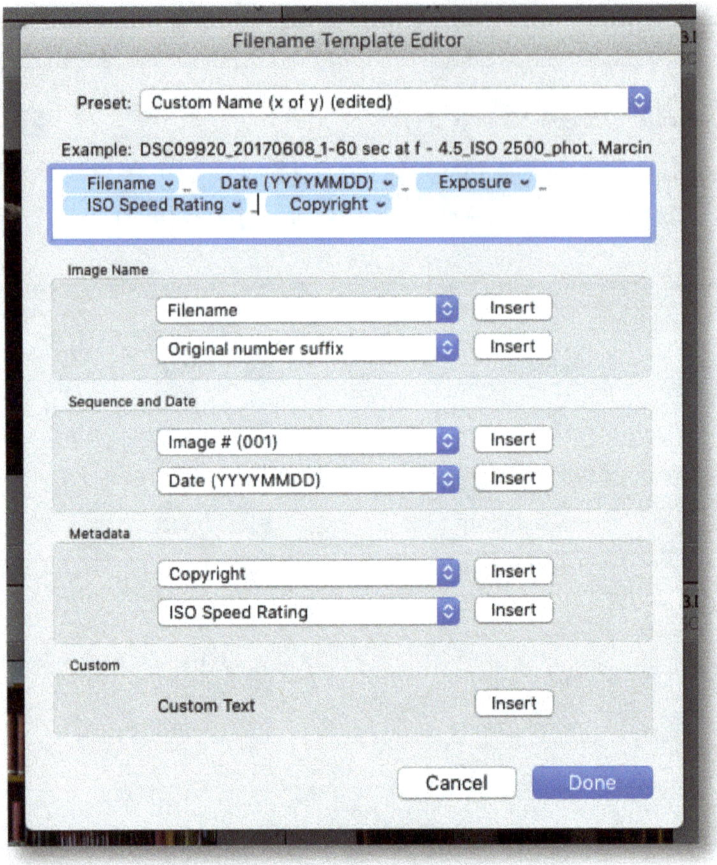

Figure 7.11 – Filename Template Editor example

Next, we will look into the **Video** menu.

Video

Lightroom offers us minimal **Video Export** options, but what's on offer is enough for any photographer who might sporadically need access to this type of functionality.

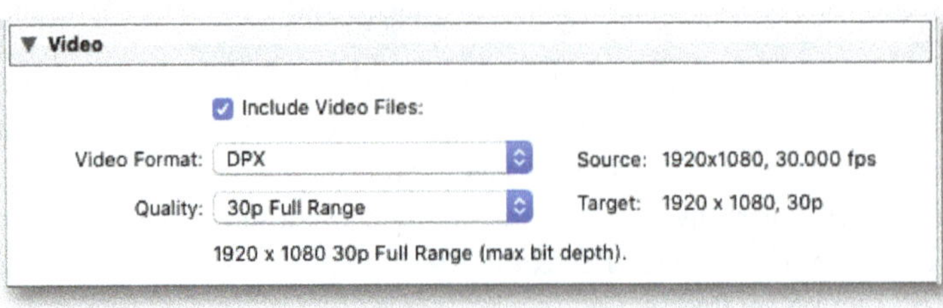

Figure 7.12 – Video

Starting with the first checkbox, we can choose whether Lightroom should include video files in the export or not. If we decide to include video files, we will have two short pull-down lists to specify **Video Format** and **Quality** of the imported video.

The **Video Format** options are very straightforward and allow us to choose between the following:

- **DPX**: The preferred, lossless format for further editing
- **H.264**: Probably the best-known video compression standard for video
- **Original, Unedited File**

For **DPX**, we can choose between three different frame rates. **H.264** offers only four vague options, from **Max** to **Low**, described in more detail once we choose any particular option. **Original, Unedited File** doesn't provide any further options.

Let's dive into the file settings now.

File Settings

We have a choice of exporting our photos in seven different file formats. With format changes, the available options also change. I'll describe each format separately.

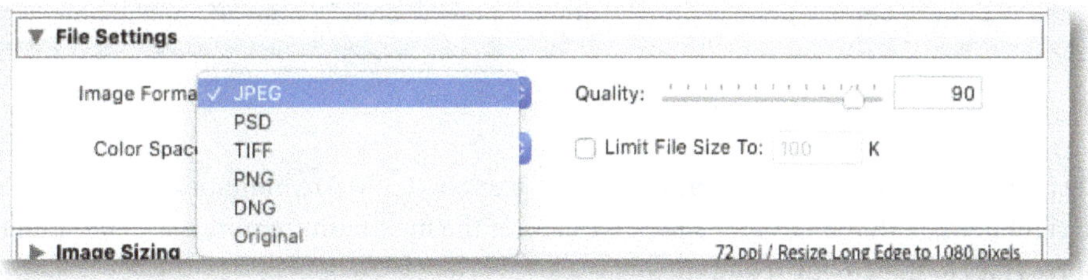

Figure 7.13 – File Settings tab

JPEG is the most widely used image format in the world. If you've ever wondered what it means, it's an abbreviation of **Joint Photographic Experts Group** – a committee of experts who created and maintain JPEG and related formats. JPG is the format that photographers use most often – whether preparing images for portfolio, print, or social media, `.jpg` will be the "go-to" format. You probably noticed that we used JPEG, JPG, and `.jpg` as alternatives to name the same thing. This is because they all describe the same thing and can be used alternately.

Quality is a rather vague measurement, but there is a massive difference in quality and file size between the original and files exported at various settings. For example, 60 MB files with **Quality** set to 100, without any resizing, and at 72 dpi will be compressed to about 10 MB. The same file set to 80 will have a size of about 5 MB, and with **Quality** set to 0, its size will be about 500 KB. When viewed in screen size, we will notice practically no difference, but zooming in to 100% will reveal a lot of artifacts and pixelation. I suggest always exporting at the "highest possible" quality, which will differ from application to application. For printing, it's always 100, but for social media and websites, we can easily use the setting of 80-90 and sometimes even less – you will have to be the judge of it yourself. Compare results side by side and choose settings that work for you.

The next available choice is **Color Space**. For anything internet-related, always use **sRGB**. In fact, use **sRGB** for anything else as well. The **sRGB** option is the most widely used color space and unless you know why you want to use any other color space, don't. You risk getting washed out, bland, and less saturated images that don't match what you saw while developing them in Lightroom. The internet can't read the full spectrum of colors that **Adobe RGB** can potentially represent. As for **ProPhoto RGB**, there are no monitors (yet?) that can display such a wide gamut of colors. You have a choice, though, and I encourage you to experiment, but for 99.99% of applications, **sRGB** is the right choice for everyone.

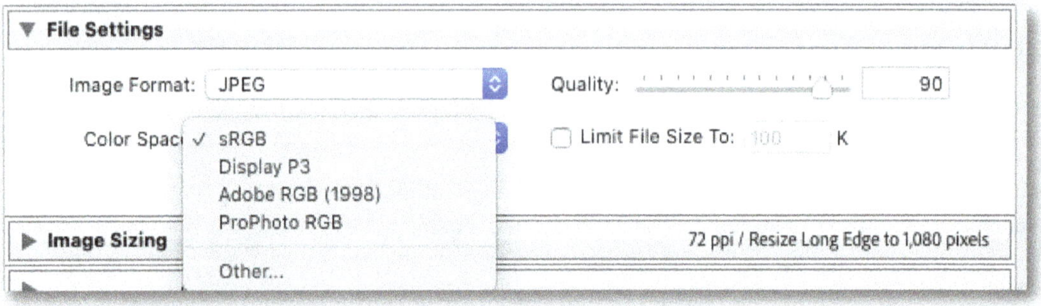

Figure 7.14 – Color Space

Limit File Size To is a great option when we need to work with file size limitations. Instead of trying to hit the right mark with the **Quality** slider, we can set the maximum required size and Lightroom will compress files to match our requirements.

PSD is the native Adobe format (Photoshop Document), and you should only use it for that. Most applications won't even be able to read it. Only use this format if you need the file to contain all the possible raw information, and you know that someone will work on it in graphics software such as Photoshop. Other than that, I would avoid it. If you must export to PSD, then you will know the difference between 8-bit and 16-bit images. 8-bit images use and work within a color space of 16,777,216 colors while 16-bit images contain 281,474,976,710,656 – this is just trivia, but if you must work outside of Lightroom and will be using PSD format, always use 16-bit images to avoid nasty surprises.

TIFF aka **Tagged Image File Format** – for **Color Space** and **Bit Depth**, please see the previous notes. Regarding compression, we choose between lossless ZIP and LZW formats; please note that the LZW format is only available for 8-bit exports.

If we want to save transparency within the file instead of filling it with white color, we must check the **Save Transparency** box. **Save Transparency** will only apply to previously imported PSD or PNG files with transparent pixels. It will also work with files such as Lightroom stitched panoramas where transparent pixels are visible around the realigned images.

PNG is great for exporting an image for web use using lossless compression. The **PNG** format supports transparency, and I use it primarily for logos and graphics. However, we don't have control over the quality of the PNG file (lossless), and we will get a rather large exported file. For example, the same 60 MB photograph I mentioned with JPEG settings, when exported as PNG, will be about 100 MB.

DNG is short for **Digital Negative Image**. **DNG** is a highly compatible raw image format, meaning an unprocessed photo directly from the camera's sensor. Unless you are using external editing software that doesn't recognize the raw format straight off your camera, I don't see a reason to export images as DNG, but please let me know if you think differently. With **Compatibility**, we can choose which Camera Raw version will be able to read our exported DNGs, set by default to the latest release, but if you intend to work with an older version, you can, at the time of writing this book, go as far back as Camera Raw 2.4 released back in 2005. **JPEG Preview** is where we choose between **Full Size**, **Medium Size**, and **None**. This will be especially useful if we plan to reimport the DNG file back into Lightroom later. Lastly, we have a choice of three boxes to check:

- **Embed Fast Load Data**: This will slightly increase the created file size, but the Develop module will open images faster.
- Next, we have **Use Lossy Compression**, which will significantly reduce the created file's size but also decrease its quality.
- Lastly, we can choose **Embed Original Raw File**, which will save the original raw data of our image embedded into the DNG information.

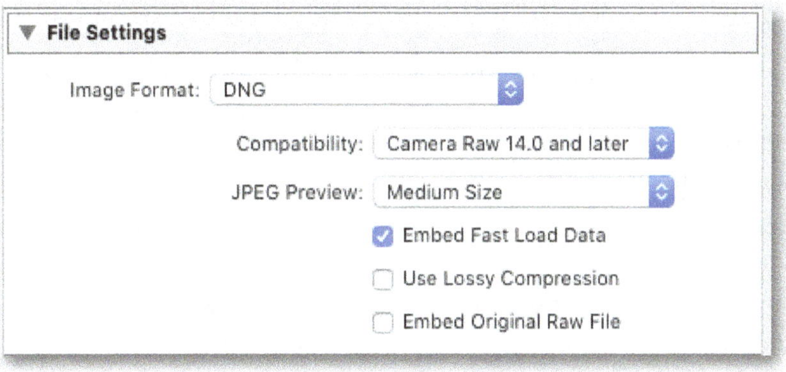

Figure 7.15 – DNG settings

Original will export a copy of the original file accompanied by a sidecar `.xmp` file containing information about any and all changes we have made so far to our photo in Lightroom.

Now that we decided on our export format, let's work on the exports' final size.

Image Sizing

Different applications work best with different formats. From submission pages requesting images within a specific MP size to alleviating too much Facebook or other social media compression by exporting in their native sizes.

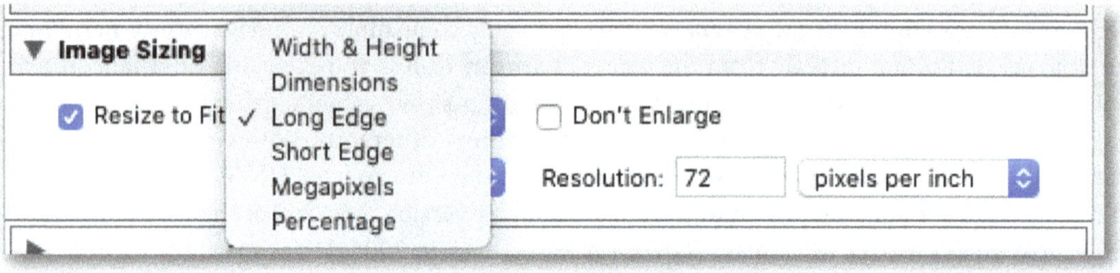

Figure 7.16 – Image Sizing

Resize to Fit offers great flexibility, and we can set the size of exported photographs with very specific rules:

- **Width & Height**: Here, we can set the maximum width and height of the exported image without changing the original aspect ratio. If we, for example, set this to *W:1500XH:1000*, Lightroom will export the image, making sure that the whole picture can fit within these dimensions and so the image will have a max height of 1000 and a max width of 1500. Imagine a box with set dimensions into which Lightroom will fit our image without rotating or cropping it.
- **Dimensions**: When we use this setting, Lightroom will apply a higher value to the longer edge and a lower value to the shorter edge. Compared to the **Width & Height** setting, it will fit the image into a box with set dimensions, rotating it if necessary for the best fit.
- **Long Edge**: With this setting, we can specify the length of the longer edge of the exported photograph. Lightroom will calculate the shorter edge's length using the exported photograph's aspect ratio.
- **Short Edge**: Similar to the Long Edge, we can specify the length of the shorter edge of the exported photograph. Lightroom will calculate the longer edge's length using the exported photograph's aspect ratio.
- **Megapixels: MP** (short for **megapixel**) count is simply the image's width in pixels multiplied by its height and divided by 1 million, rounded to the nearest number (that is, 7,264x5,440=39,516,160, 39,516,160/1,000,000=39.51616, =40 MP). When we set this to a required MP size, Lightroom will calculate the width and height, keeping the original aspect ratio.
- **Percentage**: This will export an image resized to a percentage we set, that is, if we set 10% for a 4,000x5,000 image, the resulting export will be 400x500.

Please notice the **Don't Enlarge** option - not having this box checked means that we can export images larger than our original photograph.

Lastly, we can set the print **Resolution** of exported images in **pixels per inch (ppi)** or **cm per inch**. Even though I'm a born and bred metric system user, because most print applications use ppi, I use it as well. When exporting images set for online, computer screens, and so on, I keep this at 72 ppi but for print, I usually set it to 360 (the reason for this will be explained in *Chapter 8, Get them All Out - Using the Print and Book Modules*). Some print providers might request 300 or even different values - it's always best to check what the requirements are on a print-by-print basis.

Output Sharpening

This option will provide additional sharpening to anything we already applied in the Develop process. Depending on the file's final destination, we can choose between **Sharpen For: Screen**, **Matte Paper**, or **Glossy Paper**, all with three different **Amount** settings: **Low**, **Standard**, and **High**.

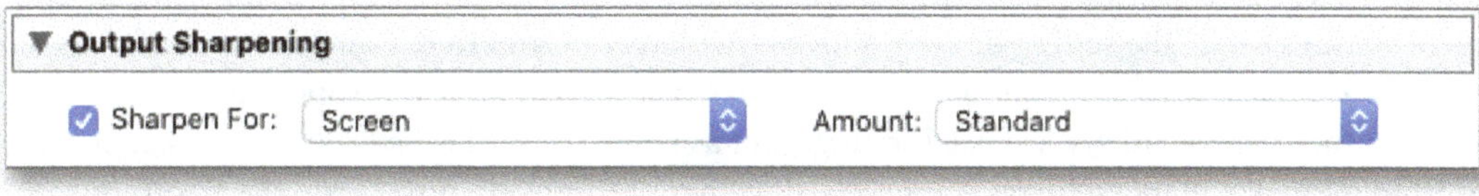

Figure 7.17 – Output Sharpening

Of course, final results will differ depending on other settings we chose, and **Low** screen sharpening will be much more prominent on a 1,080-pixel-wide export than **High** sharpening on a full resolution export. It's worth experimenting with various settings from time to time as different types of images will behave differently at various sizes and outputs, but as a rule of thumb, I keep it set to **Standard** for most types of exports.

Now it's time to explore **Metadata**.

Metadata

This tab will help us to hide or display anything we don't want to share, and I find it most important for images intended for digital, work-related distribution. Whether they are destined for websites or magazine print, we can control aspects from copyright notice to camera settings.

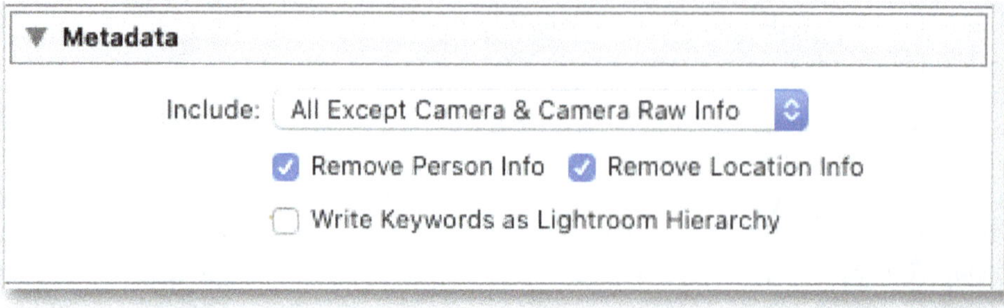

Figure 7.18 – Metadata

Diving into the **Include** menu, starting from the top of the list, we can export just the IPTC **Copyright only** metadata. This option is followed by **Copyright & Contact Info Only**. Next is my most often used setting, titled **All Except Camera and Camera Raw Info**. This setting will export **Copyright & Contact** along with every other bit of information, including keywords and captions, except information about the camera used to create the photographs and without the camera settings used. The setting directly above – **All Except Camera & Camera Raw Info** – is a bit confusing; that's why I initially skipped it. I think that, in theory, it was supposed to leave the info about the camera and discard used settings, but as far as I have checked – and I checked RAW files from all major manufacturers – it leaves all camera settings used to create the photo in the metadata. Anyway, please check it for yourself and let me know if you get different results. Lastly, we can export **All Metadata**.

In addition to the sets of info we pick from the Include list, we can control three other aspects of exported information: **Remove Person Info** (this applies to People Keywords), **Remove Location Info** (GPS coordinates), and **Write Keywords as Lightroom Hierarchy**, which is to use the "|" character to separate the **parent|child** keyword relationships within the metadata.

Next is the **Watermarking** menu.

Watermarking

After all this dry info regarding sizes, ppi, and metadata, we can finally play around with something more visual.

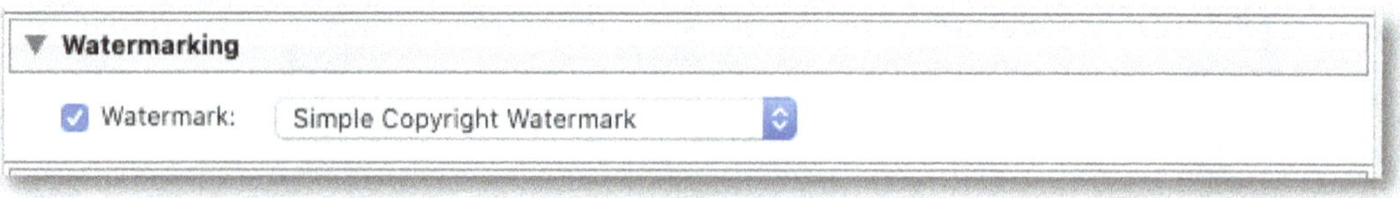

Figure 7.19 – Watermarking

Watermarking offers us three ways to approach watermarking our photographs:

- **Simple Copyright Watermark**
- **Text Watermark**
- **Graphic Watermark**

The first and quickest way to use the **Watermarking** feature is **Simple Copyright Watermark**. There are no settings associated with this option. It will place the watermark only if we have copyright information populated in the picture's metadata. Whatever we have in the **Copyright** field will be placed as a watermark in the bottom-left corner of the exported photograph using default settings. If copyright information is too long, Lightroom will cut it short.

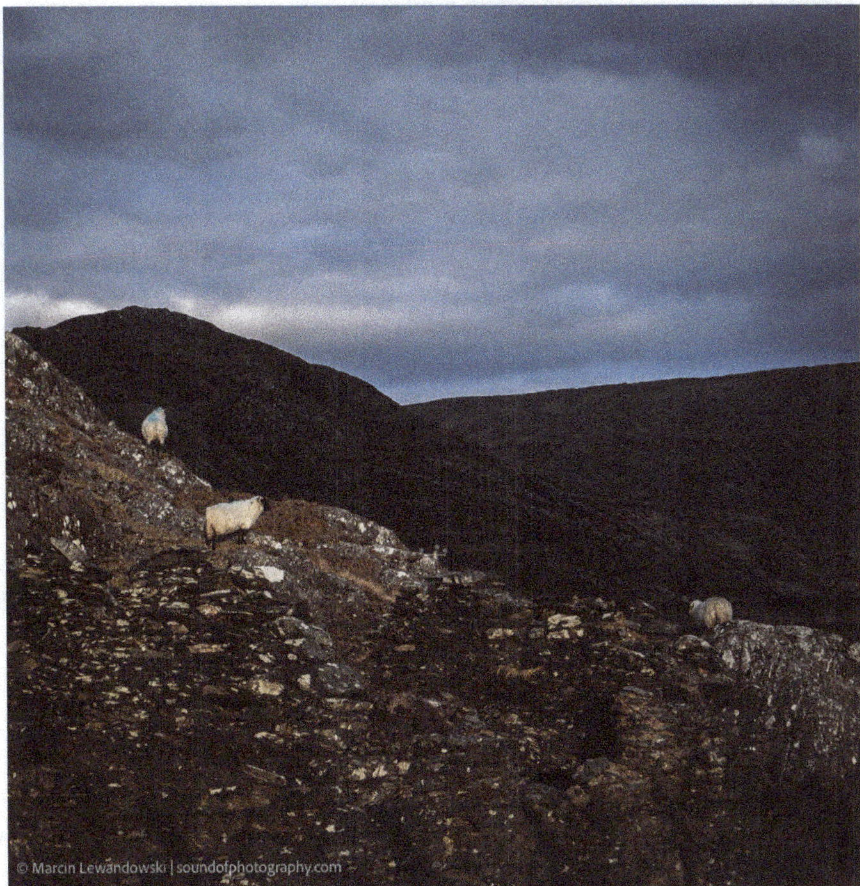

Figure 7.20 – Simple Copyright Watermark example

If we don't like the watermarks created using **Simple Copyright Watermark**, we must choose the **Edit Watermarks...** option. This will open a "hidden" **Watermark Editor** menu.

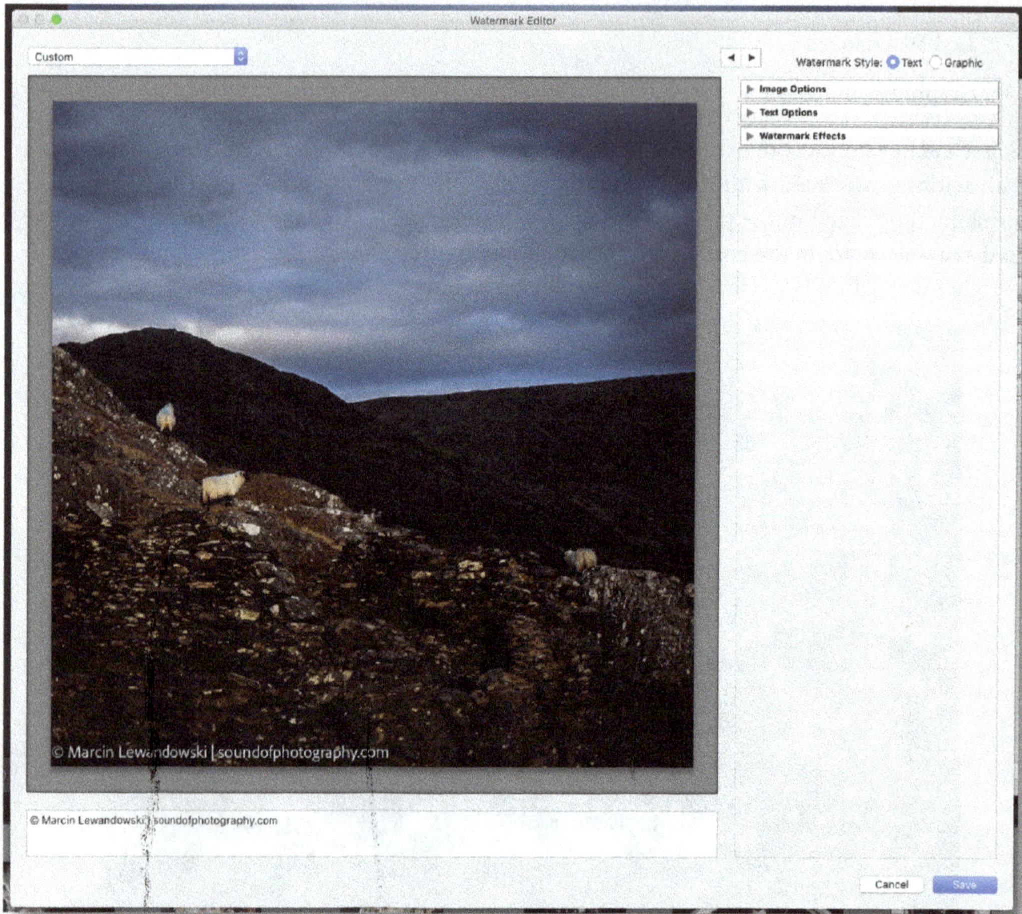

Figure 7.21 – Watermark Editor menu

Our choice is to use the **Text** or **Graphic** watermark style, and we will start with options available to tweak the **Text** version first.

First, we need the text we want to appear as a watermark. We can write it in the window just below the photograph, at the bottom of the **Watermark Editor** screen. Once we decide on that, let's move to the top-right corner within the same menu. Here, we can choose **Font**, its **Style** (if available), **Alignment**, and **Color**. Once we decide all of that, we can determine whether our text will cast a shadow. If we use the shadow, we will be able to adjust its **Opacity**, **Offset**, **Radius** (spread and feather), and **Angle**. Once we are happy with it, we can move to the **Watermark Effects** tab below. Firstly, we can change the opacity. When deciding on the size, we can choose **Proportional**, which could also read **Adjust the size**. We also select **Fit**, which will fit the text to the photo's width, and **Fill**, which will try to fill the whole height and width (this might be limited by the available sizes of the font we're using). **Inset** will create an invisible margin around our watermark. Next, we can choose where we would like the watermark to be placed with **Anchor**. Finally, we can **Rotate** the watermark in 90-degree increments.

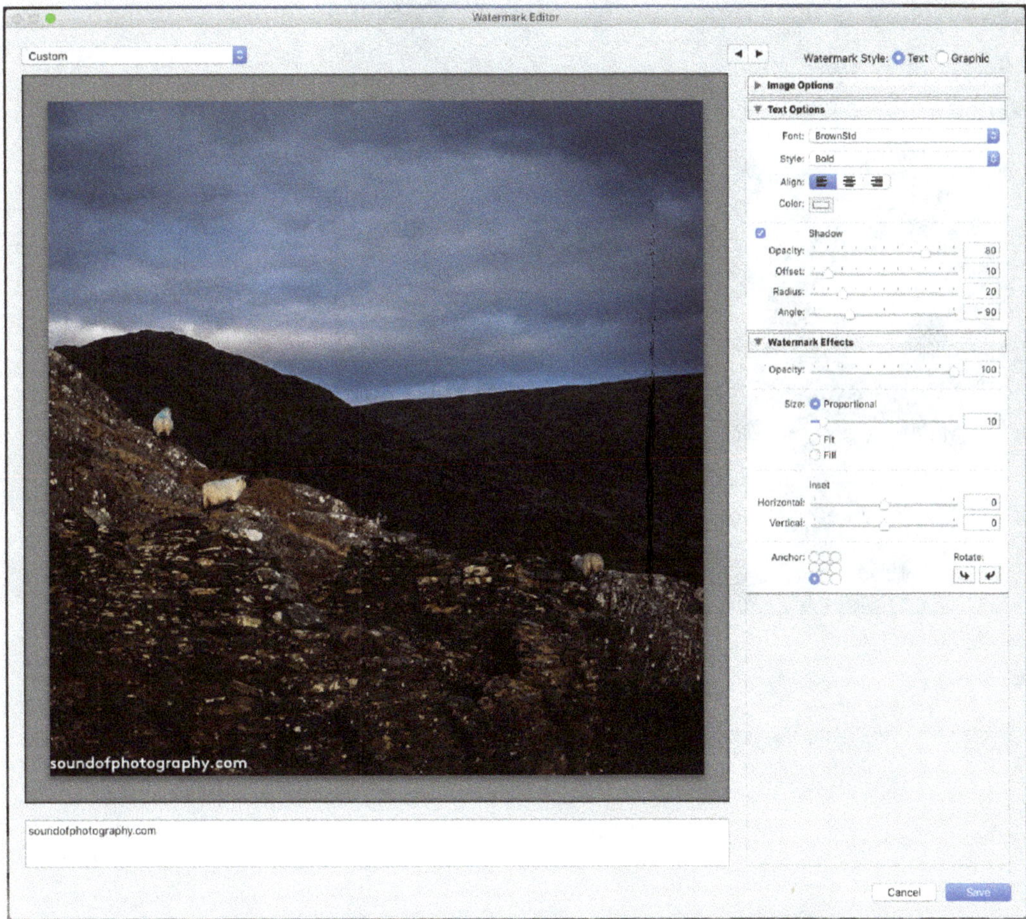

Figure 7.22 A

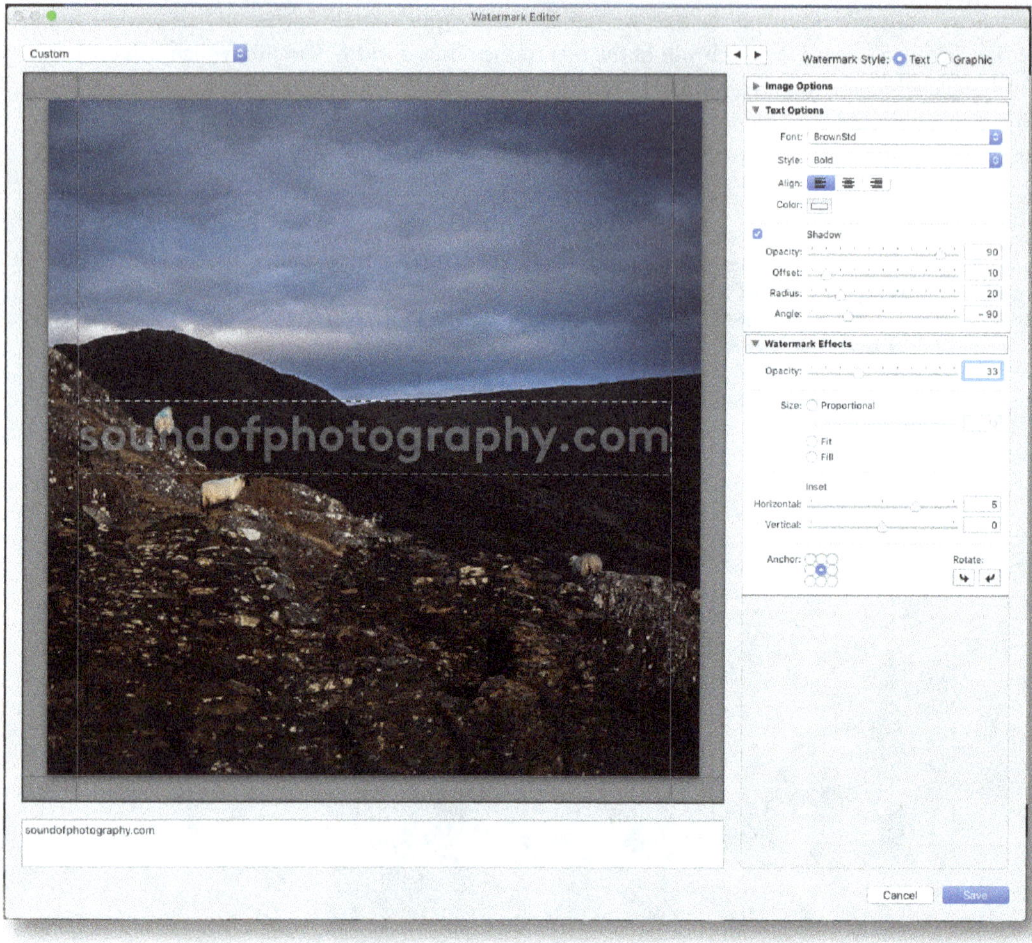
Watermark Editor
Custom
Watermark Style: Text Graphic
Image Options
Text Options
Font: BrownStd
Style: Bold
Align:
Color:
Shadow
Opacity: 90
Offset: 10
Radius: 20
Angle: -90
Watermark Effects
Opacity: 33
Size: Proportional
Fit
Fill
Inset
Horizontal: 5
Vertical: 0
Anchor:
Rotate:
soundofphotography.com
soundofphotography.com
Cancel
Save

Figure 7.22 B

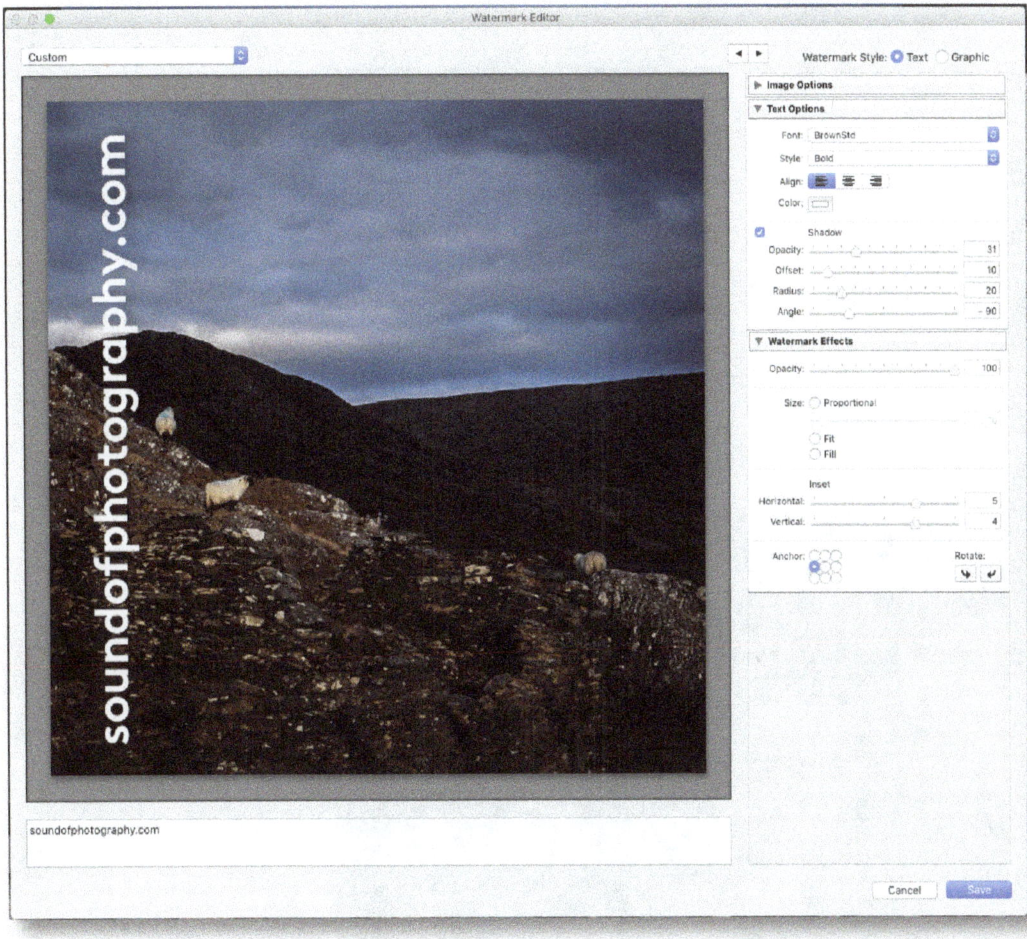

Figure 7.22 C – Text watermark examples with their settings visible on the right

If we would prefer to use a graphic image instead of text, we need to go back to the top of the editor and choose the **Graphic** option for **Watermark Style**. This will open our system window, where we can select the file we want to use. We have a choice of using either JPG or PNG formats, but since PNG supports transparency (JPG will replace transparency with white color), it is the preferred aesthetic choice. Once we pick the appropriate image, we can adjust its size, opacity, and so on, to our liking in the **Watermark Effects** tab.

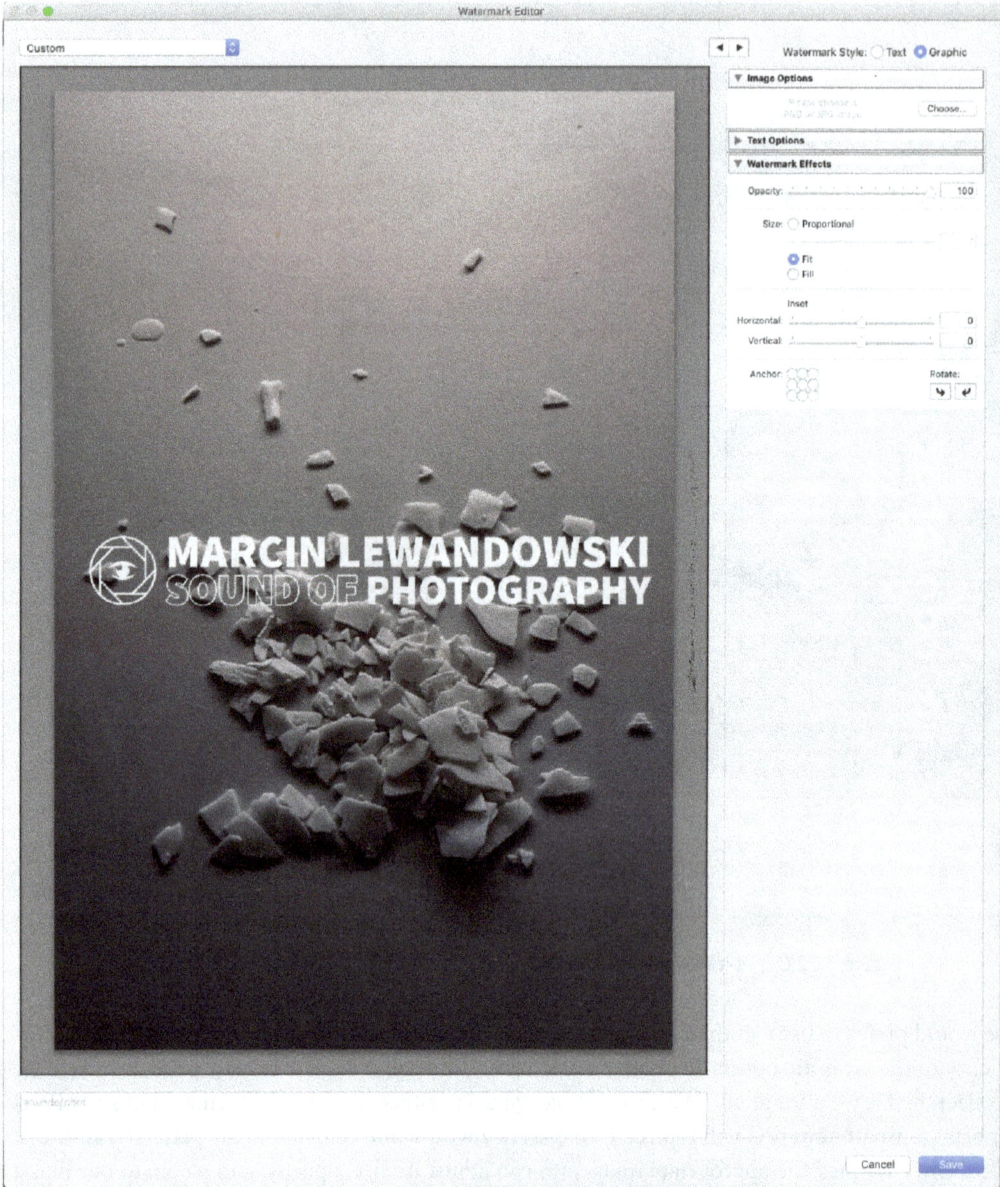
Watermark Editor
Custom
Watermark Style: Text Graphic
Image Options
Choose...
Text Options
Watermark Effects
Opacity: 100
Size: Proportional
Fit
Fill
Inset
Horizontal: 0
Vertical: 0
Anchor:
Rotate:
MARCIN LEWANDOWSKI
SOUND OF PHOTOGRAPHY
Cancel
Save

Figure 7.23 A

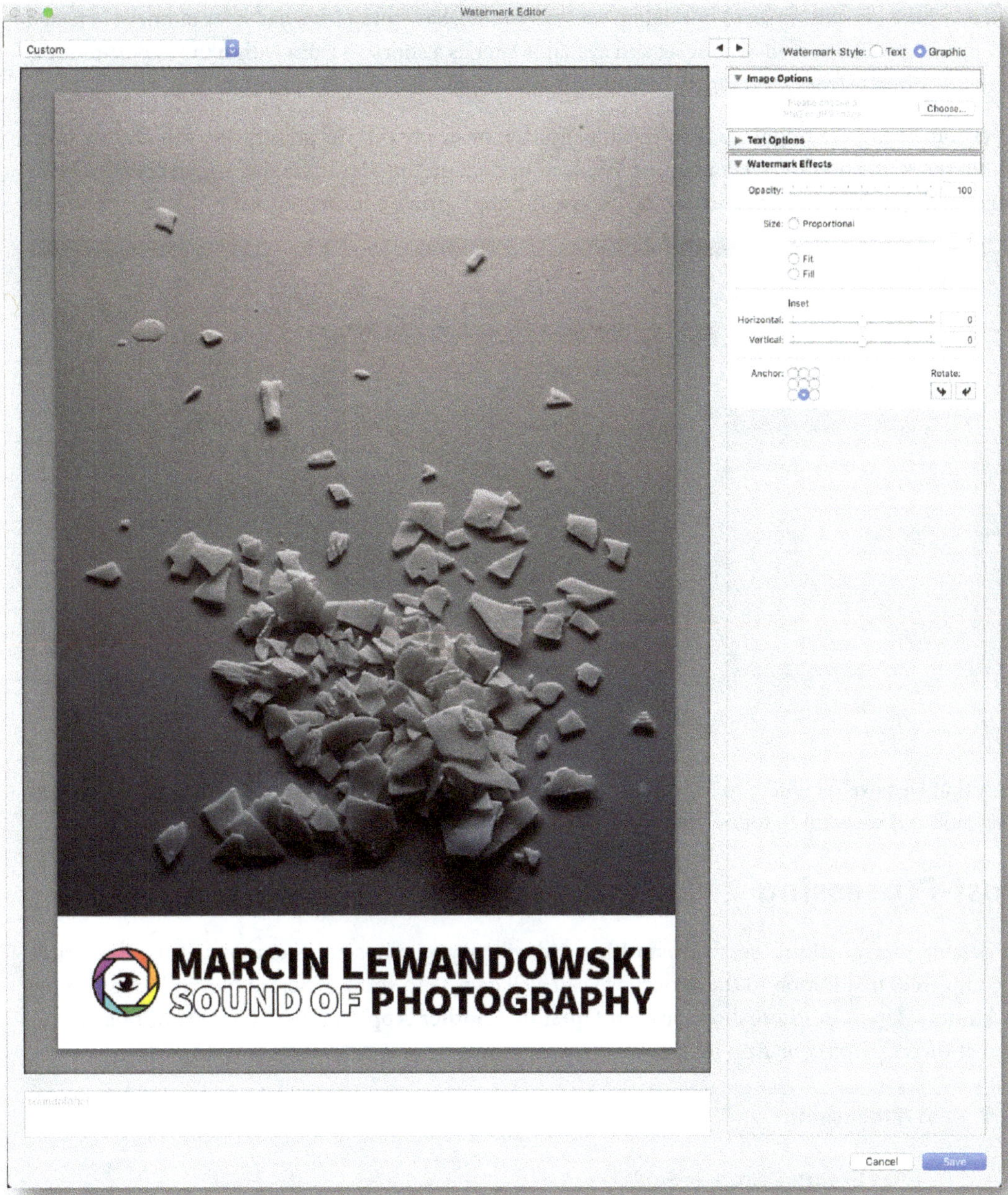

Figure 7.23 B – Graphic watermark example PNG and JPG

Whether we create a text or graphic watermark, we can check how it looks on different photographs we selected for export by clicking the left and right arrows at the top of the **Watermark Editor** window.

Once we have everything set to our liking, we need to click **Save** and pick a name for our newly created settings. This will be saved as a preset and available later as a shortcut from within the Export module as well as directly from the Library module when we right-click **Export** | **Preset**.

After some time, we might want to rename, update, or delete certain presets. We can do this from within the **Watermark Effects** window. We need to click on the pop-up menu, which contains all of our presets, in the top-right corner, and choose the appropriate action.

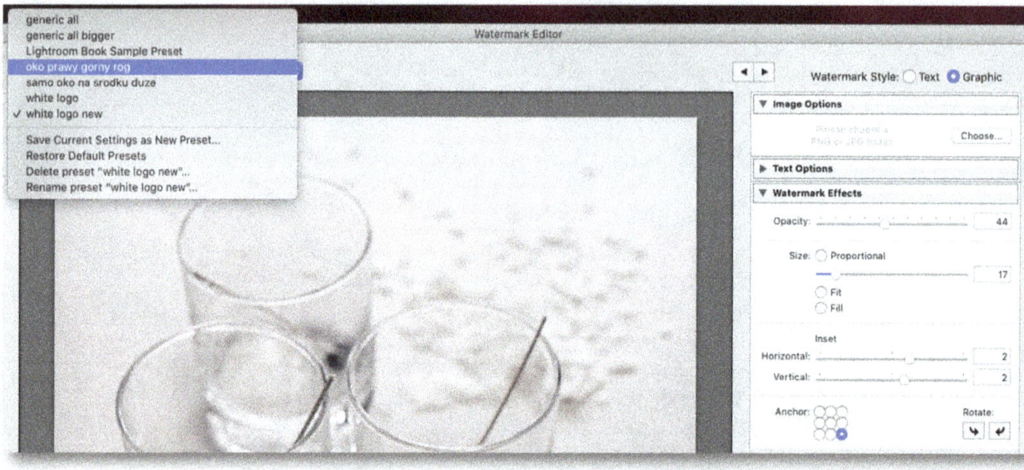

Figure 7.24 – Edit watermark presets menu

Now that we have set where to export our images and what their size and appearance will be, we can also choose if we want to follow up the export with another action.

Post-Processing

By default, this function is set to **Do nothing** and will play our chosen system sound once the export is completed. In addition to the export, we can also choose to show exported files in Finder (**Show in Finder**), **Open in Photoshop**, or even **Open in Another Application**, which we will be able to choose directly from our **App** folder.

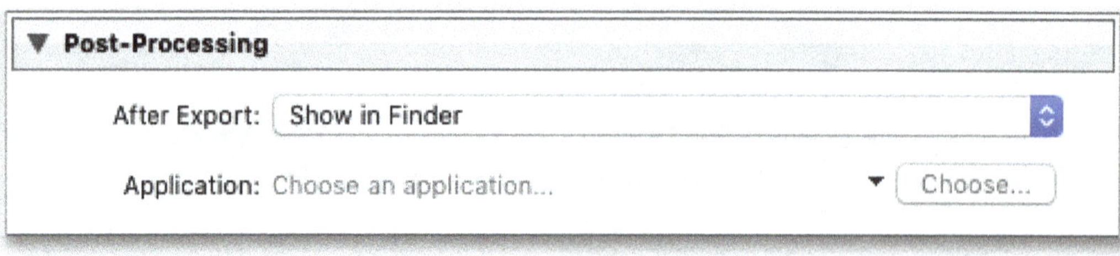

Figure 7.25 – Post-Processing

Lastly, we can use **Go to Export Actions Folder Now** and, inside it, place shortcuts to applications that we want to be opened after pictures finish exporting. If you are an advanced enough user, you can even place executable files in that folder. Anything we save in the **Export Actions** folder will be accessible to us from the **Post-Processing** list as a shortcut.

In the next section, we will learn how to save our settings as presets that can be reused whenever we need them, without the need to set up everything from scratch once more.

Creating presets

Having all of the details set up in the desired way, we can save them as a preset, which Lightroom will add to the right-side panel of the **Export** menu. To create a preset, we need to click **Add** in the bottom-left corner, and in the **New Preset** popup, choose the name and location folder of this new preset. We can either select an already existing folder, which by default is **User Presets** or select **New Folder...**. Once we have some presets available, we will be able to check the small boxes on the leftmost side of the presets, which will simultaneously export images at the chosen presets. If we want to change anything in the presets, we choose the one we want to change by clicking on its name, making all the changes to settings, and then right-clicking on it. This right-click will open an additional menu. Now we can choose **Update with Current Settings**, which will change our preset settings to reflect the changes we just made.

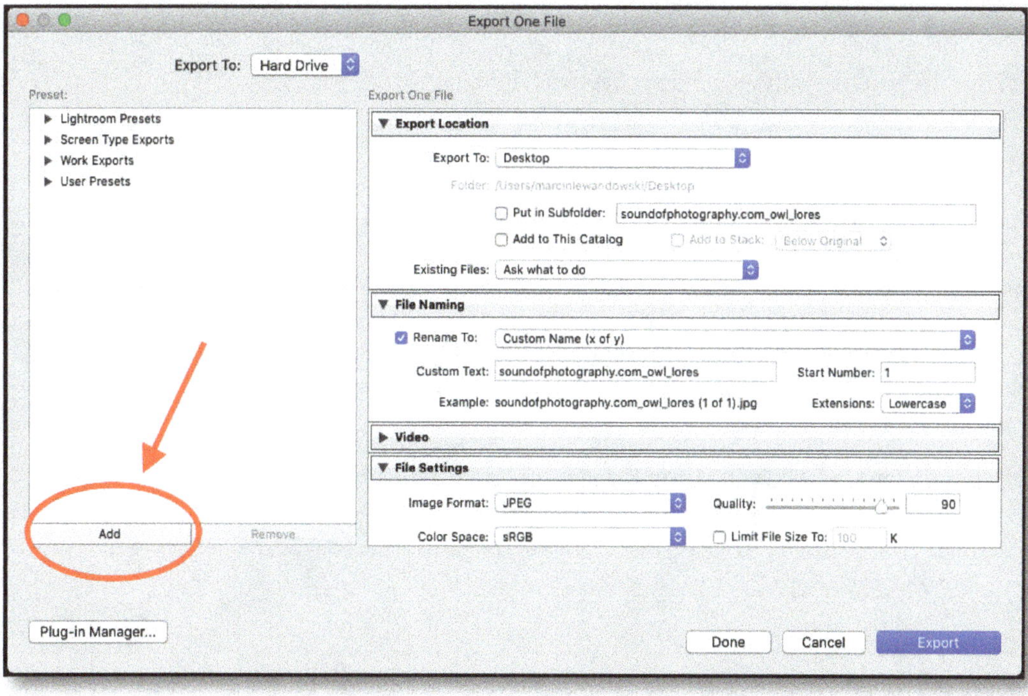

Figure 7.26 A

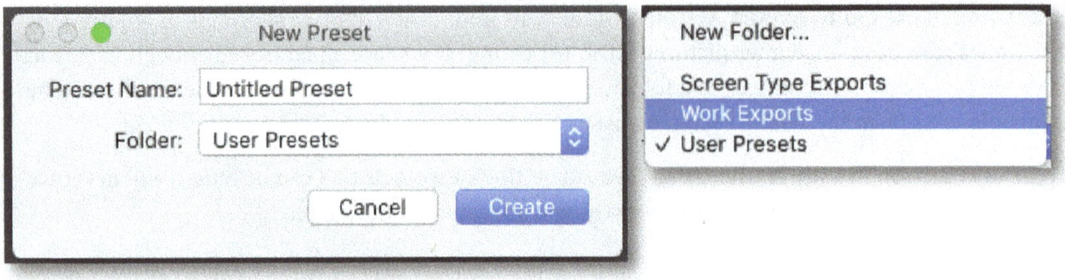

Figure 7.26 B – Adding a new preset, naming the new preset, and choosing a location folder for the new preset

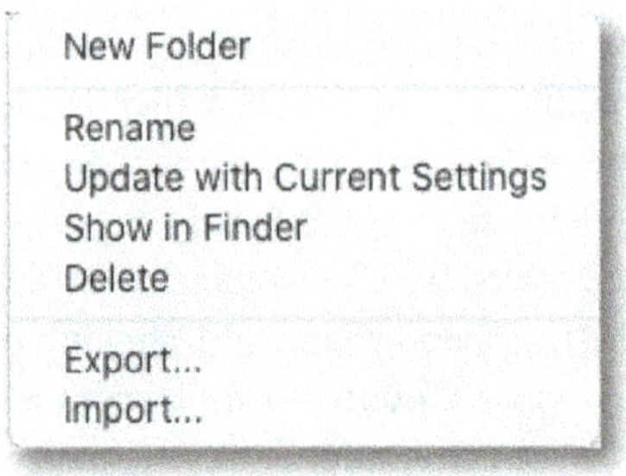

Figure 7.27 – Right-click menu to update our preset

With that, we are done with yet another chapter of this book!

Summary

What would be the point of all our complex work editing and developing photographs if we couldn't have a reliable and straightforward solution to share them. The export function within Lightroom gives us tremendous and entirely predictable results each time we click the **Export** button. Whether it's an edit from a wedding, a few pictures to print at the local shop for our mom, or unique reportage images from an event only we saw, Lightroom is there to help. It provides us with a highly personalized set of tools to export images into formats that will be easily recognizable by any machine with a screen.

In the next chapter, we will look at printing our images and designing a book.

8

Get them All Out – Using the Print and Book Modules

Prints are one of the most rewarding ways to look at photography. Lightroom offers a very streamlined way to get our pictures from the screen into the physical world with a printer between these two states. This chapter explains how to achieve the best results in preparing files for printing at home and gives you tips on preparation work when sending photographs to be printed by a service. In addition, we will look at how to work on designing a photo book layout and preparing it for print. As a bonus, we will also look at using the Print module to give you an edge in posting to social media such as Instagram.

In the second part of this chapter, we will learn about using the Book module, which will make designing our first photo book or album not only easy but also enjoyable and fun.

In this chapter, we will cover the following topics:

- A Print module overview
- Page settings
- Image settings
- Layout
- Printable information
- Branding via watermarks
- Printing to printer
- Printing to files
- A Book module overview
- Blurb and other types of books
- Book layout and layout automation
- Export for print

Exploring the Print module

Here's a quick overview of the Print module:

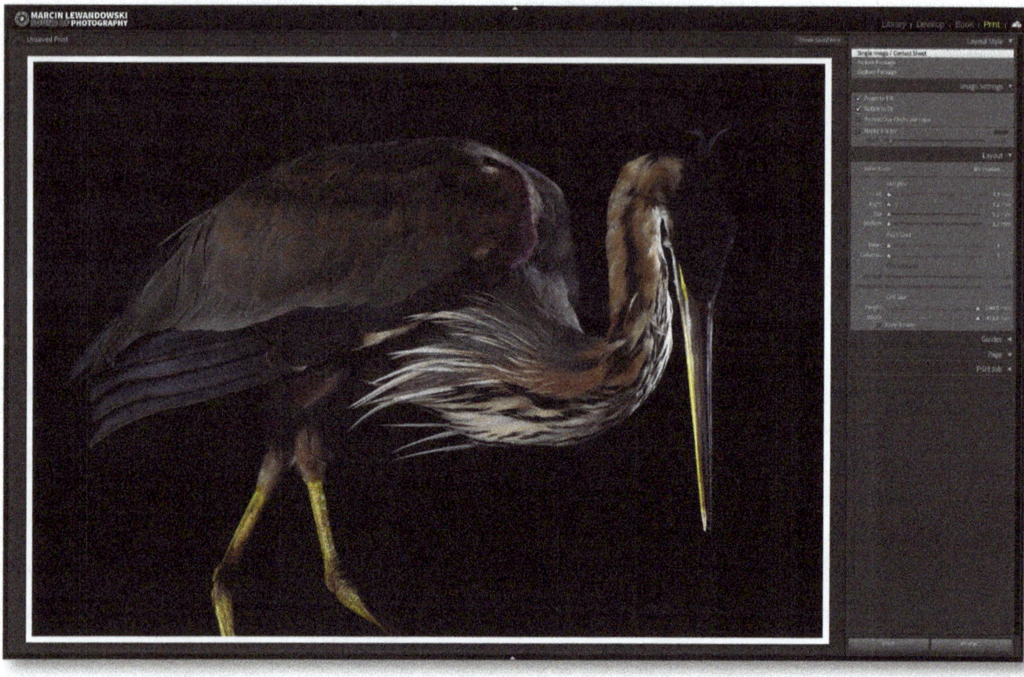

Figure 8.1 – The Print module

Let's have a look at the menus on the right side and left side of the Print module.

The right-side panel of the Print module

The right-side panel is where we will set all significant parameters of our print – from the settings managing the size and placement of our images within a sheet of paper to color management and output modes.

On the right side of the Print module, there are six tabs to work with:

- **Layout Style**
- **Image Settings**
- **Layout**
- **Guides**

- **Page**
- **Print Job**

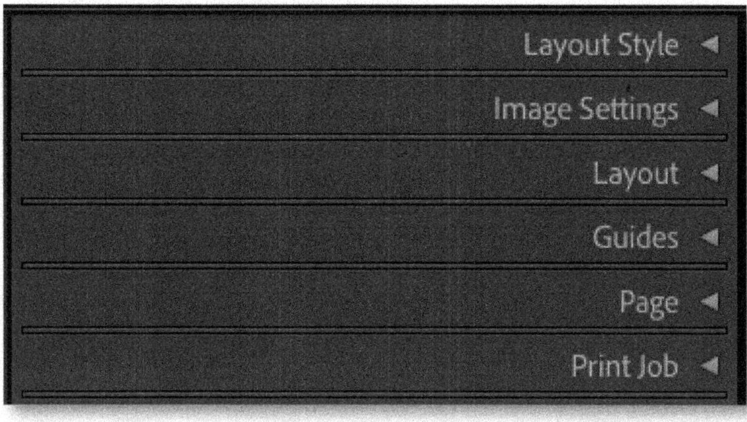

Figure 8.2 – The right-side panel of the Print module

They are relatively uncomplicated and easy to work with, making printing as enjoyable as possible. Once you learn the principles of the Print module and know your desired outcome, it will be a module that's as easy to work with as it is enjoyable to play with.

Layout Style

There are three different modes to choose from, each designed for a specific type of work:

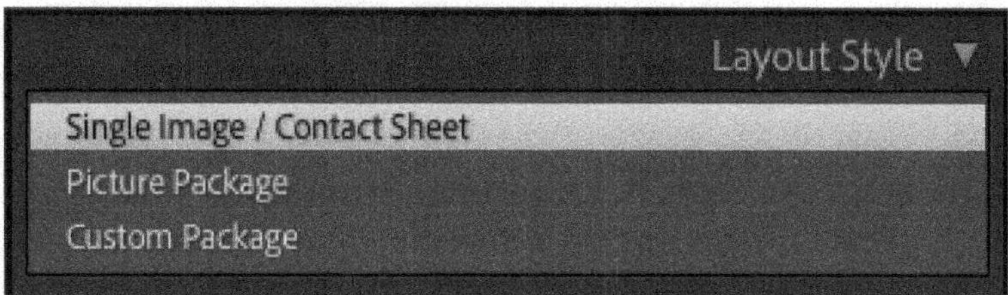

Figure 8.3 – Layout Style

- **Single Image / Contact Sheet**: In this mode, we will design a page layout for one or multiple photographs per page, all of the same size. We will choose the number of rows and columns, the space between them, and their margins. This is the "go-to" option whenever you want or need to print a photo or a series of photographs, all in the same specification. By the same specification, I mean using the same paper, matching margins, and so on.

- **Picture Package**: This mode will allow us to print the same photograph in various sizes and cropped to different aspect ratios on one or multiple pages.
- **Custom Package**: Here, we will be able to design multiple page layouts for multiple photographs in varying sizes and aspect ratios.

Once you are done with **Layout Style** and have set the **Page Setup** orientation to suit, it's time to play with all the remaining settings.

Image Settings

Let's look at the options in the **Image Settings** tab:

- **Zoom to Fill**: This setting will fill the whole image area, from margin to margin, ignoring the original aspect ratio. We can later adjust a photograph's position by dragging it up and down or left and right. This is a convenient setting if we want a uniform white border around our photograph without the need to cut anything after the image is printed.
- **Rotate to Fit**: This is a convenient option when the printed batch of images includes vertical and horizontal photos. It will rotate photographs to fill the space, so we don't end up with a vertical picture placed in the middle of a horizontal page with empty space on both sides.
- **Repeat One Photo per Page**: When we print multiple images and set our page to contain a grid of multiple image cells per page, Lightroom will fill these cells with our selected images so that each photo appears once, filling one cell. Ticking this box will fill all cells within one page with the same photograph – that is, if we want to print 10 photographs and the grid on the page contains 4 cells, we will get 4 copies of each of the selected photographs printed on each page.

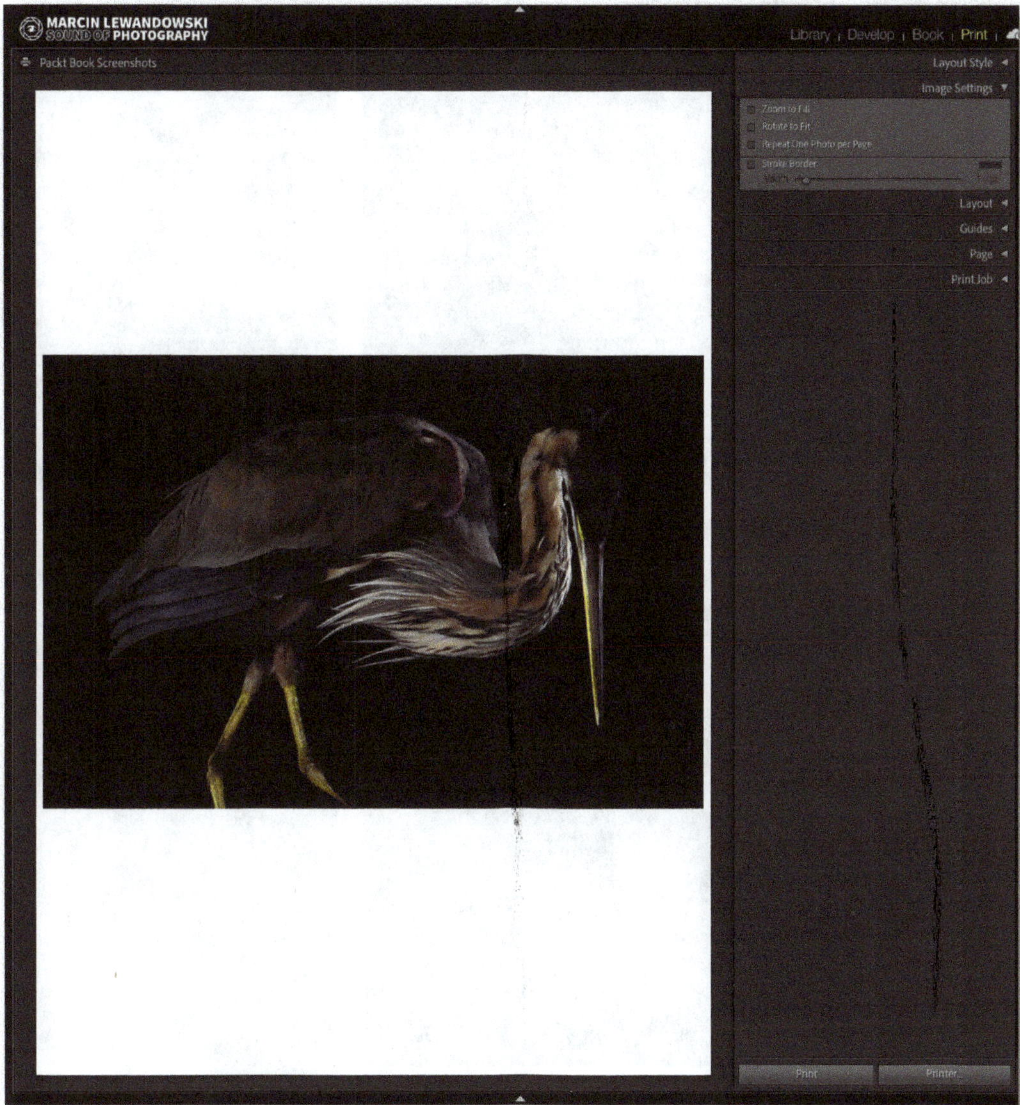

Figure 8.4 – A horizontal picture on a vertical page

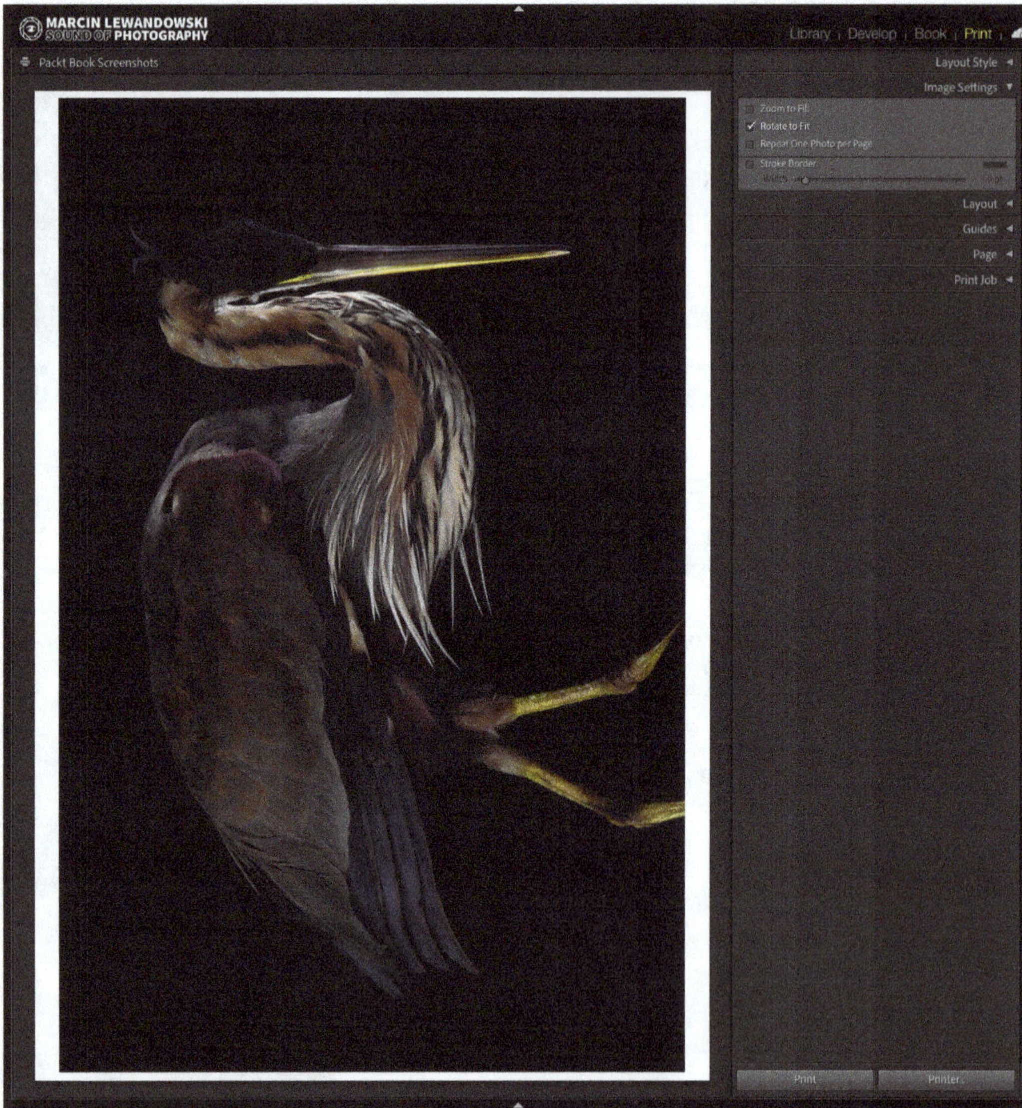

Figure 8.5 – A horizontal picture on a vertical page with Rotate to Fit selected

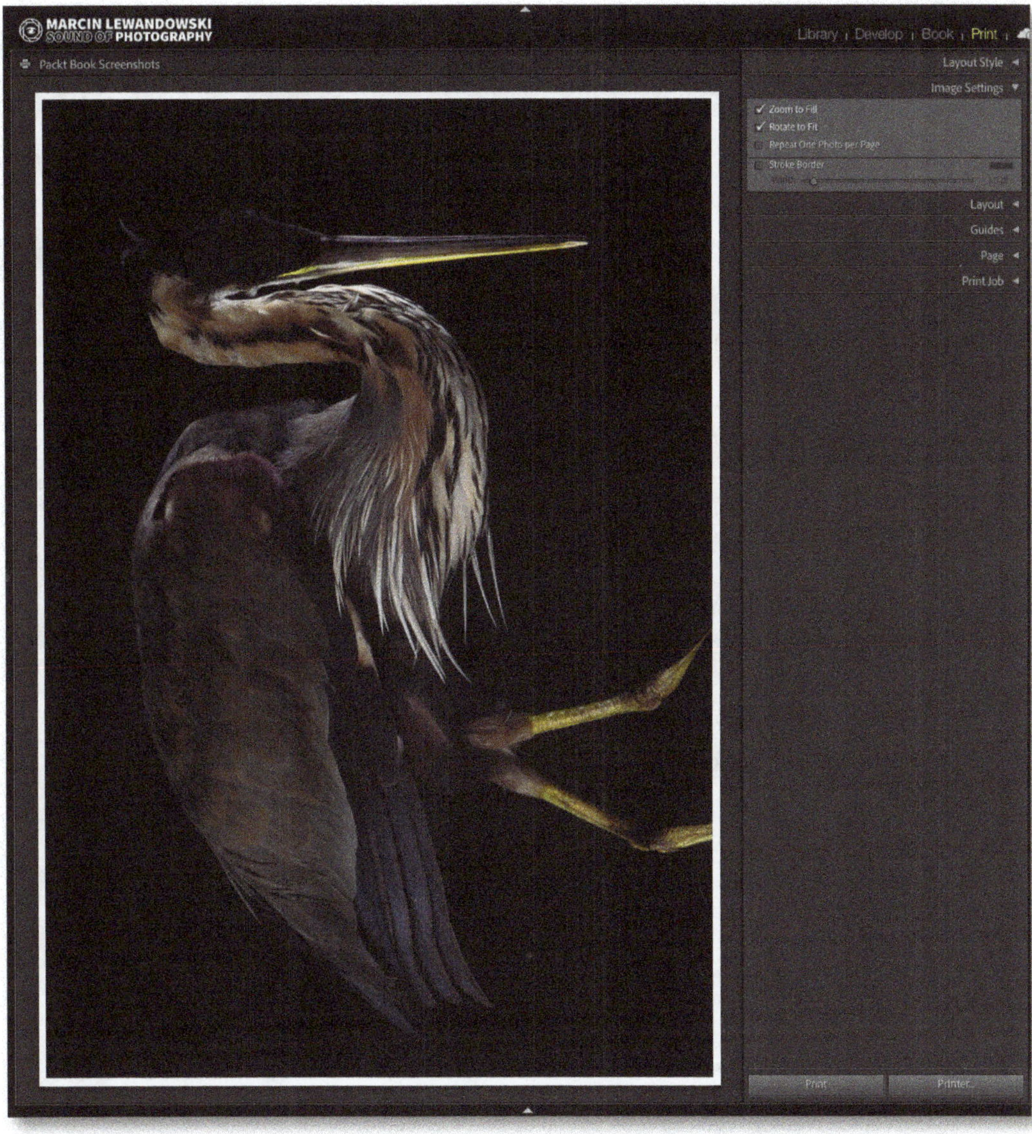

Figure 8.6 – A horizontal picture on a vertical page with Rotate to Fit and Zoom to Fill selected

- **Stroke Border:** If you would like to have a border in any color to surround your photograph, here is an easy way to do it. Once we check the **Stroke Border** box, the slider below becomes active – the **Width** slider. We can set any color border to surround our photograph. The border will be printed inside the set cell dimensions, so it will not change the size of the printed area or set margins.

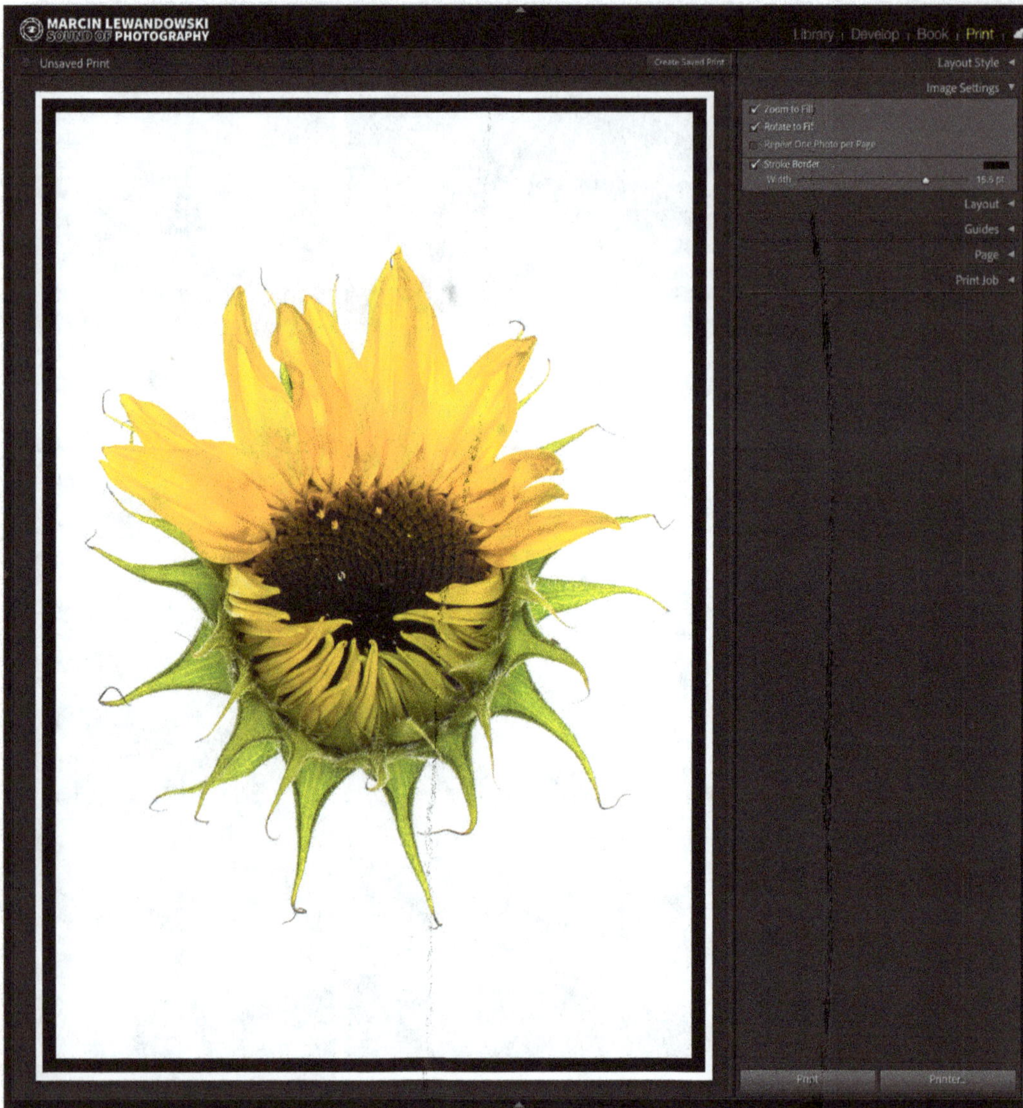

Figure 8.7 – A picture on a vertical page with Rotate to Fit, Zoom to Fill, and Stroke Border selected

Layout

Ruler Units allows us to change units to whatever we feel most comfortable with.

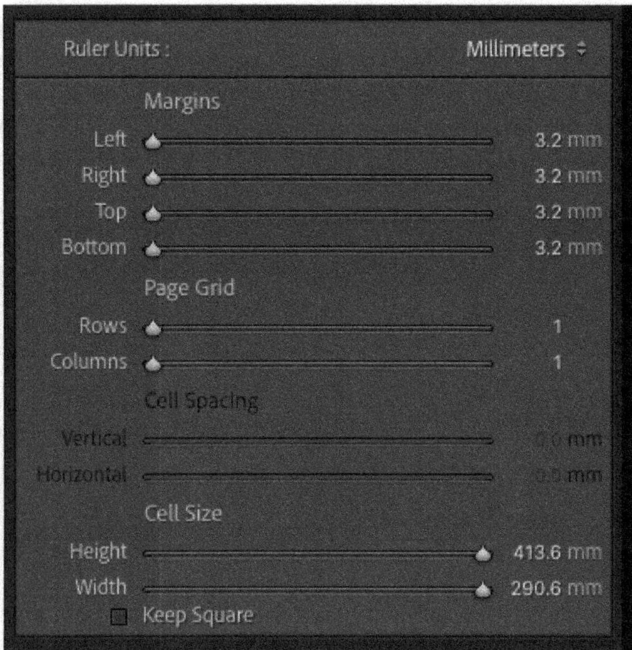

Figure 8.8 – The Layout tab

I like to work with **Millimeters**, as it's easiest to translate into print in its physical form and imagine how it will look. I can also just grab a ruler and quickly measure the distance in millimeters to better visualize it.

Margins

Here, we can set the white border surrounding our printed photograph. If we choose **Zoom to Fill** in **Image Settings**, the width of the margins will have the exact size of the frame surrounding our image. If we don't tick **Zoom to Fill**, the margins' width on the printed page will match on the short edges, with the longer edges adjusted to the inside of the set margins. Note that different printer settings for different papers fed into the printer differently might have a default value for margins that can't be reduced to **0**. If you want to print borderless, and your printer supports it, you must choose or create appropriate paper settings in the **Page Setup** menu.

Page Grid

Page Grid is a great tool if we want to print multiple images on one page. We simply specify the number of rows and columns, which will give us *rows x columns = number of pictures per page*. Once we change the value for **Rows** or **Columns**, we will be able to adjust **Vertical** and/or **Horizontal** cell spacing. For example, suppose I print multiple images per page and set them to print with the **Zoom to Fill** setting. In that case, I'll usually set **Cell Spacing** to a value that's double the value of margins. I can later cut my page, keeping the same margins around each image. We can control whether it's the same photo printed or a different photo in each grid cell with the **Repeat One Photo per Page** setting.

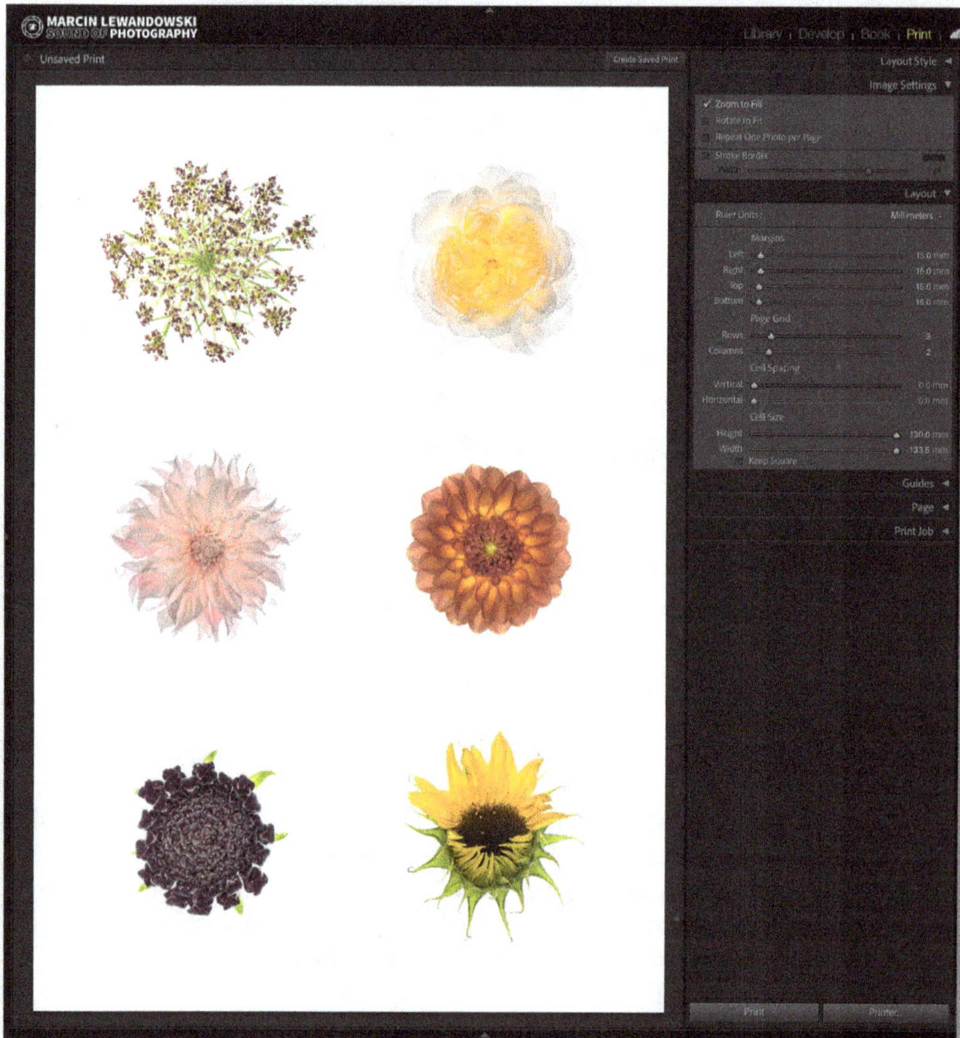

Figure 8.9 A

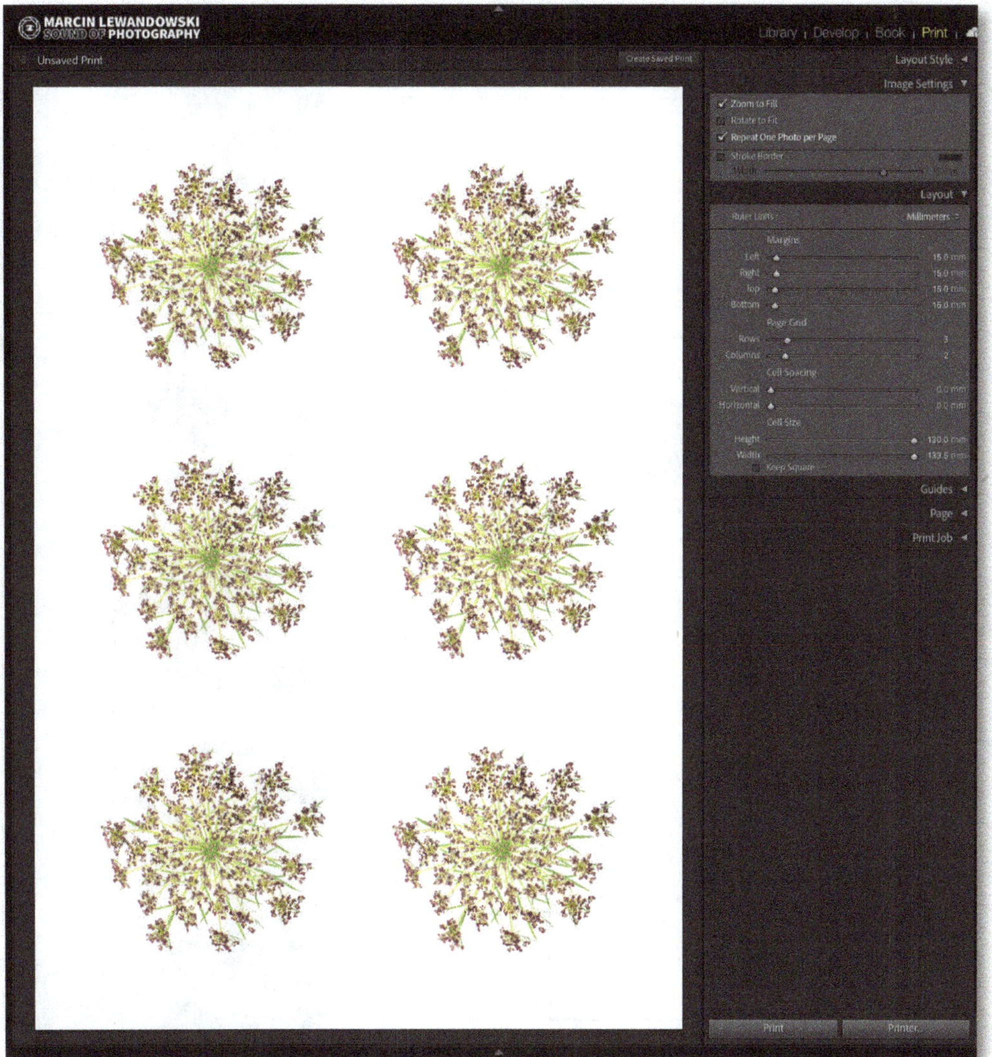

Figure 8.9 B – The first screenshot shows a three rows x two columns grid for six images. The second screenshot shows the same grid with Repeat One Photo per Page selected

Cell Size

Changing **Margins**, **Page Grid**, and **Cell Spacing** will affect the **Cell Size** setting for the photographs to be printed in. If we have actual dimensions to fit, we will be able to adjust it here. One more handy setting is **Keep Square** – checking this box will keep the cells square across the grid.

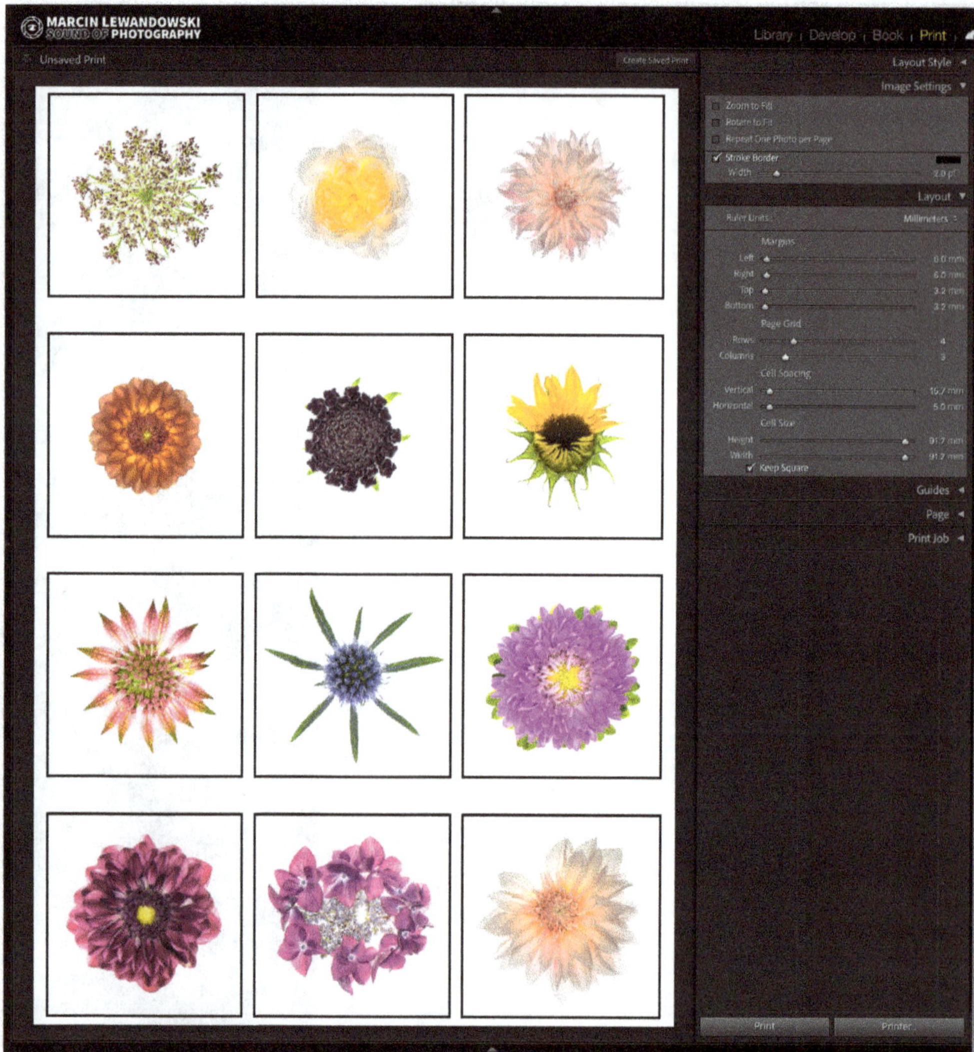

Figure 8.10 – A 4x3 grid with Keep Square and Stroke Border selected

Guides

We can turn on and off any visual guides with the **Show Guides** checkbox. Once it's enabled, we can choose which of the guides we would like to enable. Whether enabled or not, none of the guides will ever print; these are just visual aids to help us precisely lay out the page by adjusting the following options:

- **Rulers**: This appears on the top and side of the main window, showing us values in the units we chose as our **Ruler Units** in the **Layout** section.

- **Page Bleed**: This will paint in gray the unprintable border, which will depend on the paper settings.
- **Margins and Gutters**: This will visualize the grid we created with thin gray lines.
- **Image Cells**: This option will outline each image cell with a black hairline.
- **Dimensions**: Once we pick at least one image to be printed, enabling **Dimensions** will add the exact measurements of the printed area in the top-left corner of each cell containing a photograph.

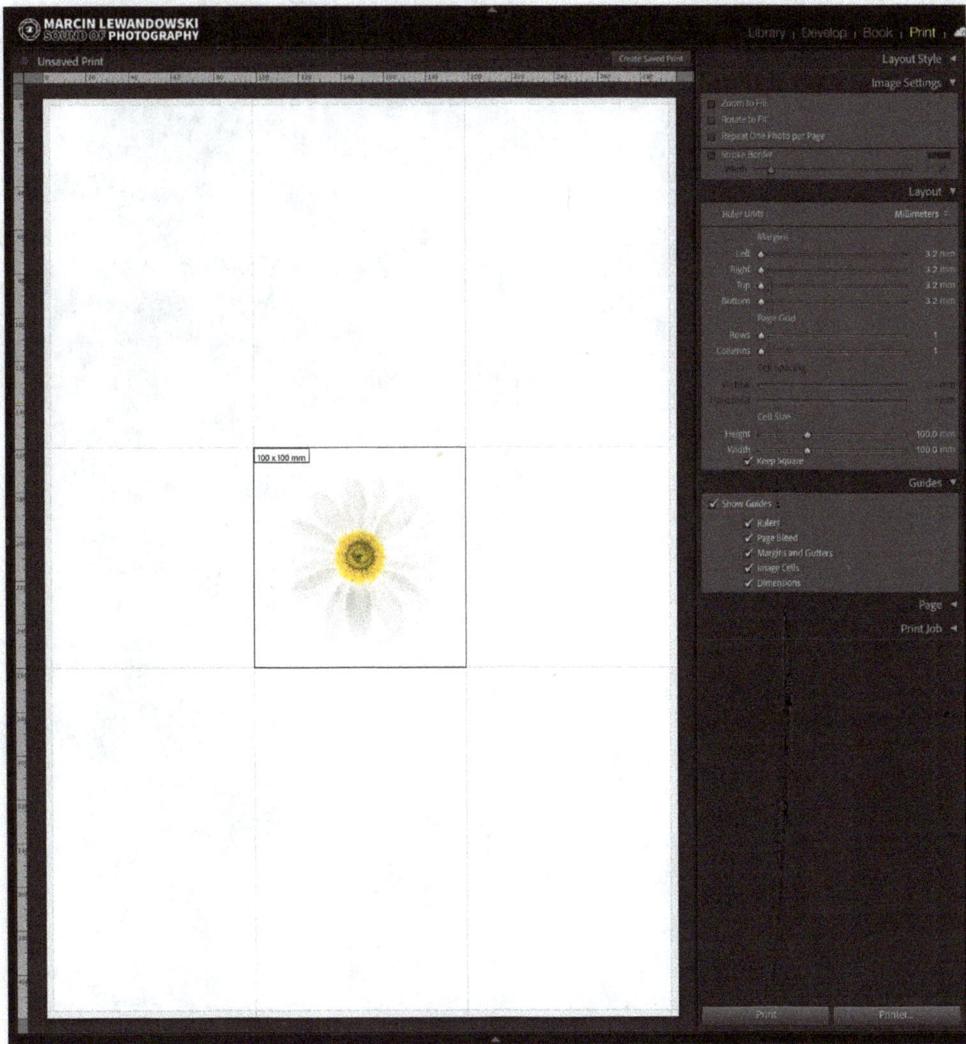

Figure 8.11 – A view with all guides enabled

Page

Here, we can add background color, a watermark, page numbers, and other information.

Page Background Color

Page Background Color will fill the entire space between the image and margins with any chosen color. We need to click on the color box on the right and select anything from the full printable color palette.

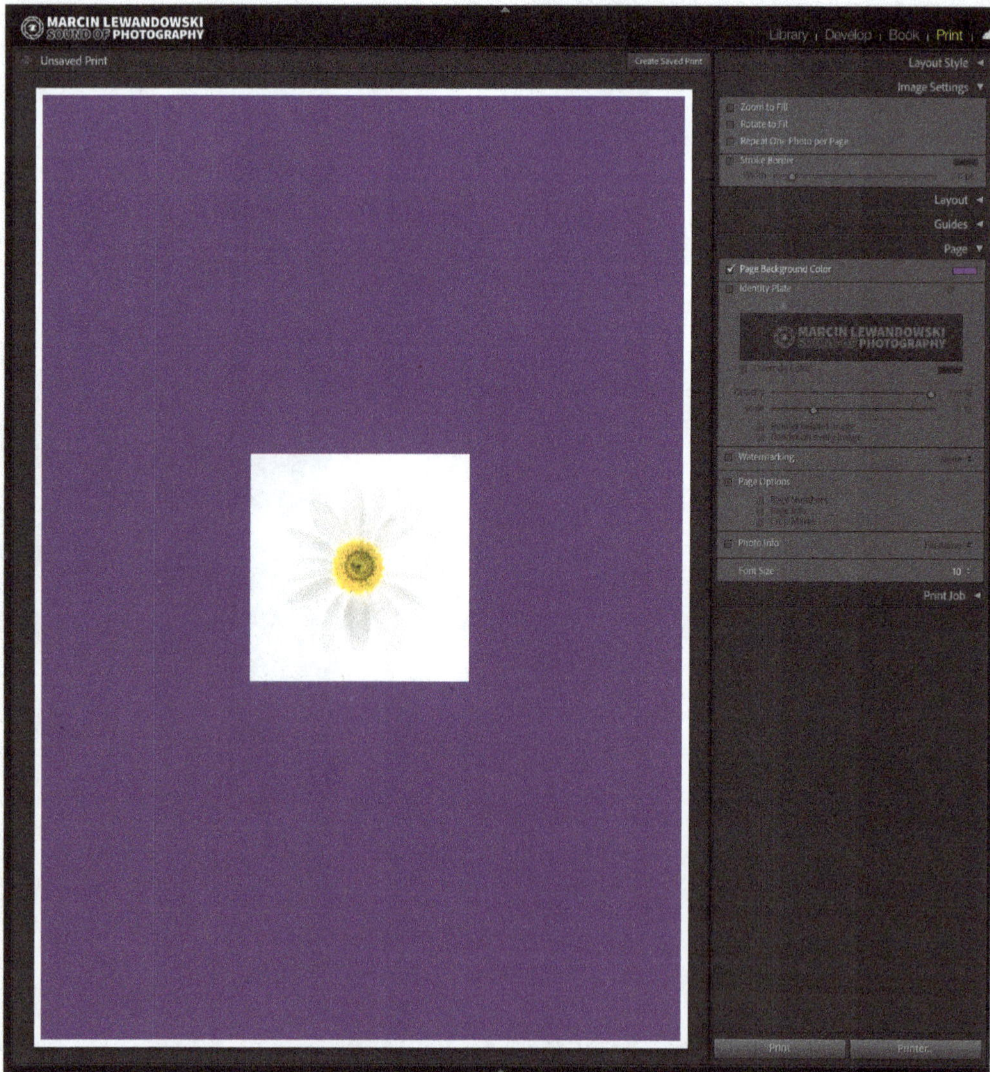

Figure 8.12 – Page Background Color enabled

Identity Plate

With this, we can add a graphic watermark to our printer page:

1. Clicking on the small gray arrow in the bottom-right corner of the blank checkerboard under the **Identity Plate** checkbox will open a list of available watermarks. The watermarks list will be empty if we are using it for the first time.
2. Clicking on **Edit** will open **Identity Plate Editor**, where we can choose a watermark we would like to use or create one. To select a readymade watermark, we must choose the **Use a graphical identity plate** option on the right, click on **Locate file**, and pick one from our drive. It's best to use files that support transparency, such as `.png`, but in the end, it will be a personal, aesthetically driven decision.
3. If we want to create a quick watermark from scratch, we can choose the **Use a styled text identity plate** option on the left and play with the available settings until we like what we see. We can choose the font, type, size, and color in the text input window.
4. Once we are happy with the changes, we need to either save this as a preset in the bottom-left corner menu or just press **OK** to use it without saving it as a preset.

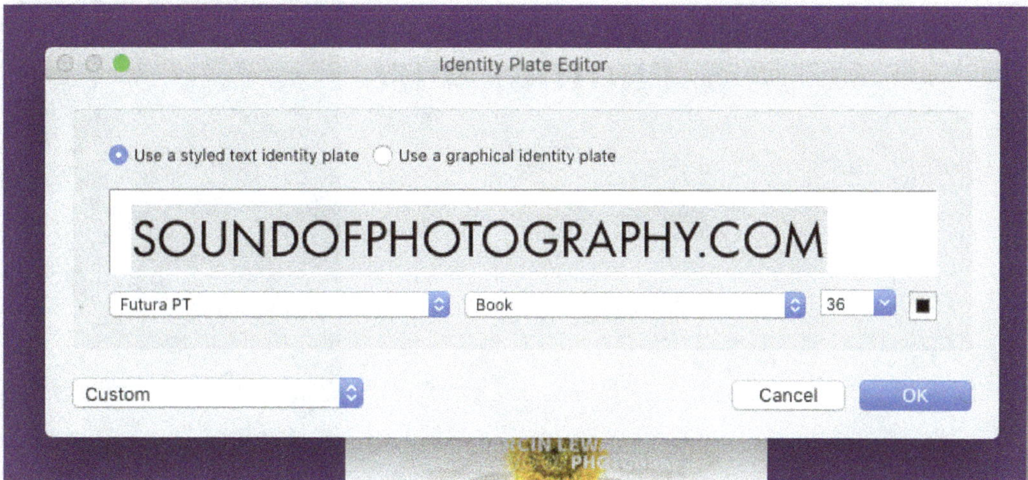

Figure 8.13 – Identity Plate Editor

With the identity plate set, we can now change its **Opacity** and **Scale** settings with two available sliders. As with most numerical values in Lightroom, we can also double-click on the value and manually input the number of our choice.

With the **Render behind image** setting, our newly created identity plate (or uploaded one) will be visible *behind the photographs.* (Imagine watermarked paper with prints glued on top.)

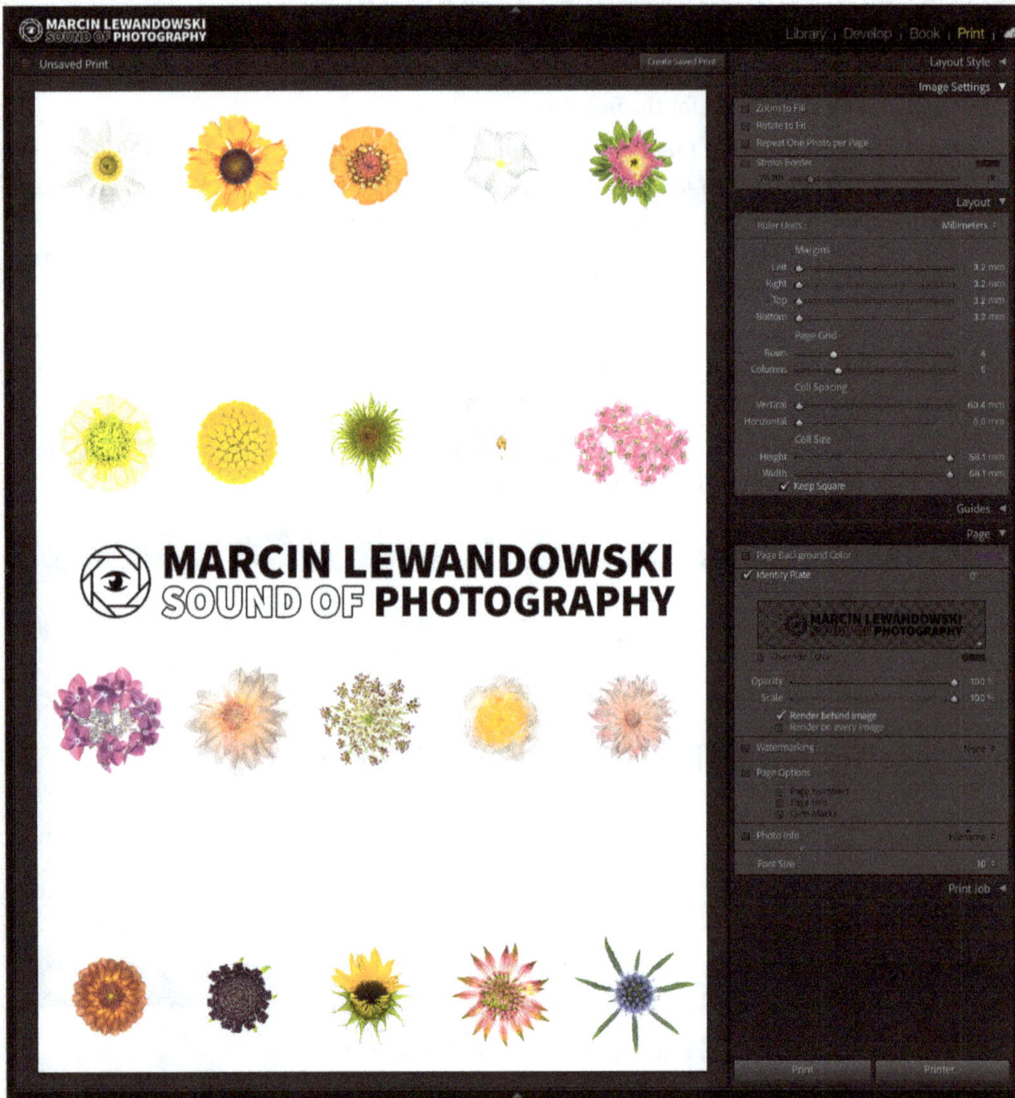

Figure 8.14 – Render behind image selected

With the **Render on every image** box unchecked, the identity plate will be placed in the middle of our print page. If we decide to check this option, it will be placed over each printed image.

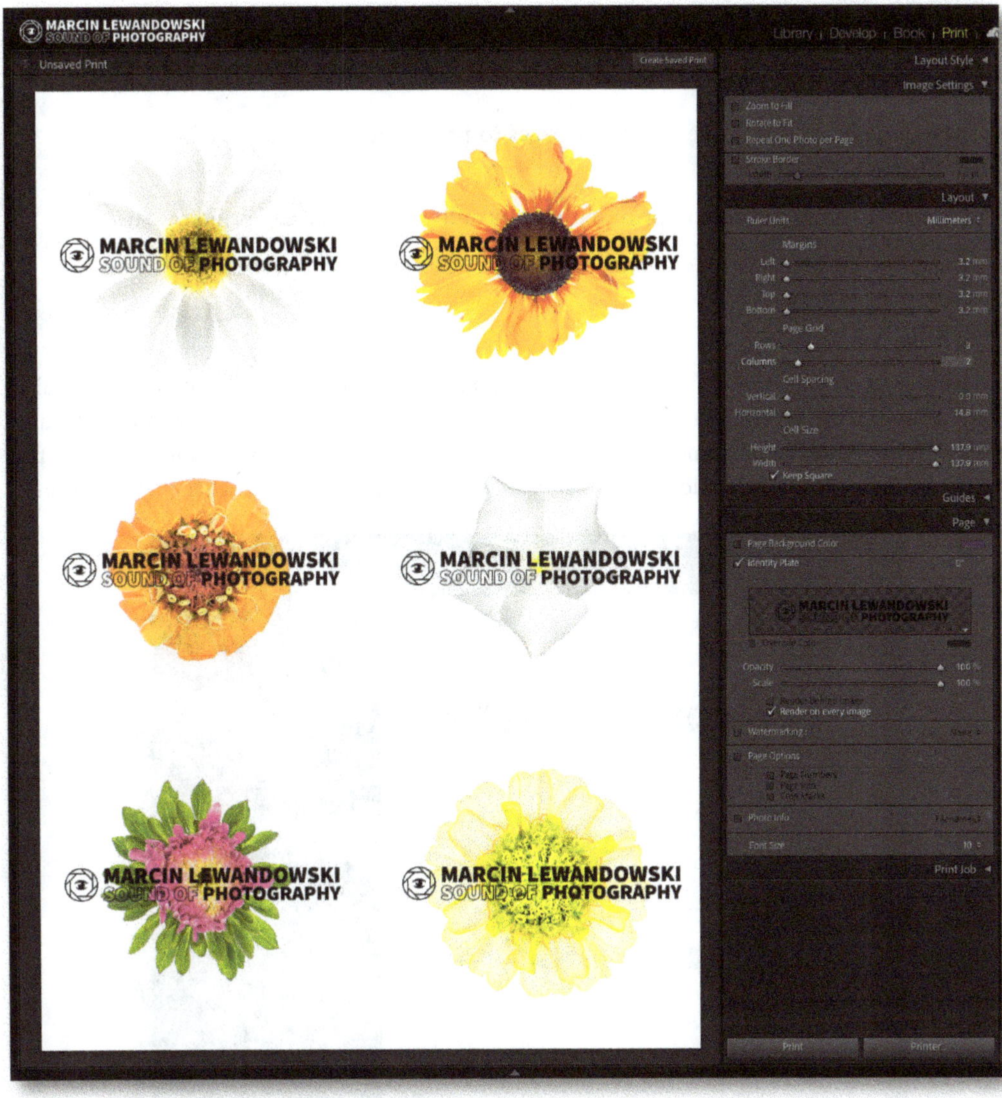

Figure 8.15 – Render on every image selected

Watermarking

Whether we choose to use an identity plate or not, we can always add a watermark. We have access to all the watermarks we created and saved as presets within the Export module. We can also create new ones by following the **Edit Watermarks...** link at the bottom of the pull-down menu located in the bottom right corner of currently selected Identity Plate. It's the same process that's used with the **Export** menu, which we learned about in the previous chapter.

Page Options

Page Options enables you to add a few potentially important pieces of information:

- **Page Numbers:** If we have numerous pages to print and would like to add numbering, we must select this option.
- **Page Info:** This info contains print settings, including the profile and printer we used.
- **Crop Marks:** Tiny hairlines helping to trim the paper to the set cell size.

Photo Info

Photo Info gives us the same capabilities as the *renaming* tool in the Export module, and we also learned about it in the previous chapter. We can change the contents of this information by clicking on **Edit...** in the **Photo Info** submenu or choosing one of the default settings. We can also select the **Font Size** setting for this information, choosing one of the values between **6** and **16** in increments of 2.

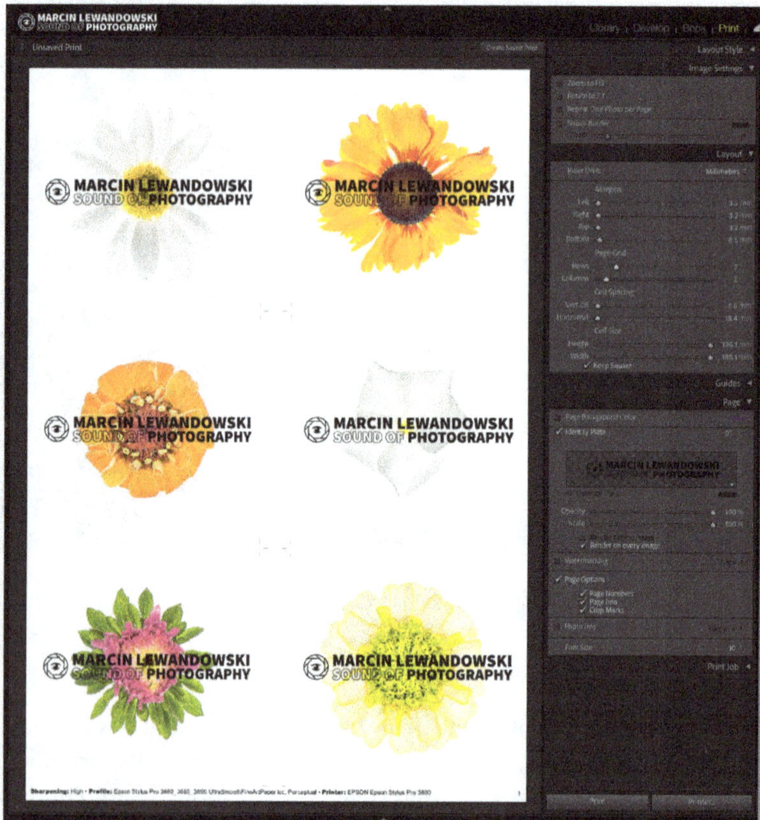

Figure 8.16 – All the page options enabled

Print Job

Last but not least, we have the menu responsible for color management and a few other bits concerning physical output.

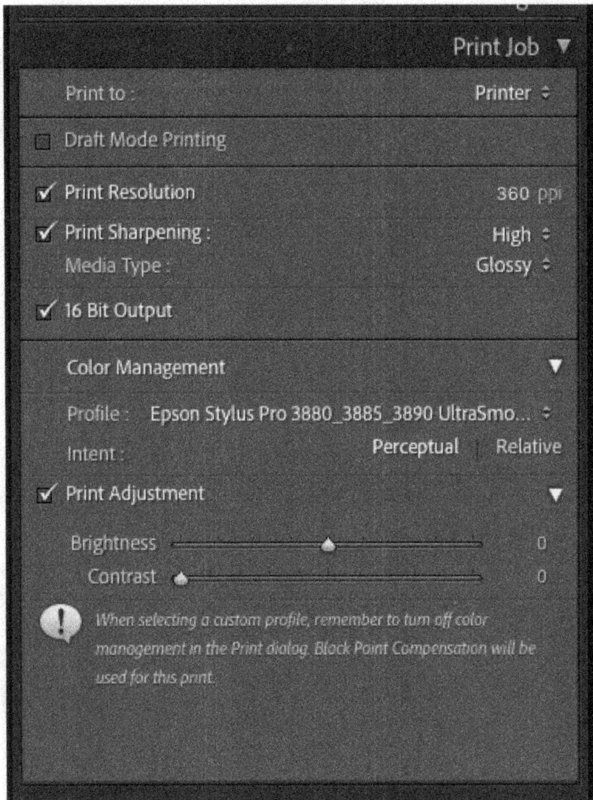

Figure 8.17 – The Print Job tab

Print to

By changing the settings of this option from **Printer** to **JPEG File**, we can export *print-ready* files in the required specification. This is not only great for sending to external print services but also can be used creatively – as an example, I used a set of presets to make a unified-looking Instagram feed.

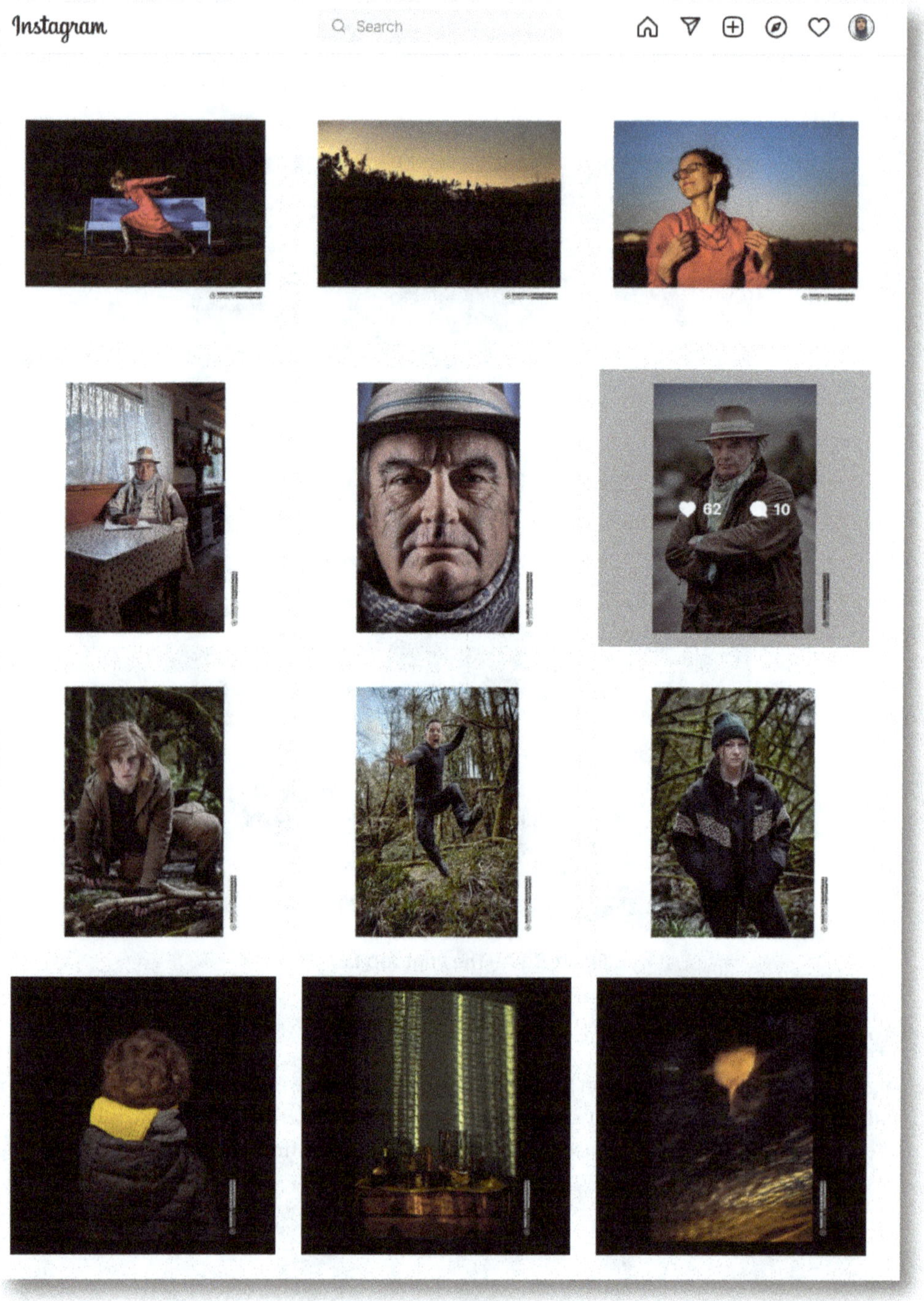

Figure 8.18 A

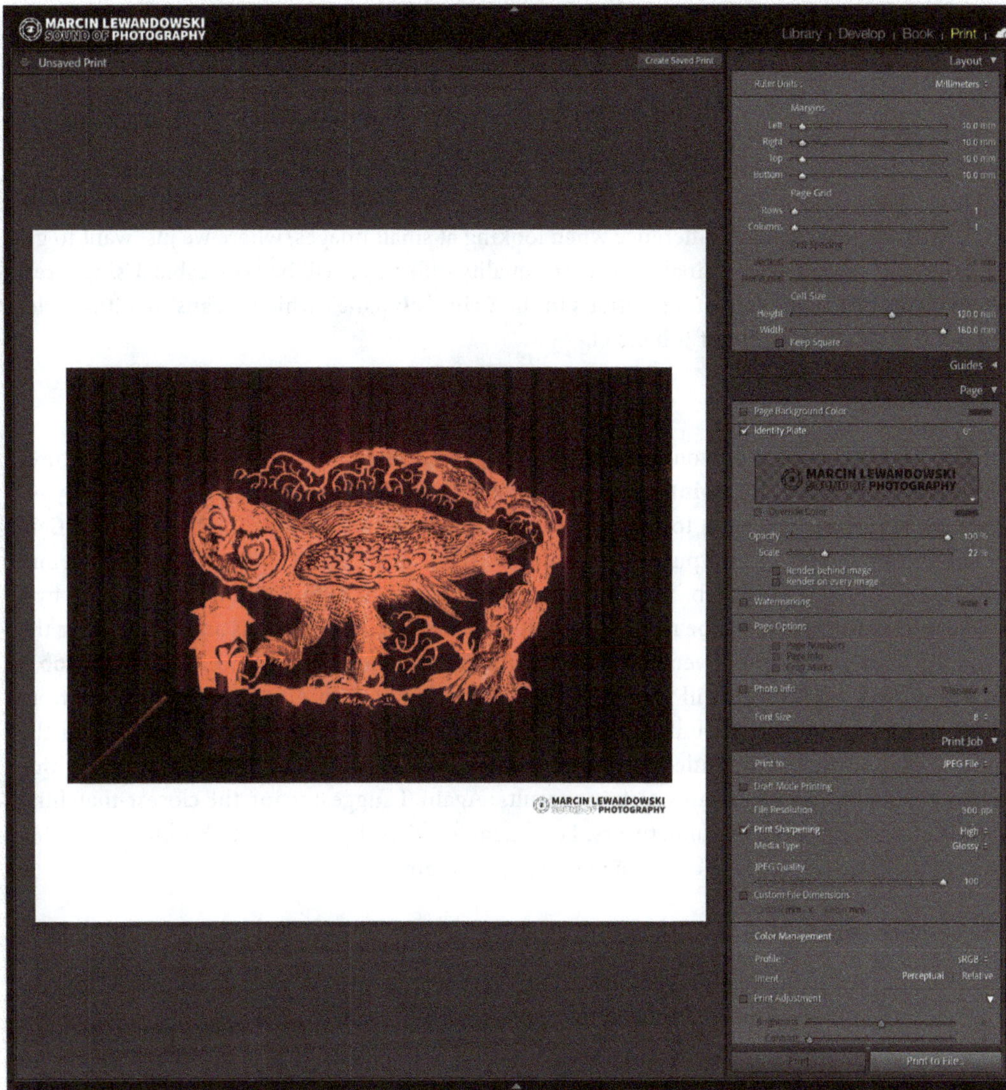

Figure 8.18 B – An Instagram feed with images printed to the file and a view of their sample Lightroom setup

But before we look into the **Print to** > **JPEG File** settings, let's go through the physical printing process.

Draft Mode Printing

First, we can choose whether we want to do draft mode printing.

This is an excellent option if the quality is not essential; instead of originals, Lightroom will send previews to the printer, which will shorten the waiting time for the prints. I suggest using it mainly for printing contact sheets and avoiding it when printing single photographs, especially when quality matters. We will not see much difference when looking at small images, where we just want to get a feel for them, but on a larger, single photo, the quality difference will be noticeable. Using **Draft Mode Printing** will blank any other options in the **Print Job** panel, which means that it disables all the other options in the **Print Job** panel.

Print Resolution

Using this field will depend on your printer, and I suggest referring to your printer manufacturer for the optimal **PPI** (short for **points per inch**) settings. To check the actual maximum PPI of your photograph in the size you want to print in, go to **Guides** > **Dimensions**. The **Dimensions** field will show the maximum PPI output at our chosen settings. You can set this to 360 for Epson and 300 for Canon as a rule of thumb. You will only see fundamental differences in print quality by a few inches. The difference will be most prevalent on pin-sharp photographs and when using the best-quality high-gloss paper. Even if **Guides** > **Dimensions** shows a PPI lower than **Print Job** > **Print Resolution**, Lightroom will upsample the image to print with the selected PPI resolution. The gist of this setting is that unless we print photos from a medium-format camera on the highest-resolution papers, intended for viewing under high-quality gallery lighting, leaving this field blank will give us more than satisfying results. Again, I suggest using the closest-matching PPI value to your printer's manufacturers. For example, when I print on my Epson Stylus 3880 Pro, I set this value to 360 and leave the math to Lightroom.

Print Sharpening

This sharpening option is applied regardless of any sharpening settings we applied in the Develop module. As it is with sharpening, you need to experiment with different settings to choose what you like. An additional selection of sharpening for the medium we are printing on will help in achieving satisfying results. I usually don't use this setting above the low level, applying any sharpening in the Develop module to the point that I'm happy with.

16 Bit Output

As you already know, 16 bits contain much more color information than 8 bits. Therefore, if your printer supports printing in 16 bits, make sure you tick this box. If you select this option for a printer that doesn't support 16-bit printing, the printing process will take much more time, but the results will remain unchanged.

Color Management

There are two main fields under this tab:

- **Profile** is where we can choose the appropriate profile for our printer/paper combination. If you have the profile on your computer but can't see it in this shortlist, click on **Other...**, which will open a complete list of all profiles installed on our computer. If the profile you are looking for is not on this list, make sure you installed the profile correctly. Paper manufacturers who provide ICC profiles will usually supply instructions on how to do that; on a Mac, it's simply a case of copying them to the ColorSync folder.
- **Intent** – **Perceptual** versus **Relative**: We already learned about the difference between **Perceptual** and **Relative** in *Chapter 6, A Detailed View of the Develop Module's Functions*. As a quick reminder, **Perceptual** converts colors in a way that will look as natural as possible for human eyes, while **Relative** will convert all of the gamut colors into the closest values that can be reproduced within the chosen destination's color space. I suggest working with **Perceptual** conversions, especially when we want all our gamut colors to look as natural as possible.

Print Adjustments

This can come in handy if we are using paper that wasn't well simulated in Soft Proofing mode. I find inaccurate soft proofing to be most often the case with matt papers or papers that are heavily textured, but I don't use **Print Adjustments** within the Print module. I prefer to create virtual copies of the photographs in question and then adjust them to achieve better prints. At the same time, I understand that you might want to use this function with hundreds of prints to make quickly. As with a few other options, it's good to be aware of it; even if we use it only once in a very long while, there will be a time when we really need it. I remember many years ago photographing a Brazilian jiu-jitsu competition and bumping contrast and brightness this way for out-of-camera JPGs to quickly produce crispier prints. It was there when I needed it and saved the day.

The two options at the bottom of the right-side panel

On the bottom of the right-side panel, we can find two additional buttons:

- **Print**
- **Printer...**

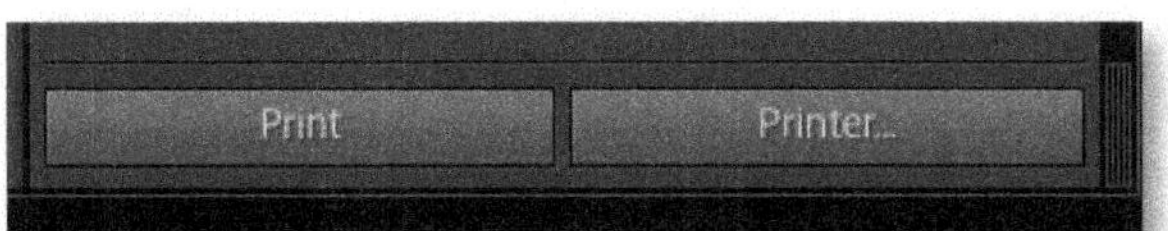

Figure 8.19 – The Print and Printer... buttons

Clicking on the **Print** button will print with the last-used settings. Unless you print image after image with the same specification, I advise never to "just hit the **Print** button." On the one hand, it's "just one page," but if that page happens to be of an expensive A2-sized paper, you might quickly regret losing time and resources. Hence the **Printer...** button offers the same functionality as **Print Settings...**, which we will discuss as one of two topics in the next part of this chapter. The main difference between these buttons is that **Printer...** offers a **Print** button at the end, and **Print Settings...** says **Save**.

Let's now have a look at the left-side panel of the Print module.

The left-side panel of the Print module

Even though the layout of the Print module is more or less the same as all other modules in Lightroom, its left side is home to a Template Browser and two buttons that will directly affect how our print will look – **Page Setup...** and **Print Settings...**. The **Print Settings...** contents will depend on the printer brand and operating system you are using, so please treat **Print Settings...** like an overview more than anything else.

Template Browser

Template Browser contains a number of default print settings that are worth browsing, even if just for inspiration.

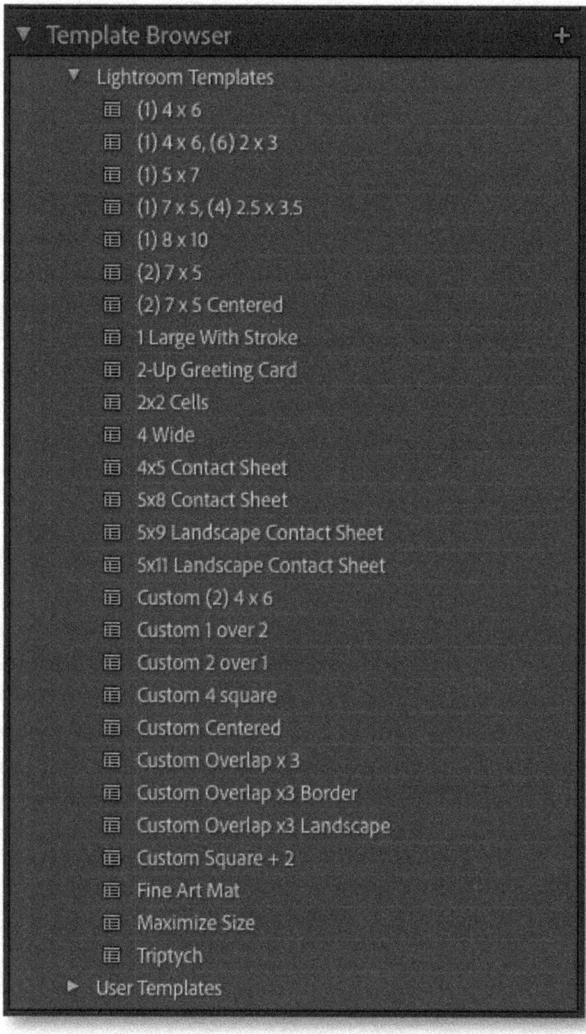

Figure 8.20 – Template Browser

Now, let's have a look at **Page Setup…** and **Print Settings…** in the next subsections!

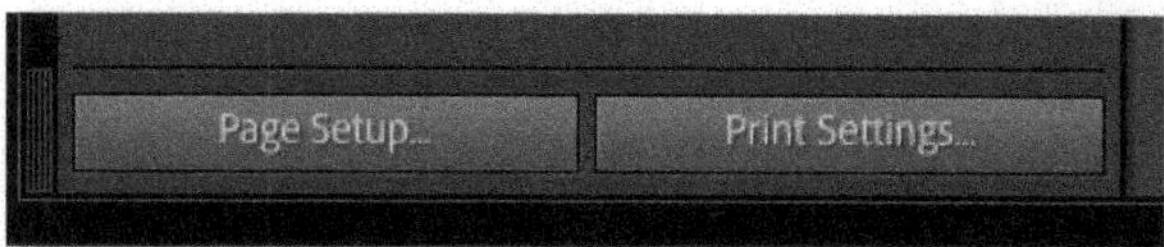

Figure 8.21 – The Page Setup… and Print Settings... buttons at the bottom of the left-side panel

Page Setup...

Page Setup... is where we will choose the paper size we want to work with.

Format For

We will choose which printer we would like to use; this is the list of all printers installed on our computer. If you can't see your printer on this list, you can follow the bottom-most option in the menu, which leads to the system menu, where you can add any missing printers. A printer being missing from this menu might also be caused by outdated drivers, firmware, and so on. Check with your computer and printer manufacturer for details. Once your operating system can see the printer, it will also be available to choose from this list, even if it's turned off and detached from the computer. Finally, we can select the **Any Printer** option. This will allow us to choose a printer at a later stage and adjust the following settings that will be default for all printers.

Paper Size

Choices on this list will depend on the size capabilities of your printer. In my setup, I use two printers - an all-in-one HP printer for office and "work-in-progress" stuff and an A2 Epson for more serious work, such as exhibition-quality prints or handmade wedding albums and books. Most of the paper sizes in the default list will have their own submenu (the ones with an arrow on the right). Depending on the printer, this submenu will offer us a choice of how we want to feed the paper into our printer. Unfortunately, some papers must be fed manually, especially really heavy or super smooth ones. Lightroom will not allow us to work with them until we specify that - this will come up when we learn about the **Print Settings...** menu. Hovering over each of the choices in this submenu will reveal a small note, showing the set print size and minimum size of the margins.

Under the selection of papers available as a default for our chosen printer, we will find an option to create custom paper sizes. We can create them in the last item in this menu, named **Manage Custom Sizes...**.

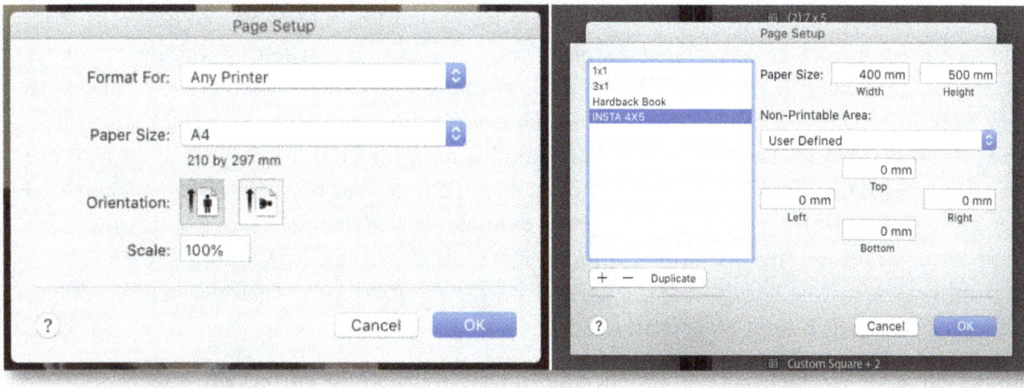

Figure 8.22

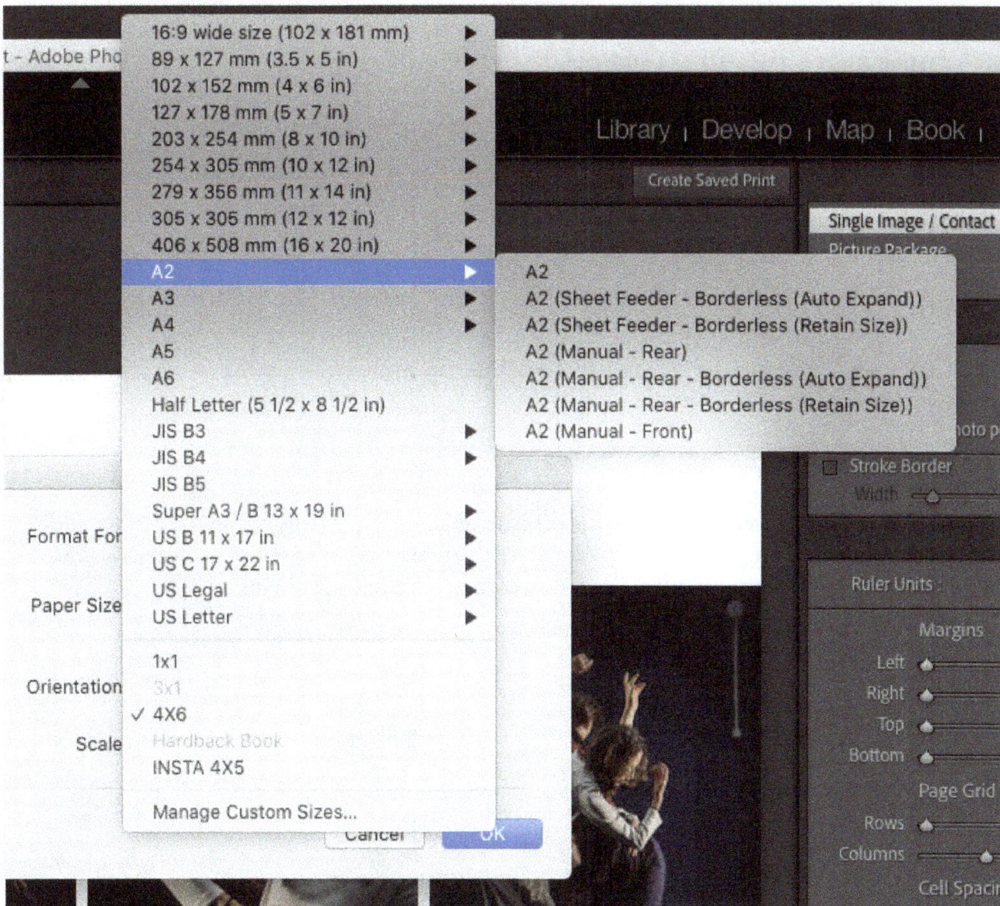

Figure 8.22 – The Page Setup… > Manage Custom Sizes… menus and an example of paper submenus

Clicking on **Manage Custom Sizes...** will open a small window where we can define custom paper size, including its non-printable margins area. To create custom settings for any paper, we need to change the width and height to the desired values and choose whether we want this to be available just for one of our printers or **User Defined**, which will make it available regardless of the printer we choose. Lastly, we can set unprintable margins for our newly set up page. Once we are happy with the dimensions, we need to click on the little plus (+) sign, and a new **Untitled** paper size will appear in the left-side list. Now, we can double-click on it to rename it. Under this list, we have two more options – the – (minus) icon, which will delete the selected paper size, and **Duplicate**, which will duplicate the currently selected paper size. Again, we will be able to change any dimensions on it and rename it.

With this done, we can finally accept (by clicking on **OK**) or cancel the current selection.

Orientation

The **OK** or **Cancel** options will lead us back to the **Page Setup** menu, where we are left with one more choice – **Orientation** > **Portrait** or **Landscape**.

Scale

Lastly, we can choose to reduce or enlarge the printout using the **Scale** option. Since we have much better control over the look of our print from within the tool tabs with the Print module, I suggest simply leaving it at 100% and clicking **OK**.

Print Settings...

Once we have set the properties of the paper we want to print on, we need to specify how our photograph will be printed.

> **Disclaimer**
> This section is just an overview of how the print settings work. Depending on the printer and operating system you are using, it will look different, giving you other options. Treat this as an outline and sketch of what you might encounter when working with **Print**.

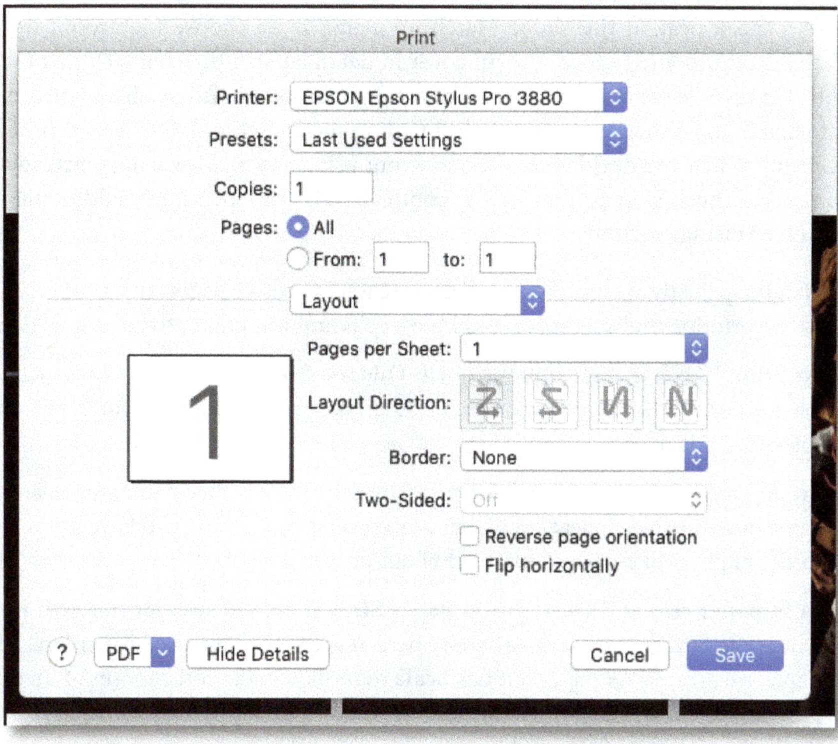

Figure 8.23 – A layout settings example

First of all, we need to choose the printer we want to use, and if we have saved any presets that apply to the job, we can choose the right one using the **Presets** dropdown. This is followed by the number of copies we want to print and the choice of pages to print, which is another standard function of any printing software.

Layout is the first in a series of menus where we can specify many additional print settings:

- **Layout**: If we wish to print more than one image onto each sheet of paper, we have the opportunity to specify it here. In addition, we can choose in what order these multiple images will be printed onto the sheet of paper, which is also represented graphically on the left side of this menu.
- **Border**: In this menu, we can add a variety of thin lines around the printed photograph, which will run around the print area we set within Lightroom. This might come in handy as cut marks if we cut for a specific frame size.
- **Two-Sided**: Lastly, if our printer can do so, we can print two-sided.

Reverse page orientation and **Flip horizontally**: With the last two checkboxes, we can tell Lightroom to print pages in reverse order or to print a mirror image. **Flip horizontally** might come in handy for applications such as iron-on transfers.

Now, let's take a sneak-peak at the **Color Matching** menu. If we choose Lightroom to manage color within the Print module (which we will cover in detail later in the chapter), this menu will be unavailable. However, if we choose a printer to manage colors, we will be able to pick the color profile of our choice. To do that, we need to select **ColorSync** and choose the desired profile from the available menu. When you decide that you want your printer to manage colors instead of using profiles, you need to check your printer's color controls. This will open a few additional options within the **Printer Settings** section:

- **Paper Handling**: Firstly, we can choose whether we want to collate pages. This is especially handy when we are printing multiple copies of photographs and want them to be arranged in sets.
- **Pages to Print**: This has three options – **All**, **Odd**, or **Even**. This is self-explanatory, and it might have an application if you want to, for example, print multiple photographs, in order, on double-sided paper.
- **Page Order**: Depending on our preference, we can choose whether photographs are printed in the same order as they appear on screen or in reverse order. This will have a reverse effect on the order of physical copies coming out of our printer.
- **Scale to fit paper size** and **Destination Paper Size**: These are settings that will resize the printed image to fit the paper size we choose here, regardless of the used paper size. Suppose, for example, we print to A3 paper but tick **Scale to fit paper size** and choose A4. In that case, it will print an A4-sized image (with the borders we set, and so on) onto an A3 page, resulting in a potentially unexpected size and borders. It's one of those settings I never choose to use, but it's essential to know where to find it to troubleshoot a potential mismatch between our screen and the printed page. Lastly, we can choose to only scale the image down, but if we don't select the **Scale to fit paper size** option, it will remain unavailable.
- **Print Cover Page**: Here, we can choose for Lightroom to print an additional page as the first or last printed page. We can choose between various texts, ranging from **Unclassified** to **Top Secret**. If you are a private investigator preparing a report, it might be just the function you need.
- **Printer Settings**: This is one of the most important pages within the **Print** menu. Here, we will set important parameters that will be instrumental in getting a predictably stunning print. Starting from the top, the page setup will be set to values we saved in the **Page Setup** menu. This will influence what paper types might be available to choose from in the **Media Type** drop-down menu, available just below it. Note that certain types of paper can't be selected. In this case, it's best to refer to the paper manufacturer's info sheet, which should provide advice on what settings should be used for the paper you are using. For example, on my Epson 3880 Pro, fine art paper options will be unavailable for paper that is set to be fed through the sheet feeder. All fine art paper options will be available once we change the paper source in **Page Setup** to manual feed. Whether we need the fine art papers or not, this menu is where we will choose the paper we will be printing on. Most good digital photographic paper manufacturers will advise suggested settings, either in the purchased box of paper or via their website. If the manufacturer of paper you want to use doesn't provide them, I

recommend choosing a setting that you think best describes the paper you are about to use. I discourage using matt inks on gloss papers, but that's a discussion that's entirely outside of the Lightroom realm. Other than that, if you have the time and resources, experiment. As much as I find both paper-specific and custom profiles accurate and easy to work with, picking something seemingly "incorrect" for a job can give us very satisfying results.

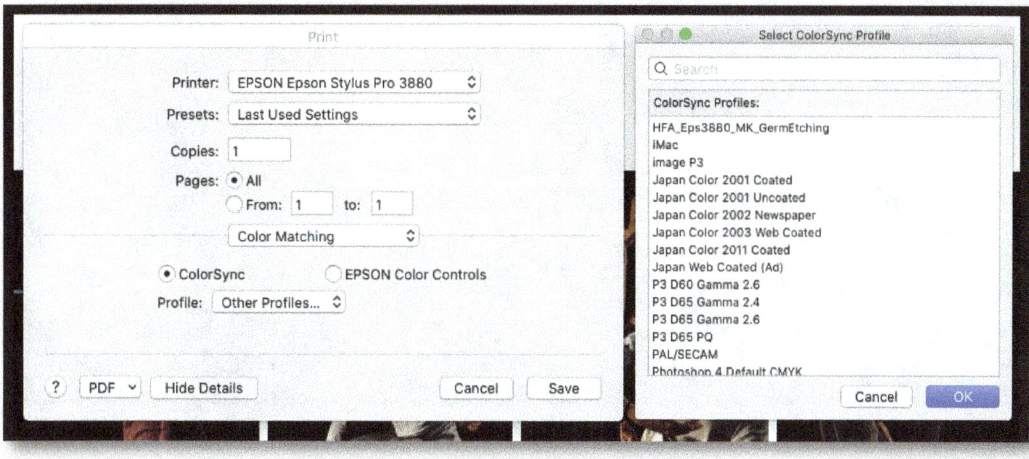

Figure 8.24 – A Color Matching menu example

You might have additional options below the media type list if you manually manage colors without using profiles. Most printers will support various output resolutions. Other menus under this tab might allow us to choose the required resolution, measured in DPI.

I want to stress again that options available within **Print Settings...** are not Lightroom settings, but I thought it might be good to include a short overview and explain what are they responsible for.

With all the information we just discussed, you should have enough confidence to make your first prints and experiment with some of the aforementioned settings. Remember that printing is like a link between the digital and physical worlds. Fine-tuning details that allow a predictable print will require more patience and double-checking before hitting that **Print** button. Once it's printed, we can't interfere with the print; we can only print the image once more. I encourage you to print photographs, even if just occasionally. There is an excellent reward in holding tactile proof of all the work we have put into creating and polishing our photographs.

The next module we will look at is the Book module, where we will be designing our own photo books.

The Book module

It's usually hard to design a book, but Lightroom makes it easy, effortless, and fun. So, let's explore the Book module.

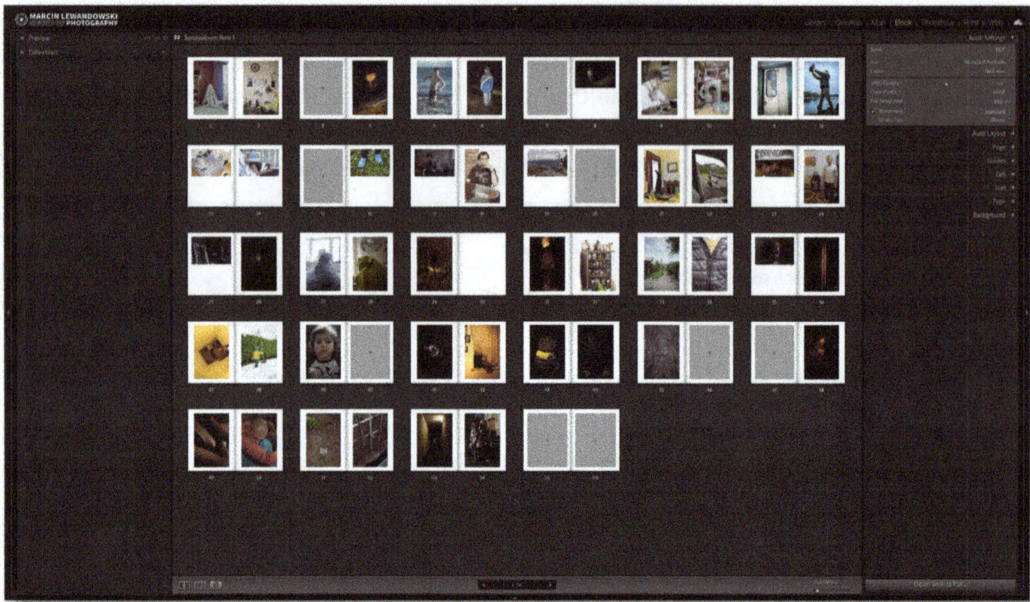

Figure 8.25 – The Book module

The left-side panel of the Book module

The left-side panel of the Book module contains **Preview** and **Collections**.

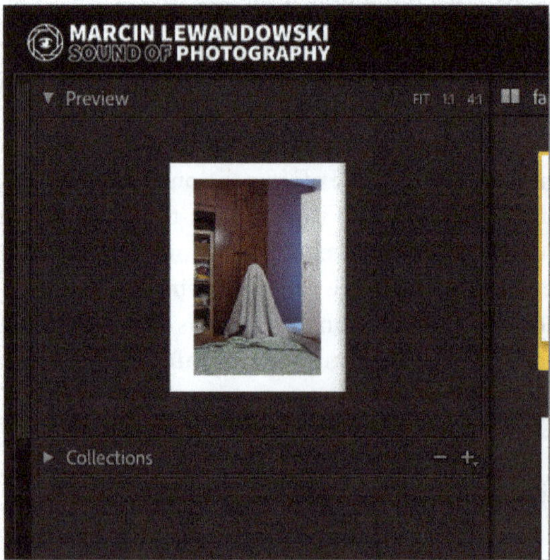

Figure 8.26 – The left-side panel

The only difference between **Preview** in the Book module, in comparison to other modules, is that instead of a single photograph, it will display the currently selected page. In addition, a delicate shadow will help us differentiate between the left- and right-side pages. **Collections** remains unchanged in comparison to the other modules.

Looking at the top, above the current page/book window, note that it says **Unsaved Book**. Opposite this notification, we have two options, **Clear Book** and **Create Saved Book**:

Figure 8.27 – The Clear Book and Create Saved Book buttons

- **Clear Book** does what it says – clears any images from the edited book and returns the layout to its default state.
- **Create Saved Book** will create a collection containing images we selected to work with and autosave any layout changes. I advise you do this every time you start working on a new book project, even if you are just playing around. I learned the hard way what happens when you don't save a book collection.

Once we click on **Create Saved Book**, Lightroom opens the **Create Book** menu, where we can choose the book's name, location, and a few other options:

- **Include only used photos** will save our book layout only with the photos we used in the book. I suggest creating a saved book at the beginning of any work in the Book module, which makes choosing this option pointless, but you might choose to work differently.
- **Make new virtual copies:** Choosing this option will create new virtual copies of all photographs we currently have in the filmstrip, unless we select the **Include only used photos** option, in which case Lightroom will create new virtual copies of the used photos only.
- **Set as target collection** and **Sync with Lightroom**: These options work precisely the same way as with other Lightroom modules.

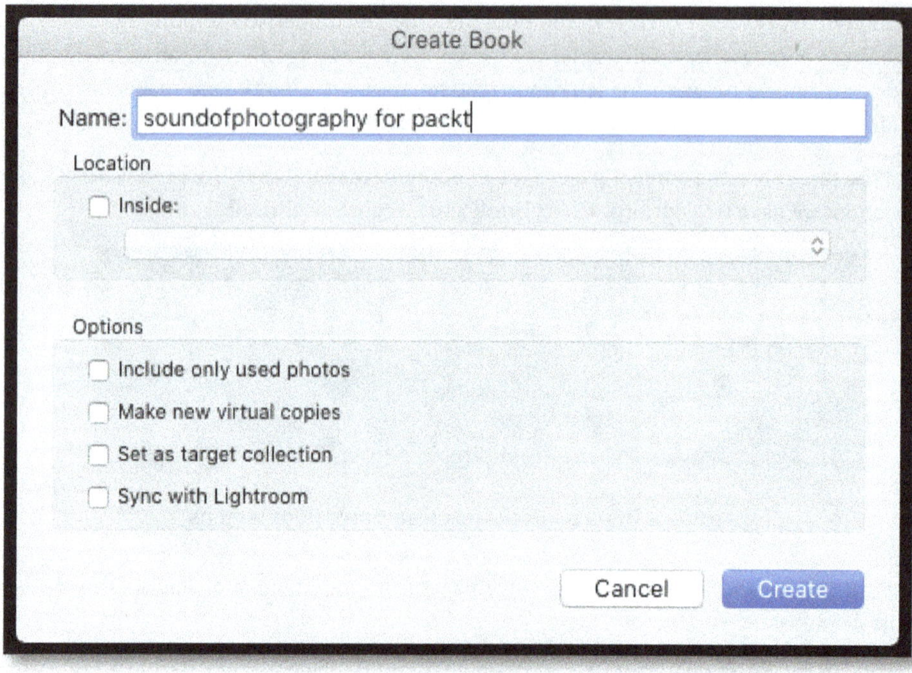

Figure 8.28 – The Create Book menu

Once we click **Create**, a new collection will appear in the **Collections** panel. What differentiates this collection from others is a small book-like icon on the left side of its name. When we view this collection in any other module than the Book module, it will have a small arrow on the right side of the name. This arrow will open our saved book directly in the Book module.

Before we dive into actual book design, it's worth noticing the navigation aids present on the bottom toolbar. On the left side, we can choose between three types of views:

- Multi-page view ("*Cmd + E*")
- Spread view ("*Cmd + R*")
- Single-page view ("*Cmd + T*")

I find the single-page view option most comfortable for designing page layouts. Once I have a few pages ready, I'll switch to spread view and see whether they flow nicely from one spread to another and whether neighboring pages look good next to each other.

Multi-page view also gives us control over the size of displayed thumbnails – a slider to control their size is present on the opposite side of the toolbar.

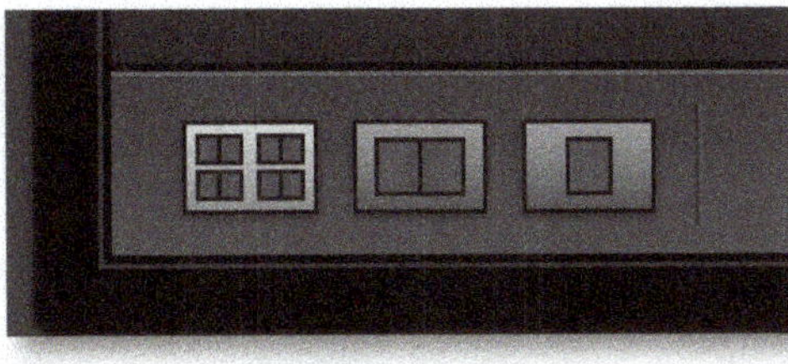

Figure 8.29 – Views

We also have access to the navigation tool in the middle of the toolbar. Arrows on the left and right will advance the book in the chosen direction by one page. Clicking in the middle will allow us to manually type in the number of the page we want to navigate to.

The functionality of the Filmstrip remains the same as throughout Lightroom.

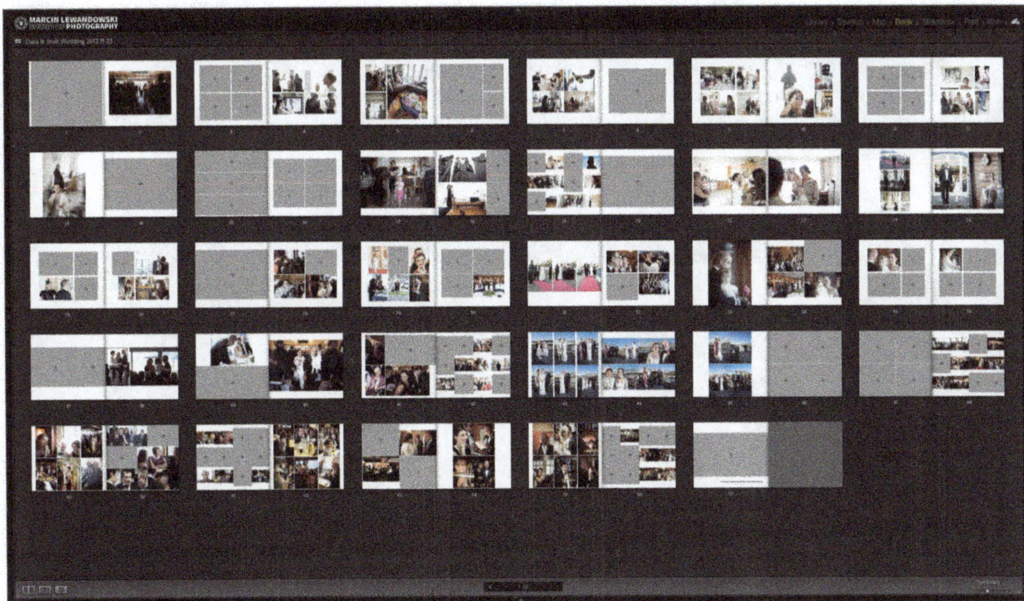

Figure 8.30 A

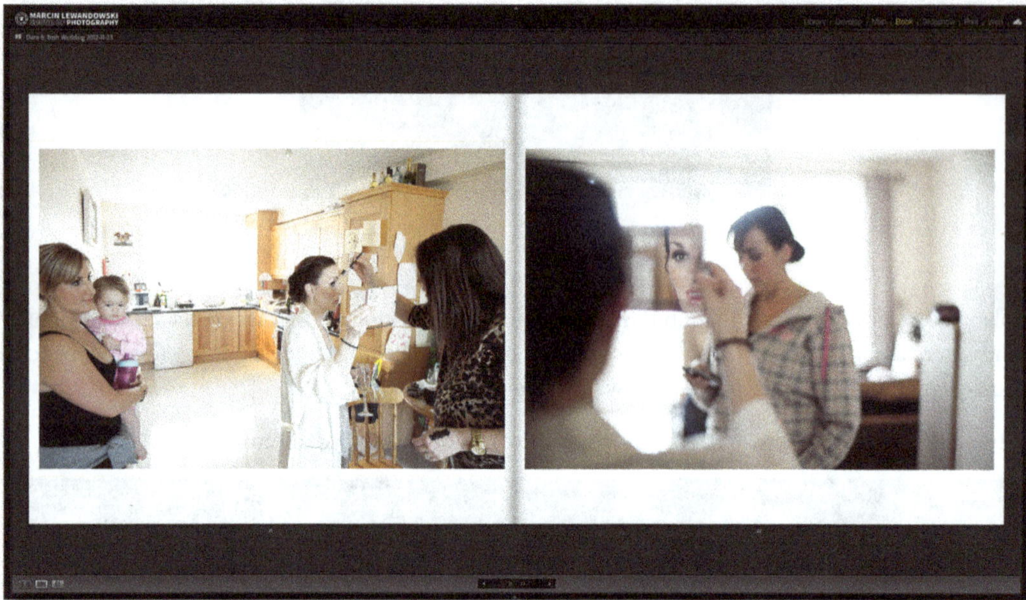

Figure 8.30 B

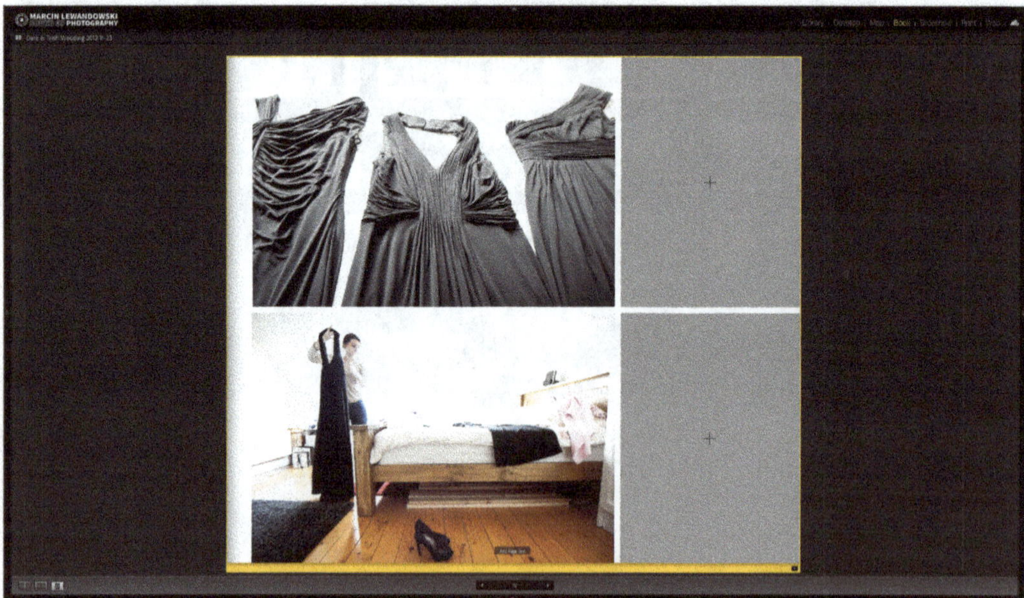

Figure 8.30 C - Multi-page view ("Cmd + E"), spread view ("Cmd + R"), and single-page view ("Cmd + T")

The right-side panel of the Book module

There are eight tabs with settings within the right-side panel of the Book module:

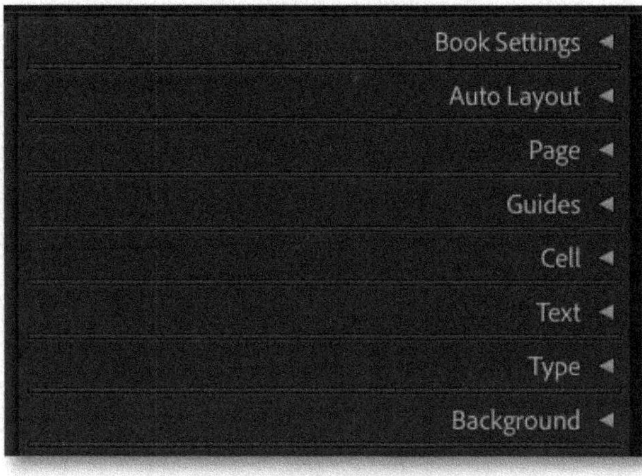

Figure 8.31 – The right-side panel's tabs

- **Book Settings**
- **Auto Layout**
- **Page**
- **Guides**
- **Cell**
- **Text**
- **Type**
- **Background**

In the remainder of this chapter, we will look at each of these tabs, but before that, I would like to give you a quick and simplified overview of how the Book module works. First of all, we will choose the size for our book, add some blank pages (or pages with a predefined layout), and drag and drop images from the Filmstrip into our pages. If we want to change the order of pages, we just drag the page (or selection of them) into a different location within a book. Once we finish the design, we either send it to print directly from Lightroom or export it as graphic files. Sound easy? Well, it is. The user interface is as friendly as other tools in Lightroom, and as long as we have an eye for sequencing, it is a great joy to even play around with it.

Now, back to the right-side panel of the Book module!

Book Settings

The first choice we need to make is what size we would like our book to have. Of course, it's possible to change the size later, but because different sizes have different aspect ratios, changing the size will interfere with the layout and composition of images on the pages.

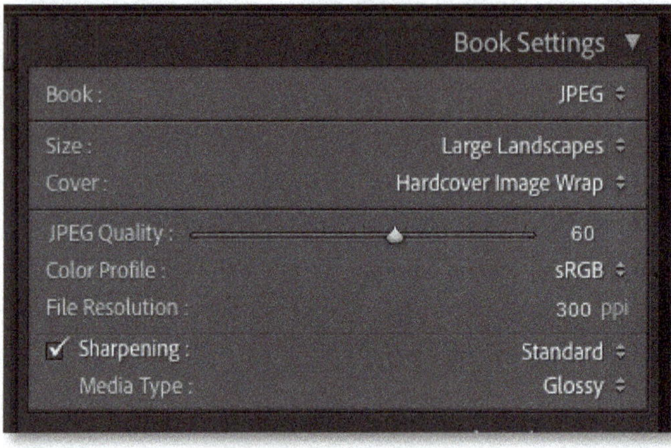

Figure 8.32 – Book Settings

To Blurb or not to Blurb

Blurb is a self-publishing platform where we can print our photo book in as few copies as *one*. It offers other services, such as design, promotion, and selling. For the purpose of our book, we will focus on the self-publishing aspect. Through seamless integration of Blurb and Lightroom, we can order the photo book we designed directly from the Book module. To do that, we must design our book in one of the three available formats:

- **Blurb Photo Book**
- **Blurb Magazine**
- **Blurb Tradebook**

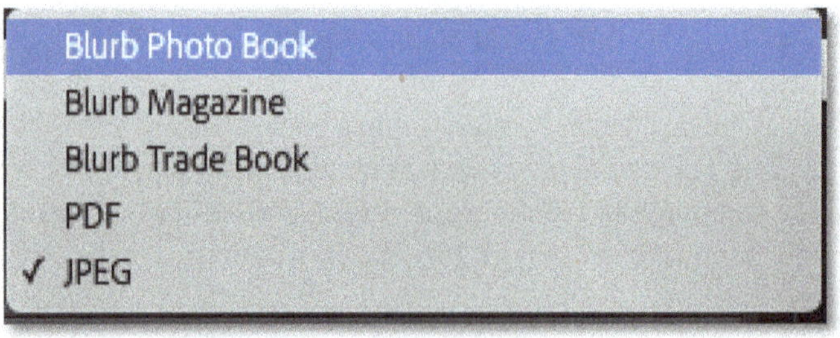

Figure 8.33 – The book options

Both of the Blurb books offer a variety of sizes and aspect ratios and a selection of different covers and papers. The most significant combination of different settings is available within the Blurb photo book. You can also choose to have a Blurb logo page included in the book, slightly decreasing the price. If you have never ordered from Blurb, I would strongly encourage you to order a small format book with a minimal number of pages in a few different variants. The more expensive papers will have a better color reproduction, but the paper choice is a matter of aesthetic preference, as your project might work best on B&W trade paper in softcover.

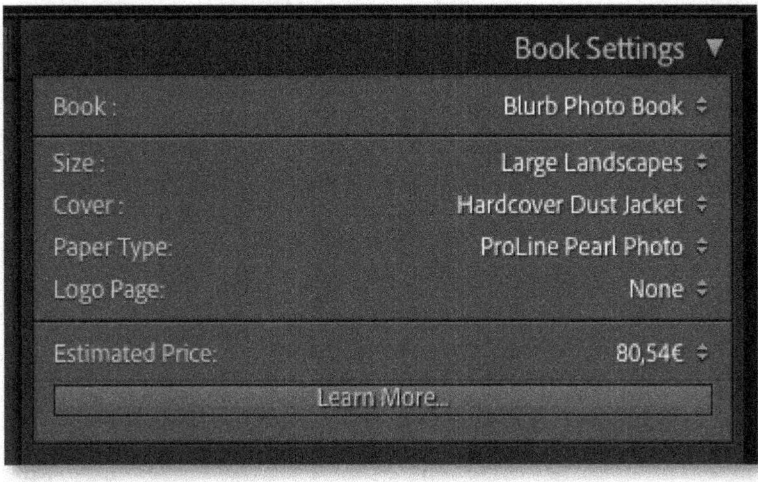

Figure 8.34 – Sample settings for Blurb Photo Book

Even if we don't plan to send a final image to Blurb, it might be handy to design the layout in one of their default sizes. They match the sizes usually found on the shelves in bookstores and news stands. These Blurb-formatted books can be exported as PDFs at the end of our design process. We will come back to that toward the end of this chapter.

Outside of the Blurb settings, we can choose to design for PDF or JPG output, with the same selection of available sizes for both of these formats. Most of the sizes can be designed in several different cover designs:

- **No Cover**: Choosing **No Cover** is quite apparent, and in this example, we will design only the book pages, ignoring the cover.
- **Hardcover Image Wrap**: This allows us to design a hardcover book.
- **Hardcover Dust Jacket**: This adds additional internal flaps on both sides, which can be filled with a combination of pictures and text.

- **Softcover**: This gives us the same design flexibility as a hardcover.

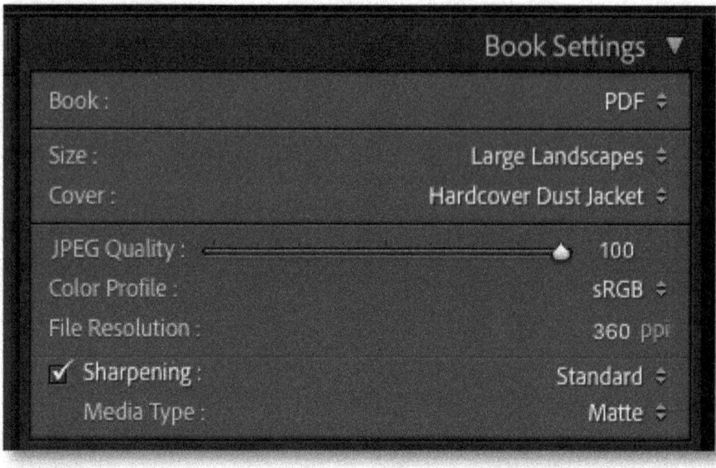

Figure 8.35 – Sample settings for a PDF book – Large Landscapes

Once we select the **Book**, **Size**, and **Cover** options, it's useful to specify the remaining technical aspects of the book in the **Book Settings** tab:

- **JPEG Quality**
- **Color Profile**
- **File Resolution**
- **Sharpening**
- **Media Type**

JPEG Quality

As with any export, setting **JPEG Quality** to 100% is a no-brainer if the quality is of the utmost priority. However, this will significantly increase the size of our final exported files. If space and size are of no issue, I suggest setting this to maximum and not looking back. This will apply the least possible amount of compression, assuring the best possible quality. If, on the other hand, we are, for example, designing this to be an e-book, then even at about 50%, we will struggle to notice significant differences. Some images might be less "crisp," losing a little bit of contrast and sharpness, but between 100% and 50% quality, we will cut the file size by up to 80%. Of course, if we don't want images to be easily reproduced, lower quality will make it harder.

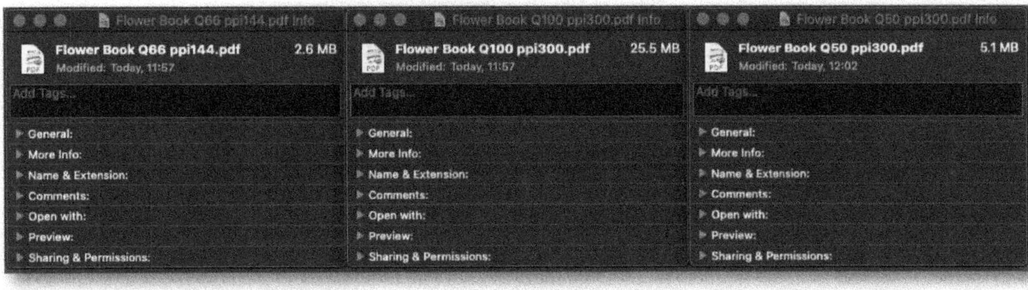

Figure 8.36 – A file size comparison at different quality (Q) and PPI settings

Color Profile

Choosing the correct settings in this tab will largely depend on the final destination for our book. If we are printing ourselves, here we can select the profile of the paper we intend to use or play it safe and choose **sRGB**, taking care of the correct profile later at the printing stage. However, if we plan to use an external service to print our book, I suggest checking with them what would be the optimal choice for our book. The nice thing about designing for printing with Blurb is that we don't need to worry about this part once we select our book format and paper.

File Resolution

You might think that "the bigger, the better," but that's not the case. Many commercial printers will not print books above 150 PPI, and we would be just wasting time and space. The Blurb settings don't ask us for this detail, so it's one less thing to worry about, but I suggest always checking requirements with the book printing service. Setting it to the maximum resolution that our printer can support is a good habit too.

Sharpening

Just as is the case with the similar setting in the Print module, we can apply varying, additional sharpening on top of any sharpening we set in the Develop module. This setting is separate for glossy and matt paper. Personally, I don't set this to higher than **Standard**, as it can produce halos in some scenarios.

These are all the book settings. Next is **Auto Layout**.

Auto Layout

As you can imagine, clicking on **Auto Layout** will take care of designing the book for us, and we can quite extensively customize this process.

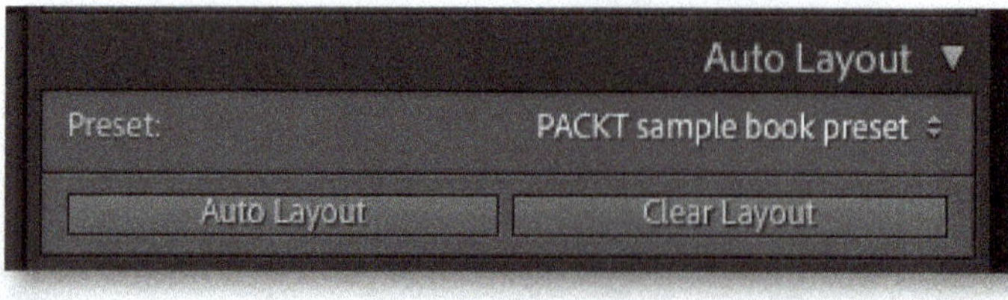

Figure 8.37 A

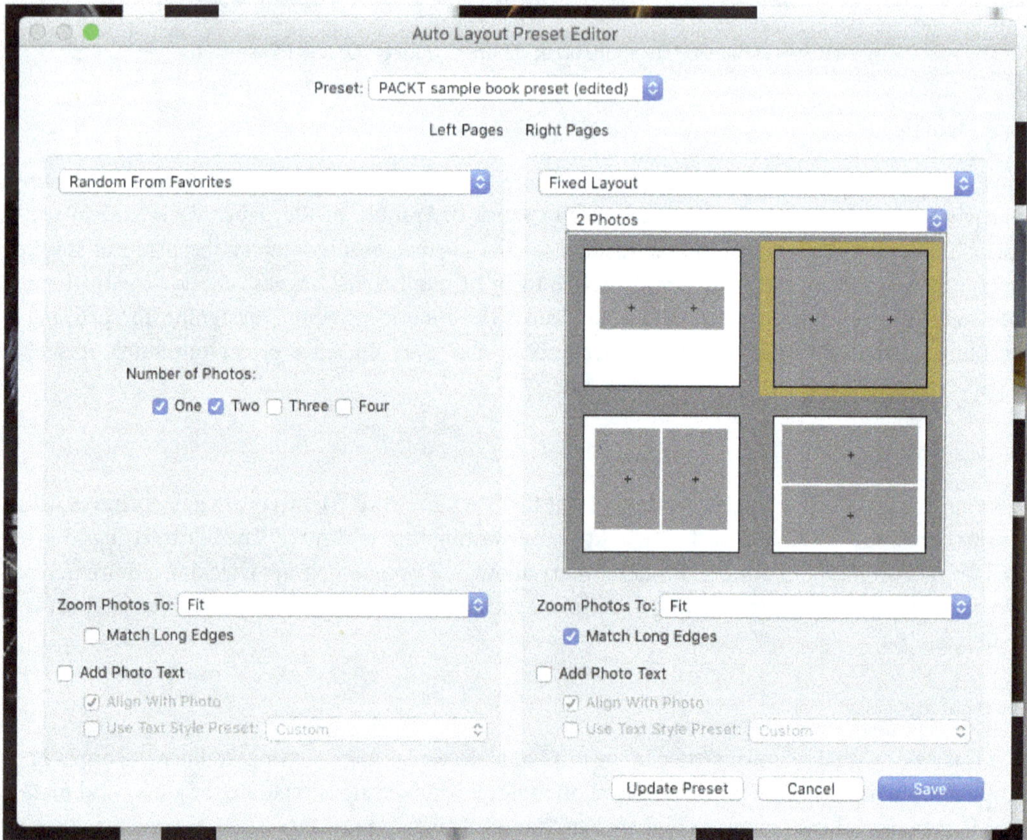

Figure 8.37 B – The Auto Layout tab and Auto Layout Preset Editor

When we click to open the **Preset** menu for the first time, we can choose from three available presets or **Edit Auto Layout Preset**. **Auto Layout Preset Editor** consists of two panels, left and right, representing each of the book's pages. We can set the layout for both pages separately by clicking on the pull-down menu and choosing a layout we like. We can also tell Lightroom to choose layouts from our favorites. (We will get to this later in the chapter when we look at manually creating the layout of each page.) Page by page is definitely my preferred way of designing a photo book. The **Auto Layout** option is here, but to be perfectly honest,

I have never used it, always preferring to create pages one by one. You might like it; it might be beneficial when creating books with a set layout across any number of pages. We can always add additional pages in any place within the book, which we will look at in the next section.

Page

This is where we can add pages and choose whether they are numbered or not.

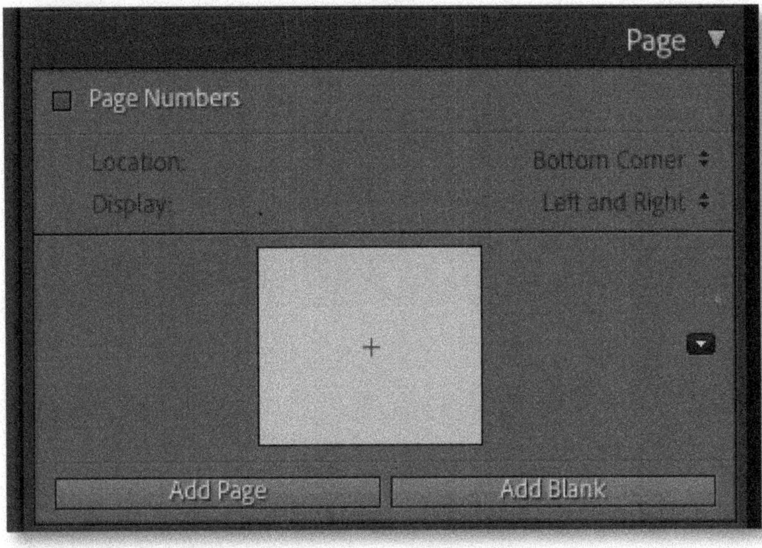

Figure 8.38 – The Page tab

The numbering menu will become available once we tick the **Page Numbers** option. We can set up where we want the page number to appear and whether we'd like it on both sides of each spread, or just on one of the pages.

When adding a page, we have two ways to do so – **Add Page** and **Add Blank**. **Add Page** will add a page with the design visible just above the buttons. We can change this layout by clicking on the small arrowhead visible on the right side of the page layout. Once we click on that small arrowhead, a list of all available arrangements will open. Here, we can choose any configuration from the quite comprehensive collection available for layouts, ranging from just 1 full-bleed photo to well over 30. We can also add any layouts to our favorites by either clicking on the small circle in the top-right corner of each layout or right-clicking and confirming our selection. Whatever we add to our favorites will be later available in the **Auto Layout** settings. **Add Blank** adds a blank page, without any layout designs.

Guides

In this tab, we can choose which guides, if any, we would like Lightroom to display on the page.

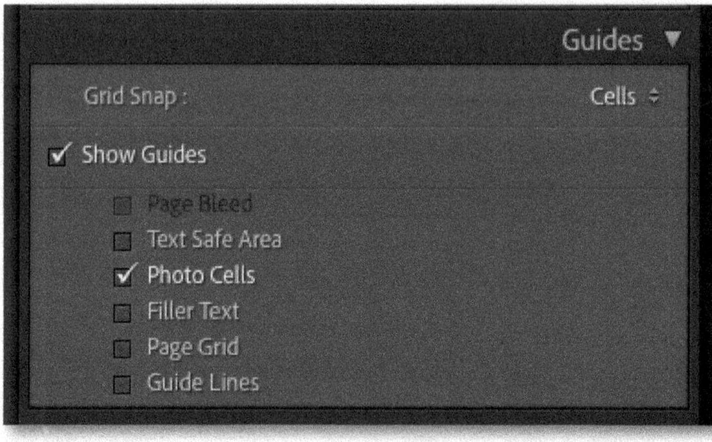

Figure 8.39 – The Guides tab

I prefer to use only **Photo Cells**, as I find everything else quite distracting, but you will have to find your own preference and best way to work. I find these especially helpful when working with text. I might come back to this tab from time to time when I change the size and layout of the photo cells, which we will learn more about in the following section.

Cell

As with most things within Lightroom, the size, shape, and positioning of the photo cells on the pages of our book are highly customizable, and the **Cell** tab is just one way to work with them.

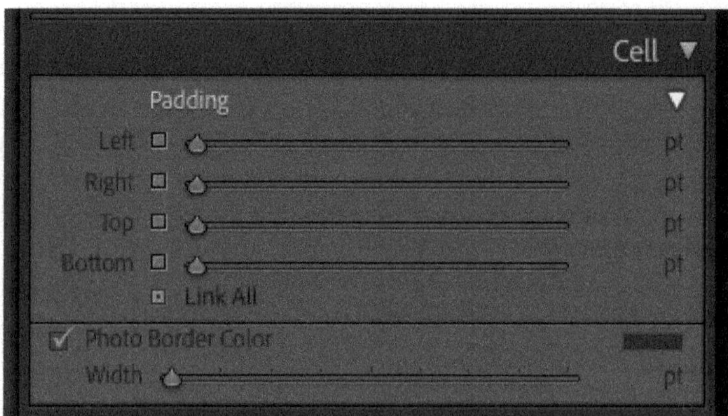

Figure 8.40 – The Cell tab

When we click on any photo cell on the book's page, it will become highlighted, and sliders in the **Cell** tab will become active. Note that each slider has a small, gray, square box next to it. These are responsible for linking settings – that is, if we have all sides linked, changing the **Padding** value of one of them will change the padding to the same value for each linked site. Padding means margins created inside the cell that we are currently editing, so for maximum flexibility and adjustability, we should start with full-bleed layouts. In the second part of this menu, we can also add a photo border, modifying its color and width.

The next two tabs, **Text** and **Type**, are responsible for working with text fields in the book, and I'm not sure why Adobe decided to split these settings into separate tabs.

Text

Photo Text must be enabled for each photo cell and page separately.

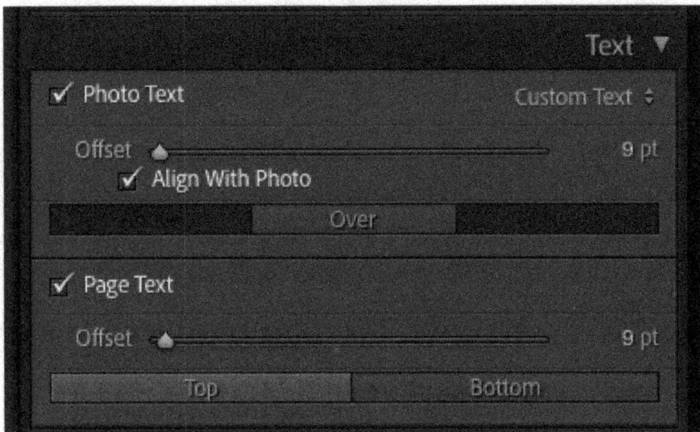

Figure 8.41 – The Text tab

Once we enable the text field, we will be able to choose whether it's positioned above, over, or under the photograph and whether we want to apply an offset to its positioning. Offsetting of the text will be limited by the text safe area, so we don't need to worry about going too far with it. We can simply adjust **Offset** to our liking without the fear of losing the text. The same rule applies to **Page Text**, but here, we can only choose whether it will appear at the top or bottom of a page.

Type

Once we have any text in our book, we can set the font type, size, and alignment within the text box.

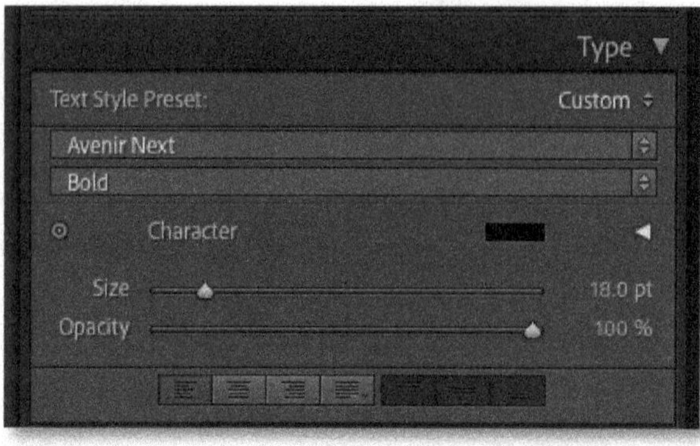

Figure 8.42 – Type tab

These are the most basic options that any text editor offers. Once we have chosen settings we like, we can save them as a preset for later use by clicking on the **Text Style Preset** menu and choosing **Save Current Settings as a New Preset**. When we change the font settings, we need to select the text we want to change, but we can also use "*Cmd*" + click on multiple text boxes and adjust settings for all of them at once. Then, every subsequent text box we have in the book will use our latest **Type** settings.

With all of the preceding tabs explained, we are left with the last one, titled **Background**.

Background

This tab allows us to change the background in our book by using one of the graphics under the **Graphic** menu.

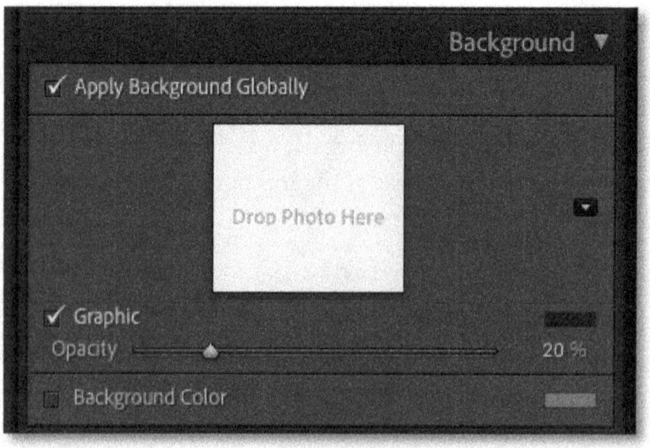

Figure 8.43 – The Background tab

It's hiding under the small arrow, which we can find next to the currently selected graphic. We can also upload our own photograph or graphic to use instead. When we check the **Apply Background Globally** box, the same graphics will appear on each book page, but we can choose a different background for each page if we don't.

A few tips and tricks not mentioned earlier in the chapter

Even though it might seem that we are limited by the templates, there are few ways to create our own layouts. First of all, we can move all picture cells around the page and adjust their size by dragging the corners of the picture cell. This is when **Page Grid** will come in handy, as we will be able to easily adjust cells to the same positions or sizes. Then, by right-clicking anywhere within the page, we can open a submenu that will allow us to save this newly created layout as a custom page. This new custom page will now be available for addition to favorites and usage throughout the book. If you would like a bit more precise control, especially for pages with multiple images, then you can use the full-bleed templates and adjust the padding, picture by picture. Let's look at an example of building a custom, symmetrical page with matching distances between photographs. First, we choose the layout for four pictures and then adjust the padding in each cell so that the padding of the external edges equals precisely half of the padding of the internal borders. In this example, the outer edges have a padding of 12 points and the inner edges have a padding of 6 points. When two cells with external padding of 6 points meet, they match the external padding of 12 points, and we have a new custom template. You can also use this trick for one, two, or three cells. I work on pages this way because Lightroom templates have much too wide padding for my liking.

When we want to move pages around, the most straightforward way is to enter a multi-page view, select the page we want to move, and drag it by the yellow border. For example, if we click and drag a picture, we will move just the photograph within its cell or even remove it off to a neighboring page.

When we want to switch the position of two images in a multi-picture grid, we can just drag one onto the other, and they will automatically swap places. To get rid of a photo from the cell, we can use "*backspace*" or right-click on it and choose to remove the picture.

Once the book is designed and ready for the world to see, all that's left is to either send it to **Blurb** or select **Export Book** to export as a **PDF** or **JPEG**. The export format will depend on the settings we picked in the **Book Settings** tab.

I hope you will find playing around with the Book module enjoyable. When it finally comes to designing someone's wedding album or a layout for your own portfolio, you will enjoy the creative process and ease of use that Adobe has built into Lightroom.

Summary

Few things feel better as a photographer than holding tactile proof of your completed work. Making prints at home and having full control over what comes out of a printer is probably the closest we can get to looking at an image slowly appearing among the darkroom chemicals. What makes a huge difference is the level of control over the outcome. The guessing game when developing and making prints from negatives could be unbearable, not to mention the "close-to-impossible" trickery involved when working with color. With the help of Lightroom's Print module, we can have reliably predictable effects that produce rewarding results each time we press the **Print** button. As for the Book module, self-publishing anything beyond a black and white "zine" was never as attainable as it is through Lightroom. Even for those who feel repulsed by actually "designing" anything, Lightroom's Book module allows them to focus on photographs themselves and play around with how they flow from page to page. The Print and Book modules are an integral part of my photography process, and even though I might use them sporadically, each time I have a chance to work with them, they always bring a broad smile to my face. I hope you will enjoy working with them as well.

9
Slideshow, Map, and Web Modules

Whether it's a presentation for a client, mailing excerpts from your portfolio, or just preparing something for friends and family, Lightroom makes preparing a slideshow as easy as pressing a button. In this chapter, we will look at the possibilities of utilizing the Maps module, even without geotagging. Lastly, we will explore the Web module, where we can create an online gallery without knowing a word of code.

In this chapter, we will cover the following topics:

- The Slideshow module
- The Map module
- The Web module

The Slideshow module

This is one of the overlooked modules in Lightroom, but it provides a handy tool for presenting and reviewing photographs.

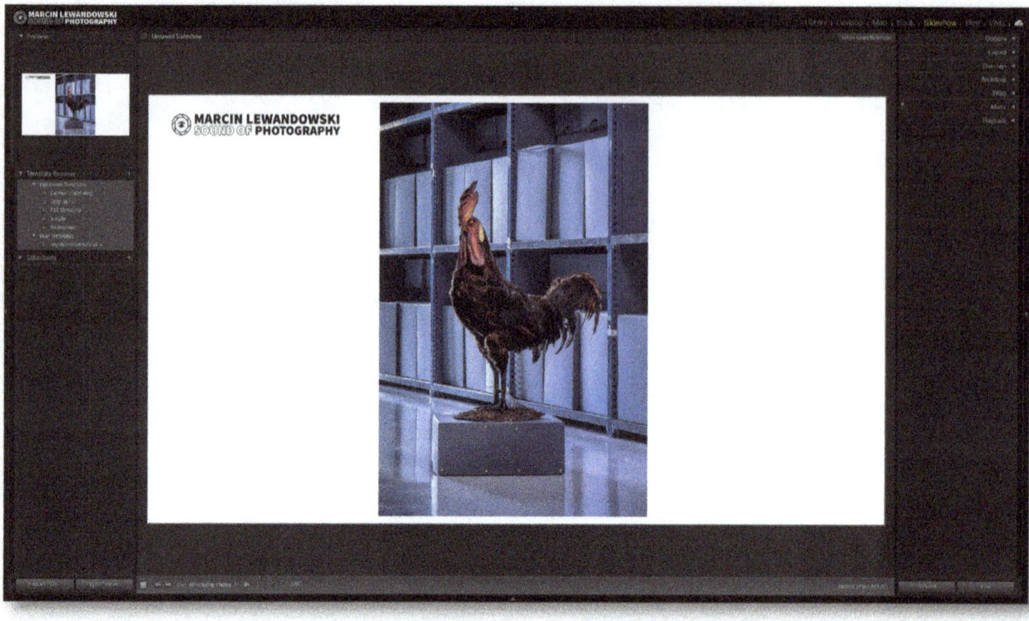

Figure 9.1 – The Slideshow module view

The left-side panel

The top of the left-side panel displays **Preview**, which, in the case of Slideshow, shows the currently viewed photograph as a miniature of the slide page.

Under **Preview**, we find two more tabs. On the bottom is the familiar **Collections** tab. In the middle sits the **Template Browser** tab with a small number of default Lightroom templates, which represent the capabilities of the Slideshow module very well. Click through them to see how much variety they offer.

At the bottom of the left panel, we can find two export buttons to which we will return after we learn about the right-side panel settings:

- **Export PDF...**
- **Export Video...**

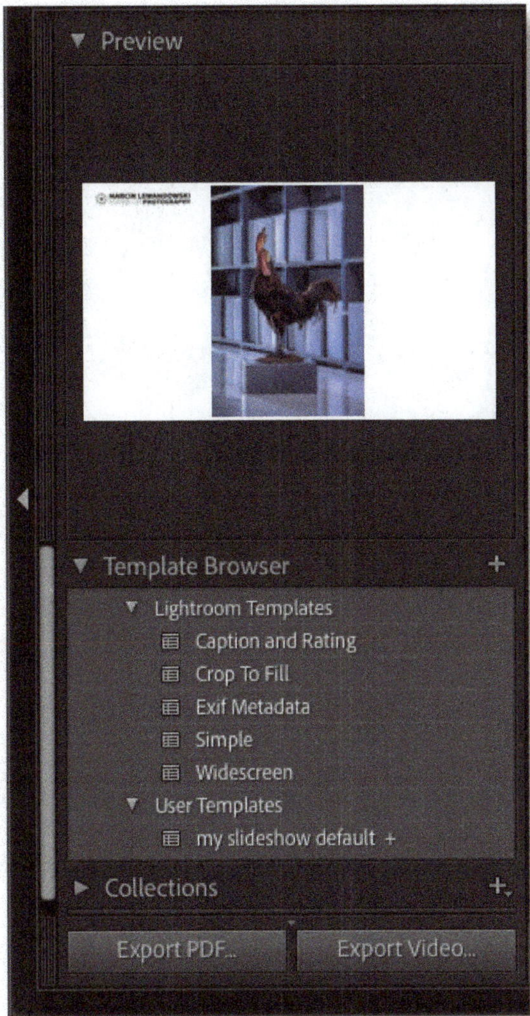

Figure 9.2 – The left-side panel detail

Right panel tabs

Let's have a look at the tabs in the right-side panel of the Slideshow module.

Options

The first tab, **Option**, has some submenus. Let's see what each of them does.

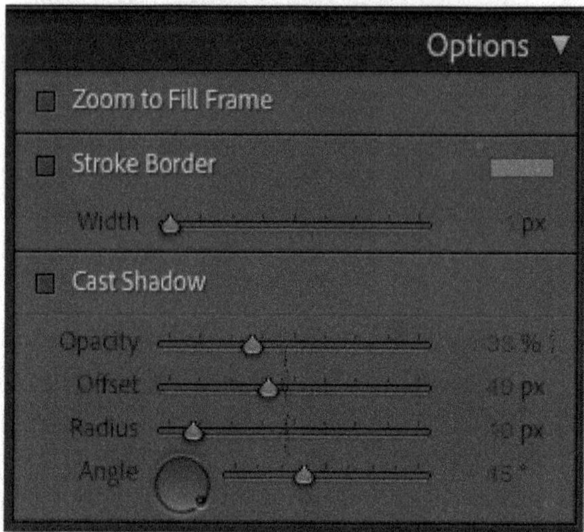

Figure 9.3 – The Options tab

Zoom to Fill Frame

This works like the **Zoom to Fill** option in the Print module. It will crop an image to the aspect ratio of the photo frame we set in the following tab titled **Layout**. Of course, it works much better with horizontal photos. Whenever I have a mixture of horizontal and vertical photos, I refrain from using the **Zoom to Fill Frame** option to keep a consistent viewing experience.

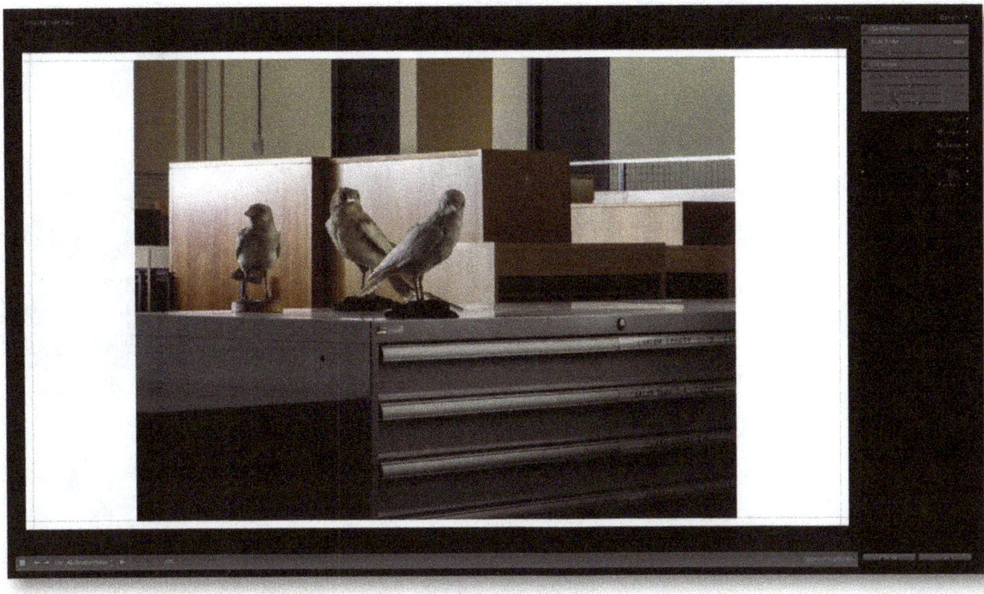

Figure 9.4 A

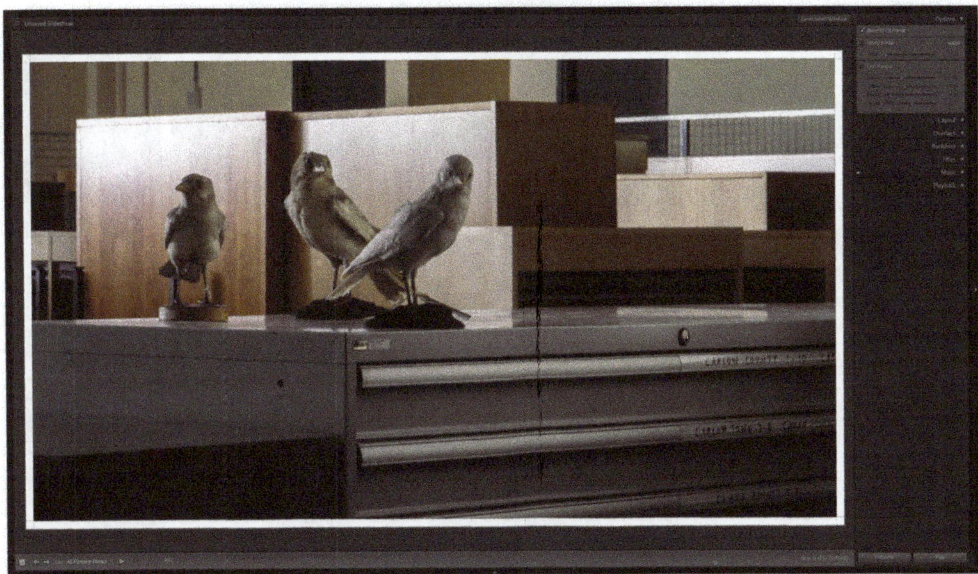

Figure 9.4 B

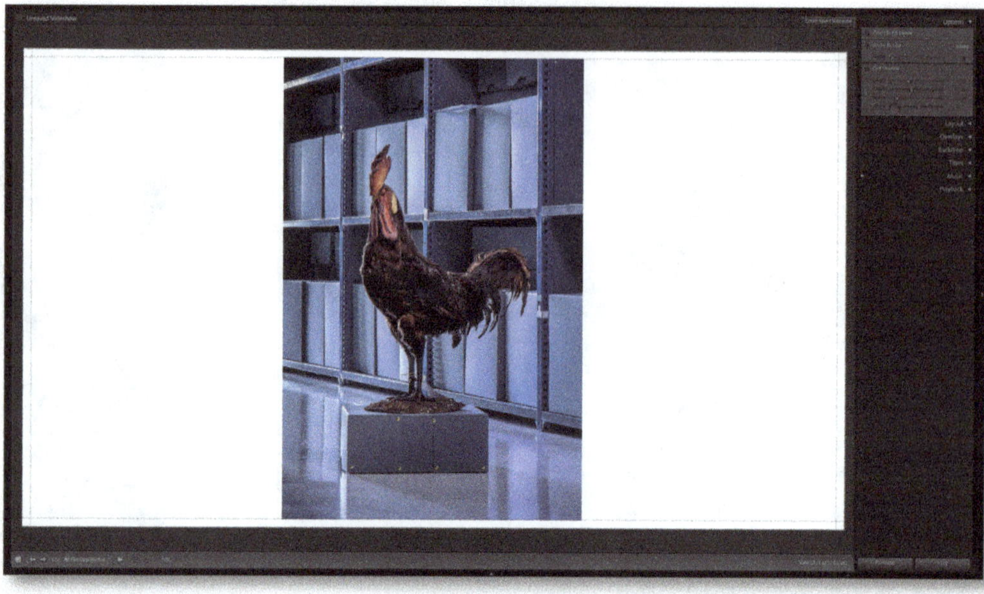

Figure 9.4 C

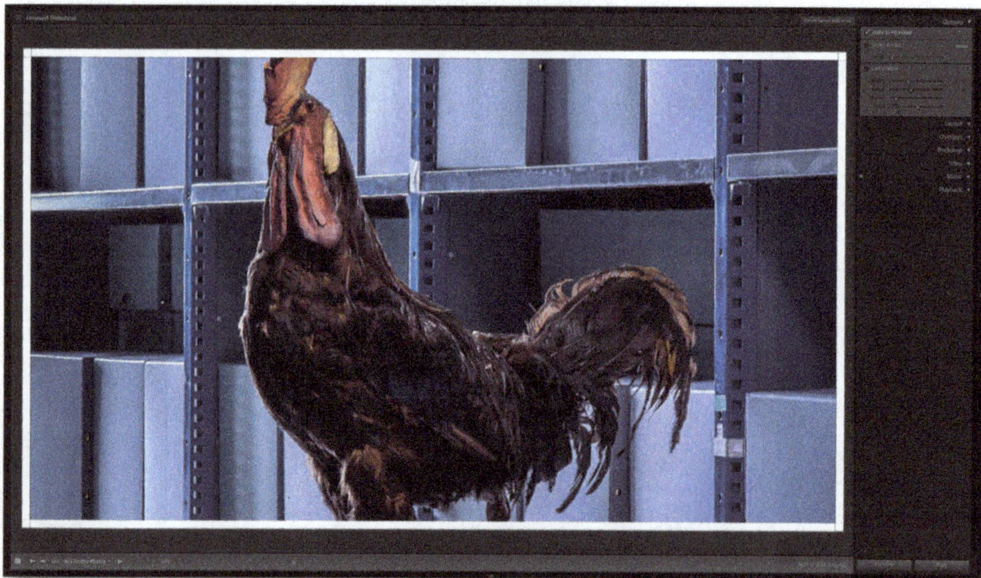

Figure 9.4 D – The first two illustrations show a horizontal photo without and with Zoom to Fill Frame enabled, followed by a vertical photo without and with Zoom to Fill Frame enabled

Stroke Border

This option will paint the border of our chosen width around the displayed image. If we select the **Zoom to Fill Frame** option, the border will match the internal part of the frame we have set.

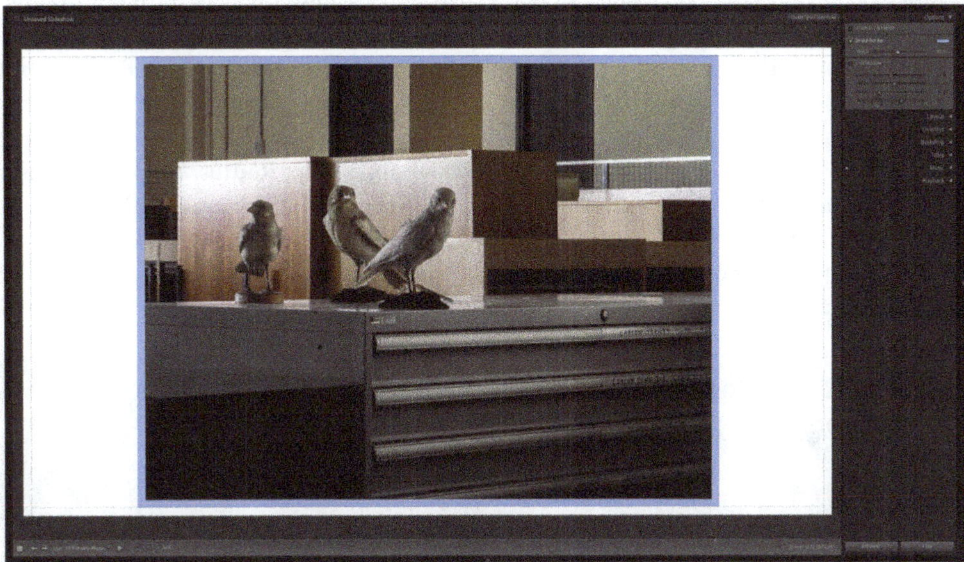

Figure 9.5 A

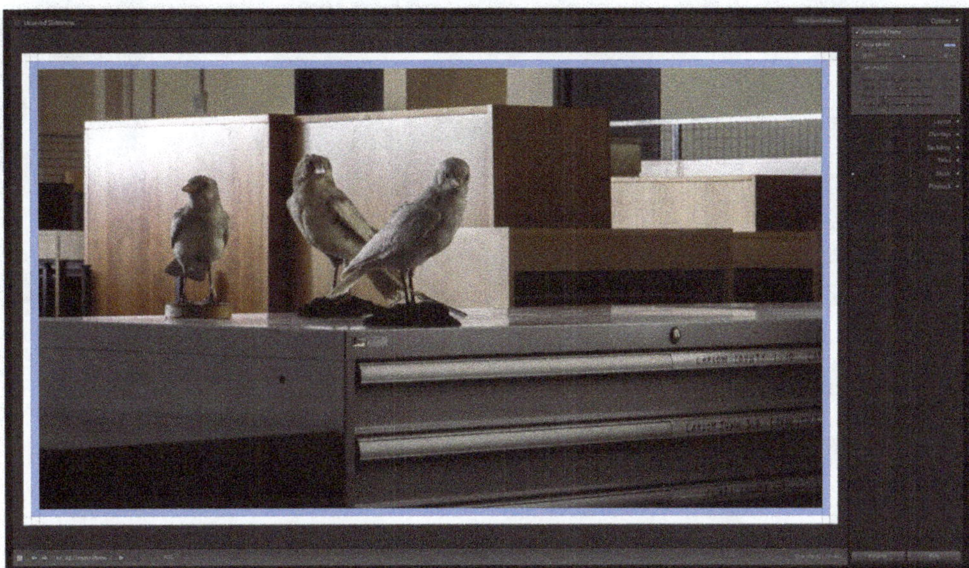

Figure 9.5 B – Stroke Border without and with the Zoom to Fill Frame enabled

Cast Shadow

The last option to play around within the **Options** tab allows us to add a little bit of a 3D feel to our slides by having them cast a shadow on the underlying page. **Opacity** is an obvious function - 100% opacity means no transparency and 0% opacity is full transparency, making it invisible. **Offset** will move the shadow from directly behind the image when it is set to 0 px, to 100 px in the direction we set in the last option of this tab, **Angle**. We can set the angle by manually inputting the value, moving the slider, or playing with the angle wheel. We can naturally mix and match these three approaches by, for example, approximately setting the wheel and then correcting to the closest rounded value. Finally, we are left with one more option, **Radius**. Think of this as a setting that's mixing spread with a feather. A **0** radius value will cast a hard, sharp-edged shadow. In contrast, a **100** radius value will display a soft shadow, with a gradient slowly dissolving into the background at a distance of 100 px. Anything in between will have a smooth edge in the width we set as the radius.

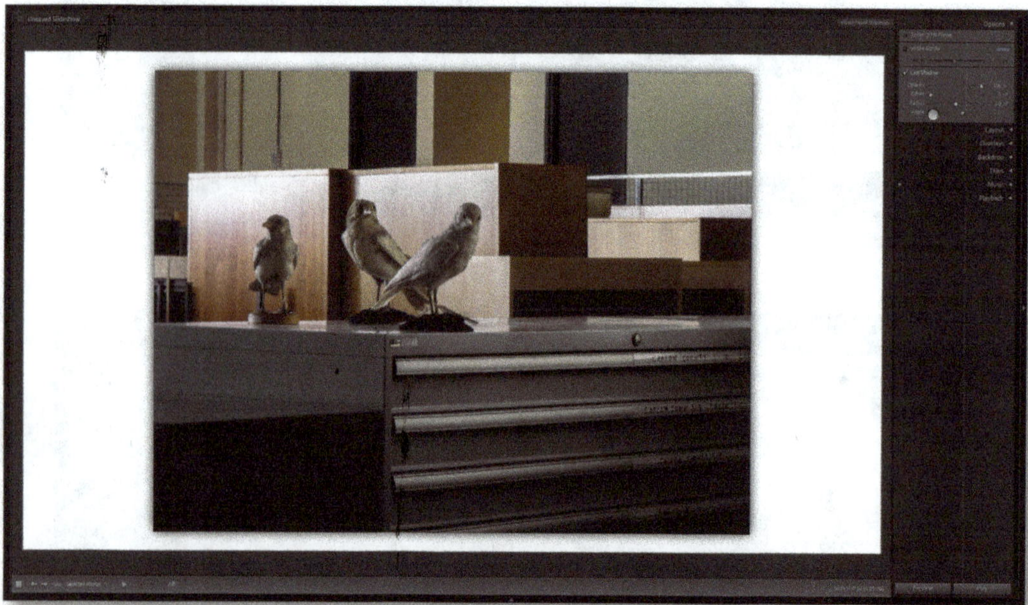

Figure 9.6 A

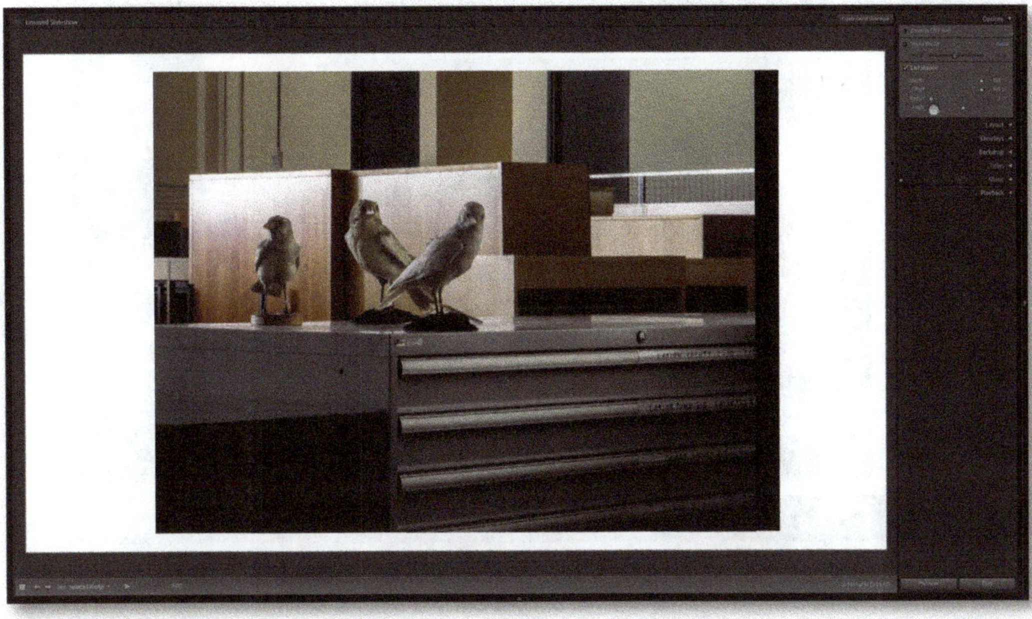

Figure 9.6 B

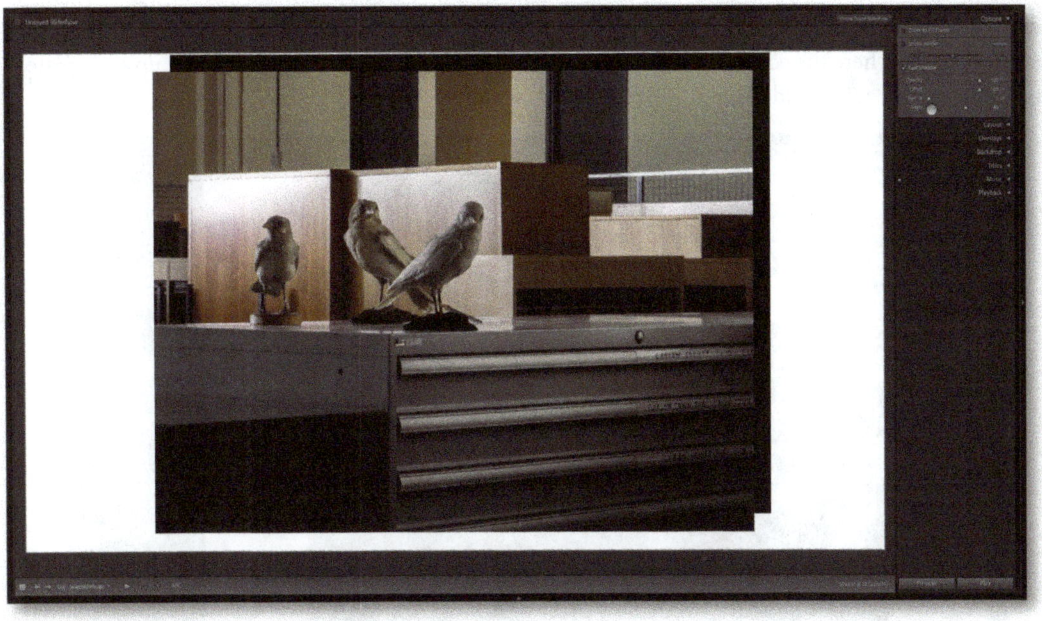

Figure 9.6 C

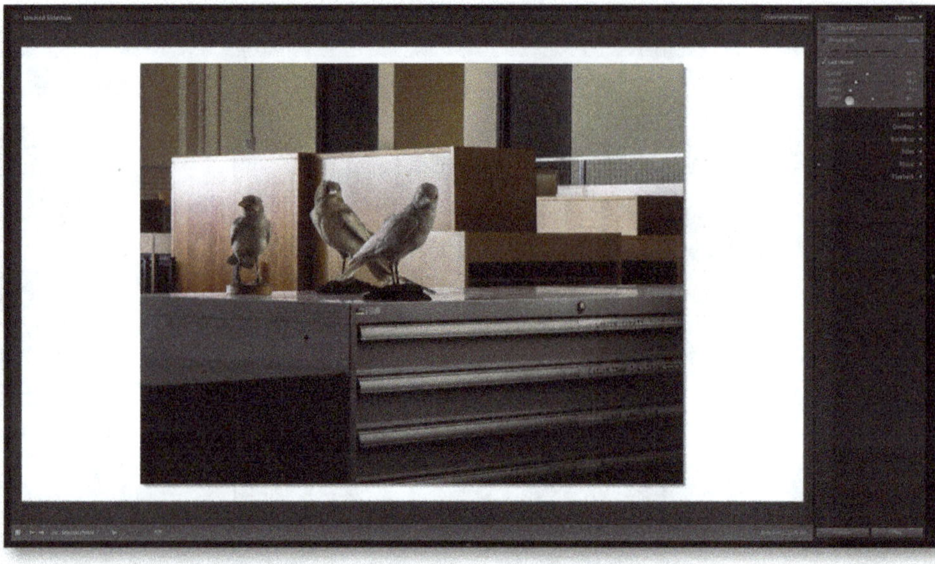

Figure 9.6 D – Examples of Cast Shadow use

Layout

Show guides can be helpful, especially when we mix vertical and horizontal images. It might help us better visualize where the edges of photographs will fall, especially when initially setting up a template for the currently edited slideshow.

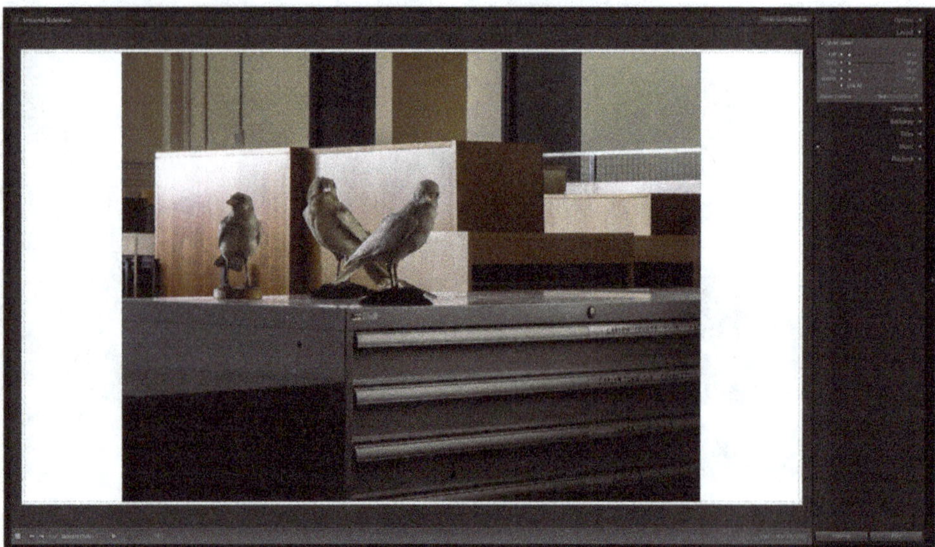

Figure 9.7 – Show Guides enabled

Setting margins can be linked so that we can adjust them simultaneously. This linking is symbolized by all of the small squares next to sliders that are highlighted in light gray. If we want to adjust the slides separately, we can either deselect the **Link All** function by clicking on the little square and choosing which side we want to modify, or we can deselect any of the boxes responsible for each side, and the selected, highlighted sides will remain linked.

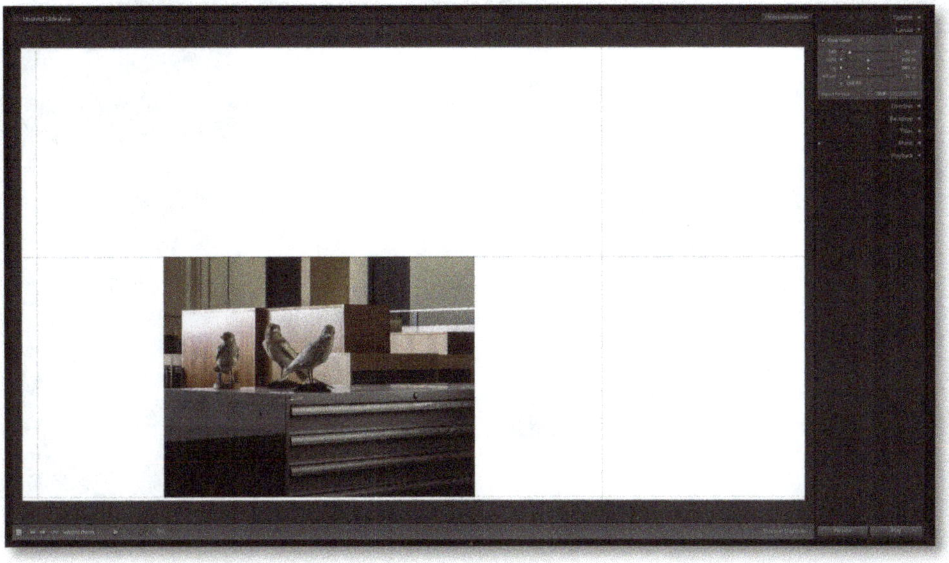

Figure 9.8 A

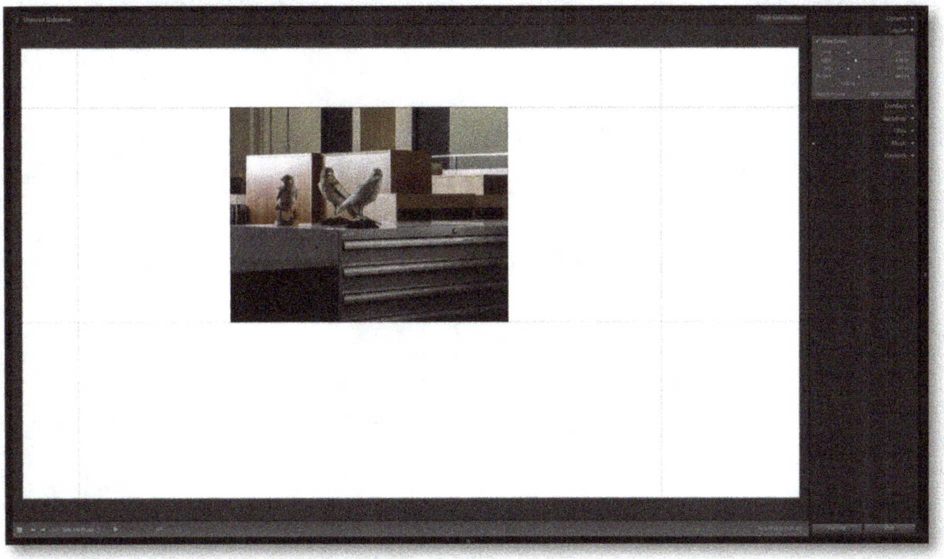

Figure 9.8 B – Disabling the linking of margins for two of the four edges and adjusting all edges separately

Aspect Preview

Many of the screens on which people will view our slideshow will have a 4:3 aspect ratio, especially work laptops. Here, we can set our desired aspect ratio to the aforementioned 4:3, wide-angle 16:9, or simply to the aspect ratio of the screen we are currently working with.

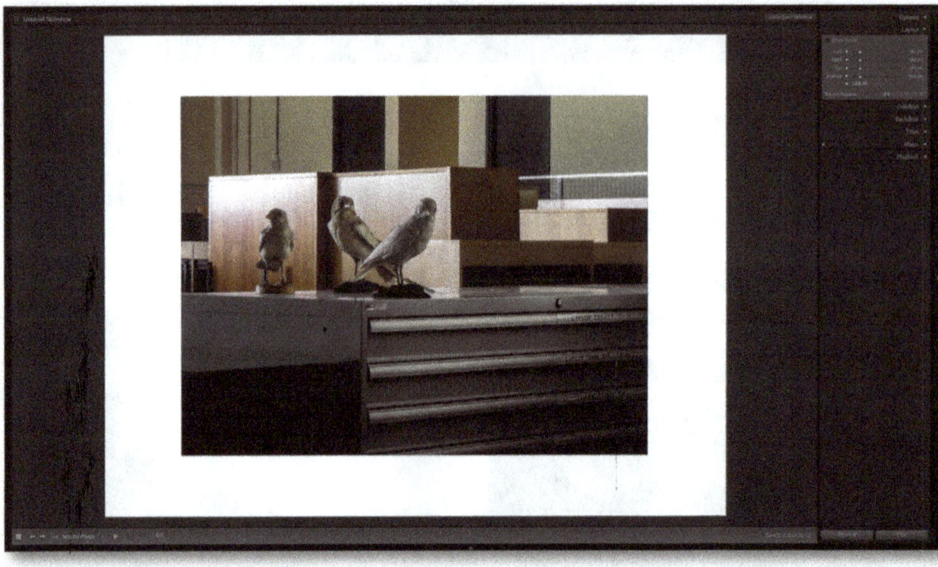

Figure 9.9 A

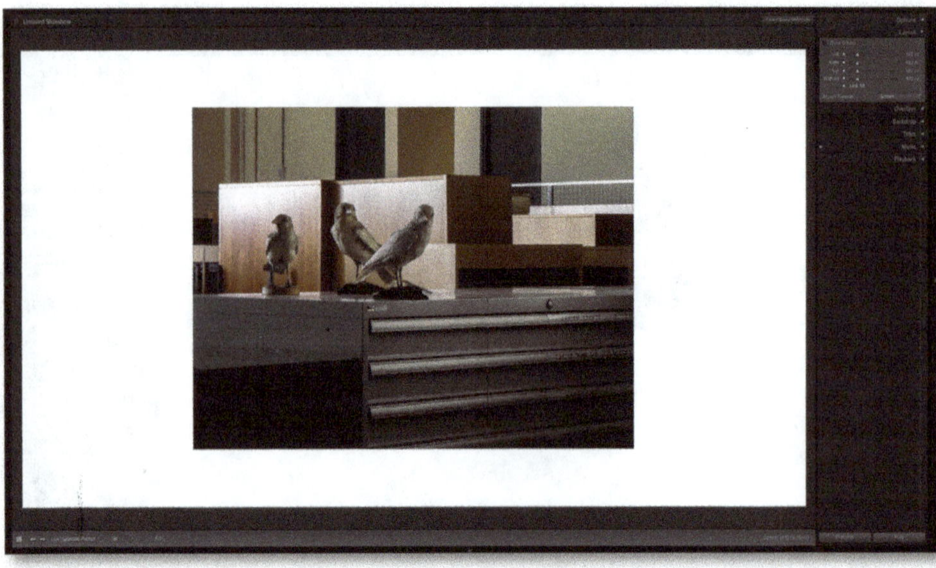

Figure 9.9 – 4:3 and 16:9 aspect ratios

Overlays

This toolset is helpful if we want to ensure that images are watermarked and that everything is strongly branded.

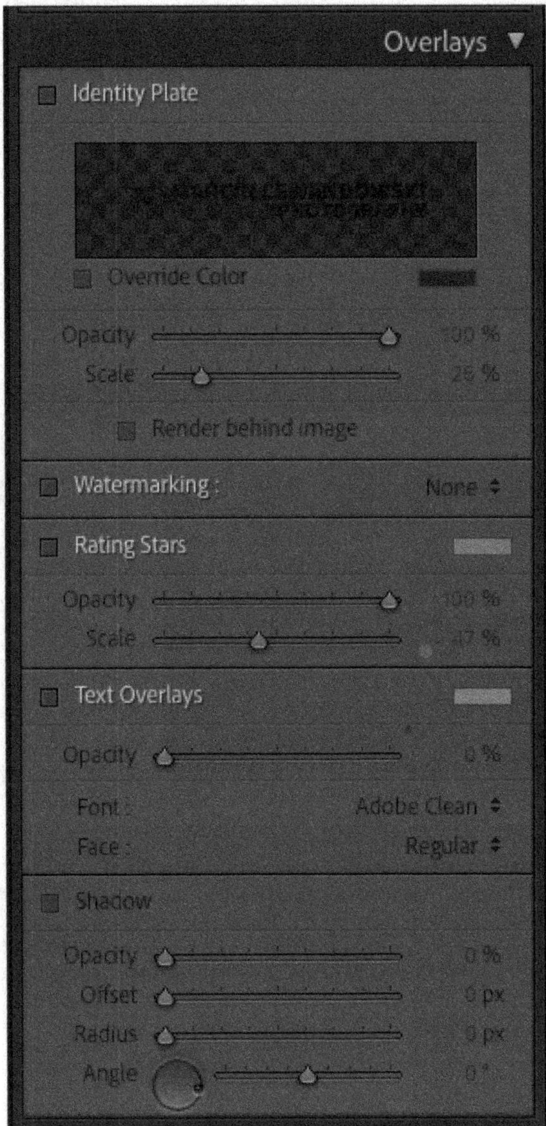

Figure 9.10 – The Overlays tab

Identity Plate

Setting an identity plate is as simple as possible, and we can choose to either upload a graphic file or create a stylized text plate. Clicking on the small arrow in the bottom-right corner of the Identity Plate window and selecting **Edit...** will open a small Identity Plate Editor. It looks just like the one we described in the Print module, as well as in the opening chapter (*Chapter 1*, *An Overview of Lightroom Classic*). When we choose to make a text identity plate, the **Override color** function under the preview will become available. We can then select any color for our identity plate without opening the Identity Plate Editor.

The next two sliders change the opacity and scale. Finally, **Render behind the image** will move the identity plate behind our image, so it's not obstructing it.

Once we have the identity plate set up, we can move it around the page slide by clicking and dragging it around. We can also change its size by dragging its sides and corners instead of working with sliders. After that, the identity plate will stay in the same position and have the same size across all slides.

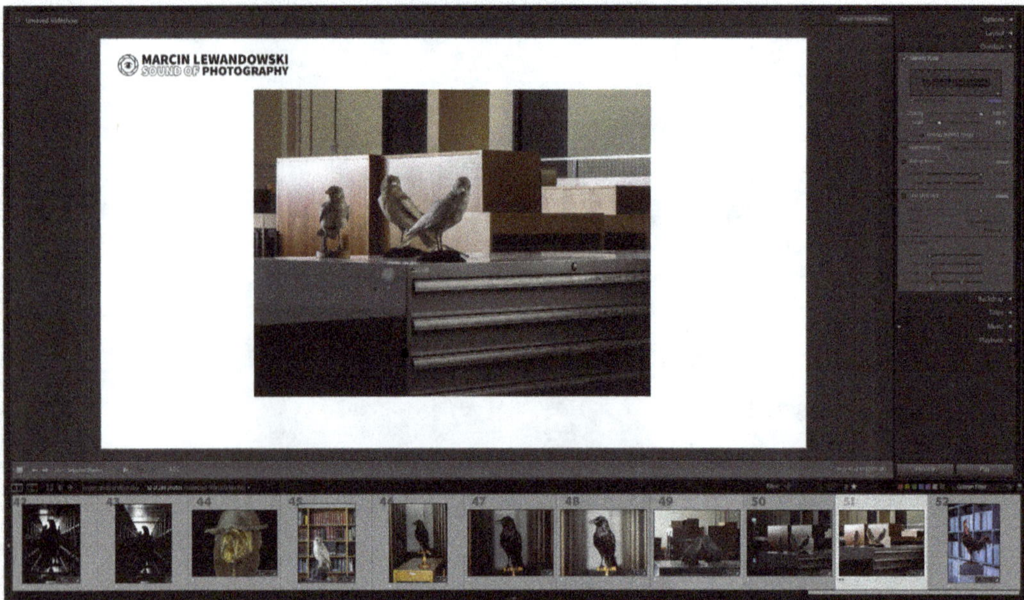

Figure 9.11 – The graphic identity plate

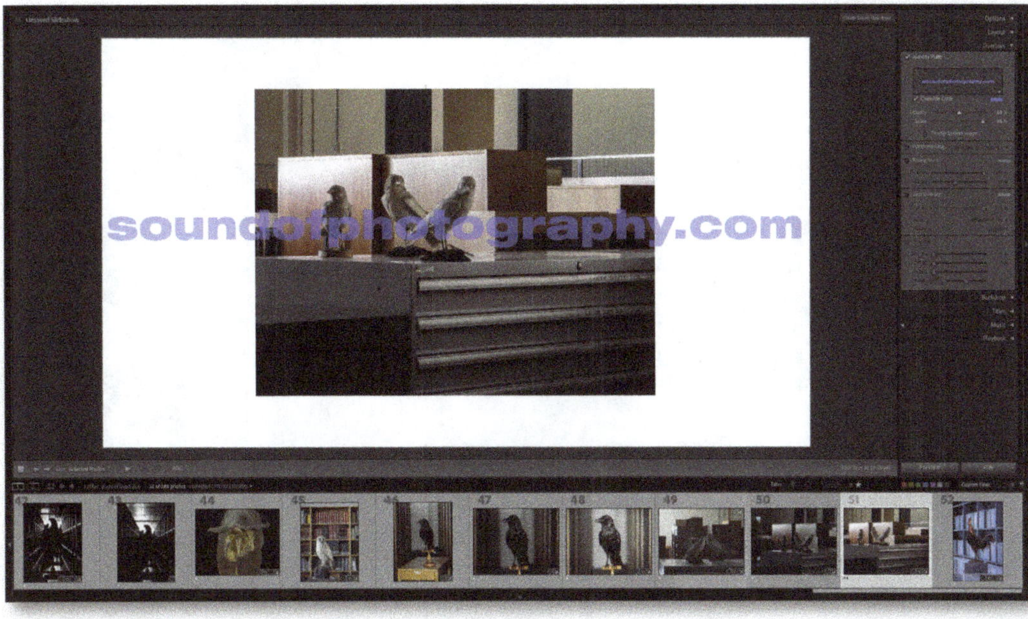

Figure 9.12 – The text identity plate at 50% opacity

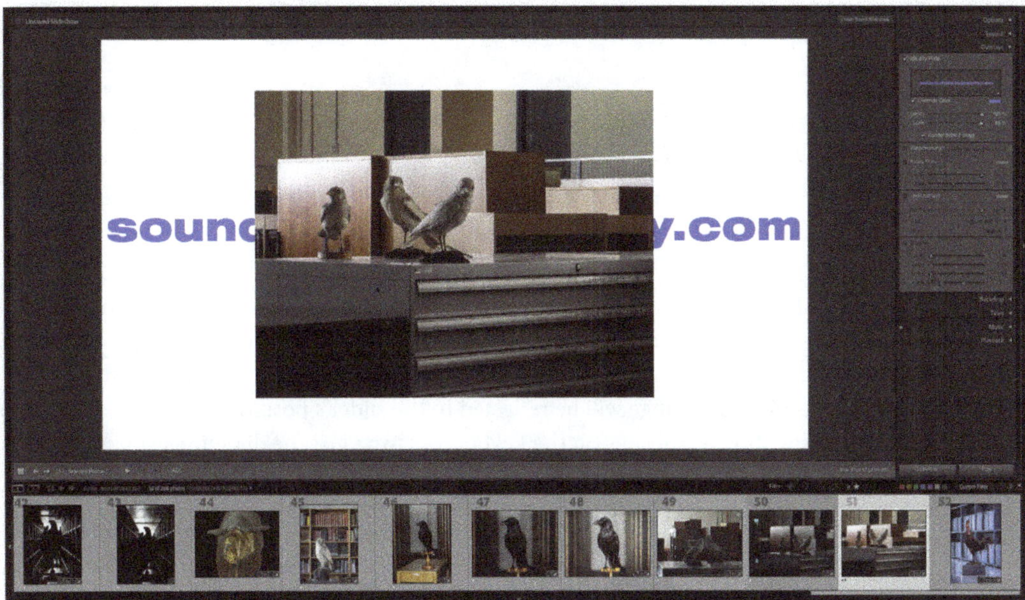

Figure 9.13 – The text identity plate at 100% opacity, rendered behind the image

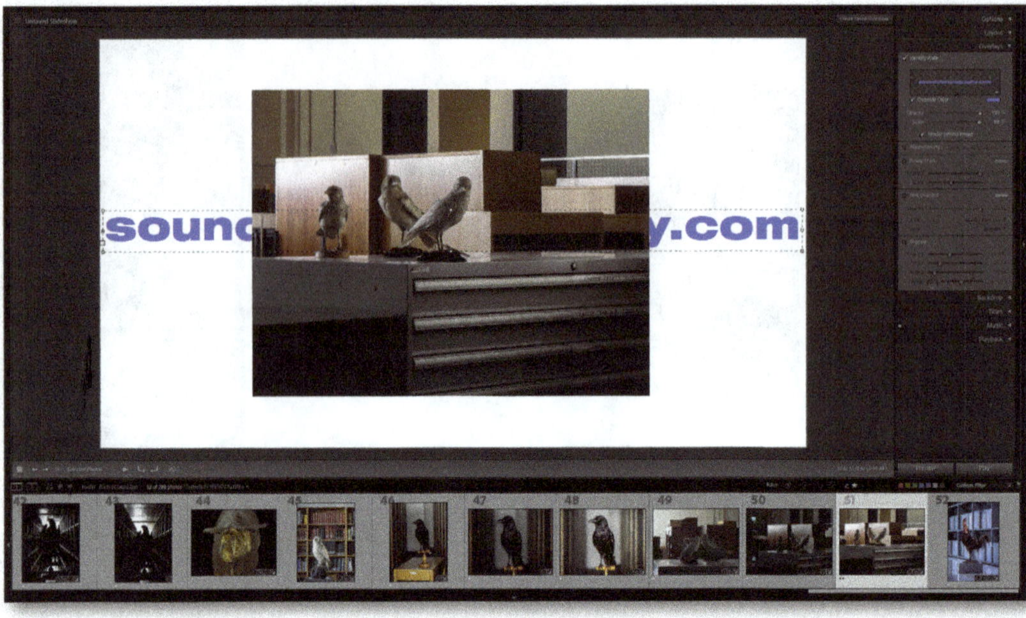

Figure 9.14 – The text Identity Plate at 100% opacity, rendered behind the image, selected, and ready to be moved and resized

Watermarking

This uses the same watermarks that we created in **Export** > **Watermark Editor** (as covered in *Chapter 7, Get Them All Out Of Lightroom - Exporting For Work and Leisure*). Choosing **Edit Watermarks** will open the Watermark Editor, where we can create a new watermark or change an existing one.

Rating Stars

Ticking this box will add our current star rating to the slides. We can choose size, color, and opacity by adjusting the sliders to our liking or by clicking and dragging the rating stars around the slide to find a position that we like. Once we have the rating selected within our slide, we can adjust its size by dragging its corners – this size change will be reflected in the slider's position. We can also move the rating around by using directional keys on the keyboard. Using just the directions will nudge it slightly. If we want to move it a bit more, we need to use "*Alt*" + "*directional keys*" – this will move it by a slightly more considerable amount. The "*Alt*" + "*directional keys*" shortcut works with any movable objects within Lightroom.

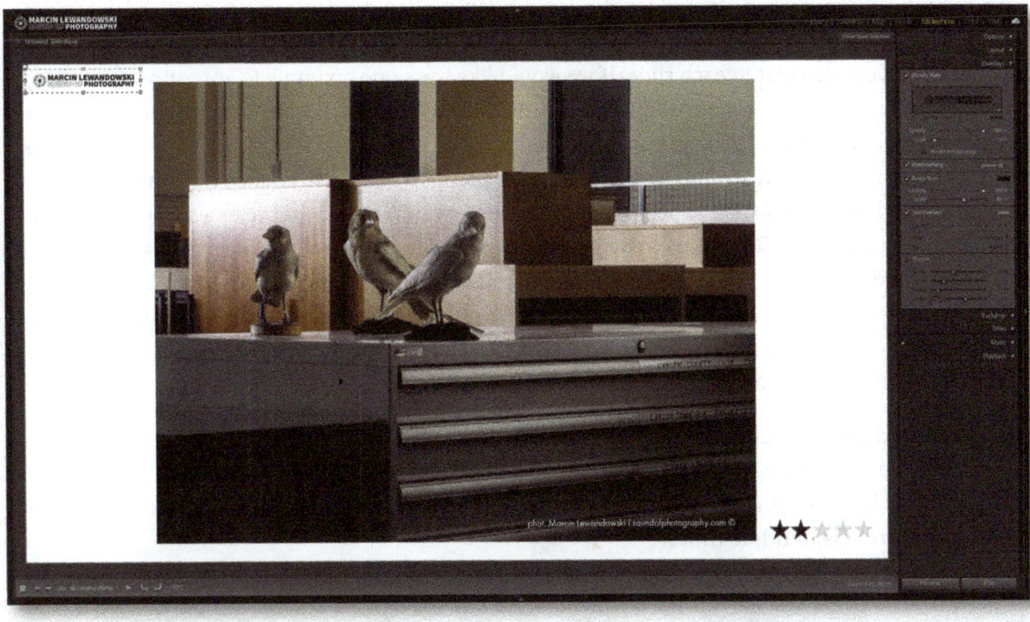

Figure 9.15 – The graphic identity plate in the top-left corner of the slide, the text watermark in the bottom-right corner of the photograph, and the rating stars in the bottom-right corner of the slide

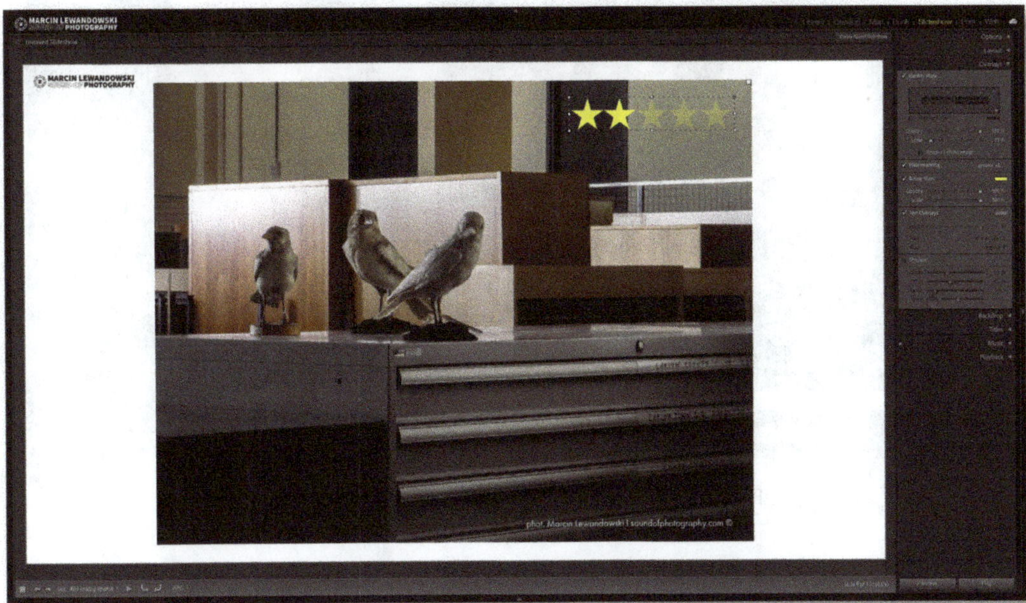

Figure 9.16 – The rating stars moved to the top-right corner of the photo, their size increased, and their color changed to yellow

Text Overlays

Here, we can add custom text to each slide. If we would like the same text note to appear on each slide, we must go to the toolbar below our slide, click on **ABC**, and choose **Custom Text** (if your toolbar is hidden, remember to use the "*T*" keyboard shortcut to make it visible). Here, we can add any text we want. This text can be moved around and scaled to our liking; we can also change the font, color, and opacity. If instead of the same text appearing on each photograph, we would prefer a separate caption, instead of choosing **Custom Text** in the **ABC** menu, we must choose one of the other available options. We can also build a template to include a full selection of parameters by selecting **Edit...** and using the Text Template Editor, where we can drag and drop a wide selection of settings available within our photographs' metadata. We can now save it as a preset available for later use or click **Done** and get back to the Slideshow module to edit our slideshow further.

Lastly, we can add a shadow and adjust it the same way we did in the top tab of this module - **Options**. There's one more thing - we can create multiple text overlays by clicking away from the current text overlay so that it is no longer selected, and by clicking the **ABC** icon on the toolbar once more. We can repeat this process multiple times.

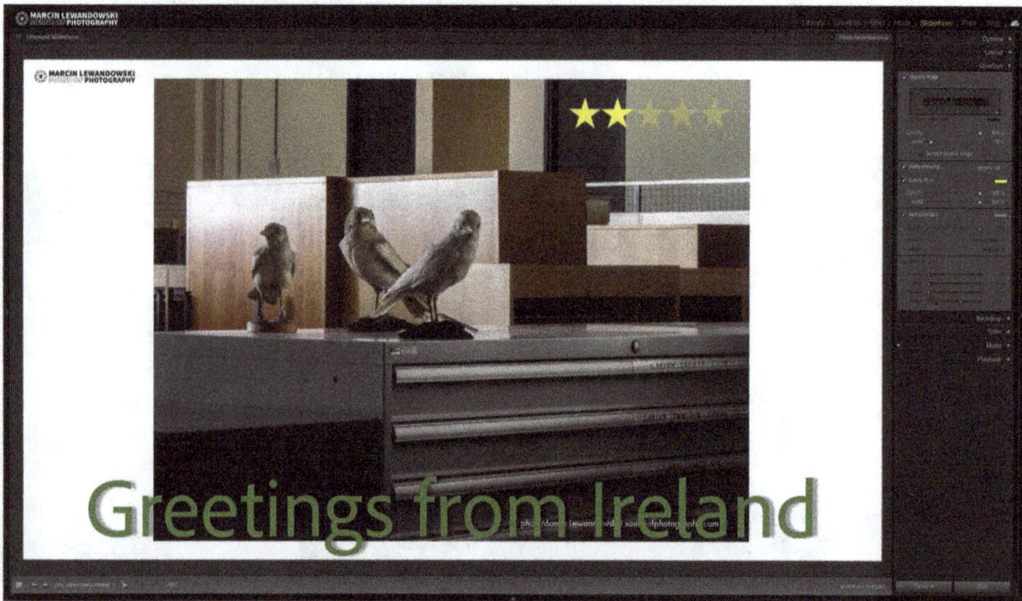

Figure 9.17 – Text overlays – manually entered

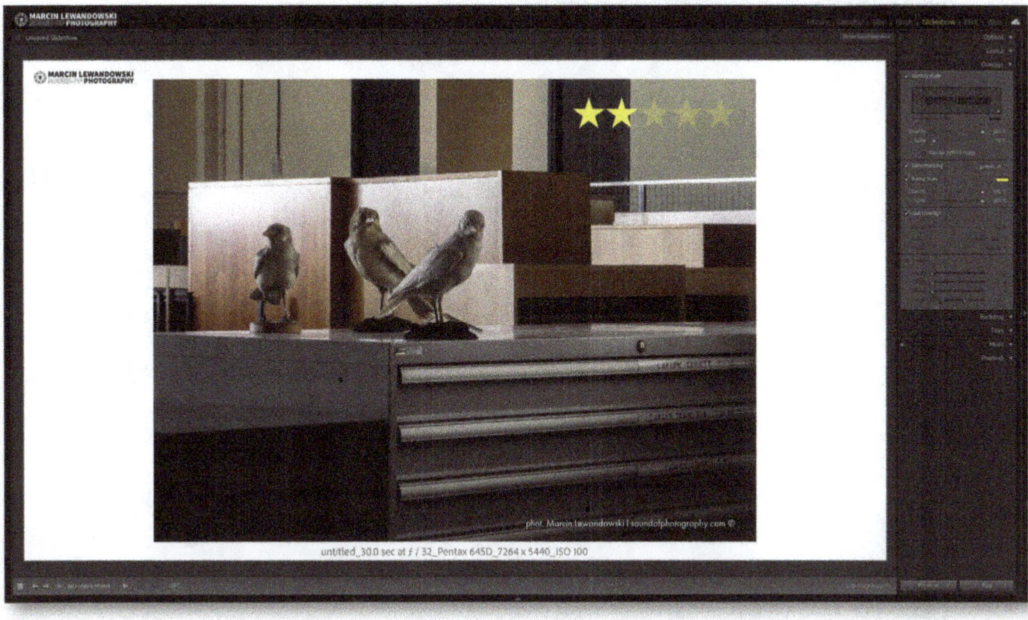

Figure 9.18 A

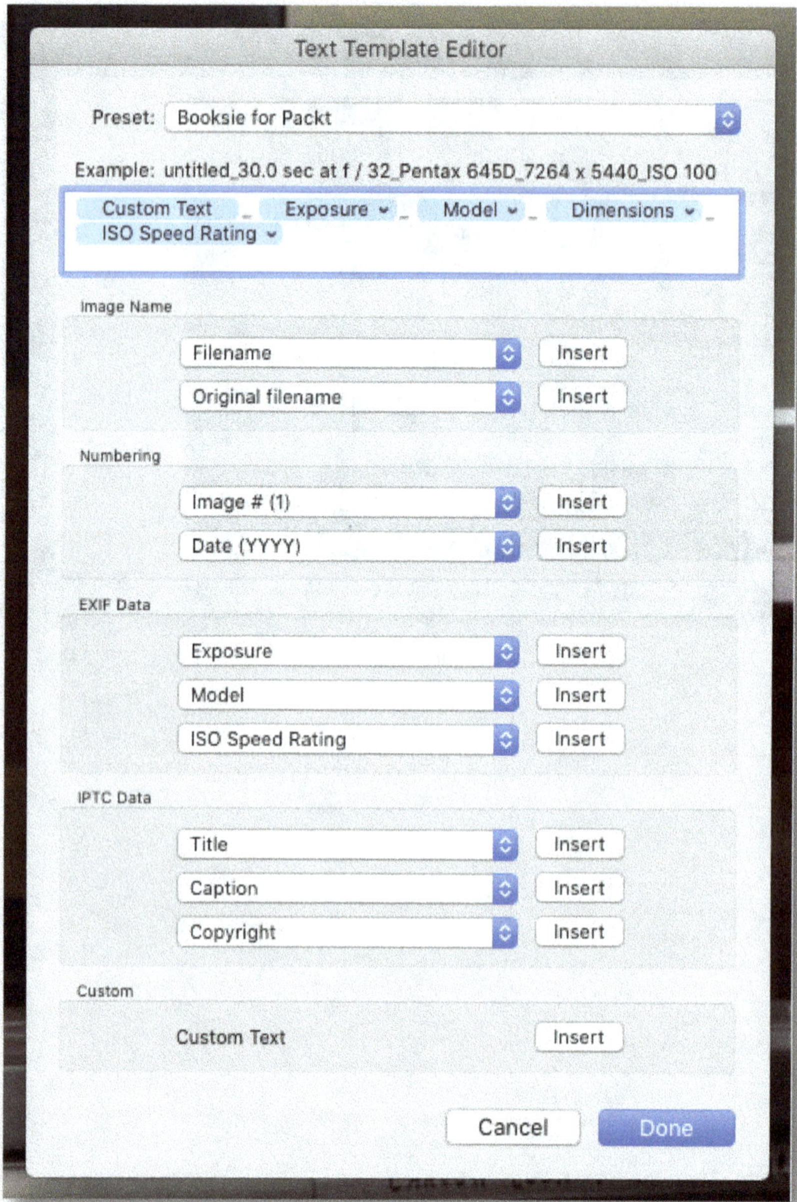

Figure 9.18 – Text overlays – a caption created from metadata, including exposure time, aperture, camera used, cropped file dimensions, and ISO setting, and a snapshot of the preceding settings in the Text Template Editor

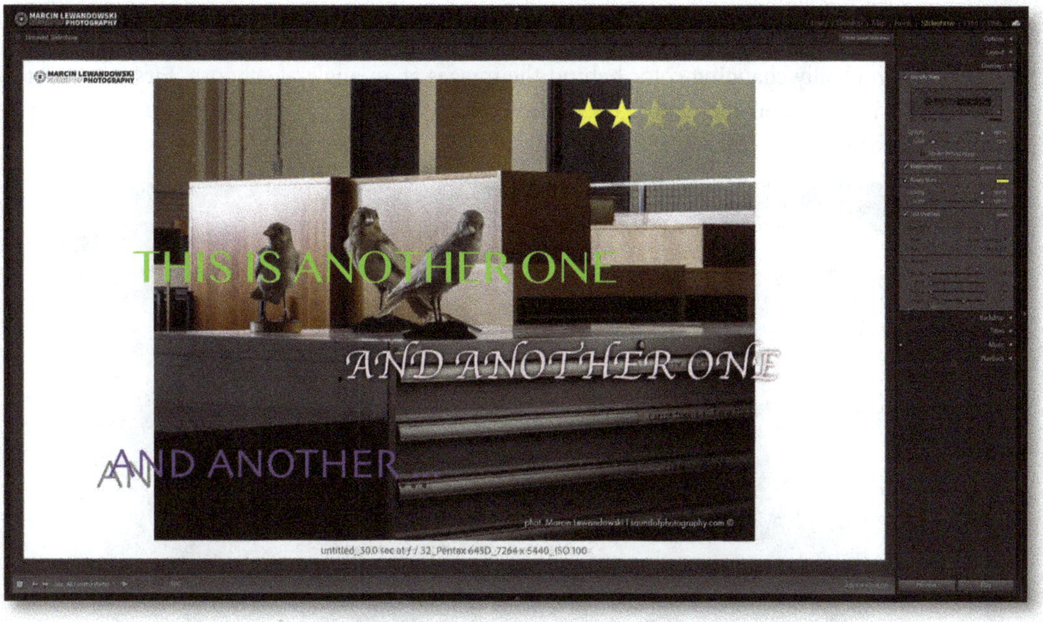

Figure 9.19 – Text overlays – multiple manually entered text fields

Backdrop

With the tools available in this tab, we can change the background for our slides, and we can do so using the following three settings.

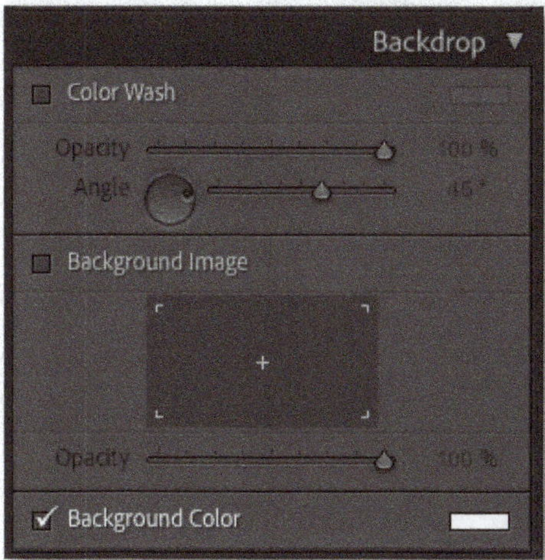

Figure 9.20 – The Backdrop tab

Color Wash

This will add a gradually changing color behind the images at an angle we choose. First, we must select the **Color Wash** option and choose the desired color. Afterward, we can play around with the opacity and angle until we are happy with the results we see.

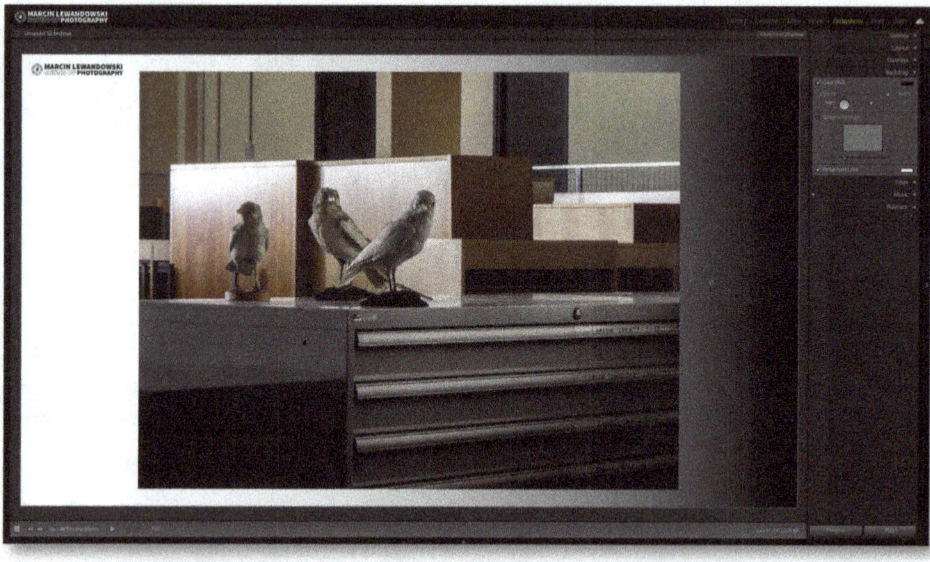

Figure 9.21 A

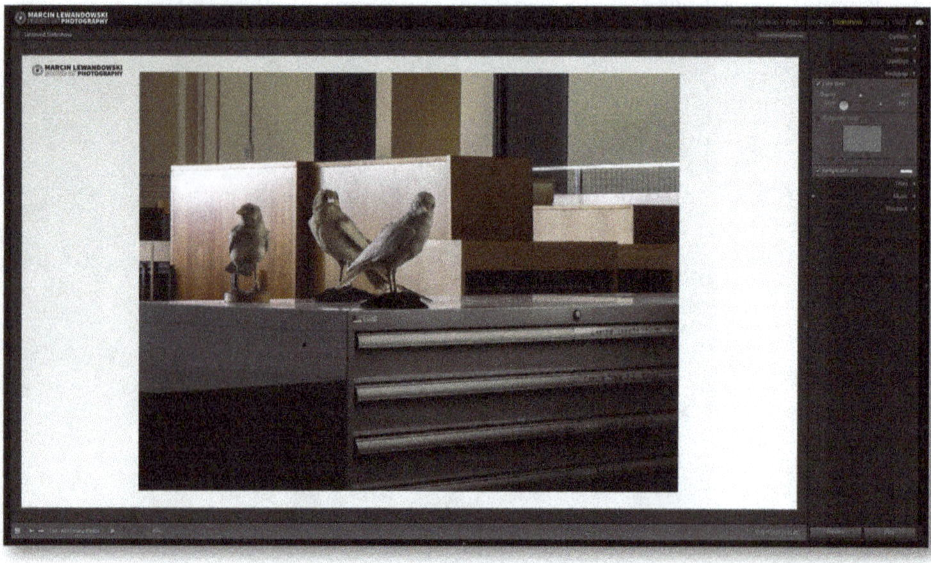

Figure 9.21 B – Color Wash examples

Background Image

Let's say we prefer to have an image instead of a plain background. In that case, we can select the **Background Image** box and drag any image from the Filmstrip into the empty box to have that image as a background for our slideshow. This will work in conjunction with **Color Wash**, and we can choose to have both, either, or none selected for a different type of look. It is all about finding a way to present images in the slideshow.

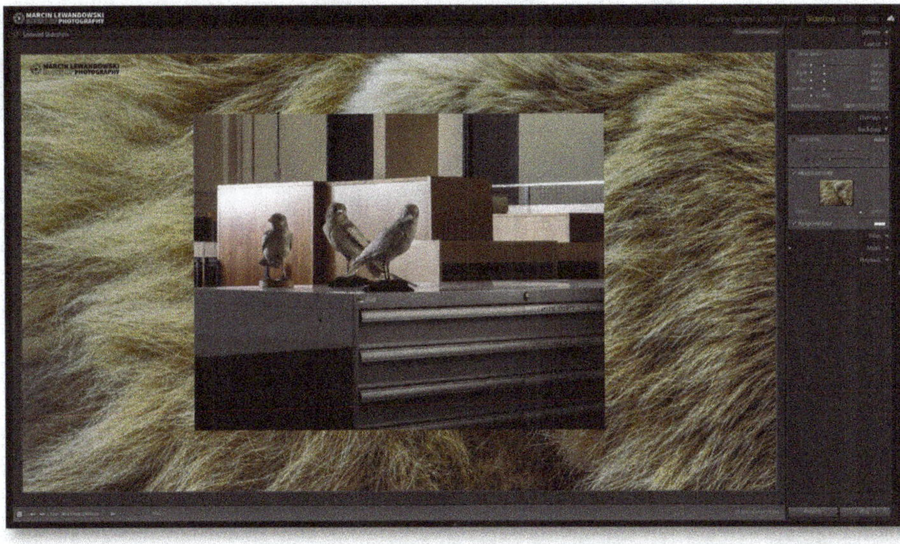

Figure 9.22 – Background Image

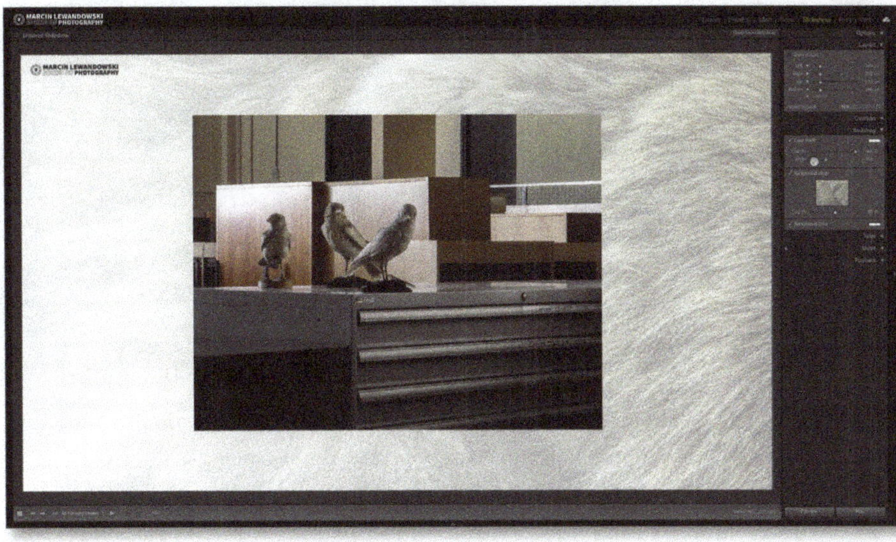

Figure 9.23 A

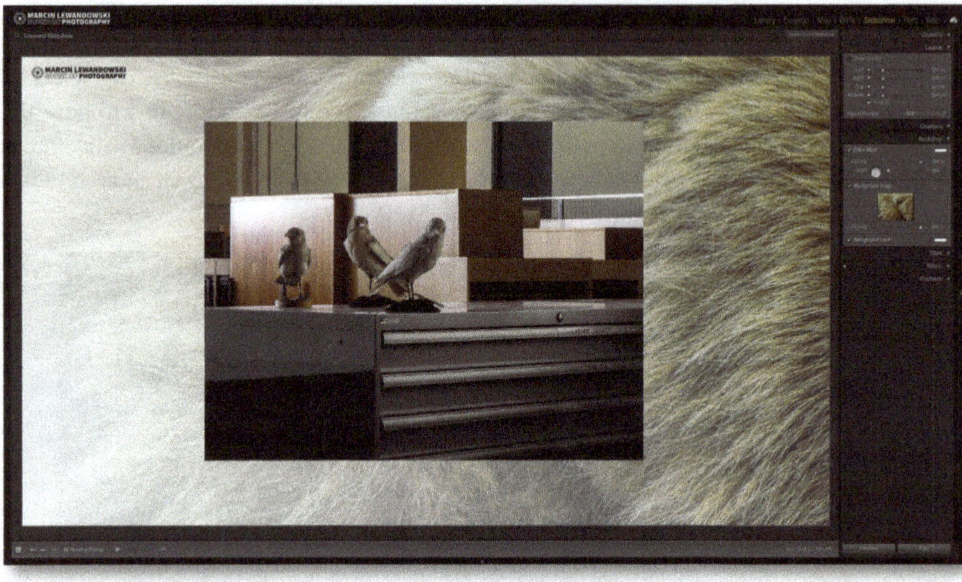

Figure 9.23 B

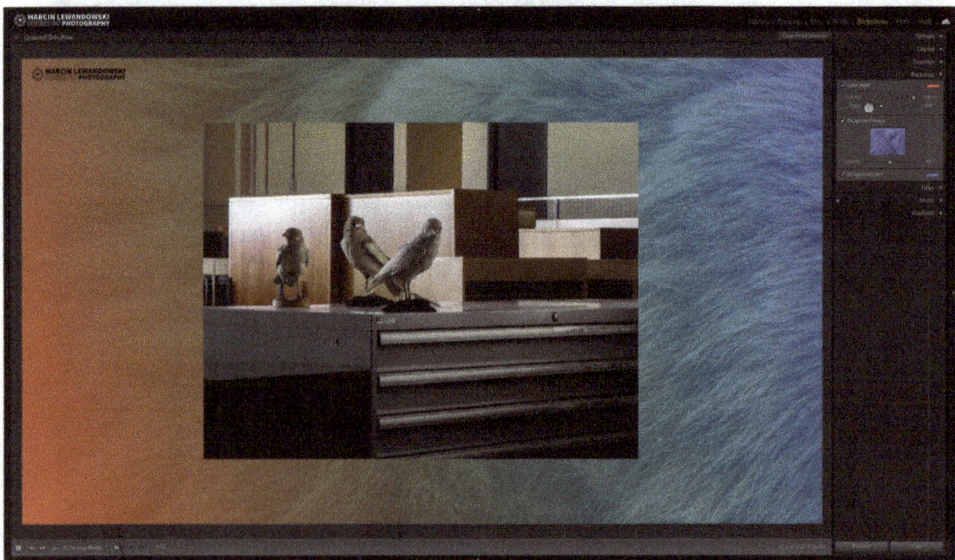

Figure 9.23 – Different Background Image and Color Wash combinations in conjunction with a blue background on the last image

Background Color

The last option in this tab is to choose a color for the background of our slides, which, as a default, will be black. Change of background color will also influence the look of the color wash and background image if their opacity is set to anything other than 100%.

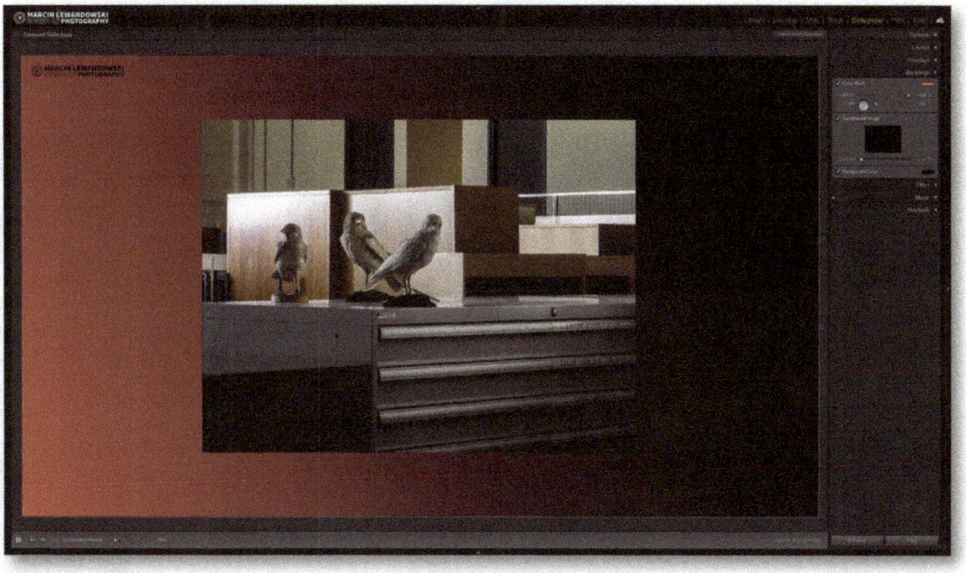

Figure 9.24 A

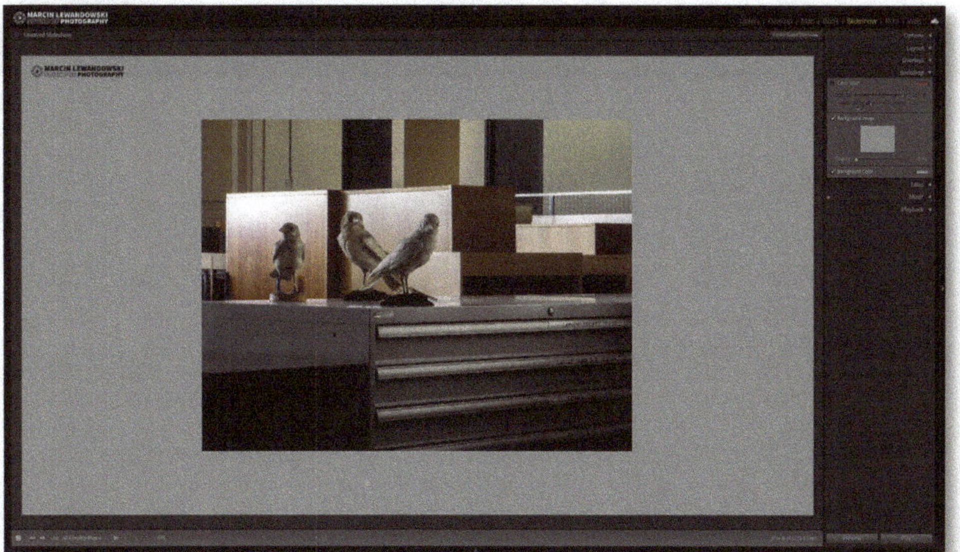

Figure 9.24 B – Background Color with and without Color Wash

Titles

We can add an extra slide at the beginning and end with a custom logo or text in the **Titles** tab. Selecting **Intro Screen** will add a chosen identity plate in the middle of the opening slide. Selecting **Ending Screen** will add an identity plate as the last slide. We can choose different background colors and identity plates for the intro and ending screens.

Additionally, if we decide to have a text identity plate instead of a graphic one, we will be able to specify the color of the text without interfering with the identity plate design we are using.

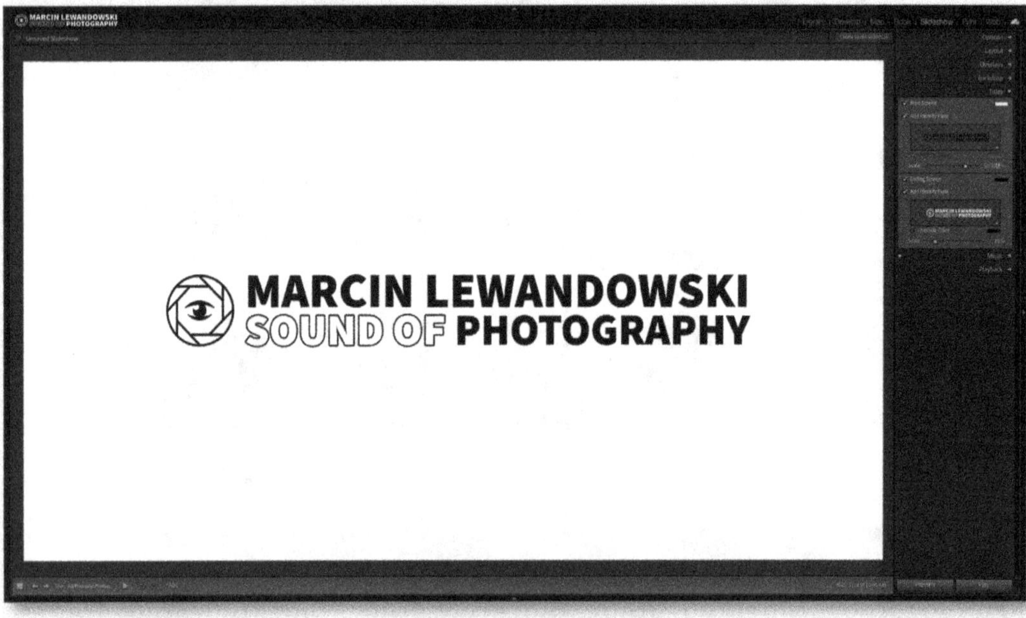

Figure 9.25 A

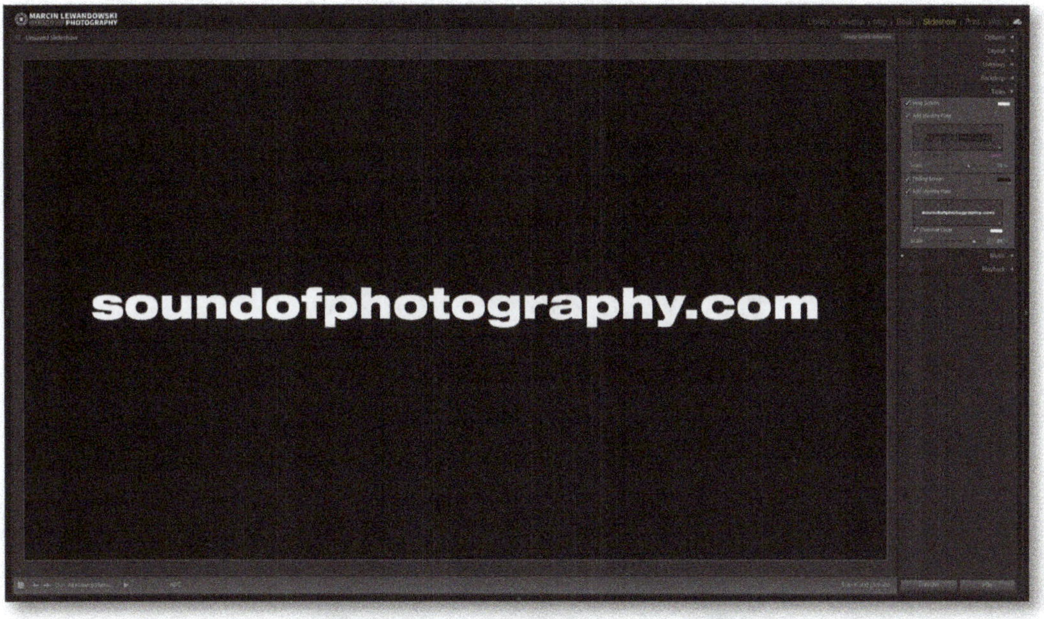

Figure 9.25 A

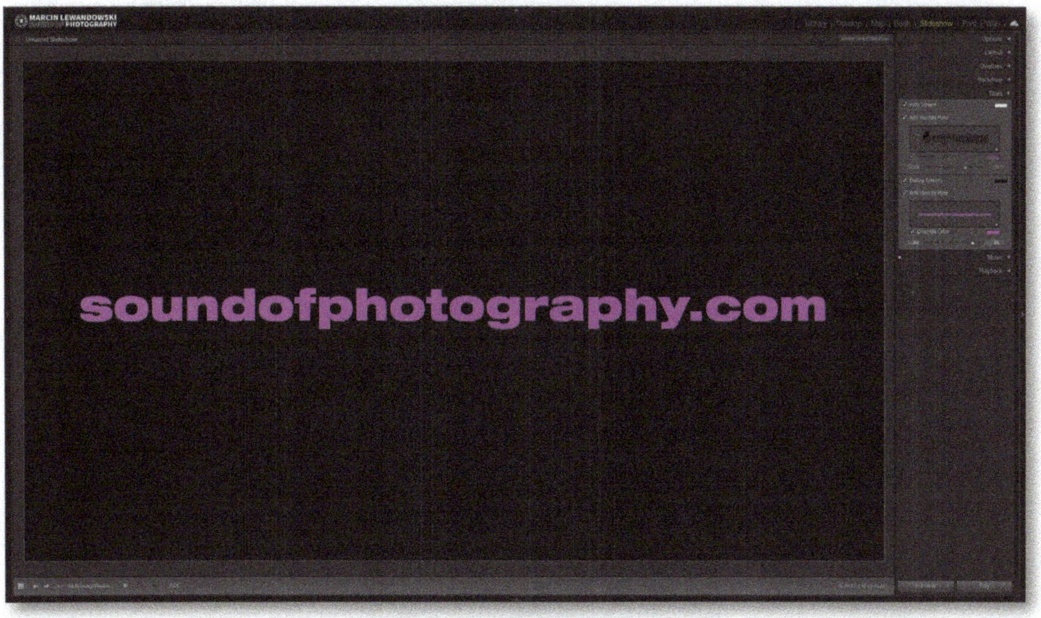

Figure 9.25 C – The graphic intro screen and text ending screen examples

Music

Here, we have an option to add music to our slideshow. We can add one track or create a whole playlist of up to 10 tracks and drag them up and down to form the desired order. To add a music track to our slideshow, we need to click on the + symbol and choose one track from our hard drive; the - symbol will do the opposite and delete the selected track.

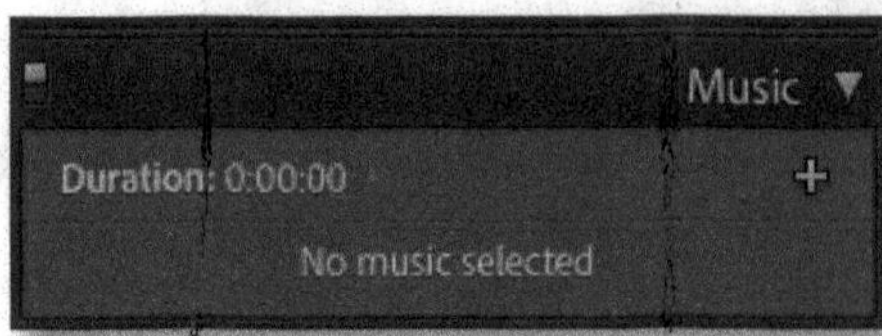

Figure 9.26 A

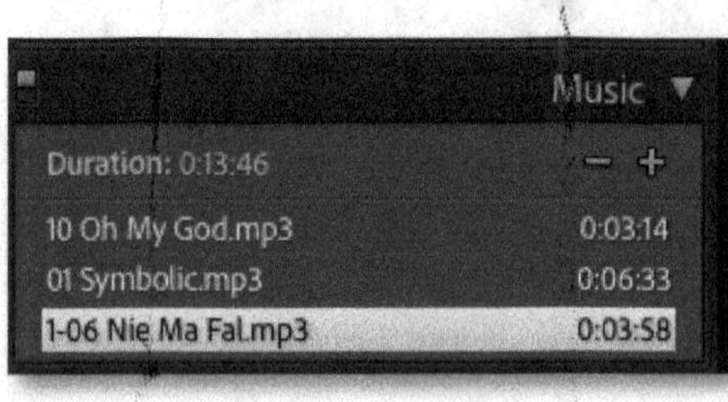

Figure 9.26 B – The Music tab – empty and with a sample playlist with three tracks

Playback

With the sequencing, look, and feel of the slideshow completed, we finally get to a tab where we can choose how the slideshow will progress from slide to slide and from the beginning to the end.

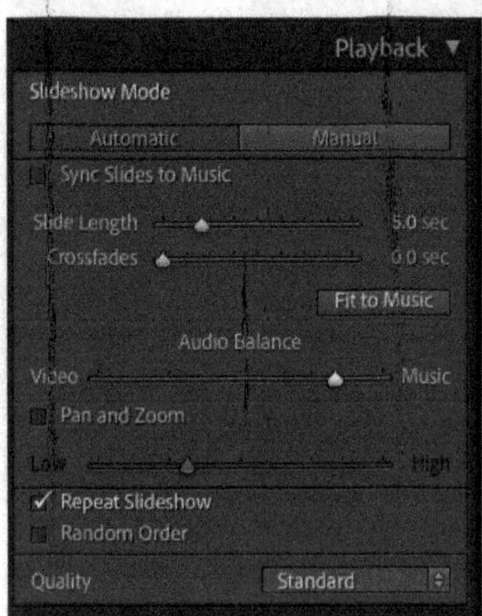

Figure 9.27 – The Playback tab

Any options we choose here will influence how the exported slideshow will work. The first two buttons (**Automatic** and **Manual**) let us decide whether we want the slides to progress automatically or only if the slideshow viewer chooses by pressing the keyboard's forward and backward arrow buttons. If we choose **Manual**, most other options will be unavailable, giving us access to choose whether we want to repeat the slideshow, run it in random order, and choose the slideshow's final quality. If we wish for the slideshow to run automatically and we already picked the soundtrack for it in the previous tab, here, we can set the slideshow to sync slides to music. When a track has a clearly defined rhythm, Lightroom might do a pretty good job keeping transition in sync with the beat, but I find both music-related features (**Sync Slides to Music** and **Fit to Music**) hit-and-miss options, making it quite unpredictable and, therefore, unreliable. Choosing this option will also not allow us to choose how long each of the slides will be shown between transitions, which is a drawback. If we decide not to use **Sync Slides to Music**, we can manually choose the slide length and how long it will crossfade between slides. We can also choose how long the crossfading transition will be between the slides. I feel that a slide length of around 4–7 seconds feels right, and I prefer a very short **Crossfade** effect or none at all. **Fit to Music** will adjust the slide length to match the duration of the music we picked. **Audio Balance** works only if we include any video clips in our slideshow. We can choose which audio will be more audible by moving the slider toward **Video** or **Music**. Lastly, we can determine whether we would like to add the **Pan and Zoom** effect and its strength. With the **Pan and Zoom** effect enabled, we can't choose which photographs will zoom in and which ones will zoom out, so if you want total control over how the slideshow is presented, you should probably leave it disabled, which is what I do. In the next part of the **Playback** tab, we can choose whether we want to repeat the slideshow, which will run it continuously, and if we would like it to run in random order. Lastly, we will choose the quality of the slideshow played from within Lightroom. It will take a lot of time for Lightroom to prepare a high-quality slideshow compared to **Draft**. If we have hundreds of photographs from a modern camera (with a high MP count), it can be a difference of many minutes, especially if we are not using a fast computer with lots of RAM and a powerful graphics card. The quality of the exported slideshow is set separately, and we will come back to it in just a moment.

The two buttons at the bottom of the right-side panel

There are two buttons at the bottom of the right panel – **Preview** and **Play**. The **Preview** button will play the slideshow in the Slide Editor window, while **Play** will play the slideshow with the whole screen filled.

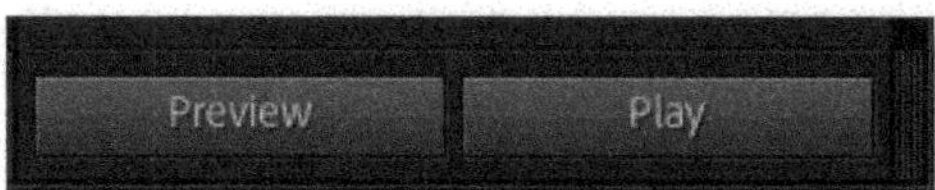

Figure 9.28 – The Preview and Play buttons

The toolbar

The toolbar (the "*t*" keyboard shortcut) offers a few additional buttons that are helpful in building our slideshow.

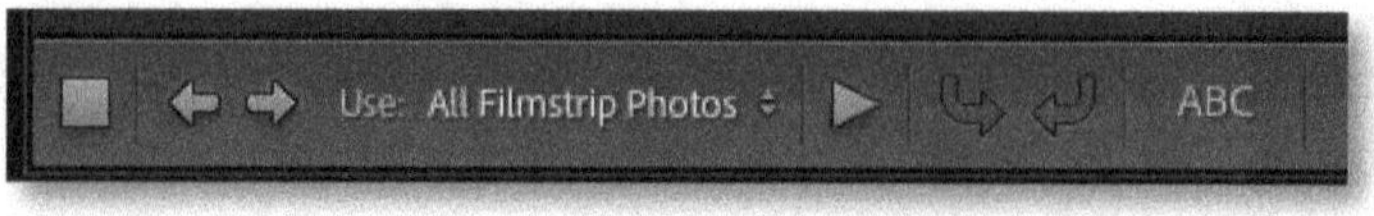

Figure 9.29 – The toolbar buttons

The toolbar buttons are as follows, from left to right:

- The square button will stop **Preview** when clicked once; after the second click, it will return to the first slide.
- The forward and backward arrows will move between slides.
- With the **Use** button, we can choose which photos available in the Filmstrip we would like to use.
- The play button will start a preview – this works exactly the same as the **Preview** button at the bottom of the right-side panel.
- The rotate buttons will rotate any add-ons, such as text or identity plates, in increments of 90 degrees.
- **ABC** is for adding text to our slides, which we have already discussed.

Exporting the slideshow

As we mentioned at the beginning, there are two buttons at the bottom of the left-side panel – **Export PDF...** and **Export Video...**.

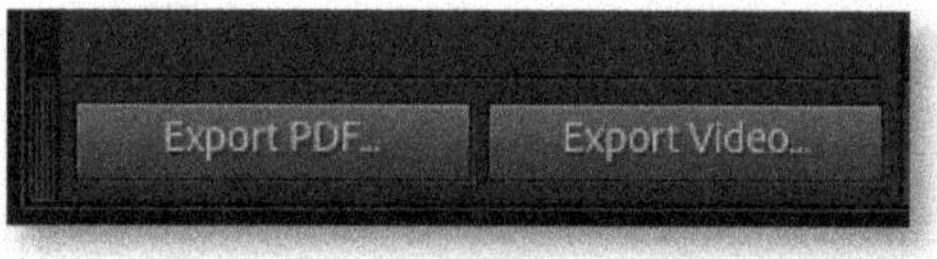

Figure 9.30 – The export buttons

Export PDF... presents us with an export menu where we can choose the quality of our exported slideshow. Choosing a higher quality will result in bigger files, while a lower quality will decrease that size. **Common Sizes** gives us a choice of commonly used **Width** and **Height** ratios, including our screen size. We can also set the width and height manually to any value we want, which will override the **Aspect Preview** value we picked in the **Layout** tab and fill the photographs with this newly chosen one. We can also choose whether we automatically want the created PDF to open in a full-screen view.

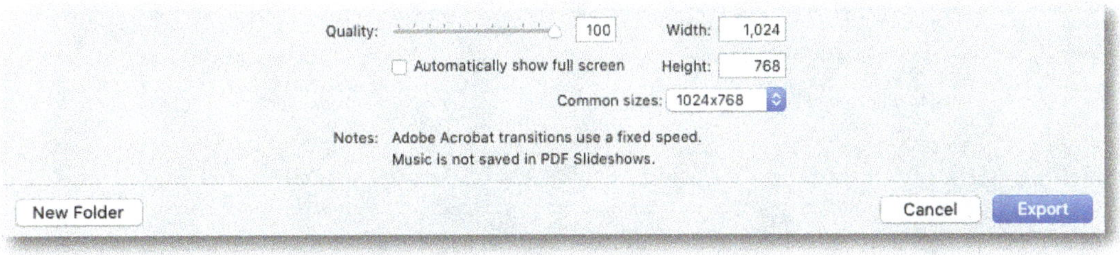

Figure 9.31 – The Export PDF… options

Export Video… offers four presets, from a low-resolution **480 x 270** preset through **720p** to full HD.

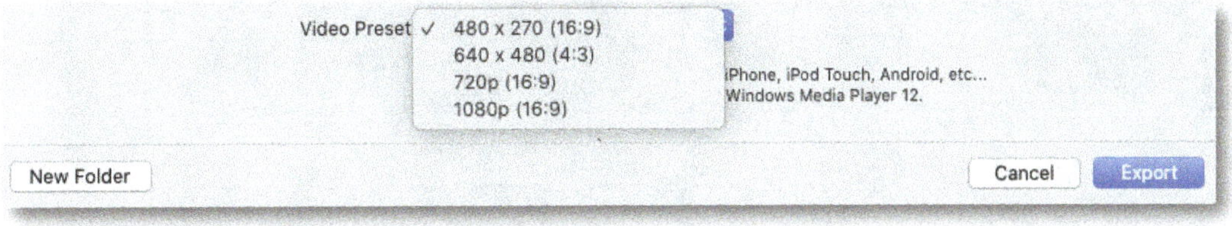

Figure 9.32 – The Export Video… options

This concludes this part of this chapter about the Slideshow module. Now, you should be confident in choosing the desired look for your slideshow, tweaking it to perfection, and exporting it in a format of your choice.

In the next part of this chapter, we will look closely at the Map module.

The Map module

The Map module welcomes us with a map of the world, which will be in its night view with no options available if we are offline. The Map module only works if we are connected to the internet.

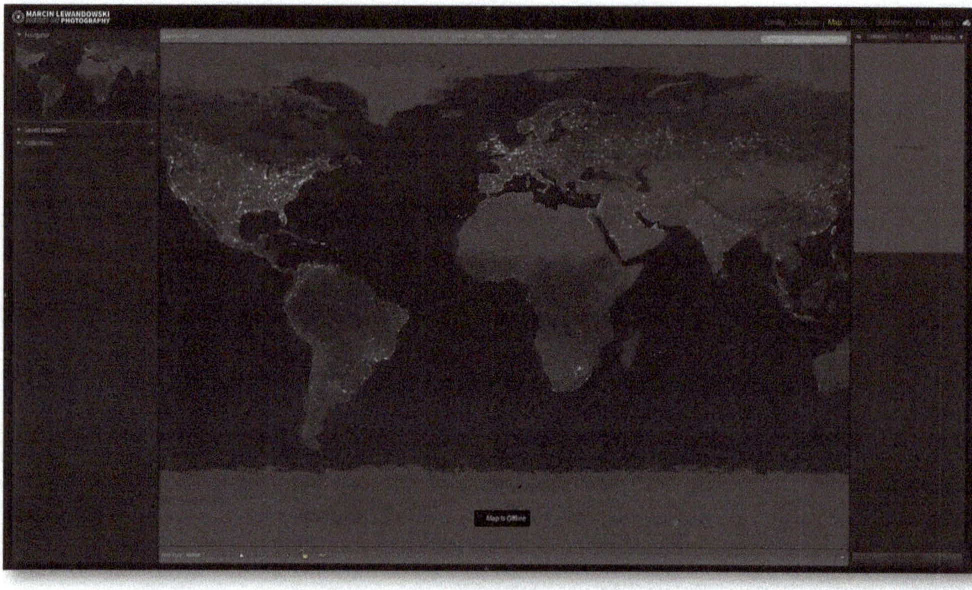

Figure 9.33 – The offline Map module

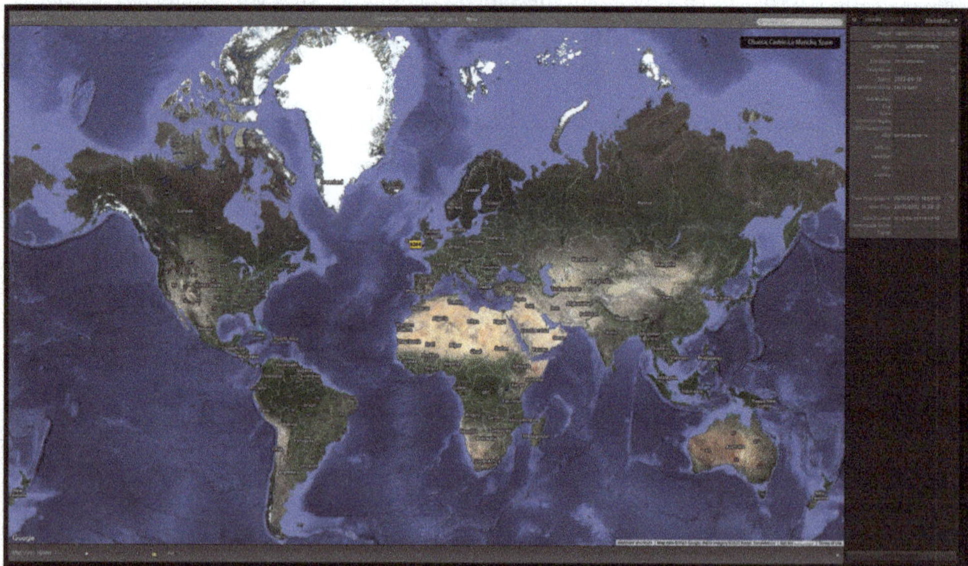

Figure 9.34 – The online Map module in Hybrid view

Left-Side Panel

Let's look at the left side of the Map module next.

Navigator

The top of the left-side panel houses the familiar **Navigator** pane. In the case of the Map module, it will display a fragment of the world map, with a white rectangle showing the area we are currently viewing in the main window.

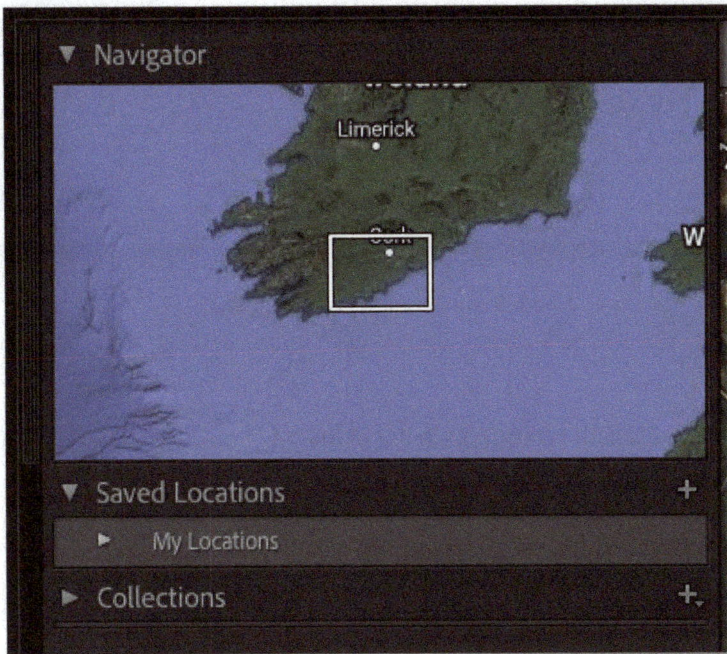

Figure 9.35 – The left-side panel tabs

Saved Locations

Saved Locations allows us to create a list of locations we want to be able to come back to quickly. To create a saved location, click on the small + symbol. This will open a **New Location** menu where we can choose the location name and folder for the new location we are creating. **Options** offers to specify the radius of this new location – it will default to the radius filling our current map view. We can also choose to make this new location private; any files within this location will never export with location information. Clicking on any location in **Saved Locations** will show a circle matching our settings for that location. Clicking on the small arrow on the right side of its name will go to that location on the map.

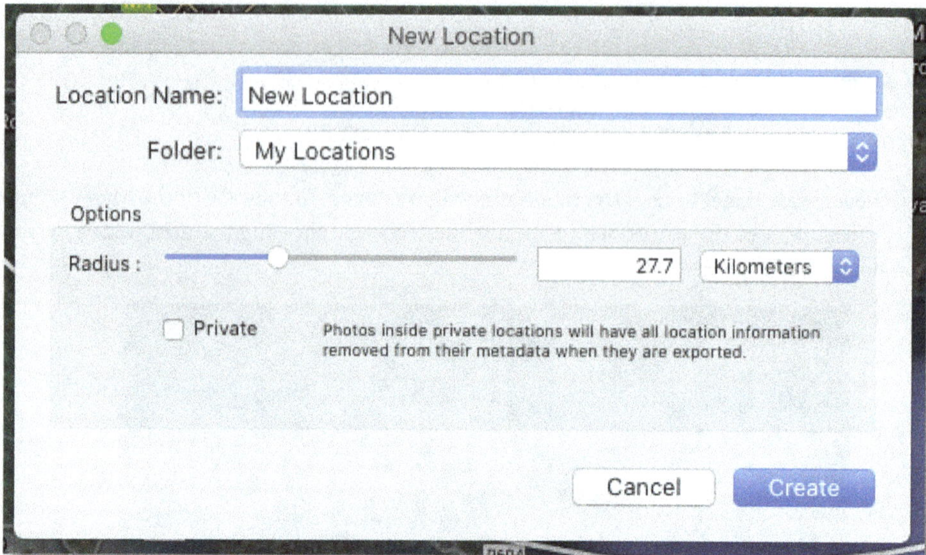

Figure 9.36 – The New Location menu

Collections

We should be very familiar with **Collections** at this point.

Location Filter

The top of the map has four options that will filter the Filmstrip photographs:

- **Visible On Map** will only show images tagged with GPS coordinates currently visible on the map.
- **Tagged** will show only images tagged with GPS coordinates.
- **Untagged** will only show photos without the GPS coordinates.
- **None** will turn off any applied filters.

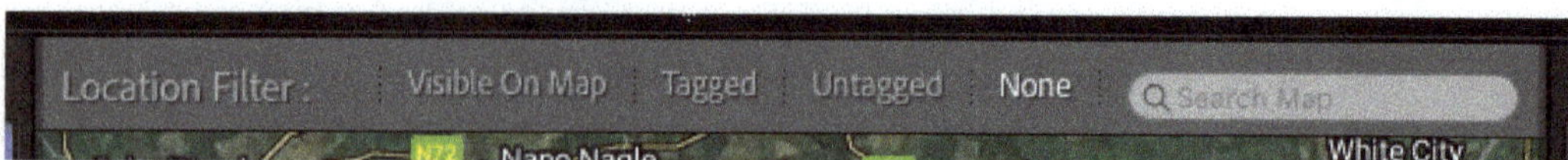

Figure 9.37 – The Location Filter menu

To see our photographs distributed on the map, we must choose a folder or a collection. The map will show any pictures with GPS coordinates as small pins in two shades of orange. Dark orange is reserved for unselected photographs (photographs not selected from the Filmstrip). The lighter shade of orange is dedicated to selected photographs (photographs selected in the Filmstrip). Clicking on any geotagged photo in the Filmstrip will open the map on that location. If, for example, we open a folder from a trip to a different city where we were taking GPS-tagged photos and we want to pinpoint a location, once we click on a picture in the Filmstrip, the map will show us the exact spot where we took the photo.

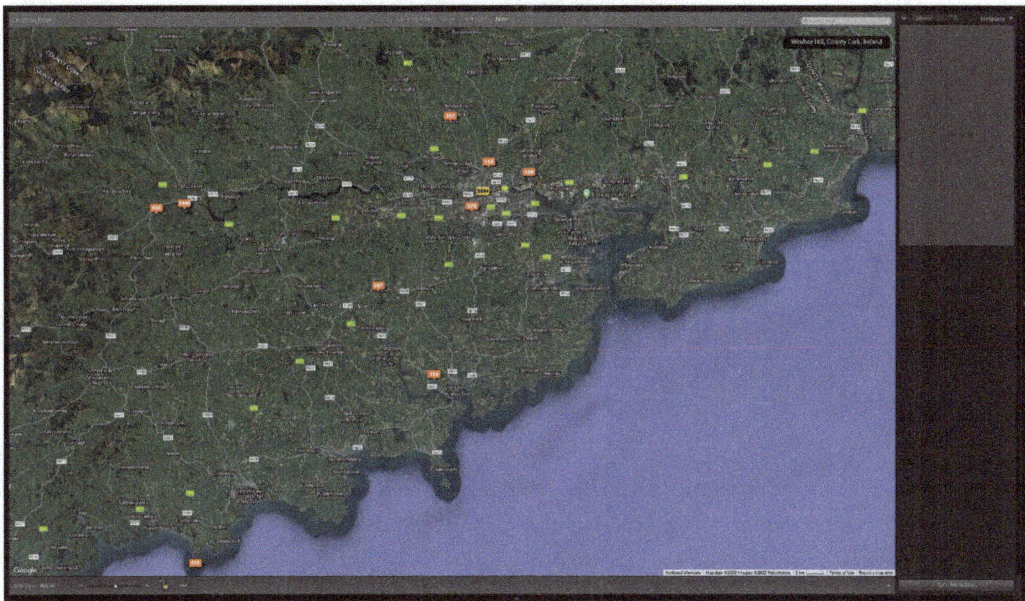

Figure 9.38 – The sample folder view on the map

We can edit the GPS coordinates of any photograph or group of photographs in a few different ways.

Clicking on the orange tag visible on the map will select photographs from the tagged location on the Filmstrip. When we press "*Backspace*" on the keyboard, Lightroom will ask us whether we want to delete coordinates for the selected photo. In case of choosing a group of photographs, Lightroom will ask whether we want to delete GPS coordinates for all of them.

Right-clicking on any tag will give us an option to create a collection or delete GPS coordinates. We can also change or delete GPS data in the metadata location, conveniently opening in the right-side panel. To change coordinates, we can either type them directly into the GPS field or, when we have several photographs selected, click on the **Sync Metadata...** button. This will sync all selected photographs' GPS with the currently active photograph.

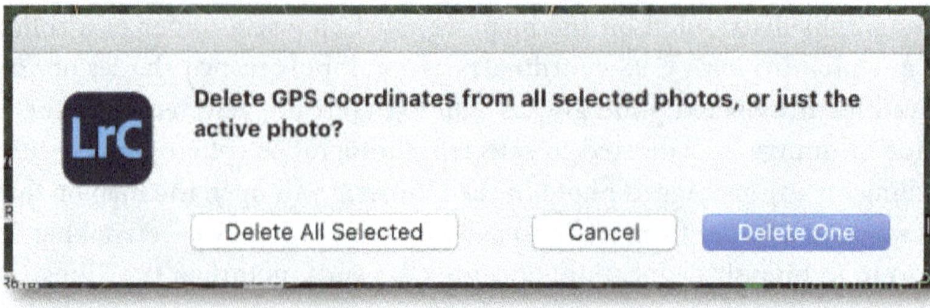

Figure 9.39 – Deleting GPS coordinates

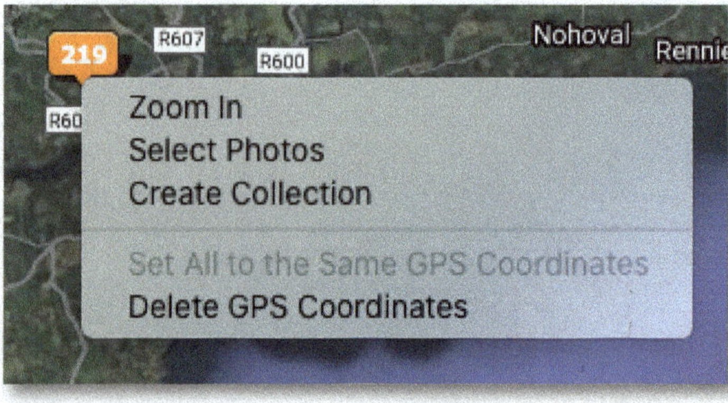

Figure 9.40 – Right-clicking on the location tag

Last but not least, we can add missing GPS coordinates to any photographs by simply dragging them from the Filmstrip onto any location on the map.

In the toolbar under the map (the "*T*" keyboard shortcut), we can choose which style of the map we could like to use. If you are using tracklogs from a third-party app, you can load them by clicking on the jagged wave button and choosing **Load Tracklog…**.

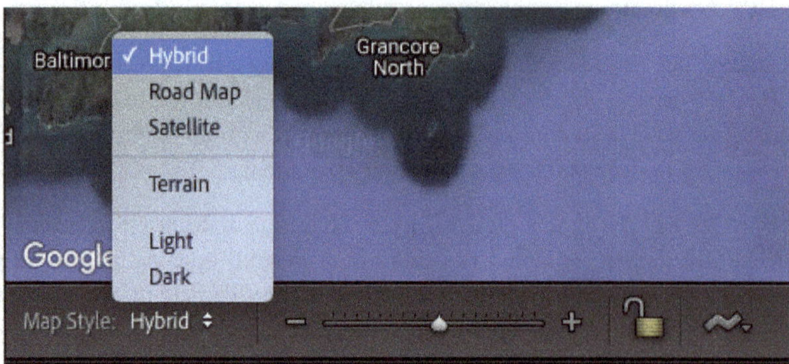

Figure 9.41 – The toolbar with the map style list opened

The preceding overview gives a good idea about working with the Map module. In the last part of this chapter, we will look at creating a simple web gallery in the Web module.

The Web module

We can build a simple web gallery in the Web module and export it as an HTML web gallery or upload it directly onto our server.

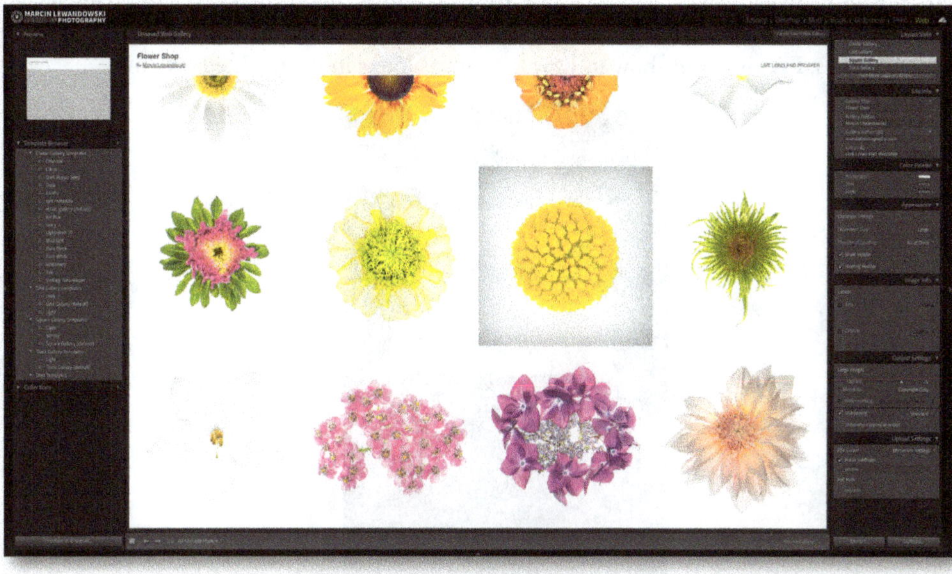

Figure 9.42 – The Web module

I'll be perfectly honest with you – there are better tools for creating web galleries, and what Lightroom has to offer might feel a bit outdated, especially when compared to what's available online, even for free. Having said this, the option to quickly build and export a web gallery (or upload directly to a server) is available directly from within Lightroom. In this chapter, we will look at the Web module's potential.

Before we start playing around with the settings, we must choose a folder or a collection of images that we want to work with and sequence them in the order we would like them to appear. In the toolbar under the main window, we can specify which photographs we would like to choose:

- **All Filmstrip Photos**
- **Selected Photos**
- **Flagged Photos**

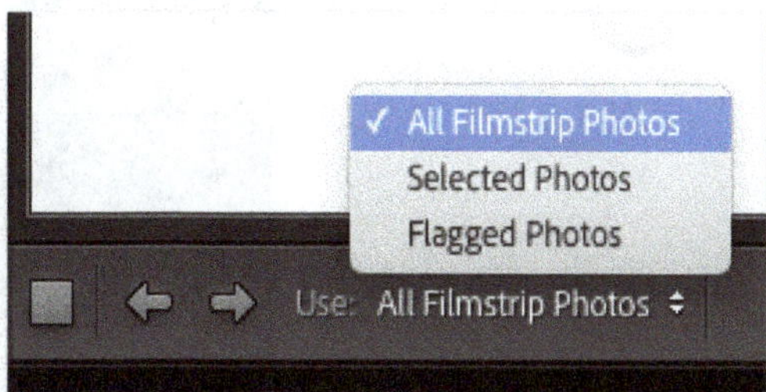

Figure 9.43 – The Use menu

We can change between these settings whenever we want and, of course, drag and drop any Filmstrip images around to form a sequence we like.

The left-side panel

The **Template Browser** option in the left-side panel of the Web module lets us choose from one of the available templates. Note that each of the different types – **Classic**, **Grid**, **Square**, and **Track Gallery** – all have one of their template's names ending with **(default)**; this is the most basic template and gives us more or less a blank canvas to work with, within each of these styles. When we hover over the template names, **Preview** will show us how the canvas looks in its unedited version.

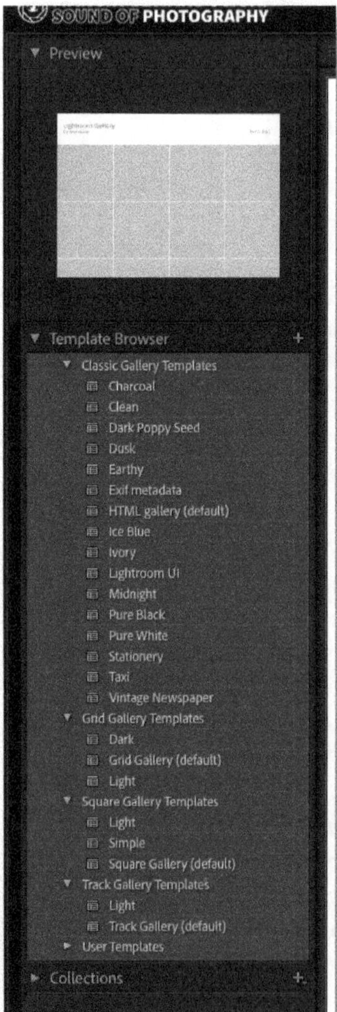

Figure 9.44 – The left-side panel

The right-side panel

Knowing that we have access to these templates, let's turn our attention to the right-side panel of the Web module and look at the tabs it contains:

- **Layout Style**
- **Site Info**
- **Color Palette**
- **Appearance**
- **Image Info**
- **Output Settings**
- **Upload Settings**

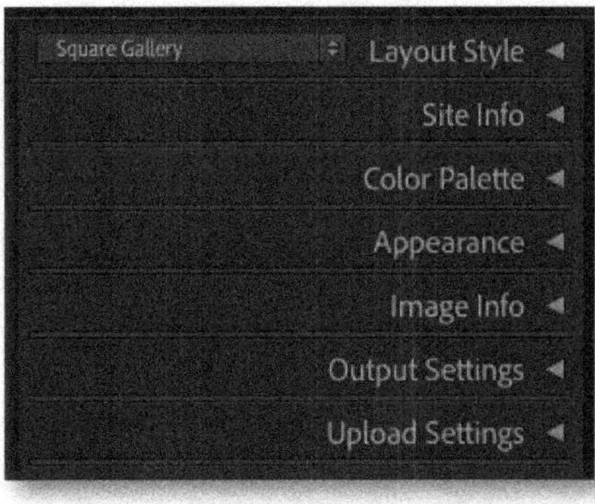

Figure 9.45 – The right-side panel tabs

The **Layout Style** tab gives us a choice between four different gallery types. These types are as follows:

- **Classic Gallery**
- **Grid Gallery**
- **Square Gallery**
- **Track Gallery**

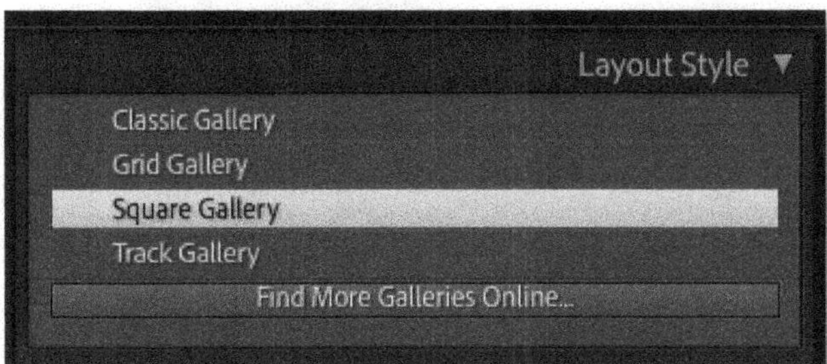

Figure 9.46 – The Layout Style tab

We will now look at the main differences and similarities between these four gallery types.

The only three tabs that will have the same settings, no matter which gallery we choose, are the following:

- **Image Info**: There are two lines of information we can add through this tab. Even though they are titled **Title** and **Caption**, they can extract whatever we want and need from a picture's metadata. For both of these settings, we can choose from a list of presets or create custom titles and captions by clicking on **Edit…**. We can build a desired string of text by inserting it from the list available in the Text Template Editor, which works on the same principle as the Filename Template Editor in the **Export** menu.
- **Output Settings**: Output settings are elementary. They allow us to set the quality of the exported images and whether metadata is exported within the pictures. We can also choose whether we want them to be watermarked and what level of sharpening we wish to apply to the exported gallery images.
- **Upload Settings**: You will only use this tab if you want to upload a created gallery directly onto your server. It might be a useful option if this is how you manage your website. All you need to do is to choose the **Configure FTP File Transfer** option, which will be a familiar list of details if you work your website this way. If you are not sure how to configure it, I suggest contacting your website provider and asking for the settings required by the **Configure FTP File Transfer** menu.

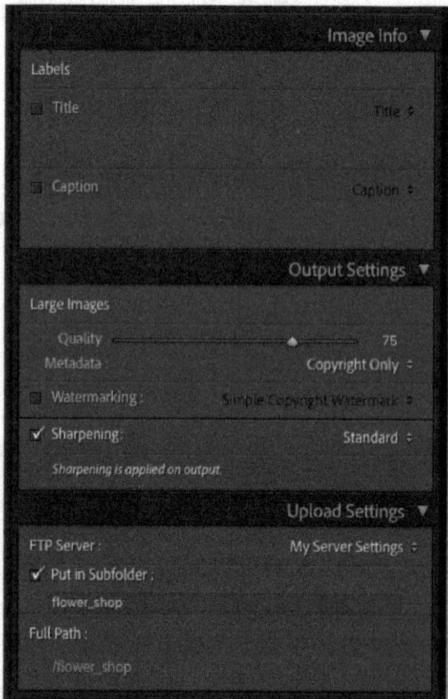

Figure 9.47 – The Image Info, Output Settings, and Upload Settings tabs

After learning about the standard settings for all four types of galleries, let's look at what the other tabs offer us in terms of gallery customization.

Classic Gallery allows the most considerable amount of information in the **Site Info** tab; it can also be set up to link our identity plate to a web address of our choice. It's also the only type of gallery allowing the use of an identity plate. **Classic Gallery** is also the only gallery that will enable us to specify the size of the grid – this can be set up in the **Appearance** tab. The minimum number of rows and columns we can set up is 3 x 3. **Color Palette** controls the coloring of each adjustable element. We can view the changes in real time and run wild, letting our inner designer go mad. **Classic Gallery** allows us also to set the image page's size (a full image that opens after clicking on a thumbnail). Unfortunately, this is a constant size, and it's not a responsive design. The image will always open and remain in the specified size, no matter what screen it is displayed on. The **Appearance** tab also allows us to set the photo borders' thickness for both the thumbnail and image pages.

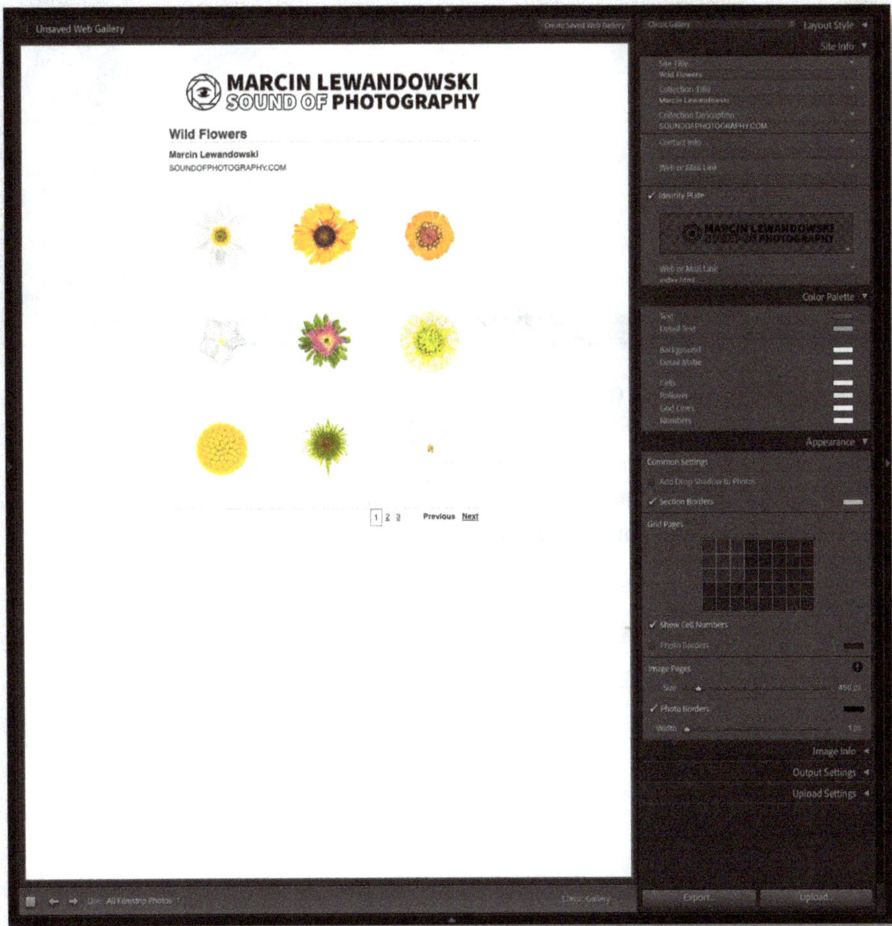

Figure 9.48 – A sample Classic Gallery view and tabs, with settings unique to the Classic Gallery

Grid Gallery offers a more simplified approach, with only three **Site Info** fields, four **Color Palette** choices, and a different approach to **Appearance**. Instead of grid size, we can choose between the pagination style and the number of items per page. We do not influence the size of the photograph displayed on the Image pages. This is a responsive design gallery; it will adjust the image to fit into any screen it is displayed on. The same responsiveness applies to the thumbnail grid.

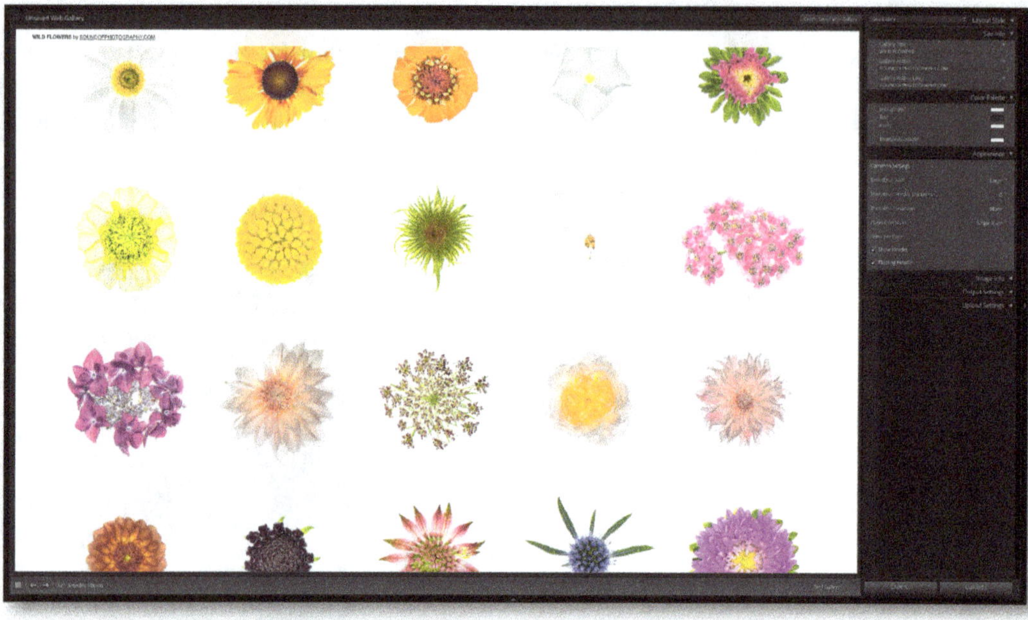

Figure 9.49 – A sample Grid Gallery with large thumbnails and floating header

Square Gallery has the least amount of settings. Thumbnails within this gallery will always appear square. The only real influence we have over the look of the thumbnails page within the Square Gallery is the size we choose for the thumbnails. As with the Grid Gallery, it's a responsive design.

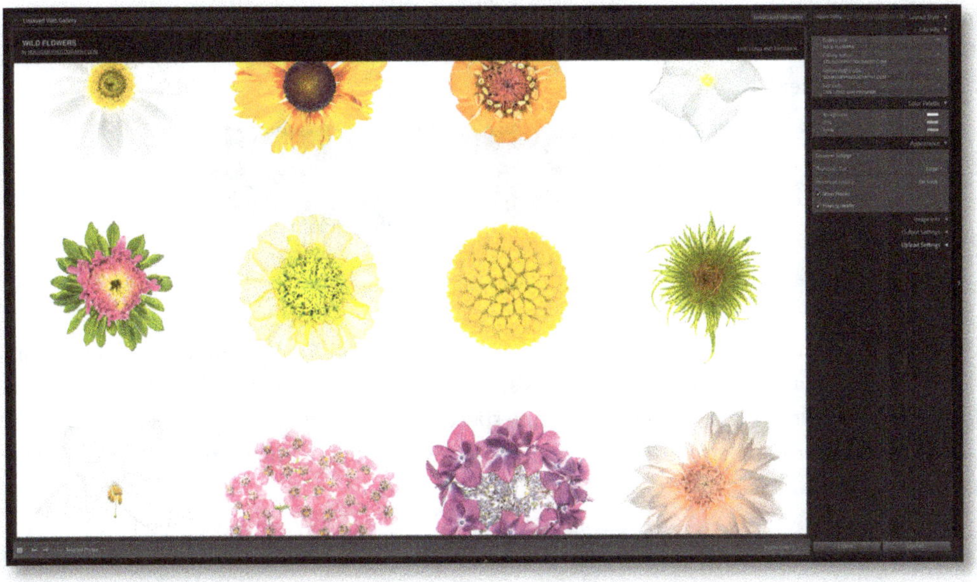

Figure 9.50 – A sample Square Gallery with large thumbnails and a floating header

The last choice is **Track Gallery**, which will display thumbnails as a uniform, continuous, and responsive flow of the images we chose for our gallery. With this design, we can only change the height and spacing of the rows with thumbnails.

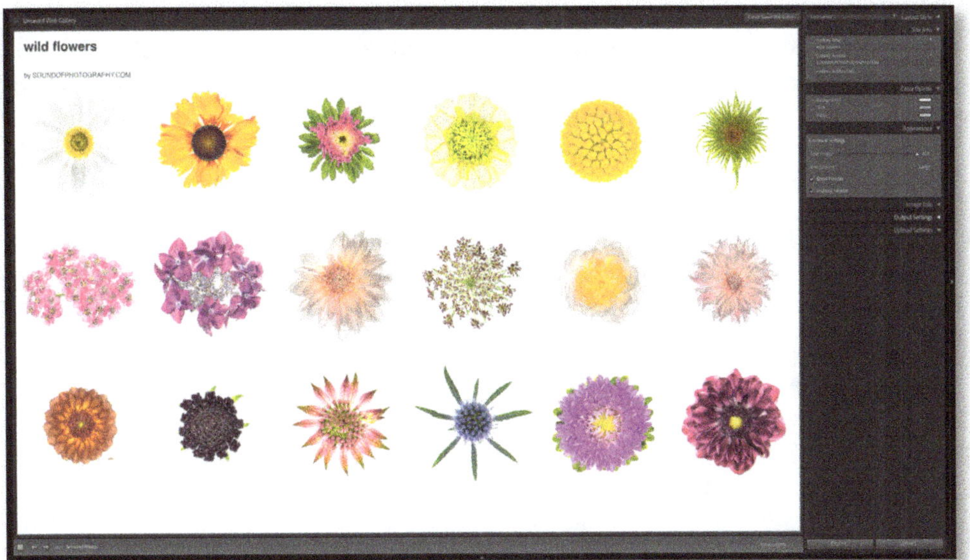

Figure 9.51 – A sample Track Gallery with the maximum size of thumbnails and the maximum spacing between rows of photos

If we want to see how our design looks and works in a browser, we can always hit the **Preview in Browser...** button at the bottom of the left-side panel, which will open the page we created in our default browser.

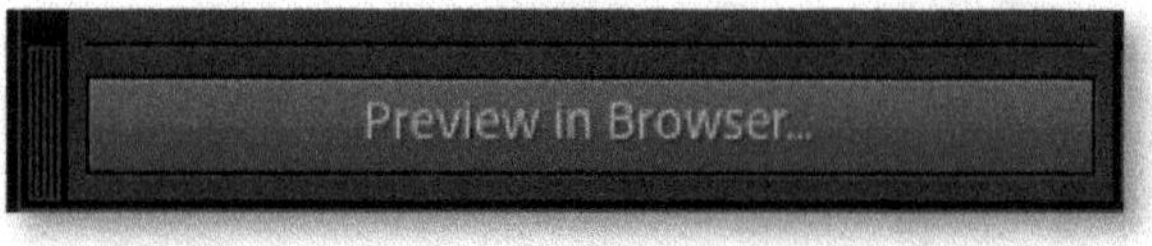

Figure 9.52 – The Preview in Browser... button

Even though it's not the latest and greatest in terms of web design, the Web module offers a simple solution with no extra added cost; all we need is some server space. We can maintain a website with no additional or hidden charges and with lighting speed, all from within the same piece of software. Once we create a user template with the design we like, we can upload new galleries to our page by clicking the **Upload...** button.

Summary

In this chapter, we learned about three modules – Slideshow, Map, and Web. Some of this information will become an indispensable part of many photographers' workflows; some of it they will never revisit. For example, I use the slideshows to look at how photographs look when viewed one after another before sending anything to clients or family and friends. I'll often sit down, relax, and watch them a few times. If anything feels out of place or unnecessary, I'll delete it from the final edit. Conversely, I practically never use the Map module, even though I see its tremendous potential. I started adding GPS positions to my work folders, but it's still just a gimmick in my workflow. Lastly, the web gallery is an option I considered at some stage, thinking that with enough tweaking, it could have a contemporary enough look, but it just didn't fit my workflow. Maybe it will fit yours.

In the next chapter, which is also the last chapter of this book, we will learn about additional Lightroom functionality, such as adding a second screen or projector and working with a tethered camera. We will also look at the basics of Lightroom CC and Lightroom for mobile. We will close the chapter with a quick look through everything that we learned throughout this book.

10

Final Notes and Summary

Welcome to the last chapter of this book! I hope you have become a well-informed Lightroom user by now and are all set to make the best out of this excellent software.

With all of the Lightroom Classic modules discussed, we can now look at the other versions that come with it as a package.

We will cover the following topics in this chapter:

- Second window
- Tethered shooting
- Lightroom
- Recapitulating the Lightroom Classic modules

Before we move on to other versions of Lightroom and finish our journey through Lightroom Classic, let's look at two items I left out earlier – second window and tethered shooting. These will be necessary for some setups.

Second window

This is a feature that gives us a second, independently managed Lightroom window. We can use it to view fullscreen images while we keep working in the main window. This window will open as a full screen if we have a second monitor attached to the computer. Once enabled, we can use the options in the **File** menu to manage the second window.

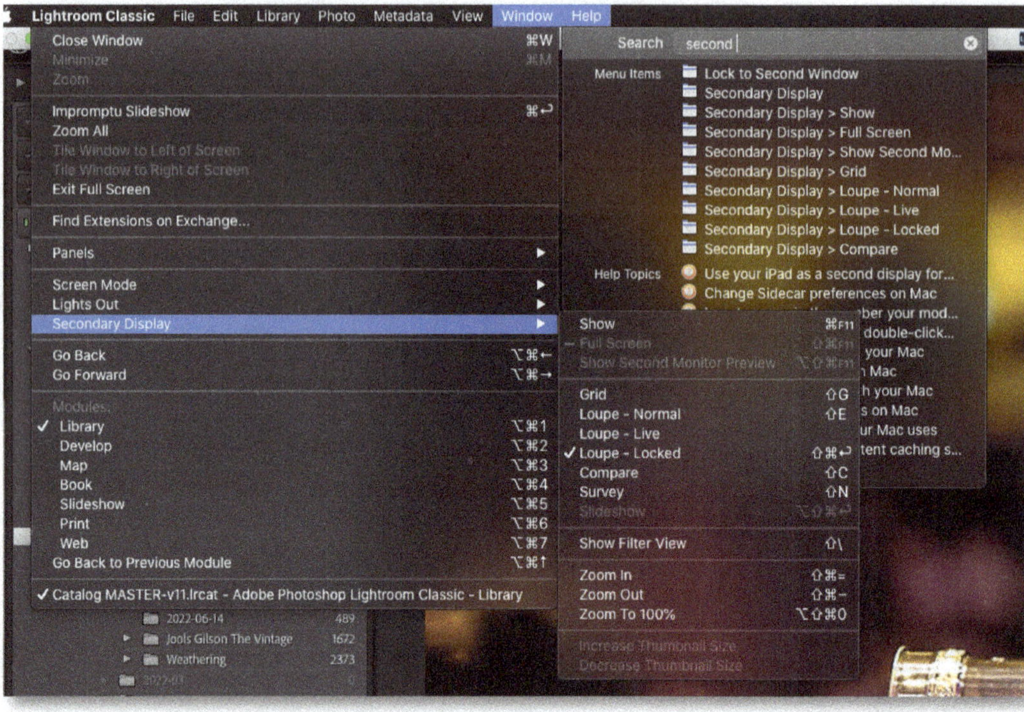

Figure 10.1 – The second window File menu options

The second window can work in four view modes but offers no tools. Tools remain part of the main window of Lightroom.

These are the available view modes:

- **Grid**
- **Loupe**
- **Compare**
- **Survey**

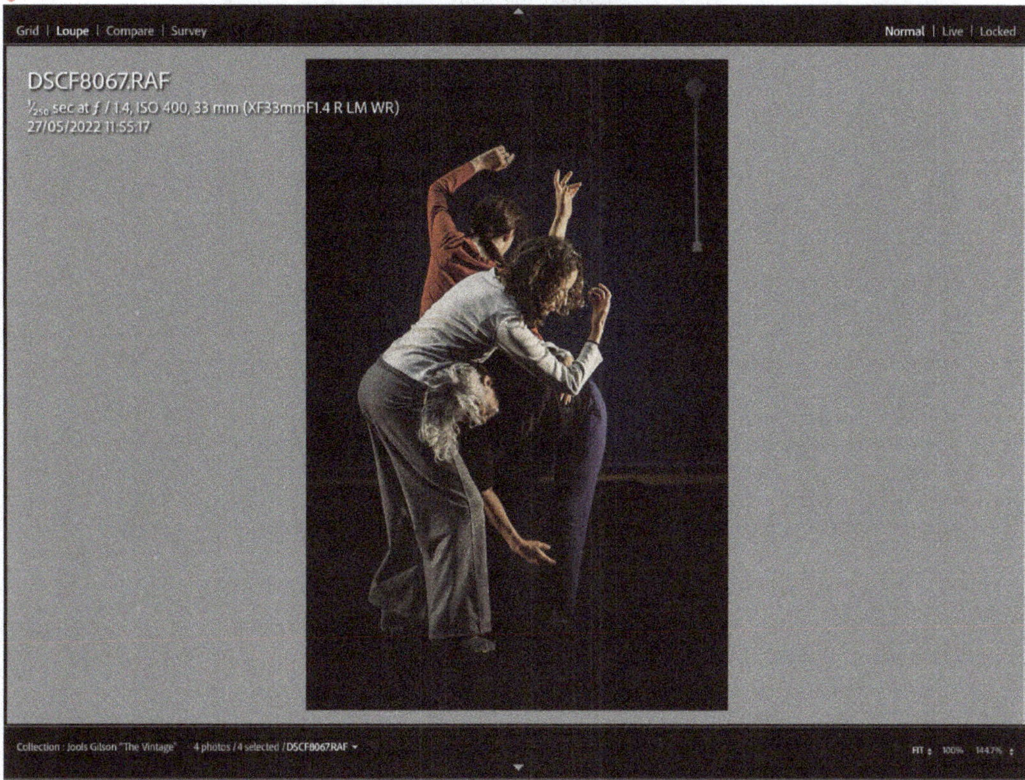

Figure 10.2 – A second window example

In addition to their standard functionality, in the **Loupe** view, we can choose between three modes:

- **Normal**
- **Live**
- **Locked**

The **Normal** view mode mirrors selections made in the main window and vice versa. The **Live** view displays the image that we are currently hovering over in the main window. Any photograph viewed in the **Locked** mode in the second window will not change with selections made in the main window. It will also remain unchanged after we move into different view modes within the second window, even if we select other photographs.

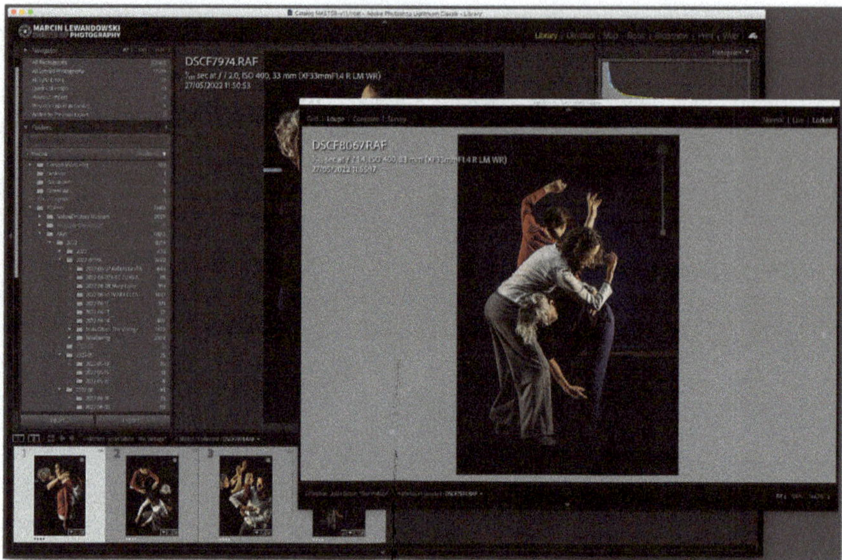

Figure 10.3 – A second window in Loupe > Locked mode example

Now, let's gain some insights into tethered capture.

Tethered capture

Tethered capture, means that our camera is tethered by a cable to the computer, where it will save the images we make while being tethered. For many Nikon and Canon camera users, this can be either a feature that comes in handy from time to time or the primary way to interact with Lightroom. A complete list of compatible cameras is available on the Adobe website. **Tethered capture** is a nonexistent feature for the unlucky users of other camera systems, such as myself, unless we use third-party plugins that offer workarounds for this lack of compatibility. Unfortunately, they are not as sleek nor as reliable. If tethered shooting is the way you work, you need a reliable solution, and if your camera is not supported, then I would suggest researching available plugins or even looking at other solutions, such as **Capture One**.

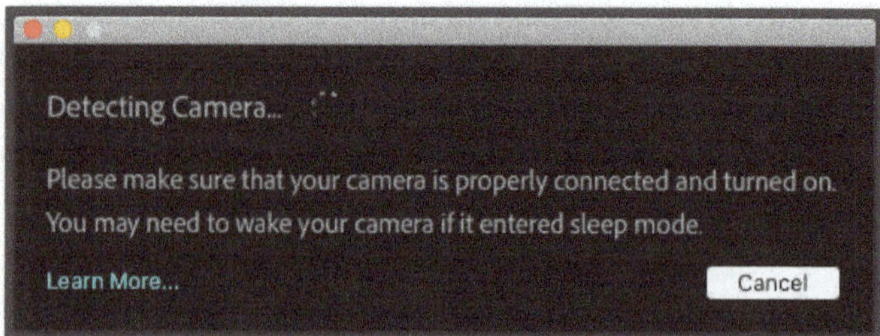

Figure 10.4 – Lightroom looking for an attached compatible camera

To start working tethered, we must connect a supported camera, turn on Lightroom, and go to **File** > **Tethered Capture** > **Start Tethered Capture**. Here, we can set the name for our session, a file-naming recipe, the destination for created files, and additional information we would like to include in the metadata. If we enable **Disable Auto Advance**, Lightroom will stop advancing to the most recently captured image.

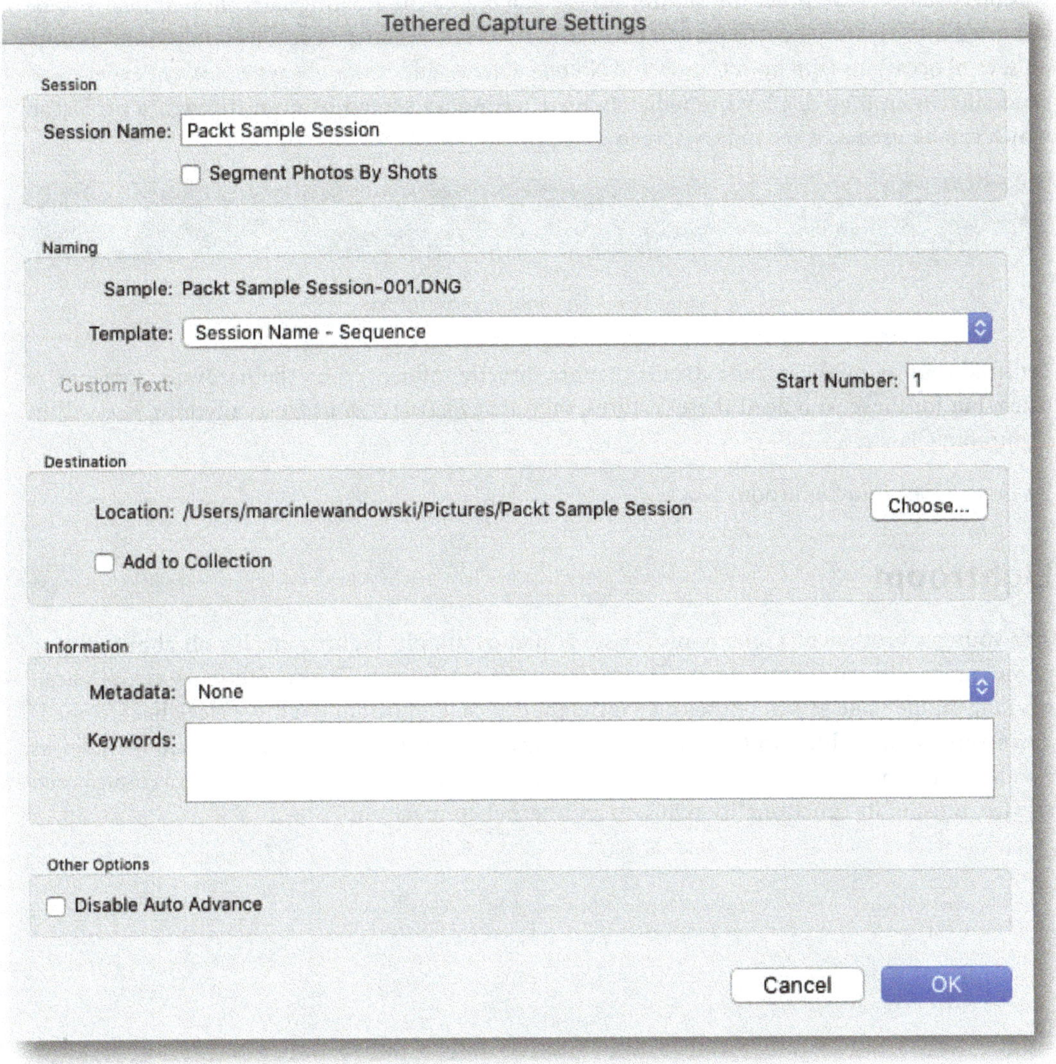

Figure 10.5 – The Tethered Capture Settings window

Once we click **OK**, Lightroom will look for a connected camera and, after a moment, display a floating control bar with a large circular button, symbolizing the shutter. The other menus give us control over our camera's basic options and allow us to immediately apply selected develop settings, just like when importing photographs. Clicking the **Live** view on the bar will display the live view from our camera in an additional window. From now on, until we end the tethered session, whenever we press the shutter on the camera or the floating bar, photographs will be imported directly into Lightroom and become available in a matter of seconds. I used this feature on several occasions with both Canon and Nikon cameras, and it was always a pleasant experience, especially when they display immediately on a secondary screen or even through a projector, which can be used as a secondary screen as well.

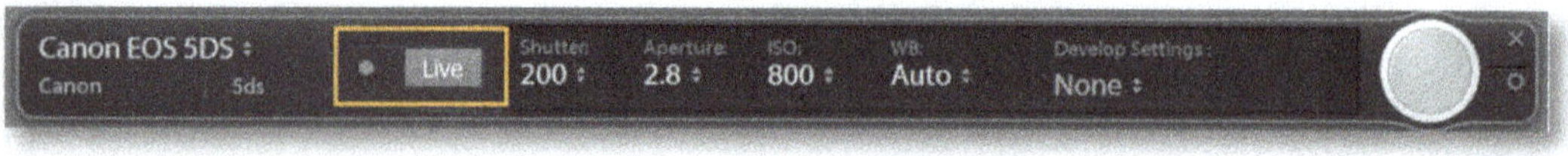

Figure 10.6 – The floating control bar

Tethered capture might include details that are directly influenced by the hardware someone is using, but for those who need these features, they are as flawless in usage as anything else within Lightroom Classic.

It's time to look into Lightroom now!

Lightroom

The younger brother of Lightroom Classic is named simply Lightroom. It's all about editing photographs without relying on copies stored on the machine we are currently using. It's about working on the same sets of photos on a different device. Lightroom is a more sleek but stripped-down version of Lightroom Classic, missing many features that Lightroom Classic includes as standard, but it also consists of a few nifty tricks that Lightroom Classic can't do. As a cloud-based service, most of its functionality relies on an internet connection.

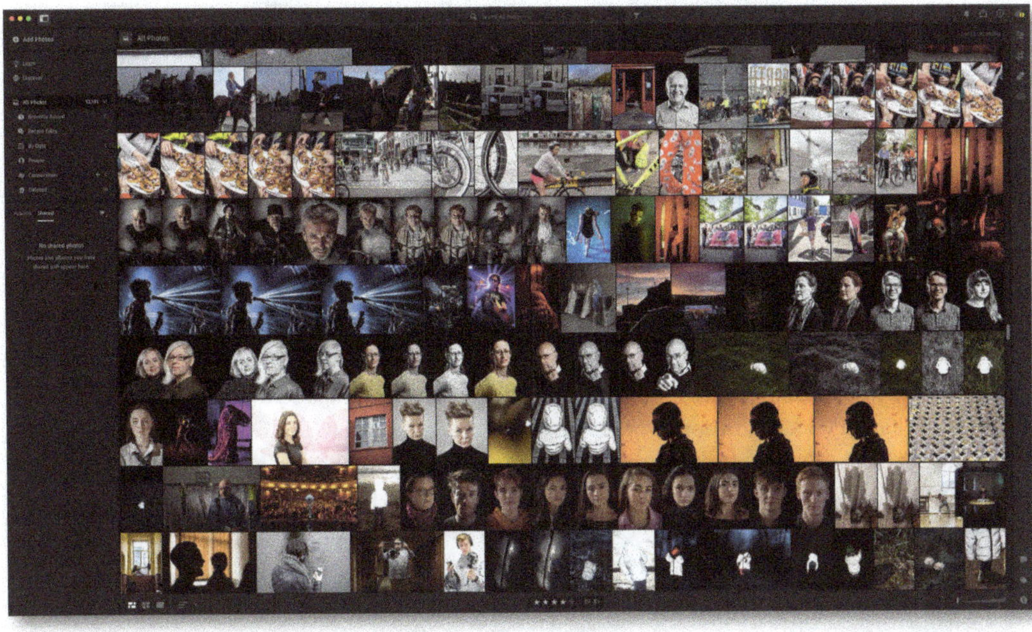

Figure 10.7 – Lightroom

The basis of Lightroom's flexibility works as follows – we create a collection in Lightroom Classic and choose for it to sync. Syncing can be done by either selecting the **Sync with Lightroom** option when creating a collection or, later, by checking the **Click to sync this Collection with Lightroom** box. We can find this box next to the collection name in the **Collection** tab. In addition to "living" on our hard drive and inside Lightroom Classic, this collection will now be available for us to edit in Lightroom. Any synced collections will be available for editing in Lightroom for mobile and Lightroom on the web through Adobe Creative Cloud, where Lightroom will upload all synced photographs.

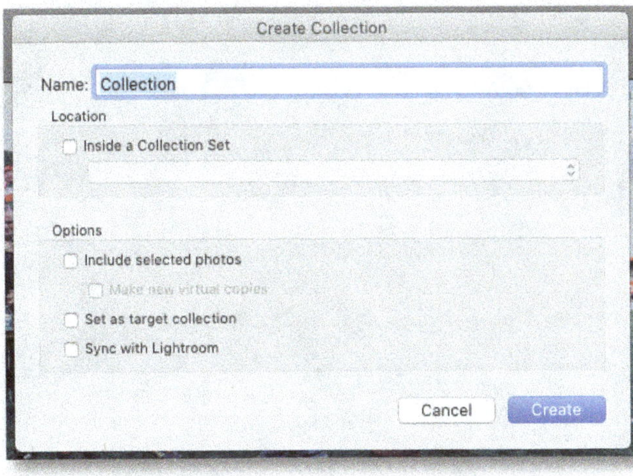

Figure 10.8 – The Create Collection menu

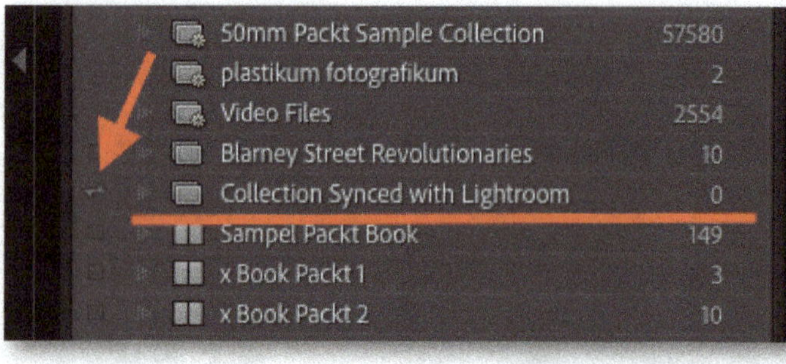

Figure 10.9 – An example of a collection synced with Lightroom

The first big and immediately noticeable difference in Lightroom (compared to Lightroom Classic) is the lack of additional tabs. Lightroom works like a hybrid of the Library and Develop module panels without the others. Its core functionality is still based around the left- and right-side panels, but they work in a slightly different way to the Lightroom Classic panels. If you feel confident with moving around Lightroom Classic, switching to Lightroom will be a breeze, as most Develop module tools are just where you would expect them to be.

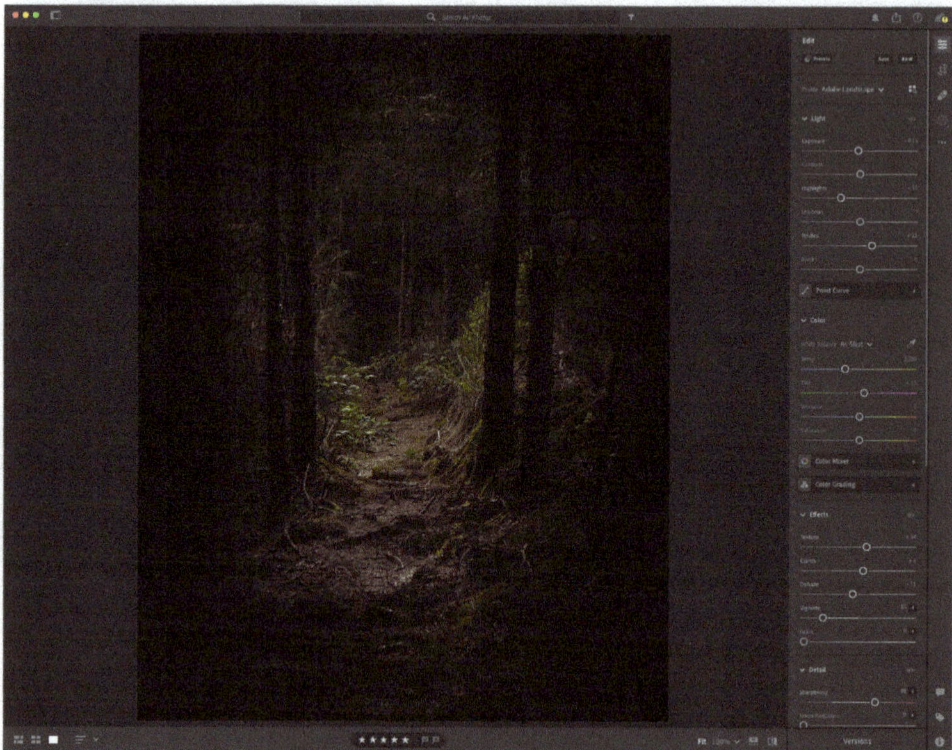

Figure 10.10 – The Edit menu, visible on the right

The left-side panel of Lightroom works like a library and gives us access to all available photographs. We can add new photos by clicking the **Add Photos** button and choosing the images or folder we want to add. Anything we add to Lightroom is automatically synced with our Adobe Creative Cloud account, making images available across all platforms. Syncing works in all directions - that is, if we develop something in Lightroom Mobile on our phone, the same settings will be visible in other Lightroom versions and vice versa.

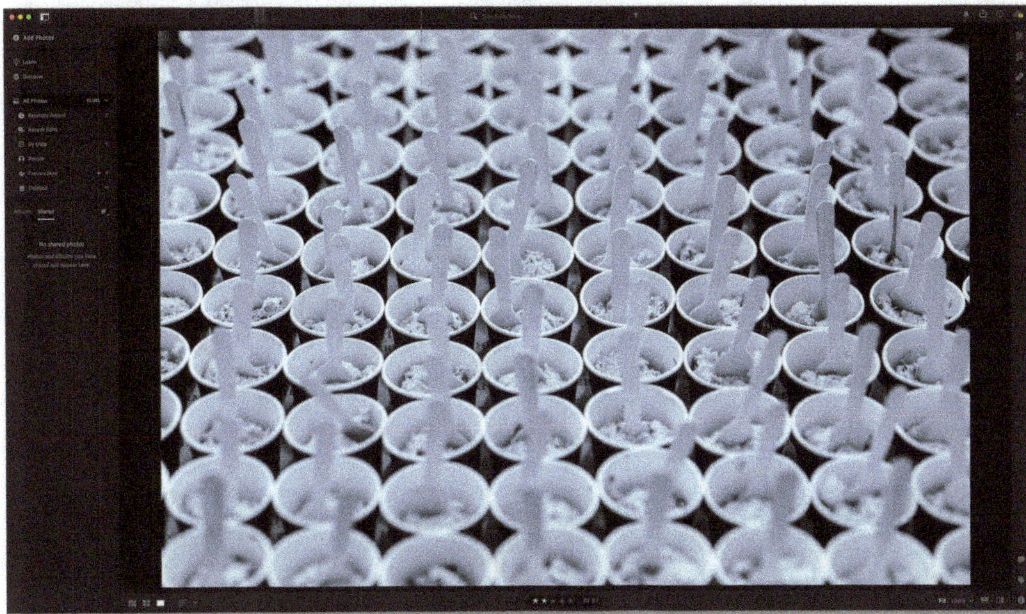

Figure 10.11 – The All Photos menu, visible on the left

One handy shortcut to remember for working in Library mode is "*P*", which will open and close the left tab. This can also be done by the button in the top-left corner of the Lightroom window. By using the familiar shortcut for entering the **Grid** view, "*G*", we will not only enter the grid but also cycle through its two available types - **photo grid** and **square grid**. A photo grid can be described as a **masonry** grid - a clear view of a stream of photographs without any notations, names, and so on. A square grid is a look more familiar to Lightroom Classic's view and includes details such as rating, flags, and its sync status. Unfortunately for us, many of the shortcuts from Lightroom Classic will not work in Lightroom or do different things - for example, "*E*" will open Develop mode while "*D*" will open a full page view, which is more or less opposite to Lightroom Classic behavior.

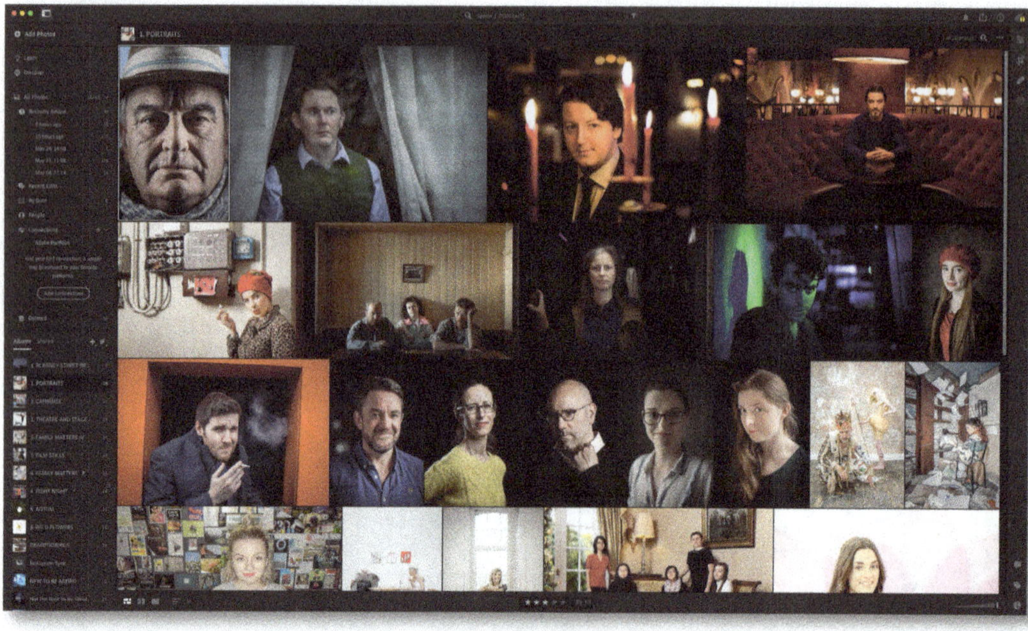

Figure 10.12 A

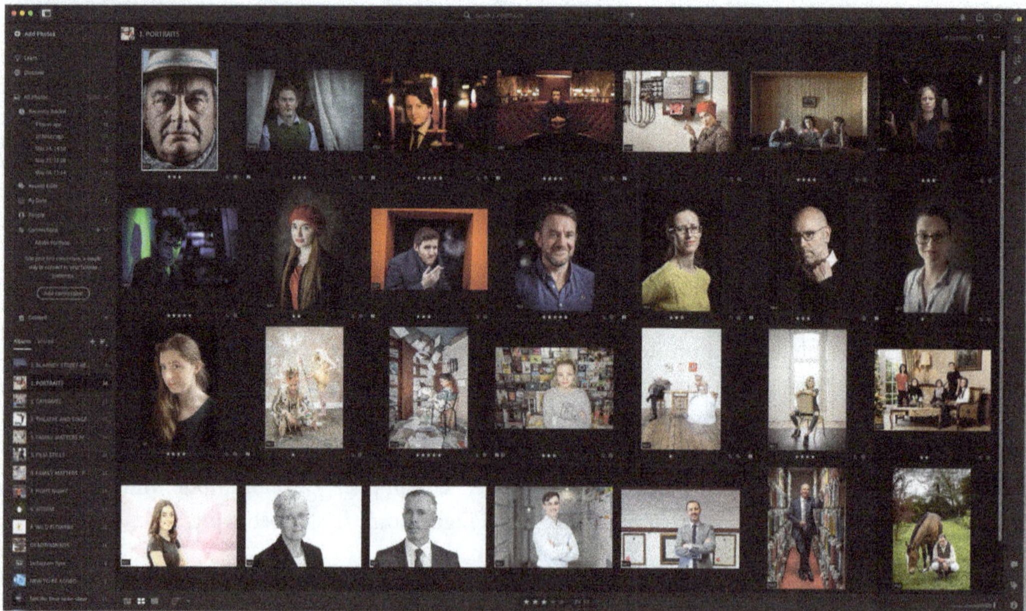

Figure 10.12 B – The photo grid and square grid views

We can enter Develop mode by using the aforementioned "*E*" shortcut, as Develop is called **Edit** in Lightroom. We can also enter **Edit** mode by clicking on one of the tool collections visible on the right side – from top to bottom, **Edit**, **Crop**, **Healing Brush**, **Masking**, and **...**, which represents *other* options. **Edit** includes most of the familiar sliders from the Develop module; they look slightly different, but they offer the same flexibility and results as the Develop settings. We won't see the familiar split into tabs and will miss a few, such as **Calibration**.

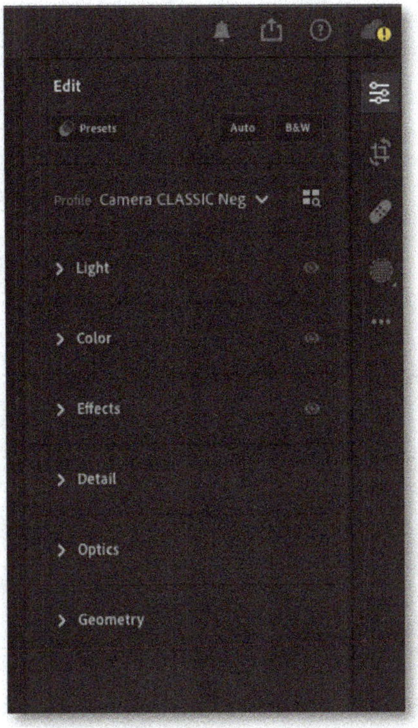

Figure 10.13 A

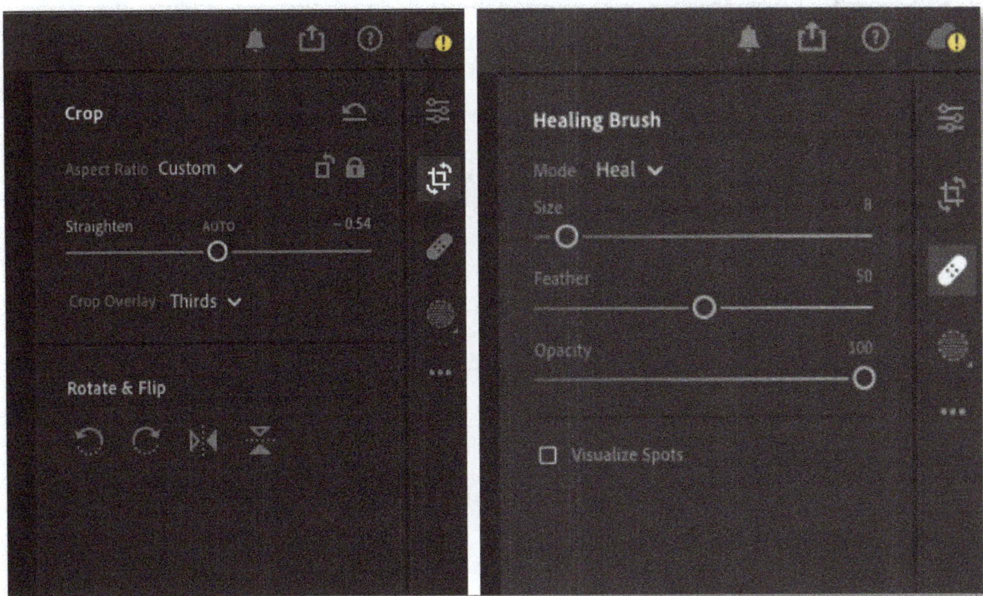

Figure 10.13 B

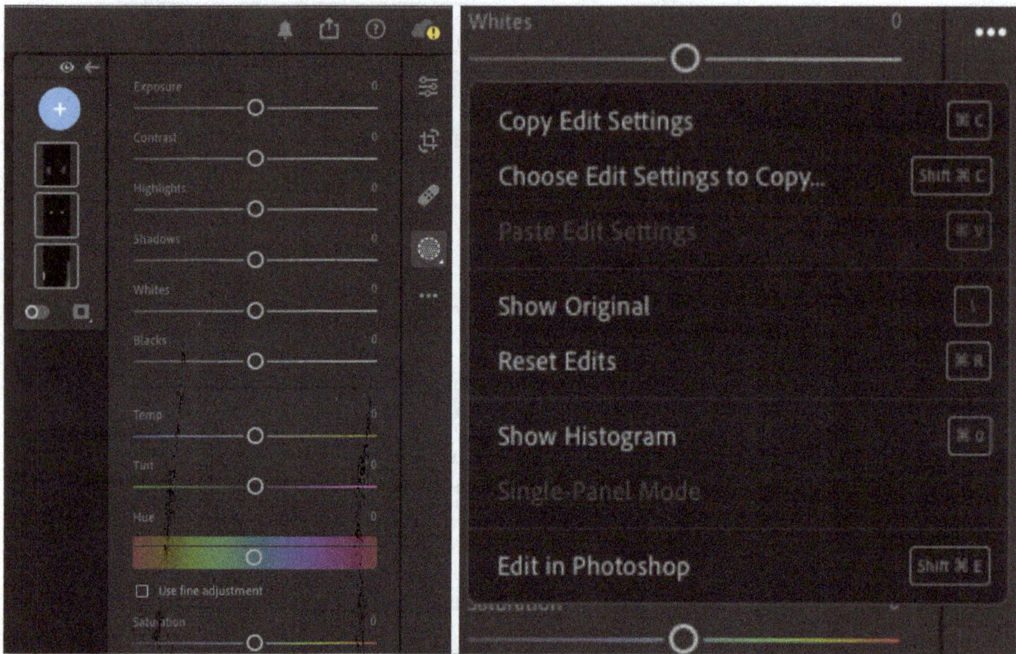

Figure 10.13 C – Edit, Crop, Healing Brush, Masking, and more options in order of appearance from the top

A feature that I miss dearly from Lightroom Classic is the **History** tab. It is replaced by the less detailed **Versions** tool, where we can create a manual snapshot with the current status of any edited photograph. Versions will also create auto versions at different stages of the editing process but won't do it at every single step, as **History** does.

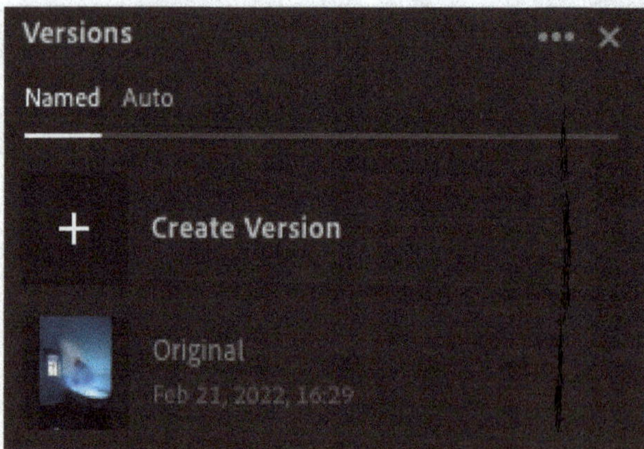

Figure 10.14 – The Versions tool

There are other differences and similarities between these two versions of Lightroom, but if you can confidently move around Lightroom Classic, Lightroom will feel like a better-looking, simplified, and natural extension. An even more straightforward transition is from Lightroom to Lightroom for mobile, which we can access in our browser.

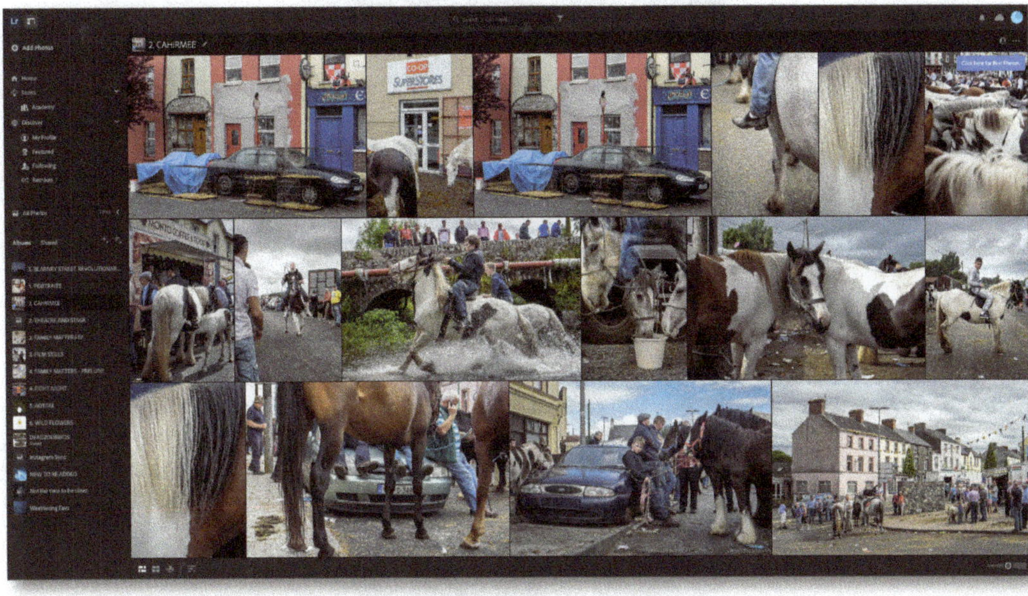

Figure 10.15 – Lightroom as seen in an internet browser

We can log in at `lightroom.adobe.com` with our Creative Cloud credentials. It has the same layout and streamlined set of tools as Lightroom. In addition, its content will be an exact match with Lightroom. This matching means that we can take our work anywhere that we have a connection to the internet and work with cloud-located files.

Even when we access Lightroom through our phone or tablet app and work with a small vertical screen, it will feel like all the tools are in the right place, with all the files available from the cloud storage. Even writing this makes me think again about how unbelievable it sounds – to be able to take some photographs with the camera, transfer them to Lightroom for mobile, and have them readily available from the cloud on any machine/device that I want to access them.

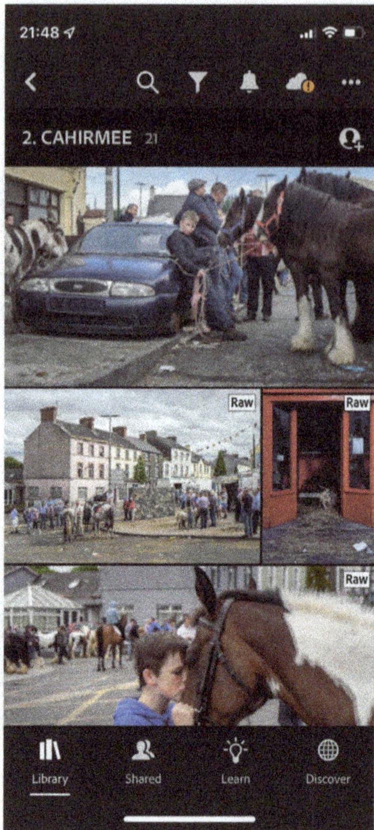

Figure 10.16 A

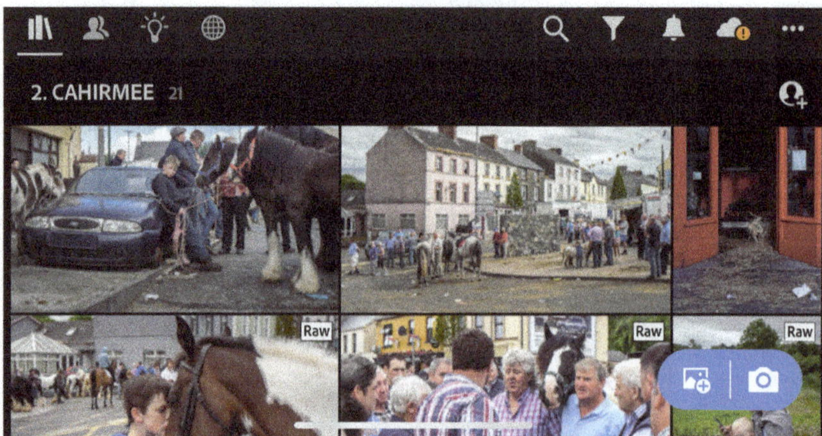

Figure 10.16 B – Lightroom for mobile as seen on a smartphone device

One fantastic feature that we have available in Lightroom, which is unavailable in Lightroom Classic (not mentioning the automatic cloud backup), is **Sensei**, an intelligent search engine. Even though I always preach that tagging and keywording images are essential if we want to find things later through deep metadata filters, with Sensei, we can type the parameters we are looking for, and it will do it for us. What's helpful is the ability to search not only for easily identifiable terms such as dates or lens models but also for abstract terms, such as `woman on a horse` or `red car`. Play around with it to see its strength in action.

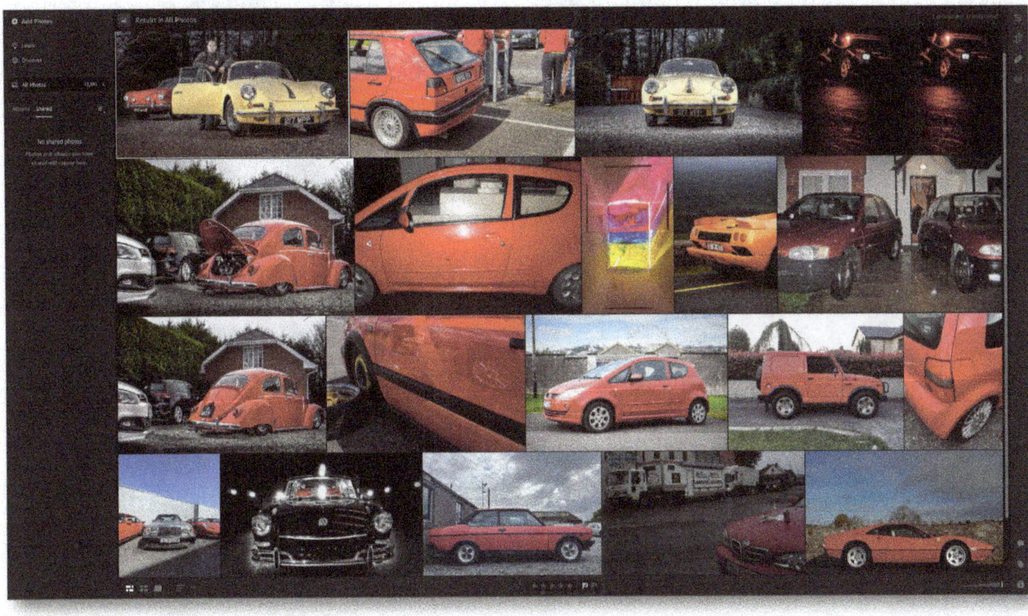

Figure 10.17 – A search for red car within my library

This quick look at cloud-based Lightroom capabilities concludes our journey through Lightroom. In the next section, also being the last part of this chapter and the book itself, we will summarize everything we have learned by glancing at each of Lightroom Classic's modules.

Recapitulating the Lightroom Classic modules

Let's start with the Library module.

The Library module

We explored the Library module in *Chapter 3, Tools Available within the Library Module*. This is where we manage our photographs. It's where each project begins and ends. We start by importing new images into Lightroom, deciding where they will be saved, and whether we want to apply any default keywords or Develop settings. We can even do a preliminary edit, picking images for import with "*P*" and rejecting them, and unselecting with "*X*". Once our new photos are imported, we can then view them as a grid ("*G*") or singular photo ("*E*"). I always call this part editing, but other photographers might call it **culling** or **selecting**. For me, personally, culling is a derogatory term in this case, and selecting describes only part of the process, and so I call it *editing*. We can create our edit, which we will later develop in a couple of different ways, from working with *1-5* star ratings through flagging "*P*", "*U*", and "*X*" (respectively, **Pick**, **Unpick**, and **Reject**) to *6-9* color labels. We can additionally aid our selections by working with metadata searches ("\"), as well as **Survey** ("*N*") and **People** ("*O*") views. Finally, we can, at any stage of the editing process, filter our results by applying any search criteria, either through the **Filter Bar** ("\") or on the top-right side of the **Filmstrip** (and with "*L*", which will enable our last-used filter). The library module is also the module where we will modify any metadata and add keywords and captions to our photographs. We can also apply simple Develop settings in the **Quick Develop** tab, including the **Auto settings** button.

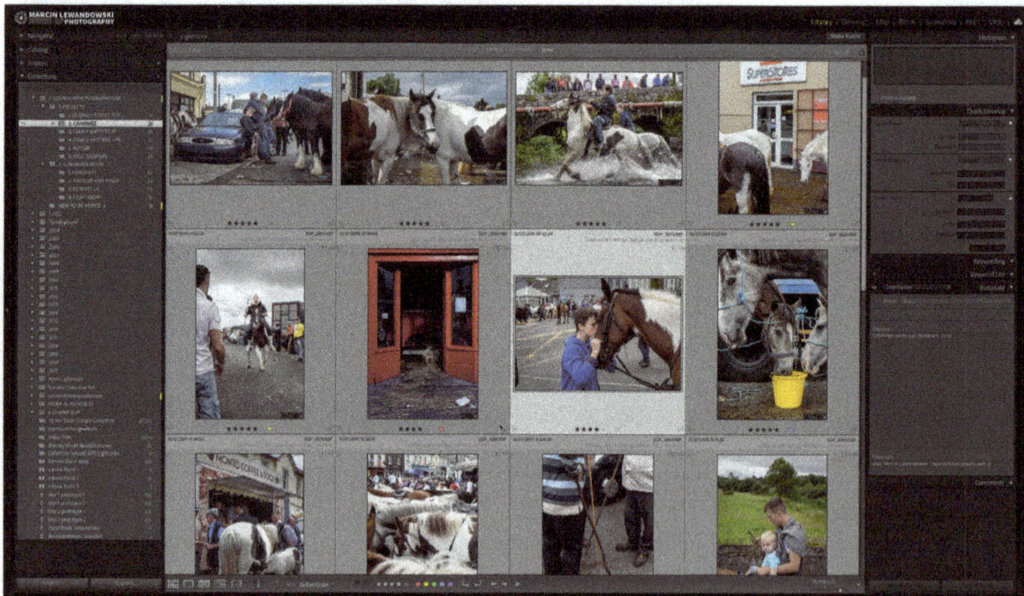

Figure 10.18 – The Library module

The Develop module

We covered the Develop module in *Chapter 5, An Introduction to the Develop Module*, and *Chapter 6, A Detailed View of the Develop Module's Functions*. Once we are happy with our edit, we can go to the next stage of working with our photographs. For that, we need to go to the Develop module ("*D*"). We will usually start in the **Basic** tab and hop to the other ones whenever we need them. To keep only one tab open at a time, we can right-click on one of them and choose the **Solo** mode. An excellent place to start is by trying the **Auto Tone** feature, which will usually produce satisfying results. We can further tweak it by working with all **Tone** sliders. Unfortunately, **Auto**

Tone doesn't fix the white balance, but we can remedy that quickly by pressing "*W*" and choosing a neutral color in our picture. From here, we can give it a bit of punch with **Presence**, and if we feel like it's still a bit bland, we can work with **Tone Curve** to bring both edges in a bit, create one of the S/M curves, or play around with color. We will go to the next tab for major and more precise shifts in color.

HSL/Color is where we get rid of a lot of unwanted color casts by desaturating unwanted ranges, darkening the skies a bit by reducing blue's luminosity, or shifting the hue of grass into a slightly different range. We can also do these operations by dragging colors directly into the photo with the selector.

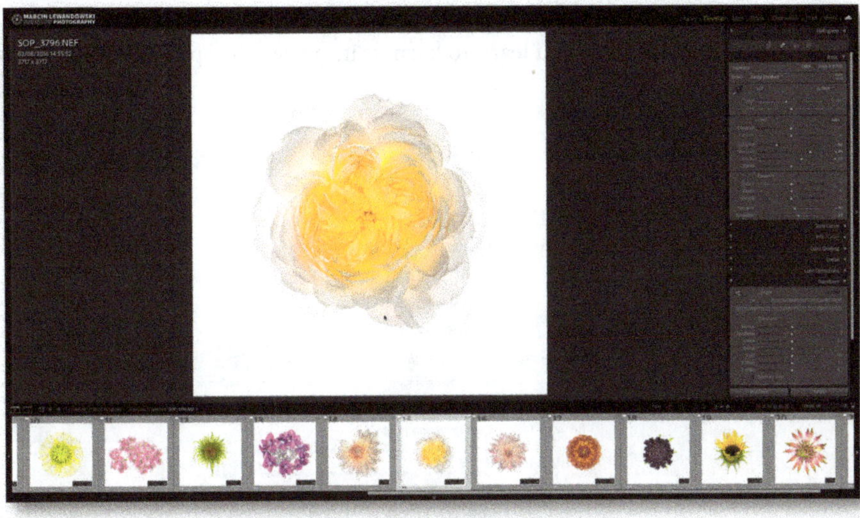

Figure 10.19 – The Develop module

Now that we have brought out all of the greatness in our photographs, we can completely change their feel by adding **Color Grading** in a luminosity area of our choice. If we want to try sepia, duotone, or even tritone, this is the place to let our imagination run wild, experiment, and have some fun. Maybe try experimenting with color wheel harmonies or add a bit of color cast using a paying client's color scheme. It's a nice tool for those special occasions when we have time to play around.

Detail is where we will add a bit more edge to our pictures, enhance their sharpness, and suppress noise. We can control all of these options and make sure we don't lose any details, making our images leap out of the screen at anyone looking.

If the lens we are using creates images that need a slight correction of any distortions, whether it is geometrical or color-related, the **Transform** tool will help us take care of it. With a good selection of manual tools and impeccable application of a built-in lens profile, **Lens Corrections** can be the first and last image correction we apply.

Before **Transform** was included in Lightroom, to straighten an image, we only had a choice between fiddling with the **Crop** tool to find a "good enough" balance or opening an image in Photoshop. Even though the **Automatic** fix that the **Transform** tool offers might sometimes be wildly inaccurate, the **Guided** tool will always be as accurate as the choices we make. After the **Basic** panel, this is often the only tab I visit when editing large batches of images after I finish the **Auto Tone** application.

Everyone needs a nice, elegant vignette from time to time, and **Effects** is the tab where we will control its strength. Tied with the **Grain** effect, **Effects** is a tab with a few creative possibilities that can strongly affect the look of a photograph.

Finally, let's come to the **Calibration** tab. This tab's use ranges from light tweaks to color behavior to wild swings of hue and saturation. Whether we like to play and experiment with colors or need to fix a stubborn color cast, this is another place where we can work on it. **Calibration** needs a bit of experimenting to get used to. Once you learn to harness its power, the applications are limitless.

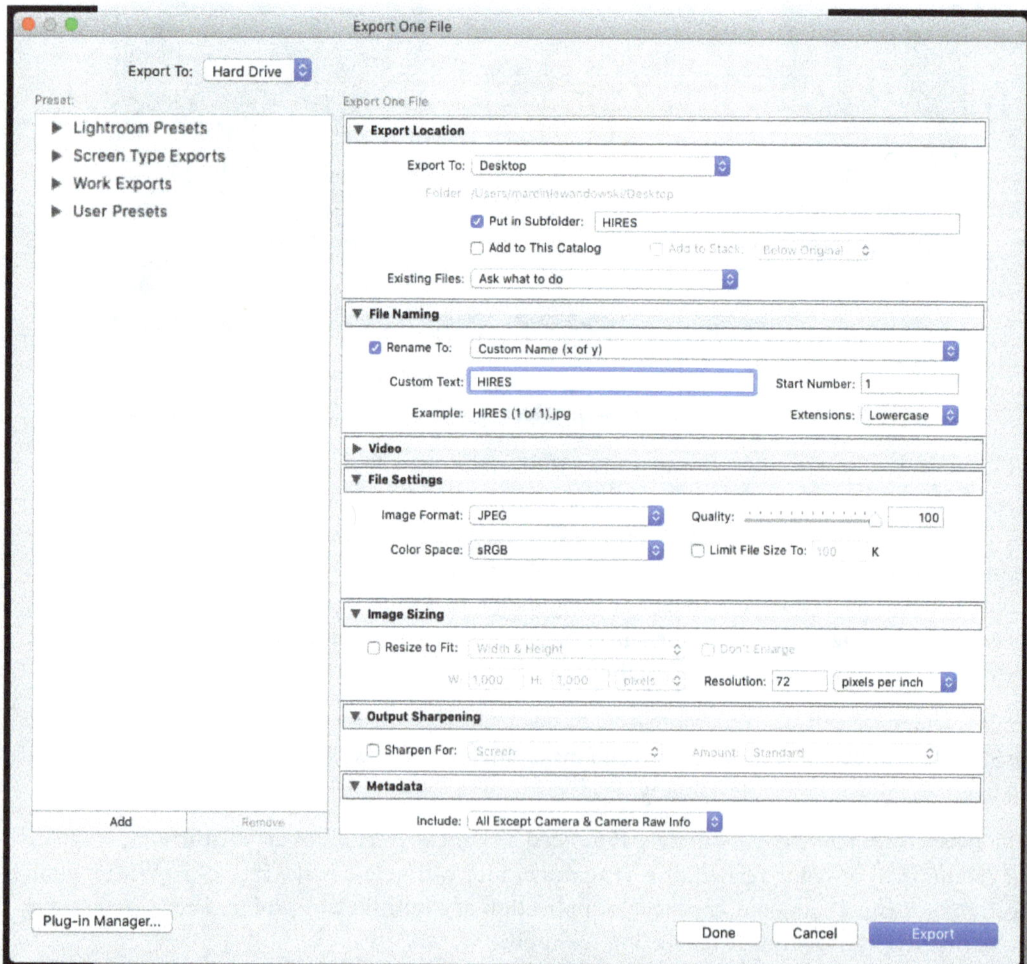

Figure 10.20 – The Export File menu

Export is probably the most often visited menu after we finish working with the Develop module. To share our images with the outside world, we must first render them in an appropriate format. The **Export** panel allows us to prepare both an optimal social media resolution and a high-resolution image for external printing. Watermarked or not, **Export** will help us present our work to the outside world.

The Map module

You can see this module as a refined "search by location" engine, which is so well designed that it can be used to our advantage in many ways. For example, as long as we have GPS data logged in our metadata, we can visually assign photographs to a timeline and location to find photographs from any place we photographed easily. So, whether we want to assess the range of the weddings we photographed, track our journeys for a travel blog, or find photographs by location, maps will help us move around folders and collections in yet another way.

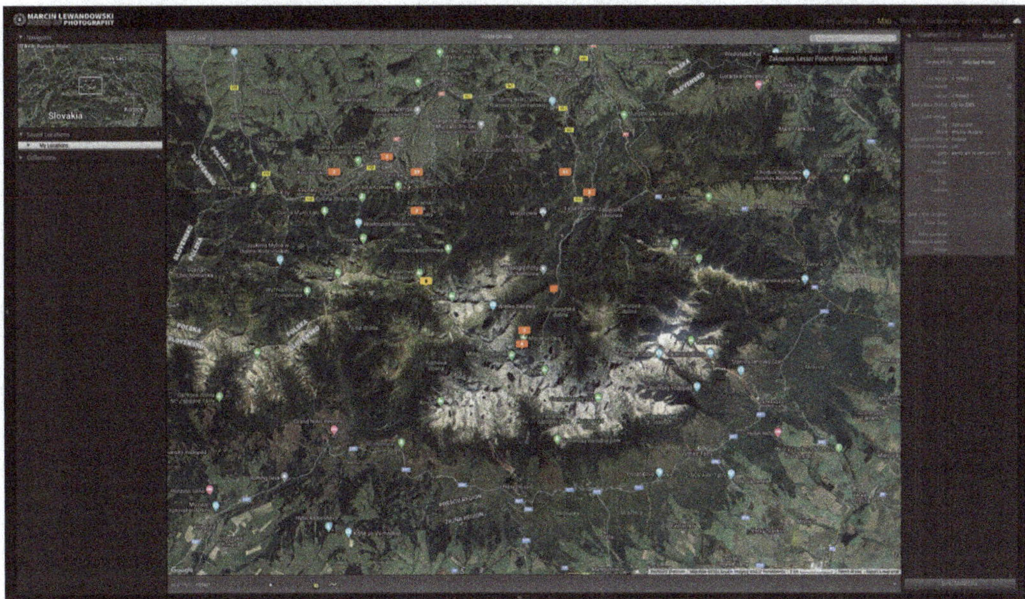

Figure 10.21 – The Map module

The Slideshow module

A slideshow is another way to present photographs digitally in a controlled manner. If we want our sequence of images to be viewed in any particular order and also control photograph distribution in a certain way, building a slideshow within Lightroom is easy and enjoyable, thanks to its simplicity and intuitiveness.

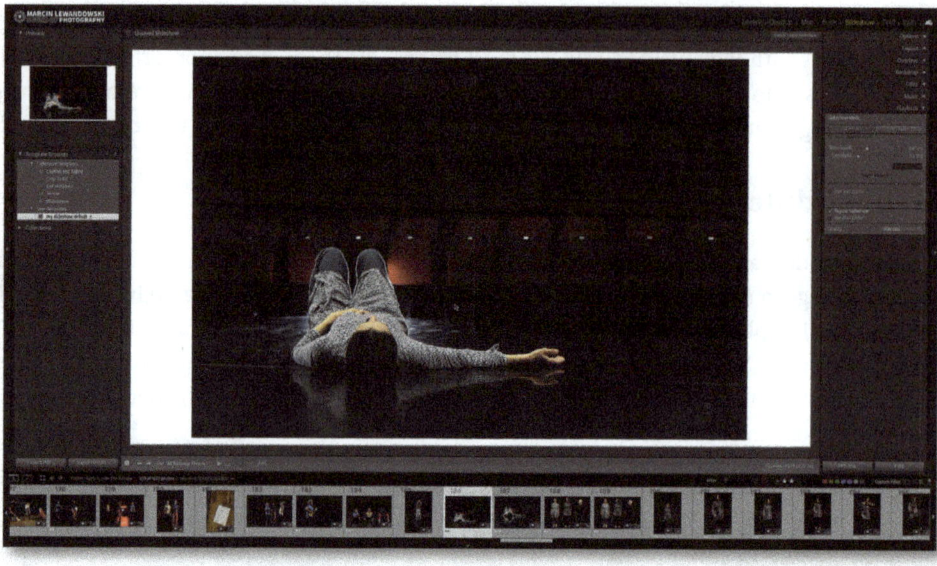

Figure 10.22 – The Slideshow module

The Web module

Finally, for the digital format anyway, we can present images to the world by creating web galleries. These can be exported directly from Lightroom without the need to use any additional FTP solution.

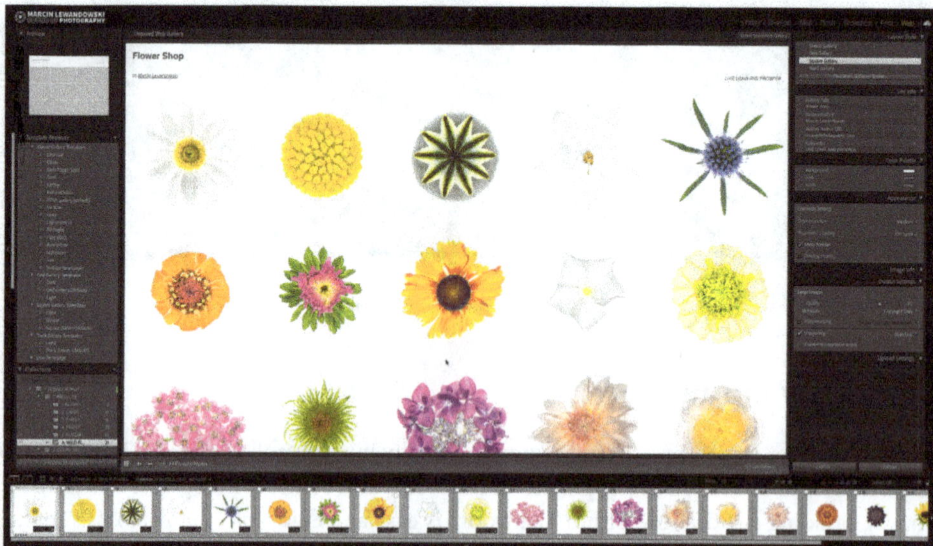

Figure 10.23 – The Web module

The Book and Print modules

As much as Lightroom Classic is a masterful tool to manage and polish our digital assets, it's also a connection to the physical world through the Book and Print modules. Designing a book can be as simple as just clicking the **Auto Layout** button or as deeply customized as we wish. From one photo per page to a seemingly random grid that we can mold to our will, we can easily design a book, prepare prints for an online service, or send images to our printer and achieve predictable, consistent results each time.

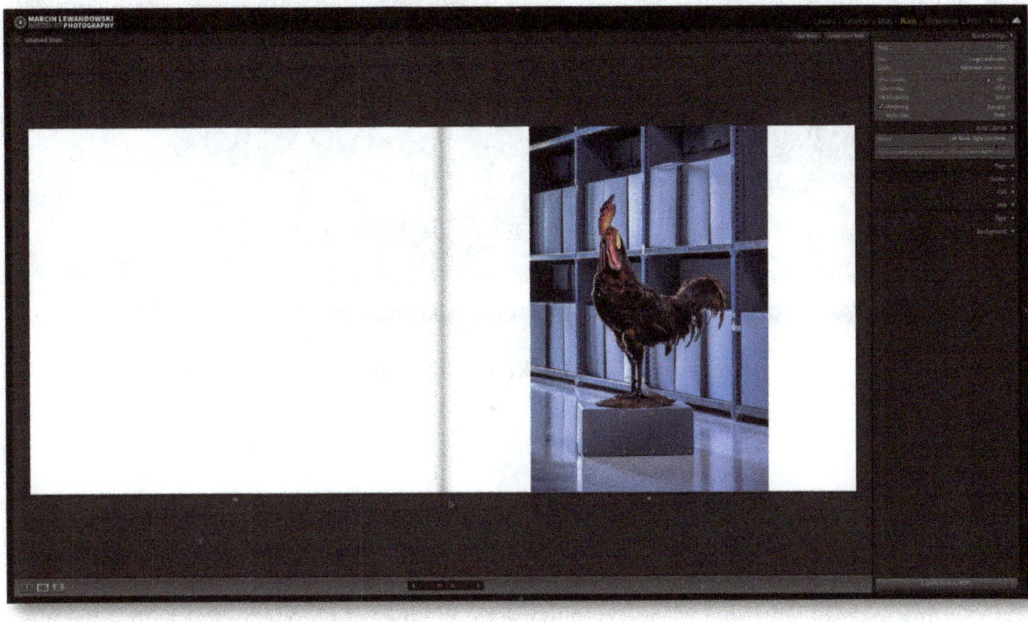

Figure 10.24 A

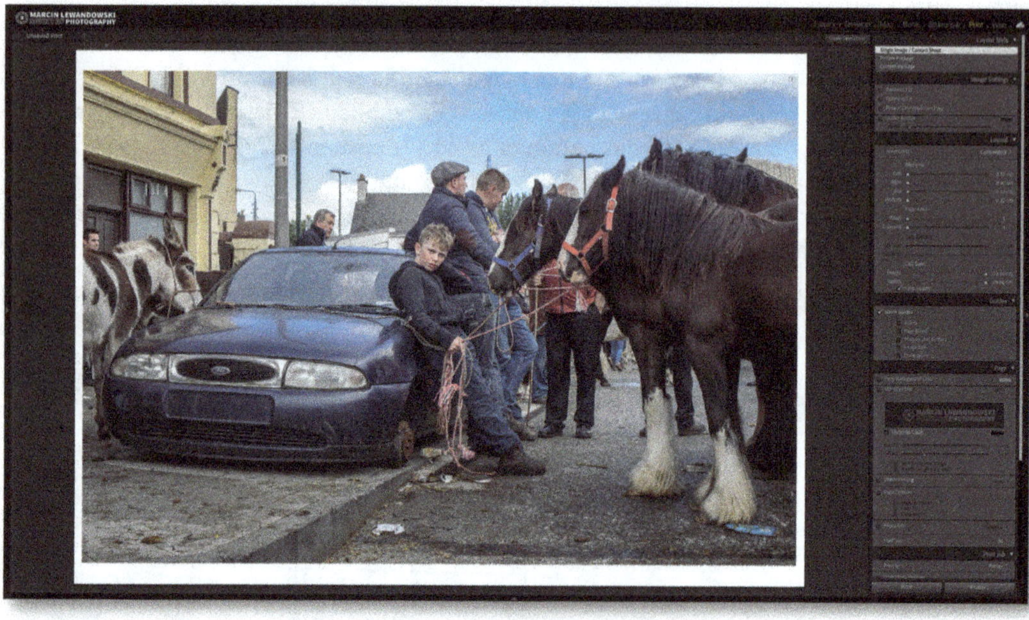

Figure 10.24 – The Book and Print modules

Summary

Lightroom is a powerful presence in any photographer's workflow, not just because it was the first software of its kind, but because, from the very beginning, it was designed with photographers in mind. Lightroom's user interface is intuitive and has multiple ways to access most functions. This flexibility makes Lightroom Classic easy to use by all types of photographers with different kinds of workflows. Every photographer can easily incorporate Lightroom Classic, whether it's a day of studio-based fashion photoshoots, a street photographer's long-running project, or to bring a bit of order to a collection of our family photographs. With many keyboard shortcuts and flexibility in arranging the workspace, Lightroom offers a streamlined user interface, focusing our experience on bare necessities without any unnecessary fluff. Lightroom Classic focuses on enabling users to adjust any parameters within their photographs so that the final images match our vision.

Thank you for joining me on this journey through the features of the best photography software available. I wish you many years of fun and a keenness to discover how much potential in your photographs can be unleashed.

Table of Keyboard Shortcuts

This comprehensive list includes all keyboard shortcuts available within Lightroom Classic. It would be tricky to learn all of them, so I've highlighted the ones I use daily:

Keys for working with panels		
Result	macOS	Windows
Show/hide side panels	*Tab*	*Tab*
Show/hide all panels	*Shift + Tab*	*Shift + Tab*
Show/hide toolbar	*T*	*T*
Show/hide the Module Picker	*F5*	*F5*
Show/hide Filmstrip	*F6*	*F6*
Show/hide the left panels	*F7*	*F7*
Show/hide the right panels	*F8*	*F8*
Toggle solo mode	*Option-click a panel*	*Alt-click a panel*
Open a new panel without closing the soloed panel	*Shift-click a panel*	*Shift-click a panel*
Open/close all panels	*Command-click a panel*	*Ctrl-click a panel*
Open/close the left panels, top to bottom	*Command + Control + 0 –5*	*Ctrl + Shift + 0 –5*
Open/close the right panels, the Library and Develop modules, top to bottom	*Command + 0–9*	*Ctrl + 0–9*
Open/close the right panels, the Slideshow, Print, and Web modules, top to bottom	*Command + 1–7*	*Ctrl + 1–7*

Keys for navigating modules		
Result	macOS	Windows
Go to the Library module	*Command + Option + 1*	*Ctrl + Alt + 1*
Go to the Develop module	*Command + Option + 2*	*Ctrl + Alt + 2*
Go to the Map module	*Command + Option + 3*	*Ctrl + Alt + 3*
Go to the Book module	*Command + Option + 4*	*Ctrl + Alt + 4*
Go to the Slideshow module	*Command + Option + 5*	*Ctrl + Alt + 5*
Go to the Print module	*Command + Option + 6*	*Ctrl + Alt + 6*
Go to the Web module	*Command + Option + 7*	*Ctrl + Alt + 7*
Go back/go forward	*Command + Option + Left Arrow/Command + Option + Right Arrow*	*Ctrl + Alt + Left Arrow/Ctrl + Alt + Right Arrow*
Go back to the previous module	*Command + Option + Up Arrow*	*Ctrl + Alt + Up Arrow*

Keys for changing views and screen modes		
Result	macOS	Windows
Enter the Library Loupe view	*E*	*E*
Enter the Library Grid view	*G*	*G*
Enter the Library Compare view	*C*	*C*
Enter the Library Survey view	*N*	*N*
Open selected photo in the Develop module	*D*	*D*
Cycle forward/backward through Lights Out mode	*L/Shift + L*	*L/Shift + L*

Keys for changing views and screen modes		
Toggle Lights Dim mode	*Command + Shift + L*	*Ctrl + Shift + L*
Cycle screen modes	*F*	*F*
Previous screen mode	*Shift + F*	
Switch between Normal and Full Screen, hide panels	*Command + Shift + F*	*Ctrl + Shift + F*
Go to Normal screen mode	*Command + Option + F*	*Ctrl + Alt + F*
Cycle info overlay	*I*	*I*
Show/hide info overlay	*Command + I*	*Ctrl + I*

Keys for using a secondary window		
Result	macOS	Windows
Open a secondary window	*Command + F11*	*F11*
Enter Grid view	*Shift + G*	*Shift + G*
Enter normal Loupe view	*Shift + E*	*Shift + E*
Enter locked Loupe view	*Command + Shift + Return*	*Ctrl + Shift + Enter*
Enter Compare view	*Shift + C*	*Shift + C*
Enter Survey view	*Shift + N*	*Shift + N*
Enter Slideshow view	*Command + Option + Shift + Return*	*Ctrl + Alt + Shift + Enter*
Enter Full Screen mode (requires a second monitor)	*Command + Shift + F11*	*Shift + F11*

Keys for using a secondary window		
Result	macOS	Windows
Show/hide the Filter bar	*Shift* + \	*Shift* + \
Zoom in/zoom out	*Command* + *Shift* + =/ *Command* + *Shift* + -	*Ctrl* + *Shift* + =/*Ctrl* + *Shift* + -

Keys for managing photos and catalogs		
Result	macOS	Windows
Import photos from the disk	*Command* + *Shift* + *I*	*Ctrl* + *Shift* + *I*
Open the catalog	*Command* + *Shift* + *O*	*Ctrl* + *O*
Open Preferences	*Command* + , (comma)	*Ctrl* + , (comma)
Open Catalog Settings	*Command* + *Option* + , (comma)	*Ctrl* + *Alt* + , (comma)
Create a new subfolder (segmented tethered capture)	*Command* + *Shift* + *T*	*Ctrl* + *Shift* + *T*
Hide/show the tether capture bar	*Command* + *T*	*Ctrl* + *T*
Create a new folder in the Library module	*Command* + *Shift* + *N*	*Ctrl* + *Shift* + *N*
Create a virtual copy (the Library and Develop modules only)	*Command* + ' (apostrophe)	*Ctrl* + ' (apostrophe)
Show in Explorer/Finder (Library and Develop modules only)	*Command* + *R*	*Ctrl* + *R*
Go to the next/previous photo in the Filmstrip	*Right Arrow*/*Left Arrow*	*Right Arrow*/*Left Arrow*
Select multiple folders or collections (in the Library, Slideshow, Print, and Web modules)	*Shift-click* or *Command-click*	*Shift-click* or *Ctrl-click*

Keys for managing photos and catalogs		
Result	macOS	Windows
Rename a photo (in the Library module)	*F2*	*F2*
Delete selected photo(s)	*Delete*	*Backspace* or *Delete*
Remove selected photo(s) from catalog	*Option + Delete*	*Alt + Backspace*
Delete the selected photo(s) and move to the Recycle Bin (Windows) or Trash (macOS)	*Command + Option + Shift + Delete*	*Ctrl + Alt + Shift + Backspace*
Delete the rejected photo(s)	*Command + Delete*	*Ctrl + Backspace*
Edit in Photoshop	*Command + E*	*Ctrl + E*
Open in another editor	*Command + Option + E*	*Ctrl + Alt + E*
Export the selected photo(s)	*Command + Shift + E*	*Ctrl + Shift + E*
Export with previous settings	*Command + Option + Shift + E*	*Ctrl + Alt + Shift + E*
Open the plug-in manager	*Command + Option + Shift +* , (comma)	*Ctrl + Alt + Shift +* , (comma)
Print the selected photo	*Command + P*	*Ctrl + P*
Open the Page Setup dialog box	*Command + Shift + P*	*Ctrl + Shift + P*

Keys for comparing photos in the Library module		
Result	macOS	Windows
Switch to Loupe view	*E* or *Return*	*E* or *Enter*
Switch to Grid view	*G or Esc*	*G or Esc*
Switch to Compare view	*C*	*C*

Keys for comparing photos in the Library module		
Result	macOS	Windows
Switch to Survey view	*N*	*N*
Switch from Grid to Loupe view	*Spacebar* or *E*	*Spacebar* or *E*
Swap select and candidate photos in Compare view	*Down Arrow*	*Down Arrow*
Make next photos select and candidate in Compare view	*Up Arrow*	*Up Arrow*
Toggle Zoom view	*Z*	*Z*
Zoom in/zoom out in Loupe view	*Command + =/Command + -*	*Ctrl + =/Ctrl + -*
Scroll up/down the zoomed photo in Loupe view (also works in the Develop and Web modules)	*Page Up/Page Down on a full-size keyboard*	*Page Up/Page Down on a full-size keyboard*
Go to the beginning/end of Grid view	*Home/End*	*Home/End*
Play an impromptu slideshow	*Command + Return*	*Ctrl + Enter*
Rotate the photo right (clockwise)	*Command +]*	*Ctrl +]*
Rotate the photo left (counterclockwise)	*Command + [*	*Ctrl + [*
Increase/decrease the Grid thumbnail size	*=/-*	*=/-*
Scroll up/down Grid thumbnails	*Page Up/Page Down on a full-size keyboard*	*Page Up/Page Down on a full-size keyboard*
Toggle cell extras	*Command + Shift + H*	*Ctrl + Shift + H*

Keys for comparing photos in the Library module		
Result	macOS	Windows
Show/hide badges	*Command + Option + Shift + H*	*Ctrl + Alt + Shift + H*
Cycle Grid views	*J*	*J*
Open the Library view options	*Command + J*	*Ctrl + J*
Select multiple discrete photos	*Command-click*	*Ctrl-click*
Select multiple contiguous photos	*Shift-click*	*Shift-click*
Select all photos	*Command + A*	*Ctrl + A*
Deselect all photos	*Command + D* or *Command + Shift + A*	*Ctrl + D*
Select only the active photo	*Command + Shift + D*	*Ctrl + Shift + D*
Deselect the active photo	/	/
Add the previous/next photo to the selection	*Shift + Left/Right Arrow*	*Shift + Left/Right Arrow*
Select flagged photos	*Command + Option + A*	*Ctrl + Alt + A*
Deselect unflagged photos	*Command + Option + Shift + D*	*Ctrl + Alt + Shift + D*
Group into a stack	*Command + G*	*Ctrl + G*
Unstack	*Command + Shift + G*	*Ctrl + Shift + G*
Toggle a stack	*S*	*S*
Move to the top of a stack	*Shift + S*	*Shift + S*
Move up in a stack	*Shift + [*	*Shift + [*

Keys for comparing photos in the Library module		
Result	macOS	Windows
Move down in a stack	*Shift +]*	*Shift +]*

Keys for rating and filtering photos		
Result	macOS	Windows
Set a star rating	*1–5*	*1–5*
Set a star rating and go to the next photo	*Shift + 1–5*	*Shift + 1–5*
Remove a star rating	*0*	*0*
Remove a star rating and go to the next photo	*Shift + 0*	*Shift + 0*
Increase/decrease a rating by one star	*]/[*	*]/[*
Assign a red label	*6*	*6*
Assign a yellow label	*7*	*7*
Assign a green label	*8*	*8*
Assign a blue label	*9*	*9*
Assign a color label and go to the next photo	*Shift + 6–9*	*Shift + 6–9*
Flag a photo as a pick	*P*	*P*
Flag a photo as a pick and go to the next photo	*Shift + P*	*Shift + P*
Flag a photo as a reject	*X*	*X*
Flag a photo as a reject and go to the next photo	*Shift + X*	*Shift + X*

Keys for rating and filtering photos		
Result	macOS	Windows
Unflag a photo	*U*	*U*
Unflag a photo and go to the next photo	*Shift + U*	*Shift + U*
Increase/decrease a flag status	*Command + Up Arrow/ Command + Down Arrow*	*Ctrl + Up Arrow/Ctrl + Down Arrow*
Cycle flag settings	*(back quote)*	*(back quote)*
Refine photos	*Command + Option + R*	*Ctrl + Alt + R*
Show/hide the Library Filter bar	\	\
Open multiple filters in the Filter bar	*Shift-click filter labels*	*Shift-click filter labels*
Toggle filters on/off	*Command + L*	*Ctrl + L*
Find a photo in the Library module	*Command + F*	*Ctrl + F*

Keys for working with collections		
Result	macOS	Windows
Create a new collection in the Library module	*Command + N*	*Ctrl + N*
Add to a Quick Collection	*B*	*B*
Add to a Quick Collection and go to next photo	*Shift + B*	*Shift + B*
Show a Quick Collection	*Command + B*	*Ctrl + B*
Save a Quick Collection	*Command + Option + B*	*Ctrl + Alt + B*
Clear a Quick Collection	*Command + Shift + B*	*Ctrl + Shift + B*

Keys for working with collections		
Result	macOS	Windows
Set as a target collection	*Command + Option + Shift + B*	*Ctrl + Alt + Shift + B*

Keys for working with metadata and keywords in the Library module		
Result	macOS	Windows
Add keywords	*Command + K*	*Ctrl + K*
Edit keywords	*Command + Shift + K*	*Ctrl + Shift + K*
Set a keyword shortcut	*Command + Option + Shift + K*	*Ctrl + Alt + Shift + K*
Add/remove a keyword shortcut from the selected photo	*Shift + K*	*Shift + K*
Enable painting	*Command + Option + K*	*Ctrl + Alt + K*
Add a keyword from a keyword set to the selected photo	*Option + 1–9*	*Alt + 1–9*
Cycle forward/backward through keyword sets	*Option + 0/Option + Shift + 0*	*Alt + 0/Alt + Shift + 0*
Copy/paste metadata	*Command + Option + Shift + C/Command + Option + Shift + V*	*Ctrl + Alt + Shift + C/Ctrl + Alt + Shift + V*
Save metadata to file	*Command + S*	*Ctrl + S*
Open the Spelling dialog box	*Command + :*	
Check spelling	*Command + ;*	
Open the Character palette	*Command + Option + T*	

Keys for working in the Develop module		
Result	macOS	Windows
Convert to grayscale	*V*	*V*
Auto tone	*Command + U*	*Ctrl + U*
Auto white balance	*Command + Shift + U*	*Ctrl + Shift + U*
Edit in Photoshop	*Command + E*	*Ctrl + E*
Copy/paste Develop settings	*Command + Shift + C/ Command + Shift + V*	*Ctrl + Shift + C/Ctrl + Shift + V*
Paste settings from the previous photo	*Command + Option + V*	*Ctrl + Alt + V*
Copy After settings to Before	*Command + Option + Shift + Left Arrow*	*Ctrl + Alt + Shift + Left Arrow*
Copy Before settings to After	*Command + Option + Shift + Right Arrow*	*Ctrl + Alt + Shift + Right Arrow*
Swap Before and After settings	*Command + Option + Shift + Up Arrow*	*Ctrl + Alt + Shift + Up Arrow*
Increase/decrease the selected slider in small increments	*Up Arrow/Down Arrow* or +/-	*Up Arrow/Down Arrow* or +/-
Increase/decrease the selected slider in larger increments	*Shift + Up Arrow/Shift + Down Arrow* or *Shift + +/ Shift + -*	*Shift + Up Arrow/ Shift + Down Arrow* or *Shift + +/Shift + -*
Cycle through Basic panel settings (forward/ backward)	. (period)/, (comma)	. (period)/, (comma)
Reset a slider	*Double-click slider name*	*Double-click slider name*
Reset a group of sliders	*Option-click group name*	*Alt-click group name*
Reset all settings	*Command + Shift + R*	*Ctrl + Shift + R*

Keys for working in the Develop module		
Result	macOS	Windows
Sync settings	*Command + Shift + S*	*Ctrl + Shift + S*
Sync settings, bypassing the Synchronize Settings dialog box	*Command + Option + S*	*Ctrl + Alt + S*
Toggle Auto Sync	*Command-click Sync button*	*Ctrl-click Sync button*
Enable Auto Sync	*Command + Option + Shift + A*	*Ctrl + Alt + Shift + A*
Match total exposures	*Command + Option + Shift + M*	*Ctrl + Alt + Shift + M*
Select the White Balance tool (from any module)	*W*	*W*
Select the Crop tool (from any module)	*R*	*R*
Constrain aspect ratio when the Crop tool is selected	*A*	*A*
Crop to the same aspect ratio as the previous crop	*Shift + A*	*Shift + A*
Crop from the center of the photo	*Option-drag*	*Alt-drag*
Cycle the Crop grid overlay	*O*	*O*
Cycle the Crop grid overlay orientation	*Shift + O*	*Shift + O*
Switch the crop between portrait and landscape orientation	*X*	*X*
Reset the crop	*Command + Option + R*	*Ctrl + Alt + R*
Select the Guided Upright tool (also works in the Library module when a photo is selected)	*Shift + T*	*Shift + T*

Keys for working in the Develop module		
Result	macOS	Windows
Select the Spot Removal tool	*Q*	*Q*
Toggle Brush between Clone and Heal modes when the Spot Removal tool is selected	*Shift + T*	*Shift + T*
Select the Adjustment Brush tool (from any module)	*K*	*K*
Select the Graduated Filter tool	*M*	*M*
Toggle Mask between Edit and Brush modes when the Graduated Filter or Radial Filter is selected	*Shift + T*	*Shift + T*
Increase/decrease the brush size	*]/[*	*]/[*
Increase/decrease brush feathering	*Shift +]/Shift + [*	*Shift +]/Shift + [*
Switch between the local adjustment brushes A and B	*/*	*/*
Temporarily switch from brush A or B to Eraser	*Option-drag*	*Alt-drag*
Paint a horizontal or vertical line	*Shift-drag*	*Shift-drag*
Increase/decrease the amount	*Drag adjustment pin right/left*	*Drag adjustment pin right/left*
Show/hide the local adjustment pin	*H*	*H*
Show/hide the local adjustment mask overlay	*O*	*O*
Cycle local adjustment mask overlay colors	*Shift + O*	*Shift + O*

Keys for working in the Develop module		
Result	macOS	Windows
Select the Targeted Adjustment tool to apply a Tone Curve adjustment	*Command + Option + Shift + T*	*Ctrl + Alt + Shift + T*
Select the Targeted Adjustment tool to apply a Hue adjustment	*Command + Option + Shift + H*	*Ctrl + Alt + Shift + H*
Select the Targeted Adjustment tool to apply a Saturation adjustment	*Command + Option + Shift + S*	*Ctrl + Alt + Shift + S*
Select the Targeted Adjustment tool to apply a Luminance adjustment	*Command + Option + Shift + L*	*Ctrl + Alt + Shift + L*
Select the Targeted Adjustment tool to apply a Grayscale Mix adjustment	*Command + Option + Shift + G*	*Ctrl + Alt + Shift + G*
Deselect the Targeted Adjustment tool	*Command + Option + Shift + N*	*Ctrl + Alt + Shift + N*
Show clipping	*J*	*J*
Rotate the photo right (clockwise)	*Command +]*	*Ctrl +]*
Rotate the photo left (counterclockwise)	*Command + [*	*Ctrl + [*
Toggle between Loupe and 1:1 Zoom preview	*Spacebar* or *Z*	*Spacebar* or *Z*
Zoom in/zoom out	*Command + =/Command + -*	*Ctrl + =/Ctrl + -*
Play an impromptu slideshow	*Command + Return*	*Ctrl + Enter*
View Before and After left/right	*Y*	*Y*
View Before and After top/bottom	*Option + Y*	*Alt + Y*
View Before and After in a split screen	*Shift + Y*	*Shift + Y*
View Before only	\	\

Keys for working in the Develop module		
Result	macOS	Windows
Create a new snapshot	*Command + N*	*Ctrl + N*
Create a new preset	*Command + Shift + N*	*Ctrl + Shift + N*
Create a new preset folder	*Command + Option + N*	*Ctrl + Alt + N*
Open Develop view options	*Command + J*	*Ctrl + J*

Keys for working in the Slideshow module		
Result	macOS	Windows
Play a slideshow	*Return*	*Enter*
Play an impromptu slideshow	*Command + Return*	*Ctrl + Enter*
Pause a slideshow	*Spacebar*	*Spacebar*
Preview a slideshow	*Option + Return*	*Alt + Enter*
End a slideshow	*Esc*	*Esc*
Go to the next slide	*Right Arrow*	*Right Arrow*
Go to the previous slide	*Left Arrow*	*Left Arrow*
Rotate a photo right (clockwise)	*Command +]*	*Ctrl +]*
Rotate a photo left (counterclockwise)	*Command + [*	*Ctrl + [*
Show/hide guides	*Command + Shift + H*	*Ctrl + Shift + H*
Export a PDF slideshow	*Command + J*	*Ctrl + J*
Export a JPEG slideshow	*Command + Shift + J*	*Ctrl + Shift + J*
Export a video slideshow	*Command + Option + J*	*Ctrl + Alt + J*

Keys for working in the Slideshow module		
Result	macOS	Windows
Create a new slideshow template	*Command + N*	*Ctrl + N*
Create a new slideshow template folder	*Command + Shift + N*	*Ctrl + Shift + N*
Save slideshow settings	*Command + S*	*Ctrl + S*

Keys for working in the Print module		
Result	macOS	Windows
Print	*Command + P*	*Ctrl + P*
Print one copy	*Command + Option + P*	*Ctrl + Alt + P*
Open the Page Setup dialog box	*Command + Shift + P*	*Ctrl + Shift + P*
Open the Print Settings dialog box	*Command + Option + Shift + P*	*Ctrl + Alt + Shift + P*
Go to the first page	*Command + Shift + Left Arrow*	*Ctrl + Shift + Left Arrow*
Go to the last page	*Command + Shift + Right Arrow*	*Ctrl + Shift + Right Arrow*
Go to the previous page	*Command + Left Arrow*	*Ctrl + Left Arrow*
Go to the next page	*Command + Right Arrow*	*Ctrl + Right Arrow*
Show/hide guides	*Command + Shift + H*	*Ctrl + Shift + H*
Show/hide rulers	*Command + R*	*Ctrl + R*
Show/hide the page bleed	*Command + Shift + J*	*Ctrl + Shift + J*
Show/hide margins and gutters	*Command + Shift + M*	*Ctrl + Shift + M*

Keys for working in the Print module		
Result	macOS	Windows
Show/hide image cells	*Command + Shift + K*	*Ctrl + Shift + K*
Show/hide dimensions	*Command + Shift + U*	*Ctrl + Shift + U*
Play an impromptu slideshow	*Command + Return*	*Ctrl + Enter*
Rotate a photo right (clockwise)	*Command +]*	*Ctrl +]*
Rotate a photo left (counterclockwise)	*Command + [*	*Ctrl + [*
Create a new print template	*Command + N*	*Ctrl + N*
Create a new print template folder	*Command + Shift + N*	*Ctrl + Shift + N*
Save print settings	*Command + S*	*Ctrl + S*

Keys for working in the Web module		
Result	macOS	Windows
Reload the web gallery	*Command + R*	*Ctrl + R*
Preview in the browser	*Command + Option + P*	*Ctrl + Alt + P*
Play an impromptu slideshow	*Command + Return*	*Ctrl + Enter*
Export a web gallery	*Command + J*	*Ctrl + J*
Create a new web gallery template	*Command + N*	*Ctrl + N*
Create a new web gallery template folder	*Command + Shift + N*	*Ctrl + Shift + N*
Save web gallery settings	*Command + S*	*Ctrl + S*

Keys for using Help		
Result	macOS	Windows
Display the current module shortcuts	*Command + /*	*Ctrl + /*
Hide the current module shortcuts	*Click*	*Click*
Go to the current module Help	*Command + Option + Shift + /*	*Ctrl + Alt + /*
Open Community Help	*F1*	*F1*

Index

D

E

F

Q

R

S

Other Books You May Enjoy

If you enjoyed this book, you may be interested in these other books by Packt:

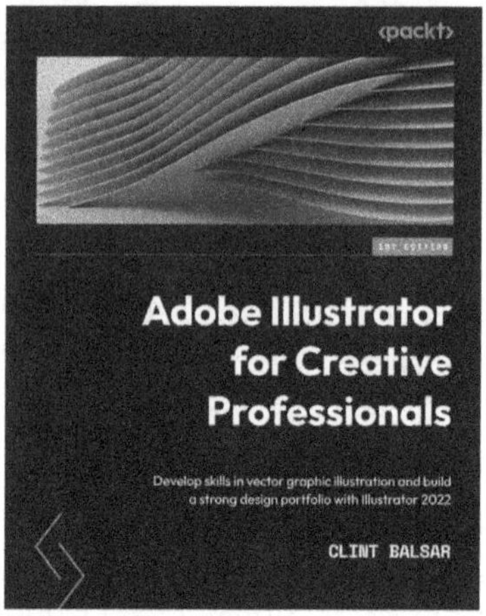

Adobe Illustrator for Creative Professionals

Clint Balsar

ISBN: 978-1-80056-925-6

- Master a wide variety of methods for developing objects
- Control files using layers and groups
- Enhance content using data-supported infographics
- Use multiple artboards for better efficiency and asset management
- Understand the use of layers and objects in Illustrator
- Build professional systems for final presentation to clients

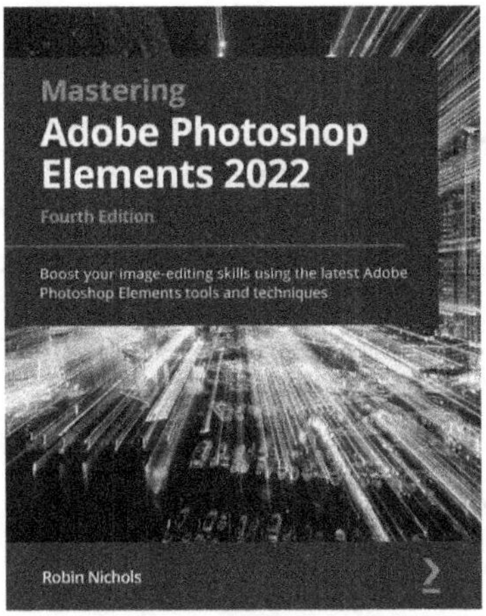

Mastering Adobe Photoshop Elements 2022 - Fourth Edition

Robin Nichols

ISBN: 978-1-80323-824-1

- Identify the five parts of Elements and set up your computer, camera, and color monitor for best results
- Import, organize, and keep track of your imported media library
- Add impressive visual effects to your work in seconds
- Develop advanced picture retouching skills
- Discover how to add text and graphic elements
- Cultivate your understanding of multi-image and multi-layered editing techniques
- Develop illustrative skills using the many drawing and design tools
- Find out how to troubleshoot your work when things don't come out the way you hoped they would

Packt is searching for authors like you

If you're interested in becoming an author for Packt, please visit `authors.packtpub.com` and apply today. We have worked with thousands of developers and tech professionals, just like you, to help them share their insight with the global tech community. You can make a general application, apply for a specific hot topic that we are recruiting an author for, or submit your own idea.

Hi!

I'am Marcin Lewandowski, author of *The Photographer's Guide to Adobe Lightroom.* I really hope you enjoyed reading this book and found it useful for increasing your productivity and efficiency in Adobe Lightroom Classic.

It would really help me (and other potential readers!) if you could leave a review on Amazon sharing your thoughts on *The Photographer's Guide to Adobe Lightroom.*

Go to the link below or scan the QR code to leave your review:

`https://packt.link/r/1801070105`

Your review will help me to understand what's worked well in this book, and what could be improved upon for future editions, so it really is appreciated.

Best wishes,

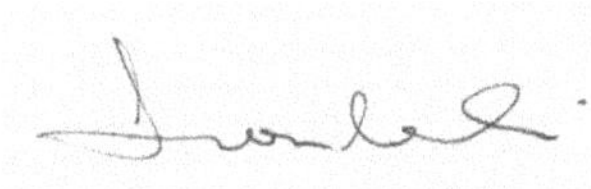

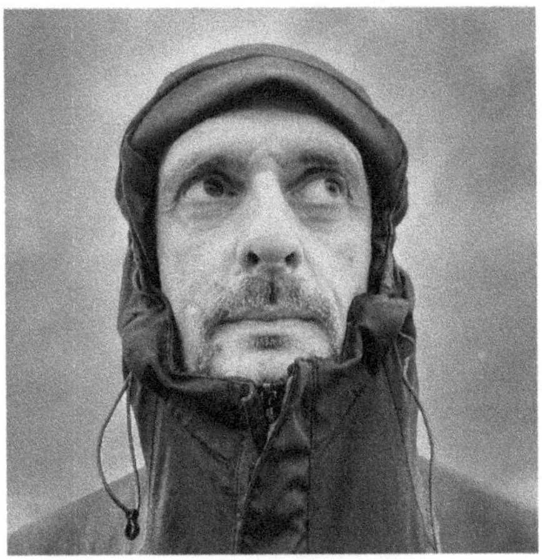

www.ingramcontent.com/pod-product-compliance
Lightning Source LLC
Chambersburg PA
CBHW082143120426
43006CB00012B/111
9781801070102